America in Modern Times

SINCE 1890

America in Modern Times

Since 1890

~

Alan Brinkley
Columbia University

Ellen Fitzpatrick
Harvard University

OVERTURE
BOOKS

The McGraw-Hill Companies, Inc.
New York   St. Louis   San Francisco   Auckland   Bogotá
Caracas   Lisbon   London   Madrid   Mexico City   Milan   Montreal
New Delhi   San Juan   Singapore   Sydney   Tokyo   Toronto

McGraw-Hill

A Division of The McGraw·Hill Companies

America in Modern Times: Since 1890

This book is printed on acid-free paper.

3 4 5 6 7 8 9 0 QWF 0 9 8 7 6 5 4 3

ISBN 0-07-007933-1

This book was set in Janson Text by Graphic World.
The editor was Lyn Uhl;
the production supervisor was Leroy A. Young.
The cover was designed by Karen K. Quigley.
Cover art: Bill Jacklin, *Fifth Avenue East Side* (1986)
The photo editor was Kathy Bendo.
Project supervision was done by Graphic World Publishing Services.
Quebecor World / Fairfield was printer and binder.

Library of Congress Cataloging-in-Publication Data
Brinkley, Alan.
    America in modern times : since 1890 / Alan Brinkley, Ellen Fitzpatrick.
      p. cm.
    Includes bibliographical references and index.
    ISBN 0-07-007933-1
    1. United States—History—20th century.   I. Fitzpatrick, Ellen F. (Ellen
Frances) II. Title.
E741.B69 1997
973.9—dc20   96-34842

http://www.mhcollege.com

About the Authors

Alan Brinkley is Professor of American history at Columbia University. He is the author of *Voices of Protest: Huey Long, Father Coughlin, and the Great Depression*, which received the American Book Award for History in 1983; *The End of Reform: New Deal Liberalism in Recession and War*; *The Unfinished Nation: A Concise History of the American People*; and *American History: A Survey*, a widely-used college textbook now in its ninth edition. He has received fellowships from the John Simon Guggenheim Foundation, the Woodrow Wilson Center for International Scholars, the National Humanities Center, the American Council of Learned Societies, and the Russell Sage Foundation. His many articles, essays, and reviews have appeared in both scholarly and nonscholarly publications.

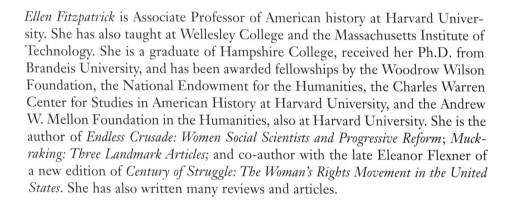

Ellen Fitzpatrick is Associate Professor of American history at Harvard University. She has also taught at Wellesley College and the Massachusetts Institute of Technology. She is a graduate of Hampshire College, received her Ph.D. from Brandeis University, and has been awarded fellowships by the Woodrow Wilson Foundation, the National Endowment for the Humanities, the Charles Warren Center for Studies in American History at Harvard University, and the Andrew W. Mellon Foundation in the Humanities, also at Harvard University. She is the author of *Endless Crusade: Women Social Scientists and Progressive Reform*; *Muckraking: Three Landmark Articles*; and co-author with the late Eleanor Flexner of a new edition of *Century of Struggle: The Woman's Rights Movement in the United States*. She has also written many reviews and articles.

Contents in Brief

Contents

Preface

As we approach the end of the twentieth century, it seems appropriate to consider as a whole the historical experiences of the American people in the last hundred years—years that may have seen greater changes and more turbulence than any other era in human history. Historians have already begun, with considerable justification, to periodize the twentieth century—to divide it into a number of relatively distinct "eras." But it is also possible to see the period since the 1890s—the period in which the United States experienced the rise and transformation of modern industrial capitalism, the emergence of America as a great world power and its often troubled efforts to adapt to that role, the growth of a powerful national government and the emergence of powerful challenges to it, the creation of a vast and pervasive national culture and the rise of searing social controversies over the place of different groups within that culture—as an era with continuing themes and consistent patterns. This book is an effort to convey both the many changes and the important continuities that have characterized American history in this extraordinary century.

Americans today look toward a new century with both considerable hope and deep anxiety. Americans in the 1890s did the same. The world of the late nineteenth century was, of course, very different from our own. Still, many of the problems that afflicted the United States then remain with us today. Earlier generations worried, as we do today, about crime; about economic instability; about immigration, pluralism, and diversity; about the costs to society (and to values) of technological and scientific progress; about changing gender roles; about the persistence of poverty and disease and homelessness; about the quality of education, the plight of children, and the condition of families; about the future of the environment; about the many divisions within the nation along lines of race, ethnicity, religion, class, and region; about the survival of freedom in the face of great centers of power; and about the question of America's identity as a nation.

At the same time, no one can look at the past century without marveling at the extraordinary accomplishments of twentieth-century Americans and the dramatic change they wrought on their society. If the men and women who tried to forecast the future at the dawn of the twentieth century could see the United States at its close, they would, to be sure, find much that would be familiar to them. But they would also likely look with incredulity at the vast wealth and power Americans have accumulated in this century; the great medical, scientific, and technological advances they have made; the remarkable expansion of personal freedom they have struggled successfully, if often controversial, to achieve.

In recounting the history of America in the twentieth century, we have sought to balance the many stories of frustration, injustice, conflict, and failure of those years with the equally important stories of generosity, progress, and success. We have tried to explain the many forces that have divided Americans, but we have tried as well to describe the equally powerful forces that have united them and made them part of a nation. We have tried to combine the "traditional" story of our nation's history—the story of politics, government, diplomacy, and war—with the "newer" stories of society and culture that explore the experiences of ordinary men and women and the broad demographic and economic changes that have shaped our world. The result, we hope, is an account of enough different approaches to and areas of American history in the last hundred years to make readers aware of its remarkable diversity. There is much drama in the history of American society over the last one hundred years, much pain, loss, triumph, and above all, determination. The record is there for all Americans to ponder and to learn from as we approach the next century.

Many people have contributed to the making of this book. We wish to thank the scholars and friends who read and commented on various versions of this manuscript, among them Theda Skocpol, Richard White, George Sanchez, Sonya Michel, William Gienapp, Dennis Skiotis, Charles Poser, Morton Keller, Jacqueline Jones, Martin Nolan, and the members of the women's writing group of which Ellen Fitzpatrick is a part. We wish to thank Thaddeus Russell, Yanek Mieczkowski, and Charles Forcey for their expert assistance with research. We acknowledge the helpful comments of the following reviewers: Ruth Alexander, Colorado State University; Robert Sellen, Georgia State University; Victor Triay, Middlesex Community Technical College; Bruce Schulman, Boston University; Paula Fass, University of California, Berkeley; Ross Evans Poulson, Augustana College; Kevin Byrne, Gustavus Adolphus College; Ira Leonard, Southern Connecticut State University; Francis Kraljic, CUNY-Kingsborough Community College; David Bernstein, California State University, Long Beach; Ronald Tobey, University of California, Riverside. And we are grateful to Peter Labella, Lyn Uhl, Monica Freedman, and Marcia Craig for supporting this project and shepherding it through the editing and publication process at McGraw-Hill.

We hope that readers of this book will feel free to write to us with comments, suggestions, and corrections (either by sending them directly to us or in care of the College Division, McGraw-Hill, 1221 Avenue of the Americas, New York, NY 10020).

Alan Brinkley
Ellen Fitzpatrick

America in Modern Times

SINCE 1890

CHAPTER ONE

A New Society

≈

Looking over the vast changes that had transformed American society in the years after 1865, many Americans of the Civil War generation justly felt they lived in a society that bore little resemblance to the one in which they had been born. "For a hundred years, between 1793 and 1893," historian Henry Adams observed, "the American people had hesitated, vacillated, swayed forward and back, between two forces, one simply industrial, the other capitalistic, centralizing, mechanical." In the 1890s, he noted regretfully, capitalism, centralization, and mechanization seemed permanently in ascendancy. "Of all the forms of society or government, this was the one he liked least," Adams wrote in his celebrated memoir, *The Education of Henry Adams* (in which he referred to himself in the third person), "but his likes or dislikes were as antiquated as the rebel doctrine of State rights."

Neither the doctrine of state rights nor a longing for decentralized government would prove as outmoded in modern America as Adams believed in 1906. Nonetheless, the patrician historian effectively described the sea change so many members of his generation felt sweeping over them in the last decades of the nineteenth century. The rapid growth of the industrial economy, the explosion in the size of American cities, and the influx of millions of immigrants had created new social problems that strained existing institutions beyond their capacities. The colossal fortunes of industrial titans stood in stark contrast to the poverty afflicting the millions who toiled long hours in factories or who lost their jobs in the boom and bust economy. But neither those great fortunes nor the widespread poverty could obscure the tangible, if often modest, gains industrial development had brought to many middle class Americans. Industrial growth improved the lives of many Americans and degraded the lives of others. Hence the ambivalence with which the nation faced its uncertain future.

THE NEW INDUSTRIAL ECONOMY

A central source of amazement and anxiety were the fast-paced dynamics of the new industrial economy. Although the roots of the late–nineteenth century boom in manufacturing reached back to the antebellum years, the scope and pace of industrial growth in the post–Civil War period far outstripped anything before it. Until the Civil War, the industrial output of the United States had lagged behind that of major European nations. By the 1890s, however, the United States was moving far ahead. The value of American manufactured goods skyrocketed, rising from less than $2 billion in 1859 to more than $13 billion at the century's end. Steel and oil scarcely existed as commercial industries in early–nineteenth century America. Even as late as 1870, the United States still manufactured under 80,000 tons of steel; oil production hovered around 3 million barrels that year. By 1890, however, both industries had been transformed. Over 4 million tons poured out of the nation's giant steel mills in 1890, while some 50 million barrels of petroleum reached the marketplace.

In one sector of the economy after another, manufacturing worked remarkable changes in the American economic landscape. The production of basic commodities such as tobacco and paper more than doubled in the 1870s and 1880s. Entirely new industries such as electricity and chemical engineering brought unfamiliar products to the market and burgeoning prosperity to the American economy. For all intents and purposes, the United States experienced a "second industrial revolution" in the post–Civil War period.

Many forces accounted for the tremendous surge in the nineteenth-century industrial economy. America had abundant natural resources. It had a vast supply of labor continually replenished by immigration. And it had a federal government eager to promote economic development and disinclined to interfere with interstate commerce. Equally important to industrial growth were ambitious entrepreneurs determined to exploit the growing domestic market for manufactured goods and the tremendous opportunities for capital accumulation in a largely unregulated economy. Significant, too, were inventive forms of corporate organization that made it possible for business leaders to raise greater sums of capital and manage much larger enterprises than ever before. Innovative technologies played an essential role in allowing entrepreneurs to make the most of nascent American industrial capabilities. Taken together all these forces spurred the American industrial economy.

Toward an Integrated National Economy—The Railroads

The emergence of a more national and interdependent economy was one of the most important developments in late–nineteenth century America. Vastly improved transportation networks were a critical part of that development. For much of the nineteenth century, ambitious American entrepreneurs had devoted extraordinary energy and immense capital to the construction of railroads and

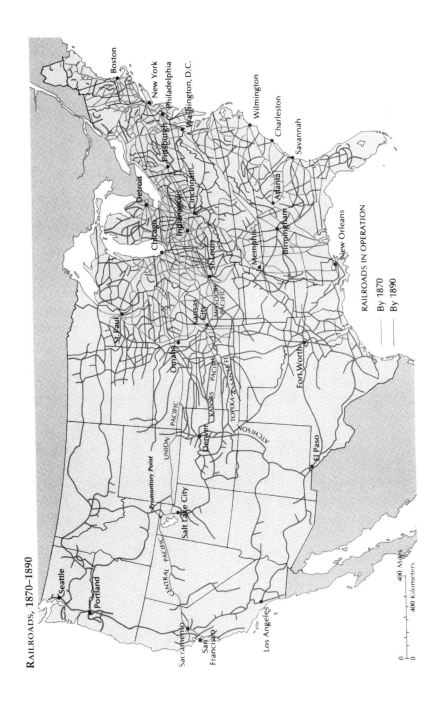

RAILROADS, 1870–1890

the digging of canals. In the post–Civil War period, rapid construction of railroad lines west of the Mississippi helped to nationalize the American railway system so that it soon overshadowed steamboats and canals. A network of railroads covering just 35,000 miles in 1865 grew dramatically during the next few decades. In the 1880s alone more than 70,000 miles of track were laid down. By 1890, the railroads covered some 164,000 miles, a workable network of overland transportation that Americans would rely upon until the automobile age.

The expansion of the railroad system bolstered the new industrial economy in several ways. The railroads gave industrialists rapid access to distant markets and to far-flung raw materials. The railroads were also the nation's biggest businesses. They stimulated the economy and spurred investment. Construction and operation of the roads required the purchase of billions of dollars worth of iron and steel, lumber and coal, as well as the employment of thousands of employees and the shipment of millions of dollars worth of freight. Finally, the railroads pioneered in creating new forms of corporate organization designed to enhance their efficiency, productivity, and profit making.

This last aspect of railroad expansion raised troubling issues for many Americans who celebrated a tradition of small independent businessmen, local, personalized markets, and self-reliant artisans and skilled laborers. The vast sums of money involved in constructing and running the railroads encouraged entrepreneurs to pool their capital, consolidate ownership, and create new administrative and financial structures to control the industry. Assisted by generous subsidies from federal, state, and local governments—as well as crucial investment from abroad—railroad tycoons such as Cornelius Vanderbilt, James J. Hill, and Collis P. Huntington began to create huge combinations that soon dominated the industry. By 1893 nearly seventy percent of railroad miles then in operation were controlled by just thirty-three firms. As the first truly modern business enterprises, the railroads provided a model of corporate organization that soon reshaped much of the American industrial economy.

In 1869 Leland Stanford wielded a silver hammer to drive in the golden spike uniting the Union Pacific and Central Pacific railroads in Utah, completing the first transcontinental railroad. The ceremony publicized the riches promised by the railroads and the brilliant engineering feats realized in the construction of the new east–west railway lines. Less visible that day were the exhausted crews of Irish immigrant and Chinese laborers who built the transcontinental railroad. The Central Pacific had met the awesome challenge of cutting a pass through the high Sierra Nevada by hiring thousands of Chinese workers whom the company paid only two thirds the going rate for unskilled white laborers. For thirteen months, Chinese laborers struggled to tunnel through the Donner Summit, enduring snow slides, bitter cold, and heavy loss of life. Irish workers on the Union Pacific lines experienced similar ordeals. The experience of these railroad workers reflected the human price many paid for industrialism's extraordinary advance.

BUILDING THE TRANSCONTINENTAL RAILROAD. To bridge the chasms of the High Sierra, the builders of the transcontinental railroads used timber trestles. Chinese laborers moved earth and built embankments to support the trestles and relied upon chisels, hammers, picks, shovels, and one-horse dump carts to do so. Although dynamite had been invented, it was not yet in wide use. Instead, the operation relied heavily on arduous manual labor. Here at Secrettown Trestle, on the western slope of the Sierra, Chinese workers labor at these tasks in 1877.

Integrating the Economy: Communication

Improved communication networks were another vital force in integrating and nationalizing the industrial economy. Many Americans found these modern communication systems attractive and alluring. Yet the emergence of new business empires in the communications industry also provided a persistent reminder of the power and, some believed, the dangers of monopoly. In addition, while many Americans celebrated the new forms of entertainment and information now available to them, others viewed the mass culture they were creating as alien and even immoral. They feared its impact on communities, families, and traditional values.

The telegraph broke many of the first barriers to a nationally integrated communications network. The telegraph pre-dated the Civil War, but it became an especially vital instrument in the workings of the late–nineteenth century industrial economy. By providing rapid communication across a vast geographical expanse, the telegraph speeded the movement and marketing of an array of goods. It permitted merchants to broker deals and plan for distribution of farm crops and manufactured goods. The telegraph proved essential to the development of commodity exchanges. It allowed brokers to buy and sell grain and cotton even as these crops were moving by rail across the United States or still growing in fields not yet ready for harvesting.

Just as deals communicated over telegraph lines relied upon the railroads for their execution, so did the railroads rely upon the telegraph to coordinate and routinize traffic on the railway lines. As the railroads spread across the country, so did telegraph lines—often in advance of train track. In 1860, some 50,000 miles of telegraph line drew together various regions of the United States. By 1880 almost 300,000 miles of telegraph line eased the transmission of over 31 million messages a year. Many of the first telegraph companies were established by the railroads; before long, railroad magnates such as Cornelius Vanderbilt, J. P. Morgan, and John Gould achieved fame for their dominant roles in the new communications industries.

The growing interdependence of communications, transportation, and the maturing industrial economy was one of the most notable features of post–Civil War society. Mail delivery became faster and cheaper as a result of railroad expansion. Before long, an entirely new form of communication hastened the long-distance transmission of information and news. When Alexander Graham Bell introduced the telephone at the 1876 Centennial Exposition in Philadelphia, many viewed his invention as little more than a delightful toy.

Before long, however, few could imagine conducting a modern, large-scale business without the telephone. The American Bell Company muscled Western Union out of the telephone business in 1879 after purchasing from Western Union the patent for telephone improvements developed by Thomas A. Edison. Through its subsidiary, American Telephone and Telegraph, the Bell Company constructed the long-distance lines that revolutionized national and international communications networks. By the 1890s AT&T had installed nearly half a million phones. In the process of planning, building, and integrating the nation's telephone systems, AT&T achieved a virtual monopoly over the industry.

Throughout the late nineteenth century, advances in communication altered forever the ways in which Americans acquired information, entertainment, and news. The introduction of the rotary press in the 1870s, halftone photoengraving in the 1880s, and speed presses in the 1890s transformed American newspapers and magazines. Vivid photographs soon competed with written and oral forms of communication. When George Eastman introduced the Kodak hand camera in 1888, he helped spark a burst of popular enthusiasm for

MUYBRIDGE'S "HORSE IN MOTION." Eadweard Muybridge's 1878 efforts to catch the "Horse in Motion" were inspired initially by the desire of a former governor of California to display the grandeur of his horses to friends abroad. By setting up a dozen cameras alongside the track, and running a string across the path of the horses to trip the camera's shutters, Muybridge captured this horse cantering in Palo Alto.

photography. In the late 1870s Eadweard Muybridge simulated moving pictures by using multiple cameras to photograph horses in motion. Two decades later, experiments with celluloid film and Edison's Kinetoscope presaged the advent of motion pictures. Fast, alluring, cosmopolitan—these new forms of communication quickened economic activity and drew American society toward a new, mass culture.

Science and Technology

The application of scientific expertise to industry produced some of the most remarkable technological feats of the late nineteenth century. Here, too, the trend was toward a more modern and more interdependent society with the familiar specter of immense organizations that overshadowed individual autonomy—this in spite of the important role brilliant inventors and entrepreneurs played in advancing science and industry.

Few inventions proved more important than the appearance in the 1880s of electricity. Charles F. Brush's arc lamp lit up city streets, and Thomas Edison's incandescent lamp (or light bulb) illuminated homes, offices, and factories. Electricity emerged as a more adaptable source of power for industry than steam. It soon revolutionized manufacturing. It illuminated American cities. It made possible electric trolleys and, eventually, subways as the basis of urban transportation.

By the turn of the century electric power was no longer a novelty. Although many Americans, especially in rural areas of the country, still lacked access to electricity, the industrial economy had come to rely increasingly upon this new source of light and energy.

Also essential to the new industrial economy were steel and oil, two products whose mass production was made possible by the application of science to industry. Using the European-invented Bessemer process for purifying molten iron and the open-hearth method for further refining steel, American engineers proved remarkably adept at mechanizing the steel industry. By the early twentieth century, giant steel mills in Pennsylvania, the Ohio River Valley, and the Great Lakes region dominated the industry. The United States had become the greatest manufacturer of steel in the world. Skyscrapers, locomotives, and endless miles of railroad track testified to the pervasive importance of steel.

Oil production also surged in the late nineteenth century as a result of technological improvements in refining and aggressive bids to uncover and exploit new oil fields. At first, oil was valued primarily for lubrication and for illumination, the latter made possible by the conversion of crude oil to kerosene. Output exceeded demand in the early years, a fact that accounted in part for brutal competition in the industry. Pennsylvania's rich oil fields provided most American petroleum in the 1860s and 1870s. But in the mid-1880s oil was discovered in northwestern Ohio; and refined oil was finding a major new market as an energy source. Baltimore, Cleveland, Pittsburgh, and New York soon boasted large refineries. At the turn of the century, the industry's reach extended nationally; seven huge companies controlled California's new and rich petroleum industry. Fresh uses of oil were now promised by the introduction of the internal combustion engine and, in 1903, the automobile.

The Industrial Workplace

New products, technologies, and industrial processes went hand in hand with the emergence of mechanization and the division of labor in the workplace. Many of the newly emergent late–nineteenth century industries were very capital intensive—that is, they used more complex and expensive technology and required fewer workers than early–nineteenth century manufacturers. To achieve economies of scale, industrialists aimed to operate large plants at full productive capacity—around the clock, if necessary. Mass production relied upon standardization, so much so that engineer Frederick Winslow Taylor undertook to make a science of production by conducting time and motion studies on workers within factories. He claimed that his theory of scientific management would increase efficiency by transforming the process of work. The goal of managers, he argued, was to control every human variable within an industry. From the shopfloor to the sales office, Taylorism attempted to speed up production and routinize manufacturing.

For many industrial workers, the drive to maximize productivity meant inhuman conditions in the factory. As late as 1910 three quarters of American steel workers still worked twelve-hour shifts; nearly a third of them put in seven-day work weeks that year. Increasing productivity rarely translated into higher wages. Wages for unskilled workers at one large Pennsylvania steel mill dropped from an average of $1.33 an hour to $1.23 between 1880 and 1900. The rates paid to skilled workers at the same plant dropped even more dramatically. The pressure to speed up work, often in dangerous factories, sent America's industrial accident rate skyrocketing.

Industrial workers also felt the impact of changes in the business organization of large industries. The self-employed artisan gave way to the wage laborer, who usually concentrated on a defined step in a long chain of manufacturing. Late–nineteenth century industrialists devoted enormous energy to creating management, distribution, and sales organizations that enhanced profits and maximized control over the conditions of a given industry. As this managerial class developed, labor's control over industry—the ability of workers to control the conditions of their own labor and to contribute to the running of the shopfloor—steadily diminished.

Corporate Consolidation

In contrast, entrepreneurs who invested heavily in creating efficient administrative and financial structures soon dominated their industries. The brilliant, aggressive, and sometimes unscrupulous tactics of the Standard Oil Company enabled John D. Rockefeller to achieve control over much of the oil industry in the 1870s. By 1880, Rockefeller monopolized ninety percent of the nation's oil refining.

Rockefeller achieved his monopoly by creating a vast business enterprise that controlled key stages in the production and distribution of oil. Rockefeller began what he once called "the great game" by building his own refinery in Cleveland. Before long he had expanded his own business and had begun buying out the refineries of his competitors. Eventually he tightened his hold on the oil industry through both vertical and horizontal integration. Horizontal integration involved combining several firms engaged in the same enterprise into a single corporation, in this case the Standard Oil Company. Rockefeller offered the low shipment rates he had negotiated with the railroads as bait to his competitors. By joining the Standard, these firms could increase their profit margins by reducing transportation costs. Some forty oil refiners had joined Rockefeller's company by 1880. The completion of a long-distance crude oil pipeline in 1879, an achievement that promised oil transportation cheaper than the railroads could provide, then prompted Rockefeller to pursue vertical integration—the ownership by a single firm of many different aspects of an industry. The oil baron and his associates began to construct their own pipelines, barrel factories, and terminal warehouses. By the late 1880s Standard Oil had begun buying up old fields and extracting crude oil from the land. They controlled the process of production and marketing from its first moment to its last.

Using the legal instrument of the trust, Rockefeller created a central administrative organization to run his growing oil empire. The shareholders of Standard's forty firms exchanged their stock for certificates in the Standard Oil Trust. Nine trustees were empowered to run the several Standard Oil Companies; the certificate holders enjoyed a share of the profits made. The trustees quickly proceeded to consolidate refining further. Soon they branched out into marketing, as well. By the early 1890s Standard Oil had become a highly centralized and fully integrated modern business enterprise. From a single office on Broadway in New York City, Rockefeller and his managers oversaw the movement of oil from the grimy fields in Pennsylvania to booming markets all over the United States and around the world. Standard Oil remained a dominant force in the industry for decades to come.

By the 1890s the word "trust" had become a synonym, to much of the public, for any large, powerful economic organization. In fact, by that time, the

JOHN D. ROCKEFELLER. John D. Rockefeller amassed previously unimaginable wealth in late–nineteenth century America through his domination of the oil industry. His vast fortune, and the business practices that enabled him to accumulate it, made Rockefeller a man both greatly admired and widely despised in turn of the century America.

holding company had already replaced the trust as the preferred means of corporate consolidation. Making use of newly liberalized New Jersey corporation laws, the holding company became a corporation whose purpose was to hold controlling stock in several other companies. Standard Oil quickly took advantage of the new law to form Standard Oil of New Jersey, a move that boosted the company's capitalization from $10 million to $100 million. Similar forms of corporate consolidation dominated other industries, including steel. Andrew Carnegie's multimillion dollar steel empire led to the formation of the first billion dollar corporation in 1901, when banker J. Pierpont Morgan purchased Carnegie's interests to create United States Steel. At its inception U.S. Steel controlled nearly two thirds of the nation's steel production.

Corporations had existed in America as early as the seventeenth century, but these earlier organizations bore little resemblance to the great trusts and holding companies that had appeared by the 1890s. The modern corporation emerged side by side with the rise of large-scale industrial production. As investors in the railroads had discovered earlier in the nineteenth century, no single individual could hope to finance, manage, and control the vast and complex enterprises that came to dominate the industrial economy. The huge capital requirements of modern industry and the erratic character of the late–nineteenth century economy encouraged the creation of large business enterprises. Ambitious industrialists, determined to maximize profit margins quickly, grasped the advantages of consolidation within the new industrial economy. Before long, many Americans viewed that ambition as greed. Many others worried openly about the fate of individuals and small producers in the new industrial economy.

THE NEW URBAN SOCIETY

Similarly alarming to many Americans was the increasingly diverse and urbanized character of their society. Although American cities had served as centers of culture and commerce since the colonial period, two aspects of American urban life underwent a fundamental shift in the final decades of the nineteenth century.

For the first time, the United States was becoming *primarily* an urban rather than an agrarian society. In 1920 the census revealed that more Americans lived in cities (defined as communities of 2,500 or more) than in rural areas—a shift heretofore unseen in the nation's history. Urban population growth strained institutions that were ill-prepared for the new demands placed upon them. Everything from sanitation systems to the instruments of politics buckled under increasing urbanization. Given the United States' deep agrarian roots, the emergence of large industrial cities, with their myriad problems, raised unsettling questions about the substance and character of American society.

Size alone did not account for the ambivalence many citizens felt toward the nation's great cities. The increasingly diverse racial and ethnic groups who peopled urban communities also provoked suspicion and even hostility among some native-born Americans. Immigration literally changed the face of American cities in the late nineteenth century. In many metropolitan areas, the foreign-born comprised a majority of urban dwellers. Struggling to adjust to a new country, an alien culture, and, often, the grueling demands of work in modern industry, immigrants shouldered enormous burdens as they tried to make their way in American society. Among their burdens was the enmity of those who saw in their arrival to American cities danger, declining moral values, and a frightful portrait of unrelenting misery.

Sources of Urban Growth

Through much of the late nineteenth century, the United States was experiencing the effects of a worldwide movement in population. In many European societies, industrialization, the disruption of agricultural society, growing population pressures, and, for Eastern European Jews, ruthless official repression through pogroms drove landless peasants, unskilled workers, and even artisans from their homes. Some moved to cities within their own countries. Many migrated to other nations around the world. The flourishing demand for unskilled labor in America's expanding industrial economy provided a powerful lure that drew millions of immigrants to the United States. New transportation and communications networks enabled immigrants to make the United States, among other countries, their destination.

From 1860 to 1890 some 10 million new arrivals entered the United States, most from such northwestern European nations as Ireland, England, Germany, and Scandinavia. Many of these immigrants settled at their ports of entry in the East and swelled the populations of New York, Boston, Baltimore, and Philadelphia, among other cities. Many others traveled west to the farming states or inland to Pennsylvania and West Virginia where they found work in the nation's coal mines. European immigrants also made their presence felt in the Far West. By 1870 the Irish outnumbered the native Mexican population in such cities as Los Angeles.

A second wave of immigration, between 1890 and 1914, had an even more profound impact on American cities. Joining a smaller number of new arrivals from Mexico, Asia, Latin America, and Canada, millions of southern and eastern European immigrants migrated to the United States between 1890 and 1914. The new immigrants, some 15 million strong, settled overwhelmingly in cities. Poverty restricted their geographical mobility; established ethnic communities and the availability of industrial work drew them to American cities.

There they were joined in an increasingly cosmopolitan and ethnically diverse setting by native-born Americans who had left rural areas in the United States for the cities. American agriculture expanded dramatically between 1860 and 1916. The number of acres under cultivation more than doubled, and the number of farms tripled. Farm production soared as new machinery and

JOURNEY TO AMERICA.   These immigrants, huddled on the steerage deck of the *S.S. Pennland,* resemble millions of others who endured the long and often arduous journey to the United States in the late nineteenth and early twentieth centuries in search of work, freedom from oppression, and a better way of life.

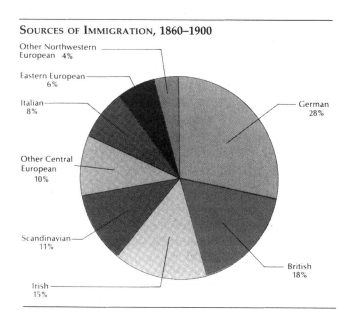

SOURCES OF IMMIGRATION, 1860–1900

Other Northwestern European 4%

Eastern European 6%

Italian 8%

Other Central European 10%

Scandinavian 11%

Irish 15%

German 28%

British 18%

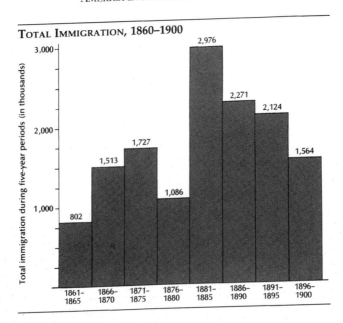

TOTAL IMMIGRATION, 1860–1900

participation in a competitive world market spurred American agriculture. But even as agriculture expanded, the number of farmers was declining. Small farmers, in particular, found it more difficult to compete in the new agricultural world. They suffered from falling farm prices, mechanization, and the consolidation of small farms into large ones; many descended into tenancy. Broken by debt, by burdensome land taxes, and by high transportation costs, thousands of farmers simply abandoned agrarian life in the hope of finding industrial opportunities in the growing cities.

Similar problems and aspirations fueled the migration of African Americans from the rural South to southern cities and to the North and the West during the 1890s. Although ninety percent of all African Americans still lived in the South in 1890, the turn of the century began a large black migration that would continue through the first half of the twentieth century and beyond. By 1900, thirty-two American cities claimed black populations of 10,000 or more. A decade later, the black populations of Washington, D.C. and New York City were the largest in the country, outstripping the major cities of the South. Wherever they migrated in the North and West, African Americans tended to settle in cities.

As was true of other racial and ethnic groups, a myriad of social, political, and economic factors fed the urban migration of African Americans. Black men and women were tyrannized by Jim Crow laws that limited their freedom, threatened by lynching and other forms of terrorism, and imprisoned in a system of economic peonage that left most black farmers hopelessly in debt. As a result, many African Americans looked to the city as an avenue of escape from oppressive social, economic, and political conditions. They also looked to cities as sources of opportunity and excitement, an appealing alternative to the isolated world of the southern farm. The promise of urban life was partially realized by the creation of strong community organizations and a vibrant urban culture in the neighborhoods where black migrants settled. Housing discrimination forced many into substandard dwellings, however, for which the new migrants paid extortionate rents. By the turn of the century, black communities in northern cities became increasingly isolated, as white migration out of those communities hardened growing patterns of residential segregation.

Black workers also could not gain access even to many of the low-paying employment opportunities in industry available to European immigrants. Some black men managed to find employment in the skilled trades in southern cities, but in the urban north discriminatory hiring practices led many employers to favor white immigrant workers. Barred from industrial jobs, many African Americans relied upon low-wage work as servants, cooks, and janitors in the service sector of the economy. Such positions were frequently gender segregated; women dominated domestic service, laundry work, and other occupations in which African Americans found it possible to find employment. As a result, black women came to outnumber black men in some cities. For white middle class families, social conventions discouraged women's work outside the home. But

AFRICAN-AMERICAN WOMEN WORKERS.   Most African-American women, both married and single, worked for wages out of economic need. Few employment opportunities were available to them, so many worked as domestic servants and laundresses, earning low wages for long hours.

the experience of working-class women, and above all of African-American women, bore little resemblance to the middle-class ideal. A majority of African-American women in northern and southern cities worked long hours for low wages, usually as servants and laundresses.

The Demands of Urban Life

The extraordinary racial, ethnic, religious, and cultural diversity of American cities made them a focal point for tensions that were inextricably linked to the emergence of the new industrial society. The cities dramatized both the alluring possibilities and the sometimes horrible realities of modern American life. Here were opportunities for wealth, consumption, and social advancement unimaginable in the nation's smallest villages and towns. Here, too, was suffering, poverty, disease, and disorder on an imposing scale. There was, of course, conflict and misery in even the most bucolic of American small towns. But those tensions were magnified a thousandfold in the nation's cities. They were sharpened, too, by the anonymity of urban life and the absence of a sense of collective responsibility that might bind together smaller and more personal communities. Rapid population growth and the resulting density of urban living would have created formidable problems in a perfectly homogeneous society. In a highly diverse one, it proved difficult to mediate the exacting demands of urban life with the diverse needs of the city's millions of inhabitants.

Housing was one of the greatest needs of late–nineteenth century cities. As thousands of new arrivals poured into the cities every day, existing structures could not begin to meet the growing demand for inexpensive lodging. In New York City, "model" tenements hastily constructed to house new city dwellers offered apartments, three or four small rooms clustered around an air shaft, to immigrant families. Bathrooms in the hallways were shared by apartment dwellers. High rents prompted some newcomers to economize by sharing their small quarters. As a result, the tenements became notorious for their overcrowding, poor sanitation, and general squalor. In 1893 just 1,200 tenements housed most of the 75,000 residents of one Lower East Side immigrant ward. In Chicago's infamous Stockyards district, some 35,000 residents were packed within a single square mile.

Such conditions created dangerous public health problems, which in turn contributed to catastrophic rates of disease in some impoverished neighborhoods. Although tuberculosis declined as a cause of mortality in the late nineteenth century, it remained a serious public health problem along with a host of other infectious diseases well into the twentieth century. Difficulties in preserving meat, keeping the water supply clean, and purifying food and milk contributed to the spread of disease. Infants and children were particularly vulnerable to infectious disease. Tainted milk, spoiled by heat or with its color "improved" by the addition of chalk or plaster of paris, poisoned young children even after pasteurization became more widespread at the turn of the century.

Poorly constructed housing, crowding, and the prevalence of wooden structures added fire to the list of possible urban calamities. By the 1890s fire protection measures had become a central feature of municipal public policy. Stricter building codes, professionalized fire departments, and the use of steel frame construction helped minimize the dangers that had razed countless buildings in the late nineteenth century. Nevertheless, fire remained a constant hazard in the crowded tenements and factories of American cities. Lax enforcement of building codes in some cities made a mockery of reforms designed to protect urban dwellers from the threat of fire.

For all the poverty endemic to late–nineteenth century cities, there were also countless signs of great wealth. Huge mansions, ornate concert halls and opera houses, grand museums, and sprawling parks offered visible evidence of the lavish lifestyles and cultural aspirations of the city's elite. Improvements in streetcars, subways, and rail transportation permitted some moderately well-to-do city dwellers to settle in suburbs that offered space, cleaner air, and even spacious lawns to those willing and able to commute. For a great many city dwellers, however, a home in the suburbs remained a still distant dream in the 1890s.

Adapting to the City

The great challenge for immigrants, newly arriving African Americans, and native-born Americans was to make a home for themselves within the teeming cauldron of the modern city. They employed a variety of strategies to recreate the most comforting elements of the communities they had left behind. Mutual aid societies, churches, social clubs, newspapers, theaters, and saloons appeared in ethnic enclaves throughout American cities. New immigrants relied upon such community resources and meeting places as they struggled to adapt to life in the United States. In southern cities, African-American men and women built an impressive infrastructure of voluntary associations and community organizations, including baseball teams, trade unions, sewing circles, literary societies, and volunteer fire departments. In all such communities, churches performed vital social functions as well.

Immigrants and African Americans also tapped large extended family networks to ease some of the strains imposed by urban living and industrial work. Although most of them established nuclear families—that is, a husband, a wife, and children—many took relatives or boarders into their homes for at least a short period of time. Others found housing near their relatives. These arrangements permitted women to share responsibilities for child care when economic necessity forced mothers to leave the home for wage work.

Some immigrant groups preferred industrial work that employed all members of the family, including small children, thereby supporting the family economy. Mexican-American women often brought their children with them to work on farms and in canning factories. The employment of Italian women in food processing plants seemed a less radical departure from traditional family roles when children came along to help out with small tasks. The employment of the entire family not only supplemented family income, it permitted women to look after their children while working for wages outside the home.

These adaptive measures could not shield the new city dwellers from the hostility of those native-born Americans who blamed them for the various evils of urban life. Certainly, there was no shortage of problems for critics to attack. Public relief agencies and private philanthropies could not begin to meet the needs of a growing number of urban poor. As a result, there were growing numbers of the indigent. Some children left alone during the day by their working parents or abandoned altogether formed rag-tag bands that begged in the city streets or resorted to petty crime. The homeless frightened many middle-class city dwellers, as men, women, and children roamed the streets scavenging for food or slept in city parks. By the 1890s, alcohol and drug abuse were widely recognized social problems. Nationwide, the murder rate rose from twenty-five murders per million people in 1880 to over 100 per million by the close of the century (about the same rate as in the 1990s). Much of the rise stemmed from the high level of violence in nonurban areas, especially the American South, with its high rates of lynching and homicides, and the West, where rootlessness and social instability created their own measure of violence. Still, the cities seemed to encapsulate many of the terrors Americans saw in modern life. And for that reason, among others, the presence of immigrants became associated in the minds of many with urban disorder, crime, and vice.

An array of solutions to the "immigrant problem" had surfaced by the turn of the century. Some native-born Americans and more assimilated immigrants favored mandatory English classes and the rapid jettisoning of old-world mores and traditions including diet, style of dress, and even religious practices. Others sought a much more aggressive approach that included restricting immigration to those who were literate. Still others supported yet more radical measures, such as legal exclusion of all immigrants. By 1894 over 500,000 had joined the American Protective Association, a rabidly anti-immigrant and anti-Catholic group committed to stopping the flow of foreigners into the United States. The APA pandered to fears that Catholic immigrants threatened the economic security of native-born Americans by taking all available jobs. Also, in 1894, a small group of prominent New England professional leaders founded the Immigration Restriction League. With Senator Henry Cabot Lodge of Massachusetts as their spokesman, the League aggressively lobbied for passage of a restrictive literary test.

The response of Congress to such pressures waxed and waned in the late nineteenth century. In 1882 the Congress caved in to strong anti-Asian sentiment among nativist Californians and approved legislation that prohibited Chinese immigration for ten years. The Chinese represented only 1.2 percent of the population of the West Coast. Nevertheless, hostility to Asian immigrants remained intense and, in 1902, Congress banned Chinese immigration again, in legislation that remained in effect well into the 1940s. An array of other laws circumscribed the rights of Chinese who were permitted to live in the United States. Restrictionists met with less success in the 1890s. President Grover Cleveland vetoed a literacy bill passed by Congress in 1897, properly noting that the bill requiring immigrants to read and write English was a thin veneer for an essentially exclusionary act. Industrialists and other employers often lobbied hard to keep open this important source of cheap labor.

Ultimately, neither restriction nor exclusion did anything to address the challenges the United States faced as a multi-cultural society. A rich racial, ethnic, religious, and cultural tapestry had been woven by decades of migration. The new industrial economy profited from the labor power of old and new migrants alike. There was no turning back to a more tranquil, less complex, and less diverse social order—if any such order had ever existed. The nation would enter the twentieth century with a diverse population, burgeoning cities, a growing industrial economy—and both the unprecedented opportunities and daunting challenges they created.

CHAPTER TWO

The Politics of Industrial Society

≈

The emergence of a mass industrial society tested American politics just as it imposed new demands on American culture and society. Revered traditions of decentralized government, individual autonomy, and localism clashed with increasing demands for regulation, reform, and public assistance. The political parties retained enormous power. Yet neither they nor the governments they controlled did much to address the growing popular concerns about the rapidly changing character of modern society. Some Americans sought to exert political influence through the formation of voluntary associations and extraparty political alliances. But they were often outmatched by the powerful corporate forces of the industrial age.

The clash between the needs of a modern industrial society and the sometimes antiquated preoccupations of organized politics created a period of volatility that strained existing governments. Although established political institutions generally survived, they were often buffeted by the turmoil of late–nineteenth century society in ways that eventually forced them to change.

PARTIES AND GOVERNMENTS

By 1890, American politics had begun to reflect the changes that had been transforming American industrial society. Conflicts over the proper role of government in regulating the industrial economy, distributing national resources, and determining social policy were becoming an increasingly visible part of public life.

The Electorate and the Party System

By world standards, the United States had a remarkably broad electorate in the final decades of the nineteenth century. In 1880 nearly 11 million men could vote in the United States, a figure that represented over eighty percent of the men of voting age. Electoral reforms in Great Britain during the same period left some forty percent of the male voting population without rights to the franchise.

But this large electorate excluded important segments of American society. Women lacked voting rights save in a few states, as did most Native Americans. In 1884, the U.S. Supreme Court ruled in *Elk* v. *Wilkins* that the Fourteenth Amendment did not confer citizenship upon Indians; only an act of Congress, the Court said, could do that. Although formally enfranchised by ratification of the Fifteenth Amendment (1870), African Americans faced formidable obstacles in exercising their newly won voting rights. Through violence, intimidation, poll taxes, literacy tests, and property requirements, white southerners succeeded by the early twentieth century in disenfranchising the vast majority of African Americans and many poor whites in the region. In the North, the use of literacy tests by some states discouraged the foreign born from voting. Chinese could not become naturalized citizens, and therefore could not vote, under the provisions of the Chinese Exclusion Act (1882).

The political parties, however, devoted their energies not to expanding the electorate but to mobilizing those who were enfranchised. This they did through the use of patronage; the invocation of party loyalty as a value in itself; the tapping of traditional regional, religious, and ethnic political affiliations; and, when necessary, through corruption. For much of the nineteenth century the electorate was almost evenly divided between Republicans and Democrats. Sixteen states could be consistently counted upon to vote Republican, fourteen states (most in the South) regularly voted Democratic. Five swing states (the most important of them New York and Ohio) determined the outcome of national elections. Results often hinged on the level of voter turnout.

From the end of Reconstruction until the late 1890s, the Republican party won the presidency in all but two national elections. But the average difference in the popular vote was a mere 1.5 percent. Between 1875 and 1895 the Republicans usually controlled the Senate, while the Democrats dominated the House. In any given election only a very few seats shifted from one party to another.

One of the great strengths of the party system was its extraordinary ability to arouse the loyalty and enthusiasm of eligible voters. Political parties did more than provide the machinery for nominating and electing candidates. Rooted in clubs, fire brigades, saloons, and other local organizations, they served as vital social and cultural institutions in many communities. The parties provided men with an opportunity to fraternize, debate public issues, and mount

CELEBRATING CLEVELAND'S ELECTION.　This drawing depicts the celebration in downtown New Orleans that followed announcement of Grover Cleveland's election to the presidency in 1884. The bonfires, fireworks, and crowds of embracing men exemplified the popular political style of the era.

impressive displays of patriotism. Partisanship sparked lively and intense contests over politics among neighbors and friends. Huge torchlight parades, marching bands, and rallies lent a festive air to political gatherings. For many nineteenth-century Americans, participation in party politics was not simply a civic duty. It was a form of entertainment and an expression of personal identity.

The parties were also bound up with deeply felt memories and understandings of recent American history. For many white southerners, the Democratic party represented the victory of tradition, region, and race over Reconstruction politics. Many northerners, white and black, viewed the Republican party as the party of Lincoln, the union, and emancipation, a bulwark against slavery and treason. Long after it receded from immediate memory, the Civil War continued to mold national politics. Religion, ethnicity, and class also played a powerful role in shaping party politics and voter enthusiasms. The majority of Catholic voters, recent immigrants, and poorer workers were drawn to the Democratic party. Northern Protestants and citizens of old stock gravitated toward the Republicans.

During the late nineteenth century, the two parties did not differ much on many of the substantive issues confronting the nation. Both supported the expansion of America's industrial economy, and neither supported far-reaching social or economic reforms. Both endorsed the principles of laissez-faire and trumpeted the virtues of self-help and individual advancement. "Neither party has any principles, any distinctive tenets," wrote British scholar James Bryce in *American Commonwealth* (1888). "Both have traditions. Both claim to have tendencies . . . All has been lost, except office or the hope of it."

Parties and Issues

There were, however, some differences between the two parties. The Democrats took a stand against centralized government at the state and federal level, but they also, at times, advocated some minimal regulation of labor conditions such as hours and wages. Support of labor often led to support of restrictions on the employment of aliens and on Chinese immigration. Such measures were designed to protect native-born American workers, an important Democratic constituency, from the plummeting wages and frequent unemployment that competition from immigrant labor often produced. But immigrants were an important part of the Democrats' constituency, too, so the party was reluctant to support broad restrictions on immigration.

The Republican party tended to favor much stricter anti-immigrant legislation than did the Democrats. It also made temperance a favored cause. Catholics and immigrants perceived the assault on alcohol as an attack on their culture and their values, and the Democratic party generally followed their lead on this issue. The Republicans continued to raise, if only rhetorically, the cause of equal rights for African Americans, while criticizing Democratic support of white supremacy. At the same time, the party became increasingly concerned about the spread of radical political sentiment, linking anarchism and socialism to the presence of immigrants and labor organizers.

Tariff reduction also divided Democrats from Republicans. The Democrats favored free trade and a lowering of duties on imported goods. They hoped to expand exports of American textiles and agricultural goods (both critical to the party's key base in the South) and to lower the price of manufactured goods to farmers. The Republicans remained fiercely protectionist. High duties on imported manufactured goods, they believed, encouraged the growth of American industry. These opposing views led to frequent skirmishes over rate schedules in the final decades of the nineteenth century. Republican ascendancy led to climbing tariff rates throughout much of the period. But the real differences between the parties were, in the end, less important than their ideological similarity. Neither represented a distinct or well-developed philosophy of politics.

The absence of sharp differences in policy did nothing to dampen voter enthusiasm. On the contrary, party politics inspired strong passions, which helps account for the extraordinarily high voter turnout among the late–nineteenth century electorate. Between 1860 and 1900, voter turnout averaged over seventy-eight percent in presidential election years. Even in nonpresidential years, from sixty to eighty percent of the voters turned out to vote for congressional candidates.

The Federal Government

Despite the high degree of political participation among enfranchised voters, the national government played a relatively modest role in the lives of most citizens. The federal bureaucracy was small, largely because the government had few responsibilities. For the most part, the government in Washington collected taxes, delivered the mail, maintained a national military, distributed public jobs, and conducted foreign policy. By the standards of today, the federal budget was very small. Most of the government's income ($567 million in 1900) came from customs duties and excise taxes. A modest income tax (two percent on self-declared incomes over $4,000) passed the Congress in 1893 only to be subsequently ruled unconstitutional by the U.S. Supreme Court in *Pollack* v. *Farmers' Loan and Trust* (1895). One justice characterized the attempt to institute this nominal income tax as an "assault on capital."

Federal expenditures rose in the late nineteenth century but seventy percent of spending was devoted to the military, to pensions, and to paying off the Civil War debt. There was little difficulty in meeting these needs. From the close of the Civil War until 1893, the federal government wound up with a substantial surplus of revenue. The problem was less one of raising money than of finding ways to spend it. In spite of the surplus, funding for social programs figured very little in the business of the federal government, with one notable exception.

From the end of the Civil War to the early twentieth century, the federal government administered and funded a broad system of pensions for Union Civil War veterans and for their widows and dependents. In 1890, thirty-four percent of the federal budget was devoted to veterans pensions. At its peak, nearly one third of all elderly Northern men, as well as countless men in others parts of the country, many widows, and dependents were receiving pensions from the United States Pension Bureau. An extensive bureaucracy, greased by patronage, was required to run the program. Only the Post Office competed with the Pension Bureau in terms of size and cost. Because there were over 60,000 post offices to run in 1890, and because postmasterships were political appointments, the Post Office was a major center of political patronage in the late nineteenth century.

A powerful anti-government sentiment blocked efforts to expand federal responsibilities further. Many influential reformers of the late nineteenth and early twentieth centuries tried to extend the Civil War pension system in ways that would have greatly enlarged the federal government's responsibility for social welfare. They wanted to create a permanent system of old age pensions for workingmen and their families; some advocated health and unemployment insurance as well. They failed to achieve these goals in part because so many people viewed the Civil War pension system as a trough of graft, corruption, and party rule. But the greater obstacle was broad opposition to any movement toward a more activist government and a national system of social spending. For much of the late nineteenth and early twentieth centuries, these anti-government views prevailed.

Limited views of the federal government also resulted in a relatively narrow, although critically symbolic, role for the president in late–nineteenth century America. Most presidents after the Civil War found themselves swamped by the demands of patronage. With nearly 100,000 government appointments to dole out, a new president spent a great deal of his time rewarding party regulars and responding to the demands of office seekers. James Garfield, who became president in 1881 after a career in Congress, once complained: "I have heretofore been treating of the fundamental principles of government, and here [in the White House]. I am considering all day whether A or B should be appointed to this or that office." The passage of the Pendleton Act in 1883, which created a national civil service system, did little to relieve the burden. The legislation required candidates for certain federal jobs to pass a written examination. It thereby reduced, although it did not eliminate, the distribution of government positions as a reward for party loyalty.

The limits on presidential power seemed to diminish the men who held the office in the last decades of the nineteenth century, as the novelist Thomas Wolfe once suggested in reflecting on his own sense of the past. "Who was Garfield, martyred man," he wrote, "and who had seen him in the streets of life? ... Who had heard the casual and familiar tones of Chester Arthur? And where was Harrison? Where was Hayes? Which had the whiskers, which the burnsides: which was which?" In truth, one President seemed to blend into the other as few national issues gave a distinctive cast to successive administrations in the late nineteenth century.

The election of Grover Cleveland in 1884 seemed a notable event because it returned the Democratic party to the White House for the first time since 1856. But few substantive political differences divided Cleveland from his opponent, Senator James G. Blaine of Maine. The latter was known to his adoring admirers as the "Plumed Knight," but thousands of other Americans saw him as a symbol of seamy party politics, "the continental liar from the state of Maine." Cleveland, on the other hand, enjoyed a modest reputation as "reform" governor of New York who had opposed corruption. An independent faction of reform-minded Republicans, known as the "mugwumps" to their critics, bolted from their party and supported Cleveland in 1884. But a heavy Catholic vote in New York proved more decisive to Cleveland's victory in a close election. Blaine's association with a Protestant clergyman who, in endorsing the Republican, referred to the Democrats as the party of "rum, Romanism, and rebellion" hurt him badly in heavily Catholic New York City. Opponents charged the senator with toleration of a slander on the Catholic church.

No one ever accused Grover Cleveland of having excessive charisma. A leader respected for his stern opposition to politicians, grafters, pressure groups, and Tammany Hall, Cleveland inspired little affection. Still he was admired in an era of restricted government for his ability to say no. Americans had a "duty" to "support the government," Cleveland reminded them, but the government had no duty "to support the people." He took a firm stand against the high protective tariff but failed to secure a bill lowering rates.

In 1888 the Republicans nominated former Senator Benjamin Harrison of Indiana, the grandson of President William Henry Harrison but an otherwise obscure candidate. Although Harrison was a protectionist, the outcome of the election, one of the most corrupt in American history, was not determined by national issues. Instead, the vagaries of party politics, money, and superior organization proved decisive to the Republican victory. Cleveland won the popular vote but lost the electoral college. It was only the second time in American history (the first was in 1876) that this had happened; it has never occurred since. For all his luck, Harrison's drab personality seemed to leave little mark on the presidency in spite of his executive skill.

Congress, more than the president, performed the important duties of government—formulating fiscal policy, appropriating funds, and, through its ever-growing structure of committees, overseeing a variety of government operations. But even here, the forces of localism muted congressional power. The passage of the Sherman Anti-Trust Act in July 1890 appeared to be an exception to that rule. By 1890 there was growing public concern that corporations were successfully evading newly adopted state laws prohibiting combinations in restraint of trade. In response to the antitrust mood, Congress outlawed "every contract, combination in the form of trust or otherwise, or conspiracy, in restraint of trade or commerce."

The Sherman Act represented a substantial symbolic step toward federal regulation of the industrial economy. But its enforcement provisions were weak, and the Justice Department exhibited little inclination to prosecute corporations for antitrust activity. Finally, in 1895, the Supreme Court of the United States eviscerated the law. In *United States* v. *E. C. Knight*, it ruled that the Sherman Act's provisions did not apply to the American Sugar Refining Company. Although the company controlled over ninety percent of sugar refining, the Court found it engaged in manufacturing, not interstate commerce. Hence Congress had no power to regulate the company.

States and Cities

At the state and municipal level, much more than in Washington, government did begin trying to address the social and economic consequences of industrialism in the final decades of the nineteenth century, with mixed results. Nearly thirty states enacted laws regulating the hours of female and child labor, although the provisions varied widely from one state to another and enforcement was usually lax. The employment of young people continued unabated in many of the nation's factories. State antitrust measures appeared with greater frequency by the century's end, but they too had little effect. A lack of uniformity, vague or disregarded enforcement provisions, and the hostility of the courts often weakened them. But the difficulty of regulating national organizations with state laws was an even larger problem. Compulsory school laws, designed not only to ensure public education but to check the spread of juvenile delinquency, met with greater success. By 1900 over thirty states and territories required all children to attend school. Still, in most areas of state-level social and economic policy, just as at the national level, a preference for decentralized government, laissez-faire, and the sanctity of private property and contracts undercut reformers' efforts to widen the regulatory power of state governments.

Municipal government also reflected the conflict between entrenched political practice and new social realities. Powerful political machines had played a central role in urban politics for much of the late nineteenth century; they were not eager to leave the scene when called upon to do so by reformers railing against their political corruption. Wars for the control of city government often followed suit, with pitched battles fought in major cities during virtually every election year. Reformers sought to "professionalize" city government by writing new city charters, drafting new election rules, tightening fiscal controls, and reducing opportunities for graft. They hoped such measures would lead to better management and governance of the increasingly complex and growing cities.

"THE BOSSES OF THE SENATE."   Cartoonist Joseph Keppler depicted "The Bosses of the Senate" in a January 1889 edition of *Puck*. Note the special wide "Entrance for Monopolists" on the right and the small "Peoples' Entrance" on the far left balcony barred and shut.

The political machines, with their powerful "bosses" at the helm, resisted most reform measures vigorously. They tapped their traditional political base of working-class and immigrant voters to very good effect. The success of the urban political machine owed a great deal to its ability to address the real needs of its constituents. A political boss' power derived from the votes he could amass for his organization. To win votes, the boss and his machine distributed favors and services. The boss' beneficence might include everything from delivering a turkey at Thanksgiving to a needy family, to finding a constituent a job on the police force or a public construction project. In many immigrant, working-class neighborhoods, this was more than most city dwellers could ever expect to receive from their city government.

The machines reaped rich rewards for their generosity. Power paid. In the late–nineteenth century city, political office holders enjoyed countless opportunities to enrich themselves when they wished. Unscrupulous office holders lined their pockets with kickbacks for building contracts, or the sale of franchises to private companies for the operation of public utilities such as street railways, waterworks, and electric light and power systems. "Don't take politics to heart," advised an urban politico in Alfred H. Lewis's novel *The Boss and How He Came to Rule* (1903). "Politics is only worth while so long as it fills your pockets. Don't tie yourself to anything. A political party is like a street car; stay with it while it goes your way."

Organizing for Political Power

The lack of substance in national party politics and the exclusion of many Americans from the electorate encouraged the proliferation of voluntary associations in the late nineteenth century. Women, who were shut out of party organizations, banned from office holding, and denied the franchise, banded together to press the cause of women's voting rights. In 1890, the two largest women's suffrage organizations—the American Woman Suffrage Association and the National Woman Suffrage Association—fused to form the National American Woman Suffrage Association. The group worked tirelessly to advance women's suffrage on the state level, but progress was slow. When Wyoming became a state in 1890, it became the first in the union to guarantee women full voting rights. Utah followed suit in 1896; Colorado and Idaho approved women's suffrage by state referenda. But no further states were added to the prosuffrage rolls until 1910. Suffrage leaders pressed on nonetheless, galvanized by the leadership of feminists such as Elizabeth Cady Stanton, Susan B. Anthony, and Carrie Chapman Catt.

Temperance reform also prompted the formation of both male and female voluntary associations. A compelling issue throughout the nineteenth century, temperance provided a forum for women's rights activists to condemn the evils of domestic violence, rape, the legal powerlessness of women, and the double moral standard that insisted on female purity while tolerating less than pure behavior in men. Temperance advocates used the prevalence of alcohol abuse as a foundation stone for a much larger edifice of social criticism. Thousands of American men and women were drawn to the cause. By 1890, the Woman's Christian Temperance Union alone had 150,000 members. The National Prohibition party, which endorsed women's suffrage, won over a quarter of a million votes in the elections of 1888 and 1892.

Although one state Prohibition party boasted that it renounced "connections with the old parties, full of dead issues, and declare for a new era, full of living virtues," the new organization never posed a fundamental threat to Republican or Democratic rule. Nonetheless, new political parties proliferated in the late nineteenth century and helped express the views of some disaffected Americans. The Greenback party, which advocated currency inflation, a graduated income tax, and railroad regulation among other causes, led to spin-offs in the 1880s, including the antimonopoly Union Labor party. Independents such as the mugwumps also challenged the authority of the parties as they rebelled against the demands of party loyalty and decried the emphasis on personalities over public issues.

Labor was among the most important of the many groups organizing for power in the late nineteenth century. For much of the nineteenth century, workers in various trades had banded together into unions to agitate for improved hours, wages, working conditions, and, perhaps most of all, recognition of their right to organize. In the immediate post–Civil War period increasing corporate consolidation spurred an earnest effort to merge workers in disparate trades into a single labor organization. The Noble Order of the Knights of Labor, founded in 1869 by Uriah Stephens, was among the most significant of these national unions.

Under the leadership of Stephens and his successor Terence V. Powderly, the Knights welcomed virtually all who "toiled," excluding only lawyers, bankers, liquor dealers, and professional gamblers. Embracing a broad reform agenda, including replacement of the wage system with a cooperative economy that favored workers, an eight-hour day, the abolition of child labor, and equal pay for equal work, the Knights amassed a membership of over 700,000 by 1886. Unlike most unions of the time, the Knights welcomed women workers into their ranks. Leonara Barry, an Irish immigrant who had worked in a New York hosiery factory, played a key role in mobilizing female laborers as head of the organization's Woman's Bureau. After 1883 African-American workers were also invited to join, although they were relegated to membership in segregated locals.

In 1881, a rival organization appeared that rejected the Knights' idea of a broadly inclusive labor union. Instead, the Federation of Organized Trade and Labor Unions of the United States and Canada, renamed the American Federation of Labor in 1886, brought together craft unions that represented largely skilled laborers. AFL leader Samuel Gompers believed a strong federation of craft unions held the best chance of matching the power of capital. His more exclusionary approach left out the majority of women workers, many racial minorities, and unskilled immigrants. Nonetheless the AFL membership grew rapidly in the 1880s and 1890s. An advocate of "pure and simple unionism," Gompers veered away from broad reform goals or affiliation with any political party; he focused instead singlemindedly on the issues of most immediacy to workers—wages, hours, working conditions, and the right to organize.

Whatever tactics labor employed, violent confrontations with capital were often the result. Employer resistance to union recognition remained strong. Deploying professional strike breakers and hired militia, large corporations fought the advance of organized labor at every turn. Among the bloodiest battles was an 1892 clash in Homestead, Pennsylvania between the AFL-affiliated Amalgamated Association of Iron and Steel Workers and the Carnegie Steel Company. Production speedups and wage cuts were the immediate causes of a walkout by steel workers at the plant. But the strike was actually the culmination of a much longer struggle between the union and management. The Amalgamated had made small but significant inroads in its campaign to organize steelworkers at Homestead. Andrew Carnegie and his chief lieutenant, Henry Clay Frick, were determined to stop the union in its tracks.

The company responded to the walkout by hiring 300 guards from the Pinkerton Detective Agency (whose principal activity was fighting unions) to help break the strike. A pitched battle between the guards and over 10,000 steel workers resulted in the deaths of several strikers and Pinkertons as well as

AT HOMESTEAD

JULY 7, 1892.

CABLEGRAM CARNEGIE TO HARRISON

SUNNINGDALE, SCOTLAND
June 12, 1892.

To BENJAMIN HARRISON,
Washington, D. C.:

The American people know a good thing when they see it. Heartiest congratulations. You deserve this triumph. ANDREW CARNEGIE.

Henry C. Frick has just Contributed $500,000 to the Republican Corruption Fund in New York

Wm. C. Hollister & Bro., Printers   148 & 150 Monroe Street, Chicago.

THE HOMESTEAD STRIKE. This 1892 political broadside, designed to mobilize workers to vote Democratic, depicts Pinkerton guards firing on unarmed workers, women, and children at the Homestead Steel Works in Pennsylvania. It attempts to lay the tragedy at the feet of the Republican party by coupling events at Homestead with a June telegram sent by Andrew Carnegie to Benjamin Harrison congratulating the latter on winning the Republican nomination. It also notes the financial contributions to the Republican party of Henry Clay Frick, Carnegie's right hand man and a critical force in efforts to crush the strike at Homestead.

countless injuries. Unable to subdue the union by itself, the company enlisted the support of the governor of Pennsylvania, who called out the state's entire national guard to protect the plant and its strike breakers. The Amalgamated struggled to keep its ranks together but, crushed by the combined weight of the government and the company, proved unable to sustain the strike. Dramatic for its intense brutality, the Homestead Strike typified many labor struggles of the time. Confronted by entrenched employers, the power of government, and a hostile judiciary, organized labor waged an exhausting struggle for power in the final decades of the nineteenth century.

THE AGRARIAN REVOLT

Out of disenchantment with the late–nineteenth century economy and disaffection with the nation's dominant political parties came one of the most powerful protest movements in American history. It was primarily an agrarian revolt, but it came to be known as "populism"—a term used to describe efforts to return power to the people.

Populism represented many things to its diverse constituency. To small farmers in the Midwest and the South, it offered some hope for reversing the apparent erosion of their economic status in the new industrial economy. For farm women, populism conferred an opportunity to join a political mass movement that broke down the isolation of rural life and held up the prospect of improving the life chances of their families. For miners in the Rocky Mountain states, populism raised the possibility of battling the "hard money" advocates who insisted on restricting the circulation of currency. For impoverished African-American tenant farmers, populism appeared to hold out a chance to battle economic oppression by using the tools of democracy. The populist movements of the late nineteenth century achieved few of these goals, but it had a major impact on its time nevertheless.

The Granger Movement

Populism had an important precursor in the Grange, a voluntary association of farmers who came together in the 1860s to provide opportunities for socializing and exchanging scientific information. Founded in 1867, the National Grange of the Patrons of Husbandry at first resembled many nineteenth century fraternal organizations in its elaborate rituals and enforced code of secrecy. But when the Depression of 1873 sent farm prices plummeting, the organization began taking on a political cast even as its membership grew exponentially. By 1875, there were over 800,000 members nationwide as well as a network of some 20,000 local lodges. Almost every state boasted a chapter of the Grange, although enthusiasm seemed greatest in the staple-producing regions of the South and the Midwest.

Rejecting "the tyranny of monopoly," the Grangers sent out a call for cooperatives designed to circumvent the rate gouging of railroads and warehouses and to enable farmers to exert greater control over marketing. A network of cooperative stores, creameries, grain elevators, warehouses, and insurance companies began to appear. Most importantly, the Grangers entered the political arena, throwing support behind politicians who supported their reform ideals and running their own candidates in third-party antimonopoly and reform campaigns. In many midwestern states, they managed to win control of the state legislatures.

The Grangers emerged as powerful advocates of state regulatory measures designed to curb the power of the railroads. As a result of their efforts, state governments passed a series of laws in the early 1870s that, among other things, set maximum freight and storage rates. They became known as "the Granger laws." In 1877, the Supreme Court of the United States upheld the constitutionality of an Illinois Granger law in *Munn v. Illinois*. The decision affirmed the right of the states to regulate private property that was used in the public interest. By 1880, the power of the Grange was waning, but it had set an important precedent, demonstrating the potential power of political organization among the nation's farmers.

THE GRANGE.   A drawing of a Grange meeting in Illinois in the late nineteenth century depicts men, and a few women with bonnets on their heads, paying rapt attention to a political orator. Signs at this rally stress familiar themes in the agrarian movement—"We are the Laborers," "Free Trade and Farmers Rights," "We Feed the World," "President, $50,000 A Year. Congressmen, 7,000 A Year. Farmers 75 cts A Week," and "Brothers Let Us Organize + Educate for Knowledge is Power."

The Alliances

In the 1880s, the most important institutional expressions of agrarian discontent were a group of regional agrarian associations known as the Farmers' Alliances. The National Farmers Alliance and Industrial Union, or the Southern Alliance, encompassing rural people in states such as Texas, Louisiana, Georgia, Alabama, and Arkansas, was the largest of these groups. At peak strength its membership numbered in the millions. The Northwestern Alliance, considerably smaller, took root in the plains states and the Midwest. More radical than the Granges, the Farmers' Alliances from the start offered a slashing critique of economic tyranny and an imaginative set of solutions to redress the grievances of the nation's farmers. They also proved extraordinarily adept at political mobilization. Alliances spread their views and recruited members by sending lecturers out into rural areas and by publishing their own newspapers. Small suballiances formed at the local level, and over time a large organizational infrastructure took form.

The Alliances were unusual for their diverse constituency. Unlike many other reform organizations of the nineteenth century, Alliance membership was mixed rather than segregated by sex. A quarter of all Southern Alliance members were women. Invited to participate fully in the organization, female members wrote for Alliance newspapers, held office, participated in decision making, and recruited new members. One Texas woman proclaimed that "the Alliance has come to redeem woman from her enslaved condition. She is admitted into the organization as the equal of her brother, and the ostracism which has impeded her intellectual progress in the past is not met with." In their support of women's education and economic equality, the Alliances tapped a reservoir of support among many farm women, who were isolated and sometimes looked down upon by genteel society. Although they did not reject all prevailing gender stereotypes, the Alliances were unusually attentive to the problems of farm women and notable for their wish to join women to the Alliance cause. According to the writer Hamlin Garland, "no other movement in history—not even the anti-slavery cause—appealed to the women like this movement here in Kansas."

Race proved a more difficult issue than gender for Alliance members. Few white members of the Southern Alliance welcomed African Americans, but that did not stop black farmers from mobilizing. In 1886, some African-American farmers began to form their own organizations modeled on, and sometimes named after, the Alliances. The Grand State Colored Alliance claimed over 1 million members by 1890. In 1889, attempts by some members of the Colored Alliance to bypass the company store in favor of Alliance cooperatives led to violence and intimidation in one Mississippi Delta town. Although the white Alliances sometimes offered rhetorical support to the Colored Alliances, relations between the two usually reflected rather than challenged the racial hierarchy of the New South.

It was not surprising that the Alliances appealed to farmers across racial lines, for chief among the organization's targets was the oppressive crop lien system. Out of the ruins of the Civil War, the defeat of slavery, and the collapse of credit in the South came a brutal economic structure that left many southern farmers caught in a web of debt, tenancy, and crippling dependency. To begin their planting season, farmers needed a source of credit to purchase seed, fertilizer, tools, and an array of other goods essential to their livelihood. In the rural South, country stores rather than banks often supplied this credit to small farmers. To secure the loan, store merchants placed a lien on the farmer's unplanted crop. When the crop came in, the farmer would be expected to repay his or her debt with interest.

This system quickly led to economic catastrophe for those—white and black—who became indebted to "the company store," which was often controlled by large landowners. Falling agricultural prices, the occasional natural disaster, extortionate interest rates, and a determination on the part of some merchants and planters to leave their tenants powerless created a situation in which farmers existed in a state of extreme vulnerability, at best. At worst, they could be plunged at a moment's notice into total impoverishment. Interest rates that exceeded 100 percent annually, and sometimes 200 percent, spelled an endless cycle of debt that left the southern farmer, as one critic put it, in "a state of helpless peonage." A two-price system at the store—one for customers paying cash, a higher one for those buying on credit—deepened the morass of debt. For many, overwhelming debt led inevitably to mortgage foreclosure and then to tenancy, as farmers lost control of their own land and wound up farming for landlords, often the same merchants who had furnished them credit in the first place. Sharecroppers (among them many black farmers) had never owned their land, but they too were often mired in debt. At harvest time, they were no nearer independence than they had been before all their work had begun.

The Alliances vowed to help farmers, in the words of one leader, "get out of debt and be free and independent people once more." In the South, that message appealed especially to white landowners of modest means, who feared they would not be able to hold onto their land in the difficult agricultural economy. On the Great Plains, Alliance members tended to be family farmers struggling to hold onto their farms under a load of debt. Like the Grange, the Alliances pursued independence by establishing their own stores, banks, processing plants, and cooperatives. It proved difficult, however, to sustain these enterprises and to overcome the resistance of local banking and business interests. More significant was their proposal to create the "subtreasury" system.

The brainchild of Alliance leader C. W. Macune, the subtreasury plan called on the federal government to create warehouses in every county that grew over $500,000 worth of agricultural products a year. There farmers could store their crops while awaiting the most favorable selling price. In the meantime, the farmer could borrow up to eighty percent of the value of the crop from the government, paying just two percent interest and a nominal charge for grading, storage, and insurance. Through the support of the federal government, farmers would be able to circumvent the furnishing merchant, who was often the only source of credit, and borrow instead from the government at a lower interest rate. The result, Macune claimed, would be an increase in the supply of currency and rising farm prices.

In 1890 some Southern Alliance members began to make support for the subtreasury system a litmus test for Democratic politicians running for office. On the Great Plains, Alliance members openly broke with the Republican party and ran candidates for office on a third party ticket. In the end, Alliance-endorsed candidates won partial or complete control of the legislatures in twelve states, six governorships, three seats in the U.S. Senate, and approximately fifty in the U.S. House of Representatives. Although many of these successful candidates were Democrats who benefited passively from Alliance endorsements, many Alliance members considered the victories evidence of political muscle.

Indeed, by 1890 the Alliances were moving more and more rapidly into national politics. A year earlier the Southern and Northwestern Alliances attempted but failed to form a loose confederation. But what they agreed upon—the importance of political engagement—ultimately proved far more significant. At a national convention in Ocala, Florida in 1890, the Alliances issued a set of demands that looked for all intents and purposes like a party platform. The "Ocala Demands" included the direct election of U.S. senators, a graduated income tax, government regulation, and, if necessary, ownership of transportation and communication systems, reduced tariffs, and the subtreasury system.

In the South, disaffection with the Democratic party, already palpable, continued to build as the Alliances made little headway in persuading the Democrats to embrace the Alliance agenda. At Alliance meetings in Cincinnati in May 1891 and St. Louis in February 1892, debate over the formation of a third party raged. Alliance leader Leonidas L. Polk exhorted those attending the St. Louis convention to turn their backs on the old standard bearers. "The time has arrived," he said, "for the great West, the great South, and the great Northwest, to link their hands and hearts together and march to the ballot box and take possession of the government . . . We want relief from these unjust oppressions, and . . . we intend to have it if we have to wipe the two old parties from the face of the earth!" Among those hearing Polk's message were Alliance men and women, former Greenbackers, members of the Knights of Labor (including Terence Powderly), temperance advocates, and woman suffragists. By the end of the St. Louis gathering, an agreement had been made to meet again in July 1892 in Omaha, Nebraska as the People's party.

The People's Party

Modeling itself after the other major political parties, the People's party approved an official set of principles and nominated candidates for the presidency and vice presidency at their first national convention in Omaha. There the similarities to the old parties seemed to end. Women orators addressed the convention, including Mary Elizabeth Lease of Kansas, famous for her fiery demand that farmers "raise less corn and more hell." The 1,400 delegates approved a platform that included familiar agrarian demands for the subtreasury "or a better system," the secret ballot, a graduated income tax, and "the free and unlimited coinage of silver and gold at the present legal ratio of sixteen to one." But the platform went beyond these then familiar causes to voice a more sweeping and radical critique of the status quo. In a bid to address the concerns of labor, the platform called for an eight-hour day and an end to the use of private armies by corporations attempting to put down strikes. The populists also endorsed not simply regulation but government ownership of the railroads and the telegraph and telephone system. These bold stands set off waves of political excitement and enthusiasm when they were presented to the convention as a whole. "The old parties go wild over their candidates," the convention chairman observed. "We go wild over our principles."

The principles, in fact, seemed more worthy of ardor than the populist's presidential and vice presidential candidates. James B. Weaver, a former Greenbacker who had been a familiar third-party candidate, led the ticket. James G. Field, a former major in the Confederate Army, was selected as the vice-presidential nominee. Weaver campaigned hard, if relatively colorlessly, in the West, the South, and across the Great Plains. But the fledgling People's party was never able to overcome the formidable obstacles to it raised by entrenched party politics. Southern Democrats, in an appeal to white racial prejudices, attacked the tentative biracial coalitions that had formed between some white and black Alliances. In some areas, the populists themselves used violence to prevent African Americans from backing anyone other than their third party candidates. Few industrial workers in the Northeast rallied to the populist cause. In the end, it proved difficult to wrest support away from the established political parties.

Even so, the birth of the People's party marked a significant moment in American political history. The Party challenged the Republican and Democratic lock on electoral politics. It offered a clear statement of political goals that was starkly different from anything either major party would consider. Further, it mobilized men and women across the nation into a powerful reform crusade. When the votes were counted, Weaver had polled more than 1 million votes, 8.5 percent of the total, and carried six mountain and plains states. For the first time since the Civil War, a third political party had won electoral votes—twenty-two in all. Nearly 1,500 populist candidates won election to seats in state legislatures. The party elected three governors, five senators, and ten congressmen. There was no national victory to celebrate in 1892, but the first test of the People's party hardly seemed a defeat.

CHAPTER THREE

The Crisis of the 1890s

~

Not since the Civil War had Americans experienced so profound a sense of national crisis as they did in the 1890s. Long-simmering grievances exploded as the nation experienced the worst depression in its history to that point beginning in 1893. Widespread labor unrest culminated in a wave of strikes in 1894 and fresh outbreaks of violence. The party system, once a symbol of post–Civil War political stability, was rocked by the challenge of populism. For all the riches industrial development had contributed to the United States, the crises of the 1890s revealed another, darker side to its dominance.

DEPRESSION AND THE INDUSTRIAL ECONOMY

The Depression of 1893 was not the nation's first experience with a slump in its economy. Instability had in fact become a predictable, if unwelcome, feature of the industrial age. In 1873 the country experienced a "panic" that did not fully recede until 1879. Three years later another less severe depression began that persisted into 1885. Waves of bank failures, collapsing businesses, wage declines, and industrial layoffs punctuated the business cycle throughout the 1870s and 1880s. But nothing prepared the American people for the severity of the Depression of the 1890s, which gave them their first real experience of mass industrial unemployment. For a growing number of citizens, optimism in the nation's future became one of the Depression's early casualties.

The Panic of 1893

The Depression began with the failure of two major corporations and a resulting plunge of the stock market in the spring of 1893. The Philadelphia and Reading Railroad collapsed first. Unable to meet payments on loans it had secured from British banks, the company declared bankruptcy. Two months later, the National Cordage Company, another industrial giant, failed as well. Taken together, the two collapsed businesses triggered a crash of the stock market that led in turn to a wave of bank failures. The resulting contraction of credit worsened economic conditions as other businesses, unable to secure credit, fell into bankruptcy. What had begun as an apparently isolated business failure soon became an economic catastrophe.

In fact, there were deeper and more long-term causes of the Depression of 1893. Since 1887 plummeting agricultural prices had weakened the purchasing power of farmers, thereby eroding the strength of the economy. Depressed economic conditions in Europe had shrunk the market for American goods abroad and resulted in a withdrawal of gold by foreign investors. The rapid expansion of the railroads and many other major industries began to outstrip market demand. The health of the American economy, and activity on Wall Street, remained highly dependent upon the railroads. Given the growing interconnectedness of its economy, the nation could ill afford serious reversals in its largest and most important corporations.

Partly as a result of the economy's interdependence, the panic that began in 1893 spread with startling speed. In six months, more than 8,000 businesses, 156 railroads, and 400 banks failed. The already declining agricultural prices fell further. By the winter of 1894, approximately twenty percent of the labor force was out of work. In the nation's major cities thousands walked the streets searching for work. Homeless men and women slept in city parks. In December of 1893 a poem in a workingman's newspaper described the "fearful line of haggard men" who haunted "each public street, / that they may chance for wife and child to get a crust to eat." A leading financial newspaper of the time described the 1893 downturn nearly as apocalyptically: "The month of August will long remain memorable in our industrial history. Never before has there been such a sudden and striking cessation of industrial activity. Nor is any section of the country exempt from paralysis." As the economic malaise reached into the lives of millions of Americans, social and political unrest began to mount.

Coxey's Army

For the many unemployed Americans, the Depression was a desperate time. Without broad-based programs of unemployment insurance or relief, men and women out of work were forced to rely on private charity, the kindness of their neighbors, mutual benefit societies, and, far more commonly, their own resourcefulness. Private charities could not begin to cope with the consequences of joblessness on a national scale. As they attempted to make the most of paltry funds, civic leaders pondered the distinction between the "deserving" poor—those idle because of social and economic conditions—and the "undeserving" poor—those who were, they believed, poor because of indolence. These debates did little to address the pressing needs of unemployed men and women, who scrambled to find odd jobs so that they could feed their families. In Massachusetts a blinding snowstorm in the winter of 1893–1894 provided momentary relief for several hundred men hired as snow shovelers to cope with the emergency.

Before long, the unemployed began to demand relief. In the fall of 1893, bands of unemployed men formed "industrial armies" some several hundred strong, clambered aboard trains in the West and rode the rails from place to place searching for work. Inspired by the idea, Ohio businessman and populist Jacob S. Coxey and his associate Carl Browne decided in 1894 to organize a living petition, "a petition in boots," that would lobby the Congress for unemployment relief. The Congress had already spurned Coxey's proposal that the government expand the currency by issuing non–interest bearing bonds. He now hoped to win support for a more ambitious bill that would inflate the money supply and pay the unemployed $1.50 a day to build roads. The public works program would, Coxey believed, provide relief to all those who needed work. To dramatize his cause, Coxey gathered an army of 100 unemployed men and women and set out for Washington on Easter Sunday in 1894.

"Coxey's Army," as the band became known, expected to pick up thousands of supporters en route to the nation's capitol for a May Day rally on the steps of Congress. With his wife and children—including his baby, Legal Tender Coxey—at his side, Coxey had gathered some 500 supporters by the time his army reached Washington. Industrial armies from various parts of the country planned to join Coxey's Army there, including one from San Francisco that numbered among its marchers the young Jack London, later a celebrated writer. Before most of these far-flung demonstrators even arrived in Washington, however, Coxey had been arrested for walking on the grass as he prepared to speak from the steps of the Capitol. A riot followed, and police herded Coxey's supporters into camps outside the Capitol where they were essentially quarantined, ostensibly to protect the public health. By August, when government officials dispersed the group, some 1,200 people had joined the army.

Coxey's demands for federal job relief fell on deaf ears in the United States Congress, but the march of Coxey's Army left an indelible impression on many who encountered this mass demonstration of the unemployed. On the long trek to Washington, supporters turned out to greet the marchers and offer provisions. In working-class towns such as Homestead, Pennsylvania, enthusiasm was especially strong. The march also attracted national attention to the plight of the unemployed, as reporters covered the dramatic appeal of Coxey's Army. In this way, middle-class and well-to-do Americans received graphic depictions of the anguish the Depression had visited upon many working people. A cub reporter named Ray Stannard Baker, who later achieved fame as a muckraking journalist,

COXEY'S ARMY. Ray Stannard Baker took this photograph of Coxey's Army as it paused at a toll gate in 1894 on its way to Washington, D.C.

described for the *Chicago Record* the pitiful suffering he had observed during the winter of 1893. The Depression had brought "unprecedented extremes of poverty, unemployment, unrest," Baker wrote. "Every day during that bitter winter the crowds of ragged, shivering, hopeless human beings in Chicago seemed to increase." Coxey's Army, Baker observed, was a "miracle" that brought to life "the prevailing unrest and dissatisfaction among the laboring classes." That unrest only deepened as the depression wore on.

The Pullman Strike

Frustration with wage cuts, industrial stagnation, and unemployment boiled over in the dramatic Pullman Strike of 1894. The strike began at the Pullman Palace Car Company, which manufactured sleeping and parlor cars for railroads at a plant near Chicago. There the company also built a 600-acre "model town" in an effort to create a stable, ordered environment for its labor force. Company-owned housing, churches, and stores dotted the town of Pullman; saloons and alcohol were conspicuous for their absence. This paternalistic community re-flected the views of George Pullman, its founder, who often referred to the workers as his "children." Chastened by the Great Railway Strike of 1877, Pullman vowed to serve as "landlord and employer" to those who worked for the Pullman Palace Car Company. Pullman was a town, the company claimed, "where all that is ugly, and discordant and demoralizing is eliminated."

The Panic of 1893 shattered Pullman's bucolic image of the town and his familial rhetoric. The entrepreneur responded to the Depression conditions by firing a third of his workers and cutting the wages of those who remained by an average of twenty-eight percent. At the same time, Pullman refused to reduce rents in his model town, which ran twenty to twenty-five percent higher than those for comparable lodging in surrounding areas. Food prices at the company store were similarly high; they were not reduced either. Wage cuts and layoffs left many workers unable to meet these costs. In desperation, a group of workers tried to persuade the corporation to restore their wages to 1892 levels. When they failed to win concessions, the workers at Pullman walked out in the spring of 1894.

The battle that followed pitted the powerful American Railway Union, an industry-wide labor organization led by Eugene V. Debs, against the Pullman

EUGENE V. DEBS. Eugene V. Debs, head of the American Railway Union, was imprisoned for his activities during the Pullman Strike. He soon became convinced socialism provided the best solution to the plight of American workers. During the early twentieth century he ran for president five times on the Socialist party ticket. His largest showing—6% of the popular vote—was in 1912.

company, a consortium of twenty-four Chicago railroads, and eventually the federal government. When Pullman declined to negotiate with the ARU, Debs ordered his union membership to refuse to work on any train that carried a Pullman car. The result was a walkout of thousands of railroad workers in twenty-seven states and territories that virtually paralyzed rail transportation running through Chicago. The railroad workers saw in the sympathy strike a powerful tool for wringing concessions from their employers.

What followed was an extraordinary intervention by the federal government and the judiciary into the battle between labor and capital. After Illinois Governor John Peter Altgeld refused to call out the state militia to break the strike, the railroads enlisted the aid of the U.S. government. President Grover Cleveland and his Attorney General Richard Olney, a former railroad lawyer, sided with the railroad operators by endorsing their contention (hotly denied by the ARU) that the strikers were interfering with delivery of the U.S. mail. At Olney's request, a federal court issued an injunction ordering the strikers back to work. "We have been brought to the ragged edge of anarchy," the Attorney General warned, "and it is time to see whether the law is sufficiently strong to prevent this condition of affairs." In cities across the nation, federal judges responded similarly with over 100 decrees against the strikers issued nationwide. Cleveland then directed U.S. troops to Chicago to restore order; riots among strikers, sympathizers, army troops, and the Chicago police broke out instead. When Debs and his associates defied the injunction, they were arrested and imprisoned.

A year later, in the case of *In re Debs* (1895), the U.S. Supreme Court upheld the injunctions and the contempt convictions against the ARU leaders. Debs's young lawyer, Clarence Darrow, argued passionately before the Court that the crushing power of industry not only justified but necessitated a workers' alliance. The Court disagreed. "The strong arm of the National Government," Justice David Brewer's majority opinion read, "may be put forth to brush away all obstructions to the freedom of interstate commerce or the transportation of the mails . . . the army of the Nation, and all its militia, are at the service of the Nation to compel obedience to its laws." Government intervention not only succeeded in breaking the strike; it forced labor activists to reconsider their tactics. After serving his six-month prison term, Debs became convinced that socialism provided the best hope for America's working people. Class-based organization had to continue at any cost. "They might as well try to stop Niagra with a feather as to crush the spirit of organization in this country," he asserted. More conservative labor leaders such as AFL President Samuel Gompers concluded otherwise. The cost of mass industry-wide sympathy strikes such as Pullman, Gompers believed, was too high. Gompers redoubled his efforts to pursue change through the more restrained tactics of the trade union movement. However labor leaders positioned themselves, few could fail to be sobered by the combined weight of law, government, and business brought down upon their movement during the Depression of 1893.

Social Criticism and Antimonopoly

The rebellion of labor had its intellectual counterpart in the fierce social criticism that surfaced during the 1890s. Hard times sharpened attacks on monopoly and attracted public attention to the critical writing of reform journalists. The 1894 publication of journalist Henry Demarest Lloyd's *Wealth Against Commonwealth* serves as a case in point. A devastating critique of the cut-throat power of monopolies, the book used public records to detail the devious workings of huge corporations, most notably the Standard Oil Company. Lloyd paid particular attention to business corruption of politics. Combination and monopoly led inexorably, Lloyd argued, to the erosion of political power among the mass of Americans. Large companies were purchasing political favors from corrupt legislators. In fact, Lloyd insisted, "the Standard has done everything with the Pennsylvania Legislature except to refine it." Describing the great industrialists as "barbarians," he viewed with amazement the accumulation of power and wealth among them. "Our great moneymakers," he wrote, "have sprung in one generation into seats of power kings do not know."

By the time Lloyd published his book, there was already a rich literature criticizing the advance of industrialization and inspiring a large following. One of the most influential studies, *Progress and Poverty*, came from lay economist and reformer Henry George in 1879. George's ideas initially took form as he was struggling to find a place for his talents as a writer and typographer in California during the depression of the 1870s. As he looked around at the stark contrast between wealth and poverty in northern California, he began to dwell upon the paradox of poverty in the midst of plenty. "This association of poverty with progress is the great enigma of our times," he wrote. "So long as all the increased wealth which modern progress brings goes but to build up great fortunes, to increase luxury and make sharper the contrast between the House of Have and the House of Want, progress is not real and cannot be permanent."

George believed increasing land values played a crucial role in producing social and economic inequality. Land values rose, he argued, not primarily from the efforts of individual owners but from population growth and from the social development that surrounded private property. In this context, the wealth accrued from rising land values constituted an "unearned increment" that rightfully belonged to the whole community. George proposed confiscating funds derived from increased market values by means of a "single tax." The program would, George believed, help destroy monopolies, distribute wealth more equitably, and eliminate poverty. Largely dismissed by academic experts, George and his ideas nevertheless developed a tremendous following in the 1880s. The single-tax movement attracted scores of middle class and laboring people, some of whom supported George in a strong but ultimately unsuccessful third party bid in the New York City mayoral race in 1886.

Edward Bellamy's utopian novel *Looking Backward* (1888) also sparked reform enthusiasm. Bellamy portrayed Boston in the year 2000 as a place transformed by a peaceful revolution, which had given birth to a new society and economy. The result strongly resembled state socialism, but Bellamy labeled the new system Nationalism. Whatever the term, the future as Bellamy described it bore none of the scars of late–nineteenth century battles between labor and capital. Abundance, productivity, and harmony pervaded the suspiciously agrarian-like environment of the modern city. Bellamy's vision had enormous appeal for many Americans in the late nineteenth century. Nationalist clubs appeared across America. Like the Single Taxers, the Bellamyites contributed to the spread of reform enthusiasm and fed the hopes of the People's party.

The writings of George, Bellamy, and Lloyd were especially significant because they shaped, and indeed helped make possible, a spirited public debate about the impact of industrialism. No single essay or piece of literature alone determined public opinion. For every critic of monopoly, the industrialists enjoyed many defenders. Rather, social criticism fed political activism, and vice versa.

THE UPHEAVAL OF DEMOCRATIC POLITICS

The social and economic unrest that accompanied the depression of the 1890s created an upheaval in American party politics. Before the Panic of 1893 had even begun, populists had mounted a potent challenge to the party system and to the ideologies that shaped it. Economic stagnation, unemployment, industrial unrest, and wide-scale hardship greatly broadened the potential appeal of the People's party. In the end, the old parties weathered the storm of populism and emerged, if not unscathed, at least triumphant. But debate continued to rage about the extent of economic equality, the distribution of power, and the workings of democratic politics.

The "Money Question"

Long before the Panic of 1893, the "money question" had become a major issue in American politics. Throughout the nineteenth century, thoughtful Americans had disagreed about how much and what kind of money should be in circulation and who should control decisions about currency. The United States financed the Civil War in part through issuing "greenbacks," paper currency that could not be converted to specie (precious metal) during the war. After the war ended, disagreement arose over what to do with the greenbacks—whether to keep them in circulation or retire them by making them convertible to gold. In 1875, Congress voted to retire the greenbacks, over the frenzied objections of farmers and others who wanted to keep cheap currency in circulation. The "greenback movement" thus became a precursor to a long battle over the currency that continued through the rest of the century. In the 1890s, as prices fell and debt mounted, pressure for an inflated currency increased.

By then, the issue had come to center on the place of silver in the nation's currency. From the time of the nation's founding, gold and silver had been recognized as money; the traditional value ratio was sixteen ounces of silver to one ounce of gold. By the 1830s the price of silver had risen so much that silver miners saw greater advantage in selling the metal on the open market rather than presenting it to the mint for coinage. In 1873, Congress discontinued the coinage of silver. At the time, their action seemed to many to be a simple recognition of reality; silver was no longer being used for coinage even before the law was passed. Before long, however, falling prices dropped the market value of silver well below the official mint ratio of sixteen to one, and made the metal available for coinage once again. Advocates of cheap money, along with silver miners, "began referring to the law as the 'crime of '73.'"

Silver now became a battle cry for many (who became known as "soft money" advocates) who endorsed an inflated currency. Although Congress remonetized silver in 1878 through the Bland-Allison Act, the issue would not die. Bound up in fundamental conflicts about access to credit, the flow of money in the American economy, the pressure of debt, and international monetary policies, currency remained a highly contentious and deeply symbolic issue in American politics. Populists embraced silver as "the people's money" and labeled gold the currency of monopolists. Financial leaders and others (known as "hard money" supporters) identified the gold standard with fiscal responsibility and stability.

The Depression of 1893 escalated tensions over the government's currency policy. To stop the flow of gold out of the U.S. Treasury, Congress repealed the Sherman Silver Purchase Act in 1894 at President Cleveland's behest. The legislation had required the Treasury to make monthly purchases of silver; the Treasury notes the government used for purchasing silver were redeemed in gold. Cleveland believed the silver purchase policy was forcing gold reserves down to fiscally irresponsible levels. But his decision to seek repeal of the Sherman Silver Purchase Act simply fanned the flames of the agrarian revolt. Southern and western Democrats railed against the president's gold policy and renewed the cry for the free coinage of silver at a ratio to gold of sixteen to one. That demand now seemed to express the fears and aspirations of many who struggled under the weight of the depression and looked for solutions in a more activist government.

The Populist Insurgency

The debate over currency had a complicated relationship to the populist insurgency. The Omaha Platform had endorsed the demand for the free and unlimited coinage of silver at a ratio of sixteen to one. As it was intended to, that position attracted silverites with little allegiance to the broader ideals of the populist movement. Many populists insisted that even unlimited coinage of silver could do little to remedy the inequalities that "the producing classes" suffered in

FEARS OF RADICALISM. Illinois Governor John Peter
Altgeld's pardoning in 1893 of three anarchists convicted
for the 1886 Haymarket bombing was still fresh in the
minds of many during the election of 1896. Altgeld led his
state's delegation to the Democratic Convention, which
was held in Chicago that year, and he had great influence
over the party's platform, which included a demand for free
silver. Far more threatening to many, however, were the
other goals Altgeld and the platform endorsed, among them
an income tax, support for labor's rights, and civil liberties.
This *Harper's Weekly* cartoon depicts Altgeld as a
deranged anarchist hiding behind the mask of the
respectable and earnest Democratic nominee for
president, William Jennings Bryan.

the new industrial economy. They feared that too close an identification with the
silver issue would detract attention from their larger message and interfere with
their efforts to broaden the new party's base.

The 1894 elections demonstrated, however, how difficult it would be to
expand the populist constituency. In Illinois, site of the Pullman Strike and
home to a vibrant reform community in Chicago, efforts to build a labor–
populist alliance failed miserably. Some industrial workers remained loyal to
the state Democratic party of Governor John Peter Altgeld, widely perceived

as a friend of labor for his pardon in 1893 of three anarchists convicted of an 1886 bombing in Chicago's Haymarket Square. Many others voted Republican in a stinging rebuke of Cleveland's handling of the depression economy. On the Great Plains and in the mountain states of the West, the Republicans surged ahead of the populists. In Kansas, long a center of populist enthusiasm, internecine warfare among devotees of the People's party, as well as a controversial populist legislative record, weakened the Party there. The populists fared much better in the South but at a high cost. By emphasizing the silver issue, populists attempted to attract middle-class Democrats who were enraged at the Cleveland administration. In some states, the populists fused with candidates from the Democratic party. In so doing, they downplayed their larger reform agenda in favor of the money question and dulled the distinctive appeal of their third party initiative.

The election of 1896 forced the hand of the populists. Postponing their convention until after the two major parties met, leaders of the People's party decided to take their cue from the actions of the Republicans and Democrats. The Republicans selected Governor William McKinley of Ohio as their presidential candidate. He accepted the mandate of his party and ran on a platform that voiced strong adherence to the gold standard.

The real drama occurred at the Democratic Convention in Chicago, the scene of an epic struggle among southern and western delegates, many of them silverites, and conservative eastern Democrats, fiercely committed to the gold standard. A divided platform committee submitted two reports to the convention. The majority report, drawn up by westerners and southerners for the most part, called for tariff reduction, an income tax, "stricter control" of trusts and railroads, and free silver. A minority report drafted by the party's eastern wing rejected free silver unless its coinage was endorsed by a highly unlikely international agreement—a position that resembled that of the Republicans.

In an electrifying moment, thirty-six-year-old William Jennings Bryan, a lawyer, journalist, and former congressman from Nebraska, mounted the podium to speak for the silver Democrats. "If they dare to come out in the open and defend the gold standard as a good thing," he proclaimed passionately, "we will fight them to the uttermost." Running his hands down from his face to mimic flowing blood, Bryan continued: "Having behind us the producing masses of this nation and the world, supported by the commercial interests, the laboring interests and the toilers everywhere, we will answer their demand for a gold standard by saying to them: 'You shall not press down upon the brow of labor this crown of thorn; you shall not crucify mankind upon a cross of gold.'" At the finish, Bryan stood before his rapt audience with his arms outstretched as if crucified. For sheer drama and oratorical power, "the cross of gold" speech had few, if any, equals in modern American political history.

The convention ended in the nomination of Bryan as the standard bearer for the Democrats. He was, and remains, the youngest person ever nominated for president by a major party. One Republican, when asked if he thought the name

WILLIAM JENNINGS BRYAN.   William Jennings Bryan
delivered one of the great speeches in American political
history at the Democratic Convention in 1896. At 36 years
old, Bryan captivated the convention with his "Cross of
Gold" speech, even though not everyone was entirely
clear about the oration's meaning.

"Boy Orator of the Platte" was an apt one for Bryan, said yes because the Platte
River in Nebraska was six inches deep and six miles wide at the mouth. But
Bryan's admirers rightly sensed the essential appeal of the young Democrat and
dubbed him "the Great Commoner." "Bryan," said one senator, "is more of a
Populist than a Democrat. . . . There was nothing left of the Democratic Party
at Chicago but the name." But in reality, Bryan's "populism" ran little deeper
than his commitment to free silver; he had no real interest in the rest of the populist agenda. His running mate, Arthur Sewell, was a banker from Maine who
both supported free silver and represented the interests of eastern Democrats.

For the populists, the choice was now one between staking a bold claim as
an alternative to the status quo or fusing with the Democrats. The heart, soul,
and future of the People's party hung in the balance. At their convention in
St. Louis, "fusionists" battled "purists," both sides employing every political
trick in their arsenals. In the end, the populists nominated Bryan for president
but rejected Sewell as his running mate and selected the Georgia populist Tom
Watson instead. Bryan had already brushed aside any suggestion of dropping
Sewell from the ticket; Watson later denounced the populist leaders who had
forged the party's ill-begotten ticket. Nor was it clear to Democratic leaders that
Bryan would profit from the populist endorsement. In defending Sewell, the
chairman of the Democratic party snidely suggested the populists "could go with
the Negroes, where they belong." The chaotic campaign that followed rang the

death knell for the populists. At the state level, populists fragmented in a thousand different directions, choosing fusion with the Democrats in some states, rejecting it in others, and in a few southern states, forging a contorted alliance with Republicans in state elections and with the Democrats for president. It became difficult to know what it meant to be a populist.

The Republican Triumph

The campaign of 1896 represented the triumph of organizational politics. Appalled at the prospect of a Bryan victory, the business and financial community contributed lavishly to the Republican campaign, which spent well over $4 million to secure victory, as opposed to the $300,000 expended by the Democrats. Ohio businessman turned party leader Marcus A. Hanna managed an unusually aggressive public relations effort. Millions of pamphlets were issued in an effort to advance a campaign steeped in "educational" politics. At the same time, the Republicans used crude polls to track voting strength. Huge corporate contributions filled the coffers of the McKinley campaign. All the while McKinley himself, as was the custom, remained aloof from the fray, speaking occasionally from his front porch in Canton, Ohio. Voters came to the candidate, including some 80,000 on a single day in September; the candidate did not go to them.

Bryan, on the other hand, stumped in twenty-seven states, speaking thirty-six times a day on some occasions. He made his case to over 5 million Americans, and he helped establish the modern form of presidential politics by violating a

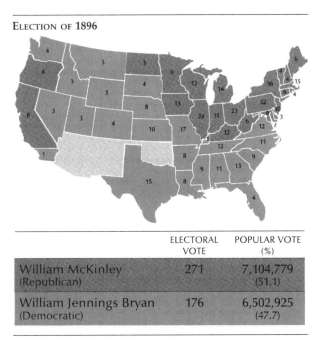

ELECTION OF 1896

	ELECTORAL VOTE	POPULAR VOTE (%)
William McKinley (Republican)	271	7,104,779 (51.1)
William Jennings Bryan (Democratic)	176	6,502,925 (47.7)

longstanding tradition by which presidential candidates remained aloof from their own campaigns (by which they "stood" for office rather than "running" for it). His approach antagonized some voters who considered his campaign undignified.

On election day, voters gave McKinley and the Republican party a decisive victory. Bryan won some 6.5 million votes, more than any previous Democrat, but they were not enough to best McKinley's 7.1 million. Although Bryan won every southern state except Kentucky and West Virginia, he fared poorly in the East and the Midwest. Traditional populist strongholds in the mountain states and on the Plains supported the Democrats. But McKinley swept the cities. Populist fusion candidates rolled up some notable victories; seven senators and thirty congressmen won on a populist, fusion, or Silver Party ticket. But in the end, the election of 1896 crushed the third-party initiative. As Tom Watson put it: "Our party, as a party, does not exist any more. Fusion has well nigh killed it. The sentiment is there, but confidence is gone." A Texas populist blamed the party's defeat on a sad collection of circumstances. "Owing to the mistakes of the past, the treachery of those we chose to lead us in 1896 and conditions over which even those had no control, we are wrecked, and cast away on strange shores." Those shores were nothing less than the triumph of Republican politics.

THE PROGRESS OF INEQUALITY

For all the political turmoil of the 1890s, many Americans drew satisfaction from the vitality of democratic politics and the efforts of competing interest groups to make use of the ballot. In an era that had seen more than its share of violence and bellicose rhetoric, there was something reassuring about the customary workings of political democracy. For some Americans, however, the decade of the 1890s tightened the noose of political, social, and economic inequality. Native Americans confronted increased efforts throughout the late nineteenth century to dissolve tribal life. The conflict resulted in a bloody show-down in 1890 at Wounded Knee. For African Americans, the decade brought a legal affirmation of segregation in the monumental 1896 U.S. Supreme Court decision *Plessy* v. *Ferguson*. In both cases, these events were symptomatic of deep-seated racial tensions in American society that would persist into the twentieth century.

Wounded Knee

The massacre at Wounded Knee marked a bloody denouement, of sorts, to decades of conflict between Native Americans and white settlers on the western frontier. By the 1890s that conflict had led to the concentration of most Indian tribes, whether of eastern origin or indigenous to the Plains and Southwest, on reservations west of the Mississippi. Administered by the Bureau of Indian Affairs, these reservations did not end the land hunger among white Americans that had led to their creation in the first place. Nor did they terminate hostilities between white settlers and the army, and the tribes. Much of the sustained warfare had ended, however, with the conclusion of the Apache wars in the 1880s. What remained were enduring problems for a nation that remained uncertain about the status of those who had first inhabited America.

The post–Civil War period brought an array of possible solutions to what whites called the "Indian problem." Renewed enthusiasm for enforced assimilation of Native American tribes surfaced among an array of interest groups. White ranchers, railroad operators, farmers, and other settlers cast covetous eyes on Indian reservations, eager for access to the tribal lands. Reformers sympathetic to the plight of the tribes viewed the Indian removal to western reservations as a form of enforced segregation from the mainstream of American society. According to these critics, collective ownership of land only furthered the isolation of Native Americans from the values, mores, and social customs of the prevailing white society. Members of the Indian Rights Association, founded in 1882, advocated a reform program of individual land ownership, the conferral of citizenship, and social integration for Native Americans. Opponents of assimilation, often stressing the lack of "civilization" among tribal groups, argued strenuously for the continued separation of Native Americans from the dominant society.

In 1887, finally, Congress approved the Dawes Severalty Act (1887), which called for dispersing tribal lands and speeding up the integration of Indians into American society. The legislation encouraged surrender of tribal holdings in exchange for individual land allotments and American citizenship. It provided for grants of 160 acres per family head, eighty acres per single adult or orphan, and forty acres to each dependent child. An important qualification, however, mandated that the new landholders would not receive full title to their lands for twenty-five years. When the Dawes Act was passed, Native American tribes held approximately 138 million acres. By the close of the century some 78 million acres remained in tribal hands. Efforts by the Bureau of Indian Affairs to administer the Act led to incidents of terrible cruelty, including attempts to rescind custody of Native American children, repress ancestral rites, and eradicate traditional modes of tribal living.

In this embattled context, a millennial religious revival emerged among some western Indians in the late 1880s. The movement began on a Nevada reservation, where a Paiute named Wovoka preached the coming of the messiah in the body of an Indian. Rich soil, clear streams, and endless herds of buffalo would renew the earth on a land inhabited by Indians. White men would be buried, while Indians who had participated in an ecstatic ritual known as the "Ghost Dance" would be reunited on earth with the spirits of their ancestors.

The prophesy and the Ghost Dance spread rapidly among many reservations, with particularly great intensity among the Sioux. Mystified and then alarmed by the duration and fervency of this religious enthusiasm, white agents called for troops to suppress the Ghost Dance among the Sioux. Several Native American leaders were singled out for tolerating the Ghost Dance. Sitting Bull, a revered Sioux leader, was killed during an altercation with Indian agents who were attempting to arrest him. Meanwhile several hundred Sioux fled to the Badlands, led by Big Foot, who became ill on the march with pneumonia and began hemorrhaging. The Seventh Cavalry caught up with the band of fleeing Indians and their weakened leader in Wounded Knee, South Dakota in December 1890. The soldiers had disarmed most of their captives when a shot was fired—whether by a Native American or a white remains a matter of dispute. Unambiguous was the massacre that quickly followed as the army's machine guns and rifles pierced the air. When it was over, more than 200 Native Americans, including many women and children, lay dead in the snow alongside some forty white soldiers.

The Massacre at Wounded Knee marked the end of the long military encounter that had pitted white soldiers against Native Americans for over a century. There would be no more pitched battles on the receding frontier. For many Native Americans, the massacre represented a final tragic act in a brutal expropriation of land and country. "I did not know then how much was ended," Black Elk later said of Wounded Knee. "I can still see the butchered women and children lying heaped and scattered all along the crooked gulch as plain as when I saw them with eyes still young. And I can see that something else died there in the

WOUNDED KNEE MASSACRE.   Soldiers bury slain Native Americans in a gulch at Wounded Knee, South Dakota after the 1890 massacre. The event marked the close of a long and bloody era in the history of white settlement and Indian removal.

bloody mud, and was buried in the blizzard. A people's dream died there." But if many Native American dreams died at Wounded Knee, the struggle to define the place of the tribes in America did not. It would continue through the twentieth century.

The Rise of Jim Crow

In the South in the late nineteenth century, state governments devised an elaborate legal structure to ensure the separation of the races. The system they constructed became known as "Jim Crow." By the early years of the twentieth century, this rigid system of social segregation, inscribed by law, reached into almost every area of southern life. Blacks and whites could not ride together in the same railroad cars, sit in the same waiting rooms, use the same washrooms, eat in the same restaurants, or sit in the same theaters. Blacks had no access to many public parks, beaches, picnic areas; many hospitals would not admit them. Much of the new legal structure did no more than confirm what had already been widespread social practice in the South since well before the end of Reconstruction. But the Jim Crow laws also stripped blacks of many of the modest social, economic, and political gains they had made in the more fluid atmosphere of the late nineteenth century.

One of the reasons for this newly vigorous effort by whites to separate the races was that the system of white supremacy they had created after the Civil War was beginning to seem unstable. The spread of railroads, the growth of industry, and the movement of black men and women from the countryside to the city had created a new dynamic in southern race relations. Older forms of control—the ability of landlords and country merchants to dominate tenants and debtors—were not easy to replicate in towns and cities. African Americans there were more independent. The Jim Crow system was in part an effort to reinforce a system of control that seemed in danger of eroding.

Many black southerners fought Jim Crow from the beginning. One area in which there was resistance was the growing web of laws segregating the railroads, which nine southern states passed between 1887 and 1891. The laws themselves came partly in response to the unwillingness of many blacks to accept railroad policies barring them from first-class cars and requiring them to surrender their seats to whites on crowded trains. Some African Americans had successfully sued for the right to travel unrestricted, so the state legislatures moved to formalize the contested railroad policies. Even then, resistance continued, as events in Louisiana made clear.

Louisiana passed a railroad segregation law in 1890 over the objections of eighteen black legislators who fought the bill. In 1892, as part of a plan devised by black leaders in New Orleans and white lawyers sympathetic to them, Homer Adolph Plessy, a black man, challenged Louisiana's Jim Crow law. Plessy boarded a white car on the East Louisiana Railroad and refused to leave when asked to do so by a conductor. Although Plessy argued that Louisiana's Jim Crow law violated the Fourteenth Amendment, Judge John H. Ferguson ruled against him. The U.S. Supreme Court agreed to hear the case on appeal.

In 1896, the Supreme Court issued its later infamous ruling in *Plessy* v. *Ferguson*. Deciding seven to one against Plessy, the Court upheld the constitutionality of Louisiana's railroad segregation law. Laws prescribing segregation, the Court found, "do not necessarily imply the inferiority of either race to the other." The enforced separation of the races, Justice Henry Brown wrote, did nothing to stamp "the colored race with a badge of inferiority. If this be so, it is not by reason of anything found in the act, but solely because the colored race chooses to put that construction upon it." As long as equal accommodations were provided, states could mandate separate accommodations. The Court also weighed in on the larger question of racial equality, and in so doing affirmed prevailing notions of white supremacy. "If one race be inferior to the other socially, the Constitution of the United States cannot put them on the same plane."

In a prescient dissent, Justice John Marshall Harlan likened the "pernicious" majority opinion to the Dred Scott case. Harlan warned that race relations would suffer for generations to come. "The present decision," he wrote,

it may well be apprehended, will not only stimulate aggressions, more or less brutal and irritating, upon the admitted rights of colored citizens, but will encourage the belief that it is possible, by means of state enactments, to defeat the beneficent purposes which the people of the United States had in view when they adopted the recent amendments of the Constitution. . . . Sixty millions of whites are in no danger from the presence here of eight millions of blacks. The destinies of the two races, in this country, are indissolubly linked together, and the interests of both require that the common government of all shall not permit the seeds of race hate to be planted under the sanction of law.

Three years later, however, when the Supreme Court ruled on segregation in public schools, Harlan saw no constitutional violation in Georgia's Jim Crow law. By that time, legalized segregation was becoming well entrenched throughout the South.

Segregation spread in tandem with efforts to disenfranchise African-American voters, thus removing a critical remedy that might have undermined the advance of social and economic inequality. In 1890, the Congress debated a bill favored by many Republicans to protect black voting rights. The proposed Federal Elections Act of 1890 provided for federal supervision of federal elections if 100 or more voters in a district so requested. The legislation, one senator warned, was "the last opportunity that will be afforded us in this generation" to make good "the pledges of the past twenty years." But the legislation died in the Senate in the face of adamant opposition from southerners. Instead, state laws restricting voting rights proliferated in the South. Among the tools of disenfranchisement were poll taxes, literacy tests, and grandfather clauses. The latter restricted voting to those whose grandfathers could vote in 1867, before the Fifteenth Amendment guaranteeing voting rights regardless of race was approved. Only whites, of course, met the stipulation. Laws that turned the Democratic primary into a white-only election also appeared in the South. The courts sanctioned, by tolerance if not explicit ruling, these efforts to strip political rights away from blacks. Congress showed little interest in intervening, and most white northerners seemed indifferent to the issue as well.

In part, the disenfranchisement laws, like the segregation laws, were a response to white fears that the system of subjugation they had erected after the war was in danger. Until the 1890s, whites had usually been able to manipulate or control the black vote. But the mobilization of hundreds of thousands of African Americans in the populist movement suggested that these voters might not be as pliant as whites had believed. Fearful they would lose control of the black vote, whites set out to take it away.

One legacy of the 1890s, therefore, was a hardening racial polarization in the South that pervaded society, politics, and the economy. Outside the South, more subtle but also destructive patterns of residential segregation, job discrimination, and racist social attitudes supported the progress of inequality. Taken together, these persistent racial conflicts would continue to bind the twentieth century nation to its nineteenth-century past.

CHAPTER FOUR

Imperialism and Expansionism

∼

A s with many other aspects of American life, the nation's relationship to
the rest of the world at the close of the nineteenth century reflected
both the United States' emergence as a modern industrial society and the
persistence of traditional values and institutions. For much of its history, the
United States had displayed a marked determination to enlarge its borders,
augment its power, and widen its geographical reach. But until the 1890s that
impulse was largely, although not entirely, directed to land that abutted the
established states. Time and again, as Americans moved south and west, the
nation annexed territory settlers had come to occupy, often adding new states to
the country in the process. Whatever conflict such expansionism entailed was
often justified by the notion of "manifest destiny," a phrase first widely used in
the 1840s to express the belief that Americans had a special mission, if not duty,
to spread their way of life across a wild and "uncivilized" frontier. In fact, the
concept conjured up millennial ideas about power and responsibility that dated
back to the Puritan migration in the seventeenth century.

By the 1890s, the boundaries of the nation within the North American continent were largely fixed. The United States had expanded west to the Pacific
Ocean, and there no longer seemed to be any real possibility of expanding south
into Mexico or north into Canada. With little potential left for territorial growth
on the continent, U.S. expansionism moved into a new phase. Expansionism in
the 1890s, the new Manifest Destiny, involved acquiring possessions separate
from the continental United States: island territories, many thickly populated,
most of which would not attract massive settlement from America, few of which
were likely to become states of the Union. Like England, France, Germany, and
other Western industrial powers, the United States looked toward the developing world as a new frontier by the end of the century. In so doing, it struggled
with the benefits and the cost of imperial power.

INTERNATIONAL FRONTIERS

For over two decades after the Civil War, the United States expanded hardly at all. By the 1890s, however, some Americans were ready—indeed, eager—to resume the course of Manifest Destiny that had inspired their ancestors to wrest an empire from Mexico in the expansionist 1840s.

The New Manifest Destiny

Several developments helped shift American attention to lands across the seas. The experience of subjugating the Native American tribes had established a precedent for exerting colonial control over dependent peoples. The concept of the "closing of the frontier," widely heralded by Frederick Jackson Turner and many others in the 1890s, produced fears that natural resources would soon dwindle and that alternative sources must be found abroad. The depression that began in 1893 encouraged some businessmen to look for new markets abroad. The bitter social protests of the time—the populist movement, the free-silver crusade, the bloody labor disputes—led some politicians to urge a more aggressive foreign policy as an outlet for frustrations that would otherwise destabilize domestic life.

Foreign trade was becoming increasingly important to the American economy in the late nineteenth century. The nation's exports had totaled about $392 million worth of goods in 1870; by 1890, the figure was $857 million and by 1900, $1.4 billion. Many Americans began to consider the possibility of acquiring colonies that might expand such markets further. "Today," Senator Albert J. Beveridge of Indiana cried in 1899, "we are raising more than we can consume. Today, we are making more than we can use. Therefore, we must find new markets for our produce, new occupation for our capital, new work for our labor."

Americans were, moreover, well aware of the imperialist fever that was raging through Europe and leading the major powers to partition most of Africa among themselves and turn eager eyes on the Far East and the feeble Chinese empire. Some Americans feared that their nation would soon be left out, that no territory would remain to be acquired. Senator Henry Cabot Lodge of Massachusetts, a leading imperialist, warned that the United States "must not fall out of the line of march."

Scholars and others found a philosophic justification for expansionism in a tortured reinterpretation of the theories of Charles Darwin. They contended that nations or "races," like biological species, struggled constantly for existence and that only the fittest could survive. For strong nations to dominate weak ones was, therefore, in accordance with the laws of nature. (This was an application to world affairs of the same distortion of Darwinism that industrialists and others had long been applying to domestic economic affairs in the form of Social Darwinism.)

One of the first to advance this argument was the popular writer John Fiske, who predicted in an 1885 article in *Harper's Magazine* that the English-speaking peoples would eventually control every land that was not already the seat of an established civilization. The experience of white Americans in subjugating the native population of their own continent, Fiske argued, was "destined to go on" in other parts of the world. Support for Fiske's position came the same year from Josiah Strong, a Congregational clergyman and champion of overseas missionary work. In a book entitled *Our Country: Its Possible Future and Its Present Crisis* (1885), Strong declared that the Anglo-Saxon "race," and especially its American branch, represented the great ideas of civil liberty and pure Christianity and was "divinely commissioned" to spread its institutions over the earth. John W. Burgess, founder of Columbia University's School of Political Science, gave the stamp of scholarly approval to imperialism. In his 1890 study *Political Science and Comparative Law*, he flatly stated that the Anglo-Saxon and Teutonic nations possessed the highest political talents. It was their duty, therefore, to uplift less fortunate peoples, even to force superior institutions on them if necessary. "There is," he wrote, "no human right to the status of barbarism."

The ablest and most effective apostle of imperialism was Alfred Thayer Mahan, a captain and later admiral in the navy. Mahan's thesis—presented in *The Influence of Sea Power upon History* (1890) and other works—was simple: Countries with sea power were the great nations of history; the greatness of the United States, bounded by two oceans, would rest on its ability to control the oceans. The prerequisites for sea power were a productive domestic economy, foreign commerce, a strong merchant marine, a navy to defend trade routes, and colonies, which would provide raw materials and markets and could serve as bases for the navy. Specifically, Mahan advocated that the United States construct a canal across the isthmus of Central America to join the oceans, acquire defensive bases on both sides of the canal in the Caribbean and the Pacific, and take possession of Hawaii and other Pacific islands. "Whether they will or no," he proclaimed, "Americans must now begin to look outward."

Mahan feared the United States did not have a large enough navy to play the great role he envisioned. But during the 1870s and 1880s, the government launched a ship-building program that by 1898 had moved the United States to fifth place among the world's naval powers and, by 1900, to third.

Controlling the Americas

James G. Blaine, who served as secretary of state in two Republican administrations in the 1880s, led early efforts to expand American influence into Latin America, where, Blaine believed, the United States must look for markets for its surplus goods. In October 1889, he helped organize the first Pan-American Congress, which attracted delegates from nineteen nations. The delegates agreed to create the Pan-American Union, a weak international organization located in Washington that served as a clearinghouse for distributing information to the member nations. But they rejected Blaine's more substantive proposals: for an inter-American customs union and arbitration procedures for hemispheric disputes.

The Cleveland administration took a similarly active interest in Latin America. In 1895, it supported Venezuela in a dispute with Great Britain over the boundary between Venezuela and British Guiana. When the British ignored American demands that the matter be submitted to arbitration, Secretary of State Richard Olney charged that Britain was violating the Monroe Doctrine. When Britain still did not act, Cleveland created a special commission to determine the boundary line; if Britain resisted the commission's decision, he insisted, the United States should be willing to go to war to enforce it. As war talk raged throughout the country, the British government finally realized that it had stumbled into a genuine diplomatic crisis and agreed to arbitration.

The Politics of Annexation

The islands of Hawaii in the mid-Pacific had been an important way station for American ships in the China trade since the early nineteenth century. By the 1880s, officers of the expanding American navy were looking covetously at Pearl Harbor on the island of Oahu as a possible permanent base for United States ships. Pressure for an increased American presence in Hawaii was emerging from another source as well: the growing number of Americans who had settled on the islands and who had gradually come to dominate their economic and political life.

In doing so, the Americans were wresting authority away from the leaders of an ancient civilization. Settled by Polynesian people beginning in about 1500 B.C., Hawaii had developed an agricultural and fishing society in which different islands (and different communities on the same islands), each with its own chieftain, lived more or less self-sufficiently. Battles among rival communities were frequent, as ambitious chieftains tried to consolidate power over their neighbors. When the first Americans arrived in Hawaii in the 1790s on merchant ships from New England, there were perhaps a half million people living there.

In 1810, King Kamehameha I established his dominance over the other chieftains on Hawaii. He welcomed American traders and helped them develop a thriving trade between Hawaii and China, from which the natives profited along with the merchants. But Americans soon wanted more than trade. Missionaries began settling there in the early nineteenth century; and in the 1830s, William Hooper, a Boston trader, became the first of many Americans to buy land and establish a sugar plantation on the islands.

The arrival of the merchants, missionaries, and planters was devastating to native Hawaiian society. The newcomers inadvertently brought infectious diseases to which the Hawaiians, like the American Indians before them, were tragically vulnerable. By the mid-nineteenth century, more than half the native population had died. By the turn of the century, disease had cut the population by more than half again. But the Americans brought other incursions as well. Missionaries worked to undermine native religion. Other white settlers introduced liquor, firearms, and a commercial economy, all of which undermined the traditional character of Hawaiian society. By the 1840s, American planters had spread throughout the islands; and an American settler, G. P. Judd, had become prime minister of Hawaii under King Kamehameha III, who had agreed to establish a constitutional monarchy. Judd governed Hawaii for over a decade.

In 1887, the United States negotiated a treaty with Hawaii that permitted them to open a naval base at Pearl Harbor. By then, growing sugar for export to America had become the basis of the Hawaiian economy as a result of an 1875 agreement allowing Hawaiian sugar to enter the United States duty-free. The American-dominated sugar plantation system that resulted not only displaced native Hawaiians from their lands but relied heavily on Asian immigrants as workers, whom the Americans considered more reliable and more docile than the natives. Indeed, finding adequate labor, and keeping it under control, was the principal concern of many planters. Some deliberately sought to create a mixed-race workforce (Chinese, Japanese, native Hawaiian, Filipino, Portuguese, and others) as a way to keep the workers divided and unlikely to challenge them.

Native Hawaiians did not accept their subordination without protest. In 1891, they elevated a powerful nationalist to the throne: Queen Liliuokalani, who set out to challenge the growing American control of the islands. But she remained in power only two years. In 1890, the United States eliminated the privileged position of Hawaiian sugar in international trade. The result was devastating to the economy of the islands, and American planters concluded that the only way for them to recover was to become part of the United States (and hence exempt from its tariffs). In 1893 they staged a revolution and called on the United States for protection. After the American minister ordered marines from a warship in Honolulu harbor to go ashore to aid the rebels, the queen yielded her authority.

A provisional government, dominated by Americans (who constituted under five percent of the population of the islands), immediately sent a delegation to Washington to negotiate a treaty of annexation. President Harrison signed an annexation agreement in February 1893. But the Senate refused to ratify the treaty, and Grover Cleveland, the new president, refused to support it. Debate over the annexation of Hawaii continued until 1898, when the Republicans returned to power and approved the agreement.

The Samoan islands, 3,000 miles south of Hawaii, had also long served as a way station for American ships in the Pacific trade. As American commerce with Asia increased, business groups in the United States regarded Samoa with new interest, and the American navy began eyeing the Samoan harbor at Pago Pago. In 1878, the Hayes administration extracted a treaty from Samoan leaders for an American naval station at Pago Pago. It bound the United States to arbitrate any differences between Samoa and other nations. Clearly, the United States now expected to have a voice in Samoan affairs.

But Great Britain and Germany were also interested in the islands, and they too secured treaty rights from the native princes. For the next ten years the three powers jockeyed for dominance in Samoa, playing off one native ruler against another, and coming dangerously close to war. Finally, the three powers agreed to create a tripartite protectorate over Samoa, with the native chiefs exercising only nominal authority. The three-way arrangement failed to halt the intrigues and rivalries of its members; and in 1899, the United States and Germany divided the islands between them, compensating Britain with territories elsewhere in the Pacific. The United States retained the harbor at Pago Pago.

THE SPANISH–AMERICAN WAR

Imperial ambitions had thus begun to stir within the United States well before the late 1890s. But a war with Spain in 1898 turned those stirrings into overt expansionism. The war transformed America's relationship to the rest of the world, and it left the nation with a far-flung overseas empire.

Crisis in Cuba

The Spanish–American War emerged out of events in Cuba, which along with Puerto Rico represented virtually all that remained of Spain's once extensive American empire. Cubans had been resisting Spanish rule since at least 1868, when they began a long but ultimately unsuccessful fight for independence. Many Americans had sympathized with the Cubans during that ten-year struggle, but the United States did not intervene.

In 1895, the Cubans rose up again. (Although their goal was an end to Spanish misrule, the island's problems were now in part a result of the Wilson-Gorman Tariff of 1894, whose high duties on sugar had prostrated Cuba's important sugar economy by cutting off exports to the United States, the island's principal market.) This rebellion produced a ferocity on both sides that horrified Americans. The Cubans deliberately devastated the island to force the Spaniards to leave. The Spanish, commanded by General Valeriano Weyler (known in the American press as "Butcher" Weyler), confined civilians in certain areas to hastily prepared concentration camps, where they died by the thousands, victims of disease and malnutrition.

The Spanish had used some of these same savage methods during the earlier struggle in Cuba without shocking American sensibilities. But the revolt of 1895 was reported more fully and floridly by the American press, which strove to create the impression that the Spaniards were committing all the atrocities, when in fact there was considerable brutality on both sides.

The conflict in Cuba came at a particularly opportune moment for the publishers of some American newspapers. Joseph Pulitzer, with his New York *World*, and William Randolph Hearst, with his New York *Journal*, were revolutionizing American journalism in the late nineteenth century by creating a new "penny press," which catered openly to a broad popular audience, lower in economic status than the traditional press. Their papers specialized in lurid and sensational news; when such news did not exist, editors were not above creating it. More traditional journalists referred to the new form as "yellow journalism." In the 1890s, Hearst and Pulitzer were engaged in a ruthless circulation war, and they saw the struggle in Cuba as a great opportunity. Both sent batteries of reporters and illustrators to the islands with orders to provide accounts of Spanish atrocities. "You furnish the pictures," Hearst supposedly told an overly scrupulous artist, "and I'll furnish the war."

A growing population of Cuban emigrés in the United States—centered in Florida, New York, Philadelphia, and Trenton, New Jersey—gave extensive support to the Cuban Revolutionary party (whose headquarters was in New York) and helped publicize its leader, José Martí, who was killed in Cuba in 1895. Later, Cuban Americans formed other clubs and associations to support the cause of *Cuba Libre*. In some areas of the country, their efforts were as important as those of the yellow journalists in generating popular support for the revolution.

The mounting storm of indignation against Spain did not persuade President Cleveland, who proclaimed American neutrality and tried to stop the agitation by Cuban refugees in New York City. But when McKinley became president in 1897, he took a stronger stand. He formally protested Spain's "uncivilized and inhuman" conduct, causing the Spanish government (fearful of American intervention) to recall Weyler, modify the concentration policy, and grant the island a qualified autonomy. At the end of 1897, with the insurrection losing ground, it seemed that American involvement in the war might be averted.

But whatever chances there were for a peaceful settlement vanished as a result of two dramatic incidents in February 1898. The first occurred when a Cuban agent in Havana stole a private letter written by Dupuy de Lome, the Spanish minister in Washington, and turned it over to the American press. It described McKinley as a weak man and "a bidder for the admiration of the crowd." This was no more than many Americans, including some Republicans, were saying about their president. (Theodore Roosevelt described McKinley as having "no more backbone than a chocolate eclair.") But coming from a foreigner, it created intense popular anger. Dupuy de Lome promptly resigned.

While excitement over the de Lome letter was still high, the American battleship *Maine* blew up in Havana harbor with a loss of more than 260 people. The ship had been ordered to Cuba in January to protect American lives and property against possible attacks by Spanish loyalists. Many Americans assumed that the Spanish had sunk the ship, particularly when a naval court of inquiry

SINKING OF THE *MAINE*.   The sinking of the U.S. battleship *Maine* in Havana harbor did much to whip up war sentiment in the United States in March 1898. Although the cause of the explosion was unclear, many leapt to the conclusion that the Spanish were responsible, particularly when encouraged in such beliefs by mass circulation newspapers such as Joseph Pulitzer's *World*, the front page of which is depicted here.

hastily and inaccurately reported that an external explosion by a submarine mine had caused the disaster. (Later evidence suggested that the disaster was actually the result of an accidental explosion inside one of the engine rooms.) War hysteria swept the country, and Congress unanimously appropriated $50 million for military preparations. "Remember the *Maine*!" became a national chant for revenge.

McKinley still hoped to avoid a conflict. But others in his administration (including Assistant Secretary of the Navy Theodore Roosevelt) were clamoring for war. In March 1898, the president asked Spain to agree to an armistice, negotiations for a permanent peace, and an end to the concentration camps. Spain agreed to stop the fighting and eliminate the concentration camps but refused to negotiate with the rebels and reserved the right to resume hostilities at its discretion. That satisfied neither public opinion nor the Congress; and a few days later, McKinley asked for and, on April 25, received a congressional declaration of war.

"A Splendid Little War"

Secretary of State John Hay called the Spanish–American conflict "a splendid little war," an opinion that most Americans—with the exception of many of the enlisted men who fought in it—seemed to share. Declared in April, it was over in August. That was in part because Cuban rebels had already greatly weakened the Spanish resistance, which made the American intervention in many respects little more than a "mopping up" exercise. Only 460 Americans were killed in battle or died of wounds, although some 5,200 perished of disease: malaria, dysentery, and typhoid, among others. Casualties among Cuban insurgents, who continued to bear the brunt of the fighting, were much higher.

And yet the American war effort was not without difficulties. United States soldiers faced serious supply problems: a shortage of modern rifles and ammunition, uniforms too heavy for the warm Caribbean weather, inadequate medical services, and skimpy, almost indigestible food. The regular army numbered only 28,000 troops and officers, most of whom had experience in quelling Indian outbreaks but none in larger scale warfare. That meant that, as in the Civil War, the United States had to rely heavily on National Guard units, organized by local communities and commanded for the most part by local leaders without military experience. The entire mobilization process was conducted with remarkable inefficiency.

There were also racial conflicts. A significant proportion of the American invasion force consisted of black soldiers. Some were volunteer troops put together by black communities (although some governors refused to allow the formation of such units). Others were members of the four black regiments in the regular army, who had been stationed on the frontier to defend white settlements against Native Americans and were now transferred east to fight in Cuba. As the black soldiers traveled through the South toward the training camps, they chafed at the rigid segregation to which they were subjected and occasionally openly resisted the restrictions. Black soldiers in Georgia deliberately made use of a "whites-only" park; in Florida, they beat a soda-fountain operator for refusing to serve them; in Tampa, white provocations and black retaliation led to a night-long riot that left thirty wounded.

THE SPANISH-AMERICAN WAR IN CUBA, 1898

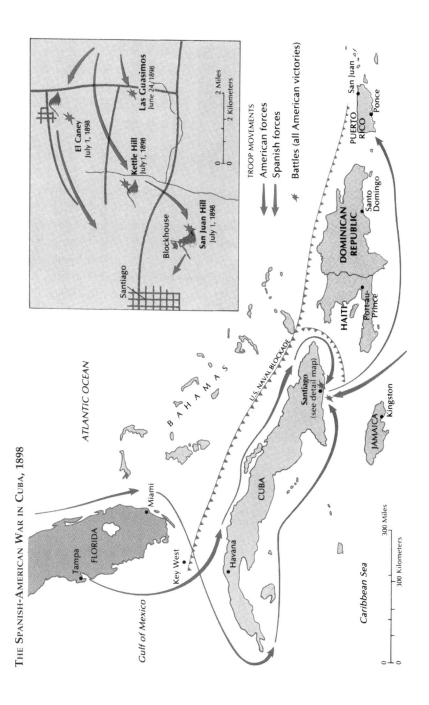

Racial tensions continued in Cuba itself, where American blacks played crucial roles in some of the important battles of the war (including the famous charge at San Juan Hill) and won many medals. Nearly half the Cuban insurgents fighting with the Americans were black and, unlike their American counterparts, they were fully integrated into the rebel army. (Indeed, one of the leading insurgent generals, Antion Maceo, was a black man.) The sight of black Cuban soldiers fighting alongside whites as equals gave American blacks a stronger sense of the injustice of their own position.

The Widening War

No agency in the American military had clear authority over strategic planning. Only the navy had worked out a coherent plan, and its objective had little to do with freeing Cuba. The assistant secretary of the navy in the McKinley administration was Theodore Roosevelt, ardent imperialist, active proponent of war, and a man uninhibited by the fact that he was a relatively minor figure in the military hierarchy. Roosevelt strengthened the navy's Pacific squadron and instructed its commander, Commodore George Dewey, to attack Spanish naval forces in the Philippines, a colony of Spain, in the event of war.

Immediately after war was declared, Dewey sailed for Manila. On May 1, 1898, he steamed into Manila Bay and completely destroyed the aging Spanish fleet stationed there. Only one American sailor died in the battle (of heat stroke), and Dewey, immediately promoted to admiral, became the first hero of the war. Several months later, after the arrival of an American expeditionary force, the Spanish surrendered the city of Manila itself. In the rejoicing over Dewey's victory, few Americans paused to note that the character of the war was changing. What had begun as a war to free Cuba was becoming a war to strip Spain of its colonies.

But Cuba remained the principal focus of American military efforts. At first, the American commanders planned a long period of training before actually sending troops into combat. But when a Spanish fleet under Admiral Pascual Cervera slipped past the American navy into Santiago harbor, on the southern coast of Cuba, plans changed quickly. The American Atlantic fleet quickly bottled Cervera up in the harbor. And the army's commanding general, Nelson A. Miles, hastily altered his strategy and left Tampa in June with a force of 17,000 to attack Santiago. Both the departure from Florida and the landing in Cuba were scenes of fantastic incompetence. It took five days for this relatively small army to be put ashore, and that with the enemy offering no opposition.

General William R. Shafter, the American commander, moved toward Santiago, which he planned to surround and capture. On the way he met and defeated Spanish forces at Las Guasimas and, a week later, in two simultaneous battles, El Caney and San Juan Hill. At the center of the fighting (and on the front pages of the newspapers) during most of these engagements was a cavalry unit known as the Rough Riders. Nominally commanded by General Leonard Wood, its real leader was Colonel Theodore Roosevelt, who had resigned from the Navy Department to get into the war and who had struggled with an almost desperate fury to ensure that his regiment made it to the front before the fighting ended. Roosevelt rapidly emerged as a hero of the conflict. His fame rested in large part on his role in leading a bold, if perhaps reckless, charge up Kettle Hill (a charge that was a minor part of the larger battle for the adjacent San Juan Hill) directly into the face of Spanish guns. Roosevelt himself emerged unscathed, but nearly a hundred of his soldiers were killed or wounded. To the end of his life, he remembered the battle as "the great day of my life."

Although Shafter was now in position to assault Santiago, his army was so weakened by sickness that he feared he might have to abandon his position, particularly once the commander of the American naval force blockading Santiago refused to enter the harbor because of mines. Disaster seemed imminent. But unknown to the Americans, the Spanish government had by now decided that Santiago was lost and had ordered Cervera to evacuate. On July 3, knowing the

THE "ROUGH RIDERS." Theodore Roosevelt (in the center) poses with his "Rough Riders" after the battle of San Juan Hill. "Rough, Rough, we're the stuff, we want to fight, and we can't get enough" was alleged to be one of the unit's favored songs. The charge that Roosevelt led up Kettle Hill was only a part of the larger battle for San Juan Hill, but the future president and his Rough Riders reaped enormous publicity for it.

effort was hopeless, Cervera tried to escape the harbor. The waiting American squadron destroyed his entire fleet. On July 16, the commander of Spanish ground forces in Santiago surrendered. And at about the same time, an American army landed in Puerto Rico and occupied it against virtually no opposition. On August 12, an armistice ended the war.

Under the terms of the armistice, Spain recognized the independence of Cuba. It ceded Puerto Rico (now occupied by American troops) and the Pacific island of Guam to the United States. And it accepted continued American occupation of Manila pending the final disposition of the Philippines.

Forging a Relationship with Puerto Rico

The annexation of Puerto Rico produced relatively little controversy in the United States—ironically, since of all the territory America acquired as a result of the Spanish–American war, Puerto Rico would be the most important to the nation's future.

The island of Puerto Rico had been a part of the Spanish empire since Ponce de Leon arrived there in 1508, and it had contained Spanish settlements since the founding of San Juan in 1521. The native people of the island, the Arawaks, gradually disappeared almost entirely, as a result of infectious diseases, Spanish brutality, and poverty. Puerto Rican society developed, therefore, with a Spanish ruling class and a large African work force for the coffee and sugar plantations that came to dominate its economy.

As Puerto Rican society became increasingly distinctive, resistance to Spanish rule began to emerge, just as it had emerged in Cuba. Uprisings occurred intermittently beginning in the 1820s; the most important of them—the so-called Lares Rebellion—was, like the others, effectively crushed by the Spanish in 1868. But the growing resistance did prompt some reforms: the abolition of slavery in 1873, representation in the Spanish parliament, and other changes. Demands for independence continued to grow, and in 1898—in response to political pressure organized by Luis Muñoz Rivera—Spain granted the island a degree of independence. But before the changes had any chance to take effect, control of Puerto Rico shifted to the United States.

American military forces occupied the island during the Spanish–American war, and they remained in control until 1900, when the Foraker Act ended military rule and established a formal colonial government: an American governor, a two-chamber legislature (the members of the upper chamber appointed by the United States, the members of the lower elected by the Puerto Rican people). The United States could amend or veto any legislation the Puerto Ricans passed. Agitation for independence continued. And in 1917, under pressure to clarify the relationship between Puerto Rico and America, Congress passed the Jones Act, which declared Puerto Rico to be United States territory and made all Puerto Ricans American citizens.

The Puerto Rican sugar industry flourished as it took advantage of the American market that was now open to it without tariffs. As in Hawaii, Americans began establishing large sugar plantations on the island and hired natives to work them; many of the planters did not even live in Puerto Rico. The growing emphasis on sugar as a cash crop, and the transformation of many Puerto Rican farmers into paid laborers, led to a reduction in the growing of food for the island. Puerto Ricans became increasingly dependent on imported food and hence became increasingly a part of the international commercial economy. When international sugar prices were high, Puerto Rico did well. When they dropped, the island's economy sagged, pushing many plantation workers—already desperately poor—into destitution. Unhappy with the instability, the poverty among natives, and the American threat to Hispanic culture, many Puerto Ricans continued to agitate for independence. Others, however, began to envision closer relations with the United States, even statehood.

The Fate of the Philippines

If the annexation of Puerto Rico produced relatively little controversy, the annexation of the Philippines was the source of a long and impassioned debate. Controlling a nearby Caribbean island fit reasonably comfortably into America's sense of itself as the hegemonic power in the Western Hemisphere. Controlling a large and densely populated territory thousands of miles away seemed different and, to many Americans, more ominous.

McKinley claimed to be reluctant to support annexation. But, according to his own accounts, he came to believe there were no acceptable alternatives. Emerging from what he described as an "agonizing night of prayer," he claimed to have received divine guidance for his decision to accept responsibility for the islands. Returning them to Spain would be "cowardly and dishonorable," he claimed. Turning them over to another imperialist power (France, Germany, or Britain) would be "bad business and discreditable." Granting the islands independence would be irresponsible; the Filipinos were "unfit for self government." The only solution was "to take them all and to educate the Filipinos, and uplift and Christianize them, and by God's grace do the very best we could by them." Growing popular support for annexation and heavy pressure from imperialist leaders of his party undoubtedly helped him reach this "decision of conscience."

The Treaty of Paris, signed in December 1898, brought a formal end to the war. It confirmed the terms of the armistice concerning Cuba, Puerto Rico, and Guam. But American negotiators startled the Spanish by demanding that they cede the Philippines to the United States, something the original armistice had not included. The Spanish objected briefly, but an American offer of $20 million for the islands softened their resistance. They accepted all the American terms.

In the United States, however, resistance was fierce. During debate over ratification of the treaty in the Senate, a powerful anti-imperialist movement arose around the country opposing acquisition of the Philippines. The anti-imperialists included some of the nation's wealthiest and most powerful figures: Andrew Carnegie, Mark Twain, Samuel Gompers, Senator John Sherman, and others. Their motives were various. Some believed simply that imperialism was immoral, a repudiation of America's commitment to human freedom. Some feared "polluting" the American population by introducing "inferior" Asians into it. Industrial workers feared being undercut by a flood of cheap laborers from the new colonies. Conservatives feared the large standing army and entangling foreign alliances that they believed imperialism would require and that they believed would threaten American liberties. Sugar growers and others feared unwelcome competition from the new territories. The Anti-Imperialist League, established by upper-class Bostonians, New Yorkers, and others late in 1898 to fight against annexation, attracted a widespread following in the Northeast and waged a vigorous campaign against ratification of the Paris treaty.

Favoring ratification was an equally varied group. There were the exuberant imperialists such as Theodore Roosevelt, who saw the acquisition of empire as a way to reinvigorate the nation, to keep alive what they considered the healthy, restorative influence of the war. Some businessmen saw opportunities in the Philippines and believed annexation would position the United States to dominate the Asian trade. And most Republicans saw partisan advantages in acquiring valuable new territories through a war fought and won by a Republican administration. Perhaps the strongest argument in favor of annexation, however, was the apparent ease with which it could be accomplished. The United States, after all, already possessed the islands.

When anti-imperialists warned of the danger of acquiring territories with large populations who might have to become citizens, the imperialists had a ready answer: The nation's longstanding policies toward Native Americans—treating them as dependents rather than as citizens—had created a precedent for annexing land without absorbing people. Senator Henry Cabot Lodge of Massachusetts, one of the leading imperialists in Congress, made the point explicitly:

> The other day . . . a great Democratic thinker announced that a Republic can have no subjects. He seems to have forgotten that this Republic not only has held subjects from the beginning, . . . but [that we have] acquired them by purchase. . . . [We] denied to the Indian tribes even the right to choose their allegiance, or to become citizens.

Other supporters of annexation argued that the "uncivilized" Filipinos "would occupy the same status precisely as our Indians. . . . They are, in fact, 'Indians'— and the Fourteenth Amendment does not make citizens of Indians."

The fate of the treaty remained in doubt for weeks, until it received the unexpected support of William Jennings Bryan, a fervent anti-imperialist. He backed ratification not because he approved of annexation but because he hoped to move the issue out of the Senate and make it the subject of a national referendum in 1900, when he expected to be the Democratic presidential candidate again. Bryan persuaded a number of anti-imperialist Democrats to support the treaty so as to set up the 1900 debate. The Senate ratified it finally on February 6, 1899.

But Bryan miscalculated. If the election of 1900 was in fact a referendum on the Philippines, as Bryan tried to make it, it proved beyond doubt that the nation had decided in favor of imperialism. Once again, Bryan ran against McKinley; and once again, McKinley won—even more decisively than in 1896. It was not only the issue of the colonies, however, that ensured McKinley's victory. The Republicans were the beneficiaries of growing national prosperity—and also of the colorful personality of their vice-presidential candidate, Colonel Theodore Roosevelt, the hero of San Juan Hill.

THE COST OF EMPIRE

The new American empire was a small one by the standards of the great imperial powers of Europe. But it created large problems. It embroiled the United States in the politics of both Europe and the Far East in ways the nation had always tried to avoid in the past. It also drew Americans into a brutal war in the Philippines.

Governance and Colonial Dependency

Three of the new American dependencies—Hawaii, Alaska, and Puerto Rico—presented relatively few problems. They received territorial status (and their residents American citizenship) relatively quickly: Hawaii in 1900, Alaska in 1912, and Puerto Rico by 1917. The navy took control of Guam and Tutuila. And some of the smallest, least populated Pacific islands the United States simply left alone.

Cuba was a thornier problem. American military forces, commanded by General Leonard Wood, remained there until 1902 to prepare the island for independence. They built roads, schools, and hospitals; reorganized the legal, financial, and administrative systems; and introduced medical and sanitation reforms. But the United States was also laying the basis for years of American economic domination of the island.

When Cuba drew up a constitution that made no reference to the United States, Congress responded by passing the Platt Amendment in 1901 and pressuring Cuba into incorporating its terms into its constitution. The Platt Amendment barred Cuba from making treaties with other nations (thus, in effect, giving the United States effective control of Cuban foreign policy); it gave the United States the right to intervene in Cuba to preserve independence, life, and property; and it required Cuba to permit American naval stations on its territory. The amendment left Cuba only nominally independent politically. And American capital, which quickly took over the island's economy, made the new nation an American economic appendage as well. American investors poured into Cuba, buying up plantations, factories, railroads, and refineries. Absentee American ownership of many of the island's most important resources was the source of resentment and agitation for decades. Resistance to "Yankee imperialism" produced intermittent revolts against the Cuban government—revolts that at times prompted U.S. military intervention. American troops occupied the island from 1906 to 1909 after one such rebellion. They returned again in 1912 to suppress a revolt by black plantation workers. As in Puerto Rico and Hawaii, sugar production— spurred by access to the American market—increasingly dominated the island's economy and subjected it to the same cycle of booms and busts that so plagued other sugar-producing appendages of the United States economy.

War in the Philippines

Americans did not like to think of themselves as imperial rulers in the European mold. Yet, like other imperial powers, the United States soon discovered—as it had discovered at home in its relations with the Native Americans—that subjugating another people required more than ideals; it also required strength and brutality. That, at least, was the lesson of the American experience in the Philippines, where American forces soon became engaged in a long and bloody war with insurgent forces fighting for independence.

The conflict in the Philippines is the least remembered of all American wars. It was also one of the longest (it lasted from 1898 to 1902) and one of the most vicious. It involved 200,000 American troops and resulted in 4,300 American deaths, nearly ten times the number who had died in combat in the Spanish–American War. The number of Filipinos killed in the conflict is still in dispute, but it seems likely that at least 50,000 natives (and perhaps many more) died. The American occupiers faced guerrilla tactics in the Philippines very similar to those the Spanish occupiers had faced prior to 1898 in Cuba. And they soon found themselves drawn into the same pattern of brutality that had outraged so many Americans when Weyler had used them in the Caribbean.

The Filipinos had been rebelling against Spanish rule even before 1898. And as soon as they realized the Americans had come to stay, they rebelled against them as well. Ably led by Emilio Aguinaldo, who claimed to head the legitimate government of the nation, Filipinos harried the American army of occupation from island to island for more than three years. At first, American commanders believed the rebels had only a small popular following. But by early 1900, General Arthur MacArthur (father of General Douglas MacArthur), an American commander in the islands, was writing: "I have been reluctantly compelled to believe that the Filipino masses are loyal to Aguinaldo and the government which he heads."

To MacArthur and others, that realization was not a reason to moderate American tactics or conciliate the rebels. It was a reason to adopt more severe measures. Gradually, the American military effort became more systematically vicious and brutal. Captured Filipino guerrillas were treated not as prisoners of war, but as murderers. Most were summarily executed. On some islands, entire communities were evacuated, the residents forced into concentration camps, while American troops destroyed their villages, farms, crops, and livestock. A spirit of savagery grew among American soldiers, who came to view the Filipinos as almost subhuman and at times seemed to take pleasure in killing almost arbitrarily. One American commander ordered his troops "to kill and burn, the more you kill and burn the better it will please me. . . . Shoot everyone over the age of 10." Over fifteen Filipinos were killed for every one wounded; in the Civil War—the bloodiest conflict in American history to that point—one person had died for every five wounded.

By 1902, reports of the brutality and of the American casualties had soured the American public on the war. But by then, the rebellion had largely exhausted itself and the occupiers had established control over most of the islands. The key to their victory was the March 1901 capture of Aguinaldo, who later signed a document urging his followers to stop fighting and declaring his own allegiance to the United States. (Aguinaldo then retired from public life and lived quietly until 1964.) Fighting continued in some places for another year, and the war revived intermittently until as late as 1906; but American possession of the Philippines was now secure.

FILIPINO PRISONERS OF WAR.   Filipino prisoners in the foreground being guarded by American soldiers near the rear. Efforts to suppress the Filipino insurrection proved far more difficult than the United States had anticipated and resulted in a longer, costlier, and more savage conflict than the Spanish–American War had been.

In the summer of 1901, the military transferred authority over the islands to William Howard Taft, who became the first civilian governor. Taft announced that the American mission in the Philippines was to prepare the islands for independence, and he gave the Filipinos broad local autonomy. The Americans also built roads, schools, bridges, and sewers; instituted major administrative and financial reforms; and established a public health system. The Philippine economy, dominated by fishing, agriculture, timber, and mining, also became increasingly linked to the economy of the United States. Americans did not make many investments in the Philippines, and few Americans moved there. But trade with the United States grew to the point that the islands were almost completely dependent on American markets.

In the meantime, a succession of American governors gradually increased Filipino political autonomy. But not until July 4, 1946, did the islands finally gain their independence.

The United States and the Far East

The acquisition of the Philippines greatly increased the already strong American interest in Asia. Americans were particularly concerned about the future of China, with which the United States already had an important trading relationship and which was now so enfeebled that it provided a tempting target for exploitation by stronger countries. By 1900, England, France, Germany, Russia, and Japan were beginning to carve up China among themselves. They pressured the Chinese government for "concessions" that gave them effective economic control over various regions. In some cases, they simply seized Chinese territory and claimed it as their own. Many Americans feared the process would soon cut them out of the China trade altogether.

Eager for a way to protect American interests in China without risking war, McKinley issued a statement in September 1898 saying the United States wanted access to China, but no special advantages there. "Asking only the open door for ourselves, we are ready to accord the open door to others." Later, Secretary of State John Hay translated those words into policy when he addressed identical messages, which became known as the "Open Door notes," to England, Germany, Russia, France, Japan, and Italy. He asked them to approve three principles: Each nation with a sphere of influence in China was to respect the rights and privileges of other nations in its sphere; Chinese officials were to continue to collect tariff duties in all spheres (the existing tariff favored the United States); and nations were not to discriminate against other nations in levying port dues and railroad rates within their own spheres. Together, these principles would allow the United States to trade freely with the Chinese without fear of interference and without having to become militarily involved in the region. They would also retain the illusion of Chinese sovereignty and thus prevent formal colonial dismemberment of China, which might also create obstacles to American trade.

But Europe and Japan received the Open Door proposals coolly. Russia openly rejected them; the other powers claimed to accept them in principle but to be unable to act unless all the other powers agreed. Hay refused to consider this a rebuff. He boldly announced that all the powers had accepted the principles of the Open Door in "final and definitive" form and that the United States expected them to observe those principles. But unless the United States was willing to resort to war, it could not prevent any nation that wanted to violate the Open Door from doing so. The Open Door notes, then, were more a statement of America's own international goals than they were a functioning agreement.

No sooner had the diplomatic maneuvering over the Open Door ended than the Boxers, a secret Chinese martial-arts society with highly nationalist convictions, launched a revolt against foreigners in China. The climax of the Boxer Rebellion was a siege of the entire foreign diplomatic corps, which huddled together in the British embassy in Beijing. The imperial powers (including the United States) sent an international expeditionary force into China to rescue the diplomats. In August 1900, it fought its way into Beijing and broke the siege.

McKinley and Hay had agreed to American participation so as to secure a voice in the settlement of the uprising and to prevent the partition of China by the European powers. Hay now won support for his Open Door approach from England and Germany and then induced the other participating powers to accept compensation from the Chinese for the damages the Boxer Rebellion had caused. Chinese territorial integrity survived, at least in name, and the United States retained access to its lucrative trade.

Toward a Modern Military

The war with Spain had revealed glaring deficiencies in the American military system. The army had exhibited the greatest weaknesses, but the entire military organization had demonstrated problems of supply, training, and coordination. Had the United States been fighting a more powerful nation, disaster might have resulted. After the war, McKinley appointed Elihu Root, an able corporate lawyer in New York, as secretary of war to supervise a major overhaul of the armed forces. (Root was one of the first of several generations of attorney–statesmen who moved easily between public and private roles and helped create what has often been called the American "foreign policy establishment.") Between 1900 and 1903, Root created a new military system.

The Root reforms enlarged the regular army from 25,000 to a maximum of 100,000. They established federal command of the National Guard, ensuring that never again would the nation fight a war with volunteer regiments over which the federal government had limited control. They sparked the creation of a system of officer training schools, including the Army Staff College (later the Command and General Staff School) at Fort Leavenworth,

ELIHU ROOT. Elihu Root, corporate lawyer turned diplomat, served as Secretary of War under President McKinley and undertook a major overhaul of the United States military in the first years of the twentieth century. He exemplified a role that would become familiar in modern America—an accomplished professional in the private sphere tapped for critical responsibilities in public life. In 1912, Root won the Nobel Peace Prize for his activities as president of the Carnegie Endowment for International Peace.

Kansas, and the Army War College at Washington. And in 1903, they established a general staff (which later became the Joint Chiefs of Staff) to act as military advisers to the secretary of war. It was this last reform that Root considered most important: the creation of a central planning agency modeled on the example of European general staffs. The Joint Chiefs were charged with many functions. They were to "supervise" and "coordinate" the entire army establishment, and they were to establish an office that would plan for possible wars. An Army and Navy Board, on which both services were represented, was to foster interservice cooperation. As a result of the new reforms, the United States entered the twentieth century with something resembling a modern military system. The country would make substantial use of it in the turbulent century to come.

CHAPTER FIVE

Origins of Progressivism

∼

D uring the final decades of the nineteenth century and the early years of the twentieth, many Americans began to seek alternatives to the harsh realities of modern industrial society. Those who offered such challenges did so in several different ways. Some used the power of the pen to identify wrongs and to argue that the nation had a moral obligation to right them. Others joined voluntary associations to address particular social and economic problems, such as child labor or urban crime, which they considered to be matters of great urgency. Still others focused on the political system in an effort to achieve broad legislative and electoral change. Taken together, these many efforts made the years from 1880 to 1920 a time of almost frenetic reform activity. The breadth of reform enthusiasm and the myriad forms it took have led historians to name the years spanning the turn of the twentieth century "the Progressive Era."

Several forces contributed to the emergence of a powerful reform impulse. The most important, perhaps, was the intrusion of large-scale industrialization into American life. Americans who had been born around the time of the Civil War had seen dramatic changes in their own lifetime. They remembered a society of small towns, close-knit communities, independent farmers, skilled artisans, and strong local elites. They saw around them now a nation of large corporate institutions, great cities, a burgeoning immigrant working class, and new patterns of authority that challenged traditional forms of community. Some of those attracted to reform yearned to recreate something of the world they felt had been lost: to preserve or restore traditional values and institutions. Others came to believe that the new economic system required new values, new institutions, and new forms of government authority if it were to function fairly and efficiently. And many people embraced parts of both these impulses. The efforts of reformers took many forms and reflected many different ideas, but together they helped shape the contours of the new society of the twentieth century.

CREATING A REFORM AGENDA

The issues that preoccupied social and political activists at the turn of the century were the products of industrial society. Brazen political corruption; perilous working conditions in factories; the brutal exploitation of children in mines, sweatshops, and factories; and a social climate that seemed to ignore, if not encourage, countless other forms of pernicious behavior and unchecked greed all became targets of reform.

Reformers brought to their task a broad range of ideas about how best to reshape their troubled society. One powerful impulse was the spirit of "antimonopoly," the fear of concentrated power and the urge to limit and disperse authority and wealth. This impulse, which had much in common with populism, appealed not only to many workers and farmers but to some middle-class Americans as well. It led to their demands that government regulate or break up trusts at both the state and national levels; and it led workers and others to conclude that they must themselves organize if they were to have any leverage in dealing with large institutions.

Another progressive impulse was a belief in the importance of social cohesion: the belief that individuals are not autonomous but part of a great web of social relationships, that the welfare of any single person is dependent on the welfare of society as a whole. That assumption produced a concern about the fraying of traditional bonds of community. It also encouraged many reformers to take an interest in the plight of particularly troubled social groups. A large number of progressive initiatives and reforms involved efforts to help poor women and children, industrial workers, immigrants, and—to a lesser extent—African Americans.

Still another impulse was a deep faith in knowledge—in the possibilities of applying to society the principles of the natural and social sciences. To some, that meant a quest for organization and efficiency. Many reformers believed that social order required intelligent social organization and rational procedures for guiding social and economic life; to them, knowledge was important for creating an efficient society. Others believed that new forms of inquiry could help Americans learn to deal more effectively with oppression and injustice; to them knowledge was important as a vehicle for making society more equitable and humane. Most progressives believed, too, that a modernized government could—and must—play an important role in the process of improving and stabilizing society. Modern life was too complex to be left in the hands of party bosses, untrained amateurs, and antiquated institutions. It required new and enhanced institutions of government, and a new breed of leaders and experts.

These varied reform impulses were not always as mutually incompatible as they seemed. Many progressives made use of all these ideas (and others), separately or in combination, as they tried to bring order and progress to their turbulent society. They sought simultaneously to preserve traditional values and to create new ideas and institutions.

The Settlement House Movement

One innovative attempt to address the plight of immigrants as well as the anonymity, lack of services, and unbridled political corruption in American cities was the settlement house movement. Inspired by English reformers, who developed the idea in the 1880s, the settlements proved enormously appealing to college-educated American men and women at the turn of the century. After the founding of the first American settlement house in 1886, Stanton Coit's Neighborhood Guild located on the Lower East Side of New York City, settlement houses appeared with amazing rapidity. By 1900 over 100 settlements had been founded in the United States; the figure soared to over 400 by 1910.

The lure of the social settlements proved particularly strong for women. This was in part because of parallel changes in late–nineteenth century women's education. After the Civil War, a virtual revolution in women's higher education occurred as several major colleges, including Vassar (1865), Smith (1875), Wellesley (1875), and Bryn Mawr (1884), opened for the express purpose of offering women a college education equivalent to that available to men. By 1890, a new generation of college-educated women had emerged who could find little outlet for their hard earned skills. Discrimination limited their access to the professions; prevailing social mores frowned upon pursuit of family and career at the same time. The settlement houses thus emerged as an ideal solution for many women who sought an active career. The settlements made use of their educations. But they also fulfilled the often-invoked ideal of women's service to society.

Although the settlements differed among themselves, they shared many characteristics. The settlement house was literally a home, located in some of the worst neighborhoods in American cities. Settlement workers deliberately sought out areas where impoverished immigrants lived devoid of even the most basic human services. There they took up residence, offering their neighbors assistance that ranged from English classes to public health clinics to reading groups to child care to an array of social activities. If the nation's best educated and most idealistic young people could extend their enthusiasm, expertise, and energy to the country's most downtrodden, the theory went, the worst evils of industrialism might be alleviated.

The settlements often served as crucibles for larger progressive reform activities as well. Jane Addams, the much revered and often emulated founder of Chicago's Hull House (established in 1889), at first avoided any involvement in local political struggles. Before long, however, she realized that the problems in the nineteenth ward, site of the Hull House community, were inseparable from the political corruption and economic exploitation she saw around her in the city. "Civic cooperation," a determined effort to build alliances between Hull House and the larger Chicago reform community, formed an important dimension of the settlement's mission by the early 1890s. With Addams's encouragement, the Hull House Men's Club directly challenged one of the city's most notoriously corrupt aldermen by running its own reform candidate.

Hull House residents often assumed prominent roles in many reform organizations, thereby tightening the connections between the settlement house and other progressive campaigns. The energetic and influential Florence Kelley, for example, served as Illinois's first state factory inspector while living at Hull House. The settlement, Jane Addams later explained, thus "became associated" not only with support for state regulation of factory working conditions, but also received "all the odium" that efforts to enforce the law provoked. Much of the labor legislation Kelley and Hull House stood behind was resisted bitterly by those who rejected the necessity for state regulation of industry. That resistance did not staunch the enthusiasm of the countless committed social activists who joined the settlement house movement.

The settlements also played an important role in advancing the wider public understanding of social problems, which was critical to progressive reform efforts. Social change depended in part, the settlers believed, upon persuading the community, and those who wielded power within it, that conditions in the cities were intolerable. The size and anonymity of the city and the rigid residential segregation of urban people along racial, ethnic, and class lines enabled middle-class Americans to turn a blind eye to the scale and depth of urban misery. Little wonder Jacob Riis, a Danish immigrant who became a police photographer and reform journalist, chose to entitle his sensational exposé of sweatshops and tenements in New York City's Lower East Side, *How the Other Half Lives* (1890).

The most idealistic of reformers, and the settlers were often among them, believed that an educated public would not tolerate the existence of such widespread desperation and poverty. For this reason, some settlements undertook extensive research projects designed to illuminate the living and working conditions in their immediate neighborhoods. Indeed, the settlements pioneered in developing the social survey in America, a technique for studying communities that would become integral to social science disciplines in the twentieth century. Few such surveys rivalled *Hull House Maps and Papers* (1895), an exhaustive study of working-class life and labor in the settlement's rough and tumble neighborhood.

It is difficult to determine how immigrants and working-class people experienced the efforts made on their behalf by the social settlements. Some clearly appreciated the services extended by the settlements and the genuine concern of the residents. There is no question that the settlements literally saved lives upon occasion and improved the circumstances of many people in desperate need. "Life began for me," one immigrant asserted, "in a social settlement." Others no doubt chafed at the middle-class values and cultural standards some settlers attempted to impose upon them. Yet not a few of the most compassionate settlement house residents came to respect and even defer to the immigrants, whose customs had seemed at first strange and abhorrent to their sensibilities. Dr. Alice Hamilton attempted to transfer the modern medical principles she had learned at the University of Michigan to the mothers who frequented the well baby clinic she began at Hull House. She later noted with amusement that "those Italian women knew what a baby needed far better than any Ann Arbor professor did."

In fact, race proved a much greater obstacle for the social settlements than ethnicity. Although Hull House was notable for its efforts to advance understanding of the "color line" that divided Chicago's black neighborhoods from its white ones, most settlements reflected rather than challenged racial boundaries. Few white settlements devoted much energy to the problems of African-American urban dwellers, even if they were not outwardly hostile to racial minorities. Only with the founding of specifically black settlement houses, such as Chicago's Wendell Phillips Settlement (1908), did the movement attend closely to the African-American community. But such settlements were relatively few. In many cities, the black church provided much of the assistance settlement houses offered in other communities.

However effective the settlements were in serving their neighborhoods, they succeeded most of all in nurturing a sense of idealism, commitment, and camaraderie among the extraordinary women and men who joined the settlement community. For the many who were unmarried, the settlements literally became their homes; their colleagues became their families. More importantly, it allowed committed social activists to join hands with others who shared their determination to promote greater economic justice and social equality. This sense of collective enterprise proved vital to advancing other progressive reform crusades.

Muckraking

One aspect of the settlement mission—increasing public awareness of social problems—formed the core of the phenomenon known as "muckraking." The term was flung at progressive-era investigative journalists in 1906 by a disgusted President Theodore Roosevelt. Worried that newspaper men and women were portraying only the evil in American society and politics, Roosevelt likened the journalists to the "man with a muckrake" in Bunyan's *Pilgrim's Progress*, who raked filth at his feet while ignoring the offer of a "celestial crown."

The press had long been an iconoclastic force in American society, but journalism developed in the late nineteenth century in ways that significantly expanded its influence. The inauguration of cheap, mass circulation magazines in the late 1880s and 1890s proved essential to the rise of muckraking. For as little as ten cents an issue, Americans of diverse social classes could have access to a consistently produced and nationally disseminated source of information, entertainment, and news. Millions of Americans, in small towns and large cities, in the Northeast and in the Far West, read the same essays and short stories; more likely, they lingered over the same lavishly drawn illustrations and increasingly striking layouts of news photography. Newspapers also expanded greatly in number and circulation in the late nineteenth century. Where newspapers were once closely tied to political parties and highly partisan in reporting the news, many became more independent by the 1890s. Certainly, journalists began to place much greater emphasis on the idea of objectivity as they became more professionalized.

The reporters who staffed the magazines and newspapers played a critical part in muckraking. Periodicals such as *McClure's Magazine* succeeded in recruiting an extraordinarily talented group of college-educated men and women whose skills as writers were matched by their interest in social issues and their sense of social responsibility. Ida M. Tarbell, Ray Stannard Baker, and Lincoln Steffens responded with gusto when asked to investigate the oil industry, the railroads, political corruption in the cities, and the problem of monopoly. Their often meticulously researched and brilliantly drawn portraits of individual political bosses and ruthless captains of industry made *McClure's Magazine* one of the most widely read periodicals of the early twentieth century. From modest beginnings, its readership soared to over 500,000 in the heyday of muckraking. The *McClure's* formula was imitated, although seldom improved upon, by countless other magazines.

But the content of the reporters' stories contributed more than did their style to the phenomenon of muckraking. Savvy editors realized there was money to be made from capitalizing on the fears and worries many Americans harbored about the character of modern industrial society. Thus, stories about the tyranny of the trusts and the conspiratorial workings of the railroads proliferated. None was more successful than Ida Tarbell's *History of the Standard Oil Company* (1904), published first in monthly installments beginning in 1902 to an avid readership. Everything from exposés of phony cancer cures to gruesome accounts of industrial accidents illustrating the greed and ruthlessness of corporations filled the pages of the magazines.

By the time Roosevelt branded them "muckrakers" in 1906, journalists such as Lincoln Steffens had achieved fame for uncovering extortion, kickbacks, and greed in some of the nation's greatest cities. Steffens's accounts of machine government and boss rule laid responsibility for these evils less on the bosses themselves than on an apathetic and immobilized citizenry who allowed these outrages to occur. The sense of moral fervor so palpable in Steffens's essays (published as *The Shame of the Cities* in 1904) was characteristic of much muckraking. The journalists frankly appealed to the public's conscience. In so doing, they helped create a climate of opinion receptive to reform crusades.

Religion and the Reform Imperative

Both the moral thrust of muckraking and the humanitarian appeal of the settlement house movement reflected the strong religious underpinnings of progressive reform ideals. Many reform activists came from families steeped in the val-

IDA M. TARBELL.   One of the great muckraking journalists of the early twentieth century, Ida M. Tarbell had grown up in the oil regions of Pennsylvania. She attended Allegheny College, studied and traveled in France, and became a writer and editor for *McClure's Magazine* in the 1890s. Her series of articles for *McClure's* on the "History of the Standard Oil Company," became a model of the fact-based, investigative journalism of the period that offered a compelling story to its readers in a superb narrative style. Tarbell's close examination of the tactics John D. Rockefeller employed to build his enormous oil empire both reflected and helped increase the widespread public attacks on the power of the trusts.

ues of evangelical Protestantism. Although some reformers moved away from religion as they entered public life, many continued to draw on Protestant traditions and beliefs in creating their critique of American industrial society. Economist Richard Ely, for example, evoked the dictates of Christianity in describing the cruelty and failings of the laissez-faire economy. "Our food, our clothing, our shelter, all our wealth," he wrote in 1894, "is covered with stains and clots of blood." For Ely the answer lay in "Christian socialism," a cooperative economic system guided by ethical values.

Religion shaped reform, too, through the growth of the "Social Gospel." By the early twentieth century, this movement within American Protestantism (and, to a lesser extent, within American Catholicism and Judaism) was focusing its attention on the redemption of the nation's cities. The Social Gospel stressed the relationship between religious principles, human salvation, and the achievement of social justice. Walter Rauschenbusch, a leading Protestant theologian who spread the Social Gospel through his influential discourses on the importance of Christian reform, stressed both the difficulty and the urgency of the task. "Let us 'go slow,'" he once wrote, "but let us hurry up about it." Both Rauschenbusch and Ely vigorously supported the American labor movement, believing cooperation among working people held the best chance of advancing social and economic equality.

The Salvation Army, which was founded in England but began operating in the United States in 1880, exemplified this fusion of religion and reform. A Christian social welfare organization with a vaguely military structure, it boasted some 3,000 "officers" and 20,000 "privates" by 1900. The organization offered both material aid and spiritual service to the urban poor. These efforts were mirrored by those of countless ministers, priests, and rabbis who left traditional parish work to serve in the troubled cities. Women, who in an earlier period might have been missionaries to foreign countries, chose to live in the settlement houses and to work with other urban social service groups instead.

Some Americans drew upon the traditions and religious principles of Roman Catholicism to support a reform agenda. Some American Catholics seized upon the 1893 publication of Pope Leo XIII's encyclical *Rerum Novarum* ("New Things") to justify their crusade for social justice. Catholic liberals such as Father John A. Ryan took to heart the Pope's warning that "a small number of very rich men have been able to lay upon the masses of the poor a yoke little better than slavery itself. . . . No practical solution to this question will ever be found without the assistance of religion and the church." For decades, Ryan worked to expand the scope of Catholic social welfare organizations.

The Social Gospel never dominated urban reform movements. Some progressives dismissed such proselytizing as irrelevant; others viewed religion as a useful, if secondary, adjunct to their own work. But the engagement of religion with reform bolstered both the ranks of progressive reformers and the moral idealism of the various movements they advanced. After a visit to a New York City slum known as Hell's Kitchen, Walter Rauschenbusch captured both the optimism and the spirituality of the Social Gospel as he observed Christian reformers hard at work among the poor: "One could hear human virtue cracking and crashing all around."

SCIENCE, REFORM, AND SOCIETY

If religious idealism demonstrated the continuity in values that tied modern American society to the nineteenth century, science seemed to set a new course for the twentieth century. By the 1890s, science had come to challenge religion as the basis of authority in modern society. Where good character, hard work, and native intelligence once seemed the critical ingredients of success, now education, scientific understanding, and technical expertise seemed to be the keys to advancement.

Science had come to signify a good deal more than a means of under-standing the natural world by 1900. Its principles were being applied to the study of society; its methods were celebrated as objective and rational techniques with wide applications in industry, education, and even politics. Many Americans embraced scientific methods as a way of unifying the disparate factions and voices in American society. A rigorous search for the truth, they believed, might well yield the political and social coherence that seemed so elusive in their time.

Science, Education, and the Professions

The increasing emphasis on scientific knowledge, expertise, and advanced train-ing fueled a drive toward professionalization in the late nineteenth century. The period brought a dramatic rise in the number of Americans engaged in adminis-trative and professional tasks as industry increasingly relied upon managers, tech-nicians, and accountants. Cities, too, needed commercial, medical, legal, and ed-ucational services on a scale hitherto unseen. New technologies required the skills of scientists and engineers who, in turn, needed educational institutions and in-structors for advanced training. By the turn of the century, those performing these services had come to constitute a distinct social group—middle-class professionals, or (as some historians have called them) a "new middle class."

Middle-class professionals were both a product of and a force in shaping new ideas about the importance of advanced education and expertise to American so-ciety. By the early twentieth century, professionals were building organizations and establishing standards to secure their position socially and economically. The ideal of professionalism had been a rather frail one in America even as late as 1880. When every patent-medicine salesman could claim to be a doctor, when every frustrated politician could set up shop as a lawyer, when anyone who could read and write could pose as a teacher, professionals carried little of the weight and influence they would later acquire. There were, of course, many skilled and responsible doctors, lawyers, and teachers, but they had no way of controlling or distinguishing themselves clearly from the amateurs, charlatans, and incompe-tents who presumed to practice their trades. Hence, professionals themselves led the way in reforming standards and strengthening training requirements.

Among the first to act was the medical profession. Throughout the 1890s, doctors who considered themselves trained professionals began forming local associations and societies. In 1901, they reorganized the American Medical Association (AMA, founded in 1847) into a national professional society. By 1920, nearly two-thirds of all American doctors were members. The AMA quickly called for strict, scientific standards for admission to the practice of med-icine, with doctors themselves serving as protectors of the standards. State and local governments responded by passing new laws that required the licensing of all physicians and that restricted licenses to those practitioners approved by the profession.

Accompanying this emphasis on strict regulation of the profession came a concern for rigorous scientific training, education, and research. In the nineteenth century, medical education was notable for its tremendous variability from place to place, its sporadic quality, and the lack of scientific merit in many of the instructional offerings. By 1900, much had changed. Medical education at a few schools—most notably Johns Hopkins in Baltimore—compared favorably with the leading institutions of Europe. Doctors such as William H. Welch at Hopkins revolutionized the teaching of medicine by moving students out of the classrooms and into laboratories and clinics. Where a nineteenth century physician might be trained without ever setting foot in a hospital, modern hospitals soon became central to the medical education of doctors. Rigorous new standards forced many smaller medical schools out of existence. Those that remained were obliged to adopt a strict scientific approach.

One casualty of professionalization was diversity among medical practitioners. In the late nineteenth century, there were many small and diverse medical schools that trained women, working-class people, and African Americans. Rising professional standards forced many of these poorly endowed institutions out of business. As professional standards tightened, medicine tended to attract white, upper-middle-class male practitioners. In 1900, there were sixteen women's medical schools in the United States and ten colleges that trained African Americans. By 1916, only two of each still existed, a development that sharply curtailed educational opportunities for women and black Americans in medicine.

Professionalization proceeded apace in other professions as well. By 1916, lawyers in all forty-eight states had established professional bar associations, and virtually all of them had succeeded in creating examining boards, composed of lawyers, to regulate admission to the profession. Increasingly, aspiring lawyers found it necessary to enroll in graduate programs, and the nation's law schools accordingly expanded greatly, both in numbers and in the rigor of the curricula. Businessmen supported the creation of schools of business administration and created their own national organizations: the National Association of Manufacturers in 1895 and the United States Chamber of Commerce in 1912. Even farmers, long the symbol of individualism, responded to the new order by forming, through the National Farm Bureau Federation, a network of agricultural organizations designed to spread scientific farming methods, teach sound marketing techniques, and lobby for the interests of their members.

Among the purposes of professionalism was to guard entry into the professions. This was only partly an effort to defend the professions from the untrained and the incompetent. Tighter admission requirements also protected those already in professions from excessive competition and lent prestige and status to their achievements. By keeping the numbers down, professionals ensured that demand for the services of existing members would remain high.

The growth of professionalism reflected the larger movement in American society toward consolidation, organization, and standardization. The new professionals were highly diverse. But they shared a commitment to organizing themselves along increasingly national lines to advance the specialized knowledge and expertise on which their professional lives relied and to enhance their status within the fluid and unstable world of the industrial era.

The Rise of the Modern University

Science also found a comfortable home in the new research universities that emerged in the last decades of the nineteenth century. Although institutions of higher education existed prior to the Civil War, few Americans attended them and most of these schools bore little resemblance to the colleges and universities of our own time. The curriculum focused on classical education; many viewed college as a training school for the ministry. After the Civil War, higher education expanded tremendously. Liberal arts colleges, including schools for women, proliferated. State universities, funded by the Morrill Land Grant Act (1862), extended opportunities for higher education to Americans across the United States. The land grant schools were explicitly designed to educate working men and women, and agricultural colleges invariably formed the core of the new nation-wide state university system. Still, higher education remained an elusive goal and a luxury for the vast majority of Americans.

The founding of Johns Hopkins University in 1876 ushered in the modern American university. Hopkins emphasized graduate research and education and, in so doing, explicitly linked the purpose of higher education to the needs of a modern industrial society. Research universities emphasized their utility to the nation in advancing scientific knowledge, furthering technical expertise, and producing a skilled professional class. In the mid-1890s, Stanford (1891) and the University of Chicago (1892) opened; and Harvard, Yale, Columbia and others experienced significant transformations.

The modern university emerged in the context of the social and political upheaval that characterized America in the 1890s; its development soon became intertwined with the tumult of modern history. Scholars eagerly contributed to the whirlwind of intellectual discourse and debate concerning the future of American society. Far from insulating themselves within an ivory tower, professors and students at several leading universities attempted to widen the boundaries of the university to encompass the world outside its door. At the University of Chicago, an Extension School opened to provide educational opportunities to working people in the city; students and faculty volunteered at Hull House and worked with municipal officials to study and resolve complex social problems. The sociologist Albion Small argued that the scholar possessed a unique ability to analyze and ameliorate the most vexing issues posed by industrialism. Through scientific research on current social and economic issues, and a stance of scholarly objectivity, academic experts would substitute what Small called "the order of investigation" for the "riot of instigation" all too common in the discourse about contemporary social policy. Scholars who ignored pressing social and economic problems, Small wrote, "are shirkers unless they grapple with these problems. It is for this that society supports us."

Universities quickly ran into problems, however, as they attempted to balance active engagement in contemporary society against a stance of neutrality and scientific objectivity. Administrators were acutely aware of the corporate interests that supported the universities and often served as their trustees. At state universities this role was frequently filled by a Board of Regents appointed by the governor and answerable to the legislature. In the midst of the Pullman Strike, economist Richard Ely was tried by the Board of Regents at the University of Wisconsin for teaching radical economics and endorsing the actions of the striking railroad workers. He was ultimately acquitted in a decision that affirmed the principle of academic freedom for all who taught at the university. But similar cases in the 1890s highlighted the dangers that seemed to arise when advocacy tempered "objectivity." Still, these chilling cases did not sever the ties that joined many professors and students to the arena of social research, reform, and social policy.

Social Science and Social Policy

The reform impulse was particularly apparent in the development of academic social science in the 1880s and 1890s. The American Social Science Association (ASSA), founded in 1865, led the way in mobilizing support for scientific efforts to address the conditions of modern industrial society. At first, the organization brought together professional scholars and amateur students of society. Professors, doctors, lawyers, and other upper-middle-class elites endorsed the accumulation of knowledge and the application of expertise as a way of eradicating crime, political corruption, poverty, urban disorder, and inefficiency. The ASSA reflected the unswerving faith of its members in the power of science to unravel the evils afflicting industrial society. As academic life became more professionalized in the 1880s and 1890s, social science developed rapidly within the new research universities.

By the turn of the century, political science, sociology, economics, and, to a much lesser extent, history emphasized the connections between social policy and the science of society. Most social scientists rejected the "hands off" stance of Social Darwinists, who ridiculed efforts to improve society by means of regulation, reform, and enlightened social policy. Instead, leading scholars stressed the environmental roots of crime, inequality, and poverty. They also demythologized the great capitalist tycoons and revealed the role of luck and privilege in creating their success. Among the most brilliant critics of capitalism was economist Thorstein Veblen, a son of Norwegian immigrants, who earned a Ph.D. at Yale. His first book, *The Theory of the Leisure Class* (1899) lampooned the behavior of wealthy elites who engaged in "conspicuous consumption"—the mindless purchase of commodities to demonstrate status within the wider community.

Race and the Debate over Education and Expertise

The importance to society of science, advanced knowledge, and educational training sparked especially sharp debate among leading African-American intellectuals at the turn of the century. The argument centered around the best way to confront the inequality that was a legacy of 200 years of slavery, economic and political repression, and racial bigotry.

In 1895, Booker T. Washington, a former slave, founder of the Tuskegee Institute, and educational leader among the black community, took a controversial stand in a speech at the Atlanta Exposition. Known as the Atlanta Compromise, Washington's argument emphasized practical education, industrial training, and economic self-sufficiency more than political agitation as the surest path to equality. "In all things that are purely social," Washington insisted, "we can be as separate as the fingers, yet one as the hand in all things essential to mutual

BOOKER T. WASHINGTON.   Born into slavery, Booker T. Washington used the knowledge he acquired at the Hampton Institute and enormous persistence and hard work to develop the Tuskegee Institute, an educational institution for African Americans that would later become Tuskegee University. His emphasis on political moderation and economic self-determination through industrial education attracted much praise from white philanthropists and admiration among some in the black community. But it also sparked controversy as his deep disagreement with Du Bois would demonstrate.

progress." Such a stance flew in the face of those who rejected any accommodation to legal and political injustice.

W. E. B. Du Bois soon became one of Washington's harshest public critics. Their backgrounds could not have differed more. Du Bois was born in Great Barrington, Massachusetts, a predominantly white New England community. He attended Fisk, and he earned a Ph.D. from Harvard in 1895. Du Bois, a brilliant student of history and sociology, was teaching at Atlanta University when he entered into the controversy with Booker T. Washington. In *The Souls of Black Folk* (1903), a meditation on race and American society, Du Bois portrayed Washington as an accomodationist who bowed to segregation by limiting the aspirations he would set before the African-American community. Du Bois believed passionately in higher education, and he militantly rejected the ever-widening racial caste system that produced political, social, and economic inequality. "Is it possible and probable," he asked, "that nine millions of men can make effective progress in economic lines if they are deprived of political rights, made a servile caste, and allowed only the most meager chance for developing

W. E. B. DU BOIS.   A penetrating critic, commentator, and
activist, W. E. B. Du Bois left an enduring mark on
American intellectual life in the twentieth century. For
much of his life, Du Bois devoted his enormous literary
and intellectual skills to analyzing, addressing, and offering
new ways of understanding race relations, the African-
American experience, and the enduring impact of
its history on American society.

their exceptional men? If history and reason give any distinct answer to these questions, it is an emphatic No."

Du Bois stressed instead the importance of college and university training. Liberal, rather than vocational, education held the best promise for racial advancement, as did full civil rights, not some day in the future but immediately. To advance these ends, Du Bois met with others who shared his views on the Canadian side of Niagara Falls (no hotel on the American side would accommodate them) in 1905. The group launched what became known as the Niagara Movement, a determined effort to secure economic, political, and social equality in part by ending segregation and discrimination in education, unions, law, and transportation. In 1909 Du Bois and some of his associates joined forces with white progressives, including Jane Addams, in founding the National Association for the Advancement of Colored People (NAACP). The Association embraced many of the principles of the Niagara Movement and hired Du Bois to edit its journal *Crisis* while serving as director of research and publicity.

All the while Du Bois continued to pursue social research that would illuminate the problem of race—"the problem," he once wrote "of the twentieth century." Du Bois conducted an exhaustive social survey of the black community in Philadelphia with the help of Isabel Eaton, a graduate student in sociology from Columbia. The resulting book, *The Philadelphia Negro* (1899), was the first major social scientific work to detail the lives of black Americans. Du Bois was far from alone among African-American leaders in blending a zest for social inquiry with his many reform activities. In 1895, Ida B. Wells-Barnett, a courageous African-American teacher and journalist, compiled *The Red Record*, a gruesome compilation and statistical analysis of lynching. Like many progressives, Wells-Barnett hoped the exposure of such hideous facts would mobilize fair-minded Americans and strengthen her crusade to eradicate lynching.

In spite of the rise of modern science, theories of race and ethnicity rooted in dubious evolutionary, hereditarian, and biologically determinist theories were far from extinct. Nonetheless they came under the attack of influential social scientists with increasing frequency. Anthropologist Franz Boas challenged prevailing wisdom in his explorations of the cultural roots of many apparent racial differences. Boas's work on "primitive man" revealed the human forces that bound together people of widely disparate origins; his studies of generational change among immigrants cast doubt on the precepts of physical anthropology. Many of his female students, including Margaret Mead, applied this critical perspective to theories that stressed the biological roots of gender differences. These social scientific studies may not have changed the minds of those who clung to biological determinism. But they provided intellectual ammunition for reformers who challenged the anti-immigrant sentiments of nativists and the restrictions placed on women's roles.

ORGANIZING FOR REFORM

New ideas about social problems and a willingness to explore the roots of poverty and inequality would have achieved little by themselves. The work of reform also required leaders and institutional structures able to translate broad theories about the problems of industrial society into specific social policies. The proliferation of voluntary associations, groups of individuals brought together by their common interests, created a powerful organizational foundation for progressive reform campaigns.

By the 1890s, industrialization had sharpened popular awareness that the nation consisted of many distinct interest groups with different, and often competing, needs and interests. If government intervened to allocate resources or uphold the claims of one group—the railroads, for example—it might well work against the interests of others, such as small landowners or local businesses. Increasing awareness of the political dynamics of modern industrial society thus affirmed the wisdom of creating interest groups. In the progressive era, voluntary associations representing particular interests thus played an increasingly important role in influencing government and advancing reform crusades.

The Women's Club Movement

Women had long formed voluntary associations to pursue religious, cultural, and civic interests; before the Civil War, they had often formed auxiliary organizations when barred from participating in male-dominated political clubs and social groups. But women's organizations came to exert particularly strong influence in the progressive era. Their influence owed much to the enormous energy of club women and to the daunting size of their organizations. During the 1880s and 1890s, a vast network of women's associations emerged, initially as an outlet for the intellectual energies and cultural interests of many middle and upper-class women. By 1892, when the General Federation of Women's Clubs was formed to coordinate the activities of local organizations, more than 100,000 members were counted among nearly 500 women's clubs. In 1900, the membership rolls swelled to over 160,000; they exceeded 1 million by 1917.

Many women's clubs focused on noncontroversial activities such as tree planting; fund raising for schools, libraries, and hospitals; and literary discussion groups. By the early twentieth century, however, clubs had become markedly more interested in social issues and politics. Ironically, the fact that women could not vote may have contributed to the clubs' political influence. As organizations of nonvoters, the women's clubs made much of their nonpartisanship. They supported no particular candidate or party; their commitment, they stressed, was only to issues of social betterment and social justice. This proved a difficult argument for politicians, immersed as they were in the machinery of party politics, to dismiss.

Club women demonstrated formidable skills as lobbyists, beginning at the state level. In the early twentieth century, the General Federation of Women's

Clubs mounted an aggressive campaign on behalf of mother's pensions—public subsidies for widowed or abandoned women who were raising small children. In state after state where women's clubs devoted their energies to lobbying state legislatures, politicians sympathetic to mothers' pensions succeeded in passing this important social welfare measure. By 1920, over 40 states had passed legislation mandating mothers' pensions, although the subsidies were usually very modest.

Indeed, the women's clubs were an important part of a reform coalition that advanced a broad range of "maternalist" social policies in the early twentieth century. Appealing to the nation's conscience by invoking the plight of mothers and children, reformers stressed that Americans shared a civic responsibility to ensure the betterment and survival of the human race. In 1912, a coalition of clubwomen and female reformers pressured Congress into establishing a Children's Bureau within the Labor Department to protect the interests of children. Protective labor laws regulating working conditions for women similarly drew upon the assumption that women, more than men, needed and deserved special care and protection.

African-American women made important contributions to the women's club movement. Although some joined associations dominated by whites, many were excluded from such groups or relegated to the margins by the white leadership. Ida Wells-Barnett recalled her disappointing experience as a member of a mixed-race women's club: "Although I was loath to accept it, I came to the conclusion . . . that our white women friends were not willing to treat us on a plane of equality with themselves." As a result, African-American women soon formed their own network of women's clubs, many of them affiliated with the National Association of Colored Women. Black women's clubs devoted themselves especially to issues of education as a means of uplift for African Americans. And they naturally displayed much greater interest in and sensitivity to the problems of racial inequality than did their white counterparts.

The Woman Suffrage Movement

At the turn of the century, the issue of woman suffrage gave rise to one of the largest organized reform movements in American history. As early as the Seneca Falls Convention in 1848, feminists publicly demanded voting rights, which they considered a prerequisite to full equality. By the 1890s, women had been agitating for the vote for over forty years, with very little to show for it. Voting rights for women seemed a radical demand to many Americans, who considered politics a male endeavor and who thought of woman's civic role chiefly in terms of motherhood, of the woman's responsibility solely to protect and nurture children, home, and family. Men and women both opposed woman suffrage on grounds that ranged from biblical injunctions (woman as a helpmate not a ruler of men) to the "peculiarities" of women's biology (their supposed tendency to faint easily and to yield to the ruling influence of their ovaries). But others strongly endorsed woman suffrage as a matter of basic liberty and equality. Although many men enthusiastically supported voting rights for women, it was women themselves who exercised control over the burgeoning late–nineteenth century suffrage movement.

In 1890, the two major suffrage associations—the American Woman Suffrage Association and the National Woman Suffrage Association—consolidated their forces and formed the National American Woman Suffrage Association (NAWSA). That same year Wyoming became the first state in the union in which women had full voting rights. Feminists then believed that an aggressive state-by-state lobbying campaign held the greatest promise for future victories. Progress was very slow, but the rolls of the woman suffrage movement continued to swell. From a membership of some 13,000 in 1893, NAWSA grew to over 100,000 by 1915. Two years later, over 2 million belonged.

Although racked by dissension, the suffrage movement displayed enormous tenacity in fighting its many opponents. Women of various social classes endorsed suffrage, but middle-class women dominated the leadership of the organizations. Over time, some of these feminists displayed a willingness to deploy virtually any argument that might persuade politicians and the wider public. Rather than emphasizing suffrage as a "natural right" all women deserved as citizens of the republic, a stance taken by Elizabeth Cady Stanton early in the history of the movement, younger suffragists frequently resorted to arguments that stressed women's "difference." Their special qualities as women—including virtue, piety, and wholesomeness—would help clean up American politics, some suffragists maintained. Others stressed women's particular commitment to peace and social justice. Such arguments made suffrage seem a less radical demand to some who had once opposed it.

Some suffragists used racism and bigotry to make their case for enfranchisement. If African-American and immigrant men, common laborers, and other "base" groups enjoyed voting rights, why shouldn't middle- and upper-class white women have the privilege? By 1906, Florence Kelley expressed disgust with the persistence of such offensive rhetoric. "I have rarely heard a ringing suffrage speech which did not refer to the 'ignorant and degraded' men, or the 'ignorant immigrants' as our masters. This is habitually spoken with more or less bitterness." Kelley was not alone among suffragists in rejecting such lines of argument; many feminists insisted that working-class women needed political rights more than virtually any other group of American women. Still, the suffrage movement at times pandered to prevailing prejudices in their determination to secure victory.

Suffragists won no further states until Washington endorsed votes for women in 1910. California followed suit in 1911; 1912 brought three additional western states into the prosuffrage ranks. The association of suffragists with the issue of temperance remained a formidable obstacle to their cause among city dwellers, Catholics, and immigrants. That some suffrage leaders expressed anti-immigrant sentiments made votes for women unpopular among many Americans.

The western states proved especially receptive to woman's suffrage. Perhaps a lack of the entrenched traditions of the East, pioneer conditions that enhanced

DATES OF WOMAN SUFFRAGE

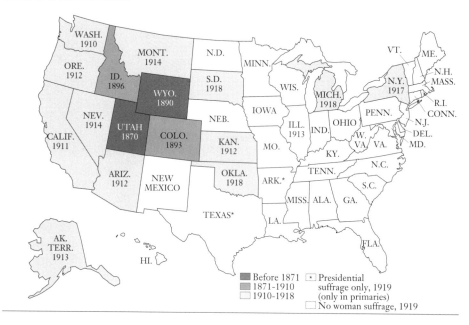

the social and economic value of women's work, and an emphasis on individualism among those who settled the frontier accounted, in part, for the progress suffragists made in the West. Sociologist Edward A. Ross argued that the paucity of women on the frontier elevated their status. "In the inter-mountain states, where there are at least two suitors for every woman, the sex becomes an upper caste to which nothing will be denied from street-car seats to ballots and public offices." Western boosters attempted to encourage family migration by boasting of the rights women enjoyed in the western states. Others embraced the notion that women's votes would limit the political influence of the mostly male immigrants in the West.

Continuing opposition in the East did little to daunt the determination of suffragists. Slowly the wall of resistance gave way in the second decade of the twentieth century. In 1913, Illinois became the first state east of the Mississippi to embrace woman's suffrage. That same year radical suffragist Alice Paul bolted from NAWSA and formed the Congressional Union. The Union devoted its energy to securing a federal constitutional amendment. Paul and her followers formed the National Woman's party in 1914. Her militance and frank determination to defeat unsympathetic congressmen alienated the more moderate leadership of NAWSA. Under the leadership of Carrie Chapman Catt, NAWSA worked instead, beginning in 1916, to promote Catt's "winning plan," a dual campaign to secure support for woman suffrage through referenda at the state level while pursuing the federal ratification campaign.

SUFFRAGE PROTEST.   Suffragists used the occasion of World War I to step up pressure on President Woodrow Wilson to support the woman suffrage amendment. Silent pickets, such as in this 1917 protest, became a familiar scene at the White House. Wilson dragged his feet, but finally in 1918 he delivered a forceful plea to the U.S. Senate to pass woman suffrage as a "war measure." Nearly another year went by before the Senate approved the measure, and not until 1920 was the nineteenth amendment granting women voting rights finally ratified.

The suffrage movement was a powerful demonstration of the strength of progressive era voluntary associations in advancing special interest politics. It is true that women represented half of the people and suffrage a great deal more than single-issue politics. Still, the combined energies of countless suffrage organizations, millions of voters, and a campaign that included everything from massive parades to hunger strikes testified to the vitality of extraparty politics. In 1920, the suffrage movement finally triumphed with the ratification of the nineteenth amendment. While not all items on the progressive reform agenda fared as well, votes for women seemed to demonstrate a potential for sweeping change in American society, progressive era social activists were determined to extend that potential further.

SOURCES OF PROGRESSIVE REFORM

Middle-class reformers, most of them from the East, dominated the public image and much of the substance of reform in the late nineteenth and early twentieth centuries. But they were not alone in seeking to improve social conditions. Working-class Americans, African Americans, westerners, even party bosses also played crucial roles in advancing some of the important reforms of the era.

Labor, the Machine, and Reform

Although the American Federation of Labor, and its leader Samuel Gompers, remained largely aloof from many of the reform efforts of the time (reflecting Gompers's firm belief that workers should not rely on government to improve their lot), some unions nevertheless played important roles in reform battles. In San Francisco, for example, workers in the Building Trades Council spearheaded the formation of the new Union Labor Party, committed to a program of reform almost indistinguishable from that of middle-class and elite progressives in the city. Corruption and ineptitude within the new party's leadership limited its effectiveness, but the party did manage to elect two of its candidates mayor. Although the workers never controlled enough votes in the state legislature to have much direct influence, other Bay Area politicians supported prolabor legislation in an effort to appeal to the party's constituency. Between 1911 and 1913, California passed a child labor law, a workmen's compensation law, and a limitation on working hours for women. Union pressures contributed to the passage of similar laws in many other states as well.

One result of such assaults on the existing parties was a change in the party organizations themselves, which attempted to adapt to new realities so as to preserve their influence. Some party machines emerged from the progressive era almost as powerful as they had entered it. In large part, this was because bosses recognized that they had to change in order to survive. Thus they sometimes allowed their machines to become vehicles of social reform. One example was New York's Tammany Hall, the nation's oldest and most notorious city machine. Its astute leader, Charles Francis Murphy, began in the early years of the century to fuse the techniques of boss rule with some of the concerns of social reformers. Murphy did nothing to challenge the fundamental workings of Tammany Hall. But Tammany began to take an increased interest in state and national politics, which it had traditionally scorned; and it used its political power on behalf of legislation to improve working conditions, protect child laborers, and eliminate the worst abuses of the industrial economy.

In 1911, a terrible fire swept through the factory of the Triangle Shirtwaist Company in New York City; 146 workers, most of them women, died. Many of them had been trapped inside the burning building because management had locked the emergency exits to prevent malingering. For the next three years, a state commission studied not only the background of the fire but the general condition of the industrial workplace. It was responding to intense public pressure from women's groups and New York City labor unions—and to less-public pressure from Tammany Hall. By 1914, the commission had issued a series of reports calling for major reforms in the conditions of modern labor.

The report itself was a classic progressive document, based on the testimony of experts, filled with statistics and technical data. Yet when its recommendations reached the New York Legislature, its most effective supporters were not middle-class progressives but two Tammany Democrats from working-class backgrounds: Senator Robert F. Wagner and Assemblyman Alfred E. Smith. With the support of Murphy and the backing of other Tammany legislators, they steered through a series of pioneering labor laws that imposed strict regulations on factory owners and established effective mechanisms for enforcement.

Western Progressives

The American West was not only the region that provided the suffrage movement with its earliest successes, it also produced some of the most notable progressive leaders of the time: Hiram Johnson of California, George Norris of Nebraska, William Borah of Idaho, and others—almost all of whom spent at least some of their political careers in the United States Senate. That was because for western states, the most important target of reform energies was not state or local governments, which had relatively little power, but the federal government, which exercised a kind of authority in the West that it had never possessed in the East.

Some of the most important issues affecting the future of the West required action above the state level. Disputes over water, for example, almost always involved rivers and streams that crossed state lines. The question of who had the rights to the waters of the Colorado River created a political battle that no state government could resolve; the federal government had to arbitrate. More significantly, perhaps, the federal government exercised enormous power over the lands and resources of the western states and provided substantial subsidies to the region in the form of land grants and support for railroad and water projects. Huge areas of the West remained (and still remain) public lands, controlled by Washington—a far greater proportion than in any states east of the Mississippi; and much of the growth of the West was (and continues to be) a result of federally funded dams and water projects.

Because so much authority in the region rested in federal bureaucracies, which state and local governments could not control, political parties in most of the West were relatively weak. That was one reason why western states could move so quickly and decisively to embrace reforms that parties did not like: among them woman suffrage, the initiative, the referendum, the recall, direct primaries. It is also why aspiring politicians were much quicker to look to Washington as a place from which they could influence the future of their region.

Varieties of Progressive Reform

More than one historian has despaired of finding any useful definition of progressivism. The reform energies of the early twentieth century were enormously varied. The reformers themselves represented no single class, region, religion, or race. The ideas that supported reforms were so disparate as to seem at times incoherent. There was, in the end, no coherent "progressive movement." There was, instead, a cluster of highly varied impulses and efforts.

But despite the enormous variety of the reform impulses of the time, despite the impossibility of finding any single definition of them, the first years of the twentieth century remain distinct for the broad effort on behalf of progressive change that swept American society. For in those years, vast numbers of Americans mobilized themselves to fight against what they considered social injustices and maladjustments and to create a better world for themselves and for their children. In the end it was their faith in the ability of society to solve its problems and brighten its future that most clearly characterized the progressive era. It was a time of great turmoil, anguish, and conflict. It was a time of great achievement and even greater hope. And it was too, a time of growing faith in the power of government to play a major role in shaping the future.

CHAPTER SIX

Reforming Politics, Mobilizing Government

~

I n the first two decades of the twentieth century, a broad array of progressive reform initiatives began to assume concrete political form. Increasingly, reformers called for more expansive government action to solve social problems and to reshape the modern industrial economy. In part, American activists were trying to bring social welfare programs to the United States that were already in virtually every Western European industrial society. By 1911 England had enacted workmen's compensation, unemployment compensation, old age pensions, and national health insurance. Germany and France also offered state welfare provisions that far exceeded the record of the United States. Many progressives hoped to emulate the European model of an emerging welfare state. But progressives were responding to other concerns as well, especially in their efforts to limit the power of the political parties and increase the authority of both the people and the "experts." Reshaping politics and government moved to the center of the progressive agenda.

Initially many progressive reformers focused on regulation and reform at the municipal level. Notable achievements were made in passing laws and ordinances governing housing, public health, safety in turn of the century cities, and in reforming urban governments. But frustration with lax enforcement and the corruption of big city political machines prompted reformers to widen their ambitions. Attempts to achieve state and federal reform soon became a persistent theme in modern American politics.

The reform initiatives of the progressive era had no single unifying theme; they were diverse in their intentions, sometimes idiosyncratic in content, often rather ambiguous in consequences. The tenor of public policy was notable for its increasing reliance on government to mediate the demands and address the needs of competing interest groups. But reformers continued to run up against powerful constraints: lingering popular beliefs in individual autonomy, in the virtues of limited government, and in competing ideas about what made for a good and just society.

THE GOOD GOVERNMENT CAMPAIGN

For many progressive reformers, enlightened, fair-minded, and efficient public policy held the only promise of countering the powerful private interests that were corrupting American society. But government at the dawn of the new century was ill prepared for the new tasks progressives wished it to perform. At every level, political institutions appeared outmoded, disorganized, and inefficient, if not blatantly corrupt. Many reformers therefore concluded that government could not be an instrument of change unless government itself first became the object of reform. At the heart of the problem, many progressives believed, were the political parties. If power could be wrested away from unscrupulous political bosses and their corrupt machines, politics might become a useful vehicle of reform. For this reason, the party system and the structure of American politics rose to the top of the reform agenda of many progressives.

Reforming City Government

The very emblem of political corruption during the progressive era was the urban political machine, the object of relentless attack by reformers throughout much of the late nineteenth century. By the 1890s, most states had already enacted ballot reform, a seemingly simple but very important challenge to the machine. As of 1910 every state in the union mandated a secret ballot except North Carolina, South Carolina, and Georgia. Under the old procedure, political parties printed their own ballots—sometimes in distinct colors to make for easy identification—which they distributed to their supporters for deposit in the ballot box on election day. This system made it easy for bosses to monitor the voting behavior of their constituents; it also posed a formidable challenge to ticket splitting—voting for candidates of different parties for different offices. The new secret ballot—or "Australian" ballot, as it was called—required state or local governments to print uniform ballots, distribute them at the polls, and make sure they were cast in secret. Ballot reform did not succeed in putting the machines out of business, but it did help chip away at their power over voters.

Reformers who made city government their target during the progressive era faced a formidable array of opponents. In addition to challenging the city bosses and their many loyalists, they were taking on a large and often well-hidden system of special interests—ranging from saloon owners and brothel keepers to corporations—that worked closely with the bosses. By 1900, oil, coal, life insurance, and other companies had joined the railroads in pouring corporate financial contributions into the coffers of innumerable political organizations. In the cities, the opportunities for graft were especially rich, a fact that heightened resistance to reform politics. Politicians who extorted money from businesses in exchange for the award of lucrative franchises had no interest in "cleaning up" or professionalizing municipal administration. Businesses counted on financial influence to ensure the quick disappearance of any unwelcome legislative measures. Each side, in other words, had an interest in courting the other, and neither saw much immediate use in the agenda of reform politics.

Although citizens often paid the price for urban political corruption in the form of higher taxes and substandard services, they did not always rally around reform candidates or measures. The boss system succeeded because it created a huge infrastructure full of rewards and punishments. Many city dwellers, recent immigrants especially, relied on the machines as a source of jobs and services. Others distrusted urban reformers, many of whom showed disdain for immigrant voters and who sometimes even seemed to be questioning their right to participate in politics. Over time, however, the reformers scored some notable successes. Their political strength grew in part because of the perceived failures of existing political leadership. The rising cost of city services, growing discontent with the parties, and even a decreasing interest in voting helped reformers wrest control in some cities from entrenched political machines.

Reform politicians soon found out, however, that electoral victories alone could not defeat the power brokers. Frustrated by their efforts to stop corruption, reform mayors such as Tom L. Johnson of Cleveland and Samuel "Golden Rule" Jones of Toledo began to demand public ownership of utilities. More common was a growing chorus of support for new administrative arrangements to govern the cities. A key innovation occurred first in Galveston, Texas, where a hurricane and tidal wave ravaged the city in 1900. The existing government could not begin to cope with the crisis. As a result of the catastrophe, prominent local businessmen and reformers succeeded in pushing a plan that called for a new city charter turning governance over to five popularly elected commissioners in 1903. The commission form of government soon spread to other cities. In 1907, Iowa approved the commission plan for large cities and coupled it with an array of reform initiatives including at-large elections for commissioners, as well as the use of the initiative, referendum, and recall as a means of increasing government accountability to voters in the city. Des Moines became the first city in the state to pursue the idea; it soon caught on in many parts of the country.

Although the commission plan streamlined and centralized city government, it did not provide a means for coordinating the work of the new administrative chiefs. As a result, reformers in some cities began to press for the appointment of professional city managers. Hired by elected city officials for their administrative expertise, city managers were expected to be nonpartisan, skilled executives capable of running the city on a day-to-day basis. Broad policy, on the other hand, was made by elected city councilors or commissioners. By the end of the progressive era, nearly 400 cities operated under the commission form of government. Over 300 had hired city managers. In both cases, reform led to the growth of a professional, nonpartisan bureaucracy.

Municipal reform programs, although promoted as a safeguard of democracy, in some ways actually limited popular participation in the municipal government. In protecting governments from the political machines, progressives were also isolating them from the people. The new nonpartisan bureaucracies often failed to inspire voter loyalty and political enthusiasm. In any case, neither reformers nor their opponents could claim complete victory. City government remained a political battleground well into the twentieth century.

State Reform

The demand for good government soon moved from city halls to state capitols. In some cases, reformers looked to the states out of frustration with the pace and scope of municipal change. In others, they drew from their victories at the city level a determination to extend the reach of reform initiatives. The corruption and inefficiency of state legislatures made them a predictable target of progressives. In the view of many reformers, the state legislatures were sinecures for the incompetent and unprincipled pawns of party bosses. One way to circumvent these corrupt politicians, reformers believed, was to increase the power of the electorate.

Two reform measures initially proposed by the populists in the 1890s—the initiative and the referendum—proved critical to the progressive bid to recapture state government. The initiative permitted reformers to bypass state legislatures by submitting new legislation directly to the voters for approval in general elections. The referendum allowed legislative measures already approved to be returned to the voters for approval or rejection. These measures increased the leverage voters could exercise over the state legislatures. But they also gave to special interest groups a powerful tool for exerting pressure on state politics. By 1918, over twenty states had enacted the initiative and the referendum.

Electoral reforms designed to break the stranglehold of the political parties over state politics also figured prominently on the agenda of progressives. A demand for the direct popular election of United States senators, a function traditionally performed by state legislatures, resulted in the approval of the Seventeenth Amendment to the constitution in 1913. The direct primary attempted to wrest away from the parties the power to control the nominations of candidates for political office through their conventions and caucuses. By 1915 almost every state in the nation had instituted primary elections for at least some offices.

Although primary elections gave voters the power to select candidates, not every voter enjoyed the privilege. In the South, the direct primary became a way further to limit black voting by tightening the noose of disfranchisement. Primary voting, some white southerners believed, would be easier to control than general elections. Although the direct primary quickly became established in southern states, the process of disfranchisement continued to virtually eradicate voting among African Americans in the region. Less well received North and South was the recall, a measure more popular in the West, that enabled voters to remove a public official from office during a special election called by citizen petition.

Progressive reform at the state level took aim not only at election rules but at the nexus between business and politics. By the early twentieth century, revelations about business corruption of politics had created considerable support in some states for new laws regulating lobbyists. By 1908, twenty-two states had banned campaign contributions by corporations; twenty-four forbade public officials from accepting free passes from railroads. In 1909, the United States Congress followed suit and outlawed corporate campaign contributions in federal elections.

The limitations such laws imposed were part and parcel of a larger regulatory movement in many states targeted at large business interests. Between 1905 and 1909, most southern states passed laws requiring the railroads to lower their freight and passenger rates. In many states where no such agencies existed, regulatory commissions were created to oversee the railroads; in other states, existing agencies were given broader mandates. The regulatory impulse directed first at transportation soon gave way in some states to insistent demands for state intervention in banking, utilities, and insurance.

Reform efforts proved most effective in states that elevated vigorous and committed politicians to positions of leadership. In New York, Governor Charles Evans Hughes mustered progressive sentiment to create a commission regulating public utilities. In California, Governor Hiram Johnson employed the new reforms to limit the political power of the Southern Pacific Railroad. In New Jersey, Woodrow Wilson, the Princeton University president elected governor in 1910, exercised executive leadership to carve away at incorporation and business laws that had earned the state its dubious distinction as "the mother of trusts."

But the most celebrated state-level reformer was Robert M. La Follette of Wisconsin. Elected governor in 1900, he helped turn his state into what reformers across the nation described as a "laboratory of progressivism." The Wisconsin progressives won approval of direct primaries, initiatives, and referenda. They regulated railroads and utilities. They passed laws governing the workplace and providing compensation for laborers injured in industrial accidents. They instituted graduated taxes on inherited fortunes and nearly doubled state levies on railroads and other corporate interests.

"Fighting Bob" La Follette, as he became known, brought a fervent, almost evangelical, commitment to reform. He used his personal magnetism to widen public awareness of progressive issues and to mobilize the energies of many previously passive citizens. Reform was not simply the responsibility of politicians, he argued, but of newspapers, citizens' groups, educational institutions, business and professional organizations, and countless other members of the public. In 1906, La Follette took his message from the statehouse of Wisconsin to the floor of the U.S. Senate. Ultimately, La Follette would find himself overshadowed by other national progressive leaders. But in the early years of the twentieth century, few men more effectively publicized the message of reform; none was as successful in blending state government and progressive politics.

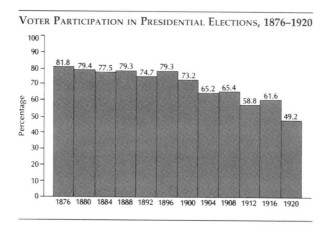

VOTER PARTICIPATION IN PRESIDENTIAL ELECTIONS, 1876–1920

Taken together, the good government movement did much to change the character of American politics. Reformers did not, of course, eliminate the political parties from American life, but they did contribute to a decline in party influence. One index of their impact was a decline in voter turnout. In the late nineteenth century, up to eighty-one percent of eligible voters routinely turned out for national elections. By the early twentieth century, turnout had begun to spiral down markedly. In the presidential election of 1900, seventy-three percent of the electorate voted. By 1912, that rate had declined to about fifty-nine percent. Voter turnout has never again reached as high as the seventy percent it had been when high levels of party loyalty mobilized broad participation.

Instead, interest groups that emerged outside the party system assumed increasing importance in American politics. In the progressive era, these professional organizations, trade associations (representing particular businesses and industries), labor unions, settlement workers, women's clubs, and countless other non-party groups helped perfect a new pattern of politics. Individuals who joined forces around a particular issue increasingly organized to influence government directly rather than through party structures.

REGULATING SOCIETY

Despite the strength of reform sentiment, many forces constrained government activism in the early twentieth century. For every interest group intent on using government to improve society, there were others determined to limit state power and preserve an unregulated economy. Progressive reformers succeeded in overcoming much resistance to reform in the early twentieth century. But compromises and accommodations often weakened their achievements.

Child Labor Reform

Child labor reform might seem to be a relatively noncontroversial item on the progressive reform agenda. By 1900, twenty-eight states had already passed some laws limiting the employment of children in industry. But enforcement provisions were often lax, and in many southern states large textile mills relied heavily upon child labor. Nearly 2 million children remained in the labor force in the early twentieth century.

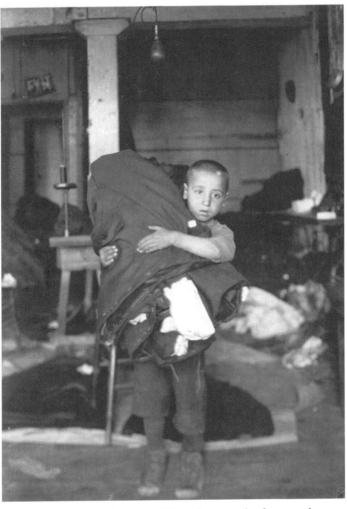

CHILD LABOR.   This Lewis Hine photograph of a young boy collecting cloth to be finished at home was taken in 1912. The child's world-weary face reflects experience far beyond his years. Efforts to curb child labor, however, ran up against powerful constraints in the early twentieth century.

As a result, reformers continued to denounce the exploitation of young children in factories. The image of stunted, maimed, and hollow-faced children, starkly portrayed in Lewis Hine's extraordinary photography, filled the pages of many magazines. In 1902 the New York Child Labor Committee was established by Florence Kelley, Lillian Wald, the founder of the Henry Street Settlement, and journalist Robert Hunter, later the author of an impassioned study entitled *Poverty* (1904). They hoped to bring together opponents of child labor in one powerful committee. At the same time, an Alabama minister named Edgar Gardner Murphy was spearheading a successful drive to pressure his state legislature to pass the South's first child labor reform statute, a feat he accomplished in 1903. In 1904, Kelley, Wald, Hunter, and other activists formed the National Child Labor Committee to lobby for legislative change. Over the next few years legal progress continued to be made as child labor laws passed in several—but by no means all—states across the country.

To circumvent the recalcitrance of states unwilling to change, Kelley and her committee proposed and lobbied for a federal law prohibiting child labor. Formidable opposition to federal intervention continued to dog these efforts. Southern textile mills fought the effort to deplete their supply of cheap labor. They also viewed child labor regulation as an unwelcome toehold by the government that might lead to further protective laws and the erosion of emerging southern industries. Other Americans trumpeted the virtues of hard work as a moral salve for even the youngest people. Politicians and industrialists who opposed child labor laws shrewdly tapped deep hostility to government interference with parental decisions about their children and their families. In the South, that message was often joined to an inflammatory "states rights" rhetoric. "Much has been said," Governor Coleman Blease of South Carolina noted in a speech that evoked both themes, "about the enactment of laws in regard to the labor in our cotton mills. These people are our people; they are our kindred; they are our friends, and in my opinion they should be left alone, and allowed to manage their own children and allowed to manage their own affairs."

In fact, many working-class families themselves opposed child labor laws because they threatened the family economy. Some relied upon their children's wages either to supplement parental earnings or to compensate for the lost earnings of an absent or sick adult. Women who brought their children to the mills or instructed them to come to the factories after school depended upon a workplace that permitted the presence of children. Before long, some children who played at the mill found themselves employed by the factory. Some preferred work to school; others did not see this as a choice and were moved by a sense of family responsibility. One young South Carolinian, who left school after second grade to help his widowed mother at the mill, later recalled: "She wanted me to go to school until I got in the fifth grade. I told her, 'You need the help worse than I need the education, because I can get it later on, or I can do without it.' And so I went to work as quick as I possibly could." Reformers who attacked parents for exploiting their own children often only antagonized the mill workers.

Despite such opposition, child labor reformers succeeded in their efforts to advance a federal child labor bill. In 1916 Congress passed the Keating-Owen Child Labor Act that barred from interstate commerce goods manufactured by children under the age of 16. The law affected only a fraction of working children, but reformers were exhilarated by their victory. Resistance to the law, however, remained stiff and constitutional tests of Keating-Owen followed quickly. Although five federal courts upheld the constitutionality of the law, the U.S. Supreme Court concluded otherwise. In *Hammer* v. *Dagenhart* (1918), the court ruled that Congress had overstepped it powers by interfering in local industry.

In many respects, child labor reform typified early twentieth century efforts to expand the power of the state. The campaign relied upon publicity, education, and extensive organization to advance the child labor issue. It sought national remedies while simultaneously pursuing change at the state level. The movement was nonpartisan, at least initially, stressing the moral foundations of child labor reform rather than political expediency. It attempted to tap an avenue to legislative change that had been successfully tested in the courts—sympathy for regulating the working conditions of "helpless" members of society (women and children, allegedly). It achieved notable success in many states, only to crash against a wall of resistance imposed by a narrow judicial vision of the federal government's rights and responsibilities.

Protecting Men and Women in the Workplace

Late nineteenth and early twentieth century reformers wanted to protect not just children, but also men and women in the workplace. The United States' extraordinarily high industrial accident rate seemed testimony enough to the necessity of some legislative action. Nearly 500,000 workers died on the job in 1906 alone. The nation's coal mines were the sites of thousands of fatal work-related accidents. In addition, the routine of accident and death was punctuated by occasional large-scale catastrophes, as in the 1911 Triangle Shirtwaist Factory fire in New York that sent 146 workers to their deaths. Without insurance, victims injured in such accidents or families who lost a loved one (and sometimes their sole means of support) were simply out of luck.

By 1910 the states had passed literally hundreds of statutes addressing the conditions of labor, including laws regulating hours, wages, occupational health, child labor, and an array of safety measures. One of the most important, and politically successful efforts to protect workingmen and -women was the campaign for workmen's compensation. While coverage varied considerably from state to state, most programs required employers to provide insurance for their workers against work-related accidents. Many employers endorsed workmen's compensation as a way of avoiding the inconvenience and expense of lengthy judicial proceedings and the prospect of state insurance programs. Workmen's compensation took root, anthropologist William Ogburn noted, some fifty years after the emergence of the working conditions that had made it necessary. Still, thirty-seven states had passed workmen's compensation acts by 1917. The success of this reform owed much to the mutual benefits that accrued to workers and employers. The legislation provided a more socially responsible and, it appeared, business-friendly method of dealing with the risks and hazards of industrial work.

The long hours industrial workers commonly put in contributed mightily to the prevalence of horrible accidents. But reformers met much greater resistance in their efforts to combat this aspect of the factory system. The courts upheld some state and municipal laws restricting the hours of work in the late nineteenth and early twentieth centuries. But in 1905, the Supreme Court of the United States swept away a New York law setting an eight-hour day for bakers in *Lochner* v. *New York*. In judging the regulation, Justice Rufus Peckham's majority opinion stressed "the freedom of master and employee to contract with each other . . . cannot be prohibited or interfered with without violating the Fourteenth Amendment's guarantee of liberty." (This sweeping protection of the sanctity of private contracts remained a cornerstone of American judicial philosophy for more than thirty years.) Because the court had upheld an 1895 Utah statute regulating the hours of miners for reasons of public health, reformers had stressed the hazards bakers endured breathing in flour day in and day out and laboring in hot bakeries long into the wee hours of the morning. The court rejected these claims in the Lochner case.

In 1908 the Supreme Court partially reversed Lochner by upholding a law limiting the hours of women workers in *Muller* v. *Oregon*. The case was notable for the brief submitted by Attorney Louis Brandeis, who defended Oregon's protective labor law. Florence Kelley, head of the National Consumers' League, worked closely with the Oregon branch of her organization in mounting a defense of the law and in shaping the Brandeis Brief, which was actually written in large part by Brandeis's sister-in-law, Josephine Goldmark, a prominent social activist. The brief marshaled prodigious social, medical, and scientific research to bolster its claim that the state had a compelling interest in safeguarding the health and well-being of women workers. The Supreme Court found merit in the argument and couched its decision in paternalist rhetoric. In speaking of women's importance to society, the Court asserted "the race needs her; her children need her; her friends need her, in a way that they do not need the other sex."

Many reformers hoped protective labor legislation for women would provide an opening wedge that would ultimately permit ever-widening state intervention on behalf of all workers. But despite growing attention to the chronic existence of unemployment in industrialized America, no serious or wide-ranging measures were enacted in the progressive era to provide insurance for the jobless. Minimum wage laws for women and children passed in fewer than a dozen states by World War I. Opposition to extending the provision to men flowed not only from business and the courts but from labor leaders such as Samuel Gompers, who feared, among other things, that a minimum would soon become a maximum wage.

Old Age and Health Insurance

Efforts to create old age and health insurance also stalled in the progressive era. Reformers who hoped to extend the Civil War pension system failed to win support for public subsidies for old age pensions. The inauguration of old age insurance in Europe did little to sway opponents in the United States. Critics looked with a jaundiced eye at the Civil War pension system and saw a fount of profligate federal spending and partisan corruption. As longevity increased, the problem of poverty among the elderly became more apparent. But federal programs of relief were almost nonexistent until the mid-twentieth century.

With the exception of mother's pensions and workmen's compensation, social welfare measures enacted in other Western industrialized nations failed to take root in American society. By 1913, nations from Great Britain to the Netherlands required some program of compulsory health insurance; other countries, including France, Italy, and Switzerland, provided state subsidies to assist workers in acquiring coverage. Most Americans, in contrast, had no coverage at all for medical or hospital costs in the early twentieth century. Those who did usually purchased their policies privately from their unions, from fraternal organizations, or from commercial insurance companies. A few employers provided health insurance to their workers, but such benefits were a distinct rarity. In 1915 the American Association of Labor Legislation (AALL) proposed a model legislative program designed to provide state health insurance for workers and their families. Financed jointly by employees, employers, and state governments, the plan provided coverage for medical bills, sick pay, and maternity benefits. Although some physicians supported the AALL model health insurance policy, opposition from the AFL, business, insurance companies, and many doctors—all suspicious of government interference in "private" matters—helped to sink the proposal. Several states debated health insurance in the progressive era but the only one to vote on the idea—California—defeated it in a state referendum by a wide margin.

Progressives thus had a mixed record in the early twentieth century on social welfare initiatives. Reformers succeeded in moving the nation toward exercising greater responsibility for workers, children, and the indigent. But strong resistance to other innovations frustrated social activists.

CONTROLLING SOCIETY

Efforts to reform politics and to widen government responsibility for social welfare were only part of the progressive agenda. There was also another reform current in the early twentieth century that expressed anxieties about personal morality, individual behavior, and social chaos. Some of the reformers who pressed for an active government in the early twentieth century sought to use the instruments of politics to control critical aspects of society. Campaigns to eliminate alcohol from the nation, to curb prostitution, regulate divorce, and create cultural unity through immigration restriction or aggressive assimilation policies gained many converts in the early years of the twentieth century. Such issues also created unlikely allies. Religious groups, conservative moralists, and progressive reformers sometimes found themselves working together—even if for different reasons—on behalf of common causes.

Temperance

Temperance was a cause that brought people across the political spectrum together in the early twentieth century. Many fundamentalist Protestants considered alcohol a moral issue and viewed drink as an instrument of the devil. Their opposition to liquor was hardly new to the progressive era. But the association of alcohol abuse with immigrants and the cities in the late nineteenth century gave an added force to these traditional criticisms of intemperance. Businessmen began to take an interest in the cause of temperance because of the effects of alcohol on their workers. Lost days of work, sickness, and lack of diligence all could be attributed, some corporate leaders maintained, to the reckless drinking habits of the working class. Temperance, they believed, would create order and efficiency in the work environment. For other reformers, alcohol abuse was less a moral issue than a blight on the family that led to domestic violence, unemployment, and impoverishment. Women reformers had long used the issue of temperance as a platform from which to condemn wife beating, marital rape, and family violence. Critics of economic privilege denounced the liquor industry as one of the nation's most sinister trusts. And political reformers, who looked on the saloon (correctly) as one of the central institutions of the machine, linked intemperance to the bosses and political corruption. Prohibition sentiment took root especially in the South, where many temperance advocates linked alcohol abuse to an array of racial problems. Bigots insisted there was a close connection between the "negro problem and the whisky problem," while Booker T. Washington viewed prohibition as a possible cure for lynching. Virtually everyone, it seemed, could find some evil in the specter of intemperance.

As a social movement, temperance dated back to the antebellum period, when both male and female reformers formed large organizations in a crusade infused with evangelical sentiment. The movement experienced a resurgence in the 1870s when the Women's Christian Temperance Union (WCTU) was founded in 1873. By 1911, the WCTU had 245,000 members and was the largest single women's organization in American history. The WCTU publicized the evils of alcohol while stressing the connection between drunkenness and the destruction of the American family, as well as the need for improved living conditions for working-men and -women.

TEMPERANCE CRUSADERS.   Artist Ben Shahn's depiction of the Women's Christian Temperance Union portrayed the reformers as elegantly dressed older women in Victorian garb gathered outside a saloon. In fact, temperance appealed to many groups of Americans as a cause to rally around.

However traditional the values it expressed, the temperance movement made ample use of the instruments of progressive reform politics. In 1893, the Anti-Saloon League added to the battle cry a demand for the legal abolition of saloons as a legislative remedy for intemperance. Gradually that demand escalated to include the complete prohibition of the sale and manufacture of alcoholic beverages everywhere in the land. With other sympathetic organizations, the Anti-Saloon League made extensive use of the initiative and referendum, political propaganda, elections, and every instrument of lobbying. By 1916, nineteen states had passed prohibition laws, and local option (whereby a community could decide to prohibit the sale of alcohol within its borders) was commonplace in every region. All this occurred despite substantial opposition from immigrant and working-class voters, and despite evidence that the country was actually experiencing a *decline* in alcohol consumption even without legislation.

America's entry into World War I, and the moral fervor it unleashed, provided the last needed push for those determined to nationalize prohibition. In 1917, with the critical support of rural fundamentalists, progressive advocates of prohibition steered a constitutional amendment through Congress outlawing the sale and manufacture of liquor. Two years later, after ratification by every state in the nation except Connecticut, New Jersey, and Rhode Island (where Catholic immigrants opposed it), the Eighteenth Amendment became law, to take effect in January 1920. Prohibition thus became one of the boldest experiments in social control in the nation's history, one that harnessed the power of the federal government to the moral imperative expressed by an array of early–twentieth century activists.

Immigration Restriction

Efforts to enact immigration reform also reflected a wish to use the power of the state to address what many believed was a national emergency. Virtually all reformers agreed that growing immigration had created serious social problems in the United States, but there was no broad agreement about the best solutions. Some progressives believed the nation needed to devote energy and financial resources to helping newcomers find housing, work, and education in their new land, and to helping them adapt to American life. Others argued that efforts at assimilation had failed miserably; the only solution now was to limit the flow of new arrivals. Still others moved back and forth between these two views, shifting their opinions frequently.

In the first decades of the century, pressure to restrict immigration mounted. New intellectual theories resurrected hereditarian views that charged immigrants with polluting the nation's racial stock. The spurious "science" of eugenics added the weight of alleged expertise to these ideas as publicists such as Madison Grant warned of the dangers of "mongrelization" in mixing Anglo-Saxon and Nordic stock with the blood of eastern Europeans, Hispanics, and Asians. In 1910 a special federal commission of "experts" chaired by Senator William P. Dillingham of Vermont endorsed the theory that newer immigrant groups—largely southern and eastern Europeans—posed a threat to American society because they could not be easily assimilated. The Dillingham Commission put its weight behind the literacy test as a means of keeping out the most ignorant. Over time, even many Americans who rejected racial arguments supported immigration restriction as a way of addressing urban problems such as overcrowding, unemployment, strained social services, and political unrest.

Immigration restriction gathered speed throughout the early twentieth century as the AFL, leading politicians, and countless other Americans endorsed at least some legislative initiative to slow, if not stop, migration. Yet powerful opponents—employers who saw immigration as a source of cheap labor, the immigrants themselves and their political representatives—managed to block the restriction movement until after World War I. At that point a nativist tide began to wash over the entire nation.

CONTROLLING CORPORATE POWER

The industrial economy itself—the power of corporations, the influence of business leaders—was always at the center of progressive concerns, and at the center of calls for government action. Most of those who supported broad state intervention in the economy and society took pains to distinguish their programs from socialism. Other Americans, however, called this model of liberal reform an ineffective set of solutions. They believed the problems of American industrial society required radical change; some came to embrace the vision of economic cooperation offered by socialism.

The Dream of Socialism

At no time in American history to that point, and rarely afterward, did radical critiques of American capitalism attract more support than they did between 1900 and 1914. Although never a force that threatened the two major political parties, the Socialist party accumulated considerable political strength during the first two decades of the twentieth century. In the election of 1900, the party had attracted the support of fewer than 100,000 voters. But after several factions coalesced to form a united Socialist party in 1901, its influence steadily grew. In 1912, its resilient leader and perennial presidential candidate, Eugene V. Debs, received nearly 1 million votes. Strongest in urban immigrant communities (particularly among Germans and Jews), socialism attracted the loyalties of substantial numbers of Protestant farmers in the South and Midwest too. Socialists won election to over 1,000 state and local offices and they enjoyed the support of such intellectuals as Lincoln Steffens, the crusading muckraking journalist, and Walter Lippmann, the brilliant young writer and social critic. Florence Kelley, Frances Willard, and many other women reformers were also attracted to socialism because of its support of labor and its pacifist stance.

Virtually all socialists agreed on the need for basic structural changes in the American economy, but they differed widely on the extent of those changes and the tactics necessary to achieve them. Some endorsed the radical goals of European Marxists; others envisioned a more moderate reform that would allow small-scale private enterprise to survive but would nationalize the major industries. Still others insisted upon the need for militant direct action.

Most conspicuous for its radicalism was the Industrial Workers of the World (IWW), a labor organization that sought to create "one big union." Known to its opponents as the "Wobblies," the IWW favored an inclusive labor movement that welcomed all workers and fought to eliminate the existing wage system. The Wobblies rejected traditional politics in favor of massive labor action. They were widely believed to have been responsible for dynamiting railroad lines and engaging in others acts of terror, although evidence to support those accusations was usually slim at best. In January of 1912, the Wobblies led a successful walkout in Lawrence, Massachusetts, when the textile mills reduced wages after the state passed a law limiting the hours of work. After violence broke out between local police and the strikers, the Wobblies attempted to evac-

uate the workers' children from the city. This incident did much to stir sentiment in favor of the strikers.

The IWW was one of the few labor organizations of the time to champion
the cause of unskilled workers. It had particular strength in the West—where a
large group of migratory laborers (miners, timbermen, and others) found it very
difficult to organize or sustain conventional unions. The Wobblies created not
just a union, but a far-flung social network that became something of a home to
workers who were otherwise largely rootless.

In 1917, another major strike by IWW timber workers in Washington and
Idaho virtually shut down production in the industry. That brought upon the
union the wrath of the federal government, which had just begun mobilizing for
war and needed timber for war production. Federal authorities imprisoned the
leaders of the union; and between 1917 and 1919 state governments passed a series of laws that effectively outlawed the IWW. The organization survived for a
time but never fully recovered.

More moderate socialists advocated peaceful change through more conventional political struggle, and they dominated the party in America. They emphasized a gradual education of the public to the need for change and patient
efforts within the system to enact it. But by the end of World War I, because the
party had refused to support the war effort and because of a growing wave of
antiradicalism that subjected the socialists to enormous harassment and persecution, socialism was in decline as a significant political force.

SOCIALIST RALLY.   Although the Socialist party initially split over
World War I, by 1917 it stood against American intervention. At this
1914 rally, socialist leader Frank Siegalman exhorts other New York
socialists to oppose the European war.

Decentralization and Regulation

Many reformers agreed with the socialists that the greatest threat to the nation's economy was excessive corporate centralization and consolidation. But they retained a faith in the possibilities of liberal reform within a capitalist system. Rather than nationalize basic industries, they hoped to restore fairness and competition to the economy. Few envisioned a return to a society of small, local enterprises; some consolidation, they believed, was inevitable. Some did argue, however, that the federal government should use its powers to break up the largest combinations and renew opportunities for competition among smaller producers. This viewpoint came to be identified particularly closely with Louis D. Brandeis, the brilliant lawyer and later Supreme Court Justice, who spoke and wrote widely (most notably in his 1913 book *Other People's Money*) about the "curse of bigness." "If the Lord had intended things to be big," Brandeis once wrote, "he would have made man bigger—in brains and character."

LOUIS D. BRANDEIS.   Well known as an advocate of progressive reform causes, Louis D. Brandeis earned a reputation as a lawyer who would forego his fees to advance public causes in which he believed. In the early twentieth century, Brandeis became known as the "people's attorney" for his advocacy of individualism, competition, and workers' right to organize. In 1916 Woodrow Wilson made Brandeis the first Jewish justice of the Supreme Court of the United States, where he served as an influential liberal jurist for 23 years.

Brandeis and his supporters opposed bigness in part because they considered it inefficient. But their opposition had a moral basis as well. It limited the ability of individuals to control their own destinies. It encouraged the abuse of power. Other progressives, however, were less enthusiastic about the virtues of competition. More important to them was efficiency, which they believed economic concentration encouraged. What government should do, they argued, was not fight "bigness," but guard against abuses of power by large institutions. It should distinguish between "good trusts" and "bad trusts," encouraging the former and disciplining the latter. Since economic consolidation was destined to remain a permanent feature of American society, continuing supervision by a strong, modernized government was essential. One of the most influential spokesmen for this emerging "nationalist" position was Herbert Croly, whose 1909 book *The Promise of American Life* became one of the most influential progressive documents.

Opinions varied widely on how the unity Croly advocated should be achieved. But increasingly, attention focused on some form of coordination or control of the industrial economy. Society must act, Walter Lippmann wrote in a notable 1914 book, *Drift and Mastery*, "to introduce plan where there has been clash, and purpose into the jungles of disordered growth." To some, that meant businesses themselves learning new ways of cooperation and self-regulation. Among the most energetic progressive reformers of the period, in fact, were businessmen determined to bring order and responsibility to finance and industry. To others, the solution was for government to play a more active role in regulating and planning economic life, not just to ameliorate problems but to anticipate future needs. One of those who came to endorse that position (although not fully until 1912) was Theodore Roosevelt, who once said: "We should enter upon a course of supervision, control, and regulation of those great corporations—a regulation which we should not fear, if necessary, to bring to the point of control of monopoly prices." Roosevelt became, for a time, the most powerful symbol of the reform impulse nationally, and a major force in shifting the attention of many progressives to the national government.

CHAPTER SEVEN

National Reform

~

The growing crusade to reshape industrial society owed much to the efforts of voluntary associations and other private organizations. It was crucially dependent on state and local political reforms. But in the end, despite the traditional American suspicion of centralized power, progressives looked to the federal government as well for solutions to the serious problems they hoped to solve. The great combinations they were attempting to combat were national in scope; only national action, reformers concluded, could effectively control the power of the trusts.

But like state and local governments, the national government—bureaucratically weak and mired in partisan politics—seemed poorly suited to serve as an agent of reform. Progressives attempted to make it more responsive to their demands. They tried to reform Congress—through the primary system, the direct election of senators, and changes in the internal rules of both Houses. But even a reformed Congress, they concluded, would be unable to provide the coherent leadership their bold agenda required. Only the president could provide the kind of moral, intellectual, and political authority reformers believed they needed. And by an unexpected twist of fate, the presidency in 1901 fell into the hands of a man who progressives quickly came to consider a model of enlightened leadership: Theodore Roosevelt.

THEODORE ROOSEVELT
AND THE MODERN PRESIDENCY

"Presidents in general are not lovable," Walter Lippmann, who had known many, said near the end of his life. "They've had to do too much to get where they are. But there was one President who was lovable—Teddy Roosevelt—and I loved him."

He was not alone. To a generation of progressive reformers, Theodore Roosevelt was more than an admired public figure; he was an idol. No president before and few after attracted such attention and devotion. Yet for all his popularity among reformers, Roosevelt was in many respects a decidedly conservative president. He earned his extraordinary popularity less because of the reforms he championed than because he brought to his office a broad conception of its powers and a sense of the presidency as a focus of national hopes and ambitions.

THEODORE ROOSEVELT.   Although short in stature, Theodore Roosevelt loomed large in the eyes of his contemporaries. Charismatic, aggressive, and determined, Roosevelt exemplified the modern progressive president with his commitment to using the power of the federal government to advance the public good.

The Youngest President

When President William McKinley suddenly died in September 1901, the victim of an assassination, Roosevelt (who had been elected vice president less than a year before) was only forty-two years old, the youngest man ever to assume the presidency. (John F. Kennedy, at forty-three, would be the youngest elected president.) Already, however, Roosevelt had achieved a reputation within the Republican party as something of a wild man. Party leaders sensed his independence and despaired of controlling him. "I told William McKinley that it was a mistake to nominate that wild man at Philadelphia," the Republican boss Marcus Hanna was reported to have exclaimed. "I asked him if he realized what would happen if he should die. Now look, that damned cowboy is President of the United States!"

Roosevelt's reputation as a wild man was a result less of the substance than of the style of his early political career. As a young member of the New York legislature, he displayed an energy seldom seen in that lethargic body. As a rancher in the Dakota Badlands (where he retired briefly after the sudden death of his first wife), he helped capture outlaws. As New York City police commissioner, he battled flamboyantly against crime, vice, and corruption. As assistant secretary of the navy, he boldly supported American expansion. As commander of the Rough Riders, he led a heroic, if militarily useless, charge in the battle of San Juan Hill in Cuba during the Spanish–American War.

But as president, Roosevelt became an advocate of cautious and moderate change. Reform, he believed, was less a vehicle for remaking American society than for preserving its essential good qualities and protecting it from those, particularly on the left, who might undermine liberty and freedom. Some progressives looked to Roosevelt to endorse far-reaching changes in the nation's social and economic policies. Although he disappointed many in those expectations, Roosevelt succeeded in making the presidency the central institution of American politics.

Government, Capital, and Labor

Roosevelt envisioned the federal government not as the agent of any particular interest but as a mediator of the public good, with the president at its center. These attitudes found expression in Roosevelt's policies toward the great industrial combinations. He was not opposed to the principle of economic concentration, but he acknowledged that consolidation produced dangerous abuses of power. He allied himself, therefore, with those progressives who urged regulation (but not destruction) of the trusts.

At the heart of Roosevelt's policy was his desire to win for government the power to investigate the activities of corporations and publicize the results. The pressure of educated public opinion, he believed, would alone eliminate most corporate abuses. Government could legislate solutions for those that remained. The new Department of Commerce and Labor, established in 1903 (later to be divided into two separate departments), was to assist in this task through its investigatory arm, the Bureau of Corporations.

Although Roosevelt was not a "trust buster" at heart, he made a few highly publicized efforts to break up combinations. In 1902, he ordered the Justice Department to invoke the Sherman Antitrust Act against a great new railroad monopoly in the Northwest, the Northern Securities Company, a $400 million enterprise pieced together by J. P. Morgan, E. H. Harriman, and James J. Hill. To Morgan, accustomed to a warm, supportive relationship with Republican administrations, the action was baffling. Hurrying to the White House with two conservative senators in tow, he told the president, "If we have done anything wrong, send your man to my man and they can fix it up." Roosevelt proceeded with the case nonetheless, and in 1904 the Supreme Court ruled that the Northern Securities Company must be dissolved. At the same time, however, Roosevelt assured Morgan and others that the suit did not signal a general campaign to dissolve trusts. Although he filed more than forty additional antitrust suits during the remainder of his presidency, Roosevelt made no serious effort to reverse the prevailing trend toward economic concentration. Many more trusts were "busted" by William Howard Taft during his presidency.

A similar commitment to establishing the government as an impartial regulatory mechanism shaped Roosevelt's policy toward labor. In the past, federal intervention in industrial disputes had almost always meant action on behalf of employers. Roosevelt was willing to consider labor's position as well. When a bitter 1902 strike by the United Mine Workers against the anthracite coal industry dragged on long enough to endanger coal supplies for the coming winter, Roosevelt asked both the operators and the miners to accept impartial federal arbitration. When the mine owners balked, Roosevelt threatened to send federal troops to seize the mines and resume coal production. The operators finally relented. Arbitrators awarded the strikers a ten percent wage increase and a nine-hour day, although no recognition of their union—less than they had wanted but more than they would likely have won without Roosevelt's intervention. Despite such episodes, Roosevelt viewed himself as no more the champion of labor than of management. On several occasions, he ordered federal troops to intervene in strikes on behalf of employers.

The Square Deal

Reform was not Roosevelt's top priority during his first years as president. He was principally concerned with winning reelection, which meant not antagonizing the conservative Republican Old Guard. By skillfully dispensing patronage to conservatives and progressives alike, by reshuffling the leadership of unstable Republican organizations in the South, by winning the support of northern businessmen while making adroit gestures to reformers, Roosevelt had all but neutralized his opposition within the party by early 1904. He won its presidential nomination with ease. And in the general election, where he faced a pallid

THE JUNGLE.   Upton Sinclair hoped his 1906 novel
The Jungle would arouse sympathy for down-trodden
industrial workers and mobilize support for socialist ideals.
In the end, most readers remembered the book for its
graphic and sickening description of sausage making in
Chicago's dirty and unregulated meat processing plants.
Like other muckraking exposés, *The Jungle* did help to
create a climate of public opinion that would support
more extensive federal regulation of industry.

conservative Democrat, Alton B. Parker, he captured over fifty-seven percent of the popular vote and lost no states outside the South. Now, relieved of immediate political concerns, he was free to display the extent (and the limits) of his commitment to reform.

During the 1904 campaign, Roosevelt boasted that he had worked in the anthracite coal strike to provide everyone with a "square deal." In his second term, he tried to extend his square deal further. One of his first targets was the powerful railroad industry. The Interstate Commerce Act of 1887, establishing the Interstate Commerce Commission (ICC), had been an early effort to regulate the industry; but over the years, the courts had sharply limited its influence. Roosevelt asked Congress for legislation to increase the government's power to oversee railroad rates. The Hepburn Railroad Regulation Act of 1906 sought to restore some regulatory authority to the government, although it was such a cautious bill that it satisfied few progressives. Some reformers were enraged. Robert La Follette, now a U.S. senator, never forgave Roosevelt for the concessions he made.

Roosevelt also pressured Congress to enact the Pure Food and Drug Act, which, despite weaknesses in its enforcement mechanisms, restricted the sale of dangerous or ineffective medicines. Upton Sinclair's powerful novel *The Jungle* appeared in 1906, featuring appalling descriptions of conditions in the meatpacking industry. This gruesome exposé did much to inflame public opinion and mobilize support for regulation of the meat industry. Roosevelt pushed for passage of the Meat Inspection Act, which ultimately helped eliminate many diseases once transmitted in impure meat. Starting in 1907, he proposed even more stringent measures: an eight-hour day for workers, broader compensation for victims of industrial accidents, inheritance and income taxes, regulation of the stock market, and others. He also started openly to criticize conservatives in Congress and the judiciary, who were obstructing these programs. The result was not only a general stalemate in Roosevelt's reform agenda, but a widening gulf between the president and the conservative wing of his party.

Conservation

Roosevelt's aggressive policies on behalf of conservation contributed to that gulf. An ardent sportsman and naturalist, he had long been concerned about the unregulated exploitation of America's natural resources and its remaining wilderness. Using executive powers, he restricted private development on millions of acres of undeveloped government land—most of it in the West—by adding them to the previously modest national forest system. When conservatives in Congress restricted his authority over public lands in 1907, Roosevelt and his chief forester, Gifford Pinchot, worked furiously to seize all the forests and many of the water power sites still in the public domain before the conservatives' bill became law.

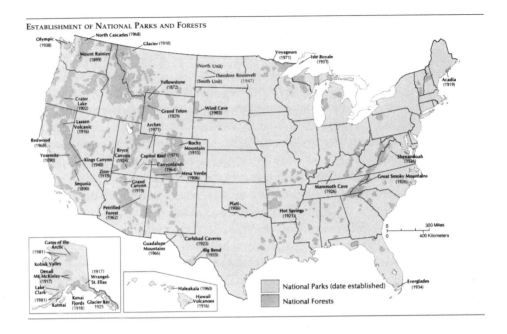

ESTABLISHMENT OF NATIONAL PARKS AND FORESTS

Roosevelt was the first president to take an active interest in the new and struggling American conservation movement, and his policies had a lasting effect on national environmental policies. More than most public figures, he was sympathetic to the concerns of the naturalists—those within the movement committed to protecting the natural beauty of the land and the health of its wildlife from human intrusion. Early in his presidency, Roosevelt even spent four days camping in the Yosemite Valley with John Muir, the nation's leading preservationist and the founder of the Sierra Club. But Roosevelt's actual policies tended to favor another faction within the conservation movement—those who believed in carefully managed development. That was in part a result of the influence of Pinchot, the first director of the National Forest Service (which he had helped create), who supported rational and efficient human use of the wilderness. The Sierra Club might argue for the aesthetic value of the forests; Pinchot insisted, in contrast, that "the whole question is a practical one." He and Roosevelt both believed that trained experts in forestry and resource management, such men as Pinchot himself, should apply to the landscape the same scientific standards that others were applying to the management of cities and industries. The president did side with the preservationists on certain issues (among them the expansion of the system of national parks), but the more important legacy of his conservation policy was to establish the government's role as manager of the continuing development of the wilderness.

The Old Guard may have opposed Roosevelt's efforts to extend government control over vast new lands. But they eagerly supported another important aspect of Roosevelt's natural resource policy: public reclamation and irrigation projects. In 1902, the president backed the National Reclamation Act, better known as the Newlands Act (named for its sponsor, Nebraska congressman Francis Newlands). It was the culmination of years of lobbying by businessmen and others from the West (through the National Irrigation Association). Frustrated by the failure of private capital and state governments to develop water resources, the Association wanted the federal government to take over such projects. The Newlands Act provided federal funds for the construction of dams, reservoirs, and canals in the West—projects that would open new lands for cultivation and (years later) provide cheap electric power. It was the beginning of many decades of critical federal aid for irrigation and power development in the western states, even though the Newlands Act (and the Bureau of Reclamation it created) had relatively little impact for more than twenty years after passage.

Economic Downturn

Despite the flurry of reforms Roosevelt was able to enact, the government still had relatively little control over the industrial economy. That became clear in 1907, when a serious panic and recession began. As in 1893, American industrial production had outrun the capacity of either domestic or foreign markets to absorb it. Once again, the banking system and the stock market had displayed pathetic inadequacies. Once again, irresponsible speculation and rampant financial mismanagement had helped to shatter a prosperity that many had come to believe was now permanent.

Conservatives blamed Roosevelt's "mad" economic policies for the disaster. And while the president naturally (and correctly) disagreed, he nevertheless acted quickly to reassure business leaders that he would not interfere with their recovery efforts. J. P. Morgan, in a spectacular display of his financial power, helped construct a pool of the assets of several important New York banks to prop up shaky financial institutions. The key to the arrangement, Morgan told the president, was the purchase by U.S. Steel of the shares of the Tennessee Coal and Iron Company, currently held by a threatened New York bank. He would, he insisted, need assurances that the purchase would not prompt antitrust action. Roosevelt tacitly agreed, and the Morgan plan proceeded. Whether or not as a result, the panic soon subsided.

Roosevelt loved being president. He had made that plain during his first moments in office, when, torn between his excitement at his new position and his distress at McKinley's death, he had written, "It is a dreadful thing to come into the Presidency in this way; but it would be a far worse thing to be morbid about it." As his years in office produced increasing political successes, as his public popularity continued to rise, more and more observers began to assume that he would run for reelection in 1908, despite the longstanding tradition of presidents serving no more than two terms.

But the panic of 1907, combined with Roosevelt's growing "radicalism" during his second term, so alienated conservatives in his own party that he might have had difficulty winning the Republican nomination for another term. In 1904, moreover, he had made a public promise to step down four years later. And so, after nearly eight energetic years in the White House, during which he had transformed the role of the presidency in American government, Theodore Roosevelt, fifty years old, retired from public life—briefly.

THE REPUBLICAN SCHISM

William Howard Taft, who assumed the presidency in 1909, had been Theodore Roosevelt's most trusted lieutenant and his hand-picked successor; progressive reformers believed him to be one of their own. But Taft had also been a restrained and moderate jurist, a man with a punctilious regard for legal process; conservatives expected him to abandon Roosevelt's aggressive use of presidential powers. By seeming acceptable to almost everyone, Taft won election to the White House in 1908 with almost ridiculous ease. He received his party's nomination virtually uncontested. His victory in the general election in November—over William Jennings Bryan, running forlornly for the Democrats for the third time—was a foregone conclusion. Taft entered the White House on a wave of good feeling.

Four years later, however, Taft would leave office the most decisively defeated president of the twentieth century, with his party deeply divided and the government in the hands of a Democratic administration for the first time in twenty years.

It had been obvious from the start that Taft and Roosevelt were not at all alike, but it was not until Taft took office that the real extent of the differences became clear. Roosevelt had been the most dynamic public figure of his age; Taft was stolid and respectable and little more. Roosevelt was an ardent sportsman and athlete; Taft was sedentary and obese—he weighed over 300 pounds and required a special, oversized bathtub to be installed in the White House. Most of all, Roosevelt had taken an expansive view of the powers of his office; Taft, in contrast, was slow, cautious, even lethargic, insistent that the president take pains to observe the strict letter of the law.

Yet even if Taft had been the most dynamic of political figures, he would still have had difficulties as president. Having come into office as the darling of progressives and conservatives alike, he soon found that he could not please them both. Gradually he found himself, without really intending to do so, pleasing the conservatives and alienating the progressives.

Conflicts with Progressives

Taft's first problem arose in the opening months of the new administration when he called Congress into special session to lower protective tariff rates, an old progressive demand. But having proposed the legislation, the president made no effort to overcome the opposition of the congressional Old Guard to it, arguing that to do so would violate the constitutional doctrine of separation of powers. The result was the feeble Payne-Aldrich Tariff, which reduced tariff rates scarcely at all and in some areas actually raised them. Progressives resented the president's passivity and were suspicious of his motives.

With Taft's standing among Republican progressives deteriorating and with the party growing more and more deeply divided, a sensational controversy broke out late in 1909 that helped destroy Taft's popularity with reformers for good. Many progressives had been unhappy when Taft replaced Roosevelt's secretary of the interior, James R. Garfield, an aggressive conservationist, with Richard A. Ballinger, a more conservative corporate lawyer. Suspicion of Ballinger grew when he attempted to invalidate Roosevelt's actions in removing nearly 1 million acres of forests and mineral reserves from the public lands available for private development.

In the midst of this mounting concern, Louis Glavis, an Interior Department investigator, charged the new secretary with having once connived to turn over valuable public coal lands in Alaska to a private syndicate for personal profit. Glavis took the evidence to Gifford Pinchot, still head of the Forest Service and a critic of Ballinger's policies. Pinchot took the charges to the president. Taft ordered his attorney general to investigate them and eventually decided they were groundless.

But Pinchot was not satisfied, particularly after Taft fired Glavis for his part in the episode. He leaked the story to the press and asked Congress to investigate the scandal. The president discharged him for insubordination, and the congressional committee appointed to study the controversy, dominated by the Old Guard, exonerated Ballinger. But progressives throughout the country supported Pinchot.

To many reformers at the time, the Pinchot–Ballinger controversy was a simple morality tale. In reality, it represented a clash between two competing visions of economic development. Pinchot represented those who wanted carefully supervised economic growth in the American West. Ballinger (himself a westerner) represented many western entrepreneurs who saw federal regulations as an impediment to their own economic ambitions. Progressives portrayed Ballinger as the defender of corporate power; in fact, Pinchot was more popular among leaders of large corporations, who generally supported his conservation policies, while Ballinger had the support of small businessmen, who had always opposed such policies.

The controversy aroused as much public passion as any dispute of its time; and when it was over, Taft had alienated the supporters of Roosevelt completely and, it seemed, irrevocably.

The Reemergence of Roosevelt

During most of these controversies, Theodore Roosevelt was far away: on a long hunting safari in Africa and an extended tour of Europe. To the American public, however, Roosevelt remained a formidable presence. His return to New York in the spring of 1910 was a major public event; and progressives noted that, although he turned down an invitation from Taft to visit the White House, he met at once with Gifford Pinchot (who had already traveled to England to see him several months before).

Roosevelt insisted that he had no plans to return to active politics, but his resolve lasted less than a week. Politicians began flocking immediately to his home at Oyster Bay, Long Island, for conferences. Roosevelt took an active role in several New York political controversies; and within a month, he announced that he would embark on a national speaking tour before the end of the summer. Furious with Taft, who had, he believed, "completely twisted around the policies I advocated and acted upon," he was becoming convinced that he alone was capable of reuniting the Republican party.

The real signal of Roosevelt's decision to assume leadership of Republican reformers was a speech on September 1, 1910, in Osawatomie, Kansas, where he outlined a set of principles that he labeled the "New Nationalism" and that made clear he had moved a considerable way from the cautious conservatism of the first years of his presidency. Social justice, he argued, was possible only through the vigorous efforts of a strong federal government whose executive acted as the "steward of the public welfare." Those who thought primarily of property rights and personal profit "must now give way to the advocate of human welfare, who rightly maintains that every man holds his property subject to the general right of the community to regulate its use to whatever degree the public welfare may require it." He supported graduated income and inheritance taxes, workers' compensation for industrial accidents, regulation of the labor of women and children, tariff revision, and firmer regulation of corporations.

Spreading Insurgency

The congressional elections of 1910 provided further evidence of how far the progressive revolt had spread. In primary elections, conservative Republicans suffered defeat after defeat, while almost all the progressive incumbents were reelected. In the general election, the Democrats, who were now offering progressive candidates of their own, won control of the House of Representatives for the first time in sixteen years and gained strength in the Senate. Reform sentiment seemed clearly on the rise; yet Roosevelt still denied that he held any presidential ambitions and claimed that his real purpose was to pressure Taft to return to progressive policies. Two events, however, changed his mind.

The first was a 1911 antitrust decision by the Taft administration. Taft had been more active than Roosevelt in enforcing the provisions of the Sherman Antitrust Act and had launched dozens of suits against corporate combinations. On October 27, 1911, the administration announced a suit against U.S. Steel, charging, among other things, that the 1907 acquisition of the Tennessee Coal and

Iron Company had been illegal. Roosevelt had approved that acquisition in the midst of the 1907 panic, and he was enraged by the implication that he had acted improperly.

Roosevelt was reluctant at first to become a candidate for president, largely because Senator Robert La Follette had been working since 1911 to secure the presidential nomination for himself. La Follette's candidacy stumbled in February 1912, however, when, exhausted and distraught about his daughter's illness, he appeared to suffer a breakdown during a speech in Philadelphia. With almost indecent haste, many of his supporters abandoned him and turned to Roosevelt, who announced his candidacy on February 22.

A Fractured Republican Party

La Follette retained some diehard support; but for all practical purposes, the campaign for the Republican nomination had now become a battle between Roosevelt, the champion of the progressives, and Taft, the candidate of the conservatives. Roosevelt scored overwhelming victories in all thirteen presidential primaries and arrived at the convention convinced that he was the choice of the party rank and file. Taft, however, remained the choice of most party leaders, whose preference was decisive.

The battle for the nomination at the Chicago convention revolved around an unusually large number of contested delegates: 254 in all. Roosevelt needed fewer than half the disputed seats to clinch the nomination, but the Republican National Committee, controlled by the Old Guard, awarded all but nineteen of them to Taft. At a rally the night before the convention opened, Roosevelt addressed 5,000 cheering supporters and announced that if the party refused to seat his delegates, he would continue his own candidacy outside the party. "We stand at Armageddon," he told the roaring crowd, "and we battle for the Lord." The next day, he led his supporters out of the convention, and out of the party. The remaining delegates then quietly nominated Taft on the first ballot.

With financial support from newspaper magnate Frank Munsey and industrialist George W. Perkins, Roosevelt summoned his supporters back to Chicago in August for another convention, to launch the new Progressive party and nominate Roosevelt as its presidential candidate. Jane Addams was one of those who placed his name in nomination, and a large number of other prominent women reformers played an active role in the new party. Roosevelt approached the battle feeling, as he put it, "fit as a bull moose" (thus giving his new party an enduring nickname). But by then, he was aware that his cause was virtually hopeless. This was partly because many of the insurgents who had supported him during the primaries refused to follow him out of the Republican party. It was also because of the man the Democrats had nominated for president.

WOODROW WILSON
AND THE NEW FREEDOM

The 1912 presidential contest was not simply one between conservatives and reformers. It was also one between two visions of social change, two different views of America's future. In the end, the campaign matched the two most important national leaders of the early twentieth century in unequal contest.

Woodrow Wilson

Reform sentiment had been gaining strength within the Democratic as well as the Republican party in the first years of the century. At the 1912 Democratic Convention in Baltimore in June, Champ Clark, the conservative Speaker of the House, was unable to assemble the two-thirds majority necessary to win the nomination because of progressive opposition. Finally, on the forty-sixth ballot, Woodrow Wilson, the governor of New Jersey and the only genuinely progressive candidate in the race, emerged as the party's nominee.

Born in Virginia and raised in Confederate Georgia and Reconstruction South Carolina, Wilson had risen to political prominence by an unusual path. An 1879 graduate of Princeton University, he attended law school and

WILSON AND TAFT.   Woodrow Wilson (seated in the left rear of the carriage) and his predecessor William Howard Taft (seated to the right) ride to the 1913 inauguration.

ELECTION OF 1912	(58.8% of electorate voting)	ELECTORAL VOTE	POPULAR VOTE (%)
Woodrow Wilson (Democratic)		435	6,293,454 (41.9)
Theodore Roosevelt (Progressive/Bull Moose)		88	4,119,538 (27.4)
William H. Taft (Republican)		8	3,484,980 (23.2)
Eugene V. Debs (Socialist)		—	900,672 (6.0)
Other parties (Prohibition; Socialist Labor)		—	235,025

for a time engaged unhappily in practice in Atlanta. But he was really more interested in politics and government, and after a few years he enrolled at Johns Hopkins University, where he earned a doctorate in political science. By virtue of his effective teaching and his lucid if unprofound books on the American political system, he rose steadily through the academic ranks until in 1902 he was promoted from the faculty to the presidency of Princeton.

There, he displayed some of the strengths and weaknesses that would characterize his later political career. A champion of academic reform, he acted firmly and energetically to place Princeton on the road to becoming a great national university. At the same time, however he displayed during controversies a self-righteous morality that at times made it nearly impossible for him to compromise. A series of such stalemates helped propel him out of academia and into politics. Elected governor of New Jersey in 1910, he brought to his new office a commitment to reform that he had already displayed as a university president; and during his two years in the statehouse, he earned a national reputation for winning passage of progressive legislation.

As a presidential candidate in 1912, he presented a brand of progressivism different from Theodore Roosevelt's New Nationalism, a program that came to be called the "New Freedom." The New Freedom differed most clearly from the New Nationalism in its approach to economic policy and the trusts. Roosevelt believed in accepting economic concentration and using government to regulate and control it. Wilson seemed to side with those who (like Brandeis) believed that bigness was both unjust and inefficient, that the proper response to monopoly was not to regulate it but to destroy it.

The presidential campaign itself was something of an anticlimax. William Howard Taft, resigned to defeat, delivered a few desultory, conservative speeches and then lapsed into silence. Roosevelt campaigned energetically (until a gunshot wound from a would-be assassin forced him to the sidelines during the last weeks before the election), but he failed to draw any significant numbers of Democratic progressives away from Wilson. In November, Roosevelt and Taft split the Republican vote; Wilson held onto the Democratic vote and won. He polled only a plurality of the popular vote: forty-two percent, to twenty-seven percent for Roosevelt, twenty-three percent for Taft, and six percent for the Socialist Eugene Debs. But in the electoral college, Wilson won 435 of the 531 votes. Roosevelt had carried only six states, Taft two, Debs none.

The Scholar as President

Wilson was a bold and forceful president. More than William Howard Taft, more even than Theodore Roosevelt, he concentrated the powers of the executive branch in his own hands. He exerted firm control over his cabinet, and he delegated real authority only to those whose loyalty to him was beyond question. Perhaps the clearest indication of his style of leadership was the identity of the most powerful figure in his administration: Colonel Edward M. House, a man who held no office and whose only claim to authority was his personal intimacy with the president.

In legislative matters, Wilson skillfully used his position as party leader and his appointive powers to weld together a coalition of conservatives and progressives who would, he believed, support his program. Democratic majorities in both houses of Congress made his task easier, as did the realization of many Democrats that the party must enact a progressive program in order to maintain those majorities.

Wilson's first triumph as president was a substantial lowering of the protective tariff. The Underwood-Simmons Tariff, passed in a special session of Congress Wilson summoned shortly after his inauguration, provided cuts substantial enough, progressives believed, to introduce real competition into American markets and thus to help break the power of trusts. The bill passed easily in the House; and despite Senate efforts to weaken its provisions, it survived more or less intact. Wilson had succeeded where Roosevelt and Taft had not. To make up for the loss of revenue under the new tariff, Congress approved a graduated income tax, which the recently adopted Sixteenth Amendment to the Constitution now permitted. This first modern income tax imposed a one percent tax on individuals and corporations earning over $4,000, with rates ranging up to six percent on incomes over $500,000.

Wilson held Congress in session through the summer to work on a major reform of the American banking system. Few doubted the necessity of change, but there were many different opinions about how best to attack the problem. Some legislators, among them Representative Carter Glass of Virginia, wanted to decentralize control of the banking system so as to limit the power of the great Wall Street financiers without substantially increasing the power of government. Others, including William Jennings Bryan and fellow agrarians, who had long detested the "money trust," wanted firm government control. Wilson endorsed a plan that divided power in the system. The government would have substantial control at the national level; the bankers would retain control at the local level. The Federal Reserve Act passed both houses of Congress and was signed by the president on December 23, 1913. It was the most important piece of domestic legislation of Wilson's administration.

The Federal Reserve Act created twelve regional banks, each to be owned and controlled by the individual banks of its district. The regional Federal Reserve banks would hold a certain percentage of the assets of their member banks in reserve; they would use those reserves to support loans to private banks at an interest (or "discount") rate that the Federal Reserve system would set; they would issue a new type of paper currency—Federal Reserve notes—which would become the nation's basic medium of trade and would be backed by the government. Most importantly, perhaps, these Federal Reserves would serve as central institutions able to shift funds quickly to troubled areas to meet increased demands for credit or to protect imperiled banks. Supervising and regulating the entire system was a national Federal Reserve Board, whose members were appointed by the president. All "national" banks were required to join the system; smaller banks were encouraged to do the same. Nearly half the nation's banking resources were represented in the system within in a year, and eighty percent by the late 1920s.

The "Attack" on Monopoly

The cornerstone of Wilson's campaign for the presidency had been his promise to attack economic concentration, most notably to destroy monopolistic trusts. By the beginning of his second year in office, however, his approach to the trusts appeared to have changed. He was moving away from his earlier insistence that government dismantle the combinations and toward a commitment to regulate them. On this issue, at least, the New Freedom was beginning to resemble the New Nationalism.

In 1914, Wilson proposed two measures to deal with the problem of monopoly. There was a proposal to create a federal agency through which the government would help business police itself—in other words, a regulatory commission of the type Roosevelt had advocated in 1912. There were, in addition, proposals to strengthen the government's power to prosecute and dismantle the trusts—a decentralizing approach more characteristic of Wilson's campaign. The two measures took shape, ultimately, as the Federal Trade Commission Act and the Clayton Antitrust Act.

The Federal Trade Commission Act created a regulatory agency of the same name that would help businesses determine in advance whether their actions would be acceptable to the government. It would also have authority to launch prosecutions against "unfair trade practices," which the law did not define, and it would have wide power to investigate corporate behavior. The act, in short, increased the government's regulatory authority significantly. Wilson signed it happily. However he seemed to lose interest in the Clayton Antitrust bill and did little to protect it from conservative assaults, which greatly weakened it. The vigorous legal pursuit of monopoly that Wilson had promised in 1912 never materialized. The future, he had apparently decided, lay with government supervision.

Complacency and Renewal

By the fall of 1914, Wilson believed that the program of the New Freedom was essentially complete and that agitation for reform should (and would) now subside. As a result, he himself began a conspicuous retreat from activism. Citing the doctrine of states' rights, he refused to support the movement for national women suffrage. Bowing to the inclinations of the many southerners in his cabinet (and perhaps also to his own southern heritage), he condoned the reimposition of segregation in the agencies of the federal government (a contrast to Theodore Roosevelt, who had ordered the elimination of many such barriers and had even taken the unprecedented step of inviting a black man, Booker T. Washington, to the White House). When congressional progressives attempted to enlist his support for new reform legislation, Wilson dismissed their proposals as unconstitutional or unnecessary.

The congressional elections of 1914, however, shattered the president's complacency. Democrats suffered major losses in the House of Representatives, and voters who in 1912 had supported the Progressive party began returning to the Republicans. Wilson would not be able to rely on a divided opposition when he ran for reelection in 1916. By the end of 1915, Wilson had begun to support a second flurry of reforms. In January 1916, he appointed Louis Brandeis to the Supreme Court, making him not only the first Jew, but the most advanced progressive ever to serve there. Later, Wilson supported a measure to make it easier for farmers to receive credit and one creating a system of workers' compensation for federal employees.

Much of this renewed effort at reform revealed that Wilson had moved even closer to the New Nationalism. He was sponsoring measures that expanded the role of the national government in important ways, giving it new instruments by which it could regulate the economy and help shape the economic and social structure. In 1916, for example, Wilson supported the Keating-Owen Act, the first federal law regulating child labor. The measure added weight to the constitutional clause assigning Congress the task of regulating interstate commerce. (It would be some years before the Supreme Court would uphold this interpretation of the clause; the Court invalidated the Keating-Owen Act in 1918.) The president similarly supported measures that used federal taxing authority as a vehicle for legislating social change. When the Court struck down Keating-Owen, a new bill attempted to achieve the same goal by imposing a heavy tax on the products of child labor. (The Court later struck it down, too.) The Smith-Lever Act of 1914 used federal spending to change public behavior by offering matching federal grants to states that agreed to support agricultural extension education.

"THE BIG STICK": THE EVOLUTION OF AMERICAN DIPLOMACY

American foreign policy during the progressive years reflected many of the same impulses that were motivating domestic reform. But more than that, it reflected the nation's new sense of itself as a world power with far-flung economic and political interests. To the general public, foreign affairs remained largely remote. Walter Lippmann once wrote: "I cannot remember taking any interest whatsoever in foreign affairs until after the outbreak of the First World War." But to Theodore Roosevelt and later presidents, this remoteness made foreign affairs even more appealing. There, the president could act with less regard for Congress or the courts. There, he could free himself from concerns about public opinion. Overseas, the president could exercise power unfettered and alone.

Roosevelt's Vision

Theodore Roosevelt was well suited, both by temperament and by ideology, for an activist foreign policy. He believed in the value and importance of using

THE WORLD'S CONSTABLE.

"THE NEW DIPLOMACY." In this 1904 *Puck* cartoon by Louis Dalrymple, Theodore Roosevelt stands tall as the world's policeman wielding the "big stick" of the new diplomacy in one hand and holding plans for arbitration in the other. The big stick is held over "less civilized" peoples from Asia and Latin America on his left while on his right, "civilized" European nations seek favors from the U.S. president.

American power in the world (a conviction he once described by citing the proverb, "Speak softly, but carry a big stick"). And he believed that an important distinction existed between the "civilized" and "uncivilized" nations of the world. "Civilized" nations, as he defined them, were predominantly white and Anglo-Saxon or Teutonic; "uncivilized" nations were generally nonwhite, Latin, or Slavic. But racism was only partly the basis of his distinction; at least as important was economic development. Roosevelt believed, therefore, that Japan, a rapidly industrializing society, had earned admission to the ranks of the civilized.

Civilized nations were, by Roosevelt's definition, producers of industrial goods; uncivilized nations were suppliers of raw materials and markets. There was, he believed, an economic relationship between the two that was vital to both of them. A civilized society, therefore, had the right and duty to intervene in the affairs of a "backward" nation to preserve order and stability—for the sake of both nations. Accordingly, Roosevelt became an early champion of the development of American sea power. By 1906, his support had enabled the American navy to attain a size and strength surpassed only by that of Great Britain (although Germany's was fast gaining ground).

The "Open Door" to the East

Roosevelt considered the "Open Door" vital for maintaining American trade in the Pacific and for preventing any single nation from establishing dominance there. (See pp. 76–77.) He looked with alarm, therefore, at the military rivalries in Asia involving Japan, Russia, Germany, and France.

In 1904, the Japanese attacked the Russian fleet at Port Arthur in southern Manchuria, a province of China that both Russia and Japan hoped to control. Roosevelt, hoping to prevent either nation from becoming dominant there, agreed in 1905 to a Japanese request to mediate an end to the conflict. Russia, faring badly in the war and already plagued by the domestic instability that twelve years later would lead to revolution, had no choice but to agree. At a peace conference in Portsmouth, New Hampshire, Roosevelt extracted from the embattled Russians a recognition of Japan's territorial gains and from the Japanese an agreement to cease the fighting and expand no further. At the same time, he negotiated a secret agreement with the Japanese to ensure that the United States could continue to trade freely in the region.

Roosevelt won the Nobel Peace Prize in 1906 for his work in ending the Russo–Japanese War. But in the years that followed, relations between the United States and Japan steadily deteriorated. Having destroyed the Russian fleet at Port Arthur, Japan now emerged as the preeminent naval power in the Pacific and soon began to exclude American trade from many of the territories it controlled.

A domestic controversy in California soon threatened Japanese–American relations again. In the process of agitating for an extension of the Chinese

Exclusion Act (see pp. 18–19), white workers in San Francisco added a demand for the legal exclusion of Japanese immigrants. Nothing came of these efforts at first. But in 1906, the school board of San Francisco voted to require all Asian schoolchildren in the city to attend a separate "Oriental School." Anti-Asian riots in California and inflammatory stories in the Hearst papers about the "Yellow Peril" further fanned resentment in Japan.

The president persuaded the San Francisco school board to rescind its edict in return for a Japanese agreement to stop the flow of agricultural immigrants into California. Then, lest the Japanese government interpret his actions as a sign of weakness, he sent sixteen battleships of the new American navy (known as the "Great White Fleet") on an unprecedented voyage around the world that included a call on Japan—to remind the Japanese of the potential might of the United States.

Controlling the Western Hemisphere

Roosevelt took a special interest in events in what he (and most other Americans) considered the nation's special sphere of interest: Latin America. Unwilling to share trading rights, let alone military control, with any other nation, Roosevelt embarked on a series of ventures into the Caribbean and South America that established a pattern of American intervention in the region that would long survive his presidency.

Crucial in shaping Roosevelt's thinking was an incident early in his administration. When the government of Venezuela began in 1902 to renege on debts to European bankers, naval forces of Britain, Italy, and Germany blockaded the Venezuelan coast. Then, German ships began to bombard a Venezuelan port amid rumors that Germany planned to establish a permanent base in the region. Roosevelt used the threat of American naval power to pressure the German navy to withdraw.

The incident helped persuade Roosevelt that European intrusions into Latin America could result not only from aggression but from instability or irresponsibility (such as defaulting on debts) within the Latin American nations themselves. As a result, in 1904 he added a new "Roosevelt Corollary" to the Monroe Doctrine. The United States, he claimed, had the right not only to oppose European intervention in the Western Hemisphere but to intervene itself in the domestic affairs of its neighbors if those neighbors proved unable to maintain order on their own.

The immediate motivation for the Roosevelt Corollary, and the first opportunity for using it, was a crisis in the Dominican Republic. A revolution had toppled the country's corrupt and bankrupt government in 1903, but the new regime proved no better able than the old to make good on the country's $22 million in debts to European nations. Using the "Roosevelt Corollary" rationale, Roosevelt established, in effect, an American receivership, assuming control of Dominican customs and distributing forty-five percent of the revenues to

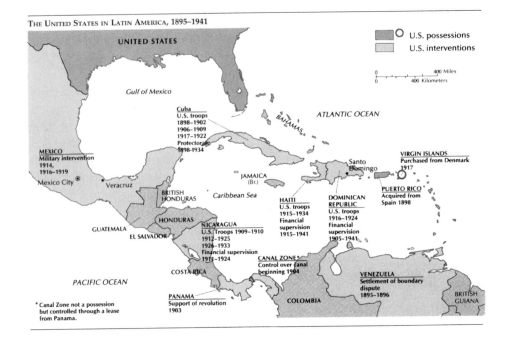

THE UNITED STATES IN LATIN AMERICA, 1895–1941

U.S. possessions
U.S. interventions

UNITED STATES

Gulf of Mexico

ATLANTIC OCEAN

BAHAMAS

Cuba
U.S. troops
1898–1902
1906–1909
1917–1922
Protectorate
1898–1934

MEXICO
Military intervention
1914,
1916–1919
Mexico City   Veracruz

JAMAICA
(Br.)

Santo
Domingo

VIRGIN ISLANDS
Purchased from Denmark
1917

BRITISH
HONDURAS   Caribbean Sea

GUATEMALA
EL SALVADOR

HONDURAS

NICARAGUA
U.S. Troops 1909–1910
1912–1925
1926–1933
Financial supervision
1911–1924

HAITI
U.S. troops
1915–1934
Financial
supervision
1915–1941

DOMINICAN
REPUBLIC
U.S. troops
1916–1924
Financial
supervision
1905–1941

PUERTO RICO
Acquired from
Spain 1898

CANAL ZONE
Control over canal
beginning 1904

VENEZUELA
Settlement of boundary
dispute
1895–1896

PACIFIC OCEAN

COSTA RICA

PANAMA
Support of revolution
1903

COLOMBIA

BRITISH
GUIANA

* Canal Zone not a possession
but controlled through a lease
from Panama.

0   400 Miles
0   400 Kilometers

the Dominicans and the rest to foreign creditors. This arrangement lasted, in one form or another, for more than three decades.

In 1902, the United States granted political independence to Cuba, but only after Cuba's new government agreed to the so-called Platt Amendment to its constitution, giving the United States the right to prevent any foreign power from intruding into the new nation. In 1906, when domestic uprisings seemed to threaten the internal stability of the island, Roosevelt reasoned that America must intervene to "protect" Cuba from disorder. American troops landed in Cuba, quelled the fighting, and remained there for three years.

The Panama Canal

The most celebrated accomplishment of Roosevelt's presidency was the construction of the Panama Canal. Creating a channel through Central America linking the Atlantic and the Pacific had been an unfulfilled dream of many nations since the mid-nineteenth century. Roosevelt was determined to achieve it.

The first step was the 1901 Hay-Pauncefote Treaty between America and Britain, cancelling an 1850 pact by which the two nations had agreed to construct any canal together. The United States was now free to act alone. The next step was to choose a site for the canal. At first, Roosevelt and many others favored a route across Nicaragua, which would permit a sea-level canal requiring no locks. But they soon turned instead to the narrow Isthmus of Panama in Colombia, the site of an earlier, failed effort by a French company to construct a channel. Although the Panama route was not at sea level (and would thus require locks), it was shorter than the one in Nicaragua, and construction was already about forty percent complete. When the French company lowered the price for its holdings from $109 million to $40 million, the United States chose Panama.

Roosevelt dispatched John Hay, his secretary of state, to negotiate an agreement with Colombian diplomats in Washington that would allow construction to begin without delay. Under heavy American pressure, the Colombian chargé d'affaires, Tomas Herran, unwisely signed an agreement giving the United States perpetual rights to a six-mile-wide "canal zone" across Colombia; in return, the U.S. would pay Colombia $10 million and an annual rental of $250,000. The treaty produced outrage in the Colombian Senate, which refused to ratify it. Colombia then sent a new representative to Washington with instructions to demand at least 20 million dollars from the Americans plus a share of the payment to the French.

PANAMA CANAL. The digging of the Panama Canal was one of the great engineering feats of modern times. Depicted here is the Culebra Cut as it looked in June 1911, some three years before the Canal's completion. The construction of the canal proved enormously costly in men, dollars, and diplomacy. Roosevelt considered the Panama Canal one of the great achievements of his presidency.

Roosevelt was furious. The Colombians, he charged, were "inefficient bandits" and "blackmailers." He began to look for ways to circumvent the Colombian government. Philippe Bunau-Varilla, chief engineer of the French canal project, was ready to help. In November 1903, he helped organize and finance a revolution in Panama. There had been many previous revolts, all of them failures, but this one had the support of the United States. Roosevelt landed troops from the *USS Nashville* in Panama to "maintain order." Their presence prevented Colombian forces from suppressing the rebellion, and three days later Roosevelt recognized Panama as an independent nation. The new Panamanian government quickly agreed to a new treaty. It granted America a canal zone ten miles wide; the United States would pay Panama the $10 million fee and the $250,000 annual rental that the Colombian Senate had rejected. Work on the canal proceeded rapidly, despite the enormous cuts and elaborate locks the construction required. It opened in 1914, three years after Roosevelt had proudly boasted to a university audience, "I took the Canal Zone and let Congress debate!"

"Dollar Diplomacy"

Like his predecessor, William Howard Taft worked to advance the nation's economic interests overseas. But he showed little interest in Roosevelt's larger vision of world stability. Taft's secretary of state, the corporate attorney Philander C. Knox, worked aggressively to extend American investments into less developed regions. Critics called his policies "Dollar Diplomacy."

The Taft-Knox foreign policy faced its severest test, and encountered its greatest failure, in the Far East. Ignoring Roosevelt's tacit 1905 agreement with Japan to limit American involvement in Manchuria, the new administration responded to pressure from American bankers and moved aggressively to increase America's economic influence in the region. In particular, Knox worked to include the United States in a consortium of Western powers formed to build railroads in China; and when the Europeans agreed, he went further and tried to exclude the Japanese from any role in Manchuria's railroads. When Japan responded by forming a loose alliance with Russia, the entire railroad project quickly collapsed.

In the Caribbean, the new administration continued and even expanded upon Roosevelt's policies of limiting European and expanding American influence in the region. That meant, Taft and Knox believed, not only preventing disorder but establishing a significant American economic presence there—replacing the investments of European nations with investments from the United States. But Dollar Diplomacy also had a more violent side. When a revolution broke out in Nicaragua in 1909, the administration quickly sided with the insurgents (who had been inspired to revolt by an American mining company) and sent American troops into the country to seize the customs houses. As soon as peace was restored, Knox encouraged American bankers to offer substantial loans to the new government, thus increasing Washington's financial leverage over the country. When the new pro-American government faced an insurrection less than two years later, Taft again landed American troops in Nicaragua, this time to protect the existing regime. The troops remained there for more than a decade.

Wilsonian Diplomacy

Woodrow Wilson entered office with little experience or interest in diplomacy. "It would be the irony of fate," he remarked shortly before assuming the presidency, "if my administration had to deal chiefly with foreign affairs." Ironic or not, Wilson faced international challenges of a scope and gravity unmatched by any president before him and few since. Although the greatest test of Wilsonian diplomacy did not occur until after World War I, many of the qualities that he would bring to that ordeal were evident in his foreign policy from his first moments in office, and particularly in his dealings with Latin America—where he continued the interventionist policies of his predecessors.

Having already seized control of the finances of the Dominican Republic in 1905, the United States established a military government there in 1916 when the Dominicans refused to accept a treaty that would have made the country a virtual American protectorate. The military occupation lasted eight years. In Haiti, which shares the island of Hispaniola with the Dominican Republic, Wilson landed the marines in 1915 to quell a revolution in the course of which a mob had murdered an unpopular president. American military forces remained in the country until 1934, and American officers drafted the new Haitian constitution, adopted in 1918. When Wilson began to fear that the Danish West Indies might be about to fall into the hands of Germany, he bought the colony from Denmark and renamed it the Virgin Islands. Concerned about the possibility of European influence in Nicaragua, he signed a treaty with that country's government ensuring that no other nation would build a canal there and won for the United States the right to intervene in Nicaragua's internal affairs to protect American interests.

But Wilson's view of America's role in the Western Hemisphere became clearest in his dealings with Mexico. For many years, under the friendly auspices of the corrupt dictator Porfirio Diaz, American businessmen had been establishing an enormous economic presence in Mexico. In 1910, however, Diaz was overthrown by the popular leader Francisco Madero, who promised democratic reform but who also seemed hostile to American businesses in Mexico. With American approval, Madero was himself deposed early in 1913 by a reactionary general, Victoriano Huerta.

The Taft administration, in its last weeks in office, prepared to recognize the new Huerta regime and welcome back a receptive environment for American investments in Mexico. Two things happened before it could do so: The new government murdered Madero, and Woodrow Wilson took office in Washington.

The new president instantly announced that he would never recognize Huerta's "government of butchers."

The problem dragged on for years. At first, Wilson hoped that simply by refusing to recognize Huerta he could help topple the regime and bring to power the opposing Constitutionalists, led by Venustiano Carranza. But when Huerta (supported by American business interests in Mexico) established a full military dictatorship in October 1913, the president became more assertive. He pressured the British to stop supporting Huerta. Then he offered to send American troops to assist Carranza. Carranza, aware that such an open alliance with the United States would undermine his popular support in Mexico, declined the offer; but he did secure the right to buy arms in the United States.

In April 1914, a minor naval incident provided the president with an excuse for more open intervention. An officer in Huerta's army briefly arrested several American sailors from the USS Dolphin who had gone ashore in Tampico. The men were immediately released, but the American admiral, unsatisfied with the apology he received, demanded that the Huerta forces fire a twenty-one-gun salute to the American flag as a public display of penance. The Mexicans refused. Wilson seized on the trivial incident as a pretext for seizing the Mexican port of Veracruz.

Wilson had envisioned a bloodless action, but in a clash with Mexican troops in Veracruz, the Americans killed 126 of the defenders and suffered nineteen casualties of their own. Now at the brink of war, Wilson began to look for a way out. His show of force, however, had helped strengthen the position of the Carranza faction, which captured Mexico City in August and forced Huerta to flee the country. At last, it seemed, the crisis might be over.

But Wilson was not yet satisfied. He reacted angrily when Carranza refused to accept American guidelines for the creation of a new government, and he briefly considered throwing his support to still another aspirant to leadership: Carranza's erstwhile lieutenant Pancho Villa, who was now leading a rebel army of his own. When Villa's military position deteriorated, however, Wilson abandoned him and finally, in October 1915, granted preliminary recognition to the Carranza regime.

By now, Wilson had created yet another crisis. Villa, angry at what he considered an American betrayal, retaliated in January 1916 by taking sixteen Americans from a train in northern Mexico and shooting them. Two months later, he led his soldiers (or bandits, as the United States preferred to call them) across the border into Columbus, New Mexico, where they killed seventeen more Americans. His goal, apparently, was to destabilize relations between Wilson and Carranza and provoke a war between them, which might provide him with an opportunity to improve his own declining fortunes.

With the permission of the Carranza government, Wilson ordered General John J. Pershing to lead an American expeditionary force across the Mexican border in pursuit of Villa. The American troops never found Villa, but they did engage in two ugly skirmishes with Carranza's army, in which forty

Mexicans and twelve Americans died. Again, the United States and Mexico stood at the brink of war. But at the last minute, Wilson drew back. He quietly withdrew American troops from Mexico; and in March 1917, having spent four years of effort and gained nothing for it but a lasting Mexican hostility toward the United States, he at last granted formal recognition to the Carranza regime.

By now, however, Wilson's attention was turning elsewhere—to the far greater international crisis engulfing the European continent and ultimately much of the world.

CHAPTER EIGHT

The Great War and the United States

⁓

The Great War, as it was known to a generation unaware that another, greater war would soon follow, began quietly in August 1914 when forces of the Austro-Hungarian Empire invaded the tiny Balkan nation of Serbia. Within weeks, it had grown into a widespread conflagration, engaging the armies of almost all the major nations of Europe and shattering forever the delicate balance of power that had maintained a general peace on that continent since the early nineteenth century. Most Americans looked on with horror as the war became the most savage in history, but also, at first, with a conviction that the conflict had little to do with them. They were wrong.

After nearly three years of attempting to affect the outcome of the conflict without becoming embroiled in it, the United States formally entered the war in April 1917. In doing so, it joined the most savage conflict in history. The fighting had already dragged on for two and a half years, inconclusive, almost inconceivably murderous, engaging not only the armies of the contending nations but their civilian populations as well. Although the American Civil War had greatly increased the ferocity and extent of combat, World War I was the first truly "total" war. It pitted entire societies against one another, and had, by 1917, left Europe exhausted and on the brink of utter collapse. By the time the war ended late in 1918, Germany had lost nearly 2 million soldiers in battle, Russia 1.7 million, France 1.4 million, and Great Britain 900,000. A generation of European youth was decimated; centuries of political, social, and economic traditions were damaged and all but destroyed.

For America, however, the war was a very different experience. As a military struggle, it was brief, decisive, and—in relative terms—without great cost. Only 112,000 American soldiers died in the conflict, half of them from disease rather than in combat. Economically, it was the source of a great industrial boom, which helped spark the years of prosperity that would follow. And the war propelled the United States into a position of international pre-eminence.

In other respects, World War I was a painful, even traumatic experience for the American people. At home, the nation became obsessed with a search not just for victory but also for social unity—a search that continued and even intensified in the troubled years following the Armistice, and that helped shatter many of the progressive ideals of the first years of the century. And abroad, once the conflict ended, the United States encountered frustration and disillusionment. The "war to end wars," the war "to make the world safe for democracy," became neither. Instead, it led directly to twenty years of international instability that would ultimately generate another great conflict.

THE ROOTS OF CONFLICT

The causes of the war in Europe—indeed the question of whether there were any significant causes at all or whether the entire conflict was the result of a tragic series of blunders—have been the subject of continued debate for nearly eighty years. What is clear is that the European nations had by 1914 created an unusually precarious international system that careened into war very quickly on the basis of what most historians agree was a minor series of provocations.

European Tensions and Precipitants

The major powers of Europe were organized by 1914 in two great, competing alliances. The "Triple Entente" linked Britain, France, and Russia. The "Triple Alliance" united Germany, the Austro-Hungarian Empire, and Italy. The chief rivalry, however, was not between the two alliances, but between the great powers that dominated them: Great Britain and Germany—the former long established as the world's most powerful colonial and commercial nation, the latter ambitious to expand its own empire and become at least Britain's equal.

The Anglo–German rivalry may have been the most important underlying source of the tensions that led to World War I, but it was not the immediate cause of its outbreak. The conflict emerged most directly out of a controversy involving nationalist movements within the Austro-Hungarian Empire. On June 28, 1914, the Archduke Franz Ferdinand, heir to the throne of the tottering empire, was assassinated while paying a state visit to Sarajevo. Sarajevo was the capital of Bosnia, a province of Austria-Hungary that Slavic nationalists wished to annex to neighboring Serbia; the archduke's assassin was a Serbian nationalist.

This local controversy quickly escalated through the workings of the system of alliances the great powers had constructed. With support from Germany, Austria-Hungary launched a punitive assault on Serbia. The Serbians called on Russia to help with their defense. The Russians began mobilizing their army on July 30, and things quickly careened out of control. By August 3, Germany had declared war on both Russia and France and had invaded Belgium in preparation for a thrust across the French border. On August 4, Great Britain—ostensibly to honor its alliance with France, but more importantly to blunt the advance of its principal rival—declared war on Germany. Russia and the Austro-Hungarian Empire formally began hostilities on August 6. Italy, the Ottoman Empire (Turkey), and other, smaller nations all joined the fighting later in 1914 or 1915. Within less than a year, virtually the entire European continent (and part of Asia) was embroiled in a major war.

Wilson and Neutrality

President Wilson called on his fellow citizens in 1914 to remain "impartial in thought as well as deed." But that was impossible, for several reasons. For one thing, many Americans were not, in fact, genuinely impartial. Some sympathized with the German cause (some German Americans, because of affection for Germany, some Irish Americans, because of hatred of Britain). Many more (including Wilson himself) sympathized with Britain. Wilson was only one of many Americans who fervently admired England—its traditions, its culture, its political system; almost instinctively, these American Anglophiles attributed to the cause of the Allies (Britain, France, Italy, Russia) a moral quality that they denied to the Central Powers (Germany, the Austro-Hungarian Empire, and the Ottoman or Turkish Empire). Lurid reports of German atrocities in Belgium and France, skillfully exaggerated by British propagandists, strengthened the hostility of many Americans toward Germany.

Economic realities also made it impossible for the United States to deal with the belligerents on equal terms. The British had imposed a naval blockade on Germany to prevent munitions and supplies from reaching the enemy. As a neutral, the United States had the right, in theory, to trade with Germany. A truly neutral course would have been either to ignore the British blockade (at the risk of conflict with England) or to stop trading with Britain as well. But while the United States could survive an interruption of its relatively modest trade with the Central Powers, it could not easily weather an embargo on its much more extensive trade with the Allies, particularly when war orders from Britain and France soared after 1914, helping to produce one of the greatest economic booms in the nation's history. So America tacitly observed the blockade of Germany and continued trading with Britain. By 1915, the United States had gradually transformed itself from a neutral power into the arsenal of the Allies.

The Germans, in the meantime, were resorting to a new and, in American eyes, barbaric tactic: submarine warfare. Unable to challenge British domination on the ocean's surface, Germany began early in 1915 to use their newly improved submarines to try to stem the flow of supplies to England. Enemy vessels, the Germans announced, would be sunk on sight. Months later, on May 7, 1915, a German submarine sank the British passenger liner *Lusitania* without warning, causing the deaths of 1,198 people, 128 of them Americans. The ship was, it later became clear, carrying not only passengers but munitions; but most Americans considered the attack what Theodore Roosevelt called it: "an act of piracy."

Wilson angrily demanded that Germany promise not to repeat such outrages and that the Central Powers affirm their commitment to neutral rights (among which, he implausibly insisted, was the right of American citizens to travel on the nonmilitary vessels of belligerents). The Germans finally agreed to Wilson's demands, but tensions between the nations continued to grow. Early in 1916, in response to an announcement that the Allies were now arming merchant ships to sink submarines, Germany proclaimed that it would fire on such vessels without warning. A few weeks later, it attacked the unarmed French steamer *Sussex*, injuring several American passengers. Again, Wilson demanded that Germany abandon its "unlawful" tactics; again, the German government relented. Lacking sufficient naval power to enforce an effective blockade against Britain, the Germans decided that the marginal advantages of unrestricted submarine warfare did not yet justify the possibility of drawing America into the conflict.

Debating War and Pacifism

Despite the president's increasing bellicosity in 1916, he was still far from ready to commit the United States to war. One obstacle was American domestic politics. Facing a difficult battle for reelection, Wilson could not ignore the powerful factions that continued to oppose intervention. His policies, therefore, represented an effort to balance the demands of those who, like Theodore Roosevelt, insisted that the nation fight to defend its "honor" and economic interests against those who, like Bryan, La Follette, and others (including many German Americans and Irish Americans hostile to Britain), denounced any action that seemed to increase the chance of war.

The question of whether America should make military and economic preparations for war provided a preliminary issue over which pacifists and interventionists could debate. Wilson, at first, sided with the antipreparedness forces, denouncing the idea of an American military buildup as needless and provocative. As tensions between the United States and Germany grew, however, he changed his mind. In the fall of 1915, he endorsed an ambitious proposal by American military leaders for a large and rapid increase in the nation's armed forces; and amid expressions of outrage from pacifists in Congress and elsewhere, he worked hard to win approval for it. He even embarked on a national speaking tour early in 1916 to arouse support for the proposal. By midsummer 1916, armament for a possible conflict was well under way.

Still, the peace faction wielded considerable political strength, as became clear at the Democratic Convention in the summer of 1916. The convention became almost hysterically enthusiastic when the keynote speaker, enumerating Wilson's accomplishments, punctuated his list of the president's diplomatic achievements with the chant, "What did we do? What did we do? . . . We didn't go to war! We didn't go to war!" That speech helped produce one of the most prominent slogans of Wilson's reelection campaign (although one the president himself never used or entirely approved): "He kept us out of war."

During the campaign, Wilson did nothing to discourage those who argued that the Republican candidate, the progressive New York Governor Charles Evans Hughes (supported by the bellicose Theodore Roosevelt), was more likely than he to lead the nation into war. And when prowar rhetoric became particularly heated, Wilson spoke defiantly of the nation being "too proud to fight." He ultimately won reelection by one of the smallest margins for an incumbent in American history: fewer than 600,000 popular votes and only twenty-three electoral votes. The Democrats retained a precarious control over Congress.

A War for Democracy

The election was behind him, and tensions between the United States and Germany were unabated. But Wilson still required a justification for American intervention that would unite public opinion and satisfy his own sense of morality. In the end, he created that rationale himself. The United States, Wilson insisted, had no material aims in the conflict. The nation was, rather, committed to using the war as a vehicle for constructing a new world order, one based on the same progressive ideals that had motivated reform in America. In a speech before Congress in January 1917, he presented a plan for a postwar order in which the United States would help maintain peace through a permanent league of nations—a peace that would ensure self-determination for all nations, a "peace without victory." These were, Wilson believed, goals worth fighting for if there was sufficient provocation. That provocation came quickly.

In January, after months of inconclusive warfare in the trenches of France, the military leaders of Germany decided on one last dramatic gamble to achieve victory. They would launch a series of major assaults on the enemy's lines in France. At the same time, they would begin unrestricted submarine warfare (against American as well as Allied ships) to cut Britain off from vital supplies. The Allied defenses would collapse, they hoped, before the United States could intervene.

The new German policy made American entry into the war virtually inevitable. Two additional events helped clear the way. On February 25, the British gave Wilson an intercepted telegram from the German foreign minister, Arthur Zimmermann, to the government of Mexico. It proposed that in the event of war between Germany and the United States, the Mexicans should join with Germany against the Americans. In return, they would regain their "lost provinces" (Texas and much of the rest of the American Southwest) to the north when the war was over. (The Germans understood that anti-American sentiment was still high in Mexico after the interventions of the previous few years.) Widely publicized by British propagandists and in the American press, the Zimmermann telegram inflamed public opinion and helped build up popular sentiment for war. A few weeks later, in March 1917, a revolution in Russia toppled the reactionary czarist regime and replaced it with a new, republican government. The United States would now be spared the embarrassment of allying itself with a despotic monarchy. The war for a progressive world order could proceed untainted.

On the rainy evening of April 2, two weeks after German submarines had torpedoed three American ships, Wilson appeared before a joint session of Congress and asked for a declaration of war:

> It is a fearful thing to lead this great peaceful people into war, into the most terrible and disastrous of all wars, civilization itself seeming to be in the balance. But the right is more precious than peace, and we shall fight for the things which we have always carried nearest our hearts—for democracy, for the right of those who submit to authority to have a voice in their own Governments, for the rights and liberties of small nations, for a universal dominion of right by such a concert of free peoples as shall bring peace and safety to all nations and make the world itself at last free.

Even then, opposition remained. For four days, pacifists in Congress carried on their futile struggle. When the declaration of war finally passed on April 6, fifty representatives and six senators voted against it.

WAR WITHOUT LIMITS

Armies on both sides in Europe were decimated and exhausted by the time of Woodrow Wilson's declaration of war. The German offensives of early 1917 had failed to produce an end to the struggle, and French and British counteroffensives had accomplished little beyond adding to the appalling number of casualties. The Allies looked desperately to the United States for help. Wilson, who had called on the nation to wage war "without stint or limit," was eager to oblige.

United States Intervention

American intervention had its most immediate effect on the conflict at sea. By the spring of 1917, Great Britain was suffering such vast losses from attacks by German submarines—one of every four ships setting sail from British ports never returned—that its ability to continue receiving vital supplies from across the Atlantic was in question. Within weeks of joining the war, the United States had begun to alter the balance. A fleet of American destroyers aided the British navy in its assault on the U-boats. Other American warships escorted merchant vessels across the Atlantic. Americans also helped sow antisubmarine mines in the North Sea. The results were dramatic. Sinkings of Allied ships had totaled nearly 900,000 tons in the month of April 1917; by December, the figure had dropped to 350,000; by October 1918, it had declined to 112,000.

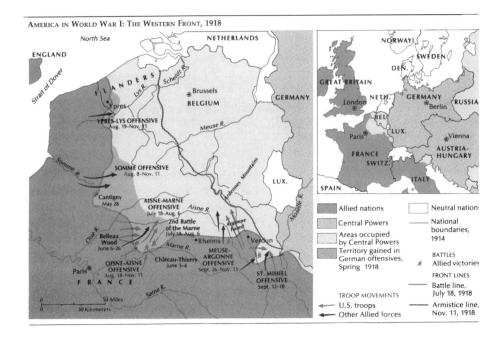

AMERICA IN WORLD WAR I: THE WESTERN FRONT, 1918

Many Americans had hoped that providing naval assistance alone would be enough to turn the tide in the war, but it quickly became clear that a major commitment of American ground forces would be necessary as well to shore up the tottering Allies. Britain and France had few remaining reserves. By early 1918, Russia had withdrawn from the war altogether. After the Bolshevik Revolution in November 1917, the new government, led by V. I. Lenin, negotiated a hasty and costly peace with the Central Powers, thus freeing additional German troops to fight on the western front.

Mobilizing the American Expeditionary Force

But the United States did not have a large enough standing army to provide the necessary ground forces in 1917. There were only about 120,000 soldiers in the army and perhaps 80,000 more in the National Guard. Neither group had any combat experience; and except for the brief experience of a few officers in the Spanish–American war two decades before and in the Mexican intervention of 1916, few commanders had any experience in battle either.

Some urged a voluntary recruitment process to raise the needed additional forces. Among the advocates of this approach was Theodore Roosevelt, now aging and ill, who swallowed his hatred of Wilson and called on him at the White House with an offer to raise a regiment to fight in Europe. Wilson refused the offer. The president and his secretary of war, Newton D. Baker, had decided, instead, that only a national draft could provide the needed men; and despite the protests of those who agreed with House Speaker Champ Clark that "there is precious little difference between a conscript and a convict," Wilson won passage of the Selective Service Act in mid-May. The draft brought nearly 3 million men into the army; another 2 million joined various branches of the armed services voluntarily. Together, they formed what became known as the American Expeditionary Force (AEF).

In some respects, it was the most diverse fighting force the United States had ever assembled. For the first time, women were permitted to enlist in the military—over 10,000 in the navy and a few hundred in the marines. They were not permitted in combat, but they served crucial auxiliary roles in hospitals and offices. Nearly 300,000 black soldiers enlisted in or were drafted into the army and navy as well. (The marines would not accept them.) And while most performed relatively menial tasks on military bases in the United States, more than 50,000 of them went to France. African-American soldiers served in segregated units under white commanders; and even in Europe, many of them were assigned to noncombat duty. But some black units fought valiantly in the great offensives of 1918. At times, African-American soldiers also lashed out, even violently, against racism. In August 1917, a group of black soldiers in Houston—subjected to continuing abuse by people in the community—used military weapons to kill seventeen whites. Retribution was quick. Thirteen black soldiers were hanged, and another forty were sentenced to life terms in military jails.

Having assembled this first genuinely national army, the War Department permitted the American Psychological Association to study them. The psychologists gave thousands of them a new test designed to measure intelligence—the "Intelligence Quotient" or "IQ" test. In fact, the tests were less effective in measuring intelligence than in measuring education; and they reflected the educational expectations of the white middle class. It is not surprising, therefore, that the largely working-class and racially mixed group of soldiers the psychologists examined performed poorly. Half the whites and the vast majority of the African Americans taking the test scored at levels that classified them as "morons." In reality, most of them were simply people who had not had very much access to education. Even so, the intelligence tests had a significant influence on the way academics, intellectuals, and others thought about the relationship between race and intelligence.

The American War Effort

The engagement of these forces in combat was intense but brief. Not until the spring of 1918 were significant numbers of American troops available for battle. Eight months later, the war was over. Under the command of General John J. Pershing, the American troops joined the existing Allied forces in turning back a series of new German assaults. In early June, they assisted the French in repelling a bitter German offensive at Chateau-Thierry, near Paris. Six weeks later, the Americans helped turn away another assault, at Rheims, farther south. By July 18, the Allies had halted the German advance and were beginning a successful offensive of their own.

On September 26, an American fighting force of over 1 million soldiers advanced against the Germans in the Argonne Forest as part of a 200-mile attack (the Meuse-Argonne Offensives) that lasted nearly seven weeks. By the end of October, they had helped push the Germans back toward their own border and had cut the enemy's major supply lines to the front.

Faced with an invasion of their own country, German military leaders now began to seek an armistice—an immediate ceasefire that would, they hoped, serve as a prelude to negotiations among the belligerents. Pershing wanted to drive on into Germany itself; but other Allied leaders, after first insisting on terms that made the agreement little different from a surrender, accepted the German proposal. On November 11, 1918, the Great War shuddered to a close.

WAR AND SOCIETY

The American experience in World War I was brief, but it had profound effects on the state, on the economy, and on society. Mobilizing an industrial economy for total war required an unprecedented degree of government involvement in industry, agriculture, and other areas. It also required, many believed, a strenuous effort to ensure the loyalty and commitment of the people.

Mobilizing the Economy

By the time the war ended, the United States government had appropriated $32 billion for expenses directly related to the conflict. This was a staggering sum by the standards of the time. The entire federal budget had seldom exceeded $1 billion before 1915, and the nation's entire Gross National Product had been only $35 billion as recently as 1910. To raise the money, the government relied on two devices. First, it launched a major drive to solicit loans from the American people by selling "Liberty Bonds" to the public. By 1920, the sale of bonds, accompanied by elaborate patriotic appeals, had produced $23 billion. At the same time, new taxes were bringing in an additional sum of nearly $10 billion—some from levies on the "excess profits" of corporations, much from new, steeply graduated income and inheritance taxes that ultimately rose as high as seventy percent in some brackets.

An even greater challenge was organizing the economy to meet war needs. The administration tried two very different approaches. In 1916, Wilson established a Council of National Defense, composed of members of his cabinet and a Civilian Advisory Commission, which set up local defense councils in every state and locality. Economic mobilization, according to this first plan, was to rest on a large-scale dispersal of power to local communities.

But this early administrative structure soon proved completely unworkable. Some members of the Council of National Defense, many of them disciples of the social engineering gospel of Thorstein Veblen and the "scientific management" principles of Frederick Winslow Taylor, urged a more centralized approach. Instead of dividing the economy geographically, they proposed dividing it functionally by organizing a series of planning bodies, each to supervise a specific sector of the economy. Thus one agency would control transportation, another agriculture, another manufacturing. The administrative structure that slowly emerged from such proposals was dominated by a series of "war boards," one to oversee the railroads, one to supervise fuel supplies (largely coal), another to handle food (a board that helped elevate to prominence the brilliant young engineer and business executive Herbert Hoover). The boards were not without weaknesses, but they generally succeeded in meeting essential war needs without paralyzing the domestic economy.

At the center of the effort to rationalize the economy was the War Industries Board (WIB), an agency created in July 1917 to coordinate government purchases of military supplies. Casually organized at first, it stumbled badly until March 1918, when Wilson restructured it and placed it under the control of the Wall Street financier Bernard Baruch. From then on, the board wielded powers greater (in theory at least) than any government agency had ever possessed. Baruch decided which factories would convert to the production of which war materials and set prices for the goods they produced. When materials were scarce, Baruch decided to whom they should go. When corporations were competing for government contracts, he chose among them. He was, it seemed, providing the centralized regulation of the economy that some progressives had long urged.

In reality, the vaunted efficiency of the WIB was something of a myth. The agency was plagued by mismanagement and inefficiency. And in the end, it was less important to the nation's ability to meet its war needs than was the sheer extent of American resources and productive capacities. Nor was the WIB, in any real sense, an example of state control of the economy. Baruch viewed himself, openly and explicitly, as the partner of business; and within the WIB, businessmen themselves—the so-called dollar-a-year men, who took paid leave from their corporate jobs and worked for the government for a token salary—supervised the affairs of the private economy. Baruch ensured that manufacturers coordinating their efforts in accord with his goals would be exempt from antitrust laws. He helped major industries earn enormous profits from their efforts. Rather than working to restrict private power and limit corporate profits, as many progressives had urged, the government was working to enhance the private sector through a mutually beneficial alliance.

The effort to organize the economy for war produced some spectacular accomplishments: Hoover's efficient organization of food supplies, William McAdoo's success in untangling the railroads, and others. In some areas, however, progress was so slow and the American fighting so brief that the war was over before many of the supplies ordered for it were ready. Even so, many leaders of both government and industry emerged from the experience convinced of the advantages of a close, cooperative relationship between the public and private sectors. Some hoped to continue and extend some version of the wartime experiments in the peacetime world.

War and Labor Militancy

This growing link between the public and private sectors extended, although in greatly different form, to labor. The National War Labor Board, established in April 1918 to resolve labor disputes, pressured industry to grant important concessions to workers: an eight-hour day, the maintenance of minimal living standards, equal pay for women doing equal work, recognition of the right of unions to organize and bargain collectively. In return, it insisted that workers forgo all strikes and that employers not engage in lockouts. Membership in labor unions increased by more than 1.5 million between 1917 and 1919.

The war provided workers with important, if usually temporary, gains. But it did not stop labor militancy. That was particularly clear in the West, where the Western Federation of Miners staged a series of strikes to improve the terrible conditions in the underground mines of the region. In Ludlow, Colorado, in 1917, workers (mostly Italians, Greeks, and Slavs) walked out of coal mines owned by John D. Rockefeller. Joined by their wives and daughters, they con-

LUDLOW MASSACRE. The wartime strike of coal miners in Ludlow, Colorado resulted in their eviction from company housing. In the depth of winter, the strikers lived in tents such as the one depicted here, until the state militia routed them. The Ludlow strike illustrated the way in which not only workers themselves, but also their families, were often mobilized—and victimized—during strikes.

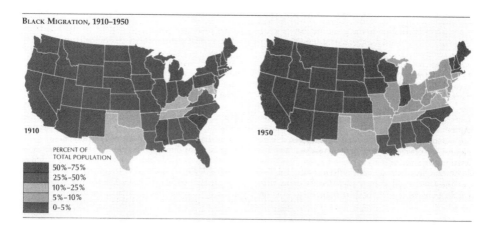

BLACK MIGRATION, 1910–1950

1910

1950

PERCENT OF
TOTAL POPULATION

50%–75%
25%–50%
10%–25%
5%–10%
0–5%

tinued the strike even after they had been evicted from company housing and had moved into hastily erected tents. The state militia was called into the town to protect the mines, but in fact (as was often the case in labor actions), it actually worked to help employers defeat the strikers. Joined by strikebreakers and others, the militia attacked the workers' tent colony; and in the battle that followed, thirty-nine people died, among them eleven children. The episode became known as the Ludlow Massacre.

Social and Economic Effects of the War

Whatever its other effects, the war helped produce a remarkable period of economic growth in the United States—a boom that began in 1914 (when European demands for American products began to increase) and accelerated after 1917 (when demand from the United States war effort fueled production). Industrial production soared, and manufacturing activity expanded in regions that had previously had relatively little of it. The shipbuilding industry, for example, grew rapidly on the West Coast. Employment increased dramatically, and because so many men were away at war, new opportunities for female, African-American, Mexican-American, and Asian workers appeared. Inflation cut into the wage increases American workers won from employers, but most workers nevertheless experienced a significant growth in income. The agricultural economy profited from the war as well. Farm prices rose to their highest levels in decades, and agricultural production increased dramatically as a result.

One of the most important social changes of the war years was the migration of hundreds of thousands of African-Americans from the rural South into northern industrial cities. It became known as the "Great Migration." Like most migrations, it was a result of both a "push" and a "pull." The push was the poverty, indebtedness, racism, and violence most blacks experienced in the South. The pull was the prospect of factory jobs in the urban North and the opportunity to live in communities where blacks could enjoy more freedom and autonomy. In the labor-scarce economy of the war years, northern factory owners dispatched agents to the South to recruit African-American workers. Black newspapers advertised the prospects for employment in the North. And perhaps most influential of all, those who migrated first sent word back to friends and families of the opportunities they encountered—one reason for the heavy concentration of migrants from one area of the South in particular cities in the North. In Chicago, for example, the more than 70,000 new black residents came disproportionately from a few areas of Alabama and Mississippi.

WOMEN WAR WORKERS.   During World War I, as in other wars, women proved vital to the home-front economy. In this photograph, women are making bullets. With much of the male work force fighting overseas, women found employment opportunities in the wartime economy that were elusive in times of peace.

The result was a dramatic growth in black communities in northern industrial cities such as New York, Chicago, Cleveland, and Detroit. Older, more established black residents of these cities were unsettled by the new arrivals, with their country ways and their revivalistic religion; some members of existing communities considered the newcomers coarse and feared that their presence would increase their own vulnerability to white racism. But the movement could not be stopped. New churches sprang up in black neighborhoods (many of them simple storefronts, from which self-proclaimed preachers searched for congregations). Low-paid black workers crowded into inadequate housing—small apartments known as kitchenettes, in which several families sometimes lived together. As the black communities expanded, they inevitably began to rub up against white neighborhoods, with occasionally violent results. In East St. Louis, Illinois, a white mob attacked a black neighborhood on July 2, 1917, burned down many houses, and shot the residents of some of them as they fled. As many as forty black people died.

For American women, black and white, the war meant new opportunities for employment. A million or more women worked in a wide range of industrial jobs that, in peacetime, were considered male preserves: steel, munitions, trucking, and public transportation. Most of them had been working in other, less well-paying jobs earlier. Among some feminists, the war inspired hopes of a lasting change in the role of women in the economy and the society. Margaret Drier Robins, an official of the Women's Trade Union League, said in 1918: "The war has created new values. Men and women are conscious that as citizens they must . . . share in the management of industry and the administration of government." But whatever changes the war brought were temporary ones. As soon as the war was over, almost all of the women working in industrial jobs once held by men quit or were fired; and in fact, the percentage of women working for wages actually declined between 1910 and 1920.

THE IDEAL OF NATIONAL UNITY

The idea of unity—not only in the direction of the economy but in the nation's social purpose—had been the dream of many progressives for decades. To them, the war seemed to offer an unmatched opportunity for America to close ranks behind a great common cause. In the process, they hoped, society could achieve a lasting sense of collective purpose. In fact, however, the search for unity produced considerable repression.

The Peace Movement

Government leaders, and many others, realized that public sentiment about American involvement in the war had been deeply divided before April 1917 and remained so even after the declaration of war.

The peace movement in the United States before 1917 had many constituencies: German Americans who opposed American intervention against Germany; Irish Americans who opposed any support for the British; religious pacifists (Quakers, Mennonites, and others); intellectuals such as Randolph Bourne, the socialist party, and the IWW, which considered the war a meaningless battle among capitalist nations for commercial supremacy—an opinion many others in America and Europe later came to share. But the most active and widespread peace activists were feminists. In 1915, Carrie Chapman Catt, a leader of the fight for woman suffrage, helped create the Woman's Peace party, with a small but active membership. As the war in Europe intensified, the party's efforts to keep the United States from intervening grew.

Women peace activists were sharply divided once America entered the war in 1917. The National American Woman Suffrage Association, the largest single women's organization, supported the war and, more than that, presented itself as a patriotic organization dedicated to advancing the war effort. Its membership grew dramatically as a result. Catt, who was among those who abandoned the peace cause, now began calling for woman suffrage as a "war measure," to ensure that woman (whose work was essential to the war effort) would feel fully a part of the nation. But many other women refused to support the war even after April 1917. Among them were Jane Addams, who was widely reviled for a time as a result, and Charlotte Perkins Gilman, a leading feminist activist.

Women peace activists shared many of the political and economic objections to the war that the Socialist party (to which some of them belonged) had articulated. But some criticized the war on other grounds as well—arguing that as wives and mothers they had a special moral basis for their pacifism. The Woman's Peace party had claimed to represent the "mother half of humanity," and a similarly maternal opposition to war shaped the position of the many women who remained in opposition after 1917.

War Propaganda and Political Repression

Government leaders were painfully aware of the continuing opposition to the war. Many believed that a crucial prerequisite for victory was to unite public opinion behind the war effort. The most conspicuous government effort to do so was a vast propaganda campaign to drum up enthusiasm for the conflict. It was orchestrated by the Committee on Public Information (CPI), under the direction of the Denver journalist George Creel, who spoke openly of the importance of achieving social unity:

> When I think of the many voices that were heard before the war and are still heard, interpreting America from a class or sectional or selfish standpoint, I am not sure that, if the war had to come, it did not come at the right time for the preservation and reinterpretation of American ideals.

The CPI supervised the distribution of innumerable tons of prowar literature (75 million pieces of printed material in all). War posters plastered the walls of offices, shops, theaters, schools, churches, and homes. Newspapers dutifully printed official government accounts of the reasons for the war and the prospects for quick victory. Creel encouraged reporters to exercise "self-censorship" when reporting news about the struggle; and although many people in the press resented the suggestion, the veiled threats that accompanied it persuaded most of them to comply.

The CPI attempted at first to distribute only the "facts," believing that the truth would speak for itself. As the war continued, however, its tactics became increasingly crude. Government-produced posters and films, at first relatively mild in tone, were by 1918 becoming lurid portrayals of the savagery of the Germans, bearing such titles as *The Prussian Cur* and *The Kaiser: Beast of Berlin*, encouraging Americans to think of the German people as something close to savages.

The government soon began more coercive efforts to suppress dissent. The CPI ran full-page advertisements in popular magazines such as the *Saturday Evening Post* urging citizens to notify the Justice Department when they encountered "the man who spreads the pessimistic stories . . . , cries for peace, or belittles our efforts to win the war." The Espionage Act of 1917 gave the government new tools with which to respond to such reports. It created stiff penalties for spying, sabotage, or obstruction of the war effort (crimes that were often broadly defined); and it empowered the Post Office to ban "seditious" material from the mails, a responsibility Postmaster General Albert Sidney Burleson accepted with great relish. Sedition, he said, included statements that might "impugn the motives of the government and thus encourage insubordination," anything that suggested "that the government is controlled by Wall Street or munitions manufacturers, or any other special interests." He included in that category all publications of the Socialist party.

More repressive were two measures of 1918: the Sabotage Act of April 20 and the Sedition Act of May 16. These bills expanded the meaning of the Espionage Act to make illegal any public expression of opposition to the war; in practice, it allowed officials to prosecute anyone who criticized the president or the government. Senator Hiram Johnson of California offered a bitter description of the provisions of the law. He said: "You shall not criticize anything or anybody in the Government any longer or you shall go to jail."

The most frequent target of the new legislation (and one of the reasons for its enactment in the first place) were such anticapitalist (and now antiwar) groups as the Socialist party and the Industrial Workers of the World. Many Americans had favored the repression of socialists and radicals even before the war; the wartime policies now made it possible to move against them with full legal sanction. Eugene V. Debs, the humane leader of the party and an opponent of the war, was sentenced to ten years in prison in 1918. Only a pardon by President Warren G. Harding in 1921 ultimately won his release. Big Bill Haywood and members of the IWW were especially energetically prosecuted. Only by fleeing

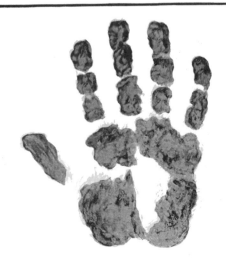

ANTI-GERMAN PROPAGANDA AND LIBERTY BONDS.   The
Liberty bond-selling program raised $23 billion dollars for
the war effort. Posters such as this one not only urged
Americans to buy the bonds in order to support the
war effort; they also depicted the Germans as savage
beasts—"Huns"—whose hands were drenched
in the blood of their victims.

to the Soviet Union did Haywood avoid a long imprisonment. In all, more than 1,500 people were arrested in 1918 for the crime of criticizing the government.

State and local governments, corporations, universities, and private citizens contributed as well to the climate of repression. Vigilante mobs sprang up to "discipline" those who dared challenge the war. A dissident Protestant clergyman in Cincinnati was pulled from his bed one night by a mob, dragged to a nearby hillside, and whipped "in the name of the women and children of Belgium." An IWW organizer in Montana was seized by a mob and hanged from a railroad bridge. A cluster of citizens' groups emerged to mobilize "respectable" members of their communities to root out disloyalty. The American Protective League, probably the largest of such groups, enlisted the services of 250,000 people who served as "agents" prying into the activities and thoughts of their neighbors, opening mail, tapping telephones, and in general attempting to impose unity of opinion on their communities. The League received government funds to support its work. Attorney General Thomas W. Gregory, a particularly avid supporter of repressing dissent, described the League approvingly as a "patriotic organization." Other vigilante organizations—the National Security League, the Boy Spies of America, the American Defense Society—performed much the same function.

There were many victims of these repressive activities: socialists, labor activists, female pacifists (some of whom were arrested and imprisoned simply for criticizing the government or capitalism). But the most frequent targets of repression were immigrants: Irish Americans because of their historic animosity toward the British and because some had, before 1917, expressed hopes for a German victory; Jews because many had expressed opposition to the anti-Semitic policies of the Russian government, until 1917 one of the Allies; and others. "Loyalist" citizens' groups policed immigrant neighborhoods and monitored meetings and even conversations for signs of disloyalty. Even some settlement house workers, many of whom had once championed ethnic diversity, contributed to such efforts. The director of the National Security League described the danger he and many others now believed ethnicity posed to the idea of "100 percent Americanism":

> the melting pot has not melted. . . . there are vast communities in the nation thinking today not in terms of America, but in terms of Old World prejudices, theories, and animosities. . . . In the bottom of the melting pot there lie heaps of unfused metal.

The greatest target of abuse was the German-American community. Its members had unwittingly contributed to their plight. In the first years of the war in Europe, some had openly advocated American assistance to the Central Powers, and many had opposed United States intervention on behalf of the Allies. But while most German Americans supported the American war effort once it began, public opinion turned bitterly hostile. A campaign to purge society of all things German quickly gathered speed, at times assuming ludicrous forms.

Sauerkraut was renamed "liberty cabbage." Hamburger became "liberty sausage." Performances of German music were frequently banned. German books were removed from the shelves of libraries. Courses in the German language were removed from school curricula; the California Board of Education called it "a language that disseminates the ideals of autocracy, brutality, and hatred." German-Americans were routinely fired from jobs in war industries lest they "sabotage" important tasks. Some were fired from positions entirely unrelated to the war, among them Karl Muck, the German-born conductor of the Boston Symphony Orchestra. Vigilante groups routinely subjected Germans to harassment and beatings, including a lynching in southern Illinois in 1918. Relatively few Americans favored such extremes, but many came to agree with the belief of the eminent psychologist G. Stanley Hall that "there is something fundamentally wrong with the Teutonic soul."

A NEW WORLD ORDER

Woodrow Wilson had led the nation into war promising a more just and stable peace at its conclusion. Well before the Armistice, he was preparing to lead the fight for what he considered a democratic postwar settlement—for a set of war aims resting on a philosophy that became known as Wilsonian internationalism.

The Fourteen Points

On January 8, 1918, Wilson appeared before Congress to present the principles for which he claimed the nation was fighting. The war aims had fourteen distinct provisions, widely known as the Fourteen Points; but they fell in three broad categories. First, Wilson's proposals contained eight specific recommendations for adjusting postwar boundaries and for establishing new nations to replace the defunct Austro-Hungarian and Ottoman Empires. Those recommendations reflected his belief in the right of all peoples to self-determination. Second, there were five general principles to govern international conduct in the future: freedom of the seas, open covenants instead of secret treaties, reductions in armaments, free trade, and impartial mediation of colonial claims. Finally, there was a proposal for a league of nations that would help implement these new principles and territorial adjustments and would resolve future controversies.

There were serious flaws in Wilson's proposals. He provided no formula for deciding how to implement the "national self-determination" he promised for subjugated peoples. He said little about economic rivalries and their effect on international relations, even though it had been such economic tensions that had been in large part responsible for the war. Nevertheless, Wilson's international vision quickly came to enchant not only much of his own generation (in both America and Europe), but members of generations to come. It reflected his belief, strongly rooted in the ideas of progressivism, that the world was as capable of just and efficient government as were individual nations; that once the international community accepted certain basic principles of conduct, and once it constructed modern institutions to implement them, the human race could live in peace.

The Fourteen Points were also an answer to the new Bolshevik government in Russia. In December 1917, Lenin had issued his own statement of war aims strikingly similar to Wilson's own. Wilson's announcement, which came just three weeks later, was in part a last-minute (and unsuccessful) effort to persuade the Bolshevik regime to keep Russia in the war. But Wilson also realized that Lenin was now a competitor in the effort to lead the postwar order. And he announced the Fourteen Points in part to ensure that the world looked to the United States, and not Russia, for guidance. "Liberalism," he said, referring to his own ideals, "is the only thing that can save civilization from chaos—from a flood of ultra-radicalism that will swamp the world. . . . Liberalism must be more liberal than ever before, it must even be radical, if civilization is to escape the typhoon."

Diplomatic and Domestic Political Resistance

Wilson was confident, as the war neared its end, that popular support would enable him to win Allied approval of his peace plan. There were, however, ominous signs both at home and abroad that his path might be more difficult than he expected. In Europe, leaders of the Allied powers were preparing to resist him even before the Armistice was signed. Most of them resented what they considered Wilson's tone of moral superiority. They had reacted unhappily when Wilson refused to make the United States their "ally" but had kept his distance as an "associate" of his European partners. They had been offended by his insistence on keeping American military forces separate from the Allied armies they were joining. Most of all, however, Britain and France, having suffered incalculable losses in their long years of war, and having stored up an enormous reserve of bitterness toward Germany as a result, were in no mood for a benign and generous peace. The British prime minister, David Lloyd George, insisted for a time that the German Kaiser be captured and executed. He and Georges Clemenceau, president of France, remained determined to the end to gain something from the struggle to compensate them for the catastrophe they had suffered.

At the same time, Wilson was encountering problems at home. In 1918, with the war almost over, Wilson unwisely appealed to American voters to support his peace plans by electing Democrats to Congress in the November elections. A Republican victory, he declared, would be "interpreted on the other side of the water as a repudiation of my leadership." Days later, the Republicans captured majorities in both houses. Domestic economic troubles, more than international issues, had been the most important factor in the voting; but because of the president's ill-timed appeal, the results damaged his ability to claim broad popular support for his peace plans.

The leaders of the Republican party, in the meantime, were developing their own reasons for opposing Wilson. Some were angry that he had tried to make the 1918 balloting a referendum on his war aims, especially since many Republicans had been supporting the Fourteen Points. Wilson further antagonized them when he refused to appoint any important Republicans to the negotiating team that would represent the United States at the peace conference in Paris.

But the president considered such matters unimportant. There would be only one member of the American negotiating team with any real authority: Wilson himself. And once he had produced a just and moral treaty, he believed, the weight of world and American opinion would compel his enemies to support him. As he sailed for Paris late in 1918, he said:

> In the name of the people of the United States, I have uttered as the objects of this great war ideals and nothing but ideals, and the war has been won by that inspiration. . . . There is a great wind of moral force moving through the world, and every man who opposes that wind will go down in disgrace.

The Paris Peace Conference

Wilson arrived in Europe to a welcome such as few men in history have experienced. To the war-weary people of Europe, he was nothing less than a savior, the man who would create a new and better world. When he entered Paris on December 13, 1918, he was greeted, some claimed, by the largest crowd in the history of France. The negotiations themselves, however, proved less satisfying.

The principal figures in the negotiations were the leaders of the victorious allied nations: Lloyd George representing Great Britain; Clemenceau representing France; Vittorio Orlando, the prime minister of Italy; and Wilson, who hoped to dominate them all. Some of Wilson's advisers had warned him that if agreement could not be reached at the "summit," there would be nowhere else to go and that it would therefore be better to begin negotiations at a lower level. Wilson, however, was adamant; he alone would represent the United States.

From the beginning, the atmosphere of idealism Wilson had sought to create was in competition with a spirit of national aggrandizement. There was, moreover, a pervasive sense of unease about the unstable situation in eastern Europe and the threat of communism. Russia, whose new Bolshevik government was still fighting "White" counterrevolutionaries, was unrepresented in Paris; but the radical threat it seemed to pose to Western governments was never far from the minds of any of the delegates, least of all Wilson himself. Indeed, not long before he came to Paris, Wilson had ordered the landing of American troops in the Soviet Union. They were there, he claimed, to help a group of 60,000 Czech soldiers trapped in Russia to escape. But the Americans soon

THE BIG FOUR IN PARIS.   Although cordial appearances were maintained at the Paris Peace Conference, serious tensions existed among the so-called "Big Four"—the leaders of the war's victorious nations. Shown here are (from left to right) David Lloyd George of Great Britain, Vittorio E. Orlando of Italy, George Clemenceau of France, and Woodrow Wilson.

became involved, both directly and indirectly, in assisting the White Russians (the anti-Bolsheviks) in their fight against the new regime. Some American troops remained as late as April 1920. Lenin's regime survived these challenges, but Wilson refused to recognize his new government nevertheless. Diplomatic relations between the United States and the Soviet Union were not restored until 1933.

In the tense and often vindictive atmosphere these competing concerns produced in Paris, Wilson was unable to win approval of many of the broad principles he had espoused: freedom of the seas, which the British refused even to discuss; free trade; "open covenants openly arrived at" (the Paris negotiations themselves were often conducted in secret). Despite his support for "impartial mediation" of colonial claims, he was forced to accept a transfer of German colonies in the Pacific to Japan, to whom the British had promised them in exchange for Japanese assistance in the war. His pledge of "national self-determination" for all peoples suffered numerous assaults. The economic and strategic demands of the great powers were constantly interfering with the principle of cultural nationalism.

Where the treaty departed most conspicuously from Wilson's ideals was on the question of reparations. As the conference began, the president opposed demanding compensation from the defeated Central Powers. The other Allied leaders, however, were intransigent, and slowly Wilson gave way and accepted the principle of reparations, the specific sum to be set later by a commission. That figure, established in 1921, was $56 billion supposedly to pay for damages to civilians and military pensions. Continued negotiations in the 1920s scaled the debt back considerably. In the end, Germany paid only $9 billion, which was still more than its crippled economy could afford. The reparations, combined with other territorial and economic penalties, constituted an effort to keep Germany not only weak but prostrate for the indefinite future. Never again, the Allied leaders believed, should the Germans be allowed to become powerful enough to threaten the peace of Europe.

Wilson did manage to win some important victories in Paris in setting boundaries and dealing with former colonies. He secured approval of a plan to place many former colonies and imperial possessions (among them Palestine) in "trusteeship" under the League of Nations—the so-called mandate system. He blocked a French proposal to break up western Germany into a group of smaller states. He helped design the creation of two new nations: Yugoslavia and Czechoslovakia. They were welded together out of, among other territories, pieces of the former Austro-Hungarian empire. Each contained an uneasy collection of ethnic groups that had frequently battled one another in the past.

But Wilson's most visible triumph, and the one of most importance to him, was the creation of a permanent international organization to oversee world affairs and prevent future wars. On January 25, 1919, the Allies voted to accept the "covenant" of the League of Nations; and with that, Wilson believed, the peace treaty was transformed from a disappointment into a success. Whatever mistakes and inequities had emerged from the peace conference, he was convinced, could be corrected later by the League.

The covenant provided for an assembly of nations that would meet regularly to debate means of resolving disputes and protecting the peace. Authority to implement League decisions would rest with a nine-member Executive Council; the United States would be one of five permanent members of the council, along with Britain, France, Italy, and Japan. The covenant left many questions unanswered, most notably how the League would enforce its decisions. Wilson, however, was confident that once established, the new organization would find suitable answers.

The Battle over Ratification

Wilson was well aware of the political obstacles awaiting him at home. Many Americans, accustomed to their nation's isolation from Europe, questioned the wisdom of this major new commitment to internationalism. Others had serious reservations about the specific features of the treaty and the covenant. After a brief trip to Washington in February 1919, during which he listened to harsh objections to the treaty from members of the Senate and others, he returned to Europe and insisted on certain modifications in the covenant to satisfy his critics. The revisions limited America's obligations to the League by ensuring that the United States would not be obliged to accept a League mandate to oversee a territory and that the League would not challenge the Monroe Doctrine. But the changes were not enough to mollify his opponents, and Wilson refused to go further. When Colonel House, his close friend and trusted adviser, told him he must be prepared to compromise further, the president retorted sharply: "I have found that you get nothing in this world that is worth-while without fighting for it." His long friendship with House ended abruptly.

Wilson presented the Treaty of Versailles (which took its name from the palace outside Paris where the final negotiating sessions had taken place) to the Senate on July 10, 1919, asking "Dare we reject it and break the heart of the world?" In the weeks that followed, he refused to consider even the most innocuous compromise. His deteriorating physical condition—he was suffering from hardening of the arteries and had apparently experienced something like a minor stroke in Paris—may have contributed to his intransigence.

The Senate, in the meantime, was raising many objections. Some senators—the fourteen so-called "irreconcilables," many of them western isolationists—opposed the agreement on principle. But other opponents, with less fervent convictions, were principally concerned with constructing a winning issue for the Republicans in 1920 and with weakening a president whom they had come to despise. Most notable of these was Senator Henry Cabot Lodge of Massachusetts, the powerful chairman of the Foreign Relations Committee. A man of stunning arrogance and a close friend of Theodore Roosevelt (who had died early in 1919, spouting hatred of Wilson to the end), Lodge loathed the president with genuine passion. "I never thought I could hate a man as I hate Wilson," he once admitted. He used every possible tactic to obstruct, delay, and amend the treaty. Wilson, for his part, despised Lodge as much as Lodge despised him. He made his feelings clear when he described his opponents in the Senate (obviously thinking primarily of Lodge) as "contemptible, narrow, selfish, poor little minds that never get anywhere."

Public sentiment clearly favored ratification, so at first Lodge could do little more than play for time. When the document reached his committee, he spent two weeks slowly reading aloud each word of its 300 pages; then he held six weeks of public hearings to air the complaints of every disgruntled minority (Irish Americans, for example, angry that the settlement made no provision for an independent Ireland). Gradually, Lodge's general opposition to the treaty crystallized into a series of "reservations"—amendments to the League covenant limiting American obligations to the organization.

Wilson might still have won approval at this point if he had agreed to some relatively minor changes in the language of the treaty. But the president refused to yield. The United States had a moral obligation, he claimed, to respect the terms of the agreement precisely as they stood. When he realized the Senate would not budge, he decided to appeal to the public.

The Tragedy of Wilson

What followed was a political disaster and a personal tragedy. Wilson embarked on a grueling, cross-country speaking tour to arouse public support for the treaty. For more than three weeks, he traveled over 8,000 miles by train, speaking as often as four times a day, resting hardly at all. Finally, he reached the end of his strength. After speaking at Pueblo, Colorado, on September 25, he collapsed with severe headaches. Canceling the rest of his itinerary, he rushed back to Washington, where, a few days later, he suffered a major stroke. For two weeks, he was close to death; for six weeks more, he was so seriously ill that he could conduct virtually no public business. His wife and his doctor formed an almost impenetrable barrier around him, shielding the president from any official pressures that might impede his recovery, preventing the public from receiving any accurate information about the gravity of his condition.

Wilson ultimately recovered enough to resume a limited official schedule, but he was essentially an invalid for the remaining eighteen months of his presidency. His left side was partially paralyzed; more important, like many stroke victims, he had only partial control of his mental and emotional state. His condition only intensified what had already been his strong tendency to view public issues in moral terms and to resist any attempts at compromise. When the Senate Foreign Relations Committee finally reported the treaty, recommending nearly fifty amendments and reservations, Wilson refused to consider any of them. When the full Senate voted in November to accept fourteen of the reservations, Wilson gave stern directions to his Democratic allies: They must vote only for a treaty with no changes whatsoever; any other version must be defeated. On November 19, 1919, forty-two Democrats, following the president's instructions, joined with the thirteen Republican "irreconcilables" to reject the amended treaty. When the Senate voted on the original version without any reservations, thirty-eight senators, all but one a Democrat, voted to approve it; fifty-five voted no.

There were sporadic efforts to revive the treaty over the next few months. But Wilson's opposition to anything but the precise settlement he had negotiated in Paris remained too formidable an obstacle to surmount. He was, moreover, becoming convinced that the 1920 national election would serve as a "solemn referendum" on the League. By now, however, public interest in the peace process had begun to fade—partly as a reaction against the tragic bitterness of the ratification fight, but more in response to a series of other crises.

POSTWAR DISCORD

Even during the Paris Peace Conference, many Americans were less concerned about international matters than about turbulent events at home. In the first months after the war, some Americans—among them workers and African Americans—set out to claim the social advances that the idealistic justifications of the conflict seemed to have promised them. But the social environment after 1918 was no longer receptive to progressive change. The American economy experienced a severe postwar recession. And much of middle-class America responded to demands for reform with a fearful, conservative hostility. The aftermath of war brought not the age of liberal reform that progressives had predicted, but a period of repression and reaction.

Economic Distress

Citizens of Washington, on the day after the Armistice, found it impossible to place long-distance telephone calls. The lines were jammed with officials of the war agencies canceling government contracts. The fighting had ended sooner than anyone had anticipated; and without warning, without planning, the nation was launched into the difficult task of economic reconversion.

At first, the wartime boom continued. But the postwar prosperity rested largely on the lingering effects of the war (government deficit spending continued for some months after the Armistice) and on sudden, temporary demands (a booming market for scarce consumer goods at home and a strong market for American products in the war-ravaged nations of Europe). The postwar boom was accompanied, moreover, by raging inflation, a result in part of the precipitous abandonment of wartime price controls. Through most of 1919 and 1920, prices rose at an average of more than fifteen percent a year.

Finally, late in 1920, the economic bubble burst, as many of the temporary forces that had created it disappeared and as inflation began killing the market for consumer goods. Between 1920 and 1921, the Gross National Product (GNP) declined nearly ten percent, 100,000 businesses went bankrupt, 453,000 farmers lost their land, and nearly 5 million Americans lost their jobs.

Labor Unrest

In this unpromising economic environment, leaders of organized labor set out to consolidate the progress they had made in the war, which now seemed in danger of being lost. The raging inflation of 1919 wiped out the modest wage gains workers had achieved during the war; many laborers were worried about job security, as hundreds of thousands of veterans returned to the workforce; arduous working conditions—such as the twelve-hour day in the steel industry—continued to be a source of discontent. Employers aggravated the resentment by using the end of the war (and the end of government controls) to rescind benefits they had been forced to concede to workers in 1917 and 1918—most notably the recognition of unions.

The year 1919, therefore, saw an unprecedented wave of strikes—more than 3,600 in all, involving over 4 million workers. In January, a walkout by shipyard workers in Seattle, Washington, evolved into a general strike that brought the entire city to a virtual standstill. The mayor requested and received the assistance of U.S. Marines to keep the city running, and eventually the strike failed. But the brief success of a general strike, something Americans associated with European radicals, made the Seattle incident reverberate loudly throughout the country.

In September, there was a strike by the Boston police force, which was responding to layoffs and wage cuts by demanding recognition of its union. Seattle had remained generally calm; but with its police off the job, Boston erupted in violence and looting. Efforts by local businessmen, veterans, and college students to patrol the streets proved ineffective; and finally Governor Calvin Coolidge called in the National Guard to restore order. (His public statement at the time that "there is no right to strike against the public safety by anybody, anywhere, any time" attracted national acclaim.) Eventually, Boston officials dismissed the entire police force and hired a new one.

In September 1919, the greatest strike in American history began, when 350,000 steelworkers in several midwestern cities walked off the job demanding an eight-hour day and recognition of their union. The steel strike was long, bitter, and violent—most of the violence coming from employers, who hired armed guards to disperse picket lines and escort strikebreakers into factories. It climaxed in a riot in Gary, Indiana, in which eighteen strikers were killed. Steel executives managed to keep most plants running with non-union labor, and public opinion was so hostile to the strikers that the AFL having at first endorsed the strike, soon timidly repudiated it. By January, the strike had collapsed. It was a setback from which organized labor would not recover for more than a decade.

The wave of strikes was a reflection of the high expectations workers had in the aftermath of a war they believed had been fought, in part, to secure their rights. It was also a reflection of the power of the forces arrayed against them. An official of the War Labor Board, observing the dismal postwar experience of unions, said in 1919: "The workers of the Allied world have been told that they were engaged in a democracy. . . . They are asking now, 'Where is that democracy for which we fought?' "

The Struggles of African Americans

The black men who had served in the armed forces during the war (367,000 of them) came home in 1919, and they marched down the main streets of the industrial cities with other returning troops. And then (in New York and other cities), they marched again through the streets of black neighborhoods such as Harlem, led by jazz bands, cheered by thousands of African Americans, worshiped as heroes. The black soldiers were an inspiration to thousands of urban blacks, a sign, they thought, that a new age had come, that the glory of black heroism in the war would make it impossible for white society ever again to treat blacks as less than equal citizens.

In fact, that black soldiers had fought in the war had little effect on white attitudes. But it did have a profound effect on black attitudes; it accentuated African-American bitterness—and increased black determination to fight for their rights. For soldiers, there was an expectation that their service would help them escape the oppression they had known before the war. For many other American blacks, the war had raised economic expectations, as they moved into industrial and other jobs vacated by white workers, jobs to which they previously had no access. Black factory workers regarded their move north as an escape from racial prejudice and an opportunity for economic gain.

By 1919, however, the racial climate had become savage and murderous. In the South, there was a sudden increase in lynchings: More than seventy blacks, some of them war veterans, died at the hands of white mobs in 1919 alone. In the North, black factory workers faced widespread layoffs as returning white veterans displaced them from their jobs. Black veterans found no significant new opportunities for advancement. Rural black migrants to northern cities encountered white communities unfamiliar with and generally hostile to them; and as whites became convinced that black workers with lower wage demands were hurting them economically, animosity grew rapidly.

The wartime riots in East St. Louis and elsewhere were a prelude to a summer of much worse racial violence in 1919. In Chicago, a black teenager swimming in Lake Michigan on a hot July day happened to drift toward a white beach. Whites on shore allegedly stoned him unconscious; he sank and drowned. Angry blacks gathered in crowds and marched into white neighborhoods to retaliate; whites formed even larger crowds and roamed into black neighborhoods shooting, stabbing, and beating passers-by, destroying homes and properties. For more than a week, Chicago was virtually at war. In the end, thirty-eight people died—fifteen whites and twenty-three blacks— and 537 were injured; over 1,000 people were left homeless. The Chicago riot was the worst but not the only racial violence during the so-called red summer of 1919; in all, 120 people died in such racial outbreaks in the space of little more than three months.

Racial violence, and even racially motivated urban riots, were not new. The deadliest race riot in American history had occurred in New York during the Civil War. But the 1919 riots were unprecedented in one respect: They did not just involve white people attacking blacks; they also involved blacks fighting back. The NAACP signaled this change by urging blacks not just to demand government protection, but also to fight to defend themselves. The poet Claude

CHICAGO RACE RIOT.   The Chicago race riot in the summer of 1919 resulted in terrible destruction and violence. Here an African American is being rounded up by mounted police and led to a zone of safety. His torn pants and swollen eye suggest that he was one of many beaten during the riot that left 38 people dead in the city.

McKay, one of the major figures of what would shortly be known as the Harlem Renaissance, wrote a poem after the Chicago riot called "If We Must Die":

Like men we'll face the murderous cowardly pack.
Pressed to the wall, dying, but fighting back.

At the same time, a black Jamaican, Marcus Garvey, began to attract a wide American following, mostly among poor urban blacks, with an ideology of black nationalism. Garvey encouraged American blacks to take pride in their own achievements and to develop an awareness of their African heritage—to reject assimilation into white society and identify with their own race and culture (which was, he claimed, superior to that of white society). His United Negro Improvement Association (UNIA) launched a chain of black-owned grocery stores and pressed for the creation of other black businesses. Eventually, Garvey began urging his supporters to leave America and return to Africa, where they could create a new society of their own. In the 1920s, the Garvey movement experienced explosive growth for a time; and the UNIA became notable for its mass rallies and parades, the elaborate uniforms of its members (and of Garvey himself), and the growth of its businesses. It began to decline, however, after Garvey was indicted in 1923 on charges of business fraud. He was deported to Jamaica two years later. But the allure of black nationalism, which he made so visible to millions of African Americans, survived in black culture long after Garvey himself was gone.

The Red Scare

To much of the white middle class at the time, the industrial warfare, the racial violence, and the demands of feminists all appeared to be frightening omens of instability and radicalism. This was in part because other evidence emerging at the same time seemed likewise to suggest the existence of a radical menace. The Russian Revolution of November 1917 made it clear that communism was no longer simply a theory, but now a powerful regime. Concerns about the communist threat grew in 1919 when the Soviet government announced the formation of the Communist International (or Comintern), whose purpose was to export revolution around the world. And in America itself, there was, in addition to the great number of imagined radicals, a modest number of real ones. The American Communist party began its life in 1919, and there were other radical groups (many of them dominated by immigrants from Europe who had been involved in radical politics before coming to America). Some of these radicals were presumably responsible for a series of bombings in the spring of 1919 that produced great national alarm. In April, the Post Office intercepted several dozen parcels addressed to leading businessmen and politicians that were triggered to explode when opened. Several of them reached their destinations, and one of them exploded, severely injuring a domestic servant of a public official in Georgia. Two months later, eight bombs exploded in eight cities within minutes of one another, suggesting a nationwide conspiracy. One of them damaged the facade of Attorney General A. Mitchell Palmer's home in Washington. In 1920, there was a terrible explosion in front of the Morgan bank on Wall Street, which killed thirty people (although only one person in the bank itself—a clerk; J.P. Morgan was in Europe at the time).

The bombings crystallized what was already a growing determination among many middle-class Americans (and within the government) to fight back against radicalism—a determination steeled by the repressive atmosphere of the war years. This antiradicalism accompanied, and reinforced, the already strong commitment among Old-Stock Protestants to the idea of "100 Percent Americanism." And it produced what became known as the Red Scare.

Antiradical newspapers and politicians now began to portray almost every form of instability or protest as a sign of a radical threat. Race riots, one newspaper claimed, were the work of "armed revolutionaries running rampant through our cities." The steel strike, the *Philadelphia Inquirer* claimed, was "penetrated with the Bolshevik idea . . . steeped in the doctrines of the class struggle and social overthrow." Nearly thirty states enacted new peacetime sedition laws imposing harsh penalties on those who promoted revolution; some 300 people went to jail as a result—many of them people whose "crime" had been nothing more than opposition to the war. There were spontaneous acts of violence against supposed radicals in some communities. A mob of off-duty soldiers in New York City ransacked the offices of a socialist newspaper and beat up its staff. Another mob, in Centralia, Washington, dragged an IWW agitator from jail and castrated him before hanging him from a bridge. Citizens in many communities removed "subversive" books from the shelves of libraries; administrators in some universities dismissed "radical" members from their faculties. Women's groups such as the National Consumers' League came under attack by antiradicals because so many feminists had opposed American intervention in the fighting in Europe.

Perhaps the greatest contribution to the Red Scare came from the federal government. On New Year's Day, 1920, Attorney General A. Mitchell Palmer and his ambitious assistant, J. Edgar Hoover, orchestrated a series of raids on alleged radical centers throughout the country. More than 6,000 people were arrested. The Palmer Raids had been intended to uncover huge caches of weapons and explosives; they netted a total of three pistols, no dynamite. Most of those arrested were ultimately released, but about 500 who were not American citizens were summarily deported.

The ferocity of the Red Scare soon abated, but its effects lingered well into the 1920s, most notably in the celebrated case of Sacco and Vanzetti. In May of 1920, two Italian immigrants, Nicola Sacco and Bartolomeo Vanzetti, were charged with the murder of a paymaster in Braintree, Massachusetts. The evidence against them was questionable; but because both men were confessed anarchists, they faced a widespread public presumption of guilt. They were convicted in a trial of extraordinary injudiciousness, before an openly bigoted judge, Webster Thayer. They were sentenced to death. Over the next several years, public support for Sacco and Vanzetti grew to formidable proportions. But all requests for a new trial or a pardon were denied. On August 23, 1927, amid widespread protests around the world, Sacco and Vanzetti, still proclaiming their innocence, died in the electric chair. Theirs was a cause that a generation of Americans never forgot. Fifty years later, the writer Katherine Anne Porter, who had demonstrated on their behalf, described the case as the "Never-Ending Wrong." It kept the bitter legacy of the Red Scare alive for many years.

A Tide of Disillusionment

On August 26, 1920, the Nineteenth Amendment, guaranteeing women the right to vote, became part of the Constitution. To the woman suffrage movement, this was the culmination of nearly a century of struggle. To many progressives, who had seen the inclusion of women in the electorate as a way of bolstering their political strength, it seemed to promise new support for reform. Yet the passage of the Nineteenth Amendment marked not the beginning of an era of reform, but the end of one.

Economic problems, feminist demands, labor unrest, racial tensions, and the intensity of the antiradicalism they helped create—all combined in the years immediately following the war to produce a general sense of disillusionment. That became particularly apparent in the election of 1920. Woodrow Wilson wanted the campaign to be a referendum on the League of Nations; and the Democratic candidates, Ohio Governor James M. Cox and Assistant Secretary of the Navy Franklin D. Roosevelt, tried to keep Wilson's ideals alive. The Republican presidential nominee, however, offered a different vision. He was Warren Gamaliel Harding, an obscure Ohio senator, whom party leaders had chosen as their nominee confident that he would do their bidding once in office. Harding offered no ideals, only a vague promise of a return, as he later phrased it, to "normalcy." He won in a landslide. The Republican ticket received sixty-one percent of the popular vote and carried every state outside the South. The party made major gains in Congress as well.

Woodrow Wilson, who had tried and failed to create a postwar order based on democratic ideals, stood repudiated. Early in 1921, he retired to a house on S Street in Washington, where he lived quietly until his death in 1924. In the meantime, for most Americans, a new era had begun.

CHAPTER NINE

The "New Era" and Its Discontents

~

The ordeals of the First World War and its aftermath gradually gave way in the 1920s to a period of remarkable growth and prosperity in the United States. Between the recession of 1921 and the crash of the stock market in 1929, Americans experienced the greatest economic boom in their history to that point. New industries appeared, cities grew, real wages rose, unemployment fell, and consumer spending soared. As a result, the American middle class expanded to include many people of once modest means who now enjoyed a much improved standard of living.

A dynamic political culture also did much to redefine American life. Political conservatism *seemed* to dominate the "New Era," and in many respects it did. But there were also significant efforts during the period to broaden the reach of government. Although the aims of reformers usually exceeded their reach, the experiments of the 1920s helped set the stage for some of the sweeping governmental initiatives of the 1930s.

For all of its excitement, energy, and accomplishment, the "New Era" also reflected the persistence of tenacious social and economic problems in the United States. The prosperity of the 1920s was real, and it enhanced the lives of millions of people. But it was not universal. Many Americans benefited from it little or not at all. Perhaps, most critically, it was short lived. After eight years, the pillars of economic prosperity came crashing down. What followed was the greatest economic depression in American history.

PROSPERITY AND THE NEW ECONOMY

A major economic expansion followed the recession of 1921–1922. American manufacturing thrived in response to growing demand, technological progress, increasing mechanization, determined efforts to rationalize industry, and government policies that promoted growth. Less visible was the survival (and even growth) of serious imbalances in the American economy and persistent inequality.

A Booming Economy

The American economy performed extremely well for much of the 1920s, particularly when compared to other leading industrialized societies. Manufacturing output rose by more than sixty percent during the decade. Per capita income grew by a third, and inflation was negligible. In 1923 a mild recession briefly stalled this pattern of growth, but when it subsided in early 1924 the economy expanded even more vigorously.

Several factors contributed to the health of the American economy during the 1920s. The debilitation of European industry in the aftermath of World War I left the United States for a short time the only truly healthy industrial power in the world. More importantly, technological innovations, the spread of mechanization, and resulting improvements in efficiency did much to spur economic growth. By the 1920s the assembly line had helped make automobiles the most important industry in the nation. The vitality of this key industry helped stimulate growth in related industries as well. Auto manufacturers purchased large quantities of steel, rubber, glass, and tools from other corporations. As automobiles proliferated, road construction expanded, too. Car owners contributed to the profits of the oil and gas industry. The increased mobility that the automobile made possible increased the demand for suburban housing. That demand contributed in turn to a boom in the construction industry.

Technological strides also helped launch new industries that became emblematic of the 1920s. Radio rapidly emerged as an important new industry within a few years of its commercial debut on election night in 1920, when KDKA in Pittsburgh began broadcasting. By 1922, some thirty radio stations were in operation. A year later 500 stations were broadcasting. The number of American homes boasting radio sets had tripled by 1924. As radio increasingly turned to advertising as a source of revenue, it helped boost other areas of the economy as well.

The motion picture industry was not new to the 1920s, but it also grew dramatically during this time, especially after the introduction of sound in 1927. Lavish motion picture "palaces" appeared in American cities, helping to make movie-going a major cultural activity that spanned much of the social spectrum. By the mid-1920s film had already become California's leading industry. Huge studios such as Metro-Goldwyn-Mayer, founded in 1924, employed thousands of people and grossed millions of dollars by the decade's end. Technology fueled the growth of countless other industries during the 1920s. Aviation, electronics, home appliances, plastics, synthetic fibers, aluminum, magnesium, oil, and electric power all grew impressively, aided by technological advances, and spurred the economic

AUTOMOBILE ASSEMBLING LINE.   Mass production in the automobile industry
contributed to the booming American economy in the 1920s. At a Chevrolet assembly
line in Flint, Michigan in 1920, early model trucks are lined up to the right
and the "409" model passenger car can be seen on the left. This plant
stayed in operation until World War II.

boom. Cheap, readily available energy—from newly discovered oil reserves, from
the expanded network of electric power, and from the nation's abundant coal
fields—further enhanced the ability of industry to produce.

Economic growth was accompanied by aggressive efforts by leading American businesses to organize and consolidate their activities further. Certain
industries—particularly those, such as steel, which were dependent on large-
scale mass production—had already moved rapidly toward concentrating
production in a few large firms. U.S. Steel, the nation's largest corporation,
was so dominant that almost everyone used the term "Little Steel" to refer to all of its competitors combined. Other industries, such as textiles,
were less dependent on technology and less susceptible to great economies
of scale. They proved more resistant to consolidation, in spite of the tire-
less efforts of many businessmen to promote it.

Where industry did consolidate, new forms of corporate organization emerged to advance the trend. By 1920 General Motors (GM) was not only the largest automobile manufacturer, but the fifth largest American corporation. It became a classic example of the modern business enterprise. Although GM's founder, William Durant, had expanded the company dramatically, he had retained an informal, personal management style. When the company foundered in the 1920 recession, however, leadership fell to Alfred P. Sloan, who jettisoned Durant's model. One colleague likened Sloan to the roller bearings manufactured at the company he had previously run: "self-lubricating, smooth, eliminates friction and carries the load." Others noted the sharp contrast between Durant's and Sloan's management styles. "Durant was a small, lively, warm man. Nearly everyone called him 'Billy.' Mr. Sloan was tall, quiet, and cool. Increasing deafness heightened his reserve. Nearly everyone called him Mr. Sloan." At GM, Sloan created a modern administrative system with an efficient divisional organization. The new system not only made it easier for GM to control its many subsidiaries; it also facilitated expansion of the company further still. Many other corporations adopted similar administrative systems.

Some industries less vulnerable to domination by a few great corporations attempted to achieve stability through cooperation rather than consolidation. National trade associations became an important means to that end. Created by various industry members to encourage coordination in production and marketing techniques, trade associations worked reasonably well in certain centralized mass-production industries. But in more decentralized industries, such as cotton textiles, their effectiveness was limited. Whatever their forms, the strenuous efforts by industrialists to curb competition reflected a strong fear of overproduction. In the midst of the booming 1920s, many industrialists well remembered how too-rapid expansion had helped produce recessions in 1893, 1907, and 1920. The great, unrealized dream of the New Era was to find a way to stabilize the economy so that such collapses would never occur again.

Labor and Inequality

Despite the dramatic economic growth and the widespread prosperity, many Americans continued to live at or near the edge of poverty. Wealth and purchasing power remained unevenly distributed in the twenties. Indeed, in some areas economic inequality appeared to be rising. In 1929 one major study concluded that more than two thirds of the American people lived at no better than the "minimum comfort level." Half of those languished at or below the level of "subsistence and poverty." In an age that celebrated efficiency, organization, and consolidation, many Americans found themselves unable to organize or protect their economic interests.

American industrial workers experienced both the successes and the failures of the 1920s with particular intensity. Most workers saw their standard of living rise during the decade; many enjoyed greatly improved working conditions, higher real wages, and a host of other benefits. Their work lives were affected, as well, by the increased attention many employers directed to the status of their labor force. Some employers in the 1920s were determined to avoid disruptive labor unrest and to forestall the growth of independent trade unions. They adopted an array of paternalistic programs that came to be known as "welfare capitalism." The great automobile manufacturer Henry Ford, for example, shortened the workweek, raised wages, and instituted paid vacations. U.S. Steel made conspicuous efforts to improve safety and sanitation in its factories. For the first time, some workers became eligible for pensions on retirement—nearly 3 million by 1926. When labor grievances surfaced despite these efforts, workers could voice them through the so-called company unions that were emerging in many industries—workers' councils and shop committees, organized by the corporations themselves.

Although welfare capitalism marked an important juncture in the long and often troubled relationship between labor and capital, its legacy was a complicated one. It brought many workers important economic benefits, but it did not help them gain any real control over their own fates. The company unions that employers often encouraged their workers to form were feeble vehicles, forbidden in most industries from raising the issues of most importance to labor. The rigid supervision and control of these unions by employers defeated the very purpose of labor organization. More critically, welfare capitalism survived only as long as industry prospered. What employers offered out of beneficence, they could also quickly take away. After 1929, with the economy in crisis, the entire system quickly collapsed.

Welfare capitalism affected only a relatively small number of workers, in any case. Most laborers worked for employers interested primarily in keeping their labor costs as low as possible. Workers as a whole, therefore, received wage increases that were proportionately far below increases in production and profits. Unskilled workers, in particular, saw their wages increase only imperceptibly—by slightly over two percent between 1920 and 1926. The average annual income of a worker remained below $1,500 a year at a time when $1,800 was considered necessary to maintain a minimally decent standard of living. Only by relying on the earnings of several family members at once could many working-class families make ends meet. And almost all such families had to live with the very real possibility of one or more members losing their jobs. Unemployment was lower in the 1920s than it had been in the previous two decades, and much lower than it would be in the 1930s. But a large proportion of the work force was out of work or working less than full time for at least some period during the decade—in part because the rapid growth of industrial technology made many jobs obsolete. The unemployment rate for the 1920s is difficult to calculate, but scholars estimate that an average of five to seven percent of the work force was without a job at any given time.

For workers who continued to look toward a strong, independent union movement as their best hope, the 1920s proved especially disappointing. The New Era was a bleak time for labor organization, in part because of the strength and effectiveness of company resistance and in part because most unions themselves were relatively conservative and were unwilling or unable to confront critical realities of the modern economy. The American Federation of Labor (AFL) remained wedded to the concept of the craft union, in which workers were organized on the basis of particular skills. It continued to make no provision for the fastest growing area of the work force: unskilled industrial workers, many of them immigrants from southern or eastern Europe. Ignored by the craft unions, such workers had few organizations of their own. In addition, the leadership of some powerful unions approached employers from a standpoint of accommodation rather than militant confrontation. William Green, who became president of the AFL in 1924, was committed to peaceful cooperation with employers and to strident opposition to communism and socialism. He frowned on strikes. Even John L. Lewis, the determined head of the United Mine Workers, insisted: "We are Americans. We cannot fight our own government." The unions themselves had little to show for their efforts at decade's end. Union membership dropped significantly during the twenties; only ten percent of industrial workers were organized as the period came to a close.

A Diverse Work Force

Women's participation in the labor force continued to grow during the 1920s, as nearly a million new women workers took jobs in the rapidly expanding clerical sector of the economy and in the professions. Their heavy concentration in what came to be called "pink-collar jobs"—low-paying service occupations—had important implications for the ability of women to improve their economic status. As secretaries, salesclerks, telephone operators, and other service personnel, very few women (no more than three percent) enjoyed the benefits, however circumscribed they might be, of union membership. Wage differentials between men and women actually grew in the 1920s as gender segregation in the labor market consigned many women to low-wage jobs and as laws designed to protect women in the workplace sometimes prevented them from gaining access to higher paid industrial employment. Even in the professions, women were usually relegated to the lower ranks. Few women scholars, for example, could hope to acquire professorships at major research universities. Many spent their entire careers as research assistants or lecturers despite having earned the advanced degrees that won their male counterparts more exalted academic positions.

For minority women, opportunities for economic and occupational mobility were especially limited. African-American women who had come north during the Great Migration from the South found it extremely difficult to find work other than domestic service. Five times as many married black women worked outside the home as did married white women. Most of them shouldered the burden of raising their children and caring for their families while spending long hours doing the same in someone else's home. In 1920, ninety percent of Pittsburgh's black working women labored as laundresses, live-in servants, and day workers. African-American women employed in industry often endured grueling working conditions. During the 1920s, one Chicago researcher noted that black women who worked in the city's slaughterhouses were placed in the "most unattractive and disagreeable department" of the factory—killing hogs "under repulsive conditions."

Such inequalities were by no means limited to women. African-American men, for example, also usually found themselves relegated to low-wage jobs in industry and barred from joining labor unions. The skilled craft unions in the AFL often actively excluded black men from their trades and organizations. African-American men were overrepresented in jobs in which the AFL took no interest—janitors, dishwashers, garbage collectors, commercial laundry attendants, domestics, and other service occupations in which organization was difficult or impossible. There was one notable exception. The Brotherhood of Sleeping Car Porters, founded in 1925, was a vigorous union, led by an African American, A. Philip Randolph, and representing a virtually all-black work force.

WORKING IN SAW MILLS. These African-American women worked in a southern sawmill in 1920. North and South, black women worked for wages in significantly greater numbers than did white women. Their uniforms appear to reflect some effort to feminize women's work clothing. But, there was nothing "feminine" about the hard work they performed in industry.

Over time, Randolph would win some significant gains for his union membership, including increased wages and shorter working hours. He also enlisted the union in battles for civil rights.

In the West and the Southwest, the ranks of the unskilled included considerable numbers of Asians and Hispanics, few of them organized, most of them actively excluded from white-dominated unions. In the wake of the Chinese Exclusion Acts, Japanese immigrants increasingly took the place of the Chinese in menial jobs in California, despite the continuing hostility of the white population. They worked on railroads, construction sites, farms, and in many other low-paying workplaces. Their wives often joined them in agricultural work. Other Japanese women during the 1920s worked for wages as domestic servants. In both settings, they worked long hours for low pay.

Over time, some Japanese managed to escape the ranks of the unskilled by forming their own small businesses or setting themselves up as truck farmers; and many of the Issei (Japanese immigrants) and Nisei (their American-born children) enjoyed significant economic success—so much so that California passed laws in 1913 and 1920 to make it more difficult for them to buy land. Other Asians, most notably Filipinos, also swelled the unskilled work force and generated considerable hostility. Anti-Filipino riots in California beginning in 1929 helped produce legislation in 1934 virtually eliminating immigration from the Philippines.

Mexican immigrants formed a major part of the unskilled work force throughout the Southwest and California. Nearly half a million Mexicans entered the United States in the 1920s, more than any other national group, increasing the total Mexican population to over a million. Most lived in California, Texas, Arizona, and New Mexico; and by 1930, most lived in cities. Large Mexican barrios—usually raw urban communities, often without even such basic services as plumbing and sewage—grew up in Los Angeles, El Paso, San Antonio, Denver, and many other cities and towns. Some residents found work locally in factories and shops; others traveled to mines or did migratory labor on farms but returned to the cities between jobs. Mexican workers, too, faced hostility and discrimination from the Anglo population of the region. Mexican women in California, for example, often earned less than their white counterparts in laundries and garment factories, even when they performed the same jobs. But there were few efforts actually to exclude Mexican workers in the West. Employers in this relatively underpopulated region needed a ready pool of low-paid, unskilled, and unorganized workers.

The "American Plan"

Whatever the weaknesses of the unions and of unorganized, unskilled workers, the strength of the corporations was the principal reason for the absence of effective labor organization. After the turmoil of 1919, many corporate leaders worked hard to spread the doctrine that unionism was somehow subversive, and that the open shop (a shop in which no worker could be required to join a union) was a crucial element of democratic capitalism. The crusade for the open shop, euphemistically titled the "American Plan," received the endorsement of the National Association of Manufacturers in 1920. It soon became a pretext for a harsh campaign of union busting across the country.

When such tactics proved insufficient to counter union power, government assistance often made the difference. In 1921, the Supreme Court upheld a lower court ruling that declared picketing illegal and supported the right of courts to issue injunctions against strikers. A year later the Justice Department intervened to quell a strike by 400,000 railroad workers. In 1924, the courts refused protection to members of the United Mine Workers Union when mine owners launched a violent campaign in western Pennsylvania to drive the union from the coal fields. Indeed, the judiciary remained largely hostile to labor during the twenties. Justice Louis Brandeis, one of the more liberal Supreme Court justices of his day, captured the mood of the courts when he observed that "neither the common law, nor the Fourteenth Amendment, confers the absolute right to strike." Employers easily secured injunctions from the courts against strikers again and again throughout the 1920s. As a result, union membership fell from more than 5 million in 1920 to under 3 million in 1929.

But dwindling success in organizing did not entirely stifle labor militancy. In the mid-twenties, when two large textile mills opened in Elizabethton, Tennessee, they quickly attracted large numbers of young, white Appalachian women eager for wages. They were not a docile labor force. As one observer noted, the women textile workers had grown up on "these farms and they had to be aggressive to live." In 1929, fed up with low wages and oppressive work rules—including supervision by management of the women's bathroom, where some workers were said to loiter for extra minutes—several hundred women workers walked out. Although the strike that followed was broken six weeks later, the events in Elizabethton reverberated into other southern textile mills and other strikes followed.

The Plight of the Farmer

Both the benefits and the costs of growth and mechanization, so apparent in industry, were visible in American agriculture during the 1920s as well. Like industry, agriculture was embracing new technologies for increasing production. The number of tractors on American farms, for example, quadrupled during the 1920s, helping to open 35 million new acres to cultivation. At the same time, agricultural production was increasing rapidly in other parts of the world. Unlike increased industrial production, increased agricultural production did not often stimulate consumer demand. The result was overproduction, a disastrous decline in food prices, and a severe drop in income for farmers beginning early in the 1920s. In 1920, farm income had been fifteen percent of the national total; by 1929, it had dropped to nine percent. The average farmer made only

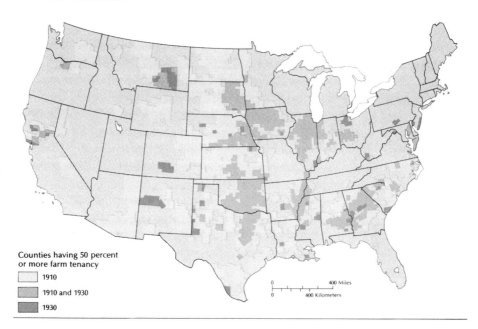

Counties having 50 percent
or more farm tenancy

1910

1910 and 1930

1930

0 ——————— 400 Miles
0 ——————— 400 Kilometers

about a quarter as much money each year in the 1920s as the average nonfarmer. More than 3 million people left agriculture in the course of the decade. Of those who remained, many were forced into tenancy—losing ownership of their lands and having to rent instead from banks or other landlords.

In response, some farmers began to demand relief in the form of government price supports. A few gravitated to such vaguely radical organizations as the Nonpartisan League of North Dakota or its successor, the Farmer-Labor party, which established a foothold as well in Minnesota and other midwestern states. Most farmers, however, were more moderate. Through such organizations as the American Farm Bureau Federation, they put increasing pressure on Congress (where farmers continued to enjoy disproportionately high representation). And while reform sentiment generally made little headway in the 1920s, farmers' organizational strength boosted the cause of agrarian reform.

One price-raising scheme in particular came to dominate agrarian demands: the idea of parity. "Parity" referred to a formula for guaranteeing farmers a fair price for their crops regardless of how national or international agricultural markets might fluctuate. In the 1920s, the formula was based on the average price of the crop during the half-decade preceding World War I (a good time for farmers) as compared with the general average of all prices during the same period. Champions of parity urged high tariffs against foreign agricultural goods and a government commitment to buying surplus domestic crops at parity and selling them abroad at whatever the market would bring.

The legislative expression of the demand for parity was the McNary-Haugen bill, named after its two principal sponsors in Congress and introduced repeatedly between 1924 and 1928. In 1926, Congress approved a bill requiring parity for grain, cotton, tobacco, and rice, but President Coolidge vetoed it. In 1928, it won congressional approval again, only to succumb to another presidential veto. Agrarian reformers were encountering one of the central political realities of the 1920s: a federal government dominated by a Republican party and Republican presidents, of firmly conservative temperament.

AN ERA OF REPUBLICAN POWER

For twelve years, beginning in 1921, both the presidency and Congress rested securely in the hands of the Republican party—a party in which the power of reformers had greatly dwindled since the pre–World War I heyday of progressivism. For most of those years, the federal government enjoyed a warm and supportive relationship with the American business community. Yet the government of the New Era was more than the passive, pliant instrument that critics often described. It also attempted to serve as an active agent of economic change.

The Presidency in the New Era

Nothing seemed more clearly to illustrate the unadventurous aspects of 1920s politics than the characters of the two men who served as president during most of the decade: Warren G. Harding and Calvin Coolidge.

Harding was elected to the presidency in 1920, having spent many years in public life doing little of note. An undistinguished senator from Ohio, he had received the Republican presidential nomination as a result of an agreement among leaders of his party who considered him, as one noted, a "good second-rater." Harding wanted to be a responsible president. He attempted to stabilize the nation's troubled foreign policy; and he displayed on occasion a vigorous humanity, as when he pardoned socialist Eugene V. Debs in 1921. But even as he attempted to rise to his office, he seemed baffled by his responsibilities, as if he recognized his own unfitness. "I am a man of limited talents from a small town," he reportedly told friends on one occasion. "I don't seem to grasp that I am President." Unsurprisingly, perhaps, Harding soon found himself delegating much of his authority to others: to members of his cabinet, to political cronies, to Congress, to party leaders. Although Harding appointed several men of real distinction to his cabinet, he lacked the strength to abandon the party hacks who had helped create his political success. One of them, Harry Daugherty, the Ohio party boss principally responsible for his meteoric political ascent, he appointed attorney general. Another, New Mexico Senator Albert B. Fall, he made secretary of the interior. Members of the so-called Ohio Gang filled important offices throughout the administration. Unknown to the public (and perhaps also to Harding), Daugherty, Fall, and others were engaged in fraud and corruption, at least some of which gradually came to light.

The most spectacular scandal involved the rich naval oil reserves at Teapot Dome, Wyoming, and Elk Hills, California. At the urging of Albert Fall, Harding transferred control of those reserves from the Navy Department to the Interior Department. Fall then secretly leased them to two wealthy businessmen and received in return nearly half a million dollars in "loans" to ease his private financial troubles. Fall was ultimately convicted of bribery and sentenced to a year in prison; Harry Daugherty barely avoided a similar fate for his part in another scandal.

In the summer of 1923, only months before Senate investigations and press revelations brought the scandals to light, a tired and depressed Harding left Washington for a speaking tour in the West and a visit to Alaska. In Seattle late in July, he suffered severe pain, which his doctors wrongly diagnosed as food poisoning. A few days later, in San Francisco, he died. He had suffered two major heart attacks. Harding was a much revered president at his death, but within months, the breadth of corruption in his administration became public. His once-good name soon became nearly synonymous with political fraud and corruption.

Harding's successor, Calvin Coolidge, was in many ways utterly different from his predecessor. Where Harding was genial, garrulous, and debauched, Coolidge was dour, silent, even puritanical. And while Harding was, if not personally corrupt, at least tolerant of corruption in others, Coolidge seemed honest beyond reproach. In other ways, however, Harding and Coolidge were similar figures. Both took an essentially passive approach to the presidency.

Like Harding, Coolidge had risen to the presidency on the basis of few substantive accomplishments. Elected governor of Massachusetts in 1919, he had won national attention with his forceful, if laconic, response to the Boston police strike that year ("There is no right to strike against the public safety, anytime, anywhere."). That was enough to make him his party's vice-presidential nominee in 1920. Three years later, after news of Harding's death reached him in Vermont, he took the oath of office from his father, a justice of the peace, by the light of a kerosene lamp on the kitchen table. It was the beginning of a skillful reinvention of Coolidge by party leaders and advisers from the advertising industry (among them advertising executive Bruce Barton). For the next five years, Coolidge built a reputation as a simple man defending country virtues, even though in reality he was a thoroughly urban man of modern sensibilities who enjoyed the company, and the comforts, of the wealthy.

CALVIN COOLIDGE.   President Coolidge was not known for humor, relaxed personal style, or affability. Here he opens the American League baseball season in the spring of 1925 by throwing out the first ball. Though the President displays only a hint of a smile, the First Lady (to his right) beams.

If anything, Coolidge was an even less active president than Harding had been, partly as a result of his conviction that government should interfere as little as possible in the life of the nation (and, most importantly, in the life of its economy) and partly as a result of his own personal lassitude. He took long naps every afternoon. ("No president of my time ever slept so much," one journalist noted.) He kept official appointments to a minimum and engaged in little conversation with those who did manage to see him. He proposed no significant legislation and took little part in the running of the nation's foreign policy. "He aspired," wrote one of his contemporaries, "to become the least President the country ever had. He attained his desire."

In 1924, Coolidge received his party's presidential nomination virtually unopposed. Running against John W. Davis, a corporate lawyer who became the 1924 Democratic candidate, he won a comfortable victory: fifty-four percent of the popular vote and 382 of the 531 electoral votes. Robert La Follette, the candidate of the reincarnated Progressive party, received 16.8 percent of the popular vote but carried only his home state of Wisconsin. Coolidge probably could have won renomination and reelection in 1928. Instead, in characteristically laconic fashion, he walked into a press room one day and handed each reporter a slip of paper containing a single sentence: "I do not choose to run for president in 1928."

The Alliance Between Business and Government

The story of Harding and Coolidge themselves, however, is only a part—and by no means the most important part—of the story of their administrations. However inept or inert the New Era presidents may have been, much of the federal government was working effectively and efficiently during the 1920s to adapt public policy to the widely accepted goal of the time: helping business and industry operate with maximum efficiency and productivity. The close relationship between the private sector and the federal government that had been forged during World War I continued, although in much altered form.

One key player in cementing the alliance between business and government was Secretary of the Treasury Andrew Mellon, a wealthy steel and aluminum tycoon with a keen appreciation for corporate needs and the intricacies of finance capitalism. Mellon devoted himself to working for substantial reductions in taxes on corporate profits and personal incomes and inheritances. Largely because of his efforts, Congress cut them all by more than half. Mellon also worked closely with President Coolidge after 1924 on a series of measures to trim dramatically the already modest federal budget. The administration even managed to retire half the nation's World War I debt.

Also central to the framing of economic policy in the Coolidge administration was its Commerce Secretary Herbert Hoover. Hoover considered himself, and was considered by others, a notable progressive. During his eight years in the Commerce Department, he constantly encouraged voluntary cooperation in the private sector as the best avenue to stability. But the idea of voluntarism did not require the government to remain passive; on the contrary, Hoover believed public institutions had a duty to play an active role in creating the new, cooperative order. Above all, Hoover championed the concept of business associationalism—the creation of national organizations of businessmen in particular industries. Through these trade associations, Hoover believed, private entrepreneurs could stabilize their industries and promote efficiency in production and marketing. Hoover strongly resisted those who urged that the government suspend the antitrust laws and sanction collusion among manufacturers to fix prices. But, he did believe that shared information and limited cooperation would keep competition from becoming destructive and thus improve the strength of the economy as a whole.

The Supreme Court in the 1920s further confirmed the business orientation of the federal government, particularly after the appointment of William Howard Taft as chief justice in 1921. In one of the most important decisions in its history, *Lochner* v. *New York* (1905), the Court had struck down a New York law limiting the number of hours bakers in New York could be required to work as an abrogation of the freedom of workers and employers to form contracts. (See p. 111.) With that decision, the Court had set a nearly impossible standard against which all future economic regulations would have to be measured.

In the 1920s, continuing along the lines the Lochner decision had laid out, the Court struck down federal legislation regulating child labor (*Baily* v. *Drexel Furniture Company*, 1922); nullified a minimum wage law for women in the District of Columbia (*Adkins* v. *Children's Hospital*, 1923); and sanctioned the creation of trade associations, ruling in *United States* v. *Maple Flooring Association* (1925) that such organizations did not violate antitrust statutes as long as some competition survived within an industry. Five years earlier, in *United States* v. *U.S. Steel*, the Court had applied the same doctrine to the monopolistic United States Steel Corporation; there was no illegal "restraint of trade," it ruled, as long as U.S. Steel continued to face any competition, no matter how slight.

The probusiness policies of the Republican administrations were not without their critics. In Congress, progressive reformers of the old school continued to criticize the monopolistic practices of big business, to attack the government's alliance with the corporate community, and to decry social injustices. Occasionally, they were able to mobilize enough support to win congressional approval of progressive legislation: the McNary-Haugen plan for farmers; an ambitious proposal to use federal funds to develop public electric power projects on the Tennessee River at Muscle Shoals; and, in 1921, the inventive Sheppard-Towner Act.

Championed by women reformers and organizations such as the General Federation of Women's Clubs, Sheppard-Towner provided federal matching funds to the states for maternal and child health programs. The recent enfranchisement of women had helped persuade Congress initially to pass the legislation, but from the start Sheppard-Towner drew the ire of bitter opponents. To the American Medical Association, the bill represented an ill-conceived and even dangerous step toward government intervention in health care and medicine. The bill, in fact, constituted a pioneering step in federal involvement with health policy by financing what was essentially a series of preventive measures. Some feminists, including Alice Paul, head of the militant National Women's Party, also criticized Sheppard-Towner for classifying all women as "mothers." Birth control activist Margaret Sanger derided the legislation's emphasis on child bearing and issued dire warnings that state health centers would simply encourage women to have more children. Over time the opposition of lobbyists, especially, had its intended impact. In 1927, Congress renewed the program for two years only. And these experiments in federally funded health care ended altogether in 1929. The fate of Sheppard-Towner did not surprise the reformers who doggedly championed the act. Throughout the 1920s progressive forces often faced an uphill battle. They usually lacked the power to override the presidential vetoes their bills almost always received.

The Democrats' Ordeal

During the 1920s the Democratic party found itself buffeted by tensions between its urban and rural factions. More than the Republicans, Democrats were a diverse coalition of interest groups, linked to the party more by local tradition than common commitment. Among those interest groups were prohibitionists, Klansmen, and fundamentalists on one side and Catholics, urban workers, and immigrants on the other. The alliance was rarely an easy one.

In 1924, the tensions among the party's diverse constituencies proved devastating. At the Democratic National Convention in New York that summer, bitter conflict broke out over the platform when the party's urban wing attempted to win approval of planks calling for the repeal of prohibition and a denunciation of the Ku Klux Klan. Both planks narrowly failed. More damaging to the party was a deadlock in the balloting for a presidential candidate. Urban Democrats supported Alfred E. Smith, the Irish-Catholic Tammanyite who had risen to become a progressive governor of New York. Rural Democrats backed William McAdoo, Woodrow Wilson's Treasury secretary (and son-in-law), later to become a senator from California. McAdoo had skillfully positioned himself to win the support of southern and western delegates suspicious of Tammany Hall and modern urban life. The convention dragged on for 103 ballots, until finally, after both Smith and McAdoo withdrew, the party settled on a compromise: the bland corporate lawyer John W. Davis, who had served as solicitor general and ambassador to Britain under Wilson. He was no match for Calvin Coolidge.

A similar schism plagued the Democrats again in 1928, when Al Smith finally secured his party's nomination for president after a much shorter and less acrimonious battle. Smith was not, however, able to unite his divided party—largely because of widespread anti-Catholic sentiment, especially in the South. He was the first Democrat since the Civil War not to carry the entire South. Outside the South, although Smith did well in the large cities, he carried no states at all except Massachusetts and Rhode Island. Smith's opponent, and the victor in the presidential election, was a man who perhaps more than any other contemporary politician, seemed to personify the modern, prosperous, middle-class society of the New Era: Herbert Hoover, widely viewed as the most progressive figure in the Republican governments of the 1920s.

Herbert Hoover, one of the great enthusiasts of modern business, entered office promising bold new initiatives to solve the nation's remaining economic

ELECTION OF 1928	(56.9% of electorate voting)	ELECTORAL VOTE	POPULAR VOTE (%)
Herbert Hoover (Republican)		444	21,391,381 (58.2)
Alfred E. Smith (Democratic)		87	15,016,443 (40.9)
Norman Thomas (Socialist)		—	267,835 (0.7)
Other parties (Socialist Workers, Prohibition)		—	62,890

AL SMITH.   Al Smith was a long way from his home state of New York when he campaigned for President in Montana in 1928. Despite the sign, Montana went to Hoover, as did most of the rest of the country, except for six states in the South as well as Massachusetts and Rhode Island.

problems. But within months of his inauguration, the nation plunged into the severest and most prolonged economic crisis in its history—a crisis that brought many of the optimistic assumptions of the New Era, among them the celebration of business, and of Hoover himself—crashing down around the new president's head.

CHAPTER TEN

A Modern Culture

~

The image of the 1920s in the American popular imagination is of an era of affluence, political conservatism, and cultural frivolity: the "Roaring Twenties," "the Jazz Age," what Warren G. Harding once called the age of "normalcy." In reality, the decade was a time of significant, even dramatic social and cultural change. During the 1920s, American popular culture seemed to reshape itself to reflect the urban, industrial, consumer-oriented society America was becoming.

At the same time, as in other eras, different Americans experienced the changes of the 1920s in very different ways. Many Americans continued to cling, some with increasing desperation, to the values and habits of their Victorian past. And so the decade saw the rise not just of an exuberant new middle-class culture, but also of a series of bitter and at times effective rebellions against the modern developments that were transforming American life. The intense cultural conflicts that characterized the 1920s were evidence of how many Americans remained outside the reach of the new, affluent consumer culture. They provided evidence, too, that some of those inside it remained unreconciled to the modernizing currents of American society.

A CULTURE FOR THE MIDDLE CLASS

The increasingly urban and consumer-oriented culture of the 1920s, and the growing mass communication network that helped disseminate it, encouraged Americans in all regions of the country to measure their lives and perceive their world in increasingly similar ways. That same culture exposed them to a new set of values that reflected the prosperity and complexity of the modern economy. But the new culture could not erase the continuing, and indeed increasing, diversity of the United States.

Mass Consumer Culture

Among the many changes industrialization produced in the United States was the creation of a mass consumer culture. By the 1920s, America was a society in which many men and women (although not, of course, all) could afford not merely the means of subsistence, but a considerable measure of additional, discretionary goods and services; a society in which people could buy items not just because of need but for pleasure. The signs of consumer spending were everywhere. Middle-class families improved their homes by purchasing new appliances such as electric refrigerators, washing machines, and vacuum cleaners. Men and women alike began to wear wristwatches and smoke cigarettes. Women especially had increased visibility as both purveyors and objects of new cultural trends. They purchased cosmetics and mass-produced fashions while figuring prominently in advertising campaigns designed to market these goods. Above all, Americans bought automobiles. By the end of the decade, there were more than 30 million cars on American roads.

No group was more aware of the emergence of consumerism (or more responsible for creating it) than the advertising industry. The first advertising and public relations firms (N. W. Ayer and J. Walter Thompson) had appeared well before World War I; but in the 1920s, partly as a result of techniques pioneered by wartime propaganda, advertising came of age. Large firms spent hundreds of thousands, and eventually millions of dollars, in yearly advertising campaigns that became a critical feature of corporate marketing and planning. Publicists no longer simply conveyed information; they sought to identify products with a particular lifestyle, to invest them with glamour and prestige, and to persuade potential consumers that purchasing a commodity could be a personally fulfilling and enriching experience. As one automobile manufacturer warned male consumers, in an advertisement that depicted an attractive woman next to the latest car model, "A Man is Known by the Car he Keeps." Companies selling personal care products emphasized their products' ability to ensure an exciting lifestyle and to create opportunities for love and romance. "You too can have the charm of a skin he loves to touch," one soap company promised.

Advertisers also encouraged the public to absorb the values of promotion and salesmanship and to admire those who were effective "boosters" and publicists. One of the most successful books of the 1920s was *The Man Nobody Knows* (1925), by advertising executive Bruce Barton. It portrayed Jesus Christ as not only a religious prophet but also a "super salesman," who "picked up twelve men from the bottom ranks of business and forged them into an organization that conquered the world." The parables, Barton claimed, were "the most powerful advertisements of all time." Barton's message was fully in tune with the new spirit of the consumer culture. Jesus had been a man concerned with living a full and rewarding life in this world; twentieth-century men and women should

"Reach for a Lucky - instead of a sweet"

LUCKY STRIKE "IT'S TOASTED" CIGARETTES

"A flavor that completely satisfies"

Billie Burke
Popular American Actress

"It's toasted"

No Throat Irritation-No Cough.

© 1929, The American Tobacco Co., Manufacturers

WOMEN IN ADVERTISING. In this 1929 advertisement, actress Billie Burke endorses cigarettes for the American Tobacco Company. The ad features Burke more than the cigarette as the lure for consumers in a style that typified the tendency in the 1920s to identify products with lifestyles.

do the same. ("Life is meant to live and enjoy as you go along," Barton once wrote.) Jesus had succeeded because he knew how to make friends, to become popular, to please others; that talent was a prescription for success in the modern era as well.

The advertising industry could never have had the impact it did without the emergence of new vehicles of communication that made it possible to reach large audiences quickly and easily. Newspapers were being absorbed into national chains. Their increasing use of press associations and news syndicates ensured that Americans across the country would read much of the same news. In addition, new or expanded mass-circulation magazines—*Time, Reader's Digest,* the *Saturday Evening Post,* and others—attracted broad, national, audiences.

Print culture began to offer Americans an array of new opportunities to widen their intellectual horizons and sharpen their mental skills. Crossword puzzles became a national intellectual pastime during the period. Simon and Schuster's first book of puzzles appeared in 1924. In less than a year, three quarters of a million puzzle books had been sold and demand continued to soar. The appearance of the Book-of-the-Month Club in 1926 helped pave the way for a "middlebrow culture," one in which "men and women, fairly civilized, fairly literate" avidly consumed the works of popular writers and critics. As more books reached more hands, Americans enjoyed new opportunities to participate in and, through their preferences, shape cultural life.

At the same time, movies were becoming an ever more popular and powerful form of mass communication. Over 100 million people saw films in 1930, as compared to 40 million in 1922. The addition of sound to motion pictures—beginning in 1927 with the first feature-length "talkie," *The Jazz Singer,* with Al Jolson—enhanced their appeal. Moviegoing provided Americans with a shared mass cultural experience available even to those of modest means. So enticing was film that movie stars emerged in the 1920s as objects of intense curiosity and fantasy. Celebrity gossip itself became an industry. The death of the popular romantic actor Rudolph Valentino in 1926 became an occasion of national mourning.

Despite the popularity of motion pictures, many Americans viewed the film industry with some ambivalence during the 1920s. An embarrassing scandal in 1921 involving the popular comedian Fatty Arbuckle produced public outrage and political pressure to "clean up" Hollywood. In response, the film industry introduced "standards" to its films. Studio owners created the Motion Picture Association, a new trade association, and hired former Postmaster General Will Hays to head it. More important, they gave Hays broad powers to review films and to ban anything likely to offend viewers (or politicians). The "Hays Office," as it became known, exercised its powers broadly and imposed on the film industry a safe, sanctimonious conformity for many years. Still, film served as an important purveyor of changing values and modern sexual mores. Movie "moderns" such as Gloria Swanson, Joan Crawford, and Clara Bow—the latter known as the "It" girl—offered a version of American womanhood on the screen that bore little resemblance to the more socially and sexually conservative messages of the pre–World War I era.

Probably the most important communications vehicle was the only one truly new to the 1920s: radio. The first commercial radio station in America, KDKA in Pittsburgh, began broadcasting in 1920; and the first national radio network, the National Broadcasting Company, was formed in 1927. By 1923, there were more than 500 radio stations, covering virtually every area of the country; by 1929, more than 12 million families owned radio sets. The radio industry, too, feared government regulation and control; the national networks, and most radio stations, monitored program content carefully and excluded controversial or provocative material. But radio was much less centralized than filmmaking. Individual stations had considerable autonomy, and even carefully monitored stations and networks could not control the countless hours of programming as effectively as the Hays office could control films. Radio programming, therefore, was more diverse—and at times more controversial and even subversive— than film.

The influence of the consumer culture, and its increasing emphasis on immediate, personal fulfillment, was visible even in religion. Theological modernists— among them Harry Emerson Fosdick and A. C. McGiffert—taught their followers to abandon some of the traditional tenets of evangelical Christianity (literal interpretation of the Bible, belief in the Trinity, attribution of human traits to the deity) and to accept a faith that would help individuals live more fulfilling lives in the present world. Perhaps even more symbolic of the consumer culture were popular preachers, new religious sects, and elaborate churches that appeared during the 1920s and that at times seemed to make of religious practice a form of entertainment. Few attracted more attention than Sister Aimee Semple McPherson, a former carnival barker turned preacher, who dispensed the wisdom of her "Four Square Gospel" from an elaborate temple in Los Angeles and through a legion of evangelists. The Four Square Gospel held, among other things, that heaven had four walls and resembled a blend of Pasadena, California and Washington, DC.

Whatever church they attended, many Americans seemed to be reassessing, however unconsciously, the place of religion in their lives. Sociologists Robert and Helen Messell Lynd made note of this fact in *Middletown* (1929), their classic study of Muncie, Indiana. Many residents of Middletown were simply not as actively engaged with religion as they once had been. "Middletown," the Lynds reported, "thinks less upon the hereafter than it did in 1890, and at the same time actively questions it little."

The New Woman

The 1920s brought important changes to the lives of many American women as modern notions of gender roles challenged decades of traditional beliefs. The image of the "flapper," that young, uninhibited icon of the twenties, captured a part of the realities of women's lives in the third decade of the twentieth century. But the more important changes were less visible and less dramatic. Women continued to confront gender segregation in the labor market, wage differentials, and restricted opportunities for work and advancement in the growing economy. Their lives in the "New Era" reflected these continuing obstacles as much as new opportunities.

The place of women in the growing world of American higher education was a good example of both change and continuity. By the 1920s college-educated women were no longer pioneers. The number of women attending college rose astronomically in the twenties. Graduates of women's colleges or coeducational colleges and universities were making their presence felt in the professions, and a growing number of women struggled to combine marriage and careers. Still, professional opportunities for women remained limited by society's assumptions (assumptions prevalent among many women as well as among most men) about what were suitable female occupations. Although there were notable success stories about female business executives, journalists, doctors, and lawyers, most professional women remained confined to such traditionally "feminine" fields as fashion, education, social work, and nursing, or to the lower levels of business management. The "new professional woman" was a vivid and widely publicized image in the 1920s. In reality, however, most employed women were nonprofessional, lower-class workers. Middle-class married women, in the meantime, remained largely in the home.

Even so, the 1920s constituted a new era for middle-class women in ways that reflected deep changes in American culture and society. In particular, the decade saw a widespread redefinition of the idea of motherhood, marriage, and female sexuality. Shortly after World War I, an influential group of psychologists—the "behaviorists," led by John B. Watson—began to challenge the long-held assumption that women had an instinctive capacity for motherhood. Instead, as the science of child development matured, the roles and responsibilities of mothers became a topic of analysis and discussion among social scientists. Maternal affection was not, many behaviorists claimed, sufficient preparation for child rearing. Instead, mothers should rely on the advice and assistance of experts and professionals in child rearing: doctors, nurses, and trained educators in nursery schools and kindergartens.

It is difficult to measure the impact of these new ideas on women's notions of mothering and, more importantly, on their actual practices of child rearing. Motherhood surely remained a central part of most women's life experience. Some fretted about the dangers of "smothering"—showering too much love on their infants and children—and heeded warnings issued by some doctors in the 1920s. Others increasingly balanced their identity as mothers with a new sense of themselves as wives and companions. Advice books promoted a new view of marriage that stressed the importance of combining emotional and physical intimacy. The emerging ideal of the "companionate marriage" rejected views of matrimony that were exclusively child centered or that denied the importance of women's sexuality. It offered support for women who thought of their sexual relationships with their husbands not simply as a means of procreation, as earlier generations had been taught to do, but as an important and pleasurable experience in its own right, as the culmination of romantic love. But, it also placed heavy responsibility for keeping romance in marriage alive on women alone; the new ideal required them to maintain their youth, vivacity, and sex appeal to keep their marriage healthy. The notion of the "companionate marriage" stressed friendship and partnership between husbands and wives, but it also encouraged women to look to marriage for an answer to most if not all of their emotional needs. It warned, as well, that men would stray if a woman did not do all she could to anticipate and meet her husband's needs. For women, marriage was supposed to be the most important part of their lives. For men, even the companionate marriage was only one significant aspect of a life enriched by other interests and activities.

Progress in the development of birth control played an important role in redefining notions of matrimony and sexuality. Attempts to control reproduction and fertility were not, of course, new to the 1920s. Private and often furtive efforts to prevent or end pregnancy dated back to ancient history. During the 1920s, however, a militant, public birth-control movement emerged. Its pioneer was Margaret Sanger, a settlement worker and public health nurse. Sanger was the sixth of eleven children born to an Irish-Catholic working-class family. Her mother, who died at forty-eight years of age, experienced eighteen pregnancies. Attracted to radical causes as a young married woman, Sanger became committed to the cause of reproductive rights in part because of the influence of Emma Goldman—a Russian immigrant and political radical who had agitated for birth control, among many other things, before World War I. Sanger began her career promoting the diaphragm and other birth-control devices in part out of a concern for working-class women, believing that large families were among the major causes of poverty and distress in poor communities. As early as 1914, she endorsed the general right of women to birth control, declaring then that "a woman's body belongs to herself alone. It does not belong to the United States of America or any government on the face of the earth."

By the 1920s, interest in birth-control had become more widespread among middle-class and upper-class women than among working-class people. And Sanger herself had become more involved with middle-class concerns. Increasingly she campaigned for "doctors-only" bills—laws that would remove government restrictions and permit physicians to offer birth-control counseling and methods to women. To make that case, Sanger embraced the arguments of eugenicists, promoters of the spurious belief that human inequalities were hereditary and that traits were specific to racial and ethnic groups. Birth control, she argued, could help prevent the "overfertility" of mentally and physically defective individuals and groups. But she also argued that birth control could improve the quality of women's lives.

Birth-control devices began to find a large market among middle-class women during the 1920s, even though contraception in many states remained

MARGARET SANGER.   Margaret Sanger leaves the Brooklyn Court of
Special Sessions after being arraigned in October 1916. With her
sister, Evelyn Byrne, Sanger had opened a birth control clinic in
Brooklyn to defy prevailing laws that made such clinics illegal.

highly restricted by law and abortion remained illegal nearly everywhere. Surveys suggested that there was widespread support among middle-class women
for contraception within the boundaries of marriage. Attitudes seemed to be
changing so rapidly that one observer predicted in 1928 that "the myth of the
pure woman is almost at an end." That sentiment troubled many leading feminists, however, some of whom had long viewed the birth-control movement with
suspicion. Certain women activists believed that birth control diminished the

importance of one of woman's most important spheres of influence, power, and authority—motherhood. Others believed wider availability of contraception primarily enhanced the privileges of men. The great suffragist Carrie Chapman Catt considered Sanger's campaign "too sordid" to merit the support of feminists; Jane Addams decried the movement's "astounding emphasis upon sex." Nonetheless, the influence of the birth-control movement spread as many American women and men welcomed the arrival of more uninhibited views of and opportunities for sex.

Shifting notions of sexual morality and the new, more secular view of womanhood had effects on women beyond the middle class. Some women concluded that in the "New Era" it was no longer necessary to maintain a rigid, Victorian female "respectability." They could smoke, drink, dance, wear seductive clothes and makeup, and attend lively parties. They could strive for physical and emotional fulfillment, for release from repression and inhibition. (The wide popularity of Freudian ideas in the 1920s—often simplified and distorted for mass consumption—contributed to the growth of these impulses.) Such assumptions became the basis of the "flapper," the modern woman whose liberated lifestyle found expression in dress, hairstyle, speech, and behavior. The "flapper" lifestyle had a particular impact on lower-middle-class and working-class single women, who were flocking to new jobs in industry and the service sector. (The young, affluent, "Bohemian" women most often associated with the "flapper" image in popular culture were, in fact, imitating a style that emerged among this larger group.) At night, such women gravitated to clubs and dance halls in search of excitement and companionship.

Despite all the changes, women remained highly dependent on men—both in the workplace, where they were usually poorly paid, and in the home. Convinced that the "new woman" was as much myth as reality, and that woman suffrage had failed to erode the existence of inequality, some American feminists during the 1920s launched efforts to remove other barriers to women's equality. In 1923 the National Woman's Party, under the leadership of Alice Paul, began to spearhead a drive to enact an amendment to the U.S. Constitution mandating that "men and women have equal rights throughout the United States and every place subject to its jurisdiction."

The Equal Rights Amendment (ERA) quickly divided the women's movement. Feminists who had devoted their efforts to improving the status of working women saw the ERA as a threat to hard-won protective labor legislation. Although the Woman's party pressed on with its campaign throughout the 1920s, it found little support in Congress (and met continued resistance from other feminist groups). Still, despite such internal divisions, women's organizations and female political activities grew in many ways in the 1920s. Responding to the suffrage victory, women organized the League of Women Voters and the women's auxiliaries of both the Democratic and Republican parties. Female-dominated consumer groups grew rapidly and increased the range and energy of their efforts.

Education and Youth

The growing secularism of American culture in the 1920s—its liberalized social values, its expanding emphasis on training and expertise—had an especially profound impact on young people. "No one understands the problem of the younger generation, then, because there is no one problem to understand," one young pundit noted in 1927. "We are not one single problem. We are a multitude of problems all different." The rise of a distinctive "youth culture" was one of the striking developments of the 1920s.

One important factor in creating the emergence of the new youth culture was the wider availability of education. During the 1920s, more people were going to school than ever before, and many were staying in school longer. High school attendance more than doubled during the decade: from 2.2 million to over 5 million students. Enrollment in colleges and universities increased three-fold between 1900 and 1930, with much of that increase occurring after World War I. In 1918, there had been 600,000 college students; in 1930, there were 1.2 million, nearly twenty percent of the college-age population. Attendance was increasing as well at trade and vocational schools and in other institutions providing the specialized training that the modern economy demanded. Schools were also beginning to perform new and more varied functions. Instead of offering instruction only in the traditional disciplines, they were providing training in modern technical skills: engineering, management, economics.

The growing importance of education contributed to a lengthening of adolescence. The very idea of adolescence as a distinct period in the life of an individual was for the most part new to the twentieth century. It resulted in large part from society's recognition that a more extended period of training and preparation was necessary and desirable before a young person was ready to move into the workplace. Schools and colleges provided adolescents with a setting in which they could develop their own social patterns, their own hobbies, their own interests and activities. An increasing number of students saw school as a place not just for academic training but for organized athletics, extracurricular activities, clubs, fraternities, and sororities—that is, as an institution that allowed them to define themselves less in terms of their families and more in terms of their peer group. Freudian psychology helped legitimize the importance of adolescence to emotional development in the eyes of many educated middle-class people.

The Decline of the "Self-Made Man"

The increasing importance of education and the changing nature of adolescence underscored one of the most important changes in twentieth-century American society: the gradual disappearance of the reality, and to some degree even the ideal, of the "self-made man." The belief that any person could achieve wealth and renown simply through hard work and innate talent had always been largely a myth; but it had had enough basis in reality to remain convincing for generations.

Beginning in the late nineteenth century and accelerating in the early twentieth, it became more difficult to believe that real success was possible through innate talent and pluck alone. Many now believed education and training were essential to advancement in the new industrial society. "The self-made manager in business," wrote *Century Magazine* in 1925, "is nearing the end of his road. He cannot escape the relentless pursuit of the same forces that have eliminated self-made lawyers and doctors and admirals."

That sense of losing control, of becoming ever more dependent on rules and norms established by large, impersonal bureaucracies, had particular significance for American men. Independence and control were integral to prevailing notions of "masculinity"; when they seemed less accessible, many looked for other ways of retaining and expressing a sense of individual achievement and autonomy. Theodore Roosevelt, for example, glorified warfare and the "strenuous life" as a route to "manhood." Other men turned to fraternal societies, to athletics, and to other settings that fostered camaraderie and their collective sense of self.

Still, the "Doom of the Self-Made Man," as *Century* described it, was a phenomenon that many people noted, feared, and regretted. Such mixed feelings were expressed in the emergence of three men as perhaps the most widely admired heroes of the New Era: Thomas Edison, the inventor of the electric light bulb and many other technological marvels; Henry Ford, the creator of the assembly line and one of the founders of the automobile industry; and Charles Lindbergh, the first aviator to make a solo flight across the Atlantic Ocean. All three men received the adulation of much of the American public. Lindbergh, in particular, became a national hero the like of which the country had never seen before. Long after Lindbergh came back to the United States from his landing in Paris, newspapers, magazines, newsreels, and radio broadcasts celebrated his accomplishments and recounted countless details about his life. Lindbergh himself claimed the wild reception he received in Paris was "the most dangerous part of the trip."

The heroes of the 1920s achieved renown for reasons that revealed a great deal about how Americans viewed the new epoch in which they were living. In reality, the accomplishments of men such as Edison, Ford, and Lindbergh represented the triumph of industry and technology. But most Americans admired them more for other reasons. All three men had achieved their astounding success without the benefit of formal education and at least in part through their own determination, imagination, and effort. They were, their admirers liked to believe, genuinely self-made men. For many Americans, these heroes served as reminders of a simpler and better past. As one writer for *American Magazine* put it, "Ever since the War there has been an outcry against 'modern' character, ideals, and morals. . . . You hear it in every stratum of society. The high-brows talk of the 'moral degeneration of the age.' The low-brows say: 'Ain't it perfectly awful!'. . . And this is the big thing Lindbergh has done: He has shown us that this talk was nothing *but* talk! He has shown us that we are *not* rotten at the core, but morally sound and sweet and

CHARLES LINDBERGH. Few Americans have been more lionized than Charles Lindbergh was in the 1920s. Here crowds look on as "Lucky Lindy" is photographed in front of his plane, the "Spirit of St. Louis."

good!" For moments, at least, the heroes of the 1920s made those who admired their accomplishments feel pride in themselves, as well.

VOICES OF A NEW GENERATION

The 1920s were also notable for a remarkable new generation of writers, artists, and critics. These men and women produced poems, essays, novels, and works of art of unusual distinction, many of which still survive at the center of American culture. In American literature, especially, the twenties brought an enormous outpouring of poetry and prose of exceptional brilliance, feeling, and clarity. The literature of the era reflected much of the diversity of the nation itself. It also reflected both the promise and the anguish of the modern age.

The Lost Generation

The generation of young artists and intellectuals who came of age in the aftermath of World War I brought a bittersweet perspective to American life and letters that led to Gertrude Stein's memorable characterization of them: "All of you young people who served in the war. You are a lost generation." Writers such as John Dos Passos and Ernest Hemingway were indeed deeply affected by their war experience and the seemingly senseless bloodletting they observed. Their sentiments were shared by many who had no direct exposure to the war and the horrors of battle. Haunted by the war, disappointed in its outcome, embittered by the failed peace, tormented by deep loneliness and alienation, many writers came to feel a profound disenchantment with modern America. That disenchantment was sharpened by what many perceived as the all-too-quick return to "business as usual" after the war—to the crassness and materialism of the New Era. For some of the most talented writers, disappointment and disillusion quickly gave way to a harsh cynicism and a contempt for American society. John Dos Passos, for example, used an occasion of public reverence and remembrance—the selection of an unknown soldier to be entombed in Washington—to express his view of the absurdity and anonymity of death in war and the futility of efforts to extract meaning from it. "In the tarpaper morgue at Chalons-sur-Marne in the reek of chloride of lime and the dead," he wrote in his novel *1919*, "they picked out the pine box that held all that was left of enie menie minie moe plenty other pine boxes stacked up there containing what they'd scraped up of Richard Roe and other person or persons unknown. Only one can go. How did they pick John Doe?" F. Scott Fitzgerald spoke for many of his contemporaries when he described "a new generation dedicated more than the last to the fear of poverty and the worship of success; grown up to find all Gods dead, all wars fought, all faiths in man shaken."

Moved in part by this deep sense of alienation, important writers and critics of the 1920s frequently adopted a role sharply different from that of many intellectuals in earlier eras. Rather than trying to influence and reform their society, they isolated themselves from it and embarked on a restless search for personal fulfillment and immediate gratification. One talented group of writers left the United States and settled in Paris, where they wrote provocative and often bitter tales of American society—what they considered its crassness, decadence, and emptiness. Ironically, their own lives often mirrored the desperation they loathed in American society. In a 1922 essay, Hemingway, a central figure in the expatriate community, contemptuously described the exodus of which he was a part: "The scum of Greenwich Village, New York, has been skimmed off and deposited in large ladlesful on that section of Paris adjacent to the Cafe Rotonde. New scum, of course, has risen to take the place of the old, but the oldest scum, the thickest scum and the scummiest scum has come across the ocean."

At the heart of the Lost Generation's critique of modern society was the belief that contemporary America no longer provided individuals with avenues by which they could achieve personal fulfillment. That sentiment found expression in, among other things, a series of savage critiques of modern society by a wide range of writers, some of whom became known as "debunkers." Among the wittiest and most sharp tongued was the Baltimore journalist H. L. Mencken. His

THE JAZZ AGE.   This cover of *McClure's Magazine* captures the libertine culture of the 1920s by depicting a flapper with her skirt above her knees dancing to the music provided by rollicking jazz musicians.

magazines—first the *Smart Set* and later the *American Mercury*—delighted in ridiculing everything most middle-class Americans valued, including religion, politics, the arts, and even democracy. Mencken could not believe, he claimed, that "civilized life was possible under a democracy," because it was a form of government that placed power in the hands of the common people, whom he ridiculed as the "booboisie." When someone asked Mencken why he continued to live in a society he found so loathsome, he replied: "Why do people go to the zoo?" Echoing Mencken's contempt was the novelist Sinclair Lewis, the first American to win a Nobel Prize in literature. In a series of savage novels—*Main Street* (1920), *Babbitt* (1922), *Arrowsmith* (1925), and *Elmer Gantry* (1927) among others—he lashed out at one aspect of modern society after another: the small town, the modern city, the medical profession, and popular religion.

Some artists and intellectuals, responding to the same feelings of disillusionment that prompted the European exodus, sought consolation in the isolated and supposedly natural communities of the American West. The colonies of artists and writers who settled in Taos and Santa Fe, New Mexico, like those in Paris and New York's Greenwich Village, frequently pursued hedonistic lifestyles replete with drinking, drugs, and casual sex. For most of these young men and women, however, the only real refuge from the travails of modern society was art. Sojourns in the Southwest inspired important works of art and literature, including two of Willa Cather's most celebrated novels, *The Professor's House* (1925) and *Death Comes to the Archbishop* (1927). By the decade's end, painter Georgia O'Keefe had discovered on a visit to Taos the place that would infuse her artistic imagination and make her one of the best known American women artists in the twentieth century.

As O'Keefe's complicated and often unhappy life clearly illustrated, the quest for fulfillment through art did not always result in personal satisfaction for modern writers and artists. But it did produce a body of work that added much luster to American culture. Among the important American writers who did significant work in the 1920s were men and women who have few equals in the annals of American letters: Hemingway, Fitzgerald, Lewis, Thomas Wolfe, Dos Passos, Ezra Pound, T. S. Eliot, Stein, Edna Ferber, Cather, William Faulkner, Eugene O'Neill.

Many intellectuals of the 1920s claimed to reject the "success ethic" that they believed dominated American life (even though many of them hoped for—and a few achieved—commercial and critical success). F. Scott Fitzgerald, for example, ridiculed the American obsession with material success in his brilliant novel *The Great Gatsby* (1925). The novel's title character, Jay Gatsby, spends his life accumulating wealth and social prestige in order to win the woman he loves. The world to which he has aspired, however, turns out to be one of pretension, fraud, and cruelty that ultimately destroys him.

Not all intellectuals of the 1920s expressed alienation and despair. Some who held deep reservations about their society responded not by withdrawing from it, but by advocating engagement and reform. John Dewey, for example, kept alive the philosophical tradition of pragmatism and appealed for "practical" education and experimentation in social policy. Charles and Mary Beard, perhaps the most influential historians of their day, stressed economic factors in tracing the development of modern society and, like other progressive reformers, emphasized the clash of economic interests as central to American history.

The Harlem Renaissance

To another group of intellectuals, the solution to contemporary problems lay neither in escapism nor in progressivism, but in an exploration of their own cultural or regional origins. During the 1920s a new generation of black intellectuals ushered in an extraordinary era in African-American culture widely described as the "Harlem Renaissance." The center of the movement could be found in the, by then, largely black community of Harlem in New York City. There, and soon elsewhere, poets, novelists, artists, and musicians drew heavily from their African roots to create work that demonstrated both to members of their own race and to the larger world the richness of the African-American voice, experience, and heritage. The poet Langston Hughes captured much of the spirit of the movement in a single sentence: "I am a Negro—and beautiful." For Hughes and many other black writers, including James Weldon Johnson, Countee Cullen, Zora Neale Hurston, Claude McKay, and Alain Locke, such self-affirmation was only one element of a compelling and alluring literary journey into the African-American experience. "The New Negro," as Alain Locke called the restless, determined, independent, and thoughtful black men and women of his day, had embarked upon a "spiritual Coming of Age."

One of the most notable features of the Harlem Renaissance was its urban character. The explosion of literary and artistic work among African Americans owed something to the large migration north that had begun not long before the First World War. Harlem especially became a center not only of a large black population but of a vibrant cultural life. Proximity to New York's publishing world proved important to the dissemination of African-American literature. As a center not only of African-American migration but of immigration from the West Indies and Africa, New York also provided an opportunity for cross-cultural exchange and a growing attention to the ties that bound black men and women around the world. From that awareness a burgeoning Pan African Movement had already emerged well before 1920.

The work the writers and artists of the Harlem Renaissance produced, like all important literature, reflected a panoply of emotions—pain, rage, joy, and hope—and a range of experiences. But unlike most other American literature, it made the black experience the heart of the tale. The city loomed large in many poems, novels and essays. "Ah stern harsh world," Claude McKay lamented in his poem "Harlem Shadows,"

that in the wretched way
Of poverty, dishonor and disgrace,
Has pushed the timid little feet of clay
The sacred brown feet of my fallen race!
Ah, heart of me, the weary, weary feet
In Harlem wandering from street to street

Zora Neale Hurston explored the richness of African-American folk tradition. She found traces of those traditions "acted out daily in a dozen streets in a

ZORA NEALE HURSTON.   Born in the black community of Eatonville, Florida, Hurston came to New York in 1925, where she soon earned recognition for her talents as a writer. Hurston studied anthropology with Franz Boas and was an avid student of folklore, which she researched in the South and the Caribbean. She wrote an autobiography and several novels that won her much critical acclaim in the 1920s and 1930s. Her work experienced a revival when she was rediscovered in the 1970s by such later novelists and critics as Alice Walker.

thousand cities and no one ever mistakes the meaning." Searing memories of the South infused the work of many writers, including that of the poet Helene Johnson, who left her readers with the haunting image of a lynching in "A Southern Road:"

A blue-fruited black gum,
Like a tall predella,
Bears a dangling figure,
Sacrificial dower to the raff,
Swinging alone,
A solemn, tortured shadow in the air.

Many African-American readers found in the varied works of the Harlem Renaissance the shock of recognition of experiences deeply felt and long held privately. Many others drew inspiration, hope, and dignity from the message of the gifted new writers and poets. They also found political inspiration. Running through the work of many African-American artists was a call for struggle, a denunciation of racial and social injustice, and a series of visions of a new society capable of erasing the stigma of racism and oppression. "If we must die, O let us nobly die," Claude McKay wrote with passion in one of his most famous poems.

So that our precious blood may not be shed
In vain; then even the monsters we defy
Shall be constrained to honor us though dead!

The Southern Agrarians

The search for meaning and self-affirmation in the 1920s also inspired the literary efforts of an influential group of white southern intellectuals. Known first as the "Fugitives" and later as the "Agrarians," these young poets, novelists, and critics sought to counter the depersonalization of industrial society by evoking the strong rural traditions of their own region and defining a distinct southern way of life. In doing so, they took aim at the cruel depiction of the South by northern critics and intellectuals as a primitive backwater. In their controversial manifesto *I'll Take My Stand: The South and the Agrarian Tradition* (1930), a collection of essays by twelve southern intellectuals, the Agrarians issued a simultaneously radical and conservative appeal for a rejection of the doctrine of "economic progress," and of the spiritual debilitation that had accompanied it. The supposedly "backward" South, they argued, could serve as a model for a nation drunk with visions of limitless growth and modernization.

In less confrontational but deeply affecting ways, southern writers offered in their essays and novels a portrait of the South that challenged the one-dimensional images painted by the region's critics. Ellen Glasgow, James Cabell, and, in 1929, Thomas Wolfe and William Faulkner helped to define a new era in southern literature. In *Look Homeward, Angel* (1929), Wolfe described the South that haunted his memory, a place in which he felt both deeply rooted and adrift. Faulkner's third novel, *Sartoris* (1929) introduced his readers to a fictional Mississippi County, Yoknapatawpha, that would dominate much of his later literature. A place of some 2,400 square miles, Faulkner's imagined county contained within its boundaries all the turmoil, passion, and tension that characterized the South as it struggled to reconcile modern culture and capitalism with agrarianism and the region's own tortured past.

The Lost Generation, the artists of the Harlem Renaissance, the Agrarians, and others who proposed alternatives to the commercial, consumer culture of their time gave evidence of how the celebration of the "New Era" often obscured deep patterns of disenchantment and alienation even among some of those best positioned to profit from its successes. The artistic rebellion, however, was only a small part of a much larger battle over the new culture.

CHAPTER ELEVEN

Battles for Tradition and Order

~

hallenges to the modern, secular culture of the 1920s spread far beyond disillusioned members of the middle class and beyond the protesting racial and regional minorities who offered alternatives to the vision of the "New Era." Modern culture had, after all, grown up alongside older, more traditional cultures, with which it continually and often bitterly competed. The older cultures often expressed the outlook of less affluent, less urban, more provincial Americans—men and women who continued to revere traditional values and customs, and who feared and resented the modernist threats to their ways of life. Over time, their convictions and fears would produce harsh cultural controversies and bruising political battles in which neither side secured a lasting victory.

CONTROLLING BEHAVIOR IN MODERN SOCIETY

Some of the fiercest battles of the 1920s centered on efforts to control the behavior of American citizens. While many people celebrated the new, sometimes libertine culture of the 1920s, others saw in the apparent excesses and decadence of the period an unraveling of American values and traditions. To them, modern trends threatened the very definition of a good society.

Prohibition

One of the most heated of the cultural battles in the 1920s focused on the use and abuse of alcohol. When the prohibition of the sale and manufacture of alcohol went into effect in January 1920, it had the support of most members of the middle class and most of those who considered themselves progressives. Within a year, however, it had become clear that the "noble experiment," as its defenders called it, was not working well. Advocates of prohibition—or "drys" as they became known—claimed correctly that the law was succeeding in reducing drinking substantially, at least in some regions of the country. But prohibition also produced conspicuous and growing violations that made it a source of considerable disillusionment and controversy, if not outright mockery and disdain, especially among "wets," who opposed the law.

Much of the trouble stemmed from the difficulty in managing federal enforcement. Prohibition was one of the most ambitious efforts to regulate social behavior ever undertaken in the United States. It soon became clear the nation was ill prepared to handle what it had set out to do. The federal government had only 1,500 agents to enforce the prohibition laws, and in many places they received little help from local police. Indeed, a bust of corrupt enforcement officials in one Indiana city resulted in the arrest of the mayor, the sheriff, a judge, a city prosecutor, and several policemen. Attempts to root out the unlawful manufacture and sale of alcoholic beverages also ran up against constitutional constraints regarding illegal search and seizure. Indeed, critics began to question

PROHIBITION BUST. Prohibition agents examine a still they seized after finding it in a cellar. The illegal sale and manufacture of alcohol remained a lively business in the 1920s despite efforts to curtail it.

whether the goal of prohibition was worth the danger to individual liberty its enforcement seemed to create.

Even more disturbing was the proliferation of crime that seemed to accompany the "noble experiment." Before long, it was almost as easy to acquire illegal alcohol in much of the country as it had once been to acquire legal alcohol. An enormous, lucrative industry had been barred to legitimate businessmen. Into the breach came organized crime—eager to amass profits, willing to flout the law, and briskly responsive to continuing consumer demand. Prohibition provided an important means of power and a bountiful source of riches to gangsters in major cities across the United States. In Chicago, Al Capone built a criminal empire based largely on illegal alcohol. He guarded it against interlopers with an army of as many as 1,000 gunmen, whose zealousness contributed to the violent deaths of more than 250 people in the city between 1920 and 1927. Gangsters and gang wars gave evidence of the growth of an "underworld," built to no small degree on the profits of illegal alcohol.

Usually law-abiding citizens found numerous ways to avoid the law. Some frequented "speakeasies"—places where liquor was illegally sold. Others turned their basements into distilleries where homemade beer and wine could be made for personal use. One 1925 study estimated that nearly 15 million gallons of wine were being made in Chicago homes every year. Those legally permitted to dispense alcohol—religious leaders, druggists, and doctors to name a few—found a growing constituency for their services. As the demand for "sacramental wine" soared, an official report acidly noted that "not more than one quarter of this wine is sacramental—the rest is sacrilegious." Evasion of the law seemed to many less a matter of concern than of comedy. Will Rogers captured the contradictions embedded in American attitudes toward prohibition when he observed: "If you think this country ain't dry, you just watch 'em vote; and if you think this country ain't wet, you just watch 'em drink."

Eventually, the contradiction between public support and private evasion became too difficult to sustain. Many middle-class progressives who had originally supported prohibition now soured on the experiment. They were joined by many immigrants who had long opposed the measure and a variety of businessmen, including hotel owners and real estate interests. But an enormous constituency of provincial, largely rural, Protestant Americans continued vehemently to defend prohibition. To them, the crusade had always carried implications far beyond the issue of drinking itself. The effort to prohibit alcohol—which many rural men and women associated with what they believed was the loose, fast, immoral new world of the city, and its Catholic, immigrant working class—reflected the determination of an older America to maintain its dominance in a society in which many felt outnumbered and increasingly marginalized.

Ultimately, however, those who sought to use prohibition as a form of protest against modern America were destined to face disappointment. As the 1920s progressed, opponents of prohibition gained steadily in influence. In 1926, voters in Montana, Nevada, Wisconsin, Illinois, and New York endorsed repeal or modification of prohibition. Numerous interest groups and voluntary associations were lobbying aggressively against the law as well. Although the "drys" hung on, they could not ultimately weather the onslaught against prohibition, particularly after the Great Depression began. Proponents liked to argue that prohibition contributed to the health of the American economy by encouraging consumers to buy manufactured goods instead of liquor. Those arguments rang hollow as the pillars of economic prosperity began to crumble in 1929 and 1930. More importantly, public opinion had by then shifted dramatically. Most Americans no longer supported the measure, and even the weight of a constitutional amendment could not prevent their growing hostility. In December 1933, the Twenty-first Amendment, which repealed the Nineteenth, brought an end to the experiment.

Although the federal government would no longer control and supervise the sale of alcohol, state and local regulations persisted, and in some cases even proliferated, after prohibition's repeal. Some states permitted only beer; others enacted various restrictions on how, when, and to whom alcohol could be sold. Native Americans, women, and welfare recipients were among the groups targeted by some restrictive laws. Most states forbade the sale of alcohol on Sunday. The passage of such regulatory measures indicated that efforts to control alcohol consumption and sales were far from dead. They also reflected the public's apparent preference for local control over more sweeping federal efforts.

Crime

However much some Americans were amused by the national flouting of prohibition, many remained deeply concerned about the larger issue of crime in the 1920s. The United States had an unenviable record on crime when compared with other industrialized Western societies. The 1929 murder rate in over thirty major American cities was almost twenty times that of England. But the growing concern about crime was less a response to a burgeoning wave of lawlessness than to a change in the character of criminal activity and to its increasing visibility in the nation's cities. Whatever the realities, many believed crime was spiralling and that society was doing too little to stop it.

How a society tries to control criminal behavior reflects the ways it understands the causes of crime. In the 1920s, many Americans clung to hereditarian theories of crime and frequently ascribed deviant behavior to the inherent inferiority of immigrants, African Americans, and an array of "degraded" social misfits. But environmental explanations of crime were steadily gaining cred-

AL CAPONE. There were many gangsters who accumulated
fortunes through a range of illegal activities including
bootlegging, prostitution, and gambling. But Al Capone
was one of the most notorious. The crime organization
he led in the 1920s piled up some $70 million in income
per year, according to federal law enforcement officials.
Capone, often known as "Scarface," lived grandly, indulging
his taste for cigars, Italian opera, tailored suits,
fine restaurants, and driving a bulletproof Cadillac.
He largely succeeded in evading the law until
convicted of federal tax evasion in 1931.

ibility as social scientists stressed the importance of unemployment, lack of
education, and restricted opportunities for social mobility as causes of criminal
behavior. During the 1920s, a new set of evils were identified as major contributors to crime: the flouting of prohibition, the automobile, drugs, lax moral
and sexual discipline, disrespect for parents, and other features of modern
culture.

Crime was a big business in the 1920s. Gambling, bootlegging, and prostitution produced billions of dollars in profits. Newspapers and magazines
lavished attention on crime stories, murder trials, and "racketeering"—the latter

word coined to describe Chicago gangsters, who made a "racket" when they gathered in the city's streets. Despite such attention, the legal system seemed to make little headway in convicting or punishing the perpetrators. Many felonies never resulted in either trial or conviction; during the 1920s prosecutors increasingly turned to plea bargaining as a means of extracting at least some form of retribution and imposing some discipline. Efforts to modernize police departments grew during the 1920s. But increasing hostility to prohibition also led to growing public scrutiny and even suspicion of law enforcement officials and national attention to charges of police brutality. Although many Americans remained concerned about the proliferation of criminal behavior within their society, few novel solutions to the problem emerged.

Nativism

Efforts to blame immigrants for the spread of criminality was evidence of how tenaciously nativism gripped many Americans. Hostility to the foreign born spawned new and successful efforts in the 1920s to stop the flow of immigration as well as brutal attempts to control those who had already arrived.

Like prohibition (which was itself in part a result of old-stock Americans trying to discipline the new immigrant population), agitation for a curb on foreign immigration to the United States had begun in the nineteenth century; and like prohibition, it had gathered strength in the years before the war largely because of the support of middle-class progressives. Such concerns had not been sufficient in the first years of the century to win passage of wide-scale curbs on immigration; but in the troubled and repressive years immediately following the war, many old-stock Americans began to associate immigration with radicalism and social disorder. As a result of such beliefs, sentiment on behalf of restriction grew rapidly.

Two bills cut an especially wide swath into the opportunities for foreign migration to the United States. In 1921, Congress passed an emergency immigration act, establishing a quota system by which annual immigration from any country could not exceed three percent of the number of persons of that nationality who had been in the United States in 1910. The quotas for southern and eastern Europeans especially were soon exhausted and illegal immigration soared. Although the new law cut legal immigration from 800,000 to 300,000 in any single year, nativists remained unsatisfied and pushed for an even harsher measure. Congress renewed the quota act in 1923, and then again in 1924 when a new restriction law took its place. The National Origins Act of 1924 cut annual immigration to 170,000 per year and mandated that the number fall even lower by 1927. (After 1927, immigration officials seldom allowed even half the number permitted by law actually to enter the country.) Now the 1890 census, rather than the 1910, would be used as a basis for determining the quota assigned to each nationality. That undercut further the migration of southern and eastern

Europeans, since fewer people from these regions had been in America in the early 1890s.

The 1924 Act also banned immigration from East Asia almost entirely. It limited arrivals to those eligible to be citizens; earlier laws had already barred all Chinese and Japanese from citizenship. The termination of Asian immigration deeply angered Japan, which understood that the Japanese were the principal target; Chinese immigration had been illegal since 1892.

What immigration there was, in other words, would heavily favor northwestern Europeans—people of "Nordic" or "Teutonic" stock. As one skeptical journal noted of the effect of the quota system, "It seems like going back to Plymouth Rock and Jamestown for a basis of restricting immigration to this great country, much of whose greatness has been wrought by immigrants since 1885."

The Rebirth of the Klan

The nativism of the 1920s extended well beyond efforts to restrict entrance into the United States. It also fostered harsh attacks and persistent harassment of groups who already lived in the country. For some defenders of an older, more homogeneous America, the growth of large communities of racially and ethnically diverse peoples, alien in speech, habits, culture, and values, came to seem a direct threat to their own way of life. Among other things, this provincial nativism helped instigate the rebirth of the Ku Klux Klan as a significant force in American society.

The first Klan, founded during Reconstruction and committed to defending white supremacy in the face of Emancipation, had died in the late 1870s. But in 1915, another group of white southerners met on Stone Mountain near Atlanta and established a new Klan. Nativist passions had swelled in Georgia and elsewhere in response to the case of Leo Frank, a Jewish factory manager in Atlanta convicted in 1914 (on very flimsy evidence) of murdering a female employee; a mob had stormed Frank's jail and lynched him. The 1915 premiere (also in Atlanta) of D. W. Griffith's film *The Birth of a Nation*, which glorified the early Klan, also helped inspire white southerners to form a new one.

At first the new Klan, like the old, was largely concerned with intimidating blacks, who according to Klan leader William J. Simmons were becoming insubordinate. And at first it remained small, obscure, and almost entirely southern. After World War I, however, concern about blacks rapidly became secondary to concern about Catholics, Jews, and foreigners. The melting pot, the Klan proclaimed, had been "a ghastly failure"—the phrase itself "coined by a member of one of the races—the Jews—which most determinedly refuses to melt." The Klan, its organizers promised, would devote itself to purging American life of impure, alien influences.

At that point, membership in the Klan expanded rapidly and dramatically, not just in the small towns and rural areas of the South, but in industrial cities in

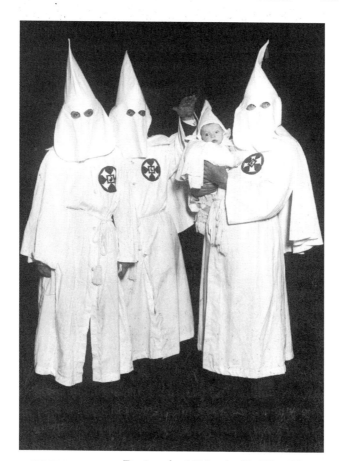

KU KLUX KLAN.   During the 1920s, the Ku Klux Klan
expanded dramatically. The Klan's elaborate rituals, secret
nighttime meetings, and hooded garb incorporated
elements of traditional fraternal organizations, even though
its reliance upon terror and violence to advance its aims
frightened many Americans. In some places, the Klan
formed women's and children's auxiliaries. Here a baby,
dressed in the Klan's robes, appears to be "baptized" into
the organization. A woman, most likely the child's mother,
stands on the far left, hidden under her robes.

the North and Midwest. Indiana had the largest membership of any state, and
there were substantial Klans in Chicago, Detroit, and other northern industrial
cities as well. The Klan was also strong in the West, with particularly large and
active chapters in Oregon and Colorado. By 1923, there were reportedly 3 million members; by 1924, 4 million. What had once seemed a distinctly southern
phenomenon had become a national force.

Despite its growing reach, the Klan differed markedly from place to place, if not in its sentiments then at least in its membership, organization, and strategy. In some communities, where Klan leaders came from the most "respectable" segments of society, the organization operated much like a fraternal society, engaging in nothing more dangerous than occasional political pronouncements. Many Klan units (or "klaverns") tried to present themselves as patriotic defenders of morality. Many established women's and even children's auxiliaries to demonstrate their commitment to the family. In other places, however, the Klan also operated as a brutal, even violent, terrorist organization, an opponent of "alien" groups, and a defender of traditional, fundamentalist morality. Some Klansmen systematically terrorized blacks, Jews, Catholics, and foreigners: boycotting their businesses, threatening their families, and attempting to drive them out of their communities. At times they also resorted to violence: public whipping, tarring and feathering, arson, and lynching.

What the Klan feared, it soon became clear, was not simply "foreign" or "racially impure" groups; it was anyone who posed a challenge to "traditional values," as the Klan defined them. Klansmen persecuted not only immigrants and blacks but those white Protestants they considered guilty of irreligion, sexual promiscuity, or drunkenness. The Klan worked to enforce prohibition; it attempted to institute compulsory Bible reading in schools; it worked to punish divorce. The Ku Klux Klan, in short, was fighting not just to preserve racial homogeneity but to defend its definition of a traditional culture against the values and morals of modernity. Its principles, Imperial Wizard Hiram Wesley Evans explained in 1926, could be summarized in its slogan: "Native, white, Protestant supremacy."

The Klan also provided its members, many of them people of modest means, with little real power in society, with a sense of community and a source of seeming authority. Its bizarre costumes, its elaborate rituals, its "secret" language, its burning crosses—all helped produce a sense of camaraderie, excitement, and cohesion. For the many women who joined Klan auxiliaries, the organization served important social functions. The Klan was as committed to defending traditional gender roles as it was to defending white supremacy and Protestant morality, but women found in the Klan opportunities for activism and political involvement while remaining within the confines of conventional female "spheres." It has been estimated that nearly a half million white Protestant women joined the Women of the Ku Klux Klan during the 1920s. Many sought to ensure that the message of the Klan found its way into neighborhoods, families, and communities. In so doing, they fused bigotry with a quest to win equal rights for white Protestant women.

The Ku Klux Klan declined quickly after 1925, when a series of internal power struggles and several sordid scandals discredited some of its most important leaders. The most damaging episode involved David Stephenson, head of the Indiana Klan, who raped a young secretary, kidnapped her, and watched her die rather than call a doctor after she swallowed poison. Although the Klan staggered on in some areas into the 1930s, by World War II it was effectively dead. (The postwar Ku Klux Klan, which still survives, is modeled on but has no direct connection to the Klan of the 1920s and 1930s.) The intolerance that the Klan so powerfully and often recklessly expressed, however, left a bitter legacy.

A New Status for Native Americans

The vision of "One-Hundred-Percent Americanism" that drove many nativist efforts in the 1920s found reflection in policy toward Native Americans. For much of the early twentieth century, public policy toward Native Americans had stressed assimilation, the importance of breaking up tribal lands, and the destruction of tribal autonomy. Widespread transfers of land to white settlers had resulted in an extensive decline in Indian land-holding during the progressive era, particularly in Oklahoma where the Five Civilized Tribes had lost much of their property.

The Citizenship Act of 1924 conferred upon all Indians born in the United States full citizenship. Native Americans who owned land had already achieved citizenship; but the 1924 legislation removed legal barriers that prevented many

APACHE INDIANS. Apaches pose outside their tent at an encampment in New Mexico, where some 600 tribesmen and women held a tribal meeting in 1919. Once one of the largest tribes in the Southwest, the Apaches largely ended their armed resistance to white settlement of their lands in 1886. Eventually thousands came to reside on reservations in New Mexico and Arizona. Although in 1925, citizenship was finally conferred upon all Native Americans born in the United States, many still viewed Indians as wards of the federal government.

from exercising their rights and privileges—although a few states continued to bar Native Americans living within tribes from the franchise until well into the 1930s. But while the Citizenship Act was a product of white determination to make Indians into mainstream "Americans," it also represented an important step in giving Indians legal rights—rights that would, ironically, later help them in their battle to preserve some autonomy within the larger society.

Despite the Citizenship Act, the belief that Indians were wards of the federal government did not yield easily. In 1924 the Bureau of Indian Affairs still held responsibility for over 300,000 Native Americans who lived on reservations, and it continued to manage huge areas of valuable property. During the late 1920s, investigations into the conduct of the Bureau of Indian Affairs led to sharp criticism of government policy. A 1929 study warned that public policies that aimed to enforce assimilation were leading to the eradication of distinctive Indian cultures and traditions. "Equality before the law," it read, "may mean annihilation." Such warnings were a first step toward a major change in Indian policy in the 1930s.

MODERNISM AND THE CLASH OF VALUES

Efforts to control behavior, define the composition of American society, and enforce homogeneity became the subject of much public discussion and political debate during the 1920s. Equally contentious and equally visible were battles over what Americans had a right to believe, learn, and teach. As a pluralist society buffeted by sweeping changes, the United States faced a daunting challenge in making room for a wide range of competing ideas and beliefs. The nation's long commitment to freedom of expression and belief remained a cornerstone of American democracy. But during the 1920s, that tolerance would be tested by a clash between those who embraced new scientific ideas and those who rejected modern theories that seemed to trample on cherished beliefs.

Education

The schools became a focal point for many controversies during the 1920s that touched on issues of cultural values, political control, and social responsibility. The issues debated ranged from the role of religious education to compulsory attendance to the teaching of foreign languages. In some states, hostility to parochial education resulted in a determined effort to mandate attendance at *public* schools. In Oregon, a coalition of groups, among them the Ku Klux Klan, succeeded in 1922 in winning passage of a bill that required public school attendance. But the law spawned fierce opposition from a range of groups, including many Catholics, other religious sects, and various business interests who did not want to see taxes for public education rise markedly. "Whose is the child?" one magazine asked. "So far as its education is concerned, Oregon has answered that it is the state's." Although the Supreme Court struck down the Oregon statute in *Pierce* v. *Society of Sisters* (1925), control over education remained a matter of intense political debate.

Conflict over public education often reflected the diverse populations the schools increasingly served. Some northern districts faced with a growing population of African-American students created separate schools for blacks, usually over the protests of black parents and local leaders. The presence of immigrant schoolchildren prompted bills that mandated only English language teaching. Who would teach also became a matter of some legislative maneuvering. It was nearly impossible for a married woman to find a teaching job in a public school; in half of the nation's cities, a female teacher who married was required to resign her position. In certain states, discrimination against Catholic and Jewish teachers kept many out of public school systems. As controversial as who would control or staff the schools was the matter of what would be taught within them. During the 1920s, several states passed laws that prescribed the teaching of particular subjects, including American history, thrifty habits, fire prevention, and kindness to animals. Some school boards went much further and mandated the teaching of certain values while banning "offensive" books and subjects altogether. Much of public education, in particular, stressed the importance of "Americanism"—defined in determinedly middle-class terms—to society.

The expansion of American public education in the 1920s offered a world of new possibilities and opportunities to many families and children. But the very value of the enterprise ensured that it would not escape the cultural conflict that was apparent elsewhere in American society.

Religious Fundamentalism

Nowhere was the clash between modernist thought and traditional belief more evident than in one of the most bitter cultural controversies of the 1920s—the place of religion in contemporary society. By 1921, American Protestantism was already divided into two warring camps. On one side stood the modernists: mostly urban, middle-class people who had attempted to adapt religion to the teachings of modern science and to the realities of their contemporary, secular society. On the other side stood the defenders of traditional faith: provincial, largely (although far from exclusively) rural men and women, fighting to maintain the centrality of religion in American life. They became known as "fundamentalists," a term derived from an influential set of pamphlets, *The Fundamentals*, published between 1910 and 1915.

Two aspects of modern society particularly grated on those who held fundamentalist beliefs. First was the move away from literal interpretation of the Bible. Closely related to this was concern about the impact of modern scientific discoveries on traditional beliefs. Above all, they opposed the teachings of

Charles Darwin, who had openly challenged the biblical story of the Creation. Human beings had not evolved from lower orders of animals, the fundamentalists insisted; they had been created by God, as described in Genesis. Not all fundamentalists rejected the theory of evolution, but many feared the power of Darwinism to undermine long-held religious beliefs.

Fundamentalism was a highly evangelical movement, interested in spreading the doctrine to new groups. Evangelists, among them the celebrated Billy Sunday, a former professional baseball player, traveled from state to state (particularly in the South and parts of the West) attracting huge crowds to their revival meetings. In sermons that mixed religious exhortation and political railing, Sunday urged his listeners to reject the worst manifestations of modernism and repent for their sins individually. "If some of you women," he instructed, "would spend less on dope and cold cream and get down on your knees and pray, God would make you prettier." Protestant modernists looked on much of this activity with condescension and amusement. But by the mid-1920s, to their great alarm, evangelical fundamentalism was gaining political strength in some states with its demands for legislation to forbid the teaching of evolution in the public schools.

The Scopes Trial

The political battle between religious fundamentalists and their opponents came to a head in 1925 in Tennessee. In March of that year, the state legislature actually adopted a measure making it illegal for any public school teacher "to teach any theory that denies the story of the divine creation of man as taught in the Bible." In fact, antievolution laws came before over twenty state legislatures in the 1920s. But Tennessee was one of the few states where such measures actually became law. The antievolution crusade reflected deeply held concerns about control over public education, the place of religion in public life, and the responsibility of the state to instill moral values shared widely within particular communities.

Predictably those larger implications made the Tennessee law a lightning rod for those who held opposing beliefs. A legal contest became inevitable, especially when the law attracted the attention of the fledgling American Civil Liberties Union. Founded in 1920 by Jane Addams, Norman Thomas, Helen Keller, and others alarmed by the repressive legal and social climate of the war and its aftermath, the ACLU was committed to defending (among other things) freedom of speech and belief. The organization offered free counsel to any Tennessee educator willing to defy the law and become the defendant in a test case. A twenty-four-year-old biology teacher in the town of Dayton, John T. Scopes, agreed to have himself arrested. And so began one of the great trials of the twentieth century.

What helped make the contest so dramatic were the charismatic figures each side brought to the contest in Dayton. The ACLU settled on the famous attorney Clarence Darrow to defend Scopes. Darrow had earned a national reputation as a fierce defender of labor activists, including Eugene V. Debs. But a year before the Scopes trial he had attracted particular attention for his brilliant defense of two young Chicago college students, Nathan Leopold and Richard Loeb, who had brutally beaten a teenager named Bobby Frank to death as an experiment to see if they could get away with it. Darrow succeeded in sparing the two youths from the death penalty by passionately arguing that they were insane. Marshaling expert testimony from psychiatrists and neurologists, he persuaded the judge to impose a sentence of life imprisonment.

As if Darrow's presence did not add drama enough to the trial, the aging William Jennings Bryan (now an important fundamentalist spokesman) announced that he would travel to Dayton to assist the prosecution. Bryan's days as a firebrand Democratic orator were long gone, but he remained a vivid symbol and determined spokesman of the nation's "plain people." More was at stake in Dayton than even the obviously weighty matters of religious belief and moral principle, Bryan argued. The case also concerned "the right of the people to have what they want in government including the kind of education they want."

The combination of issues and personalities could not help but provoke national interest. Journalists from across the country, among them H. L. Mencken,

SCOPES TRIAL. Clarence Darrow addresses the jury in this photograph from the 1925 Scopes Trial. The trial attracted enormous attention as the large number of onlookers crowded into the courtroom suggests.

flocked to Tennessee to cover the trial, which opened in an almost circuslike atmosphere. Vendors sold hot dogs and Bibles. Everyday the courthouse was packed with spectators who avidly followed the thrust and parry of the lawyers as if in a sports arena. Scopes had, of course, clearly violated the law; and a verdict of guilty was a foregone conclusion, especially when the judge refused to permit "expert" testimony by evolution scholars. Scopes was fined one hundred dollars, and the case was ultimately dismissed in a higher court because of a technicality.

Nevertheless, Darrow scored an important victory for the modernists by calling Bryan himself to the stand to testify as an "expert on the Bible." In the course of the cross-examination, which was broadcast by radio to much of the nation, Darrow made Bryan's stubborn defense of biblical truths appear foolish and finally tricked him into admitting the possibility that not all religious dogma was subject to only one interpretation. "There he stood," H.L. Mencken sneered of Bryan, "in the glare of the world, uttering stuff that a boy of eight would laugh at." Mencken claimed that Bryan was motivated by "hatred of the city men who had laughed at him so long. . . . He lusted for revenge upon them. He yearned to lead the anthropoid rabble against them." In fact, in arguing against Darrow, Bryan had given voice to concerns widely shared among many who feared modern society was destroying tradition and moral values.

In the end, the Scopes trial—or "Monkey Trial" as it became known—was a traumatic experience for many fundamentalists. Although they won the case in the courthouse, they failed miserably in the court of public opinion. Ridiculed as hicks, "yahoos," and hayseeds by many journalists, the fundamentalists also found themselves isolated and ultimately excluded from some mainstream Protestant denominations. The Scopes trial helped put an end to much of their political activism—at least, for a time. But it did not, of course, change their religious convictions. Nor did it lessen their determination to build a foundation for their ideas. Even without connection to traditional denominations, fundamentalists continued to congregate in independent churches or new denominations of their own. Over time they would establish colleges, missions, Bible schools, and publishing houses to spread the word. Far from disappearing, the views they represented remained well rooted in American society.

CHAPTER TWELVE

The Great Depression and American Society

≈

he cultural strains of the 1920s were only one sign that beneath the veneer of optimism and prosperity lay persistent and deeply-rooted problems. Even so, as the decade came to a close, optimism seemed to define the public mood. Business leaders, journalists, economists, and others expressed
unchecked confidence about the future; some political leaders blithely assured
Americans that economic hardship was firmly in the past. "We in America today,"
Herbert Hoover proclaimed in August 1928, not long before his election to the
presidency, "are nearer to the final triumph over poverty than ever before in the
history of any land. The poorhouse is vanishing from among us."

Only fifteen months later, those words would return to haunt the new president, as the nation plunged into the most severe and prolonged economic depression in its history—a depression that continued in one form or another for
a full decade, not only in the United States but throughout much of the rest of
the world. The Depression was a traumatic experience for individual Americans,
who faced unemployment, the loss of land and other property, and in some cases
homelessness and starvation. It also placed great strains on the political and social fabric of the nation. In short order, a society newly accustomed to the fast
pace, great scale, and impressive wealth produced (for some) by industrial development had to come to terms with an economic collapse equally daunting in
its speed, its impact, and its terrible costs.

THE END OF PROSPERITY

The economic decline that seemed to begin so suddenly in 1929 came as an especially severe shock because it followed so closely a period in which the economy for the most part seemed to be performing extraordinarily well. Once the
Depression was underway, signs of its impending arrival could be found in a

series of long-term factors that were gradually weakening the American economy. But most Americans overlooked hints of trouble until the economic collapse had already begun.

The Crash

The first widely visible sign of looming catastrophe was the crash of the stock-market in the fall of 1929. This proved an especially shocking event to many who routinely dabbled in the bull market at the decade's end and to investors who expected a strong return. For much of 1928 and 1929 they were not disappointed. In February 1928, stock prices began a steady ascent that continued, with only a few temporary lapses, for a year and a half. Between May 1928 and September 1929, the average price of stocks rose over forty percent. The stocks of the major industrials—the stocks that are used to determine the Dow Jones Industrial Average—doubled in value in that same period. Trading mushroomed from 2 or 3 million shares a day to over 5 million, and at times to as many as 10 or 12 million. A widespread speculative fever grew steadily more intense, particularly once brokerage firms began encouraging the mania by offering ridiculously easy credit to those buying stocks.

STOCK MARKET CRASH.   As word spread of the Stock Market Crash on October 29, 1929, crowds gathered anxiously in the streets near the New York Stock Exchange.

In the autumn of 1929, however, the market began to fall apart. On October 21, October 23, and even more seriously on October 24 ("Black Thursday") there were alarming declines in stock prices, followed by brief recoveries. One reprieve occurred on the afternoon of October 24, when J. P. Morgan and Company and other big bankers conspicuously bought up stocks in a desperate bid to restore public confidence. But on October 29, "Black Tuesday," all efforts to save the market failed. Sixteen million shares of stock were traded; the industrial index dropped 43 points; stocks in many companies became virtually worthless. In the months that followed, the market continued to decline. It remained deeply depressed for more than four years and did not fully recover for over a decade.

Popular folklore has established the stock market crash as the beginning, and even the cause, of the Great Depression. But although October 1929 might have appeared to usher in the crisis, the Depression had earlier beginnings. Its causes lay in the structure and dynamics of the American and world economy.

Origins of the Great Depression

Economists, historians, and others have argued for decades about the causes of the Great Depression, but most agree on several things. They agree, first, that what is remarkable about the crisis is not that it occurred; periodic recessions are a normal feature of capitalist economies. What is remarkable is that it was so severe and that it lasted so long. The important question, therefore, is not so much why there was a depression, but why it was such a grave one. Most observers agree, too, that a number of different factors account for the severity of the crisis, even if there is considerable disagreement about which deserves greatest weight in accounting for the economic catastrophe.

One important factor was the lack of diversification in the American economy in the 1920s. The prosperity of the era had depended excessively on a few basic industries, notably construction and automobiles. In the late 1920s, those industries began to decline. Expenditures on construction fell from $11 billion to under $9 billion between 1926 and 1929. Automobile sales fell by more than a third in the first nine months of 1929. Newer industries were emerging to take up the slack—among them petroleum, chemicals, plastics, and others oriented toward the expanding market for consumer goods—but they had not yet developed enough strength to compensate for the decline in other sectors.

A second important factor was the maldistribution of purchasing power and, as a result, a weakness in consumer demand. As industrial and agricultural production increased, the proportion of the profits going to farmers, workers, and other potential consumers was too small to create an adequate market for the goods the economy was producing. Demand was not keeping up with supply. Even in 1929, after nearly a decade of economic growth, more than half the families in America lived on the edge of or below the minimum subsistence level—too poor to buy the goods the industrial economy was producing.

As long as corporations had continued to expand their capital facilities (factories, warehouses, heavy equipment, and other investments), the economy had flourished. By 1929, however, capital investment had created more plant space than could profitably be used, and factories were producing more goods than consumers could purchase. Industries that were experiencing declining demand (construction, autos, coal, and others) began laying off workers, depleting mass purchasing power further. Even expanding industries often reduced their work forces because of new, less labor-intensive technologies; and in the sluggish economic atmosphere of 1929 and beyond, laid-off workers had difficulty finding employment elsewhere.

A third major problem was the credit structure of the economy. Many farmers were deeply in debt—their land mortgaged, and crop prices too low to allow them to pay off what they owed. Small banks, especially those tied to the agricultural economy, were in constant trouble in the 1920s as their customers defaulted on loans; many such banks failed. Large banks were in trouble, too. Although most American bankers were very conservative, some of the nation's biggest banks were investing recklessly in the stock market or making unwise loans. When the stock market crashed, many of these banks suffered losses greater than they could absorb.

A fourth factor contributing to the coming of the Depression was America's position in international trade. Beginning late in the 1920s, European demand for American goods began to decline. That was partly because European industry and agriculture were becoming more productive, and partly because some European nations (most notably Germany, under the Weimar Republic) were having financial difficulties and could not afford to buy goods from overseas. But it was also because the European economy was being destabilized by the international debt structure that had emerged in the aftermath of World War I.

The international debt structure, therefore, was a fifth factor contributing to the Depression. When the war came to an end in 1918, all the European nations that had been allied with the United States owed large sums of money to American banks, sums much too large to be repaid out of their shattered economies. That was one reason the Allies had insisted (over Woodrow Wilson's objections) on reparation payments from Germany and Austria. Reparations, they believed, would provide them with a way to pay off their own debts. But Germany and Austria were themselves in economic trouble after the war; they were no more able to pay the reparations than the Allies were able to pay their debts.

The American government refused to forgive or reduce the debts. Instead, American banks began making large loans to European governments with which they paid off their earlier loans. Thus debts (and reparations) were being paid only by piling up new and greater debts. In the late 1920s, and particularly after the American economy began to weaken in 1929, the European nations found it much more difficult to borrow money from the United States. At the same time, high American protective tariffs were making it difficult for them to sell their goods in American markets. Without any source of foreign exchange with which to repay their loans, they began to default. The collapse of the international credit structure was one of the reasons the Depression spread to Europe (and grew much worse in America) after 1931.

The Spread of Economic Misery

The stock market crash of 1929 did not so much cause the Depression, then, as help trigger a chain of events that exposed longstanding weaknesses in the American economy. During the next three years, the crisis grew steadily. Perhaps most alarmingly, each disaster—bad enough in its own right—created a ripple effect and further strained the industrial economy.

A case in point was the banking system, which began to collapse after the stock market crash. Over 9,000 American banks either went bankrupt or closed their doors to avoid bankruptcy between 1930 and 1933. Customers lost over $2.5 billion in deposits. Partly as a result of these banking closures, the nation's money supply greatly decreased. The total money supply, according to some measurements, fell by more than a third between 1930 and 1933. The declining money supply meant a decline in purchasing power, and thus deflation. Manufacturers and merchants began reducing prices, cutting back on production, and laying off workers.

Some economists argue that a severe depression could have been avoided if the Federal Reserve system had acted more responsibly. But the members of the Federal Reserve Board, concerned about protecting the Board's own solvency in a dangerous economic environment, raised interest rates in 1931, which contracted the money supply even further.

The economic collapse was so rapid and so devastating that at the time it created only bewilderment among many of those who attempted to explain it. The American gross national product plummeted from over $104 billion in 1929 to $76.4 billion in 1932—a twenty-five percent decline in three years. In 1929, Americans had spent $16.2 billion in capital investment; in 1933, they invested only a third of a billion. The consumer price index declined twenty-five percent between 1929 and 1933; the wholesale price index thirty-two percent. Gross farm income dropped from $12 billion to $5 billion in four years. By 1932, according to the relatively crude estimates of the time, twenty-five percent of the American work force was unemployed (some believe the figure was even higher); another third of the workforce experienced cuts in wages or hours or both. For the rest of the decade, unemployment averaged nearly twenty percent, never dropping below fifteen percent.

HARD TIMES

Someone asked the British economist John Maynard Keynes in the 1930s whether he was aware of any historical era comparable to the Great Depression. "Yes," Keynes replied. "It was called the Dark Ages, and it lasted 400 years." The Depression did not last 400 years. But it did bring unprecedented despair as it wreaked havoc on the economies of the United States and much of the Western world.

Unemployment and Poverty

The suffering extended into every area of American society. In the industrial Northeast and Midwest, cities were becoming virtually paralyzed by unemployment. Cleveland, Ohio, for example, had an unemployment rate of fifty percent in 1932; Akron, sixty percent; Toledo, eighty percent. Many industrial workers were accustomed to periods of unemployment, but no one was prepared for the scale and duration of the joblessness of the 1930s. Most Americans had been taught to believe that every individual was responsible for his or her own fate, that unemployment and poverty were signs of personal failure. Even in the face of national distress, many clung to such convictions. Unemployed workers walked through the streets day after day looking for jobs that did not exist. The days of idleness gave way to weeks and months and for some to years with no prospect of work in sight. An increasing number of families began turning to state and local public relief systems, just to be able to eat.

But existing relief systems, which in the 1920s had served only a small number of the indigent, proved totally unequipped to handle the new demands being placed on them. In many places, therefore, relief simply collapsed. Private charities attempted to supplement the public relief efforts, but the problem was far beyond their capabilities as well. State governments felt pressure to expand their own assistance to the unemployed; but tax revenues were declining along with everything else, and state leaders balked at placing additional strains on already tight budgets. Many public officials, moreover, believed that an extensive welfare system would undermine the moral fiber of its clients.

As a result, American cities experienced scenes that a few years earlier would have seemed almost inconceivable. Bread lines stretched for blocks outside Red Cross and Salvation Army kitchens. Thousands of people sifted through garbage cans for scraps of food or waited outside restaurant kitchens in hopes of receiving plate scrapings. Homeless men and women slept in city parks, rode the subways, and lingered in the train stations. Nearly 2 million young men (and a much smaller number of women) simply took to the roads, riding freight trains from city to city, living as nomads. "Black and white, it didn't make any difference who you were, 'cause everybody was poor," one "hobo" recalled. "Twenty-five or thirty would be out on the side of the rail, white and colored. They didn't have

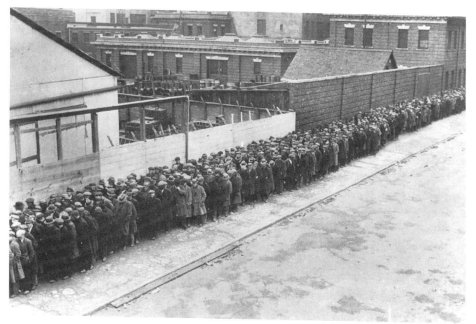

BREAD LINE.   Local charities could not begin to meet the demands imposed by the Great Depression. Nonetheless, people did not know where else to turn when poverty, hunger, and unemployment forced them to seek relief. Here a line of unemployed men, waiting to be fed, forms outside a municipal lodging house in New York City in 1930.

no mothers or sisters, they didn't have no home, they were dirty, they had overalls on, they didn't have no food, they didn't have anything."

In rural areas, conditions were in many ways worse. Farm income declined by sixty percent between 1929 and 1932. A third of all American farmers lost their land. In addition, a large area of agricultural settlement in the Great Plains of the South and West was suffering from a catastrophic natural disaster: one of the worst droughts in the history of the nation. Beginning in 1930, a large area of the nation, which came to be known as the Dust Bowl and which stretched north from Texas into the Dakotas, began to experience a steady decline in rainfall and an accompanying increase in heat.

The drought continued for a decade, turning what had once been fertile farm regions into virtual deserts. "The Dirty Thirties—the phrase was coined where we had the dust storms," one Arkansan remembered. "Everything dried up . . . the springs, the wells, the ponds, the creeks, the rivers. . . . The most valuable thing we lost was hope." In Kansas, the soil in some places was completely without moisture as far as three feet below the surface. In Nebraska, Iowa, and other states, summer temperatures averaged over 100 degrees. Swarms of grasshoppers moved from region to region, devouring what meager crops farmers were able to raise, often even devouring fenceposts or clothes hanging out to dry. Great dust storms—"black blizzards," as they were called—swept across the

DUST BOWL.   The air is thick with dust as a storm sweeps through farm country in the 1930s. Drought and heat created catastrophic conditions for farmers in the Dust Bowl region, deepening the misery of the Depression years.

plains, blotting out the sun and suffocating livestock as well as any people unfortunate or foolish enough to stay outside.

It is a measure of how productive American farmers were and how depressed the market for agricultural goods had become that even with these disastrous conditions, the farm economy continued through the 1930s to produce far more than American consumers could afford to buy. Farm prices fell so low that few growers any longer made any profit at all on their crops. As a result, many farmers, like many urban unemployed, left their homes in search of work. In the South, in particular, many dispossessed farmers, black and white, wandered from town to town, hoping to find jobs or handouts. Hundreds of thousands of families from the Dust Bowl (often known as "Okies," since many came from Oklahoma) traveled to California and other states, where they found conditions little better than those they had left. Owning no land of their own, many worked as agricultural migrants, traveling from farm to farm picking fruit and other crops at starvation wages.

Throughout the nation, problems of malnutrition and homelessness grew at an alarming rate. Hospitals observed a striking increase in deaths from starvation. Large shantytowns, known to many as "Hoovervilles," after the now discredited president, sprang up on the outskirts of cities. Homeless families lived in makeshift shacks constructed of flattened tin cans, scraps of wood, abandoned crates, and other debris. Many homeless Americans simply kept moving.

Those who managed to hang on to their jobs were far from immune to the hardships imposed by the Depression. Speed-ups designed to sustain the same level of productivity with fewer workers became commonplace in many factories. Textile workers, in particular, found it more and more difficult to make production quotas as owners "stretched out"—doubled the number of looms a worker had to tend while cutting wages at the same time. One sixteen-year-old girl wrote to Eleanor Roosevelt in 1933 describing the fate of her mother, a widow with fifteen small children who worked the looms in a South Carolina textile mill:

> In 1931–1932 they stretched out and put her on 40 looms; her average wages was 11 and 12 dollars per week. Then they stretched out to 50 and 60 looms and she couldn't make production. They turned her off and would not let her work there. She was with us little children for the mercy of the world to feed.

Coal miners, some of whom made just fifty cents for loading a seven-ton railroad car, grew accustomed to working only one or two days at a time when the owners briefly opened the mines. For the many who lived in company towns, debt mounted and the small wages earned soon disappeared at company stores, run by the mine owners. Still, even amid these grueling conditions, workers seized every opportunity for gainful employment, knowing how fleeting jobs might be in the Depression economy.

African Americans and the Depression

For African Americans, the Great Depression imposed special burdens. Many African Americans had shared very little in the prosperity of the 1920s. Indeed, poverty was so endemic among black men and women that one sharply observed: "they didn't call it a depression until white folks were out of work." But the Depression proved devastating for many African Americans despite their long experience with economic insecurity. During the Depression, black Americans experienced more unemployment, homelessness, malnutrition, and disease than they had in the past, and considerably more than most whites experienced.

As the Depression began, over half of all black Americans still lived in the South. Most were farmers. The collapse of prices for cotton and other staple crops left some with no income at all. Many left the land altogether—either by choice or because they were forced to do so by landlords who no longer found the sharecropping system profitable. Some migrated to southern cities. But there, unemployed whites believed they had first claim to all work, and some now began to take positions as janitors, street cleaners, and domestic servants, displacing the blacks who formerly occupied them.

African-American working-women, who were largely concentrated in sharecropping, domestic service, and unskilled factory work, watched with dismay as their jobs disappeared during the 1930s—"gone" as educator Nannie Burroughs put it, "to machines, gone to white people or gone out of style." Those who hung onto their jobs—nine out of ten African American women worked in domestic service or agriculture during the Depression—often experienced harsh wage cuts and grueling working conditions. Temporary or part-time work for low wages was preferable to no work at all, but the gains seemed meager for the backbreaking labor involved. A 1937 government report observed that in one Louisiana parish black women cotton pickers earned only a little more than forty dollars a year—in part because they could locate work for only a few months at a time. Some were paid just forty or fifty cents a day. In northern cities, African-American women seeking labor as domestic servants stood on street corners waiting for white employers to drive up and offer them a day's work. Some earned as little as thirty-five cents for a long day washing windows, waxing floors, ironing shirts, and performing the countless other tasks involved in household work.

As the Depression deepened, whites in many southern cities began to demand that all blacks be dismissed from their jobs. In Atlanta in 1930, an organization calling itself the Black Shirts organized a campaign with the slogan "No Jobs for Niggers Until Every White Man Has a Job!" In other areas, whites used intimidation and violence to drive blacks from jobs. By 1932, over half the African Americans in the South were without employment. And what limited relief there was went to whites first.

Unsurprisingly, therefore, many black southerners—perhaps 400,000 in all—left the South in the 1930s and journeyed to the cities of the North. There they generally found less blatant discrimination. But conditions were in most other respects little better than those in the South. In New York, black unemployment was nearly fifty percent. In other cities, it was higher. Two million African Americans were on some form of relief by 1932.

Traditional patterns of segregation and disfranchisement in the South survived the Depression largely unchallenged. But a few particularly notorious examples of racism did attract national attention. The most celebrated was the Scottsboro case. In March 1931, nine black teenagers were taken off a freight train in Alabama (in a small town near Scottsboro) and arrested for vagrancy and disorder. Later, two white women who had also been riding the train accused them of rape. In fact, there was overwhelming evidence, medical and otherwise, that the women had not been raped at all; they may have made their accusations out of fear of being arrested themselves. Nevertheless, an all-white jury in Alabama quickly convicted all nine of the "Scottsboro boys" (as they were known to both friends and foes) and sentenced eight of them to death.

The Supreme Court overturned the convictions in 1932, and a series of new trials began that attracted increasing national attention. The International Labor Defense, an organization associated with the Communist party, came to the aid of the accused youths and began to publicize the case. Later the NAACP, after some initial reluctance to associate itself with a rape case, joined the defense. The trials continued throughout the 1930s. Although the white southern juries who sat on the case never acquitted any of the defendants, most of them even-

SCOTTSBORO.   Haywood Patterson, one of the men known as the "Scottsboro boys,"
sits between his defense attorneys, Samuel Liebowitz and George Chamlee, during his
second trial in April 1933. An earlier conviction was overturned by the United States
Supreme Court on the grounds that Patterson and the others accused had not
received adequate counsel. The International Labor Defense, backed by the
Communist party, recruited well known criminal attorney Liebowitz to handle
the defense. Patterson was tried four times but his conviction was never overturned.
He died in prison at the age of thirty-nine.

tually gained their freedom. The last of the Scottsboro defendants did not leave
prison until 1950.

The Depression was a time of important changes in the role and behavior
of leading black organizations. The NAACP, for example, began to work dili-
gently to win a position for blacks within the emerging labor movement, supporting the formation of the Congress of Industrial Organizations (CIO), and
helping to break down racial barriers within labor unions. During the 1930s
several locals of the International Ladies Garment Workers Union (ILGWU)
were integrated in New York City; in Harlem some African-American women
pressers who belonged to the union were among the best-paid women workers
in the community. The Amalgamated Clothing Workers of America welcomed
black members, as did one of its affiliates, the United Laundry Workers, which
counted many African-American women among its membership. As African
Americans joined the CIO, some also helped fight the practice of using
black workers as strikebreakers. On one occasion Walter White, secretary of

the NAACP, made a personal appearance at an auto plant to implore blacks not to work as strikebreakers. Partly as a result of such efforts, more than half a million blacks were able to join the labor movement. In the Steelworkers Union, for example, African Americans constituted about twenty percent of the membership.

Hispanics and Asian Americans During Hard Times

Similar patterns of discrimination and a similar persistence of hardship characterized the experience of many Mexicans and Mexican Americans during the 1930s. The Hispanic population of the United States had been growing steadily since the early twentieth century, largely in California and other areas of the Southwest. Massive immigration from Mexico (which was specifically excluded from the immigration restriction laws of the 1920s) accounted for these trends.

In the 1930s, there were approximately 2 million Hispanics in the United States. Chicanos (as Mexican Americans are known) filled many of the same menial jobs in the West and elsewhere that blacks filled in other regions. Some farmed small, marginal tracts. Some became agricultural migrants, traveling from region to region harvesting fruit, lettuce, and other crops. But most lived in urban areas—in California, New Mexico, and Arizona, but also in Detroit, Chicago, New York, and other eastern industrial cities—and occupied the lower ranks of the unskilled labor force in such industries as steel, automobiles, and meatpacking. Even during the prosperous 1920s, it had been a precarious existence.

The Depression made things significantly worse. As in the South, unemployed English-speaking whites in the Southwest demanded jobs they once would have spurned—in this case jobs held by Hispanics. Thus Mexican unemployment rose quickly to levels far higher than those for Anglos. Some Mexicans were, in effect, forced to leave the country by officials who arbitrarily removed them from relief rolls or simply rounded them up and transported them across the border. Perhaps half a million Chicanos left the United States for Mexico in the first years of the Depression. Those who remained scrambled for work. Some Mexican-American farm workers competed for jobs as migrant workers with rural whites who had come West after losing their farms. In a break with long tradition, many Mexican-American women pursued work outside the home, often in canning factories.

Chicanos who remained in the United States during the Depression began to pour into the cities of California and the Southwest, rapidly expanding the *barrios*. They faced persistent discrimination, and they lived in a poverty comparable to that of urban blacks in the South and the Northeast. Most relief programs excluded Mexicans from their rolls or offered them benefits far below those available to whites. Hispanics generally had no access to American schools. Many hospitals refused them admission. American blacks had established certain educational and social facilities of their own in response to discrimination, but

Hispanics generally had fewer institutional supports. Some joined the American Communist party. Some turned to the Mexican consulates or to the social and economic leaders of Mexican-American communities, but with few results. Even many who possessed American citizenship found themselves treated like foreigners. There were, occasionally, signs of organized resistance by Mexican Americans themselves, most notably in California, where some formed a union of migrant farm workers. But harsh repression by local growers and the public authorities allied with them prevented such organizations from having much impact.

For Asian Americans, too, the Depression reinforced longstanding patterns of discrimination and economic marginalization. In California, where the largest Japanese-American and Chinese-American populations were, even educated Asians had always found it difficult, if not impossible, to move into mainstream professions. Japanese-American college graduates often found themselves working in family fruit stands; twenty percent of all Nisei in Los Angeles worked at such stands at the end of the 1930s. For those who found jobs (usually poorly paid) in the industrial or service economy, employment was precarious; like blacks and Hispanics, they often lost jobs to white Americans so desperate for work that they were willing to accept menial positions they once would not have considered. Japanese farm workers, like Chicano farm workers, suffered from the increasing competition for even these low-paying jobs from white migrants from the Great Plains.

In California, younger Nisei tried to challenge the obstacles facing them through politics. They organized Japanese-American Democratic Clubs in several cities, clubs that worked for, among other things, laws protecting racial and ethnic minorities from discrimination. At the same time, some Japanese-American businessmen and professionals tried to overcome obstacles by changing the Nisei themselves, by encouraging them to become more assimilated, more "American." They formed the Japanese American Citizens League in 1930 to promote their goals. By 1940, it had nearly 6,000 members.

Chinese Americans fared no better. The overwhelming majority continued to work in Chinese-owned laundries and restaurants. Those who moved outside the Asian community could rarely find jobs above the entry level. Chinese women, for example, might find work as stock girls in department stores but almost never as sales clerks. Educated Chinese men and women could hope for virtually no professional opportunities outside the world of the Chinatowns.

Hard Times for Women and Families

The Great Depression had a complicated impact on working women and their families. Many suffered deeply from the loss of their jobs, the economic insecurity their families faced, and the constant anxiety about keeping their children fed and clothed. At the same time, white women's labor force participation actually increased during the 1930s despite the economic downturn. The sectors

WOMEN IN THE WORK FORCE, 1900–1940

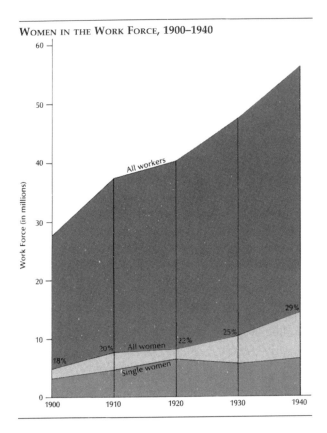

in the economy in which women were most commonly employed—clerical work, service, and sales—did not contract as much as did heavy industry, and they responded more rapidly to government recovery measures. The largest new group of female workers consisted of wives and mothers who were driven into the labor force by the need to help support their families. For African-American women, however, labor force participation declined during the Depression. A large proportion of black working women held jobs as agricultural workers or as domestics in private homes. In both cases the Depression caused a dramatic decline in opportunities for work. In addition, black women were often denied jobs in sales and clerical work. By 1940, one third of white women worked in clerical jobs, while only one percent of African-American women were similarly employed.

Both black and white women workers experienced much hostility during the Depression. Many men viewed their work as an unnecessary drain on the small pool of available jobs. Critics argued that men with families, who really needed wages, ought to be employed first during the economic emergency. Such criticism overlooked the realities of many Americans' lives. Women who were heads of household, who worked because their families could not survive without their income, and who were supporting disabled or unemployed husbands were working out of economic necessity. In addition, gender segregation in the labor market made some jobs available to women that were not available to men.

But for those who believed women did not belong in the labor force anyway, women's "unemployment" seemed an impossibility. Bills to prohibit married women from working surfaced in many state legislatures during the 1930s. Nearly eighty percent of the nation's school systems refused employment to teachers who were married, and some discharged women teachers as soon as they wed. From 1932 until 1937, it was illegal for more than one member of a family to hold a federal civil service job. Public opinion polls revealed that many Americans accepted the validity of choosing men over women for scarce jobs in the Depression economy. Indeed, one critic blamed the Depression itself on working women in 1939 as he noted "there are approximately 10 million people out of work in the United States today. There are also 10 million or more women, married and single who are jobholders. Simply fire the women, who shouldn't be working anyway, and hire the men. Presto! No unemployment. No relief rolls. No depression."

Given such attitudes, it is not surprising that many American feminists found the Depression years a time of frustration. Although economic pressures pushed more women into the work force, those same pressures helped to erode the frail support that feminists had won in the 1920s for female independence and economic equality. In the difficult years of the 1930s, such aspirations seemed to many to be less important than dealing with economic hardship. The Depression saw the virtual extinction of the National Woman's party, which had fought throughout the 1920s for the Equal Rights Amendment and for other egalitarian goals. Even more moderate feminists, committed to "protective" legislation for women, saw their influence decline—although they achieved some significant gains in the early years of the New Deal.

The economic hardships of the Depression years challenged and often changed the dynamics of American families in other ways as well. Middle-class families that had become accustomed in the 1920s to a steadily rising standard of living now found themselves plunged suddenly into uncertainty, because of unemployment or the reduction of incomes among those who remained employed. Some working-class families too had achieved a precarious prosperity in the 1920s and saw their gains disappear in the 1930s. These circumstances forced many families to retreat from the consumer patterns they had developed in the 1920s. Women often returned to sewing clothes for themselves and their families and to preserving their own food rather than buying such products in stores. Others engaged in home businesses—taking in laundry, selling baked goods, accepting boarders.

Many households expanded to include more distant relatives. Parents often moved in with their children and grandparents with their grandchildren, or vice versa. Although the divorce rate declined in the 1930s, at least part of the drop could be attributed to the expense involved in formally terminating matrimony. More common was the informal breakup of families, particularly when unemployed men left their wives and children to escape the humiliation of being unable to earn a living or deserted them at least for a time to search for work in distant cities. The marriage rate and the birth rate declined simultaneously during the Depression for the first time since the early nineteenth century. Children who grew up during the Depression could not help but feel the strains many of their parents were experiencing. Some worked to help out and in so doing learned early the value of responsibility. "It was an enormously hard life," one remembered. "But there was also a sense of great satisfaction in being a child with valuable work to do and, being able to do it well . . . to function in this world." Despite deprivation, many admired their parents for their hard work and their courage.

American Culture and the Great Depression

Although prosperity and consumerism had done much to shape American values in the 1920s, the Depression did little to alter the fundamental beliefs and values of most Americans despite the extent of the economic misery. In fact, many people responded to hard times by redoubling their commitment to familiar ideals. When sociologists Robert and Helen Merrell Lynd returned in the mid-1930s to Muncie, Indiana, the scene of their celebrated sociological study completed in the 1920s, they were struck by the persistence of values in the community. Their 1937 book *Middletown in Transition* concluded that in most respects "the texture of Middletown's culture has not changed. . . . Middletown is overwhelmingly living by the values by which it lived in 1925." Above all, the men and women of "Middletown"—and by implication many other Americans—remained committed to the traditional American emphasis on the individual.

No assumption would seem to have been more vulnerable to erosion during the Depression than the belief that the individual was in control of his or her own fate, that anyone displaying sufficient talent and industry could become a success. And in some respects, the economic crisis did work to undermine the traditional "success ethic" in America. Many people began to look to government for assistance; many blamed corporate moguls, international bankers, "economic royalists," and others for their distress. Yet the Depression did not destroy the success ethic.

The survival of the ideals of work and individual advancement was evident in many ways, not least in the reactions of those most traumatized by the Depression: conscientious working people who suddenly found themselves without employment. Some expressed anger and struck out at the economic system. Many, however, seemed to blame themselves. Nothing so surprised foreign observers of America in the 1930s than the apparent passivity of the unemployed, many of whom were so ashamed of their joblessness that they refused to leave their homes. Perhaps that was why people who continued in the 1930s to work and to live more or less as they always had found it easy at times to forget that there was an economic crisis. The Depression could be hard to see, because so many of the unemployed tended to hide themselves, unwilling to display to the world what they considered their own personal failure.

At the same time, millions responded eagerly to reassurances that they could, through their own efforts, restore themselves to prosperity and success. Dale Carnegie's *How to Win Friends and Influence People* (1936), a self-help manual preaching individual initiative, was one of the best-selling books of the decade. Carnegie's message was not only that personal initiative was the route to success; it was also that the best way for people to make something of themselves was to adapt to the world in which they lived, to understand the values and expectations of others and mold themselves accordingly. The way to get ahead, Carnegie taught, was to make other people feel important, to fit in. Harry Emerson Fosdick, a Protestant theologian who similarly preached the virtues of positive thinking and individual initiative, attracted large audiences with his radio addresses.

Not all Americans, of course, responded to the crisis of the Depression so passively. Many men and women believed that the economic problems of their time were the fault of society, not of individuals, and that some collective social response was necessary. Such beliefs found expression in politics and social action. They also found expression in American artistic and intellectual life.

Just as many progressives had become alarmed when, early in the twentieth century, they "discovered" the existence of widespread poverty in the cities, so many Americans were shocked during the 1930s at the disclosure of debilitating rural poverty. Perhaps most effective in conveying the dimensions of rural poverty was a group of documentary photographers, many of them employed by the New Deal's federal Farm Security Administration in the late 1930s, who traveled through the South recording the nature of agricultural life. Men such as Roy Stryker, Walker Evans, Arthur Rothstein, and Ben Shahn, and women such as Margaret Bourke-White and Dorothea Lange produced memorable studies of farm families and their surroundings, studies designed to reveal the savage impact of a hostile environment on its victims.

Many writers, similarly, turned away from the more personal concerns of the 1920s and devoted themselves to exposés of social injustice. Erskine Caldwell's *Tobacco Road* (1932), which later became a long-running play, was an exposé of poverty in the rural South. James Agee's *Let Us Now Praise Famous Men* (1941), with photographs by Walker Evans, was at times painfully detailed in its description of the lives of three poor rural families in the South. Richard Wright, a major African-American novelist, exposed the plight of residents of the urban ghetto in *Native Son* (1940). John Steinbeck's *The Grapes of Wrath* (1939) portrayed the trials of a migrant family in California, concluding with an open call for collective social action against injustice. John Dos Passos's *U.S.A.* trilogy (1930) explicitly attacked modern capitalism. Playwright Clifford Odets demonstrated the appeal of political radicalism in *Waiting for Lefty* (1935).

But the cultural products of the 1930s that attracted the widest popular audiences were those that diverted attention away from the Depression. The two

SHARECROPPER'S SON.   This young boy is from a sharecropping family in southeast Missouri. In 1938, a photographer caught him combing his hair as he looks into a broken mirror. Newspapers serve as wallpaper in his family's humble dwelling place.

most powerful instruments of popular culture in the 1930s—radio and the movies—provided mostly light and diverting entertainment. Although radio stations occasionally carried socially and politically provocative programs, the staple of broadcasting was escapism: comedies such as *Amos 'n Andy* (with its demeaning picture of urban blacks); adventures such as *Superman, Dick Tracy,* and *The Lone Ranger*; and other entertainment programs.

Hollywood continued to exercise tight control over its products through its resilient censor Will Hays, who ensured that most movies carried only safe, conventional messages. Even so, a few films, such as John Ford's adaptation of *The Grapes of Wrath* (1940), did explore political themes. Director Frank Capra provided a muted social message in several of his comedies—*Mr. Deeds Goes to Town* (1936), *Mr. Smith Goes to Washington* (1939), and *Meet John Doe* (1941)—which celebrated the virtues of the small town and the decency of the common people in contrast to the selfish, corrupt values of the city and the urban rich. Gangster movies portrayed a dark, gritty, violent world with which few Americans were familiar; but their desperate stories resonated with those engaged in their own difficult struggles.

More often, however, the commercial films of the 1930s were deliberately and explicitly escapist: lavish musicals such as *Gold Diggers of 1933* (whose theme song was "We're In the Money") and "screwball" comedies such as Capra's *It Happened One Night* or the many films of the Marx Brothers—films designed to divert audiences from their troubles and, often, satisfy their fantasies about quick and easy wealth.

Popular literature, similarly, offered Americans an escape from the Depression. Two of the best-selling novels of the decade were romantic sagas set in earlier eras: Margaret Mitchell's *Gone with the Wind* (1936) and Hervey Allen's *Anthony Adverse* (1933), both of them stories of tough, resilient individuals who learned to survive adversity. Leading magazines, and particularly such popular new photographic journals as *Life*, focused on fashions, stunts, and eye-catching scenery more often than on the hardships of the era. Even the newsreels distributed to movie theaters across the country tended to give more attention to beauty contests and ship launchings than to the Depression itself.

Popular culture nonetheless sometimes reflected the realities of the historical moment. This was particularly apparent in the many films that depicted outspoken women of independence during the 1930s—in the workplace, in their families, even in the wacky circumstances depicted by screwball comedies. Film stars such as Bette Davis and Katherine Hepburn, and athletes such as Babe Didrikson Zaharias, who won three medals in track and field events during the 1932 Olympics, served as emblems of vigor, determination, and self-assurance—values of great significance to many women across the country who were coping with the trying circumstances of the Depression. Few inspired greater admiration and affection than Amelia Earhart, the aviator who had been the first woman to fly across the Atlantic Ocean in 1928 and who in 1932 became the first woman to do so in a solo flight. During the 1930s, the unconventional Earhart achieved much acclaim as an American heroine, a status that only became magnified when she disappeared on a flight in 1937. Women especially seemed to revel in her impressive demonstration that women, as she put it, "can sometimes do things themselves if given the chance."

The Lure of American Radicalism

For a relatively small but important group of Americans—intellectuals, artists, laborers, the unemployed, African Americans, Mexican Americans, and others who became disenchanted with the workings of American society—the Depression produced a commitment, for a time at least, to radical politics. Some became members of the American Communist party, which achieved a size, visibility, and influence in the 1930s that it had never attained before and would never attain again. Others expressed sympathy for communist ideas without joining the party. By the standards of the rest of the world, radicalism in the United States remained relatively limited. By America's own modest standards, however, the 1930s to some degree deserved the label some commentators gave it: the "Red Decade."

For intellectuals, in particular, the left offered a compelling alternative to the lonely and difficult stance of detachment and alienation many had embraced in the 1920s. It combined a harsh critique of mainstream American society with an intense commitment to a political movement. The importance of the Spanish Civil War to many American intellectuals was a good example of how the left provided an occasion to take a principled stand on issues of great moment while giving meaning and purpose to individual lives. The battle of republicans in Spain against the Spanish fascists of Francisco Franco (who was receiving support from Hitler and Mussolini) attracted a substantial group of young Americans, more than 3,000 in all, who formed the Abraham Lincoln Brigade and traveled to Spain to join in the fight. About a third of its members died in combat. Those who survived remembered the experience with pride, as one of the great moments of their lives. Ernest Hemingway, who spent time in Spain as a correspondent, wrote in his novel *For Whom the Bell Tolls* (1940) of how the war provided those Americans who fought in it with "a part in something which you could believe in wholly and completely and in which you felt an absolute brotherhood with others who were engaged in it."

Instrumental in creating the Lincoln Brigade, and directing many of its activities, was the American Communist party. Its membership peaked at perhaps 100,000 during its heyday in the mid-1930s; and for a time it presented itself as a genuinely American organization, no more threatening or alien than any other political organization. For several years beginning in 1935, the party dropped its insistence on working completely apart from other organizations and began to advocate a democratic alliance of all antifascist groups in the United States, a "Popular Front." It began to praise Franklin Roosevelt and John L. Lewis, a powerful (and strongly anticommunist) labor leader. It adopted the slogan "Communism is twentieth-century Americanism."

The party was active in organizing the unemployed in the early 1930s and staged a hunger march in Washington, D.C., in 1931. Party members were among the most effective union organizers in many industries. And, the party was one of the few political organizations to take a firm stand in favor of racial justice; its active defense of the Scottsboro defendants was but one example of its efforts to ally itself with the aspirations of African Americans. It also helped organize a union of black sharecroppers in Alabama, which resisted—in several instances violently—efforts of white landowners and authorities to displace them from their farms.

But despite its efforts to appear a patriotic organization, the American Communist party remained closely connected to the Soviet Union, which rigidly supervised its activities. Party leaders received their orders from the Comintern in Moscow. Most members obediently followed the "party line" (although there were many areas in which communists were active for which there was no clear party line, in which members acted independently). The subordination of the party leadership to the Soviet Union was most clearly demonstrated in 1939, when Stalin signed a nonaggression pact with Nazi Germany. Moscow then sent orders to the American Communist party to abandon the Popular Front and return to its old stance of harsh criticism of American liberals; and the party's leaders in the United States immediately obeyed—although thousands of disillusioned members left the party as a result.

The Socialist party of America, now under the leadership of Norman Thomas, also cited the economic crisis as evidence of the failure of capitalism and sought vigorously to win public support for its own political program. Among other things, it attempted to mobilize support among the rural poor. The Southern Tenant Farmers Union (STFU), supported by the party and organized by a young socialist, H. L. Mitchell, tried to create a biracial coalition of sharecroppers, tenant farmers, and others to demand economic reform. Neither the STFU nor the Party itself, however, made any real progress toward establishing socialism as a major force in American politics. By 1936, in fact, membership in the Socialist party had fallen below 20,000.

There had been few times before (and few since) in American history when being part of the left seemed so respectable and even conventional among workers, intellectuals, and others. The 1930s witnessed an impressive, if temporary, widening of the ideological range of mainstream politics. But antiradicalism remained a powerful force in the 1930s as well, just as it had been during and after World War I and would be again in the 1940s and 1950s. Hostility toward the Communist party, in particular, was intense at many levels of government. Congressional committees chaired by Hamilton Fish of New York and Martin Dies of Texas investigated communist influence wherever they could find it (or imagine it). State and local governments harried and sometimes imprisoned communist organizers. White southerners tried to drive communist organizers out of the countryside, just as growers in California and elsewhere tried (unsuccessfully) to keep communists from organizing Mexican-American and other workers. These battles reflected the shared sense among radicals and their opponents that the crisis of the Great Depression made many receptive to new political ideals and messages. How American society—its institutions, it government, its people—would weather the economic downturn remained for many concerned citizens an open question. As one member of the Roosevelt administration would later reflect, "The country was aware, as it never was before, that it was on the edge of something."

CHAPTER THIRTEEN

The Struggle for Recovery

$\sim$

The unenviable task of shepherding the United States through the harrowing ordeal of the Great Depression fell first upon Herbert Hoover. When he assumed the presidency in March 1929, Hoover believed, like most Americans, that the nation's future was bright and prosperous. That expectation shaped his goals during the first six months of his administration as he attempted to expand the policies he had advocated during his eight luminous years as secretary of commerce. His goal was to complete the formation of a stable system of cooperative individualism, which would, he believed, be the key to a successful economy.

The economic crisis that began before the year was out thrust upon the president an entirely new set of problems. For most of the rest of his term, however, Hoover continued to rely on the principles that had always governed his public life. Those principles were of little help in the face of the Great Depression, and Hoover's presidency—an innovative and dynamic one in many ways—ended in failure. And so Americans turned to a new president, Franklin Delano Roosevelt.

In attempting to relieve economic suffering, restore prosperity, and reform the economy to prevent future depressions, Roosevelt transformed both the image and the reality of the national government. His broad eclectic program— the "New Deal"—was in many ways unprecedented. But it also built solidly on existing values, institutions, and practices.

CONFRONTING THE GREAT DEPRESSION

In the course of the early 1930s, Herbert Hoover's name became synonymous with the Great Depression. And, for many years after, he would be remembered as a president who served during one of the nation's greatest periods of economic suffering and did little to alleviate it. In fact, Hoover was not insensitive to the hardship many Americans were experiencing (although he often appeared to be) and to the need for the nation to act. He launched innovative programs and policies that he believed would lead to economic recovery. But he also remained true to certain basic principles that limited his range of action. Although some of Roosevelt's own advisers would later credit Hoover with introducing policies that paved the way for the New Deal, most Americans remembered him more for his caution than for his boldness in confronting the Great Depression.

Early Recovery Measures

Hoover's first response to the Depression reflected his belief that recovery depended in part upon restoring economic confidence. "The fundamental business of this country," he said the day after the stock market plummeted on "Black Thursday" in late October 1929, "that is, production and distribution of commodities, is on a sound and prosperous basis." To add substance to his claim, Hoover moved quickly to mobilize government and business in a partnership that he hoped would prevent a worsening of the economic downturn. He summoned leaders of business, labor, and agriculture to the White House and urged them to accept a program of voluntary cooperation for recovery. He implored businessmen not to cut production or lay off workers; he talked labor leaders into foregoing demands for higher wages or better hours.

At first, the president's appeals seemed to produce at least some of the cooperation he sought. But by mid-1931, economic conditions had deteriorated so much that the frail, voluntary structure he had erected quickly collapsed. Businessmen balked at keeping up full production, paying a full workforce, or investing in new plants at a time when demand for their goods was plummeting. Frightened industrialists soon began cutting production, laying off workers, and slashing wages. Hoover, committed to purely voluntary measures, was powerless to stop them.

Like his successor, Hoover attempted to use government spending as a tool for fighting the Depression. Rejecting the demands of fiscal conservatives that the government balance its own budget whatever the cost, the president proposed to Congress an increase of $423 million—then a substantial sum—in federal public works programs; and he exhorted state and local governments to engage in the "energetic yet prudent pursuit" of public construction. But unlike Roosevelt, Hoover was unwilling to fund such initiatives on a broad scale or for any long duration. While Hoover was not as committed to a balanced budget as some of his advisers, he would not tolerate deficits indefinitely. When economic conditions worsened, he became less willing to increase government spending, worrying instead about maintaining federal solvency. In 1932, at the depth of the Depression, he proposed a tax increase to help the government avoid a deficit.

Even before the stock market crash, Hoover had begun to construct a program of assistance for the troubled agricultural economy, which had been in its own depression for several years already. In April 1929, he proposed, and

Congress approved, the Agricultural Marketing Act, which established for the first time a government agency to help farmers maintain prices. A federally sponsored Farm Board would administer a budget of $500 million from which it could make loans to national marketing cooperatives or establish corporations to buy surpluses and thus raise prices. At the same time, Hoover attempted to protect American farmers from international competition by raising agricultural tariffs. The Smoot-Hawley Tariff of 1930 contained protective increases on seventy-five farm products and raised rates to the highest point in American history—to an average of fifty percent on protected commodities.

Neither the Agricultural Marketing Act nor the Smoot-Hawley Tariff, however, ultimately helped American farmers significantly. The Marketing Act relied on voluntary cooperation among farmers and gave the government no authority to do what the agricultural economy most badly needed: limit production. Hoover's call for a reduction of the wheat crop, for example, resulted in a drop in acreage of only one percent in Kansas. The Farm Board lacked sufficient funds to deal effectively with the crisis. Prices continued to fall despite its efforts. The Smoot-Hawley Tariff was an unqualified disaster—as 1,000 members of the American Economics Association had warned the president even before he signed it. It provoked foreign governments to enact trade restrictions of their own in reprisal, further diminishing the market for American agricultural goods. And it also raised rates on 925 manufactured goods, making industrial products more expensive for farmers to buy.

A Change of Direction

By the spring of 1931, Herbert Hoover's political position had deteriorated considerably. In the 1930 congressional elections, Democrats won control of the House and made substantial gains in the Senate. It was now clear that many Americans held the president personally to blame for the crisis. Shantytowns established on the outskirts of cities were labeled "Hoovervilles," old newspapers "Hoover blankets," and empty pockets "Hoover flags." In 1932, one writer borrowed the model of the Bible to write what he dubbed the 1932nd Psalm: "Hoover is my shepherd, I am in want, He maketh me to lie down on park benches, He leadeth me by still factories. . . . Yea, though I walk through the valley of soup kitchens, I am hungry." As the Depression wore on, the president remained the target of similar barbs, cruel jokes, and unrelenting personal attacks.

Progressive reformers urged the president to support more vigorous programs of relief and public spending. But Hoover resisted the idea. The president feared that federal relief programs on a large scale would soon become a paralyzing national "dole," which would undercut personal initiative, force down wages, and "endow the slackers." Instead, Hoover searched for signs of economic recovery, and for a moment in the spring of 1930 he seemed to find them. "I am convinced," he announced on May 1, 1930, "we have passed the worst and with continued effort we shall rapidly recover." Instead, the year's end brought even deeper economic woes.

Indeed, by the spring of 1931, an international financial panic had destroyed the illusion that the economic crisis was coming to an end. Throughout the 1920s, European nations had depended on loans from American banks to allow them to make payments on their debts. After 1929, when they could no longer get such loans, the financial fabric of several European nations began to unravel. In May 1931, the largest bank in Austria collapsed. Over the next several months, panic gripped the financial institutions of neighboring countries. European governments, desperate for sound assets, withdrew their gold reserves from American banks. European investors, in need of dollars to pay off their loans and protect their solvency, dumped their shares of American stocks onto the market, further depressing prices. Some European nations abandoned the gold standard and devalued their currencies, leaving the United States, which remained tied to gold, at a disadvantage in international trade. The American economy rapidly declined to new lows.

Hoover now argued that the economic crisis in the United States was not the result of problems in the American economy but of the collapse of the European financial system. He proposed a moratorium on the payment of war debts and reparations, and later on the payment of private debts as well. It was a sound proposal, but it was not enough to stop the downward slide.

By the time Congress convened in December 1931, conditions had grown so desperate that Hoover decided to support a series of measures designed to keep endangered banks afloat and protect homeowners from foreclosure on their mortgages. Most important was a bill passed in January 1932 establishing the Reconstruction Finance Corporation (RFC), a government agency whose purpose was to provide federal loans to troubled banks, railroads, and other businesses. It even made funds available to local governments to support public works projects and assist relief efforts. Unlike some earlier Hoover programs, it operated on a large scale. In 1932, the RFC had a budget of $1.5 billion for public works alone.

Nevertheless, the new agency failed to deal directly or forcefully enough with the real problems of the economy to produce any significant recovery. Because the RFC was permitted to lend funds only to those financial institutions with sufficient collateral, much of its money went to large banks and corporations. That fact prompted some critics to call the RFC a "bread line for big business." And at Hoover's insistence, it helped finance only those public works projects that promised ultimately to pay for themselves (toll bridges, public housing, and others). Its chairman, the conservative Texas banker Jesse Jones, prided himself on the solvency of his agency and followed sound, prudent banking practices. This meant that the RFC itself remained healthy by refusing to make loans to those institutions that most desperately needed them. Above all, the RFC did not have enough money to make any real impact on the Depression; and it did not even spend all the money it had. Of the $300 million available to support local relief efforts, the RFC lent out only $30 million in 1932. Of the $1.5 billion public works budget, it released only about twenty percent.

Fighting Back

For the first several years of the Depression, most Americans were either too stunned or too confused to raise many effective protests. By the middle of 1932, however, radical and dissident voices were becoming loud and pervasive. Although critics disagreed among themselves about the best course of action, they were united in their belief that present policies were failing utterly. Many groups urged the government to redress their specific needs; but most agreed on the need for immediate federal action to mend the broken economy.

Particularly vocal protests and demands came from organized American farmers. In the Midwest, farmers called for legislation, similar to the McNary-Haugen bill of the 1920s, by which the government would guarantee them a return on their crops at least equal to the cost of production. Lobbyists from the larger farm organizations pressured members of Congress to act, and some disgruntled farmers staged public protests in the capital. But neither the president nor Congress showed any signs of movement.

In the summer of 1932, a group of unhappy farm owners gathered in Des Moines, Iowa, to establish a new organization: the Farmers' Holiday Association, which endorsed the withholding of farm products from the market—in effect a farmers' strike. The strike began in August in western Iowa, spread briefly to a few neighboring areas, and succeeded in blockading several markets; but in the end it dissolved in failure. The scope of the effort was too modest to affect farm prices, and many farmers in the region refused to cooperate in any case. After several violent clashes between strikers and local authorities, the organization's leader, Milo Reno, called off the strike. Nevertheless, the uprising created considerable consternation in state governments in the farm belt and even more in Washington, where the president and much of Congress were facing a national election.

A more celebrated protest movement emerged from a less likely quarter: American veterans. In 1924, Congress had approved the payment of a $1,000 bonus to all those who had served in World War I, the money to be distributed beginning in 1945. By 1932, however, many veterans were demanding that the bonus be paid immediately. Hoover, concerned about balancing the budget, refused to comply. In June, more than 20,000 veterans, members of the self-proclaimed "Bonus Expeditionary Force" (after the "American Expeditionary Force" of World War I, in which the veterans had served) marched into Washington, built primitive camps around the city, and promised to stay until Congress approved legislation to pay the bonus. Camped out in the nation's capital, the Bonus Army dramatized the plight of the poor and the unemployed. Although a few of the veterans departed in July, after Congress had voted down

BONUS ARMY. On July 28, 1932, the U.S. Army drove the Bonus Army from its camp on lower Pennsylvania Avenue. Here troops, with rifles and fixed bayonets, advance through tear gas toward the protesting World War I veterans.

their proposal, most remained where they were. Many had lost their homes and had nowhere else to go.

The Bonus Army's continued presence in Washington was an embarrassment to President Hoover. Finally, in mid-July, he ordered police to clear the marchers out of several abandoned federal buildings in which they had been staying. A few marchers threw rocks at the police, and someone opened fire; two veterans fell dead. Hoover considered the incident evidence of dangerous radicalism. He ordered the U.S. Army to assist the police in clearing out the buildings.

General Douglas MacArthur, the army chief of staff, carried out the mission himself and greatly exceeded the president's orders. In full battle dress, he led the Third Cavalry (under the command of George S. Patton), two infantry regiments, a machine-gun detachment, and six tanks down Pennsylvania Avenue in pursuit of the Bonus Army. By his side was his deputy, Dwight D. Eisenhower. The veterans fled in terror as the troops hurled tear gas canisters and flailed at them with their bayonets. MacArthur followed them across the Anacostia River, where he ordered the soldiers to burn their tent city to the ground. More than 100 marchers were injured. One baby died.

The incident served as perhaps the final blow to Hoover's already battered political standing. Although many American newspapers (owned by conservative publishers) applauded the use of troops, much of the public was appalled. One journalist sympathetic to the marchers declared: "If the Army must be called out to make war on unarmed citizens, *this is no longer America.*" Hoover now stood confirmed as an aloof and insensitive figure, locked in the White House, uncomprehending of the distress around him. Hoover's cold and gloomy personality did nothing to challenge the public image, and some of his embattled statements at the time made his plight worse. "Nobody is actually starving," he assured reporters (inaccurately) in 1932. "The hoboes, for example, are better fed than they have ever been." The Great Engineer, the personification of the optimistic days of the 1920s, had become a symbol of the nation's failure to deal effectively with its startling reversal of fortune.

The Triumph of Roosevelt

As the 1932 presidential election approached, few people doubted the outcome. The Republican party dutifully renominated Herbert Hoover for a second term in office, but the lugubrious atmosphere of their convention made it clear that few delegates believed he could win. The Democrats, in the meantime, gathered jubilantly in Chicago to nominate the governor of New York, Franklin Delano Roosevelt.

Roosevelt had already been a well-known figure in the party for many years. A Hudson Valley aristocrat, a distant cousin of Theodore Roosevelt (a connection strengthened by his marriage in 1904 to the president's niece, Eleanor), and a handsome, charming young man, he had progressed rapidly: from a seat in the New York state legislature to a position as assistant secretary of the navy under Woodrow Wilson during World War I to his party's vice presidential nomination in 1920 on the ill-fated ticket with James M. Cox, a career path markedly similar to that of his cousin Theodore. Less than a year later, however, he was stricken with polio. He was never again able to walk without the use of crutches and braces. But as a result of indefatigable effort, much personal courage, and the constant urging of his wife and his close aide Louis Howe, he built up his physical and emotional strength and returned to politics in 1928. When Al Smith received the Democratic nomination for president that year, Roosevelt was elected to succeed him as governor. In 1930, he easily won reelection.

Roosevelt worked no miracles in New York, but he did initiate enough positive programs of government assistance to be able to present himself as a more energetic and imaginative leader than Hoover. Equally important, he avoided the inflammatory cultural issues (religion, race, prohibition) that had so divided the Democratic party in the 1920s. By emphasizing the economic grievances that most Democrats shared, he assembled a coalition within the party that enabled him to win the nomination. In a dramatic break with tradition, he flew to Chicago to address the convention in person and accept the nomination.

In the course of his acceptance speech, Roosevelt aroused the delegates with his ringing promise: "I pledge you, I pledge myself, to a new deal for the American people," giving his program a name that would long endure. Neither then nor in the subsequent campaign, however, did Roosevelt give much indication of what that program would be. Herbert Hoover's unpopularity virtually ensured Roosevelt's election; his main concern was to avoid offending voters unnecessarily.

There was, however, evidence of some important differences between Roosevelt and Hoover. Drawing from the ideas of a talented team of Columbia University professors (whom the press quickly dubbed the "Brains Trust"),

FRANKLIN DELANO ROOSEVELT. Using his dazzling smile and jaunty cigarette holder, Roosevelt captivated millions of Americans with his buoyancy and charm. As he rides in an open car near his home in Hyde Park, New York in 1937, the president appears the very picture of good health and physical vigor. Since a bout with polio as a young man in 1921, however, Roosevelt had no use of his legs. Through elaborate measures, Roosevelt largely hid his paralysis from the public.

Roosevelt endorsed during his campaign an amalgam of ideas that combined old progressive reform principles with some of the newer ideas of associationalism that had gained currency in the 1920s. He also embraced more traditional ideas; he called for a balanced budget, and he attacked Hoover for his failure to provide one. Hoover liked to insist that the Depression was international in origin and that any attempt to combat it must be international as well. Roosevelt, in contrast, portrayed the crisis as a domestic (and Republican) problem and argued that the most important solutions could be found at home. Above all, perhaps, Roosevelt's style—his dazzling smile, his floppy broad-brimmed hat, his cigarette holder held at a jaunty angle between his teeth, his skillful oratory, his lively wit—all combined to win him a wide personal popularity only vaguely related to the specifics of his programs.

In November, to the surprise of no one, Roosevelt won by a landslide. He received 57.4 percent of the popular vote to Hoover's 39.7. In the electoral college, the result was even more overwhelming. Hoover carried Pennsylvania, Connecticut, Vermont, New Hampshire, and Maine. Roosevelt won everything else. Democrats achieved majorities in both houses of Congress. It was a broad and convincing mandate, but it was not yet clear what Roosevelt intended to do with it.

The Interregnum

The period between the November 1932 election and Roosevelt's March 1933 inauguration (that long period was shortened with the 1933 passage of the Twentieth Amendment to the Constitution) was a season of growing economic crisis. In some ways, these were among the darkest days of the Great Depression. One Washington newspaperman reported: "I come home from the hill every night filled with gloom. I see on the streets filthy, ragged, desperate looking men such as I had never seen before." Across the country, conditions seemed little better. In Seattle, some families endured nights shrouded in darkness, unable to pay for candles or electricity. Jane Addams, founder of Chicago's Hull House settlement, wrote to a friend: "One has a sense of 'standing by' if only to hear the stories of the unemployed. It has been like a disaster or flood, fire or earthquake, this universal wiping out of resources." Roosevelt adviser Rexford Tugwell recorded a similar sense of alarm in his diary in December 1932. "No one can live and work in New York this winter without a profound sense of uneasiness. Never, in modern times, I should think, has there been so widespread unemployment and such moving distress from sheer hunger and cold." Although presidents-elect traditionally do not involve themselves directly in government, this was a moment of great national urgency. In a series of brittle exchanges with Roosevelt in the months following the election, Hoover tried to exact from the president-elect a pledge to maintain policies of economic orthodoxy. Roosevelt genially refused.

In February, only a month before the inauguration, a new crisis developed when the American banking system began to collapse with alarming speed. Public confidence in the banks was ebbing; depositors were withdrawing their money in panic; and one bank after another was closing its doors and declaring bankruptcy. In mid-February, the governor of Michigan, one of the states hardest hit by the panic, ordered all banks temporarily closed. Other states soon followed, and by the end of the month banking activity was restricted drastically in every state but one. Hoover again asked Roosevelt to give prompt public assurances that there would be no tinkering with the currency, no heavy borrowing, no unbalancing of the budget. "I realize," he wrote a Republican senator at the time, "that if these declarations be made by the president-elect, he will have ratified the whole major program of the Republican Administration." Roosevelt realized the same thing and again refused.

March 4, 1933, was, therefore, a day of both economic crisis and considerable personal bitterness. On that morning, Herbert Hoover, convinced that the United States was headed for disaster, rode glumly down Pennsylvania Avenue with a beaming, buoyant Franklin Roosevelt, who would shortly be sworn in as the thirty-second president of the United States. Now upon Roosevelt would fall responsibility for delivering the nation from its economic miseries. Whatever plans he had hatched remained largely shrouded in mystery. Yet despite his assumption of such awesome responsibility, Roosevelt's self-confidence was striking on inauguration day 1933. He kept his address short and offered a memorable reassurance to the nation he was about to lead: "The only thing we have to fear is fear itself."

THE NEW DEAL OF FRANKLIN ROOSEVELT

Franklin Roosevelt served longer as president than anyone else before or since, and during his twelve years in office he became more central to the life of the nation than any chief executive before him. More importantly, his administration constructed a series of programs that permanently altered the federal government and its relationship to society. "We backed into the Twentieth Century," Roosevelt adviser Gardiner C. Means later recalled, "describing our actual economy in terms of the small enterprises of the Nineteenth Century. . . . What Roosevelt and the New Deal did was to turn about and face the realities."

The New Deal was intensely controversial in its own time, and much of it remains controversial now. But almost no one questions its importance. The New Deal created many of the broad outlines of the political world we know today. It constructed the foundations of the federal welfare system. It extended national regulation over new areas of the economy. It presided over the birth of the modern labor movement. It made the government a major force in the agricultural economy. It created a powerful coalition within the Democratic party that would dominate American politics for most of the next thirty years. And it produced the beginnings of a new liberal ideology that would govern reform efforts for several decades after the war.

One thing the New Deal did not do, however, was end the Great Depression. It did help stop the disastrous downward spiral of 1933. For a time after there was a limited, if erratic, recovery in some areas of the economy. But by the end of 1939, many of the basic problems of the Depression remained unsolved. An estimated fifteen percent of the labor force was still out of work, and the gross national product was no larger than it had been ten years before.

Emergency Measures

Roosevelt's first task upon taking office was to alleviate the panic that was threatening to create chaos in the financial system. He did so in part by force of personality and in part by constructing very rapidly an ambitious and diverse program of legislation.

Much of Roosevelt's success was a result of his ebullient personality. He projected an infectious optimism that proved immensely reassuring, and he took pains to communicate his confidence to the American people through new means. He was the first president to make regular use of the radio, and his friendly "fireside chats," during which he explained his programs and plans to the people, helped build public confidence in the administration. Roosevelt held frequent informal press conferences and won the respect and the friendship of most reporters. Their regard for him was such that by unwritten agreement, no journalist ever photographed the president being carried into or out of his car or being wheeled in his wheelchair. Much of the American public remained unaware throughout the Roosevelt years that the president's legs remained completely paralyzed.

But Roosevelt could not, and did not, rely on image alone. On March 6, two days after taking office, he issued a proclamation closing all American banks for four days until Congress could meet in special session to consider banking reform legislation. So great was the panic about bank failures that the "bank holiday," as the president euphemistically described it, created a general sense of relief. Three days later, Roosevelt sent to Congress the Emergency Banking Act, a generally conservative bill (much of it drafted by holdovers from the Hoover administration) designed primarily to protect the larger banks from being dragged down by the weakness of smaller ones. The bill provided for Treasury Department inspection of all banks before they would be allowed to reopen, for federal assistance to some troubled institutions, and for a thorough reorganization of those in the greatest difficulty. A confused and frightened Congress passed the bill within four hours of its introduction. "I can assure you," Roosevelt told the public on March 12, in his first fireside chat, "that it is safer to keep your money in a reopened bank than under the mattress." Whatever else the new law accomplished, it helped dispel the panic. Three-quarters of the banks in the Federal Reserve system reopened within the next three days, and $1 billion in hoarded currency and gold flowed back into them within a month. The immediate banking crisis was over.

On the morning after passage of the Emergency Banking Act, Roosevelt sent Congress another measure—the Economy Act—designed to convince fiscally conservative Americans (and especially the business community) that the federal government was in safe, responsible hands. The act proposed to balance the federal budget by cutting the salaries of government employees and reducing pensions to veterans by as much as fifteen percent. Otherwise, the president warned, the nation faced a $1 billion deficit. Like the banking bill, this one passed through Congress almost instantly—despite heated protests from some congressional progressives.

Roosevelt also moved in his first days in office to put to rest one of the divisive issues of the 1920s. He supported and then signed a bill to legalize the manufacture and sale of beer with a 3.2 percent alcohol content—an interim measure pending the repeal of Prohibition, for which a constitutional amendment (the twenty-first) was already in process. The amendment was ratified later in 1933.

A New Deal for Agriculture

The emergency measures taken by Roosevelt in his first days in office were largely stopgaps, designed to deal with immediate crises and to buy time for more comprehensive programs and policies. The first such program was the Agricultural Adjustment Act, which Congress passed in May 1933. It reflected the demands of various farm organizations and the ideas of Henry A. Wallace, Roosevelt's progressive secretary of agriculture. Some aspects of the bill reworked long-cherished agricultural schemes (including McNary-Haugen). But more importantly, it provided a means for reducing crop production to end agricultural surpluses and halt the downward spiral of farm prices.

Under the "domestic allotment" system of the act, producers of seven basic commodities (wheat, cotton, corn, hogs, rice, tobacco, and dairy products) would decide on production limits for their crops. The government, through the Agricultural Adjustment Administration (AAA), would then tell individual farmers how much they should plant and would pay them subsidies for leaving some of their land idle. A tax on food processing (for example, the milling of wheat) would provide the funds for the new payments. Farm prices were to be subsidized up to the point of parity.

Because the 1933 agricultural season was already under way by the time the AAA began operations, the agency oversaw a large-scale destruction of existing crops and livestock to reduce surpluses. Six million pigs and 220,000 sows were slaughtered. Cotton farmers plowed under a quarter of their crop. In a society plagued by want, in which many families were suffering from malnutrition and starvation, it was difficult for the government to explain the need for destroying surpluses; the crop and livestock destruction remained controversial for many years. As one sharecropper later explained, "What bothered me about the Roosevelt time was when they come out with this business that you had to plow up a certain amount of your crop, especially cotton. I didn't understand, 'cause it was good cotton. And seein' all this cattle killed. Bein' raised with stock, to me it was kind of a human feelin' we had toward them. . . . When I listened to those cows and looked at how they were carryin' on . . . I ran up to the house and I sit up there a long time and then I went to cryin'." Beginning in 1934, however, the government used less provocative methods for limiting crop and livestock production—paying farmers for limiting their planting and breeding from the start.

The results of the AAA efforts were in many ways heartening. Prices for farm commodities did indeed rise in the years after 1933, and gross farm income increased by half in the first three years of the New Deal. The agricultural economy as a whole emerged from the 1930s stabler and more prosperous than it had been in many years. The AAA did, however, tend to favor larger farmers over smaller ones, particularly since local administration of its programs often fell into the hands of the most powerful producers in a community. New Deal farm programs actually dispossessed some struggling farmers, even if unintentionally. In the cotton belt, for example, planters who were reducing their acreage evicted tenants and sharecroppers and fired many field hands.

In January 1936, the Supreme Court struck down the crucial provisions of the Agricultural Adjustment Act, arguing that the government had no constitutional authority to require farmers to limit production. But within a few weeks the administration had secured passage of new legislation (the Soil Conservation and Domestic Allotment Act), which survived judicial scrutiny. It permitted the government to pay farmers to reduce production so as to "conserve soil," prevent erosion, and accomplish other secondary goals. It also attempted to correct one of the injustices of the original act: its failure to protect sharecroppers and tenant farmers. Now landlords were required to share the payments they received for cutting back production with those who worked their land. The new requirements, however, were largely evaded.

The administration launched other efforts to assist poor farmers as well. The Resettlement Administration, established in 1935, and its successor, the Farm Security Administration, created in 1937, provided loans to help farmers cultivating submarginal soil to relocate on better lands. But the programs never moved more than a few thousand farmers. More effective was the Rural Electrification Administration, created in 1935, which worked to make electric power available for the first time to thousands of farmers through utility cooperatives.

Although the record of New Deal agricultural programs was mixed, many farmers drew hope from the efforts of the Roosevelt administration to address the disastrous farm economy. One Iowa farmer recalled of the New Deal, "People could now see daylight and hope. It was a whole transformation of attitude. . . . It was Wallace who saved us, put us back on our feet. He understood our problems." Although the benefits of agricultural reform were distributed unevenly, it appeared to many farmers that society was finally making some headway in meeting their needs.

Plans for Industrial Recovery

Among the more daunting problems Roosevelt faced was constructing some strategy for rescuing the industrial economy, which was continuing its long downward spiral. Ever since 1931, leaders of the U.S. Chamber of Commerce and many others had been urging the government to adopt an antideflation scheme that would permit trade associations to cooperate in stabilizing prices within their industries. Existing antitrust laws clearly forbade such practices, but businesspeople argued that the economic emergency justified a suspension of the restrictions. Herbert Hoover had refused to endorse suspension of the antitrust laws. But the Roosevelt administration was more receptive.

In exchange for relaxing antitrust provisions, however, New Dealers insisted on additional provisions that would deal with other economic problems. Businesspeople would have to make important concessions to labor—recognize their right to organize and bargain collectively through unions—to ensure that the incomes of workers would rise along with prices. And to ensure that consumer buying power would not lag behind, the administration added a major program of public works spending designed to pump needed funds into the economy. The result of these and many other impulses was the National Industrial Recovery Act (NIRA), one of the most complicated pieces of legislation in American history to that point. Congress passed it in June 1933. Roosevelt, signing the bill, called it "the most important and far-reaching legislation ever enacted by the American Congress." Businesspeople hailed it as the beginning of a new era of cooperation between government and industry. Labor leaders praised it as a "Magna Carta" for trade unions.

At first, the new program appeared to work miracles. At its center was a new federal agency, the National Recovery Administration (NRA). Its director was the flamboyant and energetic Hugh S. Johnson, a retired general and successful businessman. Johnson envisioned himself as a kind of evangelist, whose major mission was to generate public enthusiasm and corporate support for the NRA. He approached his task in two ways.

First, he called on every business establishment in the nation to accept a temporary "blanket code": a minimum wage of between thirty and forty cents an hour, a maximum workweek of thirty-five to forty hours, and the abolition of child labor. The result, he claimed, would be to raise consumer purchasing power, increase employment, and eliminate the sweatshop. To generate enthusiasm for the blanket code, Johnson devised a symbol—the famous NRA Blue Eagle—which employers who accepted the provisions could display in their windows. Soon Blue Eagle flags, posters, and stickers, carrying the NRA slogan "We Do Our Part," were decorating commercial establishments in every part of the

THE BLUE EAGLE. The emblem of the National Recovery
Administration was the Blue Eagle, clutching gear works in
its left talons and thunderbolts (symbolizing electric power)
in the right. The symbol, with its accompanying slogan
"We Do Our Part," appeared in the windows of shops and
households across the country as expressions of support for
the NRA's blanket code of minimum wages, a maximum
work week of 40 hours, and an end to child labor.

country—just as parents of soldiers or purchasers of war bonds had decorated
their homes and offices with patriotic reminders during World War I.

At the same time, Johnson was busy negotiating another, more specific set
of codes with leaders of the nation's major industries. These industrial codes set
floors below which no company would lower prices or wages in its search for a
competitive advantage, and they included agreements on maintaining employment and production. He quickly won agreements from almost every major industry in the country.

From the beginning, however, the NRA encountered serious difficulties,
and the entire effort ultimately dissolved in failure. The codes themselves were

hastily and often poorly written. Administering them was far beyond the capacities of federal officials with no prior experience in running so vast a program. Large producers consistently dominated the code-writing process and ensured that the new regulations would work to their advantage and to the disadvantage of smaller firms. And the codes at times did more than simply set floors under prices; they actively and artificially raised them—at times to levels higher than was necessary to ensure a profit and far higher than market forces would have dictated. Attempts to raise wages and increase consumer purchasing power did not progress as quickly as the efforts to raise prices.

Among the most important provisions of the National Industrial Recovery Act—at least symbolically—was section 7(a). It promised workers the right to form unions and engage in collective bargaining and encouraged many workers to join unions for the first time. But section 7(a) contained no enforcement mechanisms. Hence recognition of unions by employers (and thus the significant wage increases the unions were committed to winning) did not follow. United Mine Workers' President John L. Lewis used the legislation to advance a broadscale organizing campaign in 1933, complete with placards boasting, rather dubiously, "The President Wants You To Organize." At the same time, however, many employers sought to undermine section 7(a) by forming company unions as collective bargaining units.

Problems of administration also dogged the Public Works Administration (PWA) established by the NIRA. It was designed to administer spending programs for public works projects and was directed by Secretary of the Interior Harold Ickes. But under Ickes's parsimonious administration, the PWA only gradually allowed the $3.3 billion in public works funds to trickle out. "We set for ourselves the perhaps unattainable ideal of administering the greatest fund for construction in the history of the world without scandal," Ickes explained. But his careful distribution of funds did little initially to address the goals of reducing unemployment and stimulating the economy. Not until 1938 was the PWA budget pumping an appreciable amount of money into the economy.

Perhaps the clearest evidence of the NRA's failure was that industrial production actually declined in the months after its establishment—from an index of 101 in July 1933 to seventy-one in November—despite (some argued because of) the rise in prices that the codes had helped to create. By the spring of 1934, therefore, the NRA was besieged by criticism. Businessmen were flouting its provisions, cutting wages and prices, or violating agreements on levels of production—claiming as they did so that the wage requirements of the codes (which many of them were ignoring anyway) were making it impossible to earn adequate profits. Employers were also openly ignoring the provisions requiring them to bargain with unions, and so organized labor grew increasingly hostile toward the NRA. Economists were charging that the price-fixing encouraged by the codes was undermining efforts to raise purchasing power. Reformers were complaining that the NRA was encouraging economic concentration and monopoly. A national Recovery Review Board, chaired by the famous criminal lawyer Clarence Darrow, reported in the spring of 1934 that the NRA was excessively dominated by big business and unduly encouraging of monopoly. Hugh Johnson's angry, vituperative response served only to undermine the agency's prestige even further. That fall, Roosevelt pressured Johnson to resign and established a new board of directors to oversee the NRA. Then in 1935, the Supreme Court intervened.

The constitutional basis for the NRA had been Congress's power to regulate commerce among the states, a power the administration had interpreted very broadly but that the Court continued to interpret narrowly. The case before the Court—*Schechter Poultry Corp. v. U.S.*—involved alleged NRA code violations (including the sale of diseased poultry, hence the tag "the sick chicken case") by the Schechter brothers, who operated a wholesale poultry business confined to Brooklyn, New York. The Court ruled unanimously that the Schechters were not engaged in interstate commerce and, further, that Congress had unconstitutionally delegated legislative power to the president to draft the NRA codes. It nullified the legislation establishing the agency.

Roosevelt denounced the justices for their "horse-and-buggy" interpretation of the interstate commerce clause. He was rightly concerned, for the reasoning in the Schechter case threatened many other New Deal programs as well, especially given the concurrence in the decision of some of the more progressive Supreme Court justices. Indeed, shortly after the Schecter case and two other less important but also ominous cases were decided, Justice Brandeis privately urged the president's lawyers to warn the Chief Executive: "You have heard three decisions. They change everything. The Court was unanimous. . . . The President has been living in a fool's paradise." But the destruction of the NRA itself may have been a blessing for the New Deal, providing it with a convenient way to abolish the failed experiment. "You might say," one Roosevelt adviser later offered, "NRA's greatest contribution to our society is that it proved that self-regulation by industry doesn't work." Whatever its benefits and limits, the NRA seemed to presage a much-changed role for the federal government in shaping the industrial economy. With the NRA, New Dealer Gardiner Means asserted, "laissez faire in the Nineteenth Century manner was ended." The program—both through its achievements and through its failures—suggested that "the Government had a role to play in industrial activity."

Regional Planning

The AAA and the NRA primarily reflected the beliefs of New Dealers who favored economic planning but wanted private interests (farmers or business leaders) to dominate the planning process. In some areas, however, other reformers —those who believed that the government itself should be the chief planning agent in the economy—managed to establish dominance. Their most conspicuous success, and one of the most celebrated accomplishments of the New Deal,

THE TENNESSEE VALLEY AUTHORITY

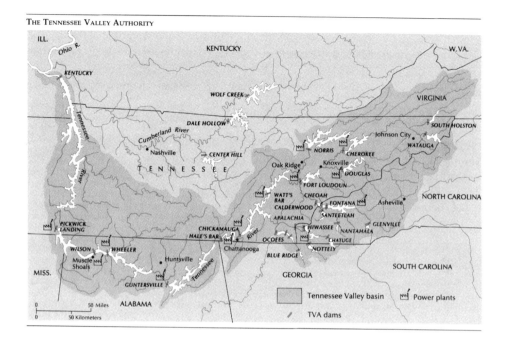

was an unprecedented experiment in regional planning: the Tennessee Valley Authority (TVA).

The TVA had its roots in a political controversy of the 1920s. Progressive reformers had agitated for years for public development of the nation's water resources as a source of cheap electric power. In particular, they had urged completion of a great dam at Muscle Shoals on the Tennessee River in Alabama—a dam begun during World War I but left unfinished when the war ended. Opposition from the utilities companies, however, had been too powerful to overcome.

But in 1932, one of the great utility empires—that of the electricity magnate Samuel Insull—had collapsed spectacularly, amid widely publicized exposés of corruption. Hostility to the utilities soon grew so intense that they were no longer able to block the public-power movement. The result was legislation supported by the president and enacted by Congress in May 1933 creating the Tennessee Valley Authority. The TVA was intended not only to complete the dam at Muscle Shoals and build others in the region, and not only to generate and sell electricity from them to the public at reasonable rates. It was also to be the agent for a comprehensive redevelopment of the entire region: for stopping the disastrous flooding that had plagued the Tennessee Valley for centuries, for encouraging the development of local industries, for supervising a substantial program of reforestation, and for helping farmers improve productivity.

Opposition by conservatives within the administration ultimately blocked some especially ambitious social planning projects proposed by the more visionary TVA administrators. But the project revitalized the region in numerous ways. It built dams and waterways. It virtually eliminated flooding in the region. It provided electricity to thousands who had never before had it. Throughout the country, largely because of the "yardstick" provided by the TVA's cheap production of electricity, private power rates declined. Still, the Authority worked no miracles. The Tennessee Valley remained a generally impoverished region despite its efforts. And like many other New Deal programs, it made no serious effort to challenge local customs and racial prejudices.

Despite such limits, and despite charges from conservatives that the TVA was socialism, the program proved enormously popular among many who lived in the region, as Roosevelt had anticipated. When asked how he would explain the character of the federal initiative, the president replied: "I'll tell them it's neither fish nor fowl but whatever it is, it will taste awfully good to the people of the Tennessee Valley." At the very least, the TVA demonstrated the power of government intervention in planning for regional development and the use and management of natural resources.

Financial Initiatives

For those who had experienced the downward slide of financial and banking institutions during the Great Depression there could be little doubt that something had to be done to prevent a recurrence. The struggling economy added a special immediacy to efforts to address money and banking policy questions. Thus financial reforms soon became a pressing matter in Roosevelt's administration. Roosevelt was not an inflationist at heart, but he soon came to consider the gold standard a major obstacle to the restoration of adequate prices. On April 18, 1933, the president made the move away from the gold standard official with an executive order. A few weeks later, Congress passed legislation confirming his decision. By itself, the partial repudiation of the gold standard meant relatively little. But both before and after the April decision, the administration experimented in various ways with manipulating the value of the dollar—by making substantial purchases of gold and silver and later by establishing a new, fixed standard for the dollar (reducing its gold content substantially from the 1932 amount).

The resort to government-managed currency—that is, to a dollar whose value could be raised or lowered by government actions according to economic circumstances—created an important precedent for future federal policies. It permanently altered the relationship between the public and private sectors. It did not, however, have any immediate impact on the depressed American economy.

Through other legislation, the early New Deal increased federal authority over previously unregulated or weakly regulated areas of the economy. The Glass-Steagall Act of June 1933 gave the government authority to curb irresponsible speculation by banks. More important, perhaps, it established the Federal Deposit Insurance Corporation, which guaranteed all bank deposits up to $2,500. In other words, even should a bank fail, small depositors would be able to recover their money. Finally, in 1935, Congress passed a major banking act that transferred much of the authority once wielded by the regional Federal Reserve banks to the Federal Reserve Board in Washington.

To protect investors in the stock market, Congress passed the so-called Truth in Securities Act of 1933, requiring corporations issuing new securities to provide full and accurate information about them to the public. Another act of June 1934 established the Securities and Exchange Commission (SEC) to police the stock market. Among other things, the establishment of the SEC was an indication of how far the financial establishment had fallen in public estimation. In earlier years, J. P. Morgan and other important financiers could have wielded enough influence to stop such government interference in the financial world. Now Morgan could not even get a respectful hearing on Capitol Hill. The criminal trials of a number of once-respected Wall Street figures for grand larceny and fraud (including the conviction and imprisonment of Richard Whitney, one-time head of the New York Stock Exchange and a close Morgan associate) eroded the public stature of the financial community still further.

Government Relief Measures

Millions of Americans were unemployed and in desperate need of assistance in 1933, and the relief efforts of private organizations and state and local governments were unable to meet the demand. The Roosevelt administration did not consider relief its most important task, but it recognized the necessity of doing something to help impoverished Americans survive until the New Deal could revive the economy to the point where relief might not be necessary.

Among Roosevelt's first acts as president was the establishment of the Federal Emergency Relief Administration (FERA), which provided cash grants to states to prop up bankrupt relief agencies. To administer the program, he chose the director of the New York State relief agency, Harry Hopkins, who disbursed the FERA grants widely and rapidly. Hopkins expressed impatience with those who counseled patient and long-term planning. "People don't eat in the long run," he said, "they eat every day." At the same time, both Hopkins and Roosevelt had misgivings about establishing a government dole. "It is probably going to undermine the independence of hundreds of thousands of families," Hopkins once lamented.

They felt somewhat more comfortable with another form of public assistance: work relief. Unlike the dole, Hopkins believed, work relief "preserves a man's morale. It saves his skill. It gives him a chance to do something socially useful." Thus when it became clear that the FERA grants would not be sufficient to pull the country through the winter, the administration established a second program: the Civil Works Administration (CWA). Between November and April, it put more than 4 million people to work on temporary projects. Some of them were of lasting value, such as the construction of roads, schools, and parks; others were little more than makework. To Hopkins, however, the important thing was pumping money into an economy badly in need of it and providing assistance to people with nowhere else to turn. This use of government spending to stimulate the economy—known at the time as "pump priming" and later as Keynesian economics—was one of the New Deal's most important contributions to public policy. But in 1933, at least, members of the administration were only vaguely aware of the broad effects of this spending on the economy as a whole.

Evidence of this limited view of the value of government spending was that most of these early relief programs had short lives. Like the FERA, the CWA was intended to be only a temporary expedient. In the spring of 1934, the president began to dismantle the agency, and he ultimately disbanded it altogether. Most economists now agree that massive and sustained government spending would have been the quickest and most effective way to end the Depression. But few policymakers in the 1930s shared that belief.

Roosevelt's favorite relief project was the Civilian Conservation Corps. Established in the first weeks of the new administration, the CCC was designed to provide employment to some of the millions of urban young men who could find no jobs in the cities and who, unemployed and restless, were raising fears of urban violence. At the same time, it was intended to advance the work of conser-

THE CIVILIAN CONSERVATION CORPS.   Firefighters in the Civilian Conservation Corps battle a blaze in the West in this photograph from the 1930s. The CCC, which provided work to millions of unemployed young men, was Roosevelt's favorite New Deal program.

vation and reforestation—goals Roosevelt had long cherished. The CCC created a series of camps in national parks and forests and in other rural and wilderness settings. There young men (women were excluded from the program) worked in a semimilitary environment on such projects as planting trees, building reservoirs, developing parks, and improving agricultural irrigation. CCC camps were segregated by race, the vast majority reserved for whites, a few open to blacks.

Mortgage relief was a pressing need for millions of farm owners and homeowners. The Farm Credit Administration, which within two years refinanced one fifth of all farm mortgages in the United States, was one response to that problem. The Frazier-Lemke Farm Bankruptcy Act of 1933 was another. It enabled some farmers to regain their land even after foreclosure on their mortgages. Despite such efforts, however, twenty-five percent of all American farm owners had lost their land by 1934. Homeowners were similarly troubled, and in June 1933 the administration established the Home Owners' Loan Corporation, which by 1936 had refinanced the mortgages of more than 1 million householders. A year later, Congress established the Federal Housing Administration to insure mortgages for new construction and home repairs—a measure that combined an effort to provide relief with a program to stimulate lasting recovery of the construction industry.

The relief efforts of the first two years of the New Deal were intended to be limited and temporary. They stressed programs that provided Americans with some assistance in getting back on their feet. And although they had the effect of significantly enlarging government responsibility for the needs of the people, they surfaced and won support in large part because they answered immediate needs posed by the Great Depression. It is true that some New Deal relief programs answered a cry for reform that dated back at least to the progressive era. Yet in stressing the importance of work, individual responsibility, and the need to avoid a permanent welfare system, they also reflected values that had long set limits on American social policies. At the same time, the New Deal relief initiatives encouraged those who hoped to put in place more sweeping social welfare measures. In the end, the creation of a permanent welfare system would be one of the New Deal's most important and lasting accomplishments.

CHAPTER FOURTEEN

Challenging the New Deal

∼

Seldom has an American president enjoyed such remarkable popularity as Franklin Roosevelt did during his first two years in office. But by early 1935, with no end to the Depression yet in sight, the New Deal was beginning to find itself the target of fierce public criticism. For many, the early New Deal restored faith and hope in the American economy and in democracy. But it also inspired larger expectations for government and fueled, among some, insistent and even radical demands for more sweeping initiatives. Also rumbling barely beneath the surface were powerful conservative currents vigorously opposed to the growth of federal power that was so integral to the New Deal. Partly in response to those who complained he was not doing enough to bring about recovery, and partly to demonstrate to those who feared he was doing too much that government action could be healthy and effective, the president launched an ambitious new program of legislation in the spring of 1935 that has often been called the "Second New Deal."

THE NEW DEAL IN TRANSITION

It was inevitable, given the persistence of the Depression and Roosevelt's attempts to challenge an array of vested interests, that his New Deal would inspire widespread criticism. What was notable about these complaints when they came, however, was the broad ideological spectrum they spanned.

Critics from the Right and Left

Some of the most strident attacks on the New Deal came from critics on the right. Roosevelt had tried for a time to conciliate conservatives and business leaders. But by the end of 1934, it was clear that the American right in general, and much of the corporate world in particular, had become irreconcilably hostile to the New Deal. So intense was conservative animosity toward the New Deal's "reckless spending," "economic crackpots," and "socialist" reforms that some of Roosevelt's critics could not even bear to say the president's name. They called him, simply and bitterly, "that man in the White House."

In August 1934, a group of the most fervent (and wealthiest) Roosevelt opponents, led by members of the Du Pont family, formed the American Liberty League, designed specifically to arouse public opposition to the New Deal's "dictatorial" policies and its supposed attacks on free enterprise. "All the big guns have started shooting," Roosevelt complained privately of the founding of the Liberty League. "Their organization has already been labeled the I CAN'T TAKE IT CLUB." The new organization generated wide publicity and caused some concern within the administration, but it was never able to expand its constituency much beyond the northern industrialists who had founded it. At its peak, membership in the organization numbered only about 125,000.

The real impact of the Liberty League and other conservative attacks on Roosevelt was not at first to undermine the president's political strength. It was, rather, to convince Roosevelt that his efforts to conciliate the business community had failed. By 1936, he no longer harbored any illusions about cooperation with conservatives. The forces of "organized money," he said near the end of his campaign for reelection, "are unanimous in their hate for me—and I welcome their hatred." At their political convention in 1936, the Republicans had, in fact, portrayed Roosevelt's New Deal as a debauched spending and taxing spree. Borrowing a theme from "Three Blind Mice," the keynote speaker, Senator Frederick Steiver, recited: "Three long years! . . . /Full of grief and tears/ Roosevelt gave us to understand/ If we would lend a helping hand/ He'd lead us to the promised land/ For three long years!" Roosevelt characterized his conservative critics as "economic royalists" who complained "we seek to overthrow the institutions of America. What they really complain of is that we seek to take away their power."

Roosevelt's critics on the left also managed to produce alarm among some supporters of the administration; but like the conservatives, they proved to have only limited strength. The Communist party, the Socialist party, and other radical and semiradical organizations were at times harshly critical of Roosevelt. A publication of the Southern Tenant Farmers' Union observed of Roosevelt in 1936 that "too often the progressive word has been the clothing for a conservative act. Too often he has talked like a cropper and acted like a planter." It was apparent to those on the left that Roosevelt's agenda differed fundamentally from their own. "Roosevelt emerged to talk about the necessity of giving people relief," one Communist organizer complained. "One thing that many do not recall was his statement that he was out to save capitalism from itself. . . . he doled out hundreds of dollars to workers, while millions were given to banks, the railroads and other industries." Still, radical organizations were sympathetic to some New Deal initiatives. And they were also uncertain about how best to combine their commitment to radical change with their fervent opposition to the growth of fascism elsewhere in the world. The Communist party, in particular, spent much of the 1930s tacitly and at times explicitly supporting the Roosevelt programs.

Popular Protest

More menacing to the New Deal than either the conventional right or left was a group of dissident political movements that defied easy ideological classification. Some were marginal "crackpot" organizations with little popular following. Others gained substantial public support within particular states and regions. Three men, however, succeeded in mobilizing genuinely national followings.

Dr. Francis E. Townsend, an elderly California physician, rose from obscurity to lead a movement of more than 5 million members with his plan for federal pensions for the elderly. According to the Townsend Plan, all Americans over the age of sixty would receive monthly government pensions of 200 dollars, provided they retired (thus freeing jobs for younger, unemployed Americans) and spent the money in full each month (which would pump needed funds into the economy). By 1935, the Townsend Plan had attracted the support of many older men and women. And while the plan itself made little progress in Congress, the public sentiment behind it helped build support for the Social Security system, which Congress did approve in 1935.

Father Charles E. Coughlin, a Catholic priest in the Detroit suburb of Royal Oak, Michigan, achieved even greater renown (and eventually great notoriety) through his weekly sermons broadcast nationally over the radio. He criticized "rapacious capitalists" for their abdication of social responsibility; and he proposed a series of monetary reforms—remonetization of silver, issuing of greenbacks, and nationalization of the banking system—that he insisted would restore prosperity and ensure economic justice. At first a warm supporter of Franklin Roosevelt, he had by 1934 become disheartened by what he claimed was the president's failure to deal harshly enough with the "money powers." In the spring of 1935, he established his own political organization, the National Union for Social Justice, which some believed was a first step toward forming a new political party. He was also displaying an apparently remarkable influence in Congress. (An avalanche of telegrams inspired by a Coughlin radio sermon was generally believed to have been responsible for the defeat in the Senate of a treaty admitting the United States to the World Court.) And he was attracting public support throughout much of the nation—primarily from Catholics, but from others as well. He was widely believed to have one of the largest regular radio audiences of anyone in America.

Most alarming of all to the administration was the growing national popularity of Senator Huey P. Long of Louisiana. Long had risen to power in his home state through his strident attacks on the banks, oil companies, and utilities,

HUEY LONG.   Among Roosevelt's most worrisome critics
was Huey Long of Louisiana who used his formidable
political and oratorical skills to challenge the president.
Long is pictured making his points at a 1934 debate in
New York City with socialist leader Norman Thomas.
Long passionately disputed the debate's resolution that
"Capitalism is Doomed and Cannot Now Be Saved
by a Redistribution of Wealth."

and on the conservative political oligarchy allied with them. Elected governor in
1928, he launched an assault on his opposition so thorough and forceful that
they were soon left with virtually no political power at all. Long dominated the
legislature, the courts, and the executive departments; and he brooked no interference. When opponents accused him of violating the Louisiana constitution,
he brazenly replied, "I'm the Constitution here now." Many claimed that he had,

in effect, become a dictator. But he also maintained the overwhelming support of the Louisiana electorate, in part because of his flamboyant personality and in part because of his solid record of conventional progressive accomplishment: building roads, schools, and hospitals; revising the tax codes; distributing free textbooks; lowering utility rates. Barred by law from succeeding himself as governor, he ran in 1930 for a seat in the U.S. Senate, won easily, and left the state government in the hands of loyal, docile allies.

Long, like Coughlin, supported Franklin Roosevelt in 1932. But within six months of Roosevelt's inauguration, Long had broken with the president. As an alternative to the New Deal, Long advocated a drastic program of wealth redistribution, a program he ultimately named the Share-Our-Wealth Plan. The government, he claimed, could end the Depression easily by using the tax system to confiscate the surplus riches of the wealthiest men and women in America, whose fortunes were, he claimed, so bloated that not enough wealth remained to satisfy the needs of the great mass of citizens. That surplus wealth would allow the government to guarantee every family a minimum "homestead" of $5,000 and an annual wage of $2,500.

Long made little effort to disguise his interest in running for president. In 1934, he established his own national organization: the Share-Our-Wealth Society, which soon attracted a large following—not only in Long's native South but in New York, Pennsylvania, parts of the Midwest, and above all California. A poll by the Democratic National Committee in the spring of 1935 disclosed that Long might attract more than ten percent of the vote if he ran as a third-party candidate, enough to tip a close election to the Republicans.

Long, Coughlin, Townsend, and other dissidents had certain concerns in common. They spoke harshly of the "plutocrats," "international bankers," and other remote financial powers who were, they claimed, not only impoverishing the nation but exercising tyrannical power over individuals and communities. They spoke equally harshly, however, of the dangers of excessive government bureaucracy, attacking the New Deal for establishing a menacing, "dictatorial" state. At the same time, they themselves wanted to use the instruments of government to provide Americans with a more secure life. They envisioned a society in which government would, through a series of simple economic reforms, guarantee prosperity to every American without exercising intrusive control over private and community activities.

To members of the Roosevelt administration, the dissident politics appeared in 1935 to have become a genuine threat to the president. An increasing number of advisers were warning Roosevelt that he would have to do something dramatic to counter their strength.

The "Second New Deal"

In the spring of 1935, Roosevelt launched a series of important new programs—widely known as the "Second New Deal"—in response both to the growing political pressures and to the continuing economic crisis. They represented, if not a new direction, at least a change in the emphasis of New Deal policy.

Perhaps the most conspicuous change was in the administration's attitude toward big business. Symbolically at least, the president was now willing openly to attack corporate interests. In March, for example, he asked Congress for a law to break up the great utility holding companies and justified it by speaking harshly of the injustices inherent in their monopolistic position. Congress did indeed pass the Holding Company Act of 1935 (known as the "death sentence" bill), but furious lobbying by the utilities resulted in amendments that sharply limited its effect.

Equally alarming to affluent Americans was a series of tax reforms proposed by the president in 1935, a program conservatives quickly labeled a "soak the rich" scheme. Apparently designed to undercut the appeal of Huey Long's Share-Our-Wealth Plan, the Roosevelt proposals called for establishing the highest and most progressive peacetime tax rates in history. Rates in the highest brackets reached seventy-five percent on income, seventy percent on inheritances, and fifteen percent on corporate incomes. In fact, the actual impact of these taxes was far less radical than the president liked to claim (as Huey Long quickly pointed out); few people made enough money to qualify for the upper brackets, and most of them were able to find ways to avoid the full tax burden in any case.

The new tax laws were more important symbolically than they were economically. They answered some demands of Roosevelt's critics on the left and gave the president the appearance of allying himself with working people against corporate interests. In the midst of debate over Roosevelt's new initiatives, Long himself delighted in portraying Roosevelt as a wily "scrootch owl." "A scrootch owl," Long explained to Congress, "slips into the roost and scrootches up to the hen and talks softly to her. And the hen just falls in love with him and the next thing you know there ain't no hen." In time, Long implied, the president's critics would suffer the same fate as the hen.

Labor Militancy

Although often portrayed as a champion of unions, Roosevelt approached the issue of labor with his characteristic caution. Still, the emergence of a powerful American labor movement was one of the most notable events of the 1930s. It occurred only partly as a consequence of government efforts to enhance and safeguard the rights of unions. Increased militancy among American workers and their leaders also played a crucial role.

During the 1920s, most workers had displayed relatively little militancy in challenging employers or demanding recognition of their unions. In the 1930s, however, many of the factors that had impeded militancy vanished or grew weaker. Above all, perhaps, business leaders and industrialists lost (at least temporarily) some of their ability to control government policies.

This was apparent in congressional approval of the Wagner Act. The Supreme Court decision in 1935 to invalidate the National Industrial Recovery Act had also erased Section 7(a) guaranteeing workers the right to organize and bargain collectively. Supporters of labor, both in the administration and in Congress, advocated quick action to restore that protection. With the president himself slow to respond, a group of progressives in Congress led by Senator Robert F. Wagner of New York introduced what became the National Labor Relations Act of 1935. The new law, popularly known as the Wagner Act, provided workers with more federal protection than Section 7(a) of the National Industrial Recovery Act had offered by providing a crucial enforcement mechanism, the National Labor Relations Board (NLRB). Under the terms of the bill, the NLRB would have power to compel employers to recognize and bargain with legitimate unions. The Board also had the power to supervise union elections and to determine who within a particular shop should comprise the collective bargaining unit. Finally, the Act gave the NLRB the power to prevent employers, and for that matter unions and employees, from engaging in unfair labor practices. The bill represented a crucial change in the relationship between labor and capital, as the mantle of the federal government was now thrown around labor's right to organize and to seek remedies against those employers who resisted it.

Both Section 7(a) of the National Industrial Recovery Act of 1933 and the Wagner Act of 1935 were passed over the strong objections of most (although not all) corporate leaders. The president himself was not entirely happy with the bill, but he signed it. That was in large part because American workers themselves—and a group of new, militant organizations representing them—had become so important and vigorous a force by 1935 that Roosevelt realized his own political future would depend in part on responding to their demands.

The growing militancy of labor seemed apparent as early as 1933 when miners, and steel and auto workers, galvanized by the New Deal's more sympathetic posture to labor, redoubled their efforts to unionize their industries. One labor organizer, noting the encouragement many workers took from the NIRA's Section 7(a), described the proliferation of new unions in steel towns this way: "You name the mill town and there was a local there, carrying a name like 'the Blue Eagle' or even 'New Deal' Local." Over a million workers participated in strikes and labor actions in 1933. But what followed in 1934 was a militancy and radicalism not seen since 1919. In several cities, large strikes led to virtual paralysis, as wildcat strikes erupted among unorganized workers sympathetic to emerging unions. When striking longshoremen clashed with police and National Guardsmen in San Francisco in July of 1934, one reporter described the scene as "close to actual war." Many workers were, it was clear, determined to make their presence felt. But it was equally clear that without stronger legal protection, their organizing drives would end in frustration. Once the Wagner Act became law, the search for more effective forms of organization rapidly gained strength in labor ranks.

The American Federation of Labor (AFL), now under the leadership of William Green, remained committed to the concept of the craft union: the idea of organizing workers on the basis of their skills. But the AFL had little to offer unskilled laborers, who now constituted the bulk of the industrial work force. During the 1930s, therefore, another concept of labor organization challenged the craft union ideal: industrial unionism. Advocates of this approach argued that all the workers in a particular industry should be organized in a single union, regardless of what functions the workers performed. All auto workers should be in a single automobile union; all steel workers should be in a single steel union. United in this way, workers would greatly increase their power.

Leaders of the AFL craft unions for the most part opposed the new concept. But industrial unionism found a number of important advocates, most prominent among them John L. Lewis, the talented, flamboyant, and eloquent leader of the United Mine Workers—the oldest major union in the country. At first, Lewis and his allies attempted to work within the AFL, but friction between the new industrial organizations Lewis was promoting and the older craft unions grew rapidly.

At the 1935 AFL convention, Lewis became embroiled in a series of angry confrontations (and one celebrated fistfight) with craft union leaders before finally walking out. "Heed this cry from Macedonia that comes from the hearts of men," Lewis had exhorted the membership in the florid, almost Shakespearean rhetoric he favored. "Organize the unorganized." His entreaty fell on deaf ears. When a leader of the Carpenter's Union, William Hutcheson, cut off the speech of an industrial union representative, Lewis rose to his feet and leveled Hutcheson with a solid blow to the jaw. Many would later date the birth of the Congress of Industrial Organizations (CIO) to the moment when Lewis threw that punch.

In fact, the critical date was a few weeks later when Lewis met with two other powerful industrial union leaders, Sidney Hillman of the Amalgamated Clothing Workers of America and David Dubinsky of the International Ladies Garment Workers' Union (ILGWU). Together they created the Committee on Industrial Organization—a body officially within the AFL but unsanctioned by its leadership that soon became Lewis's organization to lead. After a series of bitter jurisdictional conflicts, the AFL finally expelled the new committee from its ranks, and along with it all the industrial unions it represented. In response, Lewis renamed the committee the Congress of Industrial Organizations (CIO), established it in 1936 as an organization directly rivaling the AFL, and became its first president. The schism clearly weakened the labor movement in many ways. But by freeing the advocates of industrial unionism from the restrictive rules of the AFL, it gave impetus to the creation of powerful new organizations.

The CIO soon became the force behind the greatest labor organizing campaign in American history. The organization greatly enlarged the constituency of the labor movement. It proved more receptive to women and to blacks than the AFL had been, in part because women and blacks were more likely to be relegated to unskilled jobs, in part because CIO organizing drives targeted previously unorganized industries (textiles, laundries, tobacco factories, and others) where women and minorities constituted much of the work force. The CIO was also a more militant organization than the AFL. By the time of the 1936 schism, it was already engaged in major organizing battles in the automobile and steel industries.

The CIO Organizing Campaign

Even before the schism of 1936, major battles for union recognition were under way, especially in the automobile and steel industries. Out of several competing auto unions, the United Auto Workers (UAW) was gradually becoming preeminent in the early and mid-1930s. But although it was gaining recruits, it was making little progress in winning recognition from the corporations until the rank and file turned in 1936 to a radical tactic first employed early in the twentieth century by the Wobblies.

That controversial but effective technique for challenging corporate opposition was the sit-down strike. The most important of the sit-down strikes in the automobile industry occurred in Flint, Michigan in December 1936. Employees in the Fisher Body plant (a shop that manufactured the body of GM cars) simply sat down inside the factory, refusing either to work or to leave. They thus pre-

SIT-DOWN STRIKE. Workers at the Fisher Body Plant in Flint, Michigan try to keep themselves occupied during the sit-down strike of 1937. Their strike and others like it forced the hand of General Motors, who finally agreed to recognize the United Automobile Workers in March 1937.

vented the company from using strikebreakers or from carrying on business as usual in the factory. Soon the tactic spread to other locations, and by February 1937 strikers had occupied seventeen GM plants. The strikers ignored court orders and local police efforts to force them to vacate the buildings.

When Michigan's governor, Frank Murphy, a liberal Democrat, refused to call up the National Guard to clear out the strikers, and when the federal government also refused to intervene on behalf of employers, General Motors relented. The largest corporation in the United States was brought to heel by the striking automobile workers. In March 1937, GM became the first major manufacturer to recognize the UAW; other automobile companies soon did the same. "We now have a voice, and we have slowed up the speed of the line. And are now treated as human beings, not as part of the machinery," one victorious autoworker proclaimed. The sit-down strike proved effective for rubber workers and others as well, but it survived only briefly as a labor technique. Its apparent illegality aroused so much public opposition that labor leaders soon abandoned it.

In the steel industry, the battle for unionization was more difficult. In 1936, the Steel Workers' Organizing Committee (SWOC; later United Steelworkers of America) began a major organizing drive involving thousands of workers and frequent, often bitter strikes. These conflicts were notable not only for the militancy of the (predominantly male) steel workers themselves, but for the involvement of thousands of women (many of them wives or relatives of workers), who provided important logistical support for the strikers and who at times took direct action by creating a buffer between strikers and the police. (Such support had also been critical to the success of the GM strike.)

In March 1937, to the surprise of almost everyone, United States Steel, the giant of the industry, recognized the union rather than risk a costly strike at a time when it sensed itself on the verge of recovery from the Depression. But the smaller companies (known collectively as "Little Steel") were less accommodating. On Memorial Day 1937, a group of striking workers from Republic Steel gathered with their families for a picnic and demonstration in South Chicago. When they attempted to march peacefully (and legally) toward the steel plant, police opened fire on them. Ten demonstrators were killed; another ninety were wounded. Despite a public outcry against the "Memorial Day Massacre," the harsh tactics of Little Steel were successful. The 1937 strike failed and the CIO endured its first great defeat.

Still, the victory of Little Steel was one of the last gasps of the kind of brutal strikebreaking that had proved so effective in the past. In 1937 alone, there were 4,720 strikes with nearly 5 million participants. Over eighty percent of the strikes were settled in favor of the unions. By the end of the year, more than 8 million workers were members of unions recognized as official bargaining units by employers (as compared with 3 million in 1932). By 1941, that number had expanded to 10 million and included the workers of Little Steel, where employers had finally recognized the SWOC. Several million American workers now belonged to strong unions that had not even existed before the 1930s.

The Creation of Social Security

For all their benefits, and there were many, union membership did not fully protect most Americans from economic insecurity. The ravages of unemployment and the burdens of old age still had the potential to thrust many citizens who had worked hard for years into poverty. The Depression dramatized the extreme vulnerability many Americans experienced during economic downturns and renewed calls from reformers for a broad-based system of social insurance that would provide a floor under which aged and unemployed Americans could not sink. Indeed, from the first moments of the New Deal, important members of the administration, most notably Secretary of Labor Frances Perkins, had been lobbying for a system of federally sponsored social insurance for the elderly and the unemployed.

In 1935, Roosevelt gave public support to what became the Social Security Act, which Congress—after a heated battle and much dissension from Townsendites and other critics—passed the same year. Among the political casualties of the congressional debate was coverage of some of the poorest workers—farmers and domestic servants (jobs held by many African Americans)— whose inclusion some influential congressmen vigorously fought. In the end, the Social Security Act passed in 1935 did not provide universal coverage. But it was, nevertheless, the single most important piece of social welfare legislation in American history.

It established several major programs with long-range implications. For the elderly, there were two types of assistance. Those who were presently destitute could receive up to 15 dollars a month in federal assistance. More important for the future, many Americans presently working were incorporated into a pension system, to which they and their employers would contribute by paying a payroll tax and which would provide them with an income on retirement. Pension payments would not begin until 1942 and even then would provide only ten to eighty-five dollars a month to recipients. And broad categories of workers (including domestic servants and agricultural laborers, part-time and seasonal workers, many of whom were blacks and women) were excluded from the program. But the act was a crucial first step in creating the nation's most important social program for the elderly. In addition, the Social Security Act created a system of unemployment insurance, financed by a tax on employers alone, that made it possible for workers laid off from their jobs to receive government assistance for a limited period of time.

The framers of the Social Security Act wanted to create a system of "insurance," not "welfare." And so the largest programs (old-age pensions and unemployment insurance) were contributory programs to which workers and employers paid taxes; covered employees then became eligible for benefits when they were unemployed and when they retired. These programs satisfied the framers of the act, and much of the public, that the government was not creating a dole.

But the Social Security Act also made provision for some Americans who needed support but had not, in the opinion of the framers, earned it. There was no general assistance for all the needy. But there were specific programs aimed at particular groups: the elderly poor, the disabled, dependent children, and their mothers. These groups were widely perceived as genuinely unable to support themselves, and they were assumed to be small. Partly for that reason, the federal government funded them less securely than it did the more universal assistance; the Act required the states to create these programs and provided federal subsidies for them out of general revenues. But in the years to come, these public assistance programs would expand and assume dimensions that the planners of Social Security did not foresee in the 1930s. Aid to Dependent Children, renamed Aid to Families with Dependent Children (AFDC) in the 1950s, expanded to become one of the cornerstones of the modern welfare system.

The distinction built into the Social Security Act between "insurance" and "public assistance" institutionalized a set of cultural biases that would continue to influence the politics of welfare for the rest of the twentieth century. New Dealers, like most other Americans, believed that some people had "earned" social protection, either because they (or their employers) had contributed to the programs from which they drew, as was the case with old-age pensions and unemployment compensation, or because they had performed some special service to the nation, as had been the case in the past for Civil War and World War I veterans. They were entitled to earn back a portion of their contributions or to be "repaid" for services rendered to their country. Other people received benefits not because they were entitled to them by their contributions or their service but because they "needed" them. While New Dealers (and some progressive reformers before them) were willing to provide assistance to such people, they did so less generously and much more demeaningly (because of elaborate eligibility requirements) than they did for those they believed had earned social insurance. The Social Security Act continued a longstanding effort to create clear distinctions between the "undeserving" and the "deserving" poor.

New Directions in Relief

Social Security was designed primarily to fulfill long-range goals. But millions of unemployed Americans had immediate needs. To help meet those needs, the administration established in 1935 the Works Progress Administration (WPA). Like the Civil Works Administration and other earlier efforts, the WPA established a system of work relief for the unemployed. But it was much bigger than the earlier agencies, both in the size of its budget ($5 billion at first) and in the energy and imagination of its operations.

Under the direction of Harry Hopkins, the WPA kept an average of 2.1 million workers employed between 1935 and 1941. The agency was ultimately responsible for building or renovating 110,000 public buildings (schools, post offices, government office buildings) and for constructing almost 600 airports, more than 500,000 miles of roads, and over 100,000 bridges. In the process, it provided incomes to unemployed workers and stimulated the economy by increasing the flow of money into it.

The WPA also displayed remarkable flexibility and imagination in offering assistance to those whose occupations did not fit into any traditional category of relief. The Federal Writers Project of the WPA, for example, gave unemployed writers a chance to do their work and receive a government salary. The Federal Arts Project, similarly, helped painters, sculptors, and others to continue their careers. During the 1930s, one painter recalled, "artists for the first time, I dare say, had a patron—the Government—who made no aesthetic judgments at all." The Federal Music Project and the Federal Theater Project oversaw the production of concerts and plays, creating work for unemployed musicians, actors, directors, and others. This extraordinary support not only developed jobs, it kept the creative arts alive at a time when even wealthy Americans and museums were not purchasing or supporting the arts.

Other relief agencies emerged alongside the WPA. The National Youth Administration (NYA) provided work and scholarship assistance to high school- and

FEDERAL ARTS PROJECT.   Among the most imaginative programs of the Works Progress Administration was the Federal Arts Project. Along with many other creative undertakings, unemployed artists found work painting murals such as this one on the walls of the U.S. Department of the Interior. The mural depicts the oil industry as a product of nature, human intelligence, technology, and most of all, hard physical labor on the part of American working men. The latter was a frequent theme in 1930s mural art.

college-age men and women. The Emergency Housing Division of the Public Works Administration began federal sponsorship of public housing. It cleared some of the nation's most notorious slums and built instead some fifty new housing developments, containing nearly 22,000 units—most of them priced too high for those who had been displaced by slum clearance. Not until 1937, when Congress approved Senator Wagner's bill creating the United States Housing Authority, did the government begin to provide a substantial amount of housing for the truly poor.

The hiring practices of the WPA, the NYA, and other work-relief programs—like the character of the Social Security Act—revealed another important, if at the time largely unrecognized, feature of the New Deal welfare system. Men and women alike were in distress in the 1930s (as in all difficult times). But the new welfare system dealt with members of the two sexes in very different ways. For men, the government concentrated mainly on work relief—on such programs as the CCC, the CWA, and the WPA, all of which were overwhelmingly male. The WPA did provide some jobs for women, although usually in such domestic settings as sewing rooms, nursery schools, and handicraft programs. Even these few jobs tended to be quickly eliminated when WPA funds became tight.

The principal government aid to women was not work relief, but cash assistance—most notably through the Aid to Dependent Children program of Social Security, which was designed largely to assist single mothers. This disparity in treatment reflected a widespread assumption, shared even by some of the many women who helped design the programs, that men were the principal "breadwinners" and the bulk of the paid work force and that women should be treated within the context of the family. In fact, millions of women were already employed by the 1930s; and millions of women lived outside the framework of the conventional family and depended on their own earnings for survival.

The 1936 "Referendum"

The presidential election of 1936, it was clear from the start, was to be a national referendum on Franklin Roosevelt and the New Deal. And while in 1935 there had been reason to question the president's political prospects, by the middle of 1936 his reelection was virtually certain. The Republican party nominated the moderate governor of Kansas, Alf M. Landon, and produced a program that promised, in effect, to continue the programs of the New Deal—but "constitutionally," and without running a deficit. Republican conservatives seemed impotent even within their own party.

Roosevelt's dissident challengers seemed similarly powerless. One reason was the violent death of their most effective leader, Huey Long, who was assassinated in Louisiana in September 1935. Another reason was the ill-fated alliance among several of the remaining dissident leaders in 1936. Father

Coughlin, Dr. Townsend, and Gerald L. K. Smith (a henchman of Huey Long) joined forces that summer to establish a new political movement—the Union party. But the incessant squabbling among them and the colorlessness of their presidential candidate—an undistinguished North Dakota congressman, William Lemke—helped doom the new party to ineffectuality. (After its demise, two of its embittered leaders, Coughlin and Smith, moved quickly to the far right; they also became notorious for their anti-Semitism and, in Coughlin's case, overt fascist sympathies.)

The result was the greatest landslide in American history to that point. Roosevelt polled just under sixty-one percent of the vote to Landon's thirty-six percent. The Republican candidate carried only Maine and Vermont. The Democrats increased their already large majorities in both houses of Congress. The Union party received fewer than 900,000 votes. Roosevelt himself was stunned by the extent of his victory margin. "Wow!" he exclaimed as he followed the returns at his home in Hyde Park, New York by teletype. A few days later, he wrote to an American diplomat, "I am beginning to come up for air after the baptism by total immersion on Tuesday night last. The other fellow was the one who nearly drowned!"

Most significantly, the election clearly displayed the party realignment that the New Deal had produced. The Democrats now controlled a broad coalition of western and southern farmers, the urban working classes, the poor and un-employed, and the black communities of the northern cities, as well as tradi-tional progressives and committed new liberals—a coalition that constituted a substantial majority of the electorate. It would be decades before the Republican party could again produce a durable majority coalition of its own.

THE NEW DEAL IN DISARRAY

Roosevelt emerged from the 1936 election at the zenith of his popularity. Within months, however, the New Deal was mired in serious new difficulties—a result of continuing opposition, of the president's own political errors, and of major economic setbacks. What followed were bruising battles that sorely tested the president's determination and commitments and that raised questions about his political acumen. Roosevelt himself survived these troubles. But the New Deal fared less well.

The Court Fight

One of the most serious missteps involved the Supreme Court, which the 1936 mandate convinced Roosevelt he could now challenge. No program of reform, he had come to believe, could long survive the obstructionist justices, who had already struck down the NRA and the AAA and threatened to invalidate even more New Deal legislation. In February 1937, Roosevelt offered a solution. Without informing congressional leaders in advance, he sent a surprise message to Capitol Hill proposing a general overhaul of the federal court system that included, among many other provisions, the addition of up to six new justices to the Supreme Court. The courts were "overworked," he claimed, and needed additional manpower and younger blood to enable them to cope with their increasing burdens. But Roosevelt's real purpose was to give himself the opportunity to appoint new, liberal justices and change the ideological balance of the Supreme Court.

Conservatives were outraged at the "court-packing plan," and even many Roosevelt supporters were disturbed by what they considered evidence of the president's hunger for power. Still, Roosevelt might well have persuaded Congress to approve at least a compromise measure had not the Supreme Court itself intervened. Even before the court-packing fight began, the ideological balance of the Court had been precarious. Four justices consistently opposed the New Deal, and three generally supported it. Of the remaining two, Chief Justice

COURT PACKING PLAN.   This political cartoon captures the political fallout from FDR's proposed court "reorganization" plan. Even Roosevelt's own party, depicted by the donkey, is in an uproar over the court packing plan.

Charles Evans Hughes often sided with the progressives and Associate Justice Owen J. Roberts usually voted with the conservatives. Shortly after Roosevelt made his proposal, this alignment shifted.

On March 29, 1937, Roberts, Hughes, and the three progressive justices voted together to uphold a state minimum wage law—in the case of *West Coast Hotel* v. *Parrish*—thus reversing a five-to-four decision of the previous year invalidating a similar law (and suggesting the first movement away from the narrow interpretation of the interstate commerce clause that the 1905 Lochner decision had established). Two weeks later, again by a five-to-four margin, the Court upheld the Wagner Act; and in May, it validated the Social Security Act. The Court had prudently moderated its position and made the court-packing bill appear unnecessary even to some who had originally supported it. Congress ultimately defeated it.

On one level, the affair was a significant victory for Franklin Roosevelt. The Court was no longer an obstacle to New Deal reforms, particularly after some of the older justices began to retire, to be replaced by Roosevelt appointees. But the court-packing episode did lasting damage to the administration. By giving members of his own party an excuse to oppose him, he had helped destroy his congressional coalition. From 1937 on, southern Democrats and other conservatives voted against his measures much more often than in the past.

One casualty of this newly powerful conservative coalition was an ambitious plan to reorganize the executive branch of government, which Roosevelt also presented to Congress in 1937. The president promoted the measure by emphasizing its potential contribution to governmental "efficiency"; his opponents characterized it, to some degree correctly, as an effort to increase the power of the president over the federal bureaucracy. Executive reorganization, like court packing, reinforced conservative arguments that the president was aspiring to become a "dictator." The original bill failed, although a much-reduced reorganization plan passed Congress in 1939.

In 1938, the president's political situation deteriorated further. Determined to regain the initiative in his legislative battles, Roosevelt openly campaigned in several Democratic primary campaigns in spring 1938 against members of his own party who had opposed his programs. Not only was he unable to unseat any of the five Democratic senators against whom he campaigned, but his "purge" efforts drove an even deeper wedge between the administration and its conservative opponents.

Retrenchment and Recession

By the summer of 1937, the national income, which had dropped from $82 billion in 1929 to $40 billion in 1932, had risen to nearly $72 billion. Other economic indices showed similar improvements. Roosevelt seized on these improvements as an excuse to try to balance the federal budget by cutting government spending, convinced by Treasury Secretary Henry Morgenthau and many economists that the real danger now was no longer depression but inflation. Between January and August 1937, for example, he cut the WPA in half, laying off 1.5 million relief workers. A few weeks later, the fragile boom collapsed. The index of industrial production dropped from 117 in August 1937 to seventy-six in May 1938. Four million additional workers lost their jobs. Economic conditions were soon almost as bad as the bleak days of 1932–1933.

The recession of 1937 came as a terrible shock to New Dealers and others who had convinced themselves that the Depression was already over. It was a result of many factors. But to many observers at the time (including, apparently, Roosevelt), it seemed to be a direct result of the administration's unwise decision to reduce spending. And so the new crisis forced a re-evaluation of policies within the administration. The advocates of government spending as an antidote to the Depression stood vindicated, it seemed; and the notion of using government deficits to stimulate the economy established a timid foothold in American public policy. In April 1938, the president asked Congress for an emergency appropriation of $5 billion for public works and relief programs, and government funds soon began pouring into the economy once again. Within a few months, another tentative recovery seemed to be under way, and the advocates of spending pointed to it as proof of the validity of their approach.

At the same time, a group of younger liberals in the administration, who saw the recession as the result of excessively concentrated corporate power, were urging the president to launch a new assault on monopoly. In April 1938, Roosevelt sent a stinging message to Congress, vehemently denouncing what he called an unjustifiable concentration of economic power and asking for the creation of a commission to examine that concentration with an eye to major re-forms in the antitrust laws. In response, Congress established the Temporary National Economic Committee (TNEC), including representatives of both houses of Congress and of several executive agencies. At about the same time, Roosevelt appointed a new head of the antitrust division of the Justice Department: Thurman Arnold, a Yale Law School professor who soon proved to be the most vigorous (and controversial) director ever to serve in that office.

Also in 1938, the administration won approval of the Fair Labor Standards Act, which for the first time established a national minimum wage and a maximum work week. It was, in effect, the last major accomplishment of the New Deal. By the end of 1938, Roosevelt's ambitious drive for reform had essentially come to an end. Congressional opposition now made it difficult for the president to enact any major new programs. But more important, perhaps, the threat of world crisis hung heavy in the political atmosphere, and Roosevelt was gradually growing more concerned with persuading a reluctant nation to prepare for war than with pursuing new avenues of reform.

NEW DEAL LEGACIES

In the 1930s, Roosevelt's principal critics were conservatives, who accused him of abandoning the Constitution and establishing a menacing, even tyrannical state. In more recent years, the New Deal's major critics have attacked it from the left, pointing to the major problems it left unsolved and the important groups it failed to represent. A full evaluation of the New Deal must take account of both its achievements and its limits. And it must rest on an understanding of the historical moment—one that permitted much innovation but also created formidable obstacles to change.

The Idea of the "Broker State"

In 1933, many New Dealers dreamed of using their popularity and authority somehow to remake American capitalism—to produce new forms of cooperation and control that would create a genuinely harmonious, ordered economic world. By 1939, it was clear that what they had created was in fact something quite different. But rather than bemoan the gap between their original intentions and their ultimate achievements, New Deal liberals, both in 1939 and in later years, chose to accept what they had produced and to celebrate it—to use it as a model for future reform efforts.

What they had created was something that in later years would become known as the "broker state." Instead of forging all elements of society into a single, harmonious unit, as some reformers had once hoped to do, the real achievement of the New Deal was to elevate and strengthen new interest groups so as to allow them to compete more effectively in the national marketplace. And it was to make the federal government a mediator in that continuous competition—a force that could intercede when necessary to help some groups and limit the power of others.

In 1933, there had been only one great interest group with genuine power in the national economy (albeit a varied and divided one): the corporate world. By the end of the 1930s, American business found itself competing for influence with an increasingly powerful labor movement, with an organized agricultural economy, and at times with aroused consumers. In later years, the "broker state" idea would expand to embrace other groups as well: racial, ethnic, and religious minorities, women, and many others. One of the enduring legacies of the New Deal, then, was to make the federal government a protector of interest groups and a supervisor of the competition among them, rather than an instrument attempting to create a universal harmony of interests.

What determines which interest groups receive government assistance in a "broker state"? The experience of the New Deal suggests that such assistance goes largely to those groups able to exercise enough political or economic power to demand it. Thus in the 1930s, farmers—after decades of organization and agitation—and workers—as the result of militant action and mass mobilization—won from the government new and important protections. Other groups, less well organized perhaps but politically important because so numerous and visible, won more limited assistance as well: imperiled homeowners, the unemployed, the elderly, and some women.

But the interest-group democracy that the New Deal came to represent offered much less to those groups either not organized enough to demand assistance or not visible enough to arouse widespread public support. And yet those same groups were often the ones most in need of help from their government. One of the important limits of the New Deal, therefore, was its very modest record on behalf of several important social groups.

African Americans and the New Deal

One group the New Deal did relatively little to assist was African Americans. The administration was not hostile to black aspirations. On the contrary, the New Deal was probably more sympathetic to them than any previous government of the twentieth century. Eleanor Roosevelt spoke throughout the 1930s on behalf of racial justice and put continuing pressure on her husband and others in the federal government to ease discrimination against blacks. She was also partially responsible for what was, symbolically at least, one of the most important events of the decade for African Americans. When the black concert singer Marian Anderson was refused permission in the spring of 1939 to perform in the auditorium of the Daughters of the American Revolution (Washington's only major concert hall), Eleanor Roosevelt resigned from the organization and then (along with Interior Secretary Harold Ickes, another champion of racial equality) helped secure government permission for her to sing on the steps of the Lincoln Memorial. Anderson's Easter Sunday concert attracted 75,000 people and became, in effect, the first modern mass civil-rights demonstration.

The president himself appointed a number of blacks to significant secondary positions in his administration. Roosevelt appointees such as Robert Weaver, William Hastie, and Mary McLeod Bethune created an informal network of officeholders who consulted frequently with one another and who became known as the "Black Cabinet." Eleanor Roosevelt, Harold Ickes, and Harry Hopkins all made efforts to ensure that New Deal relief programs did not exclude blacks; and by 1935, perhaps a quarter of all African Americans were receiving some form of government assistance. One result was a historic change in black electoral behavior. As late as 1932, most American blacks were voting Republican, as they had since the Civil War. By 1936, more than ninety percent of them were voting Democratic—the beginnings of a political alliance that would endure for many decades.

African Americans supported Franklin Roosevelt because they knew he was not their enemy and because his programs offered economic benefits to them. But they had few illusions that the New Deal represented a millennium in American race relations. The president was, for example, never willing to risk losing the support of southern Democrats in Congress by supporting legislation to

MARIAN ANDERSON'S EASTER CONCERT. After being refused permission by the Daughters of the American Revolution to sing in their auditorium, Washington, D.C.'s only large concert hall, the great African-American female contralto instead sang at an outdoor concert at the Lincoln Memorial on April 9, 1939. Some 75,000 attended the event made possible, in part, through the intervention of First Lady Eleanor Roosevelt.

make lynching a federal crime or to ban the poll tax, one of the most potent tools by which white southerners kept blacks from voting.

New Deal relief agencies seldom challenged, and indeed usually reinforced, existing patterns of discrimination. The Civilian Conservation Corps established separate camps for blacks and whites. The NRA codes tolerated paying African Americans less than whites doing the same jobs. Blacks were largely excluded from employment in the TVA. The Federal Housing Administration refused to provide mortgages to blacks moving into white neighborhoods, and the first public housing projects financed by the federal government were racially segregated. The WPA routinely relegated African American, Hispanic, and Asian workers to the least skilled and lowest paying jobs or excluded them altogether; when funding ebbed, nonwhites, like women, were among the first to be dismissed.

The New Deal and the "Indian Problem"

Government policies toward the Indian tribes in the 1930s both continued the long-established effort to encourage Native Americans to assimilate and departed from entrenched policies. Senator Burton K. Wheeler of Montana expressed the sentiments of many members of Congress (and many other white Americans) when he said in 1934, in the midst of a hearing on an Indian reform bill, "What we are trying to do is get rid of the Indian problem rather than add to it." By that he meant that the purpose of reforms should be to reduce the numbers of Native Americans who identified themselves as members of tribes and increase the number of those who attempted to become part of the larger society and culture.

But the principal elements of federal policy in the New Deal years worked to advance a very different goal, largely because of the efforts of the extraordinary commissioner of Indian affairs in those years, John Collier. Collier was a former social worker who had become committed to the cause of the Native Americans after exposure to tribal cultures in New Mexico in the 1920s. More important, he was greatly influenced by the work of twentieth-century anthropologists who promoted the idea of cultural relativism—the idea that every culture should be accepted and respected on its own terms and that no culture is inherently superior to another. Cultural relativism was a challenge to the three-centuries-old assumption among white Americans that Indians were "savages" and that white society was inherently superior and more "civilized."

Collier promoted legislation that would, he hoped, reverse the pressures on Native Americans to assimilate and would allow them the right to retain their tribal cultures. Not all tribal leaders agreed with Collier. Indeed, his belief in the importance of preserving Indian cultures would not find its broadest support among the tribes until the 1960s. Nevertheless, Collier effectively promoted legislation—which became the Indian Reorganization Act of 1934—to advance his goals. Among other things it restored to the tribes the right to own land collectively (reversing the allotment policy adopted in 1887, which encouraged the breaking up of tribal lands into individually owned plots—a policy that had led to the loss of over 90 million acres of tribal land to white speculators and others). In the thirteen years after passage of the 1934 bill, tribal land increased by nearly 4 million acres, and Indian agricultural income increased dramatically (from under $2 million in 1934 to over $49 million in 1947).

Even with the redistribution of lands under the 1934 act, however, Indians continued to possess, for the most part, only territory that whites did not want— much of it arid, some of it desert. And as a group, they continued to constitute the poorest segment of the population. The efforts of the 1930s did not solve what some called the "Indian problem." They did, however, provide Native Americans with some tools for rebuilding the viability of their tribes.

Women and the New Deal

The New Deal was not hostile to feminist aspirations; but neither did it do a great deal to advance them. At the same time, it represented a high water mark for women's participation in government. Much of the credit for that advance belonged to the nation's First Lady, Eleanor Roosevelt, an ardent if somewhat traditional feminist who encouraged her husband to take advantage of women's long experience in social welfare as he set out to staff the New Deal. Important symbolic gestures on behalf of women followed as Roosevelt appointed the first female member of the cabinet in the nation's history, Secretary of Labor Frances Perkins. He also named more than 100 other women to positions at lower levels of the federal bureaucracy. They created an active female network within the government and cooperated with one another in advancing causes of interest to women. Molly Dewson, head of the Women's Division of the Democratic National Committee, was also influential in securing federal appointments for women as well as in increasing their role within the Democratic party. Several women received appointments to the federal judiciary. And one, Hattie Caraway of Arkansas, became the first woman ever elected to a full term in the U.S. Senate. (She was running to succeed her husband, who had died in office.)

But New Deal support for feminist aspirations operated within clear parameters, which were in part shaped by the women who participated in public life during the 1930s. Frances Perkins and many others in the administration emerged out of the feminist tradition of the progressive era. They brought to their work in government a belief that public policy needed to address women as mothers and homemakers who merited special protection. Perkins herself had been instrumental in fighting for the passage of various state laws safeguarding female workers. She opposed the National Woman's party and its goal of securing the Equal Rights Amendment because she feared the amendment would threaten the protective mechanisms that she had helped to establish. Perkins and other women reformers were instrumental in creating support for, and shaping the character of, the Social Security Act of 1935. But they built into that bill their own notion of women's special place in a male-dominated economy. The principal provision of the bill specifically designed for women—the Aid to Dependent Children program—was modeled on the state-level mother's pensions that generations of progressive women had worked to pass earlier in the century.

The New Deal generally supported the prevailing belief that in hard times women should withdraw from the workplace to open up more jobs for men. As a result, gender discrimination surfaced in the structure and work of many New Deal agencies. New Deal relief agencies, for example, offered relatively few

FRANCES PERKINS. The first woman to hold a cabinet post in the United States government, Frances Perkins was Roosevelt's Secretary of Labor. Here she receives a report from a steel construction foreman and a riveter who are building the Golden Gate Bridge in 1935.

employment opportunities for women. The NRA sanctioned gender-based discriminatory wage practices. The Social Security program excluded domestic servants, waitresses, and other occupations that were predominantly female (and in which black women were heavily represented). The record of the New Deal for women, as for African Americans, mixed signs of progress with support for continued inequality.

The New Deal and the West

One part of American society that did receive special attention from the New Deal was the American West, which benefited disproportionately from government relief and public works programs. The West received more federal funds per capita through New Deal relief programs than any other region.

Most westerners were eager for the assistance New Deal agencies provided, but their political leaders were not always as supportive. In Colorado, for example, the state legislature refused to provide the required matching funds for FERA relief in 1933. When Harry Hopkins, in response, cut Colorado off from the program, unemployed people rioted in Denver and looted food stores. Only then did the legislature reverse course and provide funding.

Just as in the South, locally administered relief programs did not challenge prevailing racial norms, so in the West New Deal programs sustained existing racial and ethnic prejudices. In several states, relief agencies paid different groups at different rates: white Anglos received the most generous aid; blacks, Native Americans, and Mexican Americans received lower levels of support. In the CCC camps in New Mexico, Hispanics and Anglos sometimes worked in the same camps; but there were frequent tensions and occasional conflicts between them.

But the main reason for the New Deal's particular impact on the West was that conditions in the region made the government's programs especially important. Federal agricultural programs had an enormous impact on the West because farming remained so much more central to the economy of the region than it did in much of the East. The largest New Deal public works programs—the great dams and power stations—were mainly in the West, both because the best locations for such facilities were there and because the West had the most need for new sources of water and power. The Grand Coulee dam on the Columbia River was the largest public-works project in American history to that point, and it provided cheap electric power for much of the Northwest. Its construction, and the construction of other, smaller dams and water projects in the region, created a basis for economic development in the region.

Without this enormous public investment by the federal government, much of the economic development that transformed the West after World War II would have been much more difficult, if not impossible, to achieve. For generations after the Great Depression, the federal government maintained a much greater and more visible bureaucratic presence in the West than in any other region.

The New Deal and the National Economy

The most frequent criticisms of the New Deal involve its failure genuinely to revive or reform the American economy. New Dealers never fully recognized the value of government spending as a vehicle for recovery, and their efforts along other lines never succeeded in ending the Depression. The economic boom sparked by World War II, not the New Deal, finally ended the crisis. Nor did the New Deal substantially alter the distribution of power within American capitalism. It had only a small impact on the distribution of wealth among the American people.

Nevertheless, the New Deal did have a number of important and lasting effects on both the behavior and the structure of the American economy. It helped elevate new groups—workers, farmers, and others—to positions from which they could at times effectively challenge the power of the corporations. It contributed to the economic development of the West and, to a lesser degree, the South. It increased the regulatory functions of the federal government

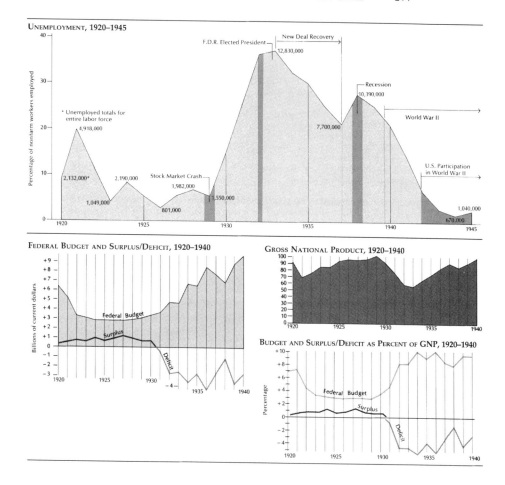

UNEMPLOYMENT, 1920–1945

FEDERAL BUDGET AND SURPLUS/DEFICIT, 1920–1940

GROSS NATIONAL PRODUCT, 1920–1940

BUDGET AND SURPLUS/DEFICIT AS PERCENT OF GNP, 1920–1940

in ways that helped stabilize previously troubled areas of the economy: the stock market, the banking system, and others. And the administration helped establish the basis for new forms of federal fiscal policy, which in the postwar years would give the government tools for promoting and regulating economic growth.

The New Deal also created the basis of the federal welfare state, through its many relief programs and above all through the Social Security system. The conservative inhibitions New Dealers brought to this task ensured that the welfare system that ultimately emerged would be limited in its impact (at least in comparison with those of other industrial nations), would reinforce some traditional patterns of gender and racial discrimination, and would be expensive and cumbersome to administer. But for all its limits, the new system marked an historic break with the federal government's traditional reluctance to offer public assistance to its neediest citizens.

The New Deal and American Politics

Perhaps the most dramatic effect of the New Deal was on the structure and be-havior of American government itself and on the character of American politics. Franklin Roosevelt helped enhance the power of the federal government as a whole. By the end of the 1930s, state and local governments were clearly of sec-ondary importance to the government in Washington; in the past, that had not always been clear. Roosevelt also established the presidency as the preeminent center of authority within the federal government. Not for many decades would Congress be able to wield as much independent power as it had in the years be-fore the New Deal. And never again would it have the same control over presi-dential authority.

Finally, the New Deal had a profound impact on how the American people de-fined themselves politically. It took a weak, divided Democratic party, which had been a minority force in American politics for decades, and turned it into a mighty coalition that would dominate national party competition for nearly forty years. It turned the attention of many voters away from some of the cultural issues that had preoccupied them in the 1920s and awakened in them an interest in economic mat-ters of direct importance to their lives. And it created among the American people at large greatly increased expectations of government—expectations that the New Deal itself did not always fulfill but that survived to become the basis of later lib-eral crusades in the postwar era.

CHAPTER FIFTEEN

The World in Crisis

~

Through most of the 1930s, the Great Depression preoccupied the American people and their leaders. In the process, it contributed to the nation's relative inattention to the growing global crisis that would soon lead to world war. America's rejection of the Treaty of Versailles and its failure to join the League of Nations presaged the independent course the country would pursue for much of the interwar period. That course would attempt, but ultimately fail, to expand American influence and maintain international stability without committing the United States to any lasting relationships with other nations.

Throughout the 1920s, those controlling American foreign policy thought they had succeeded in their cautious goals. By the end of the 1930s, however, it was clear that international stability had not been achieved. Another world war was brewing; by late 1939 it was sweeping across Europe. Now a new crisis of even more imposing dimensions confronted President Roosevelt. A longtime Wilsonian internationalist and erstwhile supporter of the League of Nations, Roosevelt nonetheless had attempted to keep America the "master of her own fate." In the end, it became impossible to ignore the threat the Nazis posed to the world. The cautious, limited American internationalism of the interwar years could not prevent American involvement in the greatest war in human history.

DIPLOMACY IN THE 1920S

Critics of American foreign policy in the 1920s often used a single word to describe the cause of their disenchantment: isolationism. Having rejected the Wilsonian vision of a new world order, they claimed, the nation had turned its back on the rest of the globe and repudiated its international responsibilities. In fact, the United States played a more active role in world affairs in the 1920s than it had at almost any previous time in its history—even if not the role the Wilsonians had prescribed.

An Agenda for Peace

It was clear when the Harding administration took office in 1921 that American membership in the League of Nations was no longer a realistic possibility. As if finally to bury the issue, Secretary of State Charles Evans Hughes secured legislation from Congress in 1921 declaring the war with Germany at an end and then proceeded to negotiate separate peace treaties with the former Central Powers. Through these treaties, American policymakers believed, the United States would receive all the advantages of the Versailles Treaty with none of the burdensome responsibilities. Hughes was, however, committed to finding something to replace the League as a guarantor of world peace and stability. He embarked, therefore, on a series of efforts to build safeguards against future wars—but safeguards that would not hamper American freedom of action in the world.

The most important of such efforts was the Washington Conference of 1921—an attempt to prevent what was threatening to become a costly and destabilizing naval armaments race among America, Britain, and Japan. Hughes startled the delegates in his opening speech by proposing a plan for dramatic reductions in the fleets of all three nations and a ten-year moratorium on the construction of large warships. He called for the actual scrapping of nearly 2 million tons of existing shipping. Far more surprising than the proposal was that the conference ultimately agreed to accept most of its terms, something that Hughes himself apparently had not anticipated. The Five-Power Pact of February 1922 established both limits for total naval tonnage and a ratio of armaments among the signatories. For every 5 tons of American and British warships, Japan would maintain 3 and France and Italy 1.75 each. (Although the treaty seemed to confirm the military inferiority of Japan, in fact it sanctioned Japanese dominance in East Asia. America and Britain had to spread their fleets across the globe; Japan was concerned only with the Pacific.) The Washington Conference also produced two other, related treaties: the Nine-Power Pact, pledging a continuation of the Open Door policy in China, and the Four-Power Pact, by which the United States, Britain, France, and Japan promised to respect one another's Pacific territories and cooperate to prevent aggression.

The Washington Conference began the New Era's effort to protect the peace (and the international economic interests of the United States) without accepting active international duties. The Kellogg-Briand Pact of 1928 concluded it. When the French foreign minister, Aristide Briand, asked the United States in 1927 to join an alliance against Germany, Secretary of State Frank Kellogg (who had replaced Hughes in 1925) proposed instead a multilateral treaty outlawing war as an instrument of national policy. Fourteen nations signed the agreement in Paris on August 27, 1928, amid great solemnity and wide international acclaim. Forty-eight other nations later joined the pact. It contained no instruments of enforcement but rested, as Kellogg put it, on the "moral force" of world opinion.

The Balance Sheet of War

The first responsibility of diplomacy, Hughes, Kellogg, and others agreed, was to ensure that American overseas trade faced no obstacles to expansion and that, once established, it would remain free of interference. Preventing a dangerous armaments race and reducing the possibility of war were two steps to that end. So were the new financial arrangements that emerged at the same time. The United States was most concerned about Europe, on whose economic health American prosperity in large part depended. Not only were the major industrial powers there suffering from the devastation World War I had produced; they were also staggering under a heavy burden of debt. The Allied powers were struggling to repay the $11 billion in loans they had contracted with the United States during and shortly after the war, loans that the Republican administrations were unwilling to reduce or forgive. "They hired the money, didn't they?" Calvin Coolidge once replied when asked if he favored offering Europe relief from their debts. At the same time, an even more debilitated Germany was attempting to pay the reparations levied against it by the Allies. With the financial structure of Europe on the brink of collapse, the United States stepped in with a solution.

Charles G. Dawes, an American banker and diplomat, negotiated an agreement in 1924 among France, Britain, Germany, and the United States under which American banks would provide enormous loans to the Germans, enabling them to meet their reparations payments; in return, Britain and France would agree to reduce the amount of those payments. Dawes won the Nobel Peace Prize for his efforts; but in fact the Dawes Plan did little to solve the problems it addressed. It was responsible for a growing American economic presence in Germany. It was also the source of a troubling circular pattern in international finance. America would lend money to Germany, which would use that money to pay reparations to France and England, which would in turn use those funds (as well as large loans they themselves were receiving from American banks) to repay war debts to the United States. The flow was able to continue only by virtue of the enormous debts Germany and the other European nations were accumulating to American banks and corporations.

Those banks and corporations were doing more than providing loans. They were becoming a daily presence in the economic life of Europe. American automobile manufacturers were opening European factories, capturing a large share of the overseas market. Other industries in the 1920s were establishing subsidiaries worth more than $10 billion throughout the continent, taking advantage of the wartime devastation of European industry, from which continental corporations had not yet recovered. Some groups within the American government warned that the reckless expansion of overseas loans and investments, many in enterprises of dubious value, threatened disaster; that the United States was becoming too dependent on unstable European economies. The high tariff barriers that the Republican Congress had erected (through the Fordney-McCumber Act of 1922) were creating additional problems, such skeptics warned. European nations, unable to export their goods to the United States, were finding it difficult to earn the money necessary to repay their loans. Such warnings fell, for the most part, on deaf ears; and American economic expansion in Europe continued until disaster struck in 1931.

The United States government felt even fewer reservations about assisting American economic expansion in Latin America. The United States had, after all, long considered that region its exclusive sphere of influence; and its investments there had become large even before World War I. During the 1920s, American military forces maintained a presence in numerous countries in the region. United States investments in Latin America more than doubled between 1924 and 1929; American corporations built roads and other facilities in many areas—partly, they argued, to weaken the appeal of revolutionary forces in the region, but at least equally to increase their own access to Latin America's rich natural resources. American banks were offering large loans to Latin American governments, just as they were in Europe; and just as in Europe, the Latin Americans were having great difficulty earning the money to repay them in the face of the formidable United States tariff barrier. By the end of the 1920s, resentment of "Yankee imperialism" was growing rapidly. The economic troubles after 1929 would only accentuate such problems.

Hoover and American Foreign Policy

After the relatively placid international climate of the 1920s, the diplomatic challenges facing the Hoover administration must have seemed ominous and bewildering. The world financial crisis that had begun in 1929 and greatly intensified after 1931 was not only creating economic distress; it was producing a dangerous nationalism that threatened the weak international agreements established during the previous decade. Above all, the Depression was toppling some existing political regimes and replacing them with powerful, belligerent governments bent on expansion as a solution to their economic problems. Hoover confronted, therefore, the beginning of a process that would ultimately lead to war, and he did so without sufficient tools for dealing with it.

In Latin America, Hoover worked studiously to repair some of the damage created by earlier American policies. He made a ten-week goodwill tour through the region before his inauguration. Once in office, he tried to abstain from intervening in the internal affairs of neighboring nations and moved to withdraw American troops from Haiti. When economic distress led to the collapse of one Latin American regime after another, Hoover announced a new policy: America would grant diplomatic recognition to any sitting government in the region without questioning the means it had used to obtain power. He even repudiated the Roosevelt Corollary to the Monroe Doctrine by refusing to permit American intervention when several Latin American countries defaulted on debt obligations to the United States in October 1931.

In Europe, the administration enjoyed few successes in its efforts to promote economic stability. When Hoover's proposed moratorium on debts in 1931 failed to attract broad support or produce financial stability, many economists and political leaders appealed to the president to cancel all war debts to the United States. Like his predecessors, Hoover refused; and several European nations promptly went into default, severely damaging an already tense international climate. American efforts to extend the disarmament agreements of the 1920s met with similar frustration. At a conference in London in January 1930, American negotiators reached agreement with European and Japanese delegates on extending the limits on naval construction established at the Washington Conference of 1921. But France and England, fearful of German resurgence and Japanese expansionism, insisted on so many loopholes as to make the treaty virtually meaningless. The increasing irrelevance of the New Era approach to diplomacy became even clearer at the World Disarmament Conference that opened in Geneva in January 1932. France rejected the idea of disarmament entirely and called for the creation of an international army to counter the growing power of Germany. Hoover continued to urge major reductions in armaments, including an immediate abolition of all "offensive" weapons (tanks, bombers) and a thirty percent reduction in all land and naval forces. The conference ultimately dissolved in failure.

The ineffectiveness of diplomacy in Europe was particularly troubling in view of some of the new governments coming to power on the Continent. Benito Mussolini's Fascist party had been in control of Italy since the early 1920s; by the 1930s, the regime was growing increasingly nationalistic and militaristic, and fascist leaders were loudly threatening an active campaign of imperial expansion. Even more ominous was the growing power of the National Socialist (or Nazi) party in Germany. By the late 1920s, the Weimar Republic, the nation's government since the end of World War I, had lost virtually all popular support; it was discredited by, among other things, a ruinous inflation. Adolf Hitler, the stridently nationalistic leader of the Nazis, was rapidly growing in popular favor. Although he lost a 1932 election for chancellor, Hitler would sweep into power less than a year later. His belief in the racial superiority of the Aryan (German) people, his commitment to providing *Lebensraum* (living space) for his "master race," his pathological anti-Semitism, and his passionate militarism — all posed a threat to European peace.

More immediately alarming to the Hoover administration was a major crisis in Asia — another early step toward World War II. The Japanese, reeling from an economic depression of their own, were concerned about the increasing strength of the Soviet Union and of Chiang Kai-shek's nationalist China. In particular, they were alarmed at Chiang's insistence on expanding his government's power in Manchuria, which remained officially a part of China but

HITLER AND MUSSOLINI. The alliance between Hitler and Mussolini was fraught with tensions. Publicly, the German and Italian dictators acted as if they were equals. Privately, Hitler treated Mussolini with contempt, and Mussolini complained constantly of being treated as an inferior in the relationship. The two are depicted here on the occasion of Mussolini's visit to Germany in late September 1937.

over which the Japanese had maintained effective economic control since 1905. When the moderate government of Japan failed to take forceful steps to counter Chiang's ambitions, Japan's military leaders staged what was, in effect, a coup in the autumn of 1931—seizing control of foreign policy from the weakened liberals. Weeks later, they launched a major invasion of northern Manchuria.

The American government had few options. For a while, Secretary of State Henry Stimson (who had served as secretary of war under Taft) continued to hope that Japanese moderates would regain control of the Tokyo government and halt the invasion. The militarists, however, remained in command; and by the beginning of 1932, the conquest of Manchuria was complete. Stimson issued stern (but essentially toothless) warnings to Japan and tried to use moral suasion to end the crisis. But Hoover forbade him to cooperate with the League of Nations in imposing economic sanctions against the Japanese. Stimson's only real tool in dealing with the Manchurian invasion was a refusal to grant diplomatic recognition to the new Japanese territories. Japan was unconcerned and early in 1932 expanded its aggression farther into China, attacking the city of Shanghai and killing thousands of civilians.

By the time Hoover left office early in 1933, it was clear that the international system the United States had attempted to create in the 1920s—a system based on voluntary cooperation among nations and on an American refusal to commit itself to the interests of other countries—had collapsed. The United States faced a choice. It could adopt a more energetic form of internationalism and enter into firmer and more meaningful associations with other nations. Or it could resort to nationalism and rely on its own devices for dealing with its (and the world's) problems. For the next six years, it experimented with elements of both approaches.

BALANCING ISOLATIONISM AND INTERNATIONALISM

The administration of Franklin Roosevelt faced a dual challenge as it entered office in 1933. It had to deal with the worst economic crisis in the nation's history; and it had to deal as well with the effects of a decaying international structure. The two problems were not unrelated. It was the worldwide Depression itself that was producing much of the political chaos throughout the globe.

Through most of the 1930s, however, the United States was unwilling to make more than the faintest of gestures toward restoring stability to the world. Like many other peoples suffering economic hardship, most Americans were turning inward. Yet the realities of world affairs were not to allow the nation to remain isolated for very long—as Franklin Roosevelt realized earlier than many other Americans.

Diplomacy in the Great Depression

From Herbert Hoover, Roosevelt inherited a foreign policy less concerned with issues of war and peace than with matters of economic policy. And although the New Deal rejected some of the initiatives the Republicans had begun, it continued for several years to base its foreign policy almost entirely on the nation's immediate economic needs.

Perhaps Roosevelt's sharpest break with the policies of his predecessor was on the question of American economic relations with Europe. Hoover had argued that only by resolving the question of war debts and reinforcing the gold standard could the American economy hope to recover. He had, therefore, agreed to participate in the World Economic Conference, to be held in London in June 1933, to try to resolve these issues. By the time the conference assembled, however, Roosevelt had already decided to allow the gold value of the dollar to fall to make American goods able to compete in world markets. Shortly after the conference convened, Roosevelt released a famous "bombshell" message repudiating the orthodox views of most of the delegates and rejecting any agreement on currency stabilization. The conference quickly dissolved without reaching agreement, and not until 1936 did the administration finally agree to new negotiations to stabilize western currencies.

At the same time, Roosevelt abandoned the commitments of the Hoover administration to settle the issue of war debts through international agreement. In effect, he simply let the issue die. Not only did he decline to negotiate a solution at the London Conference, but in April 1934 he signed a bill to forbid American banks from making loans to any nation in default on its debts. The result was to stop the old, circular system by which debt payments continued only by virtue of increasing American loans; within months, war-debt payments from every nation except Finland stopped for good.

If the new administration had no interest in international currency stabilization or settlement of war debts, it did have an active interest in improving America's position in world trade. Roosevelt approved the Reciprocal Trade Agreement Act of 1934, authorizing the administration to negotiate treaties lowering tariffs by as much as fifty percent in return for reciprocal reductions by other nations. By 1939, Secretary of State Cordell Hull, a devoted free-trader, had negotiated new treaties with twenty-one countries. The result was an increase in American exports to them of nearly forty percent. But most of the agreements admitted only products not competitive with American industry and agriculture, so imports into the United States continued to lag. Thus other nations were not obtaining enough American currency to buy more American products or to pay off debts to American banks.

America and the Soviet Union

America's hopes of expanding its foreign trade helped produce efforts by the Roosevelt administration to improve relations with the Soviet Union. The United States and Russia had viewed each other with mistrust and even hostility since the Bolshevik Revolution of 1917, and the American government—almost alone among the world's major nations—still had not officially recognized the

Soviet regime by 1933. But powerful voices within the United States were urging a change in policy—less because the revulsion with which most Americans viewed communism had diminished than because the Soviet Union appeared to be a possible source of trade. The Russians, too, were eager for a new relationship. They were hoping for American cooperation in containing the power of Japan on Russia's southeastern flank. In November 1933, therefore, Soviet Foreign Minister Maxim Litvinov reached an agreement with the president in Washington. The Soviets would cease their propaganda efforts in the United States and protect American citizens in Russia; in return, the United States would recognize the communist regime.

Despite this promising beginning, however, relations with the Soviet Union soon soured once again. American trade failed to establish a foothold in Russia, disappointing hopes in the United States; and the American government did little to reassure the Soviets that it was interested in stopping Japanese expansion in Asia, dousing expectations in Russia. By the end of 1934, the Soviet Union and the United States were once again viewing each other with considerable mistrust. And Stalin, having abandoned whatever hopes he might once have had of cooperation with America, soon began to consider making agreements of his own with the fascist governments of Japan and Germany.

Policy Toward Latin America

Somewhat more successful were American efforts to enhance both diplomatic and economic relations with Latin America through what became known as the "Good Neighbor Policy." Latin America was one of the most important targets of the new policy of trade reciprocity. During the 1930s, the United States succeeded in increasing both exports to and imports from the other nations of the Western Hemisphere by over 100 percent. Closely tied to these new economic relationships was a new American attitude toward intervention in Latin America. The Hoover administration had unofficially abandoned the earlier American practice of using military force to compel Latin American governments to repay debts, respect foreign investments, or otherwise behave "responsibly." The Roosevelt administration went further in the same direction. At the Inter-American Conference in Montevideo in December 1933, Secretary of State Hull signed a formal convention declaring: "No state has the right to intervene in the internal or external affairs of another." Roosevelt respected that pledge throughout his years in office.

The Good Neighbor Policy did not mean, however, that the United States had abandoned its influence in Latin America. On the contrary, it had simply replaced one form of leverage with another. Instead of military force, Americans now tried to use economic influence. The new reliance on economic pressures eased tensions between the United States and its neighbors considerably, eliminating the most abrasive and conspicuous irritants in the relationship. It did nothing to stem the growing American domination of the Latin American economy.

Confronting Isolationism

The first years of the Roosevelt administration marked not only the death of Hoover's hopes for international economic agreements. They marked, too, the end of any hopes for world peace through treaties and disarmament.

That the international arrangements of the 1920s were no longer suitable for the world of the 1930s became obvious in the first months of the Roosevelt presidency, when the new administration attempted to stimulate movement toward world disarmament. The arms control conference in Geneva had been meeting, without result, since 1932; and in May 1933, Roosevelt attempted to spur it to action by submitting a new American proposal for arms reductions. Negotiations stalled and then broke down on the Roosevelt proposal; and only a few months later, first Hitler and then Mussolini withdrew from the talks altogether. The Geneva Conference, it was clear, was a failure. Two years later, Japan withdrew from the London Naval Conference, which was attempting to draw up an agreement to continue the limitations on naval armaments negotiated at the Washington Conference of 1921.

Faced with a choice between more active efforts to stabilize the world or more energetic attempts to isolate the nation from it, most Americans unhesitatingly chose the latter. Support for isolationism emerged from many quarters. Old Wilsonian internationalists had grown disillusioned with the League of Nations and its inability to stop Japanese aggression in Asia; internationalism, they were beginning to argue, had failed. Other Americans were listening to the argument (popular among populist-minded politicians in the Midwest and West) that powerful business interests—Wall Street, munitions makers, and others— had tricked the United States into participating in World War I. An investigation by a Senate committee chaired by Senator Gerald Nye of North Dakota revealed exorbitant profiteering and blatant tax evasion by many corporations during the war, and it suggested (with little evidence to support the charge) that bankers had pressured Wilson to intervene in the war so as to protect their loans abroad.

Roosevelt himself shared some of the suspicions voiced by the isolationists and claimed to be impressed by the findings of the Nye investigation. Nevertheless, he continued to hope for at least a modest American role in maintaining world peace. In 1935, he proposed to the Senate a treaty to make the United States a member of the World Court—a treaty that would have expanded America's symbolic commitment to internationalism without increasing its actual responsibilities in any important way. Nevertheless, isolationist opposition (spurred by unrelenting hostility from the Hearst newspapers and a passionate broadcast by Father Charles Coughlin on the eve of the Senate vote) resulted in the defeat of the treaty. It was a devastating political blow to the president, and he would not soon again attempt to challenge the isolationist tide.

That tide seemed to grow stronger in the following months. Through the summer of 1935, it became clear that Mussolini's Italy was preparing to invade Ethiopia in an effort to expand its colonial holdings in Africa. Fearing that a general European war would result, American legislators began to design legal safeguards to prevent the United States from being dragged into the conflict. The result was the Neutrality Act of 1935.

The 1935 act and the Neutrality Acts of 1936 and 1937 that followed were designed to prevent a recurrence of the events that many Americans now believed had pressured the United States into World War I. The 1935 law established a mandatory arms embargo against both victim and aggressor in any military conflict and empowered the president to warn American citizens that they might travel on the ships of warring nations only at their own risk. Thus, isolationists believed, the "protection of neutral rights" could not again become an excuse for American intervention in war. The 1936 Neutrality Act renewed these provisions. And in 1937, with world conditions growing even more precarious, Congress passed a still more stringent measure. The new Neutrality Act established the so-called cash-and-carry policy, by which belligerents could purchase only nonmilitary goods from the United States and would have to pay cash and carry the goods away on their own vessels.

The American stance of militant neutrality gained support in October 1935 when Mussolini finally launched his long-anticipated attack on Ethiopia. When the League of Nations protested, Italy simply resigned from the organization, completed its conquest of Ethiopia, and formed an alliance (the "Axis") with Nazi Germany. Most Americans responded to the news with renewed determination to isolate themselves from European instability. Two thirds of those responding to public-opinion polls at the time opposed any American action to deter aggression.

Isolationist sentiment showed its strength once again in 1936–1937 in response to the civil war in Spain. The Falangists of General Francisco Franco, a group much like the Italian fascists, revolted in July 1936 against the existing republican government. Hitler and Mussolini supported Franco, both vocally and with weapons and supplies. Some individual Americans traveled to Spain to assist the republican cause; but the United States government joined with Britain and France in an agreement to offer no assistance to either side—although all three governments were sympathetic to the republicans.

Alarmed by the events of 1935 and 1936, Roosevelt began moving slowly and cautiously to challenge the grip of the isolationists on the nation's foreign policy. For a time, it seemed to be a hopeless cause. The United States was unable to do much more than watch as a series of new dangers emerged that brought the world closer to war.

Particularly disturbing was the deteriorating situation in Asia. Japan's aggressive designs against China had been clear since the invasion of Manchuria in 1931. In the summer of 1937, Tokyo launched an even broader assault, attacking China's five northern provinces. The United States could not, Roosevelt believed, allow the Japanese aggression to go unremarked or unpunished. In a speech in Chicago in October 1937, therefore, the president warned forcefully of the dangers that Japanese aggression posed to world peace. Aggressors, he proclaimed, should be "quarantined" by the international community to prevent the contagion of war from spreading.

The president was deliberately vague about what such a "quarantine" would mean; and there is evidence that he was contemplating nothing more drastic than a break in diplomatic relations with Japan, that he was not considering economic or military sanctions. Nevertheless, public response to the speech was disturbingly hostile. As a result, Roosevelt drew back. Although his strong words encouraged the British government to call a conference in Brussels to discuss the crisis in Asia, the United States refused to make any commitments to collective action; and the conference produced no agreement.

Only months later, another episode gave renewed evidence of how formidable the obstacles to Roosevelt's efforts remained. On December 12, 1937, Japanese aviators bombed and sank the U.S. gunboat *Panay* as it sailed the Yangtze River in China. The attack was almost undoubtedly deliberate. It occurred in broad daylight, with clear visibility; a large American flag had been painted conspicuously on the *Panay's* deck. Even so, isolationists seized eagerly on Japanese protestations that the bombing had been an accident and pressured the administration to accept Japan's apologies and overlook the attack.

The Failure of Munich

In 1936, Hitler had moved the revived German army into the Rhineland, rearming an area that France had, in effect, controlled since World War I. In March 1938, German forces marched into Austria; and Hitler proclaimed a union (or *Anschluss*) between Austria, his native land, and Germany, his adopted one. Neither in America nor in most of Europe was there much more than a murmur of opposition.

The Austrian invasion, however, soon created another crisis; for Hitler had by now occupied territory surrounding three sides of western Czechoslovakia, a region he dreamed of annexing to provide Germany with the *Lebensraum* (living space) he believed it needed. In September 1938, he demanded that Czechoslovakia cede to him part of that region, the Sudetenland, an area on the Austro-German border in which many ethnic Germans lived. Czechoslovakia, which possessed substantial military power of its own, was prepared to fight rather than submit. But it realized it could not hope to win against Germany's powerful armies without help from other European nations. It got none. Most

Western nations, including the United States, were appalled at the prospect of another war and were willing to pay almost any price to settle the crisis peacefully. On September 29, Hitler met with the leaders of France and Great Britain at Munich in an effort to resolve the crisis. The French and British agreed to accept the German demands in Czechoslovakia in return for Hitler's promise to expand no farther. "This is the last territorial claim I have to make in Europe," the Fuhrer solemnly declared. And Prime Minister Neville Chamberlain returned to England to a hero's welcome, assuring his people that the agreement ensured "peace in our time." Among those who had cabled him with encouragement at Munich was Franklin Roosevelt.

INVASION OF POLAND.   In September 1939, the German Panzer divisions that poured into Poland met with little resistance. Here some Polish citizens salute a Nazi detachment as it arrives in their town.

The Munich accords were the most prominent element of a policy that came to be known as "appeasement" and that came to be identified (not altogether fairly) almost exclusively with Chamberlain. Whoever was to blame, however, it became clear almost immediately that the policy was a failure. In March 1939, Hitler occupied the remaining areas of Czechoslovakia, violating the Munich agreement unashamedly. And in April, he began issuing threats against Poland. At that point, both Britain and France gave assurances to the Polish government that they would come to its assistance in case of an invasion; they even flirted, too late, with the Stalinist regime in Russia, attempting to draw it into a mutual defense agreement. Stalin, however, had already decided that he could expect no protection from the West; he had, after all, not even been invited to attend the Munich Conference. Accordingly, he signed a nonaggression pact with Hitler in August 1939, freeing the Germans for the moment from the danger of a two-front war.

For a few months, Hitler had been trying to frighten the Poles into submitting to German demands. When that failed, he staged an incident on the border to allow him to claim that Germany had been attacked; and on September 1, 1939, he launched a full-scale invasion of Poland. Britain and France, true to their pledges, declared war on Germany two days later. World War II had begun.

THE FAILURE OF NEUTRALITY

"This nation will remain a neutral nation," the president declared shortly after the hostilities began in Europe, "but I cannot ask that every American remain neutral in thought as well." It was a statement that stood in stark and deliberate contrast to Woodrow Wilson's 1914 plea that the nation remain neutral in both deed and thought; and it was clear from the start that among those whose opinions were decidedly unneutral in 1939 was the president himself.

Neutrality Tested

There was never any question that both the president and the majority of the American people favored Britain, France, and the other Allied nations in the contest. The question was how much the United States was prepared to do to assist them. At the very least, Roosevelt believed, the United States should make armaments available to the Allied armies to help them counteract the highly productive German munitions industry. As a result, in September 1939, he asked Congress for a revision of the Neutrality Acts. The original measures had forbidden the sale of American weapons to any nation engaged in war; Roosevelt wanted the arms embargo lifted. Powerful isolationist opposition forced him to accept a weaker revision than he would have liked; as passed by Congress, the 1939 measure maintained the prohibition on American ships entering war zones. It did, however, permit belligerents to purchase arms on the same cash-and-carry basis that the earlier Neutrality Acts had established for the sale of nonmilitary materials.

For a time, it was possible to believe that little more would be necessary. After the German armies had quickly subdued Poland, the war in Europe settled into a long, quiet lull that lasted through the winter and spring—a "phony war," some called it. The only real fighting during this period occurred not between the Allies and the Axis, but between Russia and its neighbors. Taking advantage of the situation in the West, the Soviet Union overran and annexed the small Baltic republics of Latvia, Estonia, and Lithuania and then, in late November, invaded Finland. Most Americans were outraged; but neither Congress nor the president was willing to do more than impose an ineffective "moral embargo" on the shipment of armaments to Russia. By March 1940, the Soviet advance was complete.

Whatever illusions anyone may have had about the reality of the war in Western Europe were shattered in the spring of 1940 when Germany launched an invasion to the west—first attacking Denmark and Norway, sweeping next across the Netherlands and Belgium, and driving finally deep into the heart of France. Allied efforts proved futile against the Nazi *Blitzkrieg*. One Western European stronghold after another fell into German hands. On June 10, Mussolini brought Italy into the war, invading France from the south as Hitler was attacking from the north. On June 22, finally, France fell to the German

FALL OF FRANCE.   In June of 1940, a long line of German troops marches past the Arc de Triomphe, memorial to the victories of France, as Paris falls to the Nazis.

onslaught. Nazi troops marched into Paris (and Hitler, in a brief visit, danced a jig under the Arc de Triomphe—as if to celebrate Germany's revenge for its humiliation in World War I); a new collaborationist regime assembled in Vichy; and in all Europe, only the shattered remnants of the British and French armies, rescued from the beaches of Dunkirk by an almost miraculous flotilla of military and civilian vessels, remained to oppose the Axis forces.

Roosevelt had already begun to increase American aid to the Allies. He also began preparations to resist a possible Nazi invasion of the United States. On May 16, he asked Congress for an additional $1 billion for defense (much of it for the construction of an enormous new fleet of warplanes) and received it quickly. With France tottering a few weeks later, he proclaimed that the United States would "extend to the opponents of force the material resources of this nation." And on May 15, Winston Churchill, the new British prime minister, sent Roosevelt the first of many long lists of requests for ships, armaments, and other assistance without which, he insisted, England could not long survive. Many Americans (including the United States ambassador to London, Joseph P. Kennedy) argued that the British plight was already hopeless, that any aid to the English was a wasted effort. The president, however, made the politically dangerous decision to "scrape the bottom of the barrel" to make war materials available to Churchill. He even circumvented the cash-and-carry provisions of the Neutrality Act by trading fifty American destroyers (most of them left over from World War I) to England in return for the right to build American bases on British territory in the Western Hemisphere; and he returned to the factories a number of new airplanes purchased by the American government so that the British could buy them instead.

Roosevelt was able to take such steps in part because of a major shift in American public opinion. Before the invasion of France, most Americans had believed that a German victory in the war would not be a threat to the United States. By July, with France defeated and Britain threatened, more than sixty-six percent of the public (according to opinion polls) believed that Germany posed a direct threat to the United States. Congress, aware of the change in public opinion, was becoming more willing to permit expanded American assistance to the Allies. It was also becoming more concerned about the need for internal preparations for war, and in September it approved the Burke-Wadsworth Act, inaugurating the first peacetime military draft in American history.

But while the forces of isolation may have weakened, they were far from dead. On the contrary, a spirited and at times vicious debate began in the summer of 1940 between those who advocated expanded American involvement in the war (who were termed, often inaccurately, "interventionists") and those who continued to insist on neutrality. The celebrated journalist William Allen White served as chairman of a new Committee To Defend America, whose members lobbied actively for increased American assistance to the Allies but opposed actual intervention. Others went so far as to urge an immediate declaration of war (a position that as yet had little public support) and in April created an organization of their own, the Fight for Freedom Committee. Opposing them was a powerful new lobby entitled the America First Committee, which attracted some of America's most prominent leaders. Its chairman was General Robert E. Wood, until recently the president of Sears Roebuck; and its membership included Charles Lindbergh, General Hugh Johnson, Senator Gerald Nye, and Senator Burton Wheeler. It won the editorial support of the Hearst chain and other influential newspapers; and it had at least the indirect support of a large proportion of the Republican party. (It also, perhaps inevitably, attracted a fringe of Nazi sympathizers and anti-Semites.) The debate between the two sides was loud and bitter. Through the summer and fall of 1940, moreover, it was complicated by a presidential campaign.

A Third-Term President

For many months, the politics of 1940 revolved around the question of Franklin Roosevelt's intentions. Would he break with tradition and run for an unprecedented third term? The president himself was deliberately coy and never publicly revealed his own wishes. But by refusing to withdraw from the contest, he made it virtually impossible for any rival Democrat to establish a foothold within the party. Just before the Democratic Convention in July, he let it be known that he would accept a "draft" from his party. The Democrats quickly renominated him and even reluctantly swallowed his choice of vice president: Agriculture Secretary Henry A. Wallace, a man too liberal for the taste of many party leaders.

The Republicans, again, faced a far more difficult task. With Roosevelt effectively straddling the center of the defense debate, favoring neither the extreme isolationists nor the extreme interventionists, the Republicans had few viable alternatives. Their solution was to compete with the president on his own ground. Succumbing to a remarkable popular movement (carefully orchestrated by, among others, Henry Luce, the publisher of *Time* and *Life* magazines), they nominated a dynamic and attractive but politically inexperienced businessman, Wendell Willkie. Both the candidate and the party platform took positions little different from Roosevelt's: They would keep the country out of war but would extend generous assistance to the Allies. Willkie was left, therefore, with the unenviable task of defeating Roosevelt by outmatching him in personal magnetism and by trying to arouse public fears of the dangers of an unprecedented third term. An appealing figure and a vigorous campaigner, he managed to evoke more public enthusiasm than any Republican candidate since Theodore Roosevelt. In the end, however, he was no match for Franklin Roosevelt. The election was closer than those in 1932 and 1936, but Roosevelt nevertheless won decisively. He received fifty-five percent of the popular vote to Willkie's forty-five percent, and he won 449 electoral votes to Willkie's eighty-two.

Ending Neutrality

During the last weeks of 1940, with the election behind him, Roosevelt began to make subtle but profound changes in the American role in the war. To the public, he claimed that he was simply continuing the now-established policy of providing aid to the embattled Allies. In fact, that aid was taking new and more decisive forms.

In December 1940, Great Britain was virtually bankrupt. No longer could the British meet the cash-and-carry requirements imposed by the Neutrality Acts; yet England's needs, Churchill insisted, were greater than ever. The president, therefore, suggested a method that would "eliminate the dollar sign" from all arms transactions while still, he hoped, pacifying those who opposed blatant American intervention in the war. The new system was labeled "lend-lease." It would allow the government not only to sell but to lend or lease armaments to any nation deemed "vital to the defense of the United States." In other words, America could funnel weapons to England on the basis of no more than Britain's promise to return or pay for them when the war was over. Isolationists attacked the measure bitterly, arguing (correctly) that it was simply a device to tie the United States more closely to the Allies; but Congress enacted the bill by wide margins.

With lend-lease established, Roosevelt soon faced another serious problem: ensuring that the American supplies would actually reach Great Britain. Shipping lanes in the Atlantic had become extremely dangerous; German submarines destroyed as much as a half-million tons of shipping each month. The British navy was losing ships more rapidly than it could replace them and was finding it difficult to transport materials across the Atlantic from America. Secretary of War Henry Stimson (who had been Hoover's secretary of state and who returned to the cabinet at Roosevelt's request in 1940) argued that the United States should itself convoy vessels to England; but Roosevelt decided to rely instead on the concept of "hemispheric defense," by which the United States navy would defend transport ships only in the western Atlantic—which he argued was a neutral zone and the responsibility of the American nations. By July 1941, American ships were patrolling the ocean as far east as Iceland, escorting convoys of merchant ships, and radioing information to British vessels about the location of Nazi submarines.

At first, Germany did little to challenge these obviously hostile American actions. By the fall of 1941, however, events in Europe changed their position. Nazi forces had invaded the Soviet Union in June of that year, driving quickly and forcefully deep into Russian territory. When the Soviets did not surrender, as many had predicted, Roosevelt persuaded Congress to extend lend-lease privileges to them—the first step toward creating a new relationship with Stalin that would ultimately lead to a formal Soviet-American alliance. Now American industry was providing crucial assistance to Hitler's foes on two fronts, and the navy was playing a more active role than ever in protecting the flow of goods to Europe.

In September, Nazi submarines began a concerted campaign against American vessels. Early that month, a German U-boat fired on the American destroyer *Greer* (which was radioing the U-boat's position to the British at the time). Roosevelt responded by ordering American ships to fire on German submarines "on sight." In October, Nazi submarines actually hit two American destroyers and sank one of them, the *Reuben James*, killing many American sailors. Enraged members of Congress now voted approval of a measure allowing the United States to arm its merchant vessels and to sail all the way into belligerent ports. The United States had, in effect, launched a naval war against Germany.

At the same time, a series of meetings, some private and one public, were tying the United States and Great Britain more closely together. In April 1941, senior military officers of the two nations met in secret and agreed on a joint strategy they would follow were the United States to enter the war. In August, Roosevelt met with Churchill aboard a British vessel anchored off the coast of Newfoundland. The president made no military commitments, but he did join the prime minister in releasing a document that became known as the Atlantic Charter, in which the two nations set out "certain common principles" on which to base "a better future for the world." It was, in only vaguely disguised form, a statement of war aims. It called openly for, among other things, "the final destruction of the Nazi tyranny."

By the fall of 1941, therefore, it seemed only a matter of time before the United States became an official belligerent. Roosevelt remained convinced that public opinion would support a declaration of war only in the event of an actual enemy attack. But an attack seemed certain to come, if not in the Atlantic, then in the Pacific.

Pearl Harbor

Japan, in the meantime, was taking advantage of the crisis (which had preoccupied the Soviet Union and the two most powerful colonial powers in Asia, Britain and France) to extend its empire in the Pacific. In September 1940, Japan signed the Tripartite Pact, a loose defensive alliance with Germany and Italy that seemed to extend the Axis into Asia. (In reality, the European Axis powers never developed a very strong relationship with Japan, and the wars in Europe and the Pacific were largely separate conflicts.)

Roosevelt had already displayed his animosity toward Japanese policies by harshly denouncing their continuing assault on China and by terminating a longstanding American commercial treaty with the Tokyo government. Still the Japanese drive continued. In July 1941, imperial troops moved into Indochina and seized the capital of Vietnam, a colony of France (after having demanded and received a base there a year before). The United States, having broken Japanese codes, knew that their next target would be the Dutch East Indies; and when Tokyo failed to respond to Roosevelt's stern warnings, the president froze all Japanese assets in the United States and established a complete trade embargo, severely limiting Japan's ability to purchase essential supplies (including oil). American public opinion, in part because of strong anti-Japanese prejudices developed over several decades, generally supported these forceful actions.

Tokyo now faced a choice. It would either have to repair relations with the United States to restore the flow of oil and other crucial supplies, or it would have to find those supplies elsewhere, most notably by seizing British and Dutch possessions in the Pacific. At first, the Tokyo government seemed willing to compromise. The Japanese prime minister, Prince Konoye, had begun negotiations with the United States even before the freezing of his country's assets; and in August he increased the pace by requesting a personal meeting with President Roosevelt. But the United States rebuffed these overtures. Secretary of State Hull feared that Konoye lacked sufficient power within his own government to be able to enforce any agreement, and he persuaded Roosevelt to say that he would meet with the prime minister only if Japan would give guarantees in advance that it would respect the territorial integrity of China. Konoye could give no such assurances, as Roosevelt and Hull knew, and the negotiations collapsed. In October, militants in Tokyo forced Konoye out of office and replaced him with the leader of the war party, General Hideki Tojo. With Japan's need for new sources of fuel becoming desperate, there seemed little alternative now to war.

For several weeks, the Tojo government kept up a pretense of wanting to continue negotiations. On November 20, 1941, Tokyo proposed a *modus vivendi* highly favorable to itself and sent its diplomats in Washington to the State Department to discuss it. But Tokyo had already decided that it would not yield on the question of China, and Washington had made clear that it would accept nothing less than a reversal of that policy. Hull rejected the Japanese overtures out of hand; on November 27, he told Secretary of War Henry Stimson, "I have washed my hands of the Japanese situation, and it is now in the hands of you and [Secretary of the Navy Frank] Knox, the Army and Navy." He was not merely speculating. American intelligence had already decoded Japanese messages which made clear that war was imminent, that after November 29 an attack would be only a matter of days.

But Washington did not know where the attack would take place. Most officials were convinced that the Japanese would move first not against American territory but against British or Dutch possessions to the south. American intelligence took note of a Japanese naval task force that began sailing east from the Kurile Islands in the general direction of Hawaii on November 25; a routine warning went to the United States naval facility at Pearl Harbor, near Honolulu. Officials were paying far more attention, however, to a large Japanese convoy moving southward through the China Sea. A combination of confusion and miscalculation caused the government to overlook what should have been clear indications that Japan intended a direct attack on American forces—partly because Hawaii was so far from Japan that few believed such an attack possible.

PEARL HARBOR.   The burning and twisting wreckage of the *USS Arizona* is visible after the Japanese attack on Pearl Harbor, December 7, 1941.

At 7:55 a.m. on Sunday, December 7, 1941, a wave of Japanese bombers—taking off from aircraft carriers hundreds of miles away—attacked the United States naval base at Pearl Harbor. A second wave came an hour later. Military commanders in Hawaii had taken no precautions against such an attack and had allowed ships to remain bunched up defenselessly in the harbor and airplanes to remain parked in rows in airstrips. The consequences of the raid were disastrous for America. Within two hours, the United States lost eight battleships, three cruisers, four other vessels, 188 airplanes, and several vital shore installations. More than 2,000 soldiers and sailors died, and another 1,000 were injured. The Japanese suffered only light losses.

American forces were now greatly diminished in the Pacific (although by sheer accident, none of the American aircraft carriers, the heart of the Pacific fleet, had been at Pearl Harbor on December 7). Nevertheless, the raid on Pearl Harbor did virtually overnight what more than two years of effort by Roosevelt and others had been unable to do: It unified the American people in a fervent commitment to war. On December 8, the president traveled to Capitol Hill, where he grimly addressed a joint session of Congress: "Yesterday, December 7, 1941—a date which will live in infamy—the United States of America was suddenly and deliberately attacked by the naval and air forces of the Empire of Japan." Within four hours, the Senate unanimously and the House 388 to one (the lone dissenter being Jeanette Rankin of Montana, who had voted against war in 1917 as well) approved a declaration of war against Japan. Three days later, Germany and Italy, Japan's European allies, declared war on the United States; and on the same day, December 11, Congress reciprocated without a dissenting vote. For the second time in twenty-five years, the United States was engaged in a global war.

CHAPTER SIXTEEN

Fighting a Global War

∼

T he attack on Pearl Harbor thrust the United States into the largest and most terrible war the world has ever known. World War I had cost many lives and had destroyed centuries-old European social and political institutions. But World War II created carnage and horror without precedent in human history. The war raged around the world, drawing in almost every nation in one way or another. It was fought at sea, in the air, and on land. It ended with the deployment of the atomic bomb and the unleashing of other weapons of war of unprecedented destructiveness. It has been estimated that some 60 million people died in the war—most of them civilians. Towns and cities, roads and factories, ancient cathedrals and modern buildings stood in ruins in its aftermath. By its end, World War II had changed the world as profoundly as any event of the twentieth century, perhaps of any century.

Those who served in the American armed forces during World War II endured experiences that no one else can fully measure: discomfort, loneliness, fear, horror, and at times glory. They did so willingly. And they received the gratitude of their nations. These are the men, President Bill Clinton told Americans on the fiftieth anniversary of D-Day, "who saved the world."

The war changed forever the lives of the soldiers who fought it. But it changed American society as well. Unlike the combatants, those Americans who remained at home did not experience the terrible destruction and devastation unleashed in other parts of the globe. Their cities were not bombed, their shores were not invaded, they experienced no massive dislocation. Their economy, unlike almost all others in the world, actually flourished as a result of the war. Veterans who returned home in 1945 and 1946 found their country—at least on the surface—very much like the place they had left four years before. The same could not be said of those returning to Britain, France, Germany, Italy, the Soviet Union, China, Japan, and many other nations.

321

Nonetheless, for America the war marked an important divide in its history. As the poet Archibald MacLeish noted in 1943: "The great majority of the American people understand very well that this war is not a war only, but an end and a beginning—an end to things known and a beginning of things unknown. We have smelled the wind in the streets that changes weather. We know that whatever the world will be when the war ends, the world will be different." The story of American involvement in the war, therefore, is the story of how the military forces and the industrial might of the United States helped defeat Germany, Italy, and Japan. But it is also the story of the creation of a new world, both abroad and at home.

WAR ON TWO FRONTS

Whatever political disagreements preceded American involvement in World War II, there was a striking unity of opinion once the nation had entered the war—"a unity," as one member of Congress proclaimed shortly after Pearl Harbor, "never before witnessed in this country." Even so, President Roosevelt set out to ensure that American commitment to the war effort would not waver despite the costs. "We are now in this war. We are all in it—all the way," Roosevelt instructed the nation just two days after Pearl Harbor. "Every single man, woman, and child is a partner in the most tremendous undertaking of our American history."

The "United Nations"

The partnership Americans relied upon most during the war was the one formed with its Allies. It has been said that the war was fought with British intelligence, American power, and Soviet blood. Although that sentiment grossly simplifies the complexities of the war effort, each of the Allies did, in fact, make a distinctive contribution to the war effort.

The attempt to coordinate British and American strength had begun even before Pearl Harbor when Roosevelt and Churchill had met to draft the Atlantic Charter. Shortly after the American declaration of war, the two leaders met again, in Washington, to plan Allied strategy for the war. (The Soviet Union, then engaged in fierce fighting on the eastern front in Europe but determinedly neutral in the Pacific war, did not participate in this early conference.) Through late December and then into January, British and American officials worked in what became known as the Arcadia Conference to hammer out military goals. Concerned lest the United States focus its attention primarily on defeating Japan, a tactical decision that Churchill believed might well doom the western Allies, the prime minister pressed Roosevelt to make the defeat of Germany America's first priority. Roosevelt readily agreed, despite the popular pressure in America to move quickly to avenge Pearl Harbor.

The Arcadia Conference was also notable for Allied agreements to make planning of the war a joint enterprise under the authority of a Combined Chiefs of Staff, incorporating British and American military leaders. The Allies agreed to pool their munitions and their shipping resources; administrative control over them was assigned to another joint authority. Some American military leaders chafed at the stress on sharing responsibility for strategic planning with the British. General Joseph Stilwell complained of Roosevelt, "The Limeys have his ear, while we have the hind tit." But Roosevelt partly allayed such concerns by ensuring that the Combined Chiefs of Staff had their headquarters in Washington.

Perhaps most importantly, on January 1, 1942 the United States, Britain, the Soviet Union, and 23 other nations issued a "Declaration by the United Nations." In it, the Allies affirmed commitments that Britain and America had articulated in the Atlantic Charter, most pointedly their joint mission to defeat the Axis powers. Equally critical, they promised not to make a separate peace. Together, the Allies declared, they were "now engaged in a common struggle against savage and brutal forces seeking to subjugate the world."

The first, troubled months of 1942 severely tested their unity and confidence. Despite soaring rhetoric, impressive displays of patriotism, and a dramatic flurry of activity, the Allies reeled in the face of the Axis assault. Defeat seemed a real possibility as Britain struggled to regain its footing after a near collapse in 1940, and as the Soviet Union shouldered the enormous weight of battling the Nazis on the eastern front. Also ominous, Allied strongholds in the Pacific were falling one after the other to the forces of Japan. The first task facing the United States, therefore, was less to achieve victory than to stave off defeat.

Containing the Japanese

Ten hours after the strike at Pearl Harbor, Japanese airplanes attacked the American airfields at Manila in the Philippines, destroying much of America's remaining air power in the Pacific. Three days later Guam, an American possession, fell to Japan; then Wake Island and Hong Kong. The great British fortress of Singapore in Malaya surrendered in February 1942, the Dutch East Indies in March, Burma in April. In the Philippines, American and Filipino soldiers fought desperately to hold the Bataan Peninsula in the winter of 1942 despite a lack of food and supplies.

On April 9, wasted by hunger and disease, the soldiers on Bataan surrendered to the Japanese. What followed for thousands of captured American and Filipino soldiers was a terrible "death march" toward prisoner of war camps. Along the way, nearly 10,000 died from starvation and murder. "You found all kinda bodies along the road," one American GI remembered. "Some of 'em bloated, some had just been killed. If you fell out to the side, you were either shot by the guards or you were bayoneted and left there." Incarceration in

BATAAN DEATH MARCH.   American soldiers carry the bodies of their compatriots
in slings as they march toward Bilibad Prison during the 1942
Bataan Death March in the Philippines.

terrifying prison camps followed for those who survived the march. By May 6
the island of Corregidor, once the command post of General Douglas
MacArthur himself, had surrendered as well. The soldiers on the remaining islands followed suit by June 9. This was the first wholesale surrender of American field forces in a foreign war in American history.

Faced with such defeats, American strategists planned two broad offensives to turn the tide against the Japanese. One, under the command of General
Douglas MacArthur, would move north from Australia, through New Guinea,
and eventually back to the Philippines. The other, under Admiral Chester
Nimitz, would move west from Hawaii toward major Japanese island outposts in
the central Pacific. Eventually military plans called for the two offensives to
come together in an invasion of Japan.

The Allies scored an important victory, for morale at least, in April 1942
when U.S. B25 bombers flew from the naval carrier *Hornet* on missions that
struck the heart of the enemy's homeland—Tokyo. Although the raids inflicted
minimal damage, their psychological impact on Japanese leaders was important.
They suggested a kind of vulnerability in the interior of Japan many enemy
strategists had not anticipated. A month later, the Allies achieved their first important Pacific war victory in the Battle of the Coral Sea, just northwest of

Australia. On May 7–8, 1942, American forces launched a series of air strikes against Japanese carriers that struck one light carrier, inflicted serious damage on a heavy carrier, and destroyed planes aboard another. Although the Americans lost a large carrier, the *Lexington*, they succeeded in turning back the enemy as the Japanese withdrew from a planned landing at Port Moresby, New Guinea. What was to all appearances a tactical draw was in fact a strategic victory for the United States as the Japanese retreated. The events in the Coral Sea were also notable for the unusual character of the hostilities. The two fleets never saw each other in battle; the entire action was fought by planes launched at sea from the decks of the carriers—a practice that became central to modern naval warfare.

A month later, there was a far more important turning point in the Pacific war. Determined to extend their perimeter, draw the American navy into battle, and perhaps eventually seize the Hawaiian Islands, the Japanese prepared to invade Midway Island, an American outpost about a thousand miles northwest of Hawaii. Their strategic plans were notable for their complexity and even eccentricity. While Admiral Isoroku Yamamoto himself led the Japanese combined fleet toward Midway Island, the Japanese simultaneously undertook a diversionary operation in the distant Aleutian Islands, off Alaska, and occupied two uninhabited islands.

WORLD WAR II IN THE PACIFIC

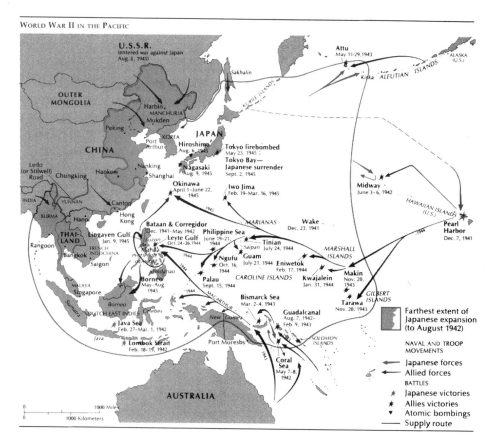

The battle for Midway was another story. For four days from June 3 to June 6, 1942, the Americans and Japanese fought bitterly for the tiny spit of land. The Japanese amassed an armada that included several battleships, aircraft carriers, over 200 airplanes, and assorted additional submarines, minesweepers, and transport craft. The American forces were much smaller in number, but two miscalculations made the Japanese vulnerable to them. First, the Japanese dispersed their fleet into several separate formations that weakened their capacity to support the main invasion group poised to strike Midway. Second, unknown to the Japanese, Admiral Nimitz had advance knowledge of the enemy strategy because the United States had cracked the Japanese naval code and used the intercepted information to plan their encounter with the enemy at Midway. Three American carriers were thus able to surprise the Japanese, by launching strikes at enemy carriers when aircraft were gathered on the decks ready for launching. A series of initial American aircraft raids failed to inflict much injury, but a second wave of dive bombers inflicted devastating damage on the enemy. When the smoke cleared, three out of four Japanese carriers were in flames. American planes sank a fourth Japanese carrier later in the battle, although not before enemy planes severely damaged the *USS Yorktown*. Despite great losses, the United States could declare a clear victory.

The Battle of Midway was of great significance to the Allied cause. By sinking four Japanese carriers, the United States managed to wrest the initiative in the Pacific war from the Japanese. They crippled planned Japanese offensive operations in the South Pacific and Indian Ocean. And although the Japanese made minor changes in their codes, they failed to prevent further intelligence interceptions that would greatly assist the Allies. The battle's most important consequence, however, was to vindicate the "Europe first" strategy. Had the Americans been defeated by the Japanese at Midway, the nation would have been forced to reconsider its commitment to focus its primary attention on the defeat of Germany. As it was, the "miracle at Midway" became a reminder of American victory for the duration of the war.

The Americans took the offensive for the first time months later in the southern Solomon Islands, to the east of New Guinea. In August 1942, American forces assaulted Guadalcanal in an effort to dislodge the Japanese who were beginning to build an airfield there. A ferocious struggle, which included terrible savagery on both sides, followed. For six months, the battle raged as U.S. Marines fought the enemy on land. In the meantime, both sides fought relentlessly for control of the seas to replenish troops and supplies that dwindled daily. Slowly, however, the tide turned in favor of the Americans. In late December, the Japanese began to abandon the island, and in early February the fight for Guadalcanal finally shuddered to a close. The young American soldiers who had fought so doggedly felt, some claimed, like old men after the savage action they had seen.

In successfully defending the Solomon Islands, American forces had denied the Japanese control over areas of the Pacific that were crucial to the Axis hopes for victory. By mid-1943, in both the southern and central Pacific, the initiative had shifted to the United States, and the Japanese advance had come to a stop. The Americans, with aid from Australians and New Zealanders, now began the slow, arduous process of moving toward the Philippines and Japan itself.

Holding Off the Germans

In the European war, the United States had less control over its military operations. It was fighting in cooperation with Britain in the West; and it was trying to conciliate its new ally, the Soviet Union, as well. Differences emerged early among the Allies about the best strategy for the defeat of Germany. Britain and the United States both envisaged a landing in western Europe, but the proposed timing failed to satisfy the Russians. The Soviet Union was shouldering (as it would throughout the war) the greatest burden in the struggle against Germany, fighting alone to drive back the Nazis in the East and suffering enormous military and civilian casualties. They wanted the Allied invasion to proceed at the earliest possible moment. They saw the establishment of a second European front as a way to ease the tremendous German pressure on them.

American strategists at first proposed starting immediately to amass a large invading force in England that would cross the Channel and confront the Germans in decisive battle in Europe. But Churchill argued that the Allies were not ready for the invasion, that they needed more time to assemble the munitions—and perhaps most critically the landing craft—they would need. A premature invasion, he warned, might fail and doom the Allied war effort. Finally, in the summer of 1942, British views prevailed. Roosevelt agreed to postpone the invasion of northwestern Europe. But the Allies were still determined to take some immediate action, and they decided to launch an offensive on the periphery of the Nazi empire in hopes that it might weaken the Germans before the great invasion of Europe.

In the fall of 1942, the British and Americans opened an offensive in North Africa against Nazi forces under the command of Field Marshall Erwin Rommel, the legendary "Desert Fox." The British Eighth Army confronted Rommel's forces at El Alamein and forced the Germans to retreat from Egypt. On November 8, Anglo-American forces landed at Oran and Algiers in Algeria and at Casablanca in Morocco—areas under the Nazi-controlled French government at Vichy—and began moving east toward Rommel. The Germans threw the full weight of their forces in Africa against the inexperienced Americans and inflicted a serious defeat on them at the Kasserine Pass in Tunisia. But under the stern command of General George S. Patton, American troops regrouped and began an effective counteroffensive. With the help of Allied air and naval power and the aid of British forces attacking from the east under Field Marshall Bernard Montgomery (the hero of El Alamein), the Allied offensive finally drove the last Germans from Africa in May 1943.

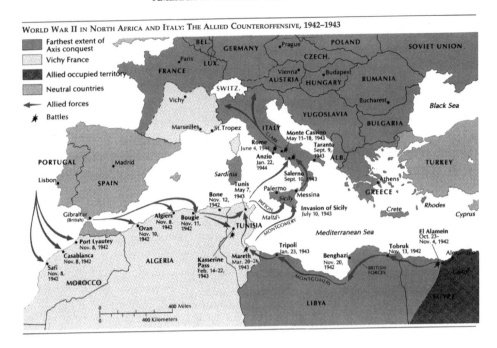

WORLD WAR II IN NORTH AFRICA AND ITALY: THE ALLIED COUNTEROFFENSIVE, 1942–1943

By then the Allies had decided to delay the planned cross-channel invasion until 1944, despite continued protests from the Soviet Union. The threat of a Soviet collapse had now diminished, for during the winter of 1942–1943, the Red Army had successfully held off the Nazis during a major German assault at Stalingrad in southern Russia. Hitler had committed enormous forces to the battle and had suffered appalling losses. Stalingrad constituted a crushing and humiliating blow to the Nazis in a winter of defeat that ultimately paralyzed the Germans' eastern offensive.

The Soviet victory had come at a terrible cost. The German siege of Stalingrad had decimated the civilian population of the city and devastated the surrounding countryside. Indeed, throughout the war, the Soviet Union absorbed losses far greater than any other warring nation—a fact that generations later continued to haunt the Russian memory and affect Soviet policy. As one Russian soldier who survived the winter offensive recalled: "Of my generation, out of a hundred who went to fight, three came back. Three percent. . . . I look at my children and grandchildren and I think: only centimeters decided whether they should be on this earth or not." His narrow escape made the soldier "recollect the phrase: 'The bullet that killed us today goes into the death of centuries and generations, killing life which didn't come to exist yet.'"

The Soviet success in beating back the German offensive provided a backdrop for discussions between Britain and America about Allied strategy. In a January 1943 meeting with Churchill in Casablanca, Roosevelt agreed to a British plan for an Allied invasion of Sicily. For many years after, there would be much debate about the wisdom of British enthusiasm for focusing attention on the Mediterranean. General Marshall opposed the invasion of Sicily, arguing that it would further delay the vital invasion of France. But the British argued that it would be far more difficult for the Germans to reinforce their armies in Italy than in France—an assumption that the long, tortured Allied campaign in Italy would subsequently challenge. On July 10, 1943, American and British soldiers landed in southeast Sicily; thirty-eight days later, they had conquered the island and were moving onto the Italian mainland. In the face of these setbacks, Mussolini's government in Rome collapsed; the dictator himself fled to northern Italy.

Mussolini's successor, Pietro Badoglio, eventually committed Italy to the Allies; but as he delayed, the Germans wrested critical positions in northern and central Italy from Italian troops. The Nazis then moved eight divisions into the country and established a powerful defensive line south of Rome. The Allied offensive on the Italian peninsula, which began on September 3, 1943, soon bogged down, especially after a serious setback at Monte Cassino that winter. In the months that followed, the fighting in Italy remained extremely harsh and exhausting as the Allies tried in vain to break the German line. For the soldiers in the Italian theater, the fighting began to resemble the terrible stalemate that had emerged during World War I. Meanwhile in Anzio, north of the German line, where the Allies had landed in January 1944, the Nazis pinned the landing forces to the beachhead and tried to push them back into the sea. The Allies resisted strenuously. Not until May 1944, however, did they succeed in resuming their northward advance in Italy. On June 4, 1944, two days before the Allied landing in Normandy, American troops liberated Rome; Allied forces moved onward in the ensuing months in an effort to drive the Germans out of central Italy.

The invasion of Italy aided the Allied war effort in several important ways. As Churchill had hoped, it cemented Allied control of the Mediterranean, tied up German forces, and permitted the Allies to establish air bases from which to launch further assaults on central Europe. But it proved extremely costly in men and resources, and it contributed to the postponement of the invasion of France by as much as a year, deeply embittering the Soviet Union. Some Russian leaders believed that the United States and Britain were deliberating delaying to allow the Russians to absorb the brunt of the fighting.

The postponement also gave the Soviets time to begin moving toward the countries of eastern Europe; and that fueled Allied fears. Roosevelt worried that without the Allied invasion of France, the Soviets might well make a separate peace with Germany. Nor did the president want to see the Soviet army move across Europe, occupying the continent while it secured victory. For these reasons, among others, Roosevelt insisted at Allied meetings in Quebec in August of 1943 that the British accept May 1, 1944 as a target date for the Allied invasion of France, which was given the codename "Operation Overlord."

America and the Holocaust

In the midst of this intensive fighting, the leaders of the American government were confronted with one of history's great horrors: the Nazi campaign to exterminate the Jews of Europe—the Holocaust. As early as 1942, high officials in Washington had incontrovertible evidence that Hitler's forces were rounding up Jews and others (including Poles, gypsies, homosexuals, and communists) from all over Europe, transporting them to concentration camps in eastern Germany and Poland, and systematically murdering them. (The death toll would ultimately reach 6 million Jews and approximately 4 million others.) News of the atrocities was reaching the public as well, and pressure began to build for an Allied effort to end the killing, or at least to rescue some of the surviving Jews.

The American government consistently resisted almost all such entreaties. Although Allied bombers flew missions within a few miles of the most notorious death camp at Auschwitz in Poland, pleas that the planes be directed to destroy the crematoria were rejected as militarily unfeasible or as an unjustifiable diversion of resources needed for more crucial operations. American officials made a similar judgment about the proposal that the Allies try to destroy railroad lines leading to the camps, even though the Air Force was already engaged in heavy bombing of industrial sites in the area.

The United States also resisted pleas that it admit large numbers of the Jewish refugees attempting to escape Europe—a pattern of refusal established well before Pearl Harbor. One ship, the *St. Louis*, had arrived off Miami in 1939 carrying nearly 1,000 escaped German Jews, only to be refused entry and forced to return to Europe. Throughout the war, the State Department did not even use up the number of visas permitted by law; almost ninety percent of the quota remained untouched. One opportunity after another to assist the imperiled Jews was either ignored or rejected. In January of 1944, the Roosevelt administration finally responded to criticism that its passivity constituted a deliberate evasion of responsibility. It created the War Refugee Board and gave it the mission of trying to evacuate Jews from Axis-occupied territories and of intervening to assist refugees. But, the agency lacked the resources and the authority to save more than a few people.

In the end, there is no way to know how many of Hitler's victims might have been saved by more forceful action on the part of the United States and Britain. But at least some lives might well have been spared had the Allies acted sooner and more decisively. The western leaders justified abandoning the Jews to their fate by concentrating their attention solely on the larger goal of winning the war. Any diversion of energy and attention to other purposes, they apparently believed, would distract them from the overriding goal of victory. They believed that even though some, at least, were fully aware of the moral gravity of the Holocaust. Churchill himself said in 1944 that "there is no doubt that this is probably the greatest and most horrible single crime ever committed in the whole history of the world." Allied troops finally reached the concentration camps in the spring of 1945, liberated those who survived and made it impossible at last for the world to ignore the magnitude of the horror. But the memory of the Holocaust—an unspeakable crime against humanity and, many believe, against God—survives still as a terrible reminder of the human capacity for evil.

THE DEFEAT OF THE AXIS

By the middle of 1943, America and its allies had succeeded in stopping the Axis advance both in Europe and in the Pacific. In the next two years, the Allies themselves seized the offensive and launched a series of powerful drives. The costs were high and the fighting fierce, but Allied operations now led inexorably toward victory.

Bombing Campaigns

By early 1944, American and British bombers were attacking German industrial installations and other targets almost around the clock, drastically cutting production and impeding transportation. Targeting problems were formidable despite the popular myth that Allied pilots could "put a bomb in a pickle barrel." American pilots conducted daylight "precision bombing" raids that managed to inflict devastating damage on some German fuel supply depots and industrial plants, but these raids ultimately proved less important for the specific targets they hit than for the psychological impact of the extraordinary damage they imposed. British fliers also began night-time saturation bombing raids that resulted in tremendous damage to major cities and the deaths of large numbers of civilians.

Especially devastating was the massive bombing of such German cities as Hamburg, Dresden, and Berlin. In July and August 1943, over 700 Allied planes dropped incendiary bombs mixed with high explosives on Hamburg, the second largest industrial city in Germany. They produced an enormous conflagration that consumed 6,000 acres of land, half the city, and killed nearly 100,000 people as buildings collapsed and fire raged out of control. Nearly a million people were left homeless. A February 1945 incendiary raid on Dresden unleashed a firestorm that destroyed three-fourths of the previously undamaged city and killed approximately 135,000 people, almost all civilians. Kurt Vonnegut, then an American prisoner of war in Dresden, described the scene the day after the bombing in his novel *Slaughter house five:* "The sky was black with smoke. The sun was an angry little pinhead. Dresden was like the moon now, nothing but minerals. The stones were hot. Everybody else in the neighborhood was dead."

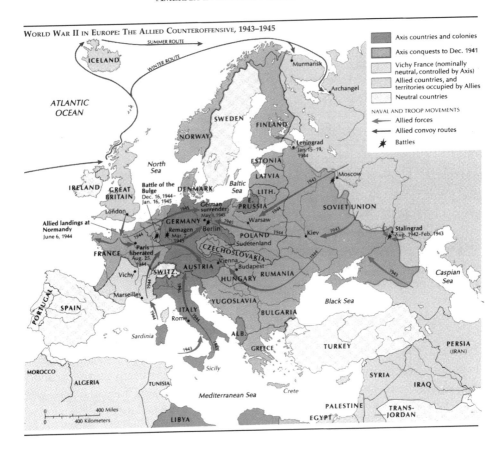

WORLD WAR II IN EUROPE: THE ALLIED COUNTEROFFENSIVE, 1943–1945

Military leaders claimed that the bombing raids destroyed industrial facilities, demoralized the population, and cleared the way for the great Allied invasion of France in the late spring. In truth, the effectiveness of much of the bombing campaign was due less to its precision than to the unrelenting pounding it inflicted on the enemy. The bombing forced the German air force (the *Luftwaffe*) to relocate much of its strength in Germany itself and to engage Allied forces in the air. The air battles over Germany considerably weakened the *Luftwaffe* and made it a much less formidable obstacle to the Allied invasion than it might once have been. But the saturation and incendiary bombings also eroded the distinction, once important to strategists, between military and civilian targets in warfare.

Operation "Overlord": The Liberation of France

By the spring of 1944, an enormous invasion force had been gathering in England for two years: almost 3 million Allied troops, including British, Canadian, and American forces, and the greatest array of naval vessels and armaments ever assembled in one place. The fear and tension were palpable among the troops in the staging areas on the morning of June 6, 1944, and among their leaders. The day before, Dwight D. Eisenhower, who served as commander, had scribbled a note to be read in the event of failure: "Our landings in the Cherbourg-Havre area have failed to gain a satisfactory foothold and I have withdrawn the troops. My decision to attack at this time and place was based on the best information available. If any blame or fault attaches to this attempt, it is mine alone." Instead, as the vast armada moved into action on the morning of June 6, one of the great triumphs of the entire Allied campaign was about to unfold.

The landing came not at the narrowest part of the English Channel, where the Germans had expected and prepared for it, but along sixty miles of the Co-tentin Peninsula on the coast of Normandy. Over 1 million Allied soldiers had been committed to the operation, and the enormous scale of the invasion soon became apparent. While airplanes and battleships offshore bombarded the Nazi defenses, 4,000 vessels landed troops and supplies on the beaches. (Three divisions of paratroopers had been dropped, chaotically but not ineffectively, behind the German lines the night before.) Fighting was intense along the beach, but the Allies' superior air and sea power, as well as the determined assault of their landing forces, gradually prevailed. By June 18, American troops had reached the port city of Cherbourg, where intense battle, accompanied by the pounding of enemy shore batteries by the 14-inch guns of Allied battleships, forced a German surrender there near the end of June. The German forces had then been dislodged from virtually the entire Normandy coast.

D-DAY. American troops disembark from a Coast Guard landing barge during the invasion of Normandy. Up ahead on Omaha Beach, the men who preceded them lie flat against the sand as German machine guns try to stop the Allied advance.

For the next month, further progress remained slow. But in late July in the battle of Saint-Lô, General Omar Bradley's First Army smashed through the German lines. George S. Patton's Third Army, spearheaded by heavy tank attacks, then moved through the gap Bradley's troops had created and began a drive into the heart of France. On August 25, Free French forces arrived in Paris and liberated the city from four years of German occupation. Eisenhower ordered two divisions of American troops to follow the French in marching into Paris, in a demonstration that German occupation of the city was truly at an end. Meanwhile, Allied forces succeeded in invading southern France. As the Nazis retreated, some key French collaborators followed them, watching the Allied occupation of France with fear and dismay. By mid-September the Allied armies had driven the Germans almost entirely out of France and had seized the city of Antwerp in Belgium.

The Battle of the Bulge

The great Allied drive came to a halt, however, at the Rhine River in the face of a refortified line of German defenses, the coldest winter ever recorded in Western Europe, and formidable Allied problems with moving supplies. In mid-December 1944, German forces struck in desperation along fifty miles of front in the Ardennes Forest. In the Battle of the Bulge (named for a large bulge that appeared in the American lines as the Germans pressed forward), German tanks drove fifty-five miles toward Antwerp before they were finally stopped at Bastogne. In the snow when the siege lifted, one soldier recalled, "dead bodies, German prisoners and burning tanks" were scattered in the forest. At the battle's end some 70,000 Americans and 80,000 Germans were dead, wounded, or unaccounted for. Nearly 8,000 Americans had been seized as prisoners of war. Still, the German gamble in deploying some of their last reserves to this arena failed. The Allies could replace the men they had lost; the Germans could not. Their offensive only hastened the Nazi defeat. Even so, the fierce fighting proved a chastening experience for the Americans. "I now live among trees," one veteran of the Battle of the Bulge reported fifty years later, "and every winter on days when the boughs are covered with snow, I think of the Ardennes."

The Battle of the Bulge ended serious German resistance in the West. Now attention shifted to the eastern front. While the Anglo-American forces had been fighting their way through France, Soviet forces had swept westward into Central Europe and the Balkans. In late January 1945, the Red Army began another great winter offensive toward the Oder River inside Germany. In early spring, they were ready to launch a final assault against Berlin. By then, American forces were pushing toward the Rhine from the west. Early in March, the First Army captured the city of Cologne, on the river's west bank. The next day, in a remarkable stroke of good fortune, the Allies discovered and seized an undamaged bridge over the river at Remagen; American troops now swarmed across the Rhine. Before long, Patton's army too had breached the river barrier. Now the Allies were within striking distance of the heart of Germany. In the following weeks the British commander, Field Marshall Montgomery, also pushed into Germany with a million troops. The Ninth Army to the north joined with the First Army to the south to complete the encirclement of German soldiers in the Ruhr by mid-April. Now surrounded, 300,000 German soldiers abandoned the fight in the largest surrender of the war. Their commander committed suicide.

The Death of Roosevelt

Amid all this fighting, a single death far from the front shocked the American people and momentarily renewed Hitler's hopes for victory. Through the war years, Roosevelt's health appeared to those who knew him well to be declining. The burden of his responsibilities showed as the president's face reflected new lines of worry and fatigue. In 1944, physicians discovered that Roosevelt was suffering from a serious heart disease; his high blood pressure revealed rapidly worsening arteriosclerosis. Publicly, the White House managed to sustain the facade that the president was healthy. To admit otherwise might have jeopardized his re-election that year to an unprecedented fourth term. Nonetheless, rumors persisted that the 62-year-old president was seriously ill.

In February 1945 at the Yalta Conference, British observers expressed shock at the deterioration in Roosevelt's appearance. "The President appears a very sick man," Churchill's personal physician reported. "I give him only a few months to live." Upon his return to Washington, Roosevelt himself sought to quiet persistent talk about his wellbeing with a quip about the far more taxing political perils he faced. "I was not ill for a second, until I arrived back in Washington, and there I heard all of the rumors which had occurred in my absence." But on April 12, 1945, at his retreat in Warm Springs, Georgia, Roosevelt died of a massive cerebral hemorrhage. For many Americans, Roosevelt had become virtually synonymous with the presidency. After dying in the midst of the war, the president was eulogized as a soldier who had fallen in battle like those he led so valiantly. His successor, Vice President Harry Truman, now assumed the burden of seeing the war to a close.

Victory in Europe

Any hopes the Germans harbored that the death of Roosevelt would somehow stall the Allies were soon thoroughly crushed. As April 1945 wound down, the German resistance collapsed on both the eastern and western fronts. By month's end the Nazis were also beating a hasty retreat in Italy, as Allied troops swarmed north toward the Alps. Italian partisans captured Mussolini and his mistress near Lake Como in northern Italy and—despite clear instructions to the contrary from Allied commanders—shot him in the back on April 28. His body was then transported to Milan and hung in a public square face downwards. The German forces who remained in Italy surrendered.

In Germany, American forces moved eastward faster than they had anticipated and could have beaten the Russians to Berlin and Prague. By then, however, the Allied conference at Yalta had reached agreement on the postwar division of Germany into several zones of occupation, each assigned to one of the Allied forces. To cross the Elbe and drive toward Berlin would have resulted in many additional casualties for the British and Americans. Eisenhower concluded there would be little advantage in doing so since the territory captured would fall within the already-designated Soviet occupation zone. The Allied high command decided instead, with some British reluctance, to halt the advance along the Elbe River in central Germany to await the Russians. That decision enabled the Soviet Union to occupy eastern Germany and Czechoslovakia and paved the way for many Cold War tensions in later years.

On April 30, as Soviet forces approached his headquarters, Adolf Hitler committed suicide in his bunker, along with his long-time mistress Eva Braun, whom he had married the day before their deaths. Hours before his death, Hitler continued to defend the achievements of his Third Reich. Powerless now to avert a Nazi defeat, he lashed out at his generals and the German people, blaming them for his own failure. In the meantime, the battle for Berlin, by one estimate, resulted in nearly a half million casualties. On May 8, 1945, the remaining German forces surrendered unconditionally. VE (Victory in Europe) Day prompted great celebrations in Western Europe and in the United States, tempered by the knowledge of the continuing war against Japan.

The Pacific Offensive

Allied strategy for the defeat of Japan had taken shape in 1944 after critical victories in the Pacific inspired hope that a successful attack on Japan might soon be possible. In February 1944, American naval forces under Admiral Nimitz won a series of victories in the Marshall Islands and cracked the outer perimeter of the Japanese Empire. Within a month, the navy had destroyed other vital Japanese bastions. American submarines, in the meantime, were decimating Japanese shipping and crippling the nation's domestic economy. By the summer of 1944, the already skimpy food rations for the Japanese people had been reduced by nearly a quarter; there was also a critical gasoline shortage.

A frustrating struggle was in progress in the meantime on the Asian mainland. The Americans, in particular, wanted to keep China in the war for both political and strategic reasons. Toward that end, Burma became a theater of war in part to ensure open supply routes to China. In 1942, the Japanese had forced U.S.

VICTORY IN EUROPE. Rumors of Germany's unconditional surrender led crowds to throng in New York's Times Square on May 7, the day before the official surrender. Despite lack of White House confirmation, those gathered celebrated the impending end of war in Europe.

General Joseph W. Stilwell out of Burma and had moved their own troops as far west as the mountains bordering on India. For a time, Stilwell supplied the isolated Chinese forces continuing to resist Japan with an aerial ferry over the Himalayas. In 1943, finally, he led Chinese and a few American troops back through northern Burma and reopened the Burma Road. By then, however, the Japanese had launched a major counteroffensive and had driven so deep into the Chinese interior that they threatened the terminus of the Burma Road and the center of Chinese government at Chungking. These difficulties turned the Allies away from their proposed plans to stage their assault on Japan from air bases in China.

Instead, Allied attention in the Pacific came to focus on a series of islands. In mid-June 1944, an enormous American armada struck the heavily fortified Mariana Islands and, after some of the bloodiest operations of the war, captured Tinian, Guam, and Saipan, 1,350 miles from Tokyo. This led to the fall of General Tojo, the leader of Japan's wartime government. But the Americans paid dearly for their victory. At Peleliu over 7,000 American soldiers were killed or wounded in the costliest amphibious assault in American history (measured in casualties). One Marine later recalled his reactions as he watched his fellows being slaughtered by machine gun fire on the beach: "We were expendable. It was difficult to accept. We come from a nation and a culture that values life and the individual. To find oneself in a situation where your life seems of little value is the ultimate in loneliness. It is a humbling experience."

On October 20, General MacArthur's troops landed on Leyte Island in the Philippines. The Japanese now used virtually their entire fleet against the Allied invaders in three major encounters—which together constituted the decisive battle of Leyte Gulf, the largest naval engagement in history. American forces held off the Japanese onslaught and sank three Japanese battleships and four carriers, as well as an array of other vessels, all but destroying Japan's capacity to continue a serious naval war.

Still, as American forces advanced closer to the Japanese mainland early in 1945, imperial forces seemed to redouble their resistance. The depth of their determination became tragically apparent in the battle of Iwo Jima. The United States viewed the tiny volcanic island, only 750 miles from Tokyo, as an ideal place to establish fighter bases for use during future assaults on the Japanese. To defend the island, the Japanese had established elaborate fortifications, many of which were underground caves. On February 16, 1945, American battleships began to bombard the shore, smoking out some Japanese gun emplacements. The U.S. Marines landed on Iwo Jima February 19 and began nearly a month of extraordinarily harsh fighting. The volcanic ash that covered the surface of the island slowed their advance. By February 24, however, a small band of resolute Marines planted an American flag atop Mt. Suribachi, a scene that gave hope to other soldiers who glimpsed the stars and stripes waving high above the battleground. The event became the source of one of the most famous photographs of World War II and was later memorialized in a monument constructed in Arlington, Virginia. By the end of March, Iwo Jima had been secured, but only after the costliest single battle in the history of the Marine Corps. The Marines suffered over 20,000 casualties. Of the 20,000 Japanese troops defending the island, only 200 were alive when the battle ended. This ferocious fighting gave support to American strategists' fears that a very high price would be extracted in the assault on Japan.

With the new B29 heavy bomber at its disposal, the Air Force began in March to launch a series of nighttime bombing raids—"a rain of death"—on the cities of Japan. Among the most devastating was the firebombing of Tokyo on the night of March 9 and in the early morning hours of the 10th. Over 100,000 people died in the firestorm; the firebombing of Tokyo was probably the single costliest event in human lives during World War II. Indeed, the U.S. Strategic Bombing Survey ventured that "probably more persons lost their lives by fire at Tokyo in a 6-hour period than at any time in the history of man." Swept by high wind, the fire destroyed everything in its path. Those watching the planes above Tokyo described scenes of eerie tranquility: B29s with their "long, glinting wings" standing out like "black silhouettes gliding through the fiery sky to

IWO JIMA. Marines from the 5th Division's 28th Regiment
plant the Stars and Stripes on Mount Suribachi after the
battle of Iwo Jima. This photograph, a reenactment
of a prior event, became one of the most famous images
of the war and the inspiration for the monument
that stands in Arlington, Virginia.

reappear farther on, shining golden against the dark roof of heaven or glittering
blue, like meteors, in the searchlight beams spraying the vault from horizon to
horizon."

Less than one month later, the Allies invaded Okinawa, the last island they
planned to take before their assault on Japan. Yet here too, on this island only
370 miles south of Japan, there was evidence of the strength of the Japanese resistance in these last desperate days. The invasion began on April 1, 1945. For
weeks, Marine and Army troops struggled to subdue the enemy. Week after
week, the Japanese sent *kamikaze* (suicide) planes against American and British
ships, sacrificing thousands of planes and pilots while inflicting substantial damage. One naval officer described the stunning sight as a *kamikaze* flew toward his
target, an American battleship off the coast of Okinawa: "Set afire and burning
fiercely he seemed to be almost on top of us and still headed for the bridge when

we got the door closed and backed into the pilot house. . . . When the scream of the plane became almost as loud as the chatter and rap of the guns, I assumed it was time to gather round and hold a little prayer meeting." When the plane hit the deck, eleven sailors died along with the pilot. The U.S. Navy sustained its highest causalities of the entire war in Okinawa.

On shore, the fighting led to widespread death and destruction. Japanese troops launched desperate nighttime attacks on the American lines. United States soldiers used flamethrowers to burn the enemy out of their caves and garrisons. The United States and its allies suffered approximately 75,000 casualties, including General Simon Buckner, who commanded the operation, before finally capturing Okinawa in late June 1945. Over 100,000 Japanese, among them tens of thousands of civilians, died in the siege.

Many Allied military planners were now convinced that the same kind of bitter fighting would await Americans in Japan itself. But others were beginning to hope that such an invasion might not be necessary. Relentless Allied attacks had badly damaged, although not entirely destroyed, the Japanese capacity to wage war. In July 1945, for example, American warships stood off the shore of Japan and shelled industrial targets (many already in ruins from aerial bombings) with impunity. The brutal firebombing of Tokyo and other Japanese cities had also damaged industrial sites and inflicted—at the very least—a major psychological blow on the Japanese homefront.

In addition, moderate Japanese leaders, who had long since decided that the war was lost, were increasing their power within the government and looking for ways to bring the war to an end. After the invasion of Okinawa, Emperor Hirohito of Japan appointed a new premier and gave him instructions to work for peace. Although the new leader could not persuade military leaders to give up the fight, he did try, along with the Emperor himself, to obtain mediation through the Soviet Union. The Russians showed little interest in playing this role, but other developments made their participation superfluous in any case.

Whether the moderates could ultimately have prevailed is a question about which historians and others continue to disagree. In any case, their efforts were ultimately irrelevant. For in mid-July, American scientists demonstrated to their government a new weapon of awesome power. On July 16, near Alamagordo, New Mexico, they conducted a successful test of an atomic bomb.

The Manhattan Project

The Manhattan Project, as the scientific endeavor to build an atomic bomb was known, grew out of concerns that the Germans were developing new weapons of extraordinary power for their war against the Allies. In 1939, scientists including the Italian physicist Enrico Fermi and the German mathematician Albert Einstein (then living in exile in America) passed word to the U.S. government that Nazi scientists had learned how to produce atomic fission in uranium. Acquiring that knowledge, they warned, was the first step toward the creation of an atomic bomb, a weapon more powerful than any ever previously devised. The United States and Britain immediately began a race to develop the weapon before the Germans did.

Over the next three years, the U.S. government secretly poured nearly $2 billion into the Manhattan Project—a massive scientific effort conducted at hidden laboratories in Oak Ridge, Tennessee; Los Alamos, New Mexico; Hanford, Washington; and other sites. (Its name had emerged earlier, when many of the atomic physicists had been working at Columbia University in New York.) Hundreds of scientists, many of them not fully aware of what they were working on, labored feverishly to complete two complementary projects. One (at Oak Ridge and Hanford) was the production of fissionable plutonium, the fuel for an atomic explosion; the other (at Los Alamos, under the supervision of J. Robert Oppenheimer) was the construction of a bomb that could use the fuel.

The scientists pushed ahead much faster than anyone had predicted. By 1944, the United States government knew that the Germans were not progressing with their own atomic bomb project. The war in Europe, in fact, ended before scientists at Los Alamos were ready to test the first bomb. But the Japanese war continued, and the scientists worked on. Just before dawn on July 16, 1945, at a place they named "Trinity," scientists gathered to witness the first atomic explosion in history. Those who saw the blast described a blinding flash of light brighter than any ever seen on earth. Physicist I. I. Rabi explained: "It blasted; it pounced; it bored its way right through you. It was a vision which was seen with more than the eye. It seemed to last forever. You would wish it would stop; altogether it lasted about two seconds . . . and we looked toward the place where the bomb had been; there was an enormous ball of fire which grew and grew and it rolled as it grew." Over the cold morning desert, now boiling from the heat of the flash, a huge billowing mushroom cloud shot up. Brilliant red, white, purple, and green colors appeared in the atmosphere. The eighteen-kiloton blast had left a crater 1200 feet in diameter. The steel tower from which the bomb had been suspended was vaporized. The blast shattered a window 125 miles away from the bomb site. As the ball of fire dispersed in the atmosphere and "washed out with the wind" the scientists made their way back to their base camp. "A few people laughed, a few people cried," J. Robert Oppenheimer recalled. "Most people were silent. I remembered the line from the Hindu scripture, the *Bhagavad-Gita*: . . . 'Now I am become Death, the destroyer of worlds.'"

The implications of the atomic bomb were momentous for human history and, as Oppenheimer's comment suggests, many of the scientists who worked on the bomb project were fully conscious of that fact. They were mindful of the war that had inspired the bomb project; their years of work had paid off. Some expressed exhilaration that "the gadget" had worked. "The war is over," a brigadier general greeted General Leslie Groves, director of the bomb project, after the blast. "Yes, after we drop two bombs on Japan," Groves responded. But some scientists, among them J. Robert Oppenheimer, were already troubled by the implications of what they had done. In the end, it would be left to others to decide when and where to deploy the terrible weapon the Manhattan Project had developed—or whether to deploy it at all.

Hiroshima and Nagasaki

News of the explosion reached American leaders at a critical juncture in the Allied war effort. Okinawa had been secured at enormous cost, long-formulated plans for an invasion of Japan were on the verge of unfolding, and word of internal dissension in Tokyo over surrender had reached the American government through decoded radio messages. President Harry S. Truman was in Potsdam, Germany, attending a conference of Allied leaders, when he received word that the atomic bomb test had succeeded. On July 26 as two unassembled bombs —code named Fat Man and Little Boy—were en route to the Pacific, Truman issued the Potsdam Declaration signed jointly by the British and Nationalist China. The document demanded the unconditional surrender of Japan, warning soberly that "the alternative for Japan is prompt and utter destruction."

Some within the Japanese government favored acceptance of the Allied ultimatum, but others resisted stubbornly. By the time the deadline Truman imposed arrived, the peace forces in Japan had not yet been able to persuade key military leaders to give up. Some Japanese still believed they could inflict such severe casualties on Allied forces when they attempted to land in Japan that the Americans would agree to a negotiated settlement on terms more favorable to the Japanese than a surrender. Others stressed the possibility that the Soviets would come through as intermediaries and produce a settlement agreeable to Japan. In the most wildly optimistic of scenarios, some hoped that the Soviet Union might actually join forces with the Japanese against the United States. The disagreement and delay contributed to tragedy. When the Japanese failed to meet the deadline, Truman ordered the military to deploy the new atomic weapons against them.

Controversy has raged for decades over Truman's decision to deploy the bomb. Critics have questioned the president's motives, his good faith, and his honesty in explaining his actions. Many have argued that the atomic attack was unnecessary, that Japan would have surrendered had the United States agreed to a settlement that would have allowed it to retain its Emperor (something which the United States ultimately permitted in any case). Others insist the Japanese would have given up anyway if the United States had waited only a few more weeks. Still others consider the American deployment of the bomb as an unacceptably immoral act. Whatever Japanese intentions, they assert, the United States should not have used a weapon with such devastating consequences for human history. For the most part, these arguments emerged in hindsight. But some made the case before the bomb was used, including one physicist who wrote to Truman shortly before the attack: "This thing must not be permitted to exist on this earth. We must not be the most hated and feared people in the world."

HIROSHIMA.   Where once a lively city stood, nothing but rubble remains. At the center of Hiroshima, depicted here, the devastation of the atomic bomb appears total.

For American and British leaders, however, there were few moral qualms about deploying the bomb. From the very beginning of the bomb project, the Allies had considered it not an abstract scientific effort, but an attempt to create a practical weapon of war. Once the bomb was successfully tested, few in authority doubted that it should now be used. Truman believed he faced a clear-cut military decision. A weapon was available that would end the war quickly; he could see no reason not to use it.

Some critics of Truman's decision have argued that motives beyond defeating Japan were at work. With the Soviet Union poised to enter the war in the Pacific, did the United States want to end the conflict quickly to forestall an expanded communist presence in Asia? Did Truman use the bomb as a weapon to intimidate Stalin, with whom he was engaged in difficult negotiations? No conclusive evidence is available to support (or definitively refute) either of these accusations.

There is, however, no question that in August 1945 the goal of an immediate end to the war figured centrally in Allied thinking. Both the British and the Soviets supported the American decision to drop the bomb on Japan. On August 6, 1945, after a few days of weather delays, an American B29, the *Enola Gay*, took off for Japan with "Little Boy" in its bomb bay. The plane dropped the atomic bomb, as planned, over the Japanese city of Hiroshima. In an instant, it completely incinerated a four-square-mile area at the center of the previously undamaged city. "Where we had seen a clear city two minutes before," one crew member aboard the *Enola Gay* recounted, "we could now no longer see the city. We could see smoke and fires creeping up the sides of the mountains." The whole "turbulent mass," another reported, "looked like lava or molasses covering the whole city, and it seemed to flow outward up into the foothills where the little valleys would come into the plain, with fires starting up all over."

On the ground, thousands died in an instant from the heat. At the center of the blast, buildings imploded, animals disappeared, every vestige of life vanished in a matter of seconds. More than 80,000 civilians died almost at once, according to later American estimates. For those who survived, a terrible quiet and a fearful darkness seemed to settle on the city. Left to the living was the herculean task of coming to terms with the physical, emotional, and material toll the atomic bomb inflicted. Some survived to find themselves maimed, burned, and blinded. Others would suffer from the crippling effects of radioactive fallout. For many who experienced it, the enormity of the event seemed to defy understanding. "I thought it might have been something which had nothing to do with the war," one survivor explained. It seemed like "the collapse of the earth which it was said would take place at the end of the world."

For many American soldiers, the bomb seemed to represent just the opposite. Aware of the enormous death toll exacted in the grueling Pacific island battles, they awaited the expected invasion of Japan acutely aware that further horror lay ahead. As writer Paul Fussell, an Army infantryman during the Second World War, explained, where one stood during the war determined much of one's reaction to Hiroshima. "I was a 21-year-old second lieutenant leading a rifle platoon. . . . When the bombs dropped and news began to circulate that . . . we would not be obliged to run up the beaches near Tokyo assault-firing while being mortared and shelled, for all the fake manliness of our facades we cried with relief and joy. We were going to live. We were going to grow up to adulthood after all."

Hiroshima stunned the government in Tokyo, which could not at first agree on how to respond to the catastrophe. The Japanese foreign minister continued his efforts to pursue negotiations with the Soviet Union, a tack that soon led to bitter disappointment. Instead of brokering a settlement, the Soviets notified the Japanese on August 8 that they, too, would be at war with Japan as of the following day. That night, just after midnight, the Soviet army attacked Manchuria. Meanwhile the United States dropped leaflets and sent radio transmissions warning the Japanese people that another bomb would soon be dropped if their country did not immediately surrender. And on August 9, an American plane deployed a second atomic weapon—this time on the city of Nagasaki—inflicting horrible damage and over 30,000 deaths on another devastated community. Finally, the Emperor intervened to break the stalemate in the cabinet, taking to the radio to ask his people to "endure the unendurable" and give up the struggle. On August 14, the Japanese government announced that it was ready to give up. On September 2, 1945, on board the American battleship *Missouri* anchored in Tokyo Bay, Japanese officials signed the articles of surrender.

The greatest and most terrible war in the history of mankind had finally come to an end. The United States emerged from it not only victorious, but in a position of unprecedented power, influence, and prestige. It was a victory, however, that few could greet with unambiguous joy. Fourteen million combatants had died in the struggle. Many more civilians had perished, from bombings, from disease and starvation, and from genocidal campaigns of extermination. The United States had suffered only light casualties in comparison with many other nations, but the cost had still been high: 322,000 dead, another 800,000 injured. And despite the sacrifices, the world continued to face an uncertain future, menaced by the new threat of nuclear warfare and by an emerging antagonism between the world's two strongest nations—the United States and the Soviet Union—that would darken the peace for many decades to come.

CHAPTER SEVENTEEN

Wartime Society and Culture

❦

"War is no longer simply a battle between armed forces in the field," an American government report of 1939 concluded. "It is a struggle in which each side strives to bring to bear against the enemy the coordinated power of every individual and of every material resource at its command. The conflict extends from the soldier in the front line to the citizen in the remotest hamlet in the rear." These statements describe very well the impact of World War II on American society.

Although the United States had experienced many wars before, not since the Civil War had the nation experienced so consuming a military experience as World War II. American armed forces engaged in combat around the globe for nearly four years. The American economy became integrally bound up with the effort to supply troops, sustain the Allied war effort, and otherwise support the waging of war in remote battlefields. Families coped with the long absence of loved ones, often by rearranging men's and women's traditional roles, at least for the time being. The war also imposed great challenges on the United States' character as a pluralist society. In all of these ways, and many others, the war had a transforming effect on American society.

THE WARTIME ECONOMY

World War II had its most profound impact on American domestic life by ending at last the Great Depression. By the middle of 1941, the economic problems of the 1930s—unemployment, deflation, industrial sluggishness—had virtually vanished in the great wave of wartime industrial expansion.

346

The Return of Prosperity

The most important agent of the new prosperity was federal spending, which after 1939 was pumping more money into the economy each year than all the New Deal relief agencies combined had done. In 1939, the federal budget had been $9 billion, the highest level it had ever reached in peacetime; by 1945, it had risen to $100 billion. Largely as a result, the gross national product soared: from $91 billion in 1939 to $166 billion in 1945. Personal incomes in some areas grew by as much as 100 percent or more. In the face of a wartime shortage of consumer goods, many wage earners diverted much of their new affluence into savings. That practice would later help keep the economic boom alive in the postwar years.

The impact of government spending was perhaps most dramatic in the West, which had long relied heavily on federal largesse. The West Coast, naturally, became the launching point for most of the naval war against Japan; and the government created large manufacturing facilities in California and elsewhere to serve the needs of the military. Altogether, the government made almost $40 billion worth of capital investments (factories, military and transportation facilities, highways, power plants) in the West during the war, more than in any other region. Ten percent of all the money the federal government spent between 1940 and 1945 went to California alone. Other western states also shared disproportionately in war contracts and government-funded capital investments. By the war's end, forty-five percent of California's personal income was derived from the federal government.

The activities of one important entrepreneur, Henry J. Kaiser, illustrate the extent and character of the western economic boom. During the 1930s, Kaiser's construction companies had built some of the great western dams. In the process, he became a great favorite of many members of the Roosevelt administration. During the war, Kaiser singlehandedly steered billions of federal dollars and funds into vast capital projects in the West. He helped build the infrastructure to support major centers for shipbuilding, steel, magnesium, and aluminum production.

Kaiser also pioneered in providing health care plans for the over 125,000 war workers he employed in California. Even before the war, he had begun to provide medical assistance to his employees. But the war sharpened his determination and led Kaiser to mount an aggressive public relations campaign in favor of prepaid health insurance programs. At Kaiser's shipbuilding plants, medical clinics were established to provide extensive services ranging from preventive care to free house calls to emergency and specialist services—benefits Kaiser believed added to his workers' productivity and to the success of his business. During the war, Kaiser ran the largest prepaid health program in the nation, an achievement that earned him the enmity of the American Medical Association, who doggedly opposed what they derided as "contract medicine." The Association threatened to expel doctors who worked for the Kaiser plan and in the end fought Kaiser in the courts, where they received a stunning rebuke from the judicial system. The innovative health care program inaugurated during the war by Kaiser provided at least some workers with a valued fringe benefit for their service in the wartime economy, a benefit that became part of many union contracts in the postwar years.

By the end of the war, the economy of the Pacific Coast and, to a lesser extent, other areas of the West had been transformed. The Coast had become the center of the growing American aircraft industry. New yards in southern California, Washington State, and elsewhere made the West a center of the shipbuilding industry. Los Angeles, formerly a medium-sized city notable chiefly for its film industry, now became a major industrial center as well. Once a lightly industrialized region, parts of the West were now among the most important manufacturing areas in the country. A part of the country that had once lacked adequate facilities to support substantial economic growth now stood poised to become the fastest growing region in the nation after the war.

Labor During the War

The war had an ambiguous impact on American workers. The economic growth it created lifted millions of workers out of unemployment and poverty; but the war also produced conflict between organized labor's desire to advance the status of working men and women, by strikes if necessary, and the nation's demand for a stable labor force devoted first and foremost to the needs of war production. In addition, an astronomical industrial accident rate cost the lives of thousands of workers on the home front who labored on complex machinery many were not experienced in operating. Indeed, by one estimate, casualties among industrial workers in 1942–1943 exceeded that of American soldiers in battles by a ratio of twenty to one.

Among the more stunning developments of the war was the way in which it eliminated almost overnight the terrible rates of unemployment of the 1930s. Instead, the war created a serious labor shortage. The armed forces removed over 15 million men and women from the civilian work force at the same time that the demand for labor was rising rapidly. Nevertheless, the civilian work force increased by almost twenty percent during the war. The 7 million who had previously been unemployed accounted for some of the increase; the employment of many people previously considered inappropriate for the work force—the very young, the elderly, and most importantly, several million women—accounted for the rest.

The war also gave an enormous boost to union membership, which rose from about 10.5 million in 1941 to over 13 million in 1945. But it created important new restrictions on the ability of unions to fight for their members' demands. Not long after the attack on Pearl Harbor in December 1941, Roosevelt established the War Labor Board (WLB) in an effort to enlist the cooperation of labor and industry in ensuring the smooth working of the wartime economy. The government was principally interested in preventing inflation and keeping production moving without disruption. It managed to win important concessions from union leaders on both scores. One was the so-called Little Steel formula, which set a fifteen percent limit on wage increases. Another was the "no-strike" pledge, by which unions agreed not to stop production in wartime. In return, the government provided labor with a "maintenance-of-membership" agreement, which ensured that the thousands of new workers pouring into unionized defense plants would be automatically enrolled in the unions. The agreement ensured the continued health of the union organizations, but in return workers had to give up the right to demand major economic gains during the war.

Organized labor responded to the war with outspoken patriotism. The new head of the CIO, Phillip Murray, exhorted his membership to "heed the call of the Commander in Chief and Work, Work, Work, PRODUCE, PRODUCE,

WORKING FOR VICTORY.   A welder works on a ship nearing completion during World War II. Aside him a propaganda poster celebrates the virtues of free labor in American society. Organized labor exhorted their members to devote themselves to war production, but some wildcat strikes broke out during the war among the rank and file who chafed at rising corporate profits and price increases.

PRODUCE." Still many rank-and-file union members, and some local union leaders, resented the restrictions imposed on them by the government and the labor movement hierarchy. They observed with dismay the rise in profits accrued by many corporations and wartime price increases even as their wages lagged behind, chained to the "Little Steel formula." Despite the no-strike pledge, there were nearly 15,000 work stoppages during the war, mostly wildcat strikes unauthorized by the union leadership.

Labor militancy was especially evident among coal miners. In 1942, eighty coal towns in Pennsylvania struggled in the face of rising food costs (one estimate pegged the increase at 125 percent) and grueling and dangerous working conditions. For their pains, mine workers earned only an average of forty dollars per week, considerably less than workers in other industries that posed fewer dangers and provided better working conditions. On January 1, 1943 anthracite mine workers in Pennsylvania walked out, defying their union's leaders and a back to work order by the War Labor Board. John L. Lewis, the United Mine Workers' president, then changed course and supported his membership. Lewis harshly attacked the "miserably stupid Little Steel formula for chaining labor to the wheels of industry without compensation for increased costs, while other agencies of government reward and fatten industry by charging increased costs to the public purse."

What followed was a series of strikes, including four national labor actions, that provoked the wrath of industry and government. The War Labor Board charged that Lewis gave "aid and comfort to our enemies"—a none too subtle suggestion of treason—while the military newspaper, the *Stars and Stripes*, denounced Lewis for his presumed selfishness: "Speaking for the American soldier—John L. Lewis, damn your coal-black soul." Even liberal journals such as the *Nation* attacked Lewis and his striking workers, arguing that their walkout "was irresponsible and unpatriotic and unjustified, no matter what the miners' grievances." Nonetheless the miners stood firm. When industry and government threatened to send in troops to break the strike or even draft striking workers into the Army, the miners brazenly faced the threat down. "What will they do" they responded to the threat to bring soldiers into the mines, "dig coal with their bayonets?"

In May 1943 Congress reacted to the unrest by passing, over Roosevelt's veto, the Smith-Connally Act (or War Labor Disputes Act). The legislation required unions to wait thirty days between calling a strike and actually beginning it (a so-called cooling-off period). It empowered the president to seize a struck war plant. And, it made it a crime for union officials to advocate strikes in defense plants. Even so, coal miners continued to challenge the "Little Steel formula." In November 1943, they finally won a wage increase in an important concession from the federal government.

But the costs of success were high. By the winter of 1943 a civilian coal shortage, to which the miners' strike had only partially contributed, left many Americans on the East Coast without adequate heating supplies for the winter.

When they turned to fuel coordinator Harold Ickes for assistance, he blamed the shortage on the unusual demands of the war. "We can fuel all of the people some of the time," he said, "and fuel some of the people all the time. But in war we can't fuel all of the people all of the time." Many others, however, blamed organized labor. A railroad strike that winter forced Roosevelt to seize some of the nation's rail lines. In the end, the railway workers, too, won important wage concessions. But, public animosity toward labor rose rapidly during the rest of the war, and many states passed laws to limit union power.

Stabilizing the Boom and Financing the War

The fear of deflation, the central concern of the 1930s, gave way during the war to concerns about inflation, particularly after prices rose twenty-five percent in the two years before Pearl Harbor. In October 1942, Congress grudgingly responded to the president's request and passed the Anti-Inflation Act, which gave the administration authority to control prices, wages, salaries, and rents throughout the country. Enforcement of these provisions was the task of the Office of Price Administration (OPA), led first by Leon Henderson and then by Chester Bowles. In part because of the office's success, inflation was a much less serious problem during World War II than it had been during World War I.

Even so, the OPA was never popular. There was widespread resentment of its controls over wages and prices. And there was only grudging acquiescence in its complicated system of rationing scarce consumer goods: coffee, sugar, meat, butter, canned goods, shoes, tires, gasoline, and fuel oil. Black-marketing and overcharging grew to proportions far beyond OPA policing capacity. One OPA study concluded in 1944 that some fifty-seven percent of American businesses failed to observe price controls.

From 1941 to 1945, the federal government spent a total of $321 billion—twice as much as it had spent in the entire 150 years of its existence to that point, and ten times as much as the cost of World War I. The national debt rose from $49 billion in 1941 to $259 billion in 1945. The government borrowed about half the revenues it needed by selling $100 billion worth of bonds. It raised much of the rest by radically increasing income taxes through the Revenue Act of 1942, which established a ninety-four percent rate for the highest brackets and, for the first time, imposed taxes on the lowest income families as well. To simplify collection, Congress enacted a withholding system of payroll deductions in 1943.

Wartime Production

The search for an effective mechanism to mobilize the economy for war began as early as 1939 and continued for nearly four years. One failed agency after another attempted to bring order to the mobilization effort. Finally, in January 1942, the president responded to widespread criticism by creating the War

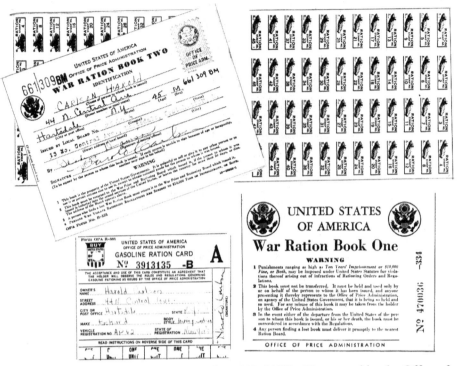

RATIONING.   A sample of rations books from World War II prepared by the Office of Price Administration (OPA). Ration Book One warns of the stiff penalties that could be imposed for violating ration regulations—10 years in jail, a $10,000 fine or both.

Production Board (WPB), under the direction of former Sears Roebuck executive Donald Nelson. In theory, the WPB was to be a "superagency," with broad powers over the economy. In fact, it never had as much authority as its World War I equivalent, the War Industries Board. And the genial Donald Nelson never displayed the administrative or political strength of his 1918 counterpart, Bernard Baruch.

Throughout its troubled history, therefore, the WPB found itself constantly outmaneuvered and frustrated. It was never able to win control over military purchases; the Army and Navy often circumvented the board entirely in negotiating contracts with producers. It was never able to satisfy the complaints of small business, which charged (correctly) that most contracts were going to large corporations. Gradually, the president transferred some of the WPB's authority to a new office located within the White House: the Office of War Mobilization, directed by former Supreme Court Justice and South Carolina Senator James F. Byrnes. But the OWM was only slightly more successful than the WPB.

Despite the administrative problems, the war economy managed to meet almost all the nation's critical war needs. Enormous new factory complexes sprang up in the space of a few months, many of them funded by the federal government's Defense Plants Corporation. An entire new industry producing synthetic rubber emerged to make up for the loss of access to natural rubber in the Pacific. By the beginning of 1944, American factories were, in fact, producing more than the government needed. Their output was twice that of all the Axis countries combined. There were even complaints late in the war that military production was becoming excessive, that a limited resumption of civilian production should begin before the fighting ended. The military staunchly and successfully opposed almost all such demands.

WAR AND DIVERSITY

In addition to the imposing military and economic challenges it raised, the war placed new strains on the nation's social fabric, calling into question many traditions of racial, ethnic, and gender identity. For some groups straining against longstanding social and cultural restrictions, the war created opportunities to press their case for equality and opportunity. For others, most notably Japanese Americans, the war produced new levels of oppression. The war itself created few lasting solutions to the problems of racial and ethnic prejudice and sexual inequality, but it helped ensure that America would not be able to ignore those problems much longer.

African Americans and the War

During World War I, many African Americans had eagerly seized the chance to serve in the armed forces, believing that their patriotic efforts would win them an enhanced position in postwar society. They had been cruelly disappointed. As World War II approached, blacks were again determined to use the conflict to improve their position in society. This time, however, they actively pressed demands for economic justice and political equality from the start.

One of the most important initiatives occurred in the summer of 1941 when A. Philip Randolph, president of the Brotherhood of Sleeping Car Porters (a union with a predominantly black membership), began to insist that the government require companies receiving defense contracts to integrate their work forces. The demand stemmed from evidence of widespread racial discrimination in defense industries. Aircraft factories routinely excluded African Americans, or segregated black and white workers. In the construction industry, thousands of African-American craftsmen were denied work despite a vocal attempt by many companies to recruit skilled workers. Randolph, along with Walter White of the NAACP and T. Arnold Hill of the National Urban League, pressed the issue on President Roosevelt at a meeting in 1940. Despite his evident sympathy, Roosevelt offered only vague assurances that he would explore their grievances.

When five months had lapsed with no sign of action from the president, Randolph formed the idea of organizing a massive march on Washington by

African Americans to dramatize their call for jobs in defense factories and for integration of the armed forces. Randolph's promise to bring 100,000 black demonstrators to Washington produced great anxiety in the Roosevelt administration. Roosevelt was afraid both of the possibility of violence and of the certainty of political embarrassment. Many intermediaries, including First Lady Eleanor Roosevelt, attempted to persuade Randolph to cancel the march in exchange for modest concessions. But Randolph rejected these appeals. Instead, he seized on the idea of an executive order banning discrimination, which had surfaced in one high level New Deal conference. With that goal in mind, Randolph met Roosevelt face to face in late June 1941.

The meeting had important consequences. Roosevelt rejected the idea of integrating the armed forces, stressing the problems such an order would create given the likelihood of impending war. Instead he urged Randolph to accept his personal assurance that the chief executive would work hard to persuade industry to integrate their labor force voluntarily. Randolph did not flinch. Instead, he calmly told Roosevelt that he had come "to ask you to say to white workers and to management that we are American citizens and should be treated as equals. We ask no special privileges; all we ask is that we be given equal opportunities with all other Americans for employment on those industries that are doing work for the government." This could be accomplished, Randolph stressed, if

A. PHILIP RANDOLPH.   A. Philip Randolph is pictured with Eleanor Roosevelt and New York Mayor Fiorello LaGuardia a year after the war's end. During the war, Randolph had pressured Roosevelt into addressing discrimination against African Americans with some limited, though highly symbolic, success.

the president made it "a requirement of any holder of a government contract that he hire his workers without regard to race, creed, or color." Moved both by the moral weight of Randolph's plea and by his fear of the consequences of ignoring it, Roosevelt instructed three assistants to draft an Executive Order which, after some delay, he then signed. Randolph responded by cancelling the March on Washington.

Executive Order 8802 turned out to be largely a symbolic victory. It did ban discrimination by management and labor in industries that held defense contracts. And, it mandated the establishment of a Fair Employment Practices Committee to investigate discrimination against blacks in war industries. However, the FEPC's enforcement powers, and thus its effectiveness, were severely limited. As complaints began to come in, the committee found itself hamstrung in its efforts to mediate disputes between workers and the industries that employed them. In its entire history, the FEPC never recommended cancellation of a defense contract for racial discrimination. Its own chairman asserted at one public hearing in Alabama that "there is no power in the world—not even in all the mechanized armies of the earth, Allied and Axis—which could now force the southern white people to the abandonment of the principle of social segregation." Still, despite its disappointing performance, the creation of the FEPC created an important precedent. For the first time in many years, the federal government had intervened publicly and institutionally on behalf of equality for African Americans and had issued an unequivocal statement condemning racial discrimination.

The demand for labor in war plants greatly increased the migration of blacks from the rural areas of the South into industrial cities—a migration that continued for more than a decade after the war and brought many more African Americans into northern cities than the first Great Migration of 1914–1919 had done. Of the more than six million African Americans who left the South for the North between 1910 and 1970, five million came after 1940.

The migration had profound consequences for African Americans. It permitted many of them to improve their economic conditions. It also helped create an infrastructure of community organizations and church groups that would provide a foundation for the burgeoning postwar civil rights movement. Finally, it drew attention to extensive de facto segregation outside the South, as racial discrimination soon confronted many of the new migrants who searched for employment and housing opportunities in northern cities. At times that hostility resulted in violence, as a major race riot in 1943 demonstrated. On a hot June day in Detroit, a series of altercations between blacks and whites at a city park escalated into a full-scale riot. Two days of violence left thirty-four people dead, twenty-five of them blacks, and over 500 wounded. Both the mayor and the governor blamed the city's African-American community for the riot.

Despite such signs of conflict and tension, the leading black organizations redoubled their efforts during the war to challenge segregation. The Congress of Racial Equality (CORE), organized in 1942, mobilized mass popular resistance to discrimination in a way that the older, more conservative organizations had never done. Randolph, Bayard Rustin, James Farmer, and other, younger black leaders helped organize sit-ins and demonstrations in segregated theaters and restaurants. In 1944, they won a much-publicized victory by forcing a Washington, D.C. restaurant to agree to serve blacks.

Pressure for change was also growing within the military. At first, the armed forces maintained their traditional practice of limiting blacks to the most menial assignments, keeping them in segregated training camps and units, and barring them entirely from the Marine Corps and the Army Air Corps. Gradually, however, military leaders were forced to make adjustments—in part because of public and political pressures, but also because they recognized that these forms of segregation were wasting manpower. By the end of the war, the number of black servicemen had increased sevenfold, to 700,000; some training camps were at least partially integrated; blacks were serving on ships with white sailors; and more African-American units were being sent into combat. These changes created tensions of their own. In some of the partially integrated army bases—Fort Dix, New Jersey, for example—riots occasionally broke out when African Americans protested having to serve in segregated divisions. Substantial discrimination survived in all the services until well after the war. But within the military, as within the society at large, the traditional pattern of race relations was slowly eroding.

Native Americans and the War

For Native Americans, the war also gave evidence of new opportunities and of the persistence of racial tensions. Approximately 25,000 Native Americans performed military service during World War II. Many of them served in combat (among them Ira Hayes, one of the men who raised the American flag at Iwo Jima and became part of the legendary photograph and, later, war memorial). Others worked as "code-talkers," working in military communications and speaking their own languages (which enemy forces would be unlikely to understand) over the radio and the telephones.

The war also made its presence felt in the lives of those Native Americans who remained civilians. Little war work reached the tribes, and government subsidies dwindled. These developments increased the pressures for assimilation. As many talented young people left the reservations—some to serve in the military, even more (over 70,000) to work in war plants—contact with white society increased in ways that also spurred assimilation. For some, such exposure awakened a taste for the material benefits of life outside the reservations. It has been estimated that the average income of Indian households tripled during World War II. These improved economic conditions encouraged some Indians to remain in western cities when the war was over. Others found that employment opportunities that had been available to them during the fighting became unavailable once the war was won; many returned to the reservations.

The wartime emphasis on national unity undermined support for the revitalization of tribal autonomy that the Indian Reorganization Act of 1934 had launched. New pressures emerged to eliminate the reservation system and require the tribes to assimilate into white society—pressures so severe that John Collier, the energetic director of the Bureau of Indian Affairs who had done much to promote the reinvigoration of the reservations, resigned in 1945.

Mexican-American War Workers

World War II played an important role in enlarging the Mexican-American population. Large numbers of Mexican workers entered the United States during the war in response to labor shortages on the Pacific Coast, in the Southwest, and eventually in almost all areas of the nation. Indeed, Mexicans formed the second largest group of migrants to American cities (after blacks) in the 1940s. In Los Angeles, the population of Mexicans grew to nearly 400,000 during the war. Some migration was shaped by an agreement between the American and Mexican government in 1942 by which *braceros* (contract laborers) would be admitted to the United States for a limited time to work at specific jobs. American employers in some parts of the Southwest began actively recruiting Hispanic workers.

The war also influenced the kinds of work Mexican immigrants did. During the Depression, many Mexican farm workers had been deported to make room for desperate white workers. The wartime labor shortage caused farm owners to begin hiring them again. More important, however, Mexicans were able for the first time to find significant numbers of factory jobs. And over 300,000 Mexican Americans served in the United States military.

The sudden expansion of Mexican-American neighborhoods created tensions and occasionally conflict in some American cities. White residents of Los Angeles became alarmed at the activities of Mexican-American teenagers, many of whom were joining street gangs (*pachucos*). The gang members were particularly distinctive because of their style of dress, which featured long, loose jackets with padded shoulders, baggy pants tied at the ankles, long watch chains, broad-brimmed hats, and greased, ducktail hairstyles. (It was a style borrowed in part from fashions in Harlem.) The outfit was known as a "zoot suit." For those who wore them, as for many adolescents, their style of dress became a symbol of rebellion against and defiance toward conventional, white, middle-class society.

Eventually, the rebellion of these young Mexican Americans led to confrontation. As Los Angeles newspapers decried a non-existent crime wave supposedly created by Mexicans, an ordinance cleared the City Council that banned the wearing of zoot suits. The law permitted law enforcement officials to sweep through the barrios of Los Angeles and arrest, search, or detain Mexicans virtually at will. The Los Angeles county sheriff insisted that Mexicans had "a biological pre-disposition to criminal tendencies." In 1942, the apparently accidental death of a young man named Jose Diaz led to the arrest of twenty-two young Mexicans who were accused of murdering him. Over half of them were convicted and sentenced to life imprisonment on flimsy evidence before their convictions were overturned two years later.

In June 1943, animosity toward the "zoot suiters" produced a four-day riot in Los Angeles, after a rumor circulated that a group of Mexicans had beaten a white American serviceman. Several white soldiers stationed in the city joined with other white Angelenos and retaliated by indiscriminately beating young Mexicans wearing zoot suits. In subsequent days other riots followed in nearby southern Californian communities. The city police did little to restrain the white rioters in Los Angeles, who grabbed Hispanic teenagers, tore off and burned their clothes, cut off their ducktails, and beat them. But when Hispanics tried to fight back, the police moved in and arrested them. One soldier who observed the scene was horrified by the bloodshed, beatings, and rioting. "This is a form of class war," he concluded.

Chinese Americans and the War

For Chinese Americans, World War II produced a reversal, to some extent, of the blatant rejection many faced in American society earlier in the twentieth century. In fact, the American military alliance with China during World War II significantly enhanced both the legal and social status of Chinese Americans. In 1943, partly to improve relations with the government of China, Congress finally repealed the Chinese Exclusion Acts, which had barred almost all Chinese immigration since 1892. President Roosevelt, in supporting the reform, invoked the demands of the war as he urged the Congress to end exclusion. "By the repeal of the Chinese exclusion laws, we can correct a historic mistake and silence the distorted Japanese propaganda." The legislation that passed, however, did not entirely eliminate restrictions of Chinese immigration. The new quota for Chinese immigrants was minuscule (105 a year). Still, a substantial number of Chinese women—over 4,000 in a three-year period—managed to gain entry into the country through other provisions covering war brides and fiancées. And, perhaps most significantly, permanent residents of the United States of Chinese descent were finally permitted to become citizens.

Racial animosity toward the Chinese by no means disappeared during the war, but it did decline—in part because government propaganda and popular culture both began presenting positive images of the Chinese (partly to contrast them with the Japanese). As Chinese Americans (like African Americans and other previously marginal groups) began taking jobs in war plants and other booming areas suffering from labor shortages, they moved out of the relatively isolated world of the Chinatowns. The war offered an important opportunity for economic mobility as many Chinese gained access to higher-wage jobs than the service positions they had so often occupied in the American economy. On the West Coast and in the East, Chinese men and women labored in aircraft factories and shipyards. Indeed, some fifteen percent of shipyard workers in the San Francisco area in 1943 were Chinese.

Chinese Americans displayed a deeply felt patriotism in countless ways during World War II. The day after Pearl Harbor, and the formation of the United States–China alliance, a newspaper in San Francisco's Chinese community published a letter to "Mr. Hitler, Hirohito & Co." that boasted: "Chinatown is proud to be a part of Freedom's legion in freeing all the decent people of the world." The entire Chinese community in most cities worked hard and conspicuously for the war effort. A higher proportion of Chinese Americans (twenty-two percent of all adult males) were drafted than of any other national group. To men of our generation," one Chinese American explained, "World War II was the most important historic event of our times. For the first time we felt we could make it in American society."

The Internment of Japanese Americans

World War I had produced in America a virtual orgy of hatred, vindictiveness, and hysteria, as well as widespread and flagrant violations of civil liberties. World War II did not. The government barred from the mails a few papers it considered seditious, among them Father Coughlin's anti-Semitic and profascist *Social Justice*; but there was no general censorship of dissident publications. A few Nazi agents and American fascists were jailed; but there was no major assault on people suspected of sympathizing with the Axis. The most ambitious effort to punish domestic fascists, a sedition trial of twenty-eight people, ended in a mistrial, and the defendants went free. Unlike during World War I, the government generally left socialists and communists (most of whom strongly supported the war effort) alone.

Nor was there much of the ethnic or cultural animosity that had shaped the social climate of the United States during World War I. Americans continued to eat sauerkraut without calling it "liberty cabbage." They displayed little hostility toward German and Italian Americans. Instead, they seemed to share the view of their government's propaganda: that the enemy was less the German and Italian people than the vicious political systems to which they had been subjected.

But there was a glaring exception to the general rule of relative ethnic tolerance: the treatment of the small, politically powerless group of Japanese Americans. From the beginning, Americans adopted a different attitude toward their Asian enemy than they did toward their European foes. They attributed to the Japanese people certain racial and cultural characteristics that made it easier to hold them in contempt. The Japanese, both government and private propaganda encouraged Americans to believe, were a devious, malign, and cruel people. The infamous attack on Pearl Harbor seemed to many to confirm that assessment.

This racial animosity soon extended to Americans of Japanese descent. There were not many Japanese Americans in the United States—only about

127,000, most of them concentrated in a few areas in California. About a third of them were unnaturalized, first-generation immigrants (Issei); two thirds were naturalized or native-born citizens of the United States (Nisei). The Japanese in America, like the Chinese, had long been the target of ethnic and racial animosity; and unlike members of European ethnic groups, who had encountered similar resentment, Asians seemed unable to dispel prejudice against them no matter how assimilated they became. Many white Americans continued to consider Asians (even native-born citizens) "foreigners" who could never become "real" Americans. Partly as a result, much of the Japanese-American population in the West continued to live in close-knit, to some degree even insular, communities. Nativists used the existence of such communities as further evidence that the Japanese were, as they should be, outsiders to American life, alien and potentially menacing.

Pearl Harbor inflamed longstanding suspicions and transformed them into active animosity. Wild stories circulated about how the Japanese in Hawaii had helped sabotage Pearl Harbor and how Japanese Americans in California were conspiring to aid an enemy landing on the Pacific Coast. There was no evidence to support any of these charges; but according to Earl Warren, then attorney general of California, the apparent passivity of the Japanese Americans was more evidence of the danger they posed. Because they did nothing to allow officials to gauge their intentions, Warren claimed, it was all the more important to take precautions against conspiracies.

There was some public pressure in California to remove the Japanese "threat," but on the whole, popular sentiment was more tolerant of the Nisei and Issei (and more willing to make distinctions between them and the Japanese in Japan) than was official sentiment. The real impetus for taking action came from the government. Secretary of the Navy Frank Knox, for example, said shortly after Pearl Harbor that "the most effective fifth column work of the entire war was done in Hawaii," a statement that later investigations proved to be entirely false. General John L. DeWitt, the senior military commander on the West Coast, claimed to have "no confidence in [Japanese-American] loyalty whatsoever." When asked about the distinction between unnaturalized Japanese immigrants and American citizens, he said, "A Jap is a Jap. It makes no difference whether he is an American citizen or not."

In February 1942, in response to pressure from military officials like DeWitt and Knox and West Coast political leaders like Warren (and over the objections of the attorney general and J. Edgar Hoover, the director of the FBI), the president authorized the army to "intern" the Japanese Americans. He created the War Relocation Authority (WRA) to oversee the project. More than 100,000 people (Issei and Nisei alike) were rounded up, told to dispose of their property however they could (which often meant simply abandoning it), and taken to what the government euphemistically termed "relocation centers" in the "interior."

In fact, they were facilities little different from prisons, many of them located in the western mountains and the desert. "Suddenly," one evacuee recalled,

EVACUATING JAPANESE AMERICANS. During World War II, anxiety about the loyalty of Americans of Japanese ancestry resulted in the evacuation and internment of more than 100,000 Japanese residing in the United States. Most were American citizens. The experience of gathering up one's belongings, abandoning home and property, and moving to "relocation" centers was painful and disorienting, as this photograph of an evacuation center in San Francisco in 1942 suggests.

"you realized that human beings were being put behind fences just like on the farm where we had horses and pigs in corrals." Conditions in the internment camps were not brutal, but they were harsh, uncomfortable, and—at first at least—disorienting. As one of those interned later recalled: "We did not know where we were. No houses were in sight, no trees or anything green—only scrubby sagebrush and an occasional low cactus, and mostly dry, baked earth." Government officials, on the other hand, talked of the internment centers as places where the Japanese could be socialized and "Americanized," much as many officials had at times considered Indian reservations places for training Native Americans to become more like whites.

But like Indian reservations, the internment camps were more a target of white economic aspirations than of missionary work. The governor of Utah, where many of the internees were located, wanted the federal government to turn over thousands of Japanese Americans to serve as forced laborers. Washington did not comply, but the WRA did hire out many inmates as agricultural laborers.

The internment never produced significant popular opposition. For the most part, once the Japanese were in the camps, other Americans (including their former neighbors on the West Coast) largely forgot about them—except to make strenuous efforts to acquire the property they had abandoned. Even so, conditions slowly improved beginning in 1943. Some young Japanese Americans left the camps to attend colleges and universities (mostly in the East—the WRA continued to be wary of letting Japanese return to the Pacific Coast). Others were permitted to move to cities to take factory and service jobs (although again, not on the West Coast). Some young men joined and others were drafted into the American military; a Nisei army unit fought with distinction in Europe. In 1944, the Supreme Court ruled in *Korematsu* v. *U.S.* that the relocation was constitutionally permissible. In another case the same year, it barred the internment of "loyal" citizens, but it left the interpretation of loyalty to the discretion of the government.

Nevertheless, by the end of 1944, most of the internees had been released; and early in 1945, they were finally permitted to return to the West Coast—where they faced continuing harassment and persecution, and where many found their property and businesses irretrievably lost. For many years following, survivors of the camps and their descendants attempted to direct national attention to the injustice they had endured and the economic losses they had sustained. A report by the Presidential Commission on the Wartime Relocation and Internment of Civilians issued in 1983 finally agreed. The internment, the report asserted, "was not justified by military necessity" but rather shaped by "race prejudice, war hysteria and a failure of political leadership." The report went on to conclude: "A grave injustice was done to American citizens and resident aliens of Japanese ancestry, who without individual review or any probative evidence against them, were excluded, removed and detained by the United States during World War II." In 1988 Congress voted to award reparations in the form of a single $20,000 cash payment to those internees who were still alive, a number that represented approximately half of those who were relocated and interned during the war years.

WOMEN, WAR, AND THE FAMILY

World War II affected women and the family in ways that few Americans could have anticipated before the war began. The demands of the wartime economy for new workers made it necessary for employers to turn to women, including many who had not worked for wages before. The absence of wage-earning men in many families made it necessary for women to work to support themselves and their children. As in many other areas of American life, gender roles felt the transforming effects of war.

Women and Wage Work

The participation of women in the American labor force had been growing throughout much of the twentieth century. But until World War II, most white women who worked were single and young. (Married African-American women with children had long worked for wages.) World War II altered these patterns in striking ways. Some 6 million new women workers joined the labor force during the war. Of these new workers, sixty percent were thirty-five-years-old or older, and seventy-five percent were married. One third of the new women workers had children under fourteen at home. Overall, the number of women in the work force increased by nearly sixty percent during World War II. Women accounted for a third of paid workers in 1945 (as opposed to a quarter in 1940).

The war did more than simply expand the number of women working for wages, however. It also redefined, at least temporarily, the kinds of work many women did, drawing them into roles from which they had previously been largely barred, either by custom or by law. Most notably, many women obtained high-wage work in industrial jobs that were once the nearly exclusive domain of men. The shortage of available male workers resulted in the hiring of women as ship riveters, keel binders, crane operators, stevedores, and tool and die makers, among other traditionally male jobs. More commonly, women found work in aircraft factories and defense plants, where they worked on assembly lines.

In the end, however, most women workers during the war were employed not in factories but in service-sector jobs. Above all, they worked for the government, whose bureaucratic needs expanded dramatically alongside its military and industrial needs. Washington, in particular, was flooded with young female clerks, secretaries, and typists—known as "government girls"—most of whom lived in cramped quarters in boarding houses, private homes, and government dormitories and worked long hours in the war agencies. Public and private clerical employment for women expanded in other urban areas as well, creating high concentrations of young women in places largely depleted of young men. The result was the development of distinctively female communities, in which women, often separated for the first time from home and family, adjusted to life in the work force through their association with other female workers.

Reconfiguring Gender Roles

Women have played important roles on the home front in all American wars. But World War II was especially important for the ways in which it reshaped traditional gender roles and stereotypes. The War Manpower Commission churned out an enormous amount of propaganda that both challenged and confirmed

WOMEN'S WAR WORK. "Rosie the Riveter," memorialized in a popular song and a drawing prepared for the *Saturday Evening Post* by Norman Rockwell, served as a symbol of women war workers who assumed unorthodox jobs in industry to take up the slack from absent male workers. These real-life "Rosies" were welders at a war production plant in New Britain, Connecticut. The war provided many women with lucrative jobs in industry that had long been closed to them. After demobilization, however, many "Rosies" lost these higher paying jobs and returned to more traditional women's employment.

many traditional images of women's proper roles. Suddenly a woman's "proper place" was not necessarily in the home—it was in the workplace, laboring for victory. At the same time, however, government films encouraged women to believe that warwork was not dissimilar to housework; both were well within the reach of women's innate competence. "Instead of cutting the lines of a dress, this woman cuts the pattern of aircraft parts," a narrator explained in one such movie, *The Glamour Girls of '43*.

The best-known symbol of women war workers was Rosie the Riveter, sketched by Norman Rockwell for a 1943 cover of the *Saturday Evening Post.* Decked out in overalls, her chest studded with victory pins, protective goggles perched high on a curly head of red hair, Rosie seemed at once the all-American girl and a vigorous, even brawny, specimen of the nation's toughest and most hard-working industrial craftsmen. A popular song told the story of Rosie the Riveter, who "kept a sharp lookout for sabotage, sitting up there on the fuselage. That little frail can do, more than a male can do." Women of independence and courage also appeared in films and even comic strips. The first episode of *Wonder Woman* by Charles Moulton appeared in 1941. "At last, in a world torn by the hatred and wars of men," Moulton wrote, "appears a *woman* to whom the problems and feats of men are mere child's play."

But while economic and military necessity eroded some objections to women's presence in the workplace, many obstacles and prejudices remained. Most factory owners continued to categorize jobs by gender. Female work, like male work, was also categorized by race: black women were usually assigned more menial tasks, and paid at a lower rate, than their white counterparts. Most African-American women, for instance, found it difficult to enter the higher-wage industrial jobs newly open to women during the war, even though twice as many black women were working in industry during the war than had been working there before 1941.

In addition to gender segregation and racial discrimination, the workplace also reflected the persistence of traditional ideas about men's and women's roles. Recruiting materials that described women's factory work as akin to household work reflected stereotypical views of women's capacities. Many employers treated women in the war plants with a combination of solicitude and patronization, which was helpful to them in some respects but was also an obstacle to winning genuine equality within the work force. Important wage differentials among men and women industrial workers still existed despite urging from the National War Labor Board that men and women be paid equally for equal work. Finally, even the most fervent official advocacy of new economic roles for women stressed the temporary nature of the wartime emergency. Most men, at least, assumed that when the war was over, women would return to their domestic sphere.

Still, women did make important inroads in the workplace during the war. They joined unions in substantial numbers, and they helped erode at least some of the prejudice, including the prejudice against mothers working, that had previously kept many of them from paid employment. Women had been working in industry for over a century, but during the war many new women workers gained a measure of confidence in themselves and an appreciation for wage work that they did not leave behind. "They were hammering away that the woman who went to work did it temporarily to help her man," one nurse recalled. "I think a lot of women said, Screw that noise. 'Cause they had a taste of freedom, they had a taste of making their own money, a taste of spending their own money, making their own decisions. I think the beginning of the women's movement had its seeds right there in World War Two." Although many years would pass before the women's movement provided a means for organizing those who shared such sentiments, the war left an important impression on an entire generation of women, as well as the sons and daughters they helped to raise.

War and the American Family

Women's new opportunities for wage work during the war produced new problems and concerns in American society. Many mothers whose husbands were in the military had to combine working with caring for their children. The scarcity of childcare facilities or other community services meant that some women had no choice but to leave young children—often known as "latch-key children" or "eight-hour orphans"—at home by themselves. Although federal funds were provided for some childcare centers under the Lanham Act (1943), very few women defense workers were able to take advantage of the limited assistance provided. The nation appeared to adapt readily to the necessity for women to leave the home and enter the workplace. But far less apparent was any systematic effort to address the need for childcare that the female entry into the workplace made inevitable. Many women were themselves uneasy with the idea of daycare and preferred to rely, when possible, upon their mothers and their extended families to watch over their children. But many women were left to shoulder by themselves the burdens that the combination of motherhood and wage work imposed.

Although little was done to address the need for childcare, much public discussion and debate focused on the American family during the war years. Social critics and public officials expressed anxiety that the family was deteriorating as a result of women's work. FBI Director J. Edgar Hoover warned that the absence of women from the home was fueling a vicious circle of neglect and crime. "There must be no absenteeism among mothers," Hoover insisted. "Her patriotic duty is not on the factory front. It is on the home front." Fear of juvenile delinquency grew especially pronounced as young boys appeared to be engaging in petty crime at a rapidly rising rate. For many children, however, the distinctive experience of the war years was not crime but work. More than a third of all teenagers between the ages of fourteen and eighteen were employed late in the war, causing some reduction in high school enrollments.

The return of prosperity and the coming of the war helped increase the rate and lower the age of marriage. Some couples married quickly before the husbands shipped out; when the men returned, many met newborn sons and daughters for the first time. They thus adjusted to marriage and children simultaneously. Others were eager to marry and begin their families as soon as they were demobilized. The war made life seem tenuous, and the lure of the stability of family proved especially powerful. Some of these young marriages were unable to survive the pressures of wartime separation, and the divorce rate rose rapidly. More notably, the birth rate began to rise precipitously—the first sign of what would become the great postwar "baby boom."

WAR AND THE NEW DEAL

The war's transforming impact on economy and society was no less evident in the arena of politics. When the war began, the New Deal already appeared to be in eclipse. The political casualties sustained by Roosevelt during the court-packing debacle, the recession of 1937, the growing suspicion of organized labor—all these things and many more suggested an underlying shift in the political winds. Still, it was not entirely clear when the war began what would happen to New Deal initiatives and ideas. For many American liberals, the war led to a reassessment of cherished beliefs and ideals. When the war was over, New Deal reform bore little resemblance to the spirited and idealistic movement that took form early in the 1930s.

"Dr. Win-the-War"

Late in 1943, Franklin Roosevelt publicly suggested that "Dr. New Deal," as he called it, had served its purpose and should now give way to "Dr. Win-the-War." The statement reflected the president's own genuine shift in concern: that victory was now more important than reform. But it reflected, too, the political reality that had emerged during the first two years of war. Liberals in government were finding themselves unable to enact new programs. They were even finding it difficult to protect existing ones from conservative assault.

Within the administration itself, many liberals found themselves displaced by the new managers of the wartime agencies, who came overwhelmingly from large corporations and conservative Wall Street law firms. But the greatest threat came from conservatives in Congress, who seized on the war as an excuse to do what many had wanted to do in peacetime: dismantle many of the achievements of the New Deal. They were assisted by the end of mass unemployment, which decreased the need for such relief programs as the Civilian Conservation Corps and the Works Progress Administration (both of which were abolished). They were assisted, too, by their own increasing numbers. In the congressional elections of 1942, Republicans gained forty-seven seats in the House and ten in the Senate. Roosevelt continued to talk bravely at times about his commitment to social progress and liberal reform, in part to bolster the flagging spirits of his traditional supporters. But increasingly, the president quietly accepted the defeat or erosion of New Deal measures in order to win support for his war policies and peace plans. He also accepted the changes because he realized that his chances for reelection in 1944 depended on his ability to identify himself less with domestic issues than with world peace.

The Election of 1944

Republicans approached the 1944 election determined to exploit what they believed was resentment of wartime regimentation and privation and unhappiness with Democratic reform. They nominated as their candidate the young and vigorous governor of New York, Thomas E. Dewey. Roosevelt was unopposed within his party; but Democratic leaders pressured him to abandon Vice President Henry Wallace, an advanced New Dealer and hero of the CIO, and replace him with a more moderate figure. Roosevelt reluctantly acquiesced in the selection of Senator Harry S. Truman of Missouri. Truman was not a prominent figure in the party, but he had won acclaim as chairman of the Senate War Investigating Committee (known as the Truman Committee), which had compiled an impressive record uncovering waste and corruption in wartime production.

The conduct of the war was not an issue in the campaign. Instead, the election revolved around domestic economic issues and, indirectly, the president's health. The president was, in fact, gravely ill. It may not be too much to say that he was dying. But the campaign seemed momentarily to revive him. He made several strenuous public appearances late in October, which dispelled popular doubts about his health and ensured his re-election. That he had succeeded was apparent on election day. "It is going to be a census rather than an election," Harry Hopkins predicted to a British diplomat. When the votes came in, it was not the landslide some New Dealers anticipated. But Roosevelt won handily, capturing 53.5 percent of the popular vote to Dewey's forty-six percent and winning 432 electoral votes to Dewey's ninety-nine. Democrats lost one seat in the Senate, gained twenty in the House, and maintained control of both.

The Eclipse of Reform

Despite the robust support Roosevelt received in the election of 1944, there would be no return to the broad interest in domestic reform and the imaginative array of programs that had characterized his first term. President Roosevelt continued to speak of the importance of federal activism in ensuring the economic well-being of the American people. He spoke in 1944 of "a second Bill of Rights under which a new basis of security and prosperity can be established for all." In fact, the older agenda of liberal reform appeared to inspire little enthusiasm as the war came to a close.

Many liberals who had stood behind the New Deal shifted their attention to new concerns during the war. As the world confronted the bloody consequences of totalitarian regimes, few liberals felt comfortable pressing a vision of a powerful state. The antimonopoly critique of the early New Deal also rang hollow as businessmen and finance capitalists played an important role in mobilizing national resources to sustain the war effort. Instead, those who embraced the goal of liberal reform focused more attention on stabilizing the American economy and helping it grow. Active fiscal policy and other programs designed to produce full employment were important means toward that end.

By 1945, the concerns that had animated reform in the 1930s had not disappeared. But they now reflected the nation's experience with a decade of depression, a period of vibrant reform, and total war. In the postwar years, prosperity and progress would remain central themes in American political life. Those goals would be much influenced by a new sense of the United States' role in the world.

CHAPTER EIGHTEEN

Waging Peace

∾

T he defeat of the Axis powers, most Americans believed, was a great victory for freedom and the prospects for international stability. Yet even before the end of World War II, tensions between the United States and the Soviet Union, who had been fighting as allies, began to darken the prospects for peace. Once the hostilities were over, those tensions grew quickly. And before long the two nations were locked in what became known as a "Cold War"—a tense and dangerous rivalry that would cast its shadow over international affairs for more than forty years. The Cold War also had profound effects on American domestic life, ultimately producing the most corrosive outbreak of antiradical hysteria of the century. America in the postwar years enjoyed enormous power in the world and great prosperity at home. It also experienced uncertainty and upheaval.

THE COLD WAR

Few issues in twentieth-century American history have aroused more debate than the question of the origins of the Cold War. Some have claimed that Soviet duplicity and expansionism created the international tensions, others that American provocations and imperial ambitions were at least equally to blame. Most historians agree, however, that wherever the preponderance of blame may lie, both the United States and the Soviet Union contributed to the atmosphere of hostility and suspicion that quickly clouded the peace.

Historical Tensions

In retrospect, the enmity between the Soviet Union and the United States after war seems less surprising than their wartime alliance. For throughout the decades before the war, the two nations had viewed each other with deep mutual mistrust and sometimes outright hostility.

The reasons for American hostility toward the Soviet Union were both obvious and many. As early as the 1890s, the two nations clashed over Russian efforts to develop parts of Manchuria, a goal some American diplomats saw as antithetical to the American interest in keeping Asian markets open for competition. Another source of hostility was World War I and the decision of the new Soviet regime in 1917, in one of its first official acts, to negotiate a separate peace with Germany. That left the West to fight the Central Powers alone.

In addition, the ideological underpinnings of the Soviet state ran directly counter to the ideas and values celebrated by American capitalism and democracy. The Soviet Union had called openly and continually for world revolution and the overthrow of capitalist regimes (even if it did little before World War II actively to advance that goal). Finally, there were the realities of the totalitarian state Stalin had overseen. The Stalinist policies and purges of the 1930s and 1940s—among them a brutal campaign of extermination against real and imagined opponents of the regime—had caused the deaths of millions of people. Knowledge of these events caused understandable revulsion in the West. Stalin, like Hitler, was one of the great tyrants of modern history; and in 1939, these two tyrants had agreed to the short-lived Nazi-Soviet Pact, freeing Germany to launch World War II.

Soviet hostility toward the United States had deep roots as well. The United States had opposed the Russian revolution in 1917 and had sent troops into Russia at the end of World War I to work, Soviet leaders believed, to overthrow their new government. Furthermore, the West had excluded the Soviet Union from the international community throughout the two decades following World War I; Russia had not been invited to participate in either the Versailles Conference in 1919 or the Munich Conference in 1938. The United States had refused to recognize the Soviet government until 1933, sixteen years after the revolution. The Soviet Union viewed such attempts to marginalize it, even to deny its integrity as a state, as acts of deep hostility. Finally, just as most Americans viewed communism with foreboding and contempt, so did most Russian communists harbor deep suspicions of and a genuine distaste for industrial capitalism. There was, in short, a powerful legacy of mistrust on both sides.

Postwar Visions

In some respects, the experience of World War II helped to soften that mistrust. Both the United States and the Soviet Union tended to depict each other during the war less as a dangerous potential foe than as a brave and dauntless ally. Americans expressed open admiration for the courage of Soviet forces in withstanding the Nazi onslaught and began to describe Stalin not as the bloody ogre of the purges but as the wise and persevering "Uncle Joe." The Soviet government, similarly, praised both the American fighting forces and the wisdom and courage of Franklin Roosevelt.

In other respects, however, the war deepened the gulf between the two nations. The Soviet invasion of Finland and the Baltic states late in 1939, once the war with Germany had begun in the West, angered many Americans. So did Soviet wartime brutality—not only toward the fascist enemies but toward supposedly friendly forces such as the Polish resistance fighters. Stalin harbored even greater resentments toward the American approach to the war. Despite repeated assurances from Roosevelt that the United States and Britain would soon open a second front on the European continent, thus drawing German strength away from the assault on Russia, the Allied invasion did not finally occur until June 1944, more than two years after Stalin had first demanded it. In the meantime, the Russians had suffered appalling casualties—some estimates put them as high as 20 million. It was a small step for Stalin to believe that the West had deliberately delayed the invasion to force the Soviets to absorb the brunt of fighting the Nazis.

At the heart of the tensions between the Americans and the Soviets in the 1940s, however, was a fundamental difference in the way the great powers envisioned the postwar world. The vision many Americans embraced was one first openly outlined in the Atlantic Charter in 1941, and later popularized through a 1943 book by Wendell Willkie entitled *One World.* It foresaw a world in which nations abandoned their traditional belief in military alliances and spheres of influence and governed their relations with one another through democratic processes. An international organization would serve as the arbiter of disputes and the protector of every nation's right of self-determination. The United States also called for an open economic world, in which it would have free access to international markets—particularly in Europe, which Americans assumed would rebuild along capitalist lines after the war.

Roosevelt publicly embraced much of the "One World" vision, and he devoted considerable energy to making the case to the American people for the participation of the United States in a new postwar international order. In his 1945 State of the Union message, Roosevelt issued a stern warning: "In our disillusionment after the last war, we gave up the hope of achieving a better peace because we had not the courage to fulfill our responsibilities in an admittedly imperfect world. We must not let that happen again, or we shall follow the same tragic road again—the road to a third world war." At the same time, Roosevelt believed that Britain, the Soviet Union, the United States, and perhaps to a lesser extent China ought to play especially important roles in postwar international relations. Whatever his public rhetoric, privately he remained a realist who understood the postwar world would be shaped by the major powers. But he also believed that a new international organization—ultimately embodied in the United Nations—would provide a means of arbitrating differences among the Great Powers peacefully.

The Soviet Union viewed the postwar world very differently. Stalin had signed the Atlantic Charter, but the Soviet Union was determined to create a secure sphere for itself in eastern Europe as protection against possible future aggression from the West. Having twice been invaded by Germany through Poland, the Soviet Union intended to forestall that eventuality from ever occurring again. Controlling Poland and destroying the ability of the Germans to wage war figured prominently on the Soviet postwar agenda. Although the British soon would condemn what they viewed as contemptible expansionism by the Soviet Union, they too were not entirely enamored of Roosevelt's "One World" vision. Britain had always been uneasy about the implications of the self-determination ideal for its own enormous colonial empire. Both Churchill and Stalin tended to envision a postwar structure in which the great powers would control areas of strategic interest to them, and in which something vaguely similar to the traditional European balance of power would re-emerge.

These differences of opinion were particularly important because the "One World" vision Roosevelt promoted had, by the end of the war, become a fervent commitment among many Americans. Thus when Britain and the Soviet Union began to balk at some of the goals the United States was advocating, the debate seemed to become more than a simple difference of opinion. It became an ideological struggle for the future of the world. By the end of the war, Roosevelt was able to win at least the partial consent of Winston Churchill to his principles. But although he believed at times that Stalin would similarly relent, he never managed to steer the Soviets from their determination to control eastern Europe and from their vision of a postwar order in which each of the great powers would dominate its own sphere of influence. Gradually, the differences between these two positions would turn the peacemaking process into a form of warfare, fought not with guns but with threats, bellicose rhetoric, and at times, actively hostile actions hidden behind the thin veneer of diplomacy.

Wartime Diplomacy

Serious strains began to develop in the alliance with the Soviet Union as early as 1942, a result of Stalin's irritation at delays in opening the second front and his resentment of the Anglo-American decision to invade North Africa before Europe. In this deteriorating atmosphere, Roosevelt and Churchill met in Casablanca, Morocco, in January 1943 to discuss Allied strategy. (Stalin had declined Roosevelt's invitation to attend.) The two leaders could not accept Stalin's most important demand—the immediate opening of a second front—but they tried to reassure him by announcing they would accept nothing less than the unconditional surrender of the Axis powers. It was a signal that the Americans and British would not negotiate a separate peace with Hitler and leave the Soviets to fight on alone.

In November 1943, Roosevelt and Churchill traveled to Teheran, Iran, for their first meeting with Stalin. By now, however, Roosevelt's most effective bargaining tool—Stalin's need for American assistance in his struggle against Germany—was almost gone. The German advance against Russia had failed;

Soviet forces were now launching their own westward offensive. Meanwhile, new tensions had emerged in the alliance as a result of the refusal by the British and Americans to allow any Soviet participation in the creation of a new Italian government following the fall of Mussolini. To Stalin, at least, the "One World" doctrine already seemed to be a double standard: America and Britain expected to have a voice in the future of eastern Europe, but the Soviet Union was to have no voice in the future of the West.

Nevertheless, the Teheran Conference seemed in most respects a success. Roosevelt and Stalin established a cordial personal relationship. Stalin agreed to an American request that the Soviet Union enter the war in the Pacific soon after the end of hostilities in Europe. Roosevelt, in turn, promised that an Anglo-American second front would be established within six months. All three leaders agreed in principle to a postwar international organization and to efforts to prevent a resurgence of German expansionism.

On other matters, however, the origins of future disagreements were already visible. Most important was the question of the future of Poland. Roosevelt and Churchill were willing to agree to a movement of the Soviet border westward, allowing Stalin to annex some historically Polish territory. But on the nature of the postwar government in the portion of Poland that would remain independent, there were sharp differences. Roosevelt and Churchill supported the claims of the Polish government-in-exile that had been functioning in London since 1940; Stalin wished to install another, procommunist exiled government that had spent the war in Lublin, in the Soviet Union. The three leaders avoided a bitter conclusion to the Teheran Conference only by leaving the issue unresolved.

The Yalta Conference

For more than a year after Teheran, the Grand Alliance among the United States, Britain, and the Soviet Union alternated between high tension and warm amicability. In the fall of 1944, Churchill flew by himself to Moscow for a meeting with Stalin to resolve issues arising from a civil war in Greece. In return for a Soviet agreement to cease assisting Greek communists, who were challenging the British-supported monarchical government, Churchill consented to a proposal whereby control of some parts of eastern and central Europe would be divided between Britain and the Soviet Union. "This memorable meeting," Churchill wrote to Stalin after its close, "has shown that there are no matters that cannot be adjusted between us when we meet together in frank and intimate discussion." To Roosevelt, however, the Moscow agreement was evidence of how little the Atlantic Charter principles seemed to mean to his two most important allies.

In February 1945, Roosevelt joined Churchill and Stalin for a great peace conference in the Soviet city of Yalta. The meeting began in an atmosphere of some gloom. The American president, his health visibly failing, sensed resistance to his internationalist dreams. The British prime minister, already dismayed by Stalin's willingness to make concessions and compromises, warned even before the conference met that "I think the end of this war may well prove to be more disappointing than was the last." Stalin, whose armies were now only miles from Berlin, was aware of how much the United States still wanted his assistance in the Pacific. He was confident and determined.

On a number of issues, the Big Three reached mutually satisfactory agreements. In return for Stalin's promise to enter the war against Japan, Roosevelt agreed that the Soviet Union should receive the Kurile Islands north of Japan; that it should regain southern Sakhalin Island and Port Arthur, both of which Russia had lost in the 1904 Russo–Japanese War; and that it could exercise

THE BIG THREE AT YALTA.   Churchill, Roosevelt, and Stalin meet in the Soviet Crimea at Yalta to discuss the shape of the postwar order in February 1945. Churchill and Stalin were alarmed by President Roosevelt's gaunt appearance and his apparent weariness during the meeting—evidence of physical deterioration that would lead to the president's death two months later. By the end of the Allied leaders' next meeting— at Potsdam, Germany, in July—only Stalin would remain in power. By then, Truman had succeeded Roosevelt, and Clement Atlee had succeeded Churchill as prime minister of Great Britain after Atlee's Labour party won a postwar election.

some influence (along with the government of China) in Manchuria. The negotiators also agreed to accept a plan for a new international organization, a plan that had been hammered out the previous summer at a conference at Dumbarton Oaks, in Washington, D.C. The new United Nations would contain a General Assembly, in which every member would be represented; a Security Council, with permanent representatives of the five major powers (the United States, Britain, France, the Soviet Union, and China), each of which would have veto power; and temporary delegates from several other nations. These agreements became the basis of the United Nations charter, drafted at a conference of fifty nations that opened in San Francisco on April 25, 1945. The United States Senate eventually ratified the charter in July by a vote of eighty to two (a striking contrast to the slow and painful defeat it had administered to the charter of the League of Nations twenty-five years before).

On other issues, however, the Yalta Conference either left fundamental differences unresolved or papered them over with weak and unstable compromises. Fundamental disagreement remained about the postwar Polish government. Stalin, whose armies now occupied Poland, had already installed a government composed of the procommunist "Lublin" Poles. Roosevelt and Churchill insisted that the pro-western "London" Poles be allowed a place in the Warsaw regime. Roosevelt wanted a government based on free, democratic elections—which both he and Stalin recognized the pro-western forces would win. Stalin agreed to a vague compromise. He promised to offer an unspecified number of places in the government to pro-western Poles, and he consented to hold "free and unfettered elections" in Poland. He made no commitment to a date for them. They did not take place for more than forty years.

Nor was there agreement about the future of Germany. Stalin wanted to impose $20 billion in reparations on the Germans, of which Russia would receive half. Roosevelt and Churchill agreed only to leave final settlement of the issue to a future reparations commission. A more important difference was in the way the leaders envisioned postwar German politics and society. In 1944, Roosevelt and Churchill had met in Quebec and had agreed to a plan, crafted by the American secretary of the treasury, Henry Morgenthau, for the "pastoralization" of Germany—dismantling its industry and turning it into a largely agricultural society. By the time of the Yalta meeting, however, Roosevelt had changed his mind. He seemed now to want a reconstructed and reunited Germany—one that would be permitted to develop a prosperous, modern economy while remaining under the careful supervision of the Allies. Stalin wanted a permanent weakening of Germany.

The final agreement was, like the Polish accord, vague and unstable. The United States, Great Britain, France, and the Soviet Union would each control its own "zone of occupation" in Germany—the zones to be determined by the position of troops at end of the war. Berlin, the German capital, was already well inside the Soviet zone. But because of its symbolic importance, it would itself be divided into four sectors, one for each nation to occupy. At an unspecified date, the nation would be reunited; but there was no agreement on how the reunification would occur. As for the rest of Europe, the conference produced a murky accord on the establishment of interim governments "broadly representative of all democratic elements." They would be replaced ultimately by permanent governments "responsible to the will of the people" and created through free elections. Once again, no specific provisions or timetables accompanied the agreements.

The Yalta accords, in other words, were less a settlement of postwar issues than a set of loose principles that sidestepped the most divisive issues. Roosevelt, Churchill, and Stalin returned home from the conference each apparently convinced that he had signed an important agreement. But the Soviet interpretation of the accords differed so sharply from the Anglo-American interpretation that the illusion endured only briefly. In the weeks following the Yalta Conference, Roosevelt watched with growing alarm as the Soviet Union moved systematically to establish procommunist governments in one eastern European nation after another and as Stalin failed to make the changes in Poland that the president believed he had promised. But Roosevelt did not abandon hope. He continued to believe the differences could be settled to the day he died.

AN EMBATTLED PEACE

Harry S. Truman, who became president upon Roosevelt's death, had almost no familiarity with international issues. Nor did he share Roosevelt's faith in the flexibility of the Soviet Union. Roosevelt had believed that Stalin was, essentially, a reasonable man with whom an ultimate accord could be reached—a belief he was beginning to question at the time of his death, but one he had not yet abandoned. Truman, in contrast, sided with those in the government (and there were many) who considered the Soviet Union fundamentally untrustworthy and viewed Stalin himself with suspicion and loathing.

Potsdam

Truman had been in office only a few days before he decided to "get tough" with the Soviet Union. Stalin had made what the new president considered solemn agreements with the United States at Yalta. The United States would insist that he honor them. Dismissing the advice of Secretary of War Stimson that the Polish question was a lost cause and not worth a world crisis, Truman met on April 23 with Soviet Foreign Minister Molotov and sharply chastised him for violations of the Yalta accords. "I have never been talked to like that in my life," a shocked Molotov reportedly replied. "Carry out your agreements and you won't get talked to like that," said the president.

In fact, Truman had only limited leverage with which to compel the Soviet Union to carry out its agreements. Russian forces already occupied Poland and much of the rest of Eastern Europe. Germany was already divided among the conquering nations. The United States was still engaged in a war in the Pacific and was neither able nor willing to engage in a new conflict in Europe. Truman insisted that the United States should be able to get "85 percent" of what it wanted, but he was ultimately forced to settle for much less.

He conceded first on Poland. When Stalin made a few minor concessions to the pro-western exiles, Truman recognized the Warsaw government, hoping that noncommunist forces might gradually expand their influence there. Until the 1980s, they were not able to do so. Other questions remained, above all the question of Germany. To settle them, Truman went to Potsdam, in Russian-occupied Germany, in mid-July to meet with Churchill (who was replaced as prime minister by Clement Atlee in the midst of the negotiations) and Stalin. Truman reluctantly accepted adjustments of the Polish–German border that Stalin had long demanded; he refused, however, to permit the Russians to claim any reparations from the American, French, and British zones of Germany. The result, in effect, was to confirm that Germany would remain divided, with the western zones eventually united into one nation, closely allied with the United States, and the Russian zone surviving as another nation, with a pro-Soviet, communist government. Soon, the Soviet Union was siphoning between $1.5 and $3 billion a year out of its zone of occupation.

The China Problem

Central to American hopes for an open, peaceful world policed by the great powers was a strong, independent China. But even before the war ended, the American government knew that those hopes faced a major, perhaps insurmountable obstacle: the Chinese government of Chiang Kai-shek. Chiang was generally friendly to the United States, but he had few other virtues. His government was corrupt and incompetent. His popular legitimacy was feeble. And Chiang himself lived in a world of almost surreal isolation, unable or unwilling to face the problems that were threatening to engulf him. Ever since 1927, the nationalist government he headed had been engaged in a prolonged and bitter struggle with the communist armies of Mao Zedong. So successful had the communist challenge grown that Mao was in control of one fourth of the population by 1945.

At Potsdam, Truman had managed to persuade Stalin to recognize Chiang as the legitimate ruler of China; but Chiang was rapidly losing his grip on his country. Some Americans urged the government to try to find a "third force" to support as an alternative to either Chiang or Mao. A few argued that America should try to reach some accommodation with Mao himself. Truman, however, decided reluctantly that he had no choice but to continue supporting Chiang. That was in part because of the strength in the United States of forces committed to him, including the formidable publisher of *Time* and *Life* magazines, Henry Luce, the son of Chinese missionaries and an inveterate defender of Chiang. The pro-Chiang forces came to be known as the "China Lobby," and for thirty years they helped shape American policy toward Asia.

In the last months of the war, American forces diverted attention from the Japanese long enough to assist Chiang against the communists in Manchuria. For the next several years, as the long struggle between the nationalists and the communists erupted into a full-scale civil war, the United States continued to send money and weapons to Chiang, even as it was becoming clear his cause was lost. But Truman was not prepared to intervene more directly to save the nationalist regime.

Instead, the American government was beginning to consider an alternative to China as the strong, pro-western force in Asia: a revived Japan. Abandoning the restrictive occupation policies of the first years after the war (when General Douglas MacArthur had governed the nation), the United States lifted all limitations on industrial development and encouraged rapid economic growth in Japan. The vision of an open, united Asia had given way, as in Europe, to an acceptance of the necessity of developing a strong, pro-American sphere of influence.

The Containment Doctrine

By the end of 1945, the Grand Alliance of World War II was in shambles, and with it any realistic hope of a postwar world constructed according to the Atlantic Charter ideals Roosevelt and others had supported. Instead, a new American policy was slowly emerging. Rather than attempting to create a unified, "open" world, the West would work to "contain" the threat of further Soviet expansion. The United States would be the leading force in that effort.

The new doctrine emerged in part as a response to events in Europe in 1946. In Turkey, Stalin was trying to win some control over the vital straits to the Mediterranean. In Greece, communist forces were again threatening the pro-Western government; the British had announced they could no longer provide assistance. Faced with these challenges, Truman decided to enunciate a firm new policy. In doing so, he drew from the ideas of the influential American diplomat George F. Kennan, who earlier that year had warned from Moscow, in a famous cable known as the "long telegram," (and later in an article published under the pseudonym "X" in *Foreign Affairs*) of the Soviet threat to American postwar goals. The United States, Kennan argued, faced in the Soviet Union "a political force committed fanatically to the belief that with the U.S. there can be no permanent modus vivendi." The only answer for the United States, then, was "a long-term, patient but firm and vigilant containment of Russian expansive tendencies."

On March 12, 1947, Truman appeared before Congress and used Kennan's warnings as the basis of what became known as the Truman Doctrine. "I believe," he argued, "that it must be the policy of the United States to support free peoples who are resisting attempted subjugation by armed minorities or by out-side pressures." In the same speech he requested $400 million—part of it to bol-ster the armed forces of Greece and Turkey, another part to provide economic assistance to Greece. Congress quickly approved the measure.

The American commitment ultimately helped ease Soviet pressure on Turkey and helped the Greek government defeat the communist insurgents. More important, it established a basis for American foreign policy that would survive for over forty years. On the one hand, the Truman Doctrine was a way of accommodating the status quo: It accepted that there was no immediate likelihood of overturning the communist governments Stalin had established in eastern Europe. On the other hand, the Truman Doctrine was a strategy for the future. Communism was an innately expansionist force, the new theory argued, and it must be contained within its present boundaries. Its expansion anywhere could be a threat to democracy everywhere because, as Secretary of State Dean Acheson argued, the fall of one nation to communism would have a "domino effect" on surrounding nations. It would, therefore, become the policy of the United States to assist pro-western forces in struggles against communism whether that struggle directly involved the Soviet Union or not.

Rebuilding Europe

An integral part of the containment policy was a proposal to aid in the economic reconstruction of western Europe. There were many motives: humanitarian concern for the European people; a fear that Europe would remain an economic drain on the United States if it could not quickly rebuild and begin to feed itself; a desire for a strong European market for American goods. But above all, American policymakers believed that unless something could be done to strengthen the shaky pro-American governments in the nations of western Europe, they might fall under the control of their rapidly growing domestic communist parties.

Important initial steps toward supporting economic reconstruction took place at the Bretton Woods Conference in 1944, when the United State estab-lished the International Monetary Fund (IMF) and the World Bank. The orga-nizations were capitalized at over $7 billion each and were authorized to make loans to promote international recovery, investment, trade, and a stable world currency. Although the organizations emerged out of Anglo-American plans, the United States provided the lion's share of the funds and therefore expected to have a deciding role in what was done with them. The Soviets attended the Bret-ton Woods Conference, but they chose not to participate in either fund. Some elected officials grumbled, but Congress approved the plan in July 1945 by a large margin.

After the war, these initial moves to address European economic recovery were joined by a far more ambitious plan. In a June 1947 speech at Harvard University, Secretary of State George C. Marshall announced a program to provide economic assistance to all European nations (including the Soviet Union) that would join in drafting a program for recovery. Although Russia and its eastern satellites quickly and predictably rejected the plan, sixteen western European nations eagerly participated. Whatever domestic opposition there was largely vanished after a sudden coup in Czechoslovakia in February 1948 established a Soviet-dominated communist government there. By now public opinion polls in the United States revealed a widespread popular belief that the Soviet Union appeared to be seeking world domination. Partly as a result, a conservative Congress approved in April 1948 the creation of the Economic Cooperation Administration, the agency that would administer the Marshall Plan, as it became known. Over the next three years, the Marshall Plan channeled over $12 billion of American aid into Europe, helping to spark a substantial economic revival. By the end of 1950, European industrial production had risen sixty-four percent, communist strength in the member nations had declined, and opportunities for American trade had revived.

GEORGE C. MARSHALL AT HARVARD, 1947. Secretary of State George C. Marshall is escorted through Harvard Yard en route to the commencement ceremony, where he received an honorary degree. Later that day, in a speech to Harvard alumni, he presented the Truman administration's proposal to aid in the postwar reconstruction of Europe. Its official name was the European Recovery Program, but it was better known as the Marshall Plan.

Protecting National Security

That the United States had fully accepted a continuing commitment to the containment policy became clear in 1947 and 1948 when Congress enacted a series of measures to maintain American military power at near wartime levels. In 1948, at the president's request, Congress approved a new military draft and revived the Selective Service System. In the meantime, the United States, having failed to reach agreement with the Soviet Union on international control of nuclear weapons, redoubled its own efforts in atomic research, elevating nuclear weaponry to a central place in its military arsenal. The Atomic Energy Commission, established in 1946, became the supervisory body charged with overseeing all nuclear research, civilian and military alike.

Particularly important was the National Security Act of 1947, which created several new instruments of foreign policy. A new Department of Defense would oversee all branches of the armed services, combining functions previously performed by the war and navy departments. A National Security Council (NSC), operating out of the White House, would advise the president on foreign and military policy. A Central Intelligence Agency (CIA) would be responsible for collecting information through both open and covert methods and, as the Cold War continued, for engaging secretly in political and military operations overseas on behalf of American goals. The National Security Act, in other words, gave the government (and particularly the president) expanded powers with which to pursue the nation's international aims. It centralized in the White House control that had once been widely dispersed; it enabled the president to take warlike actions without an open declaration of war; it created vehicles by which the government could at times act politically and militarily overseas behind a veil of secrecy; and it created the framework for the subsequent growth of the national security state.

The Road to NATO

At about the same time, the United States was also moving to strengthen the military capabilities of western Europe. Convinced that a reconstructed Germany was essential to the hopes of the West, Truman reached an agreement with England and France to merge the three western zones of occupation into a new West German republic (which would include the American, British, and French sectors of Berlin, even though that city lay well within the Soviet zone.) Stalin interpreted the move as a direct challenge to his hopes for a subdued Germany and a docile Europe. He was especially alarmed because, at almost the same moment, he was facing a challenge from inside what he considered his own sphere. The government of Yugoslavia, under the leadership of Marshall Josip Broz Tito, broke openly with the Soviet Union and declared the nation an unaligned communist state. The United States offered Tito assistance.

Stalin responded quickly to the American plans for Germany. On June 24, 1948, he imposed a tight blockade around the western sectors of Berlin. If

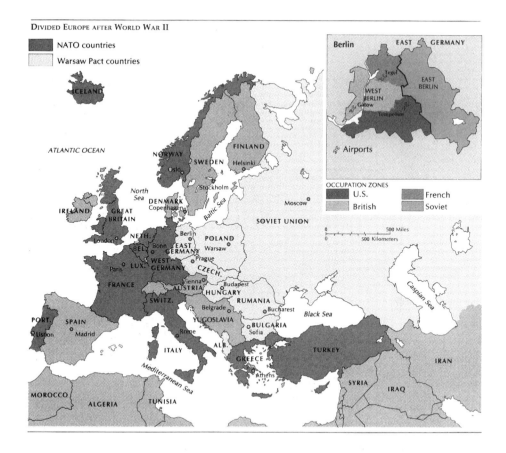

DIVIDED EUROPE AFTER WORLD WAR II

NATO countries

Warsaw Pact countries

ICELAND

ATLANTIC OCEAN

NORWAY
Oslo
SWEDEN
Helsinki
FINLAND
Stockholm
North Sea
DENMARK
Copenhagen
Baltic Sea
Moscow
SOVIET UNION

IRELAND
GREAT BRITAIN
London
NETH.
Berlin
BEL.
Bonn
EAST GERMANY
Warsaw
POLAND
Paris
LUX.
WEST GERMANY
Prague
CZECH.
FRANCE
Vienna
AUSTRIA
Budapest
HUNGARY
SWITZ.
Belgrade
Bucharest
RUMANIA
Black Sea
Caspian Sea

PORT.
SPAIN
Lisbon
Madrid
YUGOSLAVIA
Rome
BULGARIA
Sofia
ITALY
ALB.
TURKEY
IRAN
GREECE
Athens
SYRIA
IRAQ
Mediterranean Sea

MOROCCO
ALGERIA
TUNISIA

Berlin
EAST GERMANY
Tegel
EAST BERLIN
WEST BERLIN
Gatow
Tempelhof

Airports

OCCUPATION ZONES
U.S.
British
French
Soviet

0   500 Miles
0   500 Kilometers

Germany was to be officially divided, he was implying, then the country's western government would have to abandon its outpost in the heart of the Soviet-controlled eastern zone. Truman refused to do so. "We are in Berlin by the terms of the agreement," Truman asserted, "and the Russians have no right to get us out by either direct or indirect pressure." Unwilling to risk war through a military response to the blockade, the president instead ordered a massive airlift to supply the city with food, fuel, and other necessities. The airlift continued for more than ten months, transporting nearly 2.5 million tons of material, keeping a city of 2 million people alive, and transforming West Berlin into a symbol of the West's resolve to resist communist expansion. In the spring of 1949, Stalin lifted the now ineffective blockade. And in October, the division of Germany into two nations—the Federal Republic in the West and the Democratic Republic in the East—became official.

The crisis in Berlin accelerated the consolidation of what was already in effect an alliance among the United States and the countries of Western Europe. On April 4, 1949, twelve nations signed an agreement establishing the North Atlantic Treaty Organization (NATO) and declaring that an armed attack against one member would be considered an attack against all. The NATO countries

THE BERLIN AIRLIFT.   Children standing amid the rubble of postwar Berlin gather to
watch American planes bringing food and supplies to their beleaguered city in 1948.
The Soviet blockade of West Berlin was intended to force the western
allies to abandon the city, but it only increased their resolve, and
that of the Berliners themselves.

would, moreover, maintain a standing military force in Europe to defend against
what many believed was the threat of a Soviet invasion. The American Senate
quickly ratified the treaty, which fused European nations that had been fighting
one another for centuries into a strong and enduring alliance. It also spurred the
Soviet Union to create an alliance of its own with the communist governments
in eastern Europe—an alliance formalized in 1955 by the Warsaw Pact.

The Hardening of Tensions

For a time, Americans believed that their initial achievements had turned the tide
of the battle against communism. But a series of events in 1949 eroded that confidence and launched the Cold War in new directions. Deeply alarming was the
collapse of Chiang Kai-shek's nationalist government in China, which occurred
with startling speed in the last months of 1949. Chiang fled with his political allies and the remnants of his army to the offshore island of Formosa (Taiwan), and
the entire Chinese mainland came under the control of a communist government

that many Americans believed to be an extension of the Soviet Union. Few policymakers shared the belief of many members of the China Lobby that the United States should now commit itself to the rearming of Chiang Kai-shek. But neither would the United States recognize the new communist regime, which created the People's Republic of China on October 1, 1949. The Chinese mainland would remain almost entirely closed to the West for a generation. The United States, in the meantime, would devote increased attention to the revitalization of Japan as a buffer against Asian communism, ending the American occupation in 1952.

The year 1949 also brought an end to the American atomic monopoly. An announcement in September that the Soviet Union had successfully exploded its first atomic weapon, years earlier than predicted, shocked and frightened many Americans. Meanwhile in the highest levels of the United States government a debate was already underway about whether to pursue production of a hydrogen

THE CHINESE REVOLUTION.   Chinese troops march through
the city of Beijing in 1949, carrying banners and accompanied
by a propaganda truck carrying a portrait of Mao Zedong.
The triumph of communist forces in China alarmed many
Americans; the United States did not recognize the People's
Republic of China and Mao's regime until the 1970s.

bomb, a thermonuclear weapon that would be at least ten times as destructive as the bombs dropped on Hiroshima and Nagasaki. Although an advisory committee of the Atomic Energy Commission recommended in January 1950 against the new bomb, Truman decided to approve development of it. "It is part of my responsibility as Commander in Chief of the Armed Forces," the President announced, "to see to it that our country is able to defend itself against any possible aggressor."

Forced to make a series of momentous decisions amid rapidly changing world and domestic events, Truman called for a thorough review of American foreign policy. The result was a National Security Council report, commonly known as NSC-68, which recommended an important shift in the American position. The April 1950 document argued that the United States could no longer rely on other nations to take the initiative in resisting communism. It must itself establish firm and active leadership of the noncommunist world. And it must move to stop communist expansion anywhere it occurred, regardless of the intrinsic strategic or economic value of the lands in question.

Perhaps most significantly, the report called for a major expansion of American military power, with a defense budget almost four times the previously projected figure. The United States and its allies needed to amass military strength "to a point at which the combined strength will be superior . . . , both initially and throughout a war, to the forces that can be brought to bear by the Soviet Union and its satellites." In 1949 Truman had proposed a reduction in military spending for 1950 and 1951. Now he was faced with a stark choice: increase military preparedness and defense spending or, NSC-68 warned, face the potential "destruction not only of this Republic but of civilization itself."

As Truman pondered the report in the summer of 1950, North Korea invaded South Korea. That event erased whatever remaining doubts the president may have had about the wisdom of the new approach to foreign policy. NSC-68, he directed, should be considered "a statement of policy to be followed over the next four or five years." Programs designed to realize its objectives should "be put into effect as rapidly as feasible." In the aftermath of Truman's decision, and amid U.S. intervention in Korea, American military spending increased threefold. The trend proved a lasting one, as defense expenditures remained high for the next 40 years. But the more important result of NSC-68, and the shift in policy it helped create, was to establish the United States clearly and decisively—in its own mind at least—as the policeman of the world.

CHAPTER NINETEEN

Cold War America

~

International crises were not the only frustrations Americans encountered in the aftermath of World War II. The United States in the late 1940s faced the formidable challenge of adapting its wartime economy to the new demands of peace. It also experienced a series of wrenching crises in trying to adapt its domestic political life to the escalating demands of the Cold War.

THE FAIR DEAL

Despite all the weighty diplomatic decisions President Truman faced in the middle to late 1940s, he decided as well to address the unfinished business of the New Deal—to launch a program of reform that would, he believed, complete the structure Roosevelt had begun. Within days of the Japanese surrender, Truman proposed a broad "twenty-one point" reform agenda in a message to Congress. It called for federal housing assistance, a rise in the minimum wage, tax reform, farm aid, broader unemployment insurance, and an invigorated Fair Employment Practices Committee. "We want to see the time come when we can do the things in peace that we have been able to do in war," he had said in July 1945. "If we can put this tremendous machine of ours . . . to work for peace, we can look forward to the greatest age in the history of mankind."

Truman soon faced formidable problems in advancing his goals for American society. Gone were the Depression conditions that had made the New Deal so popular. Instead, there were new obstacles and challenges that undermined Truman's reform initiatives.

A Peacetime Economy

One immediate problem was economic reconversion—shifting the nation's economy from war production to peacetime activity. The bombs that destroyed Hiroshima and Nagasaki ended the war months earlier than almost anyone had predicted. As a result, the nation was propelled suddenly into a process of adapting to peace. The lack of planning was soon compounded by a growing popular impatience for a return to "normal" economic conditions—which meant an end to such wartime restrictions as rationing and price controls. Under intense public pressure, the Truman administration attempted to hasten economic reconversion, despite dire warnings by many planners and economists. The result was a period of great economic instability.

But the problems of the postwar economy were not the ones most Americans had feared. There had been many predictions that peace would bring a return of Depression unemployment, as war production ceased and returning soldiers flooded the labor market. But no general economic collapse occurred in 1946—for several reasons. Government spending dropped sharply and abruptly, to be sure; $35 billion of war contracts were canceled at a stroke within weeks of the Japanese surrender. But increased consumer demand soon compensated. Consumer goods had been generally unavailable during the war, so many workers had saved a substantial portion of their wages and were now ready to spend. A $6 billion tax cut pumped additional money into general circulation. The Servicemen's Readjustment Act of 1944, better known as the GI Bill of Rights, provided economic and educational assistance to veterans, increasing spending even further.

This flood of consumer demand ensured that there would be no new depression, but it did contribute to more than two years of serious inflation. During that period prices rose at rates of up to fifteen percent annually. In the summer of 1946, the president vetoed an extension of the wartime Office of Price Administration's authority, thus eliminating price controls. (He was opposed not to the controls, but to congressional amendments that had weakened the OPA.) Inflation soared to twenty-five percent before he relented a month later and signed a bill little different from the one he had rejected.

Compounding the economic difficulties was a sharp rise in labor unrest, driven in part by the impact of inflation. By the end of 1945, there had already been major strikes in the automobile, electrical, and steel industries. In April 1946, John L. Lewis again led the United Mine Workers out on strike, shutting down the coal fields for forty days. Fears grew rapidly that without vital coal supplies, the entire nation might virtually grind to a halt. Truman finally forced the miners to return to work by ordering government seizure of the mines. But in the process, he pressured mine owners to grant the union most of its demands, which he had earlier denounced as inflationary. Almost simultaneously, the nation's railroads suffered a total shutdown—the first in the nation's history—as two major unions walked out on strike. Truman lashed out bitterly at the unions. Although he was "a friend of labor," Truman said, he could not tolerate a situation in which labor leaders could "completely stifle our economy and ultimately destroy our country." In the end, Truman faced down the striking workers. By threatening to use the army to run the trains, Truman pressured them back to work after only a few days.

The problems of reconversion fell particularly hard on the millions of women and minorities who had entered the work force during the war. With veterans returning home and looking for jobs in the industrial economy, employers viewed many women, African Americans, Hispanics, Chinese, and other war workers as temporary employees who ought to give up their jobs to make room for returning soldiers. Some war workers left the work force voluntarily, including women who wanted to return to their homes to care for their returning husbands and for their children. But as many as eighty percent of women workers wanted to continue working. Many lost the jobs they had gained during the war but managed to remain in the work force. Postwar inflation, the pressure to meet the rising expectations of a high-consumption society, and the rising divorce rate (which left many women responsible for their own economic well-being) all combined to create a high demand for paid employment among women. As they found themselves excluded from industrial jobs, women workers instead moved into other areas of the economy (above all, the service sector). Virtually all black, Hispanic, and Asian males needed to remain in the work force as well. Most did so, but often in less skilled and less lucrative jobs than those they had occupied during the war.

Repudiating the Fair Deal

Despite problems with economic reconversion, Truman remained committed to enacting domestic reform measures. Indeed within weeks of announcing his "twenty-one point plan" he added several other ambitious proposals: federal aid to funding for the St. Lawrence Seaway (which was to link the Great Lakes to the Atlantic Ocean), nationalization of atomic energy, and perhaps most significantly, national health insurance. The latter had been a dream of welfare-state liberals for decades, but one deferred in 1935 when the Social Security Act was written. In unveiling such sweeping plans, the president was declaring an end to the wartime moratorium on liberal reform. He was also symbolizing, as he later wrote, "my assumption of the office of President in my own right."

But most of Truman's domestic programs (which he later labeled the "Fair Deal") fell victim to the same public and congressional conservatism that had crippled the last years of the New Deal. Indeed, that conservatism seemed to be intensifying. At the same time, the president was losing the confidence of much of the public—and even of many liberals. Truman was subject to daily criticism in the press; he fared little better among elected officials in Washington. Increasingly his critics portrayed Truman as bumbling and ill fitted for the momentous responsibility of the American presidency. Invidious comparisons between Truman and Franklin Roosevelt worsened the president's plight. One joke, which began with the question of what Roosevelt would do if he were still alive, ended with the punch line: "I wonder what Truman would do if he were alive."

By October 1946 public opinion polls indicated that only forty percent of Americans approved of the president's performance. Before long even that dismal approval rating had sunk to only thirty-two percent. The president himself privately expressed frustration with the pressures of office—"I would rather be *anything* than president," he told his press secretary in 1946. To his mother he confessed, "When I make a mistake it's a good one." As the November 1946 congressional elections approached, the Republicans made use of a simple but devastating slogan "Had Enough?" When the votes were counted, the Republican party had won control of both houses of Congress.

The new Republican Congress quickly moved to reduce government spending and chip away at New Deal reforms. The president bowed to what he claimed was the popular mandate to lift most remaining wage and price controls, and Congress moved further to deregulate the economy. Inflation rapidly increased. When a public outcry arose over the soaring prices for meat, Senator Robert Taft of Ohio, perhaps the most influential Republican conservative in Congress, advised consumers to "Eat less," and added, "We have got to break with the corrupting idea that we can legislate prosperity, legislate equality, legislate opportunity." True to the spirit of Taft's words, the Republican Congress quickly applied what one congressman described as a "meat-axe to government frills." It refused to appropriate funds to aid education, increase Social Security, or support reclamation and power projects in the West. It defeated a proposal to raise the minimum wage. It passed tax measures that cut rates dramatically for high-income families and only slightly for those with lower incomes. Only vetoes by the president finally forced a more progressive bill.

The most notable action of the new Congress was its assault on the Wagner Act of 1935. Conservatives had always resented the new powers the legislation had granted unions; and the labor difficulties during and after the war had sharply intensified such resentments. The result was the Labor-Management Relations Act of 1947, better known as the Taft-Hartley Act. It made illegal the so-called closed shop (a workplace in which no one can be hired without first being a member of a union). And although it continued to permit the creation of so-called union shops (in which workers must join a union after being hired), it permitted states to pass "right-to-work" laws prohibiting even that. Repealing this provision, the controversial Section 14(b), remained a goal of the labor movement for decades. The Taft-Hartley Act, like the wartime Smith-Connally Act, also empowered the president to call for a "cooling-off" period before a strike by issuing an injunction against any work stoppage that endangered national safety or health. Outraged workers and union leaders denounced the measure as a "slave labor bill." Truman vetoed it. But both houses easily overruled him the same day.

The Taft-Hartley Act did not destroy the labor movement, as many union leaders had predicted. But it did damage weaker unions in relatively lightly or-

ganized industries such as chemicals and textiles; and it made much more difficult the organizing of workers who had never been union members at all, especially women, minorities, and most workers in the South.

The Election of 1948

Despite the 1946 election results, Truman and his advisers still believed the
American public was not ready to abandon the achievements of the New Deal.
As they planned strategy for the 1948 campaign, therefore, they placed their
hopes on an appeal to enduring Democratic loyalties. Throughout 1948,
Truman proposed one reform measure after another. He again endorsed housing programs, a rise in the minimum wage from forty to seventy-five cents, farm
support, aid to education, and national health insurance.

Most remarkably, on February 2 he sent the first major civil-rights program
of the century to the Congress. Noting that "not all groups enjoy the full privileges of citizenship," Truman asserted that "the federal government has a clear
duty to see that all the Constitutional guarantees of individual liberties and equal
protection under the law are not denied or abridged anywhere in the Union."
Truman asked for passage of a federal law against lynching, a ban on the poll tax,
protection of voting rights, a ban on discrimination in interstate travel, a new
Fair Employment Practices Commission, the end of racial discrimination in the
military, and redress of the wrongs inflicted on Japanese Americans who had
been interned during the war "solely because of their racial origin." Many of
these proposals had come from the report of a presidential Civil Rights Commission that had made a deep impression on Truman. When southern Democratic congressmen heaped criticism on Truman for his civil-rights program, the
president reminded one that he himself had Confederate ancestors and was thoroughly familiar with "Jim Crowism." But, Truman continued, "my very stomach
turned over when I learned that Negro soldiers, just back from overseas, were
being dumped out of army trucks in Mississippi and beaten. Whatever my inclinations as a native of Missouri might have been, as president I know this is bad.
I shall fight to end evils like this."

While Congress ignored or defeated all of Truman's reform proposals, the
president built campaign issues for the fall. There remained, however, the problem of the public's perceptions of Truman himself—the assumption among much
of the electorate that he lacked stature, that his administration was weak and inept. Also troubling were deep divisions within the Democratic party. At the Democratic Convention that summer, two factions abandoned the party altogether.
Southern conservatives reacted angrily to Truman's proposed civil-rights bill and
to the approval at the convention of a civil-rights plank in the platform (engineered by Hubert Humphrey, the mayor of Minneapolis). They walked out and
formed the States' Rights (or "Dixiecrat") party, with Governor Strom Thur-
mond of South Carolina as its presidential nominee. At the same time, the party's
left wing formed a new Progressive party, with Henry A. Wallace as its candidate.

Wallace supporters objected to what they considered the slow and ineffective domestic policies of the Truman administration, but they resented even more the president's confrontational stance toward the Soviet Union. It attracted the support of, among others, those on the left sympathetic to communism.

In addition, many Democratic liberals unwilling to leave the party attempted to dump the president in 1948. The Americans for Democratic Action (ADA), a coalition of liberals, tried to entice Dwight D. Eisenhower, the popular war hero, to contest the nomination. Only after Eisenhower had refused did liberals bow to the inevitable and accept the nomination of Truman. The Republicans, in the meantime, had once again nominated Governor Thomas E. Dewey of New York, whose substantial re-election victory in 1946 had made him one of the nation's leading political figures. Austere, dignified, and presumably competent, he seemed to offer an unbeatable alternative to the president. Polls showed Dewey with an apparently insurmountable lead in September, so much so that some opinion analysts stopped taking surveys. Dewey conducted a subdued, statesmanlike campaign and tried to avoid antagonizing anyone.

Only Truman, it seemed, believed he could win. As the campaign gathered momentum, he became ever more aggressive, turning the fire away from himself and toward Dewey and the "do-nothing, good-for-nothing" Republican Congress, which was, he told the voters, responsible for fueling inflation and abandoning workers and common people. To dramatize his point, he used his acceptance speech at the Democratic convention to call Congress into special session in July and give it a chance, he said, to enact the liberal measures the Republicans had recently written into their platform. Congress met for two weeks and, predictably, did almost nothing.

The president traveled nearly 32,000 miles and made 356 speeches, delivering blunt, extemporaneous attacks on his opponents. He had told Alben Barkley, his running mate, "I'm going to fight hard. I'm going to give them hell." And he was true to his word. He called for repeal of the Taft-Hartley Act, increased price supports for farmers, and strong civil-rights protection for blacks. (He was the first president ever to campaign in Harlem.) He sought, in short, to recreate much

ELECTION OF 1948	(53% of electorate voting)	ELECTORAL VOTE	POPULAR VOTE (%)
Harry S. Truman (Democratic)		303	24,105,695 (49.5)
Thomas E. Dewey (Republican)		189	21,969,170 (45.1)
Strom Thurmond (States' Rights)		39	1,169,021 (2.4)
Henry A. Wallace (Progressive)		—	1,156,103 (2.4)
Other candidates (Socialist, Prohibition, Socialist Labor, Socialist Workers)		—	272,713

ELECTION OF TRUMAN.   Few pundits believed Truman would beat Dewey in the election of 1948. Public opinion polls showed Truman lagging far behind his opponent. In this famous photograph, Truman exuberantly displays the Chicago Tribune's erroneous headline reporting the results of the election. In fact, Truman had defeated Dewey in a narrow victory.

of Franklin Roosevelt's New Deal coalition. To the surprise of virtually everyone, including nearly all the polls, media pundits, and political experts, he succeeded. On election night, he won a narrow but decisive victory: 49.5 percent of the popular vote to Dewey's 45.1 percent (with the two splinter parties dividing the small remainder between them), and an electoral margin of 303 to 189. Democrats, in the meantime, regained both houses of Congress by substantial margins. It was the most dramatic upset in the history of presidential elections.

The Fair Deal Revived

Despite the Democratic victories, the Eighty-first Congress was little more hospitable to Truman's Fair Deal reform than its Republican predecessor had been. But Truman did win some important victories, to be sure. Congress raised the legal minimum wage from forty cents to seventy-five cents an hour. It approved an important expansion of the Social Security system, increasing benefits by seventy-five percent and extending them to 10 million additional people. And it passed the National Housing Act of 1949, which provided for the construction of 810,000 units of low-income housing accompanied by long-term rent subsidies. (Inadequate funding plagued the program for years, and it reached its initial goal only in 1972.)

But on other issues—national health insurance and aid to education among them—Truman made no progress. Nor was he able to persuade Congress to accept the civil-rights legislation he proposed in 1949. Southern Democrats filibustered to kill the bill. Truman did proceed on his own to battle several forms of racial discrimination. He ordered an end to discrimination in the hiring of government employees. He began to dismantle segregation within the armed forces. And he allowed the Justice Department to become actively involved in court battles against discriminatory statutes. The Supreme Court, in the meantime, signaled its own growing awareness of the issue by ruling, in *Shelley* v. *Kraemer* (1948), that the courts could not be used to enforce private "covenants" meant to bar blacks from residential neighborhoods. The achievements of the Truman years made only minor dents in the structure of segregation, but they were the tentative beginnings of a federal commitment to confront the problem of racism.

There was less to celebrate in Truman's attempt to advance national health insurance. Through much of his presidency Truman had endorsed the importance of ensuring that all Americans had access to decent medical care and security from the ravages of catastrophic illness. His program to redress existing shortcomings called for the creation of more hospitals, greater support for public health, maternal and child health programs, federal aid for medical research and education, and most sweepingly, prepaid health insurance for all Americans. The program would be funded, Truman proposed, by a four percent increase in the Social Security tax raised through payroll deductions. Those not covered by Social Security would be covered by general federal funds.

Although Congress failed to act on the legislation when Truman first proposed it, the president renewed his call for action during the 1948 campaign and in his first State of the Union address after his re-election. What followed was a bitter debate in which the American Medical Association fiercely resisted the President's reform program. The AMA denounced national health insurance as "socialized medicine," characterized it as an attack on the free enterprise system, and charged that the government was attempting to control the medical profession. The organization devoted over $3 million to lobbying against national health insurance. Part of their campaign included public relations messages designed to "educate" the public about dangers they claimed a mandated federal program would pose. Whether because of such lobbying or for other reasons, the public in fact displayed little enthusiasm for Truman's program. In 1949, polls indicated that only thirty-six percent of Americans favored the legislation.

Health insurance slowly made headway, nonetheless, but as private rather than public programs. Voluntary programs increased, and many unions succeeded in winning coverage as a fringe benefit. By 1950, some fifty-one percent of Americans had coverage for hospital charges, although fewer than fifteen percent had insurance that covered in-hospital physician fees. Fewer than 3 million American workers were covered by negotiated health insurance plans in 1948; by 1954 that figure had risen to some 12 million. As more large employers provided some form of health coverage to their employees, commercial insurance companies also became much more involved in providing health-related plans. But the voluntary programs and commercial insurance plans left many Americans without coverage; and the cost of insurance for those within the covered pool steadily grew.

Despite the failure of national health insurance, there was significant progress in spurring hospital construction. The Hill-Burton Act passed by Congress in 1946 provided the states with federal money to build both public and private hospitals. Between 1947 and 1971, Hill-Burton would result in almost 30 billion dollars devoted to hospital construction, and a significant expansion of the number of hospital beds in the United States.

These measures fell far short, however, of what Truman had envisioned. Not until 1965 did the federal government provide national health insurance—and then only for the aged. The roots of that later success were evident to President Lyndon Johnson, who traveled to Independence, Missouri to sign the bill in Truman's presence. "You have made me a very, very happy man," the eighty-one-year-old former president would tell Lyndon Johnson.

THE KOREAN WAR

Truman's domestic policies had a difficult time from the beginning in competing against the growing national obsession with the Soviet threat in Europe. In 1950, a new and more dangerous element of the Cold War emerged and all but killed hopes for further Fair Deal reform. On June 24, 1950, the armies of communist North Korea swept across their southern border in an invasion of the pro-western half of the Korean peninsula to the south. Within days, they had occupied much of South Korea, including Seoul, its capital. Many Americans believed that the Soviet Union had engineered the North Korean invasion. Almost immediately, the United States committed itself to the conflict: the first military engagement of the cold war.

A Divided Country

The Korean War reflected a kind of political instability that was far from uncommon in the post–World War II period. Both the United States and the Soviet Union had sent troops into Korea by the end of 1945, and neither was willing to leave. Instead, they divided the nation, supposedly temporarily, along the thirty-eighth parallel. The Russians finally departed in 1949, leaving behind a communist government in the North with a strong, Soviet-equipped army. The Americans left a few months later, handing control to the pro-western government of

Syngman Rhee, anticommunist but only nominally democratic. He had a relatively small military, which he used primarily to suppress internal opposition.

The relative weakness of the South offered a strong temptation to nationalists in the North Korean government who wanted to reunite the country. The temptation grew stronger early in 1950 when the American government implied that it did not consider South Korea within its own "defense perimeter." The role of the Soviet Union in initiating the invasion remains unclear, but the Soviets supported the offensive once it began.

The Truman administration responded quickly. On June 27, 1950, the president ordered limited American military assistance to South Korea; and on the same day he appealed to the United Nations to intervene. The Soviet Union was boycotting the Security Council at the time (to protest the council's refusal to recognize the new communist government of China) and was thus unable to exercise its veto power. As a result, American delegates were able to win United Nations agreement to a resolution calling for international assistance to Syngman Rhee's government in South Korea. On June 30, the United States ordered its own ground forces into Korea, and Truman appointed General Douglas MacArthur to command the UN operations there. (Several other nations provided assistance and troops, but the "UN" armies were, in fact, overwhelmingly American.)

The intervention in Korea was the first expression of the newly expansive American foreign policy outlined in NSC-68. But the administration soon went beyond NSC-68 and decided that the war would be an effort not simply at containment but also at "liberation." After a surprise American invasion at Inchon in September had dislodged the North Korean forces from the South and sent them fleeing back across the thirty-eighth parallel, Truman gave MacArthur permission to pursue the communists into their own territory. His aim, as an American-sponsored UN resolution proclaimed in October, was to create "a unified, independent and democratic Korea."

The Costs of Invasion

For several weeks, MacArthur's invasion of North Korea proceeded smoothly. On October 19, the capital, Pyongyang, fell to the UN forces. Victory seemed near, until the new communist government of China—alarmed by the movement of American forces toward its border—intervened, as it had been threatening to do. By November 4, eight divisions of the Chinese army had entered the war. The UN offensive stalled and then collapsed. Through December 1950, outnumbered American forces fought a bitter, losing battle against the Chinese divisions, retreating at almost every juncture. Within weeks, communist forces had pushed the Americans back below the thirty-eighth parallel once again and had captured the South Korean capital of Seoul a second time. By mid-January 1951, the UN armies had stalled the North Korean advance; and by March, the UN armies had managed to regain much of the territory they had recently lost, taking back Seoul and pushing the communists north of the

THE KOREAN WAR, 1950–1953

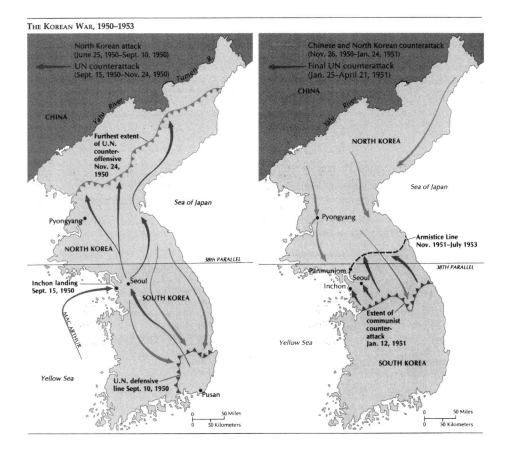

thirty-eighth parallel once more. But with that, the war degenerated into a protracted stalemate.

From the start, Truman had been determined to avoid a direct conflict with China, which he feared might lead to a new world war. Once China entered the war, he began seeking a negotiated solution to the struggle; and for the next two years, he insisted that there be no wider war. But he faced a formidable opponent in General MacArthur, who resisted any limits on his military discretion. The United States was fighting the Chinese, he argued. It should, therefore, attack China itself, if not through an actual invasion, then at least by bombing communist forces massing north of the Chinese border. In March 1951, he indicated his unhappiness in a public letter to House Republican leader Joseph W. Martin that concluded: "There is no substitute for victory." His position had wide popular support.

The Martin letter came after nine months during which MacArthur had resisted Truman's decisions and balked at the president's orders not to make his objections public. The release of the Martin letter, therefore, struck the president as intolerable insubordination. On April 11, 1951, he relieved MacArthur of his command.

KOREAN WAR.   As American soldiers march toward engagement with the enemy, South Korean women and children flee in the opposite direction. The Korean War, precipitated by a North Korean invasion of South Korea, reflected the contradictory pressures of the Cold War as the United States struggled both to stop communist aggression and, at the same time, to limit the scale of military intervention.

There was a storm of public outrage. Sixty-nine percent of the American people supported MacArthur, a Gallup poll reported. When the general returned to the United States later in 1951, he was greeted with wild enthusiasm. His televised farewell appearance before a joint session of Congress—which he concluded by saying "Old soldiers never die, they just fade away"—attracted an audience of millions. Public criticism of Truman finally abated somewhat when a number of prominent military figures, including General Omar Bradley, publicly supported the president's decision. But substantial hostility toward Truman remained.

In the meantime, the Korean stalemate continued. Negotiations between the opposing forces began at Panmunjom in July 1951, but the talks—and the war—dragged on until 1953.

Limited Mobilization

Just as the war in Korea produced only a limited American military commitment abroad, so it created only a limited economic mobilization at home. Still, the government did try to control the wartime economy in several important ways.

First, Truman set up the Office of Defense Mobilization to fight inflation by holding down prices and discouraging high union wage demands. When these cautious regulatory efforts failed, the president took more drastic action. Railroad workers walked off the job in 1951, and Truman ordered the government to seize control of the railroads. That helped keep the trains running, but it had no effect on union demands. Workers ultimately got most of what they had demanded. In 1952, during a nationwide steel strike, Truman seized the steel mills, citing his powers as commander in chief. But in a six to three decision, the Supreme Court ruled that the president had exceeded his authority, and Truman was forced to relent. A long and costly strike followed, and the president's drastic actions appeared to many to have been both rash and ineffective.

The Korean War gave a significant boost to economic growth by pumping new government funds into the economy at a point when many believed a recession was about to begin. But the war had other, less welcome effects. It came at a time of rising insecurity about America's position in the world and intensified anxiety about communism. As the long stalemate continued, producing 140,000 American dead and wounded, frustration turned to anger. The United States, which had recently won the greatest war in history, seemed unable to conclude what many Americans considered a minor border skirmish in a small country. Some began to believe that something must be deeply wrong—not only in Korea but within the United States as well. Such fears contributed to the rise of the second major campaign of the century against domestic communism.

THE CRUSADE AGAINST COMMUNISM

The question of why so many Americans came to believe that their government, and their nation, were riddled with communist subversives remains a subject of much controversy among historians. No single factor explains why these concerns by the early 1950s had reached the point of near hysteria. There are, nonetheless, several factors that clearly played a part in fueling the campaign against domestic enemies.

Communism itself was obviously one factor in fueling the fears of Americans. Stalin's atrocities, the expansionism of the Soviet Union in the postwar period, and perhaps most notably, American setbacks in the battle against communism (the Korean stalemate, the "loss" of China, the Soviet development of an atomic bomb) certainly made fertile ground for those who would plant suspicions about domestic communism. The idea of a communist conspiracy within

American borders, aided and abetted by traitors and spies, offered a convenient explanation of why the United States had not always prevailed in the Cold War abroad. But other important factors, rooted in events in American domestic politics, contributed to the rise of the anticommunist fervor as well.

Early Investigations

At least initially, a good deal of the anticommunist furor emerged out of infighting among the Democratic and Republican parties and their battles for political control in the late 1940s. Beginning in 1947 (with Republicans temporarily in control of Congress), the House Committee on Un-American Activities (HUAC) held widely publicized investigations to prove that, under Democratic rule, the government had tolerated (if not actually encouraged) communist subversion. The committee turned first to the movie industry, arguing that communists had infiltrated Hollywood and tainted American films with propaganda. Writers and producers, some of them former communists, were called to testify. Several who became known as "friendly witnesses" agreed to cooperate with the committee and in their testimony named associates and colleagues who, they claimed, had been involved in left-wing politics. Others refused to cooperate with what they viewed as an inquisition. Among them were several leading directors and screenwriters known as the "Hollywood Ten." When these men declined to answer questions about their own political beliefs and those of their colleagues, they were jailed for contempt. As the investigations continued, others were barred from employment in Hollywood when the film industry, attempting to protect its imperiled public image, adopted a blacklist of those of "suspicious loyalty."

More alarming to the public was HUAC's investigation into charges of disloyalty leveled against a former high-ranking member of the State Department, Alger Hiss. In 1948, Whittaker Chambers, who admitted he had once been a communist agent and was now a conservative editor at *Time* magazine, told the committee that Hiss had passed classified State Department documents through him to the Soviet Union in 1937 and 1938. When Hiss sued him for slander, Chambers produced microfilms of the documents (called the "pumpkin papers," because Chambers had kept them hidden in a pumpkin in his garden) that he claimed Hiss had given to the Soviets. Hiss could not be tried for espionage because of the statute of limitations (a law that protects individuals from prosecution for most crimes after seven years have passed). But largely because of the relentless efforts of Richard M. Nixon, a freshman Republican congressman from California and a member of HUAC, Hiss was convicted of perjury and served several years in prison. The Hiss case not only discredited a prominent young diplomat; it cast suspicion on a generation of liberal Democrats and made it possible for many Americans to believe that communists had actually infiltrated the government.

The Federal Loyalty Program

Partly to protect itself against Republican attacks and partly to encourage support for the president's foreign policy initiatives, the Truman administration in 1947 initiated a widely publicized program to review the loyalty of federal employees. Truman himself had some doubts about the program. He believed that America was "perfectly safe so far as communism is concerned—we have far too many sane people." But he yielded to political pressures when he issued Executive Order 9835 establishing the Federal Employees Loyalty and Security Program. Although precedents for such screenings existed during war, no such program had ever been enacted in peacetime.

The program had two important elements. First, it gave the attorney general authority to draw up a list of subversive organizations. Membership in or even support for listed groups could then be used to determine the "loyalty" of federal employees. Second, the program provided the means for the federal government to investigate its own employees for suspicion of political subversion.

THE PUMPKIN PAPERS.   According to Whittaker Chambers, these hollowed out pumpkins held microfilms of classified State Department papers passed to him by Alger Hiss. Chambers claimed Hiss had passed the "pumpkin papers," as they were called, through him to the Soviet Union.

In August 1950, the president went further and authorized sensitive agencies to fire people deemed no more than "bad security risks." By 1951, more than 2,000 government employees had resigned under pressure, and 212 had been dismissed.

Whatever Truman's political intentions, the employee loyalty program seemed to add legitimacy to those leveling accusations of subversion against the government. The anticommunist frenzy quickly grew so intense that even a Democratic Congress felt obliged to bow to it. In 1950, Congress passed the McCarran Internal Security Act, which required all communist organizations to register with the government and publish their records while creating additional restrictions on "subversive" activity. Truman vetoed the bill. Congress easily overrode his veto.

The Rosenberg Case

The anticommunist crusade reached new levels of intensity with revelations of an alleged conspiracy within the United States to pass atomic secrets to the Soviet Union. Many believed the plot accounted for the Soviet success in creating an atomic weapon in 1949, earlier than most Americans had expected. In 1950, Klaus Fuchs, a young British scientist, seemed to confirm those fears when he testified that he had delivered to the Russians details of the manufacture of the American bomb. The case ultimately settled on an obscure New York couple, Julius and Ethel Rosenberg, members of the Communist party, whom the government claimed had been the masterminds of the conspiracy. The case against them rested in large part on testimony by Ethel's brother, David Greenglass, a machinist who had worked on the Manhattan Project. Greenglass admitted to channeling secret information to the Soviet Union through other agents (including Fuchs). His sister and brother-in-law had, he claimed, planned and orchestrated the espionage. The Rosenbergs denied any part in the conspiracy, but they were convicted and, on April 5, 1951, sentenced to death. A worldwide movement in support of the Rosenbergs took form in the next two years; many legal appeals were also filed on their behalf to no avail. They died in the electric chair on June 19, 1953, proclaiming their innocence to the end.

All these factors—the HUAC investigations, the Hiss trial, the loyalty investigations, the McCarran Act, the Rosenberg case—combined with concern about international events to create a fear of communist subversion that by the early 1950s seemed to have gripped virtually the entire country. State and local governments, the judiciary, schools and universities, and labor unions all sought to purge themselves of real or imagined subversives. A pervasive fear settled on the country—not only the fear of communist infiltration but the fear of being suspected of communism. It was a climate that made possible the rise of an extraordinary public figure, whose behavior at any other time might have been dismissed as preposterous.

McCarthyism

Joseph McCarthy was an undistinguished, first-term, Republican senator from Wisconsin when, in February 1950, he suddenly burst into national prominence. In the midst of a speech in Wheeling, West Virginia, he raised a sheet of paper and claimed to "hold in my hand" a list of 205 known communists currently working in the American State Department. No person of comparable stature had ever made so bold a charge against the federal government; and in the weeks to come, as McCarthy repeated and expanded on his accusations (and altered his numbers accordingly), he emerged as the nation's most prominent leader of the crusade against domestic subversion.

Within weeks of his charges against the State Department, McCarthy was leveling accusations at other agencies. After 1952, with the Republicans in control of the Senate and McCarthy the chairman of a special subcommittee, he conducted highly publicized investigations of subversion in many areas of the government. His unprincipled assistants, Roy Cohn and David Schine, sauntered arrogantly through federal offices and American embassies overseas looking for evidence of communist influence. One hapless government official after another appeared before McCarthy's subcommittee, where the senator belligerently and often cruelly badgered witnesses and destroyed public careers. McCarthy never produced solid evidence that any federal employee was a communist. But a growing constituency adored him nevertheless for his coarse, "fearless" assaults on a government establishment that many considered arrogant, effete, even traitorous. Republicans, in particular, rallied to his claims that the Democrats had been responsible for "twenty years of treason," that only a change of parties could rid the country of subversion. McCarthy, in short, provided his followers with an issue into which they could channel a wide range of resentments: fear of communism, animosity toward the country's "Eastern establishment," and frustrated partisan ambitions.

For a time, McCarthy intimidated all but a few people from opposing him. Even the highly popular Dwight D. Eisenhower, running for president in 1952, did not dare speak out against him, although he disliked McCarthy's tactics and was outraged at, among other things, McCarthy's attacks on General George Marshall. Instead, as Eisenhower campaigned with McCarthy in Wisconsin he joined the attack on communist subversion in government, stressing the damage that had been done by Democratic administrations who "had poisoned two decades of our national life" by tolerating communism. A disgusted Harry Truman expressed dismay that Eisenhower did not publicly defend General Marshall. "I thought he might make a good president," Truman said of Eisenhower after his Wisconsin speech, "but that was a mistake. In this campaign he has betrayed almost everything I thought he stood for." Eisenhower, Truman insisted, "knows or he ought to know, how completely dishonest Joe McCarthy is. He ought to despise McCarthy; just as I expected him to—and just as I do."

The Republican Revival

Instead, public frustration over the stalemate in Korea and popular fears of internal subversion combined to make 1952 a bad year for the Democratic party. Truman, whose own popularity had diminished almost to the vanishing point, wisely withdrew from the presidential contest. The party united instead behind Governor Adlai E. Stevenson of Illinois. Stevenson's dignity, wit, and eloquence made him a beloved figure to many liberals and intellectuals. But those same qualities seemed only to fuel Republican charges that Stevenson lacked the strength or the will to combat communism sufficiently. McCarthy described him as "soft" and took delight in deliberately confusing him with Alger Hiss.

NIXON AND EISENHOWER.   General Eisenhower greets his running mate Richard Nixon, shortly after Nixon's "Checkers" speech explaining alleged financial improprieties. Though privately critical of Nixon, Eisenhower stood by him. The two men went on to crush the Democratic ticket of Stevenson and Kefauver in the election of 1952.

Stevenson's greatest problem, however, was the Republican candidate opposing him. Rejecting the efforts of conservatives to nominate Robert Taft or Douglas MacArthur, the Republicans turned to a man who had no previous identification with the party: General Dwight D. Eisenhower, military hero, commander of NATO, president of Columbia University in New York. He chose as his running mate the young California senator who had gained national prominence through his crusade against Alger Hiss: Richard M. Nixon.

Eisenhower and Nixon were a powerful combination in the autumn campaign. While Eisenhower attracted support through his geniality and his statesmanlike pledges to settle the Korean conflict (at one point dramatically promising to "go to Korea" himself), Nixon effectively exploited the issue of domestic subversion. After surviving early accusations of financial improprieties (which he effectively neutralized in a famous television address, the "Checkers speech"), Nixon went on to launch harsh attacks on Democratic "cowardice," "appeasement," and "treason." He spoke derisively of "Adlai the appeaser" and ridiculed Secretary of State Dean Acheson for running a "cowardly college of communist containment." And he missed no opportunity to publicize Stevenson's early support for Alger Hiss as opposed to Nixon's own role in exposing Hiss. Eisenhower and Nixon both made effective use of allegations of corruption in the Truman administration and pledged repeatedly to "clean up the mess in Washington."

The response at the polls was overwhelming. Eisenhower won both a popular and electoral landslide: fifty-five percent of the popular vote to Stevenson's forty-four percent, 442 electoral votes to Stevenson's eighty-nine. Republicans gained control of both houses of Congress for the first time in two decades. The election of 1952 ended twenty years of Democratic government. And, while it might not have seemed so at the time, it also signaled the end of some of the worst political turbulence of postwar era.

CHAPTER TWENTY

The Culture of Postwar Prosperity

~

During the 1950s the United States enjoyed a period of exceptional abundance that shaped the nation's social, economic, and even physical landscape in profound ways. Postwar prosperity helped produce a widespread sense of national purpose and self-satisfaction. And it permitted many Americans to live in much greater comfort and with a much stronger sense of personal security than they ever had before.

As throughout American history, not everyone shared equally, or even at all, in the postwar prosperity. Many people lagged far behind the vaunted middle-class standard of living that some Americans now considered virtually a birthright and trumpeted as the "American Dream." In fact more than 30 million Americans lived in poverty in the early 1950s. Significant minorities—most prominently the ten percent of the American people who were African American, but also Hispanics, Asians, and others—continued to suffer social, political, and economic discrimination. American women, too, faced significant obstacles to personal and professional fulfillment.

Indeed, the very things that made America so successful in the 1950s also contributed over time to a restlessness with the nation's enduring social problems. Gunnar Myrdal, a Swedish sociologist who spent several years studying American social problems, wrote in 1944: "American affluence is heavily mortgaged. America carries a tremendous burden of debt to its poor people." Ultimately, the paradox of poverty and inequality among plenty helped move the nation into more turbulent times in the 1960s. Even in the culture of prosperity, signs of problems to come were already visible.

THE ROOTS OF PROSPERITY

Perhaps the most striking feature of American society in the 1950s and early 1960s was the booming, almost miraculous, economic growth that made even

406

the heady 1920s seem pale by comparison. It was a better balanced and more widely distributed prosperity than that of thirty years earlier. It was not, however, as universal as some Americans liked to believe.

Economic Growth

By 1949, despite the continuing problems of postwar reconversion, an economic expansion had begun that would continue with only brief interruptions for almost twenty years. Between 1945 and 1960, the gross national product grew by 250 percent, from $200 billion to over $500 billion—a striking rebuke to the widespread predictions in 1945 that the GNP would decline once the demands of war production ended. Unemployment, which during the Depression had averaged between fifteen and twenty-five percent, remained at about five percent or lower throughout the 1950s and early 1960s. Inflation, in the meantime, hovered around three percent a year or less.

The causes of this growth were varied. Government spending, which had ended the Depression in the 1940s, continued to stimulate growth through public funding of schools, housing, veterans' benefits, welfare, and the $100 billion interstate highway program, which began in 1956. Above all, there was military spending. Economic growth peaked (averaging 4.7 percent a year) during the first half of the 1950s, when military spending was highest because of the Korean War. In the late 1950s, with spending on armaments in decline, the annual rate of growth declined by more than half, to 2.25 percent.

Technological progress also contributed to the boom. Advances in production techniques and mechanical efficiency helped boost worker productivity more than thirty-five percent in the first decade after the war, a rate far higher than that of any previous era. The development of electronic computers, which first became commercially available in the mid-1950s, began to improve the performance of some American corporations. And technological research and development itself became an increasingly important sector of the economy, expanding the demand for scientists, engineers, and other highly trained experts.

The fruits of this scientific and technological research were especially evident in the developing computer industry. The first computers were created by scientists and engineers working for the military during World War II, primarily to help decipher enemy codes. After the war, the International Business Machines Corporation (IBM) and scientists at Harvard developed a more advanced computer, the Mark I, which also served military needs. By 1954, however, IBM and other companies were developing computers for non-military use by government agencies and, more important, private business. Although most Americans did not come into direct and regular contact with computers until the 1980s, the new machines were having a substantial effect on the economy long before then.

The postwar "baby boom" also contributed to economic growth. During World War II, the national birth rate began to reverse a long pattern of decline

EARLY IBM COMPUTER.   One of the early computers built by International Business Machines (IBM), this Naval Ordinance Research Calculator (NORC) was composed of vacuum tubes, resistors, condensers and crystal rectifiers arranged in circuits. Created for the navy, the machine was heralded for its "tremendous speed"—plodding, though it was, by the standards of later computers.

as more young Americans started families. The baby boom peaked in 1957. The nation's population rose almost twenty percent in the decade, from 150 million in 1950 to 179 million in 1960. Americans with large, young families proved to be avid consumers in the postwar economy.

In addition, the rapid expansion of suburbs—whose population grew forty-seven percent in the 1950s, more than twice as fast as the population as a whole—helped stimulate growth in several important sectors of the economy. The number of privately owned cars (more essential for suburban than for urban living) more than doubled in a decade, sparking a great boom in the automobile industry. Demand for new homes helped sustain a vigorous housing industry. The construction of roads, which was both a cause and a result of the growth of suburbs, stimulated the economy as well.

Because of this unprecedented growth, the economy grew nearly ten times as fast as the population in the thirty years after the war. And while that growth was far from equally distributed, it affected most of society. The average American had over twenty percent more purchasing power in 1960 than in 1945, and more than twice as much as during the prosperous 1920s. By 1960, per capita in-

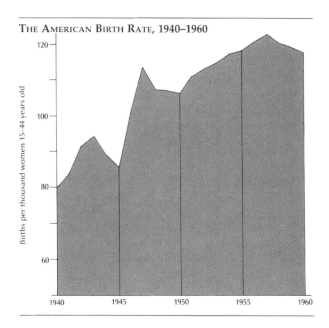

THE AMERICAN BIRTH RATE, 1940–1960

come (the average income for every individual man, woman, and child) was over 1,800 dollars—500 dollars more than it had been fifteen years before. Family incomes had risen even more. The American people had achieved the highest standard of living of any society in the history of the world.

The Growth of the American West

No region of the country experienced more dramatic changes as a result of the new economic growth than the American West. Its population expanded dramatically; its cities boomed; its industrial economy flourished. Before World War II, most of the West had been, economically at least, an appendage of the great industrial economy of the East—providing it with raw materials and agricultural goods. By the 1960s, some parts of the West had emerged as among the most important (and populous) industrial and cultural centers of the nation.

As during World War II, much of the growth of the West was a result of federal spending and investment—spending on the dams, power stations, highways, and other infrastructure developments that made economic development possible; and the military spending that continued to flow disproportionately to factories in California and Texas, many of them built with government funds during the war. But other factors played a role as well. The enormous increase in automobile use after World War II (a result, among other things, of suburbanization and improved highway systems) gave a large stimulus to the petroleum industry and contributed to the rapid growth of oil fields in Texas and Colorado, and the metropolitan centers serving them: Houston, Dallas, and Denver.

State governments in the West invested heavily in their universities. The University of Texas and University of California systems, in particular, became among the nation's largest and best; as centers of research, they helped attract technology-intensive industries to the region. Climate contributed as well. Once they had the infrastructure (and, most important, the water supplies) to sustain large populations, and once air-conditioning became widely available, southern California, Nevada, and Arizona, in particular, attracted many migrants from the East because of their warm, dry, and sunny climates. The growth of Los Angeles after World War II was an especially remarkable phenomenon. More than ten percent of all new businesses in the United States between 1945 and 1950 began in Los Angeles. The population of the city exploded to make the city one of the largest in the country by 1960.

New Economic Theories

The exciting (and to some surprising) discovery of the power of the American economy contributed to the confident, at times complacent tone of much American political life in the 1950s. During the Depression, politicians, intellectuals, and others had often questioned the viability of capitalism. In the 1950s, those doubts seemed to disappear. The postwar economy became a source of national confidence in several ways.

One was the belief that Keynesian economics made it possible for government to regulate and stabilize the economy without intruding directly into the private sector. The British economist John Maynard Keynes had argued as early as the 1920s that by varying the flow of government spending and managing the supply of currency, the state could stimulate the economy to cure recession and dampen growth to prevent inflation. The experience of the last years of the Depression and the first years of the war had seemed to confirm this argument. And by the mid-1950s, Keynesian theory was rapidly becoming a fundamental article of faith—not only among professional economists but among much of the public. The most popular economics textbook of the 1950s and 1960s, Paul Samuelson's *Economics*, imbued generations of college students with Keynesian ideas. Armed with these fiscal and monetary tools, economists now believed, it was possible for the government to maintain a virtually permanent prosperity. The dispiriting boom and bust cycle that many had long believed to be a permanent feature of industrial capitalism could now be banished for-ever. Never again would it be necessary for the nation to experience another Depression.

If any doubters remained, they found ample evidence to dispel their misgivings during the brief recessions the economy experienced during the era. When the economy slackened in late 1953, Secretary of the Treasury George M. Humphrey and the Federal Reserve Board worked to ease credit and make money more readily available. The economy quickly recovered, seeming to confirm the value of Keynesian tactics (even though Humphrey and the Board did not explicitly endorse them). A far more serious recession began late in 1957 and continued for more than a year. This time, the Eisenhower administration ignored the Keynesians and adopted such deflationary tactics as cutting the budget. The slow, halting nature of the recovery, in contrast with the rapid revival in 1954, seemed further to support the Keynesian philosophy.

In addition to the belief in the possibility of permanent economic stability was the equally exhilarating belief in permanent economic growth. As the economy continued to expand far beyond what any observer had predicted was possible only a few years before, more and more Americans assumed that such growth knew no bounds. A comforting thought in itself, this assumption also made possible a new outlook on social and economic problems. In the 1930s, many Americans had argued that the elimination of poverty and injustice would require a redistribution of wealth—a limitation on the fortunes of the rich and a program to distribute income and wealth more fairly. By the mid-1950s, most reformers abandoned the scarcity model that focused on equitably distributing a limited supply of wealth, resources, and income. Instead they came to believe that the solution to economic deprivation lay in increased production. The affluent would not have to sacrifice in order to eliminate poverty. The nation would simply have to generate more abundance, thus raising the quality of life of even the poorest citizens to a level of comfort and decency.

The Keynesians never managed to remake federal economic policy entirely to their liking. Political obstacles consistently limited the ability of even the most committed Keynesians to use fiscal and monetary policies as they wished; and the increasingly complex modern economy did not always respond as quickly to Keynesian policies as the theory behind them suggested it should. Still, the new economics gave many Americans a confidence in their ability to solve economic problems that previous generations had never developed.

Capital and Labor

Centralization, which had been a conspicuous feature of industrial capitalism since the late nineteenth century, continued and even accelerated after World War II. There were more than 4,000 corporate mergers in the 1950s. A relatively small number of large-scale organizations continued to control an enormous proportion of the nation's economic activity. This was particularly true in industries benefiting from government defense spending. As during World War II, the federal government tended to award military contracts to large corporations. In 1959, for example, half of all defense contracts went to only twenty firms. But the same pattern repeated itself in many other areas of the economy, as corporations moved from being single-industry firms to becoming diversified conglomerates. By the end of the decade, half the net corporate income in the nation was going to only slightly more than 500 firms, or one-tenth of one percent of the total number of corporations.

A similar consolidation occurred in the agricultural economy. Increasing mechanization reduced the need for farm labor, and the agricultural work force declined by more than half in the two decades after the war. Mechanization also endangered one of the most cherished American institutions: the family farm. By the 1960s, relatively few individuals could any longer afford to buy and equip a modern farm; and much of the nation's most productive land had been purchased by financial institutions and corporations.

Corporations enjoying booming growth attempted to stave off strikes that interfered with their operations. Since the most important labor unions were now so large and entrenched that they could not easily be suppressed or intimidated, business leaders made important concessions to them. As early as 1948, Walter Reuther, president of the United Automobile Workers, obtained a contract from General Motors that included a built-in "escalator clause"—an automatic cost-of-living increase pegged to the consumer price index. In 1955, Reuther persuaded the Ford Motor Company to provide a guaranteed annual income to auto workers. A few months later, steelworkers in several corporations won a guaranteed annual salary as well. By the mid-1950s, factory wages in all industries had risen substantially, to an average of eighty dollars per week. Some workers also now received substantial additional benefits, among them health insurance and paid vacations.

By the early 1950s, in other words, large labor unions had developed a new kind of relationship with employers, a relationship sometimes known as the "postwar contract." Workers in steel, automobiles, and other large unionized industries received generous increases in wages and benefits; in return, the unions tacitly agreed to refrain from raising other issues—issues involving control of the workplace and a voice for workers in the planning of production. The postwar "contract" had the support of the National Labor Relations Board, whose mediators (many drawing from their experience in World War II) believed the purpose of labor relations was to maintain industrial peace and promote the general health of the economy, not to defend or expand the "rights" of workers. The contract served the corporations and the union leadership well; many rank-and-file workers, however, resented the abandonment of efforts to give them more control over the conditions of their labor.

Also troubling were the number of industrial jobs in some major industries that disappeared as a result of the new technologies that automated production. Even as the labor movement enjoyed impressive successes in winning better wages for its members, its share of the labor force dropped—from an all-time high of thirty-six percent in 1953 to thirty-one percent by the end of the decade. After a crucially important, but fleeting, time of growth, organized labor faced retrenchment.

Still, the economic successes of the 1950s helped pave the way for a reunification of the labor movement. In December 1955, the American Federation of Labor and the Congress of Industrial Organizations ended their twenty-year rivalry and merged to create the AFL-CIO, under the leadership of George Meany. But success also bred stagnation and corruption in some union bureaucracies. In 1957, the powerful Teamsters Union became the subject of a congressional investigation; and its president, David Beck, was charged with the misappropriation of union funds. Beck ultimately stepped down to be replaced by Jimmy Hoffa, whom government investigators pursued for nearly a decade before finally winning a conviction against him (for tax evasion) in 1967. The union that had spearheaded the industrial movement in the 1930s, the United Mine Workers, similarly, became tainted by violence and suspicions of corruption. John L. Lewis's last years as head of the union were plagued by scandals and dissent within the organization. His successor, Tony Boyle, was convicted of complicity in the 1969 murder of Joseph Yablonski, the leader of a dissident faction within the union.

While the labor movement enjoyed significant success in winning better wages and benefits for workers already organized in strong unions, the majority of laborers who were as yet unorganized made fewer advances. Total union membership remained relatively stable, at about 16 million, throughout the 1950s. Lack of growth reflected in part a shift in the work force from blue-collar to white-collar jobs, as well as new obstacles to organization. The Taft-Hartley Act and the state right-to-work laws that it spawned made it more difficult to create new unions, or new units of existing unions, powerful enough to demand recognition from employers.

In the American South, in particular, impediments to unionization remained enormous. The CIO had launched a major organizing drive in the South shortly after World War II, targeting the poorly paid workers in textile mills in particular.

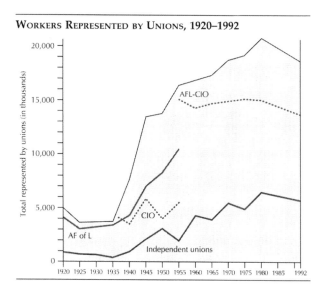

WORKERS REPRESENTED BY UNIONS, 1920–1992

But "Operation Dixie," as it was called, was a failure—as were most other organizing drives there during the postwar period. Antiunion sentiment appeared so powerful in the South—not just among employers, but also among politicians, the press, local police, and many others—that almost all organizing drives encountered crushing and usually fatal resistance.

A PEOPLE OF PLENTY

Among the most striking developments of the postwar era was the rapid extension of a middle-class life style and outlook to large groups of the population previously insulated from it. Several things contributed to the homogenizing of American middle-class culture in the 1950s. The new prosperity of social groups previously living on the margins, the growing availability of and fascination with consumer goods, the rise of television, and perhaps above all, the massive population movement from the cities to the suburbs all played a part in shaping middle-class culture. During the 1950s the American middle class appeared to be a larger, more powerful, more homogeneous, and more dominant force than it had ever been before.

The new prosperity, in fact, inspired some Americans to see abundance, and a set of middle-class values associated with it, as the key to understanding the American past and the American character. Leading intellectuals argued that American history had been characterized by a broad "consensus." "However much at odds on specific issues," the historian Richard Hofstadter wrote in *The American Political Tradition* (1948), Americans have "shared a belief in the rights of property, the philosophy of economic individualism, the value of competition; they have accepted the economic virtues of capitalist culture as necessary qualities of man." David Potter, another leading American historian of the era, published an influential examination of "economic abundance and American character" in 1954. He called it *People of Plenty*. For the American middle class in the 1950s, at least, it seemed an appropriate label.

The Consumer Culture

At the center of middle-class culture in the 1950s, as it had been for many decades before, was consumerism. Increased prosperity, the growing variety and wide availability of new products, and the adeptness of advertisers helped create an insistent demand for products that fueled the consumer culture. The growth of consumer credit, which increased by 800 percent between 1945 and 1957 through the development of credit cards, revolving charge accounts, and easy-payment plans also fed consumption. Prosperity revived the American love affair with the automobile; Detroit responded to the boom with ever-flashier styling and accessories. Consumers also found themselves drawn to new products such as dishwashers, garbage disposals, television, "hi-fis," and (later) stereos. To a

THE SUBURBAN CONSUMER. This 1953 advertisement for a Whirlpool washing machine shows one of the many consumer appliances that were then moving within reach of the average American consumer. Women were a particularly important target of advertisers, as this picture suggests; and manufacturers tried to associate their products with the comfortable, middle-class suburban lifestyle to which women in the 1950s were encouraged to aspire.

striking degree, the prosperity of the 1950s and 1960s was consumer, as opposed to investment, driven.

National marketing and advertising made possible the rapid spread of great national consumer crazes. For example, children, adolescents, and even some adults became entranced in the late 1950s with the "hula hoop"—a large plastic ring kept spinning around the waist. The popularity of the Walt Disney–produced children's television show, The *Mickey Mouse Club* created a national demand for related products such as Mickey Mouse watches and hats. It also helped produce the stunning success of Disneyland, an amusement park near Los Angeles that recreated many of the characters and events of Disney entertainment programs. The Disney technique of turning an entertainment success into an effective tool for marketing consumer goods was not an isolated event. Other entertainers and producers soon began to do the same.

The Suburban Nation

A third of the nation's population lived in suburbs by 1960. The growth of suburbs resulted not only from increased affluence, but from important innovations in home building, which made single-family houses affordable to millions of new people. The most famous of the suburban developers, William Levitt, came to symbolize the new suburban growth with his use of mass-production techniques to construct a large housing development on Long Island, near New York City. This first "Levittown" (there would later be others in New Jersey and Pennsylvania) consisted of several thousand two-bedroom Cape Cod-style houses, with identical interiors and only slightly varied facades, each perched on its own concrete slab (to eliminate excavation costs), facing curving, treeless streets. Levittown houses sold for under $10,000 and they helped meet the enormous postwar demand for housing, which had been developing during more than a decade of very little construction. Young couples—often newly married war veterans eager to start a family, assisted by low-cost, government-subsidized mortgages provided by the GI Bill and other federal programs—rushed to purchase the inexpensive homes, not only in the Levittowns but in similar developments that soon began appearing throughout the country.

Why did so many Americans want to move to the suburbs? One reason was the enormous importance postwar Americans placed on family life after five years of war in which families had often been separated or otherwise disrupted. Suburbs provided families with larger homes than they could find (or afford) in the cities and thus made it easier to raise larger numbers of children. They allowed privacy. They offered security from the noise and dangers of urban living. They created space for the new consumer goods—the cars, boats, appliances, outdoor furniture, and other products—that advertisers helped persuade many middle-class Americans they needed for fulfillment.

For many Americans, suburban life also helped provide a sense of community that some found it difficult to find in large, crowded, impersonal urban areas. In later years, the suburbs would come under attack for their supposedly stifling conformity, homogeneity, and isolation. But in the 1950s, many people were attracted by the idea of living in a community populated largely by people of similar age and background and found it easier to form friendships and social

LEVITTOWN.   This aerial view of Levittown, a vast postwar suburban development on Long Island, shows its carefully laid out streets with their identically designed houses. Communities such as Levittown had enormous appeal for many young middle-class families after World War II, who needed affordable housing and wanted to raise their children in the comfort of the suburbs.

circles there than in the city. Women in particular often valued the presence of other nonworking mothers living nearby to share the tasks of child raising.

Another factor motivating white Americans to move to the suburbs was race. In an era when the African-American population of most cities was rapidly growing, many white families fled to the suburbs to escape the integration of urban neighborhoods and schools. There were some African-American suburbs. But most black families remained in the cities or the countryside. That was in part because suburban housing was too costly, too distant from employment opportunities, and too far removed from public transportation for people of limited means. Suburbs were often also closed to African Americans (and other minorities, including Jews) through discriminatory selling practices and racial "covenants." Even prosperous black families often could not acquire homes in wealthy suburbs because of formal and informal barriers.

Many suburban neighborhoods appeared to be very homogeneous. But they were far from uniform. A famous study of one Levittown revealed a striking variety of occupations, ethnic backgrounds, and incomes there. Still, the Levittowns and inexpensive developments like them ultimately became the homes of mainly lower-middle-class people one step removed from the inner city. Other, more affluent suburbs became enclaves of wealthy families. Around virtually every city, a clear hierarchy emerged of upper-class suburban neighborhoods and more modest ones, just as such gradations had emerged years earlier among urban neighborhoods.

The Suburban Family

For professional men (who tended to work in the city, at some distance from their homes), suburban life generally meant a rigid division between their working and personal worlds. For many middle-class women, it meant an increased isolation from the workplace. The enormous cultural emphasis on family life in the 1950s strengthened popular prejudices against women entering the professions or occupying any paid job at all. Many middle-class husbands considered it demeaning for their wives to be employed. And many women themselves shied away from the workplace when they could afford not to work for wages, in part because prevailing ideas about motherhood encouraged women to stay at home with their children.

One of the most influential books of the postwar era was a famous guide to child rearing: Dr. Benjamin Spock's *Baby and Child Care*, first published in 1946 and reissued repeatedly for decades thereafter. Dr. Spock took a child-centered approach to raising babies, as opposed to the parent-centered theories of many previous childcare experts. Mothers, he instructed, should devote their energies to helping their children learn and grow and realize their potential. All other considerations, including the mother's own physical and emotional requirements, were subordinate. Dr. Spock at first envisioned only a very modest role for fathers in the process of childrearing, although he changed his views on this (as on many other issues) over time.

Thus, many American women faced heavy pressures—both externally and internally imposed—to remain in the home and concentrate on raising their children. Some women, however, had to balance these pressures against other, contradictory ones. As expectations of material comfort rose, many middle-class families needed a second income to maintain the standard of living they desired. As a result, the number of married women working outside the home actually increased in the postwar years—even as the social pressure for them to stay out of the workplace grew. By 1960, nearly a third of all married women were part of the paid work force. Many women thus balanced competing and, at times, conflicting popular expectations.

The experiences of the 1950s worked in some ways to diminish the power of feminism, which some argue ebbed to its lowest point in nearly a century. But they also produced conditions that would very soon create the most powerful feminist movement in American history. The increasing numbers of women in the workplace did much to spur growing demands for equality—at home, on the job, in politics and society—that would become central to the feminist crusades of the 1960s and 1970s.

The 1950s also saw a surge in women's voluntary activities and associations. Many middle-class women who were homemakers became involved in public life through their work with such organizations as the League of Women Voters, the Red Cross, YWCAs, and PTAs. By the late 1950s and early 1960s, some participated actively in more political movements, including civil-rights crusades and anti-nuclear demonstrations, some of them organized by mothers. In all of these associations, women gained organizational and political skills that would later be useful in supporting feminist causes. The growing frustrations of still other women, both in the home and the workplace, created a heightened demand for female professional opportunities that would do much to spur the women's liberation movement.

The Birth of Television

Television, perhaps the most powerful medium of mass communication in history, was central to the culture of the postwar era. Experiments in broadcasting pictures (along with sound) had begun as early as the 1920s, but commercial television appeared only shortly after World War II. It experienced a phenomenally rapid growth. In 1946, there were only 17,000 television sets in the country; by 1957, there were 40 million—almost as many sets as there were families. More people owned television sets, according to one report, than refrigerators (a statistic strikingly similar to one in the 1920s that revealed more people owning radios than bathtubs).

The television industry emerged directly out of the radio industry. All three of the major networks of the 1950s and 1960s—the National Broadcasting Company, the Columbia Broadcasting System, and the American Broadcasting Company—had begun their lives as radio companies. The television business, like radio, relied upon advertising. The need to attract advertisers determined most programming decisions; and in the early days of television, sponsors often played a direct, powerful, and continuing role in determining the content of the programs they chose to sponsor. Many early television shows came to bear the names of the corporations that paid for them: the *GE Television Theater*, the *Chrysler Playhouse*, the *Camel News Caravan*, and others. Proctor and Gamble and other companies actually produced daytime serials known as "soap operas," because their sponsors were almost always companies making household goods targeted at women.

The impact of television on American life was rapid, pervasive, and profound. By the late 1950s, television news had replaced newspapers, magazines, and radios as the nation's most important vehicle of information. Television

THE BIRTH OF TELEVISION. Popular culture in America was transformed during the post-World War II era with the advent of commercial television. Here two young people watch one of the many popular shows of the period, *Hopalong Cassidy*, on the family television.

advertising helped create a vast market for new fashions and consumer goods. Televised athletic events gradually made professional and college sports one of the important sources of entertainment (and one of the biggest businesses) in America. Television entertainment programming, almost all of it controlled by the three national networks (and their corporate sponsors), replaced movies and radio as the principal source of diversion for American families.

Much of the programming of the 1950s and early 1960s created a common image of American life—an image that was predominantly white, middle-class, and suburban. That image was epitomized by such popular situation comedies as *Ozzie and Harriet* and *Leave It to Beaver*. Programming also reinforced the concept of gender roles that many Americans embraced unthinkingly. Situation comedies, in particular, almost always showed families in which, as the title of one of the most popular put it, *Father Knows Best*, and in which women were almost always mothers and housewives striving to serve their children and please their husbands. Often however, the programs cleverly transmitted a more subtle message. In programs such as *Donna Reed*, the apparently deferential mother was actually a woman of great sensitivity and intelligence who exerted the real power in the suburban family. The wacky situations in which Lucille Ball found herself in *I Love Lucy* often revolved around her character's desire to escape domesticity, find a decent job, and contribute to the family income.

Television also conveyed other more complex images: the gritty, urban working-class families in Jackie Gleason's *The Honeymooners;* the childless show-business family of the early *I Love Lucy;* the unmarried professional women in *Our Miss Brooks* and *My Little Margie.* Television did not seek only to create an idealized image of a homogeneous suburban America. It also sought to convey experiences at odds with that image, but to convey them in warm, unthreatening terms—taking social diversity and cultural conflict and domesticating them, turning them into something benign and even comic.

Yet television also, inadvertently, created conditions that could accentuate social conflict. Even those unable to share in the affluence of the era could, through television, acquire a vivid picture of how the rest of their society purportedly lived. Families of limited means or children with an absent parent, whether through death, divorce, or some other misfortune, sometimes measured themselves against the idealized world presented in television families. Real life rarely resembled the world men, women, and children inhabited on television. At the same time that television was reinforcing the homogeneity of the white middle class, it also contributed to a sense of alienation and powerlessness among groups excluded from the world it portrayed.

Science and Space

In 1961, *Time* magazine chose as its "man of the year" not an individual but "the American Scientist." It was an indication of the widespread fascination with which Americans in the age of atomic weapons viewed science and technology. Major medical advances accounted for much of that fascination. Jonas Salk's vaccine to prevent polio, which the federal government provided to the public free beginning in 1955, virtually eliminated polio from American life in a few short years. Other dread diseases such as diphtheria and tuberculosis also all but vanished from society (at least for a time) as new drugs and treatments emerged. Infant mortality declined by nearly fifty percent in the twenty-five years after the war; the death rate among young children fell significantly as well (although both such rates were lower in western Europe). Average life expectancy in those same years rose by five, to seventy-one years.

Other innovations reinforced the American veneration of science and technology: the jet plane, the computer, synthetics, new types of commercially prepared foods, and, especially, developments in aerospace and aviation. Nothing better illustrated the nation's reverence for scientific expertise than the popular enthusiasm for the American space program. The program began in large part because of the Cold War. When the Soviet Union announced in 1957 that it had launched a satellite—Sputnik—which was orbiting the earth in outer space, the American government (and much of the American public) reacted with alarm, as if the Soviet achievement were evidence of massive American failure. Strenuous efforts began to improve scientific education in the schools, to develop more research laboratories, and above all, to speed the development of America's own exploration of outer space.

The centerpiece of that exploration was the manned space program, established in 1958 with the selection of the first American space pilots, or "astronauts," who quickly became the nation's most revered heroes. On May 5, 1961, Alan Shepard became the first American launched into space (several months after a Soviet "cosmonaut," Yuri Gagarin, had made a similar, and longer, flight). John Glenn (later a United States senator) became the first American to orbit the globe on February 2, 1962 (again, only after Gagarin had already done so). For John F. Kennedy, the space program seemed the last great frontier. He committed the nation to landing a man on the moon before the end of the 1960s. Although Kennedy himself did not live to see the fulfillment of his promise, in the summer of 1969 Neil Armstrong and Edwin Aldrin became the first men to walk on the surface of the moon.

For nearly two decades the manned space program was a source of enormous pride and great interest to many Americans. The optimism and faith in the

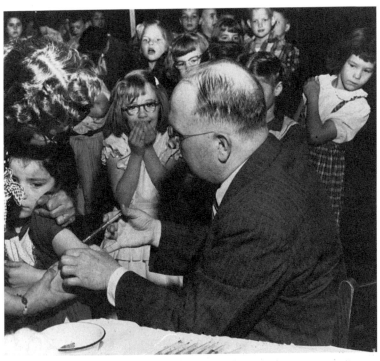

SALK VACCINE.   The invention of a vaccine against polio by Jonas Salk was one of the most exciting medical breakthroughs of the postwar period. In 1955, the federal government sponsored national inoculation of children with the new Salk vaccine. Among the first to receive the shots were these school children in Lancaster, Pennsylvania who apparently viewed the event with mixed emotions.

ALAN SHEPARD.   The first American launched into space,
Alan Shepard was caught by this photographer just
moments before his capsule was sealed. Shepard's brief 302
mile suborbital flight on May 5, 1961 was the first of the
Project Mercury Program.

National Aeronautics and Space Administration (NASA), which ran the program, was badly damaged, however, by the tragic explosion of the *Challenger* space shuttle on January 28, 1986. The worst disaster in the history of the American manned space program claimed the lives of a crew that included Christa McAuliffe, a young public school teacher who had been selected for the honor of being the first ordinary citizen to participate in the space program. Until that moment, Americans had sometimes questioned the expense of the space program; but few had doubted the evidence it gave of American scientific genius, technological know-how, and daring.

The Organized Society

The growing emphasis on scientific expertise and rationalization had its institutional counterpart in large-scale organizations and bureaucracies, which greatly increased their influence over American life in the postwar era. White-collar workers came to outnumber blue-collar laborers for the first time, and an increasing proportion of them worked in corporate settings with rigid hierarchical structures. Industrial workers also confronted large bureaucracies both in the workplace and in their own unions. Consumers discovered the frustrations of bureaucracy in dealing with the large national companies from whom they bought goods and services. More and more Americans were becoming convinced that the key to a successful future lay in acquiring the specialized training and skills necessary for work in large organizations, where every worker performed a particular, well-defined function.

The American educational system responded to the demands of this increasingly organized society by experimenting with changes in curriculum and philosophy. Elementary and secondary schools gave increased attention to the teaching of science, mathematics, and foreign languages—all of which educators considered important for the development of skilled, specialized professionals. The National Defense Education Act of 1958 (passed in response to the Soviet Union's Sputnik success) provided federal funding for development of programs in those areas. Universities in the meantime expanded their curricula to provide more opportunities for students to develop specialized skills. The idea of the "multiversity"—a phrase coined by Clark Kerr, the chancellor of the University of California at Berkeley, to describe his institution's curricular diversity—represented a commitment to making higher education a vehicle for training specialists in a wide variety of fields.

As in earlier eras, Americans reacted to these developments with ambivalence. Harsh criticism of the debilitating impact of bureaucratic life on the individual slowly became one of the central themes in popular and scholarly debate in the postwar period. William H. Whyte, Jr., produced one of the most widely discussed books of the decade: *The Organization Man* (1956), which attempted to describe the special mentality of the worker in a large, bureaucratic setting. Self-reliance, Whyte claimed, was losing place to the ability to "get along" and "work as a team" as the most valuable trait in the modern character. Sociologist David Riesman made similar observations in *The Lonely Crowd* (1950), in which he argued that the traditional "inner-directed" man, who judged himself on the basis of his own values and the esteem of his family, was giving way to a new "other-directed" man, more concerned with winning the approval of the larger organization or community.

A group of young poets, writers, and artists generally known as the "beats" (or, by derisive critics, as "beatniks") became the most caustic critics of bureaucracy, and of middle-class society in general. They produced slashing attacks on what they considered the sterility and conformity of American life, the meaninglessness of American politics, and the banality of popular culture. Allen Ginsberg's dark, bitter poem *Howl* (1955) decried the "Robot apartments! invincible suburbs! skeleton treasuries! blind capitals! demonic industries!" of modern life.

Jack Kerouac produced what may have been the central document of the Beat Generation in his novel *On the Road* (1957), an account of a cross-country automobile trip that depicted the rootless, iconoclastic lifestyle of Kerouac and his friends.

Other, less starkly alienated writers also used their work to express misgivings about the enormity and impersonality of modern society. Saul Bellow produced a series of novels—*The Adventures of Augie March* (1953), *Seize the Day* (1956), *Herzog* (1964), and others—that chronicled the difficulties American Jewish men had in finding fulfillment in the modern urban world. J. D. Salinger wrote in *The Catcher in the Rye* (1951) of a prep-school student, Holden Caulfield, who could not find anything in society—school, family, friends, city—that seemed genuine and worthy of admiration or commitment.

THE "OTHER AMERICA"

It was relatively easy for white, middle-class Americans in the 1950s to believe that the world they knew—a world of economic growth, personal affluence, and cultural homogeneity—was the world virtually all Americans knew; that the values and assumptions they shared were ones that most other Americans shared, too. But such assumptions were false. Even within the middle class, there was considerable restiveness among women, intellectuals, and many others who found the consumer culture somehow unsatisfying, even stultifying. More important, large groups of Americans remained outside the circle of abundance and shared neither the affluence nor, in many cases, the values of the middle class.

Outside the Affluent Society

In 1962, the socialist writer Michael Harrington published an influential book called *The Other America*, in which he chronicled the continuing existence of poverty in America. The conditions he described were not new. Only the attention he brought to them was.

The great economic expansion of the postwar years reduced poverty dramatically. But it did not eliminate it. At any given moment in the first two decades after World War II, more than a fifth of all American families (over 30 million people) continued to live below what the government defined as the poverty line in 1960 (down from a third of all families fifteen years before.) Many millions more lived just above the official poverty line but with incomes that gave them little comfort and no security.

Many of the poor experienced poverty intermittently and temporarily. Eighty percent of those classified as poor at any particular moment were likely to have moved into poverty relatively recently and might move out of it again as soon as they found a job—an indication of how unstable employment could be at the lower levels of the job market. But approximately twenty percent of the poor were people for whom poverty was a prolonged, debilitating experience, from which there was no easy escape. That included approximately half the nation's elderly and a large proportion of African Americans and Hispanics. Native Americans constituted the single poorest group in the country, a result of government policies that had undermined the economies of the reservations and had driven many Indians into cities, where some lived in a poverty worse than that they had left.

This hard-core poverty rebuked the assumptions of those who argued that economic growth would eventually lead everyone into prosperity, that, as many claimed, "a rising tide lifts all boats." It was a poverty that the growing prosperity of the postwar era seemed to affect hardly at all, a poverty, as Harrington observed, that appeared "impervious to hope."

Rural Poverty

Among those on the margins of the affluent society were many rural Americans. In 1948, farmers had received 8.9 percent of the national income; in 1956, they received only 4.1 percent. In part, this decline reflected the steadily shrinking farm population; in 1956 alone, nearly ten percent of the rural population moved into or was absorbed by cities. But it also reflected declining farm prices. Because of enormous surpluses in basic staples, commodity prices fell thirty-three percent in those years, even though national income as a whole rose fifty percent at the same time. Even many farmers who managed to survive economically experienced substantial losses of income at the same time that the prices of many consumer goods rose.

Not all farmers suffered equally as a result of these conditions. On the contrary, some substantial landowners weathered, and even managed to profit from, the changes in American agriculture. Others moved from considerable to only modest affluence. But the agrarian economy did produce substantial numbers of genuinely impoverished people. African-American sharecroppers and tenant farmers were shrinking in number, but those who remained lived at or below subsistence level throughout the rural South—in part because of the mechanization of cotton picking beginning in 1944, in part because of the development of synthetic fibers that reduced demand for cotton generally. (Two-thirds of the cotton acreage of the South went out of production between 1930 and 1960.)

Migrant farmworkers, a group concentrated especially in the West and Southwest and containing many Mexican-American and Asian workers, lived in similarly dire circumstances. In rural areas without much commercial agriculture—such as the Appalachian region in the East, where the decline of the coal economy reduced the one significant source of support for the region—whole communities experienced desperate poverty, increasingly cut off from the market economy. All these groups were vulnerable to malnutrition and even starvation.

The Inner Cities

As white families moved from cities to suburbs in vast numbers, more and more inner-city neighborhoods became vast repositories for the poor, "ghettos" from which there was no easy escape. The growth of these neighborhoods owed much to a vast migration of African Americans out of the countryside (where the cotton economy was in decline) and into industrial cities. More than three million black men and women moved from the South to northern cities between 1940 and 1960, many more than had made the same journey during the Great Migration during and after World War I. Chicago, Detroit, Cleveland, New York, and other eastern and midwestern industrial cities experienced a great expansion of their black populations—both in absolute numbers and, even more, as a percentage of the whole, since so many whites were leaving for the suburbs at the same time.

Similar migrations from Mexico and Puerto Rico expanded poor Hispanic neighborhoods in many American cities at the same time. Nearly a million Puerto Ricans moved into American cities (the largest group to New York) between 1940 and 1960. Mexican workers crossed the border in Texas and California and swelled the already substantial Latino communities of such cities as San Antonio, Houston, San Diego, and Los Angeles (which by 1960 had the largest Mexican-American population of any city in the United States, approximately 500,000 people).

Why these inner-city communities, populated largely by racial and ethnic minorities, remained so poor in the midst of growing affluence has been the subject of considerable, and very heated, debate. Some analysts have stressed the structural impediments to mobility many of the inner-city poor faced. A lack of jobs, training programs, and decent wages, combined with persistent inequality and racial prejudice, fueled persistent poverty. Other critics have insisted that the new migrants were at least in part victims of their own pasts; that the work habits, values, and family structures they brought with them from their rural homes were poorly adapted to the needs of the modern, industrial city. Still others have focused on the inner city itself—its crippling poverty, its lack of strong educational or service institutions, its crime, its violence, its apparent hopelessness. These conditions, they argue, created a "culture of poverty" that is reproduced generation after generation in a relentless cycle that offers no easy escape from those trapped within it.

Whatever the reasons, it is indisputable that inner cities were filling up with poor minority residents at the same time that the unskilled industrial jobs they were seeking were diminishing. Employers relocated factories and mills from old industrial cities to new locations in suburbs, smaller cities, and even abroad—places where labor was cheaper and other costs were lower. Even in the factories that remained, automation reduced the number of unskilled jobs. The economic opportunities that had helped earlier immigrant groups rise up from poverty were unavailable to most of the postwar migrants. At the same time, historic patterns of racial discrimination in hiring and housing doomed many members of these communities to continuing, and in some cases increasing, poverty.

For many years, the principal policy response to the poverty of inner cities was "urban renewal": the effort to tear down buildings in the poorest and most degraded areas. In the twenty years after World War II, urban renewal projects destroyed over 400,000 buildings, among them the homes of nearly 1.5 million people. In some cases, urban renewal provided new public housing for poor city residents—some of it considerably better than the housing they left. More often, however, urban renewal was better at eliminating "blights" than at helping the people who lived in them. In many cases, urban renewal projects replaced "slums" with middle- and upper-income housing (part of an often futile attempt to keep middle-class people from leaving the inner city), office towers, commercial buildings, or—in Los Angeles—a baseball stadium for the Los Angeles Dodgers, recently relocated from Brooklyn, on the site of a Mexican *barrio*.

Inner-city poverty also appeared to contribute greatly to a rising juvenile crime rate. Indeed, "juvenile delinquency" remained one of the few results of poverty that middle-class Americans discussed and worried about with any consistency. A 1955 book, *One Million Delinquents*, called juvenile crime a "national epidemic" and described the existence of a troubling inner-city youth subculture, peopled by embittered, rebellious adolescents with no hope of advancement and no sense of having a stake in the structure of their society.

For much of the 1950s, the persistence of crime, inequality, and poverty struck a discordant note in American society. Many Americans turned a blind eye to such problems and to the manifestations of unrest increasingly apparent in the nation's cities. Before long, however, one of the most powerful social movements in the twentieth century would force the nation to confront the persistence of injustice in contemporary society. However much critics liked to characterize the 1950s as an "age of conformity," those years also gave rise to a powerful civil rights movement that would soon transform American society.

CHAPTER TWENTY-ONE

The Fight for Racial Justice

≈

The early postwar period—a period often characterized as one of stability and conformity—gave rise to one of the great social movements in American history. Throughout the twentieth century, African Americans had engaged in a long struggle to gain equal rights in American society. Amid much discouragement, generation after generation sought privileges that most Americans enjoyed simply by virtue of being citizens. But they faced formidable barriers, a result of a long history of economic, political, and social discrimination. Formal, legalized segregation remained entrenched in the American South at midcentury. In the rest of the nation, less visible but often equally pernicious forms of racial prejudice were a part of life for many African Americans.

Throughout American history, black men and women had employed many different strategies, tactics, and ideas to overcome the injustices they faced. But the 1950s became an important watershed in the long drive for racial equality. A civil rights movement of tremendous force, power, and determination began to challenge the very roots of racial oppression in American society. Before the decade was over, the segregation by law that many white Americans had defended or had tolerated for decades was suddenly on the defensive. More subtle forms of racial prejudice, and the persistence of inequality, would also become matters of national debate and, for some, priority.

RACIAL INEQUALITY AT MIDCENTURY

By the mid-twentieth century, African Americans had achieved some important milestones in the long quest for an end to racial discrimination and for equality of opportunity. The agitation of leaders from W. E. B. DuBois in the early twentieth century to A. Philip Randolph in the 1940s, and the long commitment of groups such as the NAACP and, later, the Congress of Racial Equality (founded in 1942) had done much to expose the history, character, and dynamics of inequality. They had also demanded concrete legal and political changes in American society.

There was no question that the life fortunes of many African Americans had improved vastly by midcentury. The booming wartime economy and postwar prosperity had boosted the standard of living for countless black workers and their families. Migration had provided some with a better way of life, a route out of some of the worst conditions imposed by segregation. Rising challenges to racial discrimination were succeeding in leveling some barriers to integration. The integration of the military, important court decisions, Randolph's success in pressuring the federal government, and even such symbolic events as Jackie Robinson's celebrated integration of major league professional baseball in 1947 suggested that sweeping change was in the wind.

At the same time, racial discrimination and oppression were still the norm in American society at midcentury. The remaining barriers to equality were steep. Most obvious was the tradition of legalized segregation in the South—a way of life that stifled opportunities for and inflicted great pain on black Americans, poisoned race relations, and prevented the exercise of basic constitutional rights.

Poverty and Inequality

One of the most important sources of racial oppression in mid-twentieth century America was the persistence of severe economic inequality. During the 1930s, the crop lien system had largely collapsed as a result of the Great Depression and New Deal agricultural policies. The growing availability of new mechanized agricultural technology in the early 1940s—most notably tractors and the mechanical cotton picker—further hastened the demise of sharecropping. But tenant farming was by no means extinct in the United States by 1950. Many white planters, most notably in Mississippi, spurned the mechanical devices and continued to rely on tenant farm labor. Nor had the economic changes in southern agriculture necessarily improved the standard of living for the impoverished white and black farmers who had been caught in the lien system. Some former tenants left the land and found good industrial jobs in southern and northern cities. But many others found only menial jobs in industry, while still others became migrant workers and engaged in an exhausting and endless struggle to piece together a living wage. Black migrants traveled up and down the Mississippi Valley and the East Coast as the season and the needs of the economy dictated, just as migrants had been doing for many years in the West.

Most African Americans who remained in the rural South continued to work for white land owners. In Clarendon County, South Carolina, where one of the first challenges to school segregation would be mounted, seven out of ten residents in 1950 were African Americans. Virtually all lived on farms and made

PICKING COTTON. This photograph of African-American men picking cotton in Mississippi was taken in 1957. Such workers were paid around 2 1/2 cents per pound of cotton picked—or $5 a day.

their livings through agricultural work. Most were tenant farmers. White citizens, the majority absentee landlords, owned nearly eighty-five percent of the farm land in Clarendon County. Two thirds of those who lived in Clarendon County survived on less than 1,000 dollars a year. For most, life was shaped by grinding poverty.

Public education in Clarendon County also reflected gross inequality. Most Africans Americans in the county did not have more than four grades of schooling. Children who did attend were taught in segregated schools that, for black children, were often little more than falling-down shanties. The taxpayers in the county spent approximately 179 dollars for every white child attending a public school in 1949–1950 and 43 dollars for each black pupil. Many defended the system by arguing that whites paid more taxes and therefore deserved better schools. These conditions—although especially terrible in Clarendon County— were far from uncommon in the American South at midcentury. In Mississippi, nearly ninety percent of nonwhite families lived below the poverty level as late as 1960. Only seven percent of African Americans had completed high school. In 1964 the state of Mississippi was spending an average of under 23 dollars per black school pupil and approximately 82 dollars per white schoolchild.

Voting

African Americans might have sought remedies for such injustices in the political system, but here, too, the legacy of Jim Crow laws was strong. The great majority of southern blacks had no access to the ballot. Some legal challenges to restrictive voting laws had succeeded in the early twentieth century, and the Supreme Court had outlawed a system that restricted primary voting to whites only in 1944. But many discriminatory practices survived. The selective use of poll taxes and literacy clauses continued to prevent or discourage the registration of black voters. In 1940, only three percent of eligible black voters in the South were registered. Some officials frankly admitted that they employed any tactic necessary to disqualify black voters, including open defiance of the courts. In Mississippi, one election official explained turning away an African American who had attempted to vote in the primary by saying that "in the southern states it has always been a white primary, and I just couldn't conceive of this darkey going up there to vote."

By the late 1950s, much had changed. But some eighty percent of potential black voters in the South still were not registered. As late as 1962 in five Mississippi counties with black residential majorities, not a single African American was a registered voter. Active efforts to stifle black demands for voting rights actually grew stronger as those demands increased. In parts of the South, whites used considerable violence to uphold prevailing customs.

The Realities of Segregation

Segregation of the races remained the most visible manifestation of inequality at midcentury. Signs reading "white" and "colored" directed the races to separate drinking fountains, restrooms, and sections of movie theaters (for black Americans, usually the balcony). Segregation in transportation, housing, health care, public accommodations, school, and work was the norm throughout the American South. Outside the South, African Americans faced less formal but still corrosive racial discrimination in cities, clubs, labor unions, professions, housing, and countless other areas of life. In 1947, twenty-four hospitals run by the Veterans Administration maintained separate wards for black patients; nineteen such hospitals in the South had no facilities at all for black veterans. In the 1960s civil rights activists were still attempting to force the desegregation of hospitals that denied beds to African Americans and staff appointments to black physicians.

Prevailing attitudes reflected the persistence of racial bigotry. Surveys conducted at midcentury suggested that increasing numbers of white Americans supported desegregation. And by 1956 the vast majority of white Americans surveyed rejected the view that black Americans were intellectually inferior to whites. But that did not always mean support for specific desegregation efforts. When white Americans were asked in a 1958 survey whether they would move if a black person moved next door to them, nearly sixty percent said no. But

SEGREGATION. Signs directing African-American men and women to separate facilities were commonplace in the American South. Here a young African-American man waits in the "colored" section of a bus station. Once aboard the bus, he would have been expected to occupy a seat in a "colored only" section to the rear of the vehicle. One of the crucial challenges to Jim Crow laws mandating segregation would occur in public transportation.

when asked what their response would be if "great numbers" of blacks moved into the neighborhood, over fifty percent replied that they would definitely leave their homes. Such responses reflected continued, if not growing, discomfort as white and black Americans confronted some of the manifest problems in American race relations. And in the South, there was relatively little evidence in polls, or elsewhere, of even this limited commitment to racial equality.

CHALLENGING SEGREGATION IN EDUCATION

The challenge to segregation in the 1950s focused early on the nation's public school system. The Supreme Court's 1896 decision in *Plessy* v. *Ferguson* provided the legal bulwark for segregation for half a century. But the Plessy decision had sanctioned segregation where the races were provided with equal facilities despite separation by race. However, segregated schools, and the funds provided for them, were usually grossly unequal. In the 1930s and 1940s, the NAACP succeeded on a number of occasions in demonstrating to the courts that certain segregated educational facilities were not, in fact, equal. But not until the 1950s would a challenge to the entire concept of "separate but equal" be successfully mounted.

Brown v. Board of Education

The case that succeeded in finally overturning *Plessy* v. *Ferguson* decision was *Brown* v. *Board of Education of Topeka, Kansas.* The Brown decision was the culmination of many decades of effort by black opponents of segregation. Particularly important were a group of talented lawyers, many of them trained at Howard University in Washington by the great legal educator Charles Houston, who worked to fight segregation through the NAACP's Legal Defense Fund. Thurgood Marshall, William Hastie, James Nabrit, and others spent years filing legal challenges to segregation in one state after another, nibbling at the edges of the system, and accumulating precedents to support their assault on the "separate but equal" doctrine itself. In one day in 1950, the Supreme Court sustained three challenges to segregation mounted by Marshall and his associates. In none of these decisions, however, did the Court revisit and strike down the Plessy decision.

The goal then became to secure an unambiguous ruling that would demolish the entire intellectual and legal edifice that upheld the "separate but equal" doctrine. Beginning in late 1949 and 1950, Marshall and his colleagues started to mount several challenges against school boards in various parts of the country including Delaware, South Carolina, Virginia, the District of Columbia, and Kansas. Their complaints argued segregation's inherent inequality. The Kansas suit was filed against the Board of Education of Topeka, Kansas by the NAACP on behalf of Oliver Brown. Brown's eight-year-old daughter Linda had to travel several miles to a segregated public school every day, even though she lived virtually next door to a white elementary school.

When these various challenges to school segregation came before the Supreme Court of the United States, they were all docketed under the name of Oliver Brown—hence giving the case its name. Oral arguments in the cases were heard in late December of 1952. Thurgood Marshall and the other NAACP lawyers presented familiar data to demonstrate inequitable expenditures for black and white public education. But they went further this time. Marshall introduced new studies by social scientists that demonstrated, he argued, that not only were there no differences in the learning potential of black and white schoolchildren (challenging a claim long used to defend school segregation), but that segregation did irreparable harm to black schoolchildren. In an eloquent closing argument James Nabrit, who argued for the plaintiffs in the District of Columbia, summarized the position of the NAACP: "We submit that in this case, in the heart of the nation's capital, in the capital of democracy . . . there is no place for a segregated school system. This country cannot afford it, and the Constitution does not permit it, and the statutes of Congress do not authorize it."

Marshall's opponent, the South Carolina lawyer John W. Davis (who had been the 1924 Democratic nominee for president) argued passionately that the Court had no reason to question the logic of the Plessy decision. He ridiculed the social scientific findings presented by the plaintiffs. And he invoked the importance of states rights, local rule, and custom in his efforts to dissuade the justices from tampering with segregation. "Is it not the height of wisdom," he asked the Court, that education "should be left to those most immediately affected by it, and that the wishes of the parents, both white and colored, should be ascertained before their children are forced into what may be an unwelcome contact?"

The Court was divided on how to decide the case, and most pointedly about whether to overturn the Plessy decision. They thus instructed the parties to return for reargument. But before reargument occurred in December of 1953,

A VICTORY IN BROWN V. BOARD OF EDUCATION. George E. C. Hayes (*left*), Thurgood Marshall (*center*) and James Nabrit, Jr. (*right*) smile with evident pride on the steps of the United States Supreme Court after learning the Court had sustained their challenge to school segregation in *Brown* v. *Board of Education.* The May 17, 1954 landmark decision represented a crucial victory in the long battle to dismantle legalized segregation.

Chief Justice Fred Vinson died and had been replaced by President Eisenhower's nominee, former California governor Earl Warren. Vinson had opposed overturning Plessy, but Warren felt differently. Further, he pressed hard for the Court to hand down a unanimous decision in the case. To do otherwise, he believed, would invite resistance. For months after reargument, the Court failed to make a ruling. But finally, on May 17, 1954, the Court spoke. "We conclude," Chief Justice Warren said as he read the unanimous decision, "that in the field of public education the doctrine of 'separate but equal' has no place. Separate educational facilities are inherently unequal. . . . Any language in *Plessy* v. *Ferguson* contrary to these findings is rejected."

The following year, in May 1955, the Court issued another decision, popularly known as "Brown II," that addressed the question of how to implement desegregation (although the words "desegregation" and "segregation" never appeared in the ruling). This time the Court rejected the NAACP's position, which had insisted upon immediate desegregation. Instead, the decision took a more gradual approach to implementing the 1954 order. The court gave local school boards the responsibility of drawing up desegregation plans, and it ordered federal district courts to supervise compliance. No date was set for achieving desegregation. The court asked only that "the defendants make a prompt and reasonable start at full compliance" and—in a phrase subject to much interpretation—that the schools be desegregated "with all deliberate speed." The justices had said that segregation was wrong; but they left it to communities and lower-level officials and judges to decide how to eliminate it.

Massive Resistance

What followed was a painful struggle in many states and localities to come to terms with school desegregation, a process that still continues. In some communities, for example Washington, D.C., compliance came relatively quickly and quietly. In many of the border states, desegregation had begun in 1954 shortly after the announcement of the first Brown decision. Several hundred school districts in ten states had started peacefully to integrate their school systems. When Brown II was announced, however, momentum slowed perceptibly.

Strong local opposition (what came to be known in the South as "massive resistance") helped produce long delays and bitter conflicts in many communities. Some school districts ignored the ruling altogether. Others attempted to circumvent it with purely token efforts at integration. More than 100 southern members of Congress signed a "Declaration of Constitutional Principles" in 1956 denouncing the Brown decision as an unwarranted—indeed illegal—intervention in local and state affairs by the federal government. They urged their constituents to defy the Brown decision. Southern governors, mayors, local school boards, and nongovernmental pressure groups (including hundreds of White Citizens' Councils) all worked to obstruct desegregation. The "pupil placement laws" that many school districts enacted allowed school officials to place students in schools according to their scholastic abilities and social behavior. Such laws were transparent devices for maintaining segregation; but in 1958, the Supreme Court (in *Shuttlesworth* v. *Birmingham Board of Education*) refused to declare them unconstitutional.

By the fall of 1957, only 684 of 3,000 affected school districts in the South had even begun to desegregate their schools. In those that had complied, white resistance often produced angry mob actions and at times, violence. Many white parents simply withdrew their children from the public schools and enrolled them in all-white "segregation academies"; some state and local governments diverted money from newly integrated public schools and used it to fund the new, all-white institutions. The Brown decision, far from ending segregation, had launched a prolonged battle between federal authority and state and local governments.

The Eisenhower administration was not eager to commit itself to that battle. The president himself had greeted the Brown decision with skepticism and once said it had set back progress on race relations "at least fifteen years." "It's all very well to talk about school integration," Eisenhower added,"—if you remember you may also be talking about social *dis*integration." More pointedly, Eisenhower refused to endorse the Supreme Court decision publicly. But events in the South forced the administration's hand.

Little Rock

In September 1957, Eisenhower faced a case of direct state defiance of federal authority. Federal courts had ordered the desegregation of Central High School in Little Rock, Arkansas, a process that was to begin with the admission of nine African-American students to a school attended by some 2,000 white pupils. Other educational institutions in Arkansas had already begun the process of desegregation peacefully, some even before the Brown decision. In addition, many facilities in Little Rock had been integrated by the mid 1950s, including the city's bus and park system. The head of the NAACP in Little Rock, Daisy Bates, praised the community in 1954 as a "liberal southern city." Some local white-run newspapers wrote sympathetically of desegregation. There was reason to believe, in short, that desegregation plans might go forward in the city without incident.

Instead the desegregation of Central High School soon became a crisis with national implications. As the date for the admission of the black students approached, local white citizen organizations began whipping up popular opposition. The governor of the state, Orval Faubus, was in the midst of a re-election campaign and chose to seize upon the desegregation order to galvanize support among white voters. The night before Central High was due to open in September 1957, Faubus indicated he would defy the desegregation order, citing the need to maintain order and prevent violence. (In fact, no violence had been expected, although it soon followed Faubus's act of defiance.) The governor called in the Arkansas National Guard to "protect" the school. When the nine black pupils arrived on September 4, they were met by the guard who announced that "Governor Faubus has placed this school off limits to Negroes." Elizabeth

LITTLE ROCK–1957. Elizabeth Eckford, one of nine African Americans admitted as part of a plan to desegregate Little Rock's Central High School, met a mob shouting epithets when she arrived at the school on September 4, 1957. To the left, Arkansas National Guardsmen called out by Governor Faubus to "protect" the school, stand by watching.

Eckford, the first African American to try to enter the school, was greeted with shouts and racial slurs—including the chilling cry "Lynch her!"—from an angry white crowd. With bayonets poised, the guardsmen prevented the black students from entering the high school.

The federal district court immediately issued a decree demanding that their desegregation order be enforced unless Faubus could produce some compelling reason to the contrary. Again the students attempted to enter Central High; again they were met at the door by National Guardsmen who barred them from entering. By now the Justice Department and President Eisenhower were forced to confront the situation. The Justice Department filed a petition for an injunction to require desegregation plans to continue and to remove the National Guardsmen. President Eisenhower privately attempted to persuade Faubus to stop his resistance, but to no avail. On September 20, a federal court issued the injunction and ordered the removal of the Guard. Faubus announced that he would comply, but then left the state for a long weekend.

On Monday September 23, the "Little Rock Nine," as the black students became known, entered the school amid a hostile crowd estimated to be near 1,000. "What I felt inside," one of the students later recalled, "was stark raving fear—terrible, wrenching, awful fear. . . . I had known no pain like that because I did not know what I had done wrong. You see, when you are fifteen years old and someone's going to hit you or hurt you, you want to know what you did wrong. Although I knew the differences between black and white, I didn't know the penalties one paid for being black at that time." Although police safely escorted the pupils through the crowd, a melee occurred outside the high school. A mob of angry white protesters, supplemented by segregationists who had traveled to Little Rock from other parts of the South, gathered, taunting the students and shouting racial epithets. When the black pupils actually entered the building, one screamed, "They're in the school! Oh my God, they're in the school!" Some white students began to file out, encouraged by the shouts of protesters who yelled through the windows, "Don't stay in there with them."

The disturbance led city authorities to remove the black students for their own safety. Little Rock's mayor then turned to the Eisenhower administration for assistance. Federal troops, he asserted, were needed to prevent violence and to restore order. Eisenhower had little choice but to deal head on with this defiance of a federal court order. At stake now was not just peace, order, and a desegregation plan; the situation represented a challenge to the authority of the federal government. On September 24, Eisenhower federalized the Arkansas National Guard and sent U.S. army troops from the 101st Airborne Division to Little Rock to restore order. The troops were not there, Eisenhower stressed later that evening to the nation, to "enforce integration, but to prevent opposition by violence to orders of a court." Whatever "personal opinions" some Americans might hold regarding the Brown decision, Eisenhower explained, could not justify mob action. The following day the troops led the first black students into Central High. Tensions remained, and the National Guardsmen stayed in the school for the remainder of the year—this time to protect the black students. But Central High had been desegregated.

"MOVING ON TO VICTORY"

The challenge to school segregation was a critical milestone in the burgeoning civil rights movement. But it was only one of many simultaneous efforts to advance toward racial justice. Throughout the South, African Americans and white sympathizers began to challenge the humiliating practices and traditions that were central to segregation. With considerable courage and growing mass mobilization, those who participated in the civil rights movement sought to dismantle, brick by brick, the solid walls of segregation.

The Montgomery Bus Boycott

On December 1, 1955, Rosa Parks, an African-American seamstress and an active member of the local chapter of the NAACP, was arrested in Montgomery, Alabama, when she refused to give up her seat on a city bus to a white passenger. Although the vast majority of the passengers using the city bus lines in Montgomery were black, they were forced to pay their fare at the front of the bus, then walk to the rear door and enter there. In addition, when the white sections near the front of the bus were filled, black passengers were expected to give up their seats and stand so that white passengers could ride comfortably. These demeaning practices had become a way of life for many black and white passengers. But for many African Americans who complied, they were a daily indignity that was hard to tolerate.

In 1943, Mrs. Parks had refused to enter a segregated bus by the back entrance. Now the very same bus driver who had put her off the bus then for that infraction loomed over her. "If you don't stand up, I'm going to have to call the police and have you arrested," he said. "You may do that," Mrs. Parks replied calmly. Parks was arrested and taken to the city jail. Soon word spread among Montgomery's black community that Mrs. Parks had been detained.

Although on that particular day, Mrs. Parks had decided spontaneously to resist the order to move because she was tired, resistance to segregation in public transportation was not new in 1955, even in Montgomery. In the early 1950s some African Americans in Baton Rouge, Louisiana, had attempted to integrate city bus lines, organizing a short-lived boycott in the process. In Montgomery in 1953, a young English professor at a local black college, Jo Ann Robinson, had also attempted to mobilize fellow members of the Women's Political Council, a group of black professional women, after a humiliating instance in which Robinson had been berated by a white bus driver for sitting in the all-white section. Robinson, civil rights activist E. D. Nixon, and members of the Women's Political Council had then tried to persuade the city commissioners to end segregation on the buses, but to no avail. By 1955, the Council, which Jo Ann Robinson now led, was planning a boycott of the city bus lines. Three times in 1955 other women in Montgomery had been arrested for refusing to leave their seats. But although civil rights activists hoped to use one such incident to challenge the segregation law, none of these cases, for various reasons, seemed entirely suitable to serve as a test case.

When Rosa Parks resisted, however, the moment appeared ripe for broad-scale action. Mrs. Parks was a highly respected, even revered woman in the Montgomery African-American community with much experience in the civil rights movement. (The summer before her act of defiance, she had attended an inter-racial workshop at the Highlander Folk School in Tennessee designed to assist activists in their efforts to change and improve race relations.) E. D. Nixon persuaded Mrs. Parks to permit her arrest to be made into a test case for desegregation. Together, Nixon, Jo Ann Robinson, and the Women's Political Council began to mobilize a mass boycott of the city's bus lines. They printed over 35,000 handbills asking the black citizens of Montgomery not to ride the buses "to work, to town, or anywhere." Crucial to the outcome was the support of black ministers, among them Reverend Martin Luther King, Jr., the young pastor of the Dexter Avenue Church and new to Montgomery. King and his fellow ministers spoke from their pulpits about the bus boycott's significance and the importance of compliance.

When the city bus lines rolled on the first day of the boycott, they were virtually empty of black riders. A sign tacked up at a bus stop captured the spirit of the moment. "PEOPLE DON'T RIDE THE BUSES TODAY. DON'T RIDE IT FOR FREEDOM." Soon a group of ministers and civil rights activists met and formed an organization, the Montgomery Improvement Association, to work toward keeping up the boycott's momentum. At a mass meeting, King—who had agreed (after some initial reluctance) to serve as head of the Montgomery Improvement Association—exhorted Montgomery's black citizens to seize the momentum of the boycott and force an end to segregation. "One of the great glories of democracy is the right to protest for right," he said in one of his first major public speeches. "If you will protest courageously and yet with dignity and Christian love, when the history books are written in future generations the historians will pause and say, 'There lived a great people—a black people—who injected new meaning and dignity into the veins of civilization.' This is our challenge and our responsibility."

The Montgomery bus boycott lasted for 381 days despite considerable hardship to the working people of the African-American community. Black workers who needed to commute to their jobs (the largest group consisted of female domestic servants) formed carpools to ride back and forth to work, or simply walked, at times over long distances. The boycott put economic pressure not only on the bus company (a private concern) but on many Montgomery merchants. The bus boycotters found it difficult to get to downtown stores and tended to shop instead in their own neighborhoods. Merchants complained they were losing millions of dollars as the boycott wore on. Day in and day out, week after week, for over a year, most African Americans in Montgomery did not ride on the city's bus system. In June 1956 a federal district court responded to cases filed by several Montgomery women and ruled against segregation on the bus

MONTGOMERY BUS BOYCOTT. African Americans walk to work through the streets of Montgomery during the bus boycott. The boycott lasted for over a year until the courts ruled that segregation on common carriers was unconstitutional.

lines. Segregation on "common carriers," they held, violated the equal protection clause of the Fourteenth Amendment. In November, the Supreme Court affirmed the court's decision. Segregation on the buses, the justices ruled, was unconstitutional. The boycotters had won.

Among the most important accomplishments of the Montgomery bus boycott was its success in demonstrating the effectiveness of the boycott as a form of protest. Another was its elevation to prominence of Martin Luther King, Jr., who was destined to become one of the great figures in modern American history. The son of a prominent Atlanta minister, King had attended Crozier Theological Seminary and Boston University, where he earned a Ph.D. in theology. Despite his initial reluctance to become a civil rights activist, he soon became consumed by the movement.

King's approach to black protest was based on the doctrine of nonviolent civil disobedience—that is, of passive resistance even in the face of direct attack. He drew from the teachings of Mahatma Gandhi, the Indian nationalist leader; from Henry David Thoreau; and from Christian doctrine. And he embraced an approach to racial struggle that captured the moral high ground for his supporters. He urged African Americans to engage in peaceful demonstrations; to allow themselves to be arrested, even beaten, if necessary; and to respond to hate with love. For the next thirteen years—as leader of the Southern Christian Leadership Conference, an inter-racial group he helped found shortly after the bus boycott—he was highly influential and widely admired, surely the most visible leader in the civil rights movement.

But King's celebrated role—crucial though it was—should not overshadow the extraordinary contributions men and women from all walks of life made to the civil rights movement. Some of the great heroes and heroines were people who never gave speeches, never appeared in headlines, never received any public recognition. The domestic servants who walked instead of rode Montgomery's buses, the young schoolchildren who faced taunts and jeers in the battle for school desegregation, the countless men and women who attended rallies, ran printing presses, marched, and silently demonstrated—all helped make possible the civil rights movement. The movement they joined soon spread throughout the South and throughout the country. Soon after Montgomery, bus boycotts occurred in Tallahassee, Florida, as well as Birmingham and Mobile, Alabama.

Civil Rights Legislation

For the most part, the pressure for change came from African Americans who used the courts and, increasingly, boycotts and other demonstrations to move the public and the institutions of government. But white leaders also began to respond to black demands. Their support was slow to emerge and often grudging when it came. But the national political leadership was gradually moving on the issue of race. President Eisenhower completed the integration of the armed forces, which he had originally opposed. His attorney general pushed the president to support a broad civil rights bill. In 1957, Congress passed the first civil rights legislation since the end of Reconstruction. Majority leader Lyndon Baines Johnson of Texas played an important role in shepherding this compromise bill through the Senate.

Both Eisenhower and Johnson felt particularly strongly about emphasizing voting rights in the legislation, and they helped block more ambitious bills. The law the president signed established a Civil Rights Division within the Justice Department and authorized the attorney general to file injunctions against the infringement of voting rights. The bill also created a Commission on Civil Rights that had powers to investigate and report on civil rights violations. In the end, however, the Civil Rights Act of 1957 was a weak bill, with few mechanisms for enforcement. Two years after it had passed, obstacles to black voter registration still appeared largely intact. The Civil Rights Commission seemed unable to do much to change the discriminatory practices it uncovered.

In 1958, some fifty bombings of black churches, synagogues, and schools occurred in the South. President Eisenhower continued to assure white southerners that he did not support active intervention in desegregation by the federal government, but he also expressed abhorrence of violence and lawlessness by extremists. When a synagogue in Atlanta was bombed in 1958, for example, Eisenhower said in a news conference: "I was raised to respect the word 'Confederate'—very highly, I might add—and for hoodlums such as these to describe themselves as any part or relation to the Confederacy of the mid-nineteenth century is, to my mind, a complete insult to the word." As politicians attempted to balance the concerns of conservative white southern voters with their sense that the civil rights challenge could not be spurned, civil rights activists recognized that much of the momentum for reform would have to come from a mass, grassroots social movement.

Causes of the Civil Rights Movement

Given the many periods of struggle against racial injustice, it is worth asking why such an unprecedentedly powerful movement emerged in the 1950s and early 1960s—and not earlier or later. Several factors helped spur African-American protest in the postwar years. There was, first, the legacy of World War II itself, which had provided considerable momentum to the struggle against inequality. Millions of black men and women had served in the military or worked in war plants during the war. African-American leaders had invoked that record of service to demand change, and the government, however haltingly, had responded. There was, in fact, considerable continuity between the civil rights crusades of the 1940s and those of the 1950s.

The black migration that the war and the collapse of sharecropping helped produce was another important factor in fueling the civil rights movement. When African Americans moved from farms to southern cities, they escaped the isolation of rural life and the close supervision and often harsh control of many white planters. They also created a strong infrastructure of urban churches, community organizations, and social and professional groups. That infrastructure would eventually play a crucial role in the civil rights movement. Migration

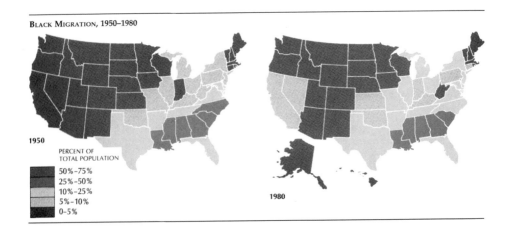

BLACK MIGRATION, 1950–1980

1950

PERCENT OF
TOTAL POPULATION

50%–75%
25%–50%
10%–25%
5%–10%
0–5%

1980

also encouraged some African Americans to challenge the entrenched traditions of segregation. The willingness to pull up stakes, to change one's life, and to take new risks affirmed for many a new sense of freedom and possibility. Finally, northern migration made African Americans a vital factor in post–World War II American politics. The ability of African Americans in northern cities to vote and to create their own political organizations prompted many party leaders to attend more closely to their demands.

The growth of an urban black middle class, which had been developing for decades but which expanded rapidly after the war, also proved important to civil rights activism in the postwar period. A powerful group of leaders, including ministers, educators, professionals, and students at black colleges and universities (which had grown significantly in the previous decades), provided tremendous force to the movement. These men and women with education, a strong stake in society, and often a sense of generational boldness felt increasingly empowered to challenge the racial caste system. Their actions built momentum and provided cohesion as the civil rights movement unfolded. They helped ensure that the message of protest would be heard nationally.

In addition to the forces that were inspiring African Americans to mobilize, there were other forces at work encouraging many white Americans to support the movement once it began. Some whites simply acted on a conviction that the racial injustices in American society were not compatible with democracy. The Cold War made racial injustice particularly embarrassing for those who believed that American society ought to provide a model to the world of democratic institutions. Labor unions with substantial black memberships played an important part in supporting (and funding) the civil rights movement. White ministers and churches also responded to the religious appeal that was so central to the movement. Finally, white business leaders North and South began to see the wisdom of challenging segregation. Efforts to prompt northern businesses to invest in the South and relocate industry there prompted some southern business leaders to support modifications of segregation.

Whatever its causes, the civil rights movement had become by 1960 a force that had already done much to change the contours of American society. It would continue to expand as the United States moved into the turbulent 1960s.

CHAPTER TWENTY-TWO

Eisenhower Republicanism

≈

D wight D. Eisenhower was the least experienced politician to serve in the White House in the twentieth century. He was also among the most politically successful presidents of the postwar era. At home, he pursued essentially moderate policies, avoiding most new initiatives but accepting the work of earlier reformers. Abroad, he continued and even intensified American commitments to oppose communism but brought to some of those commitments a measure of restraint that his successors did not always match. Eisenhower served in the presidency during a time when the United States was at peace and enjoying economic prosperity. His tenure as president also coincided with rising social and political pressures that he largely avoided but that his successors would have to grapple with for many years to come.

THE HERO AS PRESIDENT

Eisenhower was the first Republican elected to the presidency since 1928. He showed no special interest in the reform agenda that had so absorbed his two immediate predecessors. Nor, as a man who had seen more than his share of bloodletting and the horrible costs of war, was he inclined to pursue an actively interventionist foreign policy. "The trouble with Eisenhower," General Douglas MacArthur complained privately on the eve of the president's election, "is that he doesn't have the guts to make a policy decision. He never did have the guts and he never will." He made this complaint after Eisenhower had responded coolly to MacArthur's suggestion that the president order atomic weapons dropped on North Korea and a full-scale bombing campaign against China to end the Korean War. Some interpreted Eisenhower's caution in both the domestic and international arenas as evidence of timidity and lack of vision. Many others admired Eisenhower's inclination to conciliate conflicting interest groups and to proceed cautiously, although firmly, in the Cold War. But there could be little doubt that Eisenhower enjoyed tremendous popularity. He would be among the few postwar presidents to serve out two full terms.

From the Army to the White House

Eisenhower came to the presidency a celebrated military hero of the Second World War. His parents had been pacifists, and it may have seemed in some measure an act of rebellion when their young son chose to attend West Point for his education. But if so, it was one of a very few rebellious acts in a life committed to working smoothly and effectively within established institutions. Eisenhower did well, but not spectacularly, at the Military Academy; he graduated in 1915, determined to make a successful career in the army.

Although Eisenhower sought overseas combat duty in World War I, he spent most of the war in the United States as a commander of training camps. The war ended a week before he was due to arrive in Europe. A man of considerable personal warmth and shrewd political sense, Eisenhower caught the attention of the right officers early on and rose rapidly through the ranks. By 1933, General Douglas MacArthur had selected Eisenhower as his administrative assistant.

When war broke out in Europe again, Eisenhower quickly earned a series of important commands. In December 1941 he became the chief aide to General George Marshall, Army Chief of Staff. By 1942 his effective work in military planning led to his appointment as commander of Allied forces in North Africa. Not long after that, he became the Supreme Allied Commander in Europe, charged with leading the great invasion of the continent. Before World War II, Eisenhower had never commanded troops in battle. By 1944, he was in command of the greatest invasion force in history.

His fame derived less from brilliant contributions to military strategy—others were far more distinguished than he in that respect—than from his great aptitude for organizing men, resources, and military power and from his tremendous appeal as a public figure. British General Bernard Montgomery's dismissive assessment of Eisenhower's World War II performance—"nice chap, no soldier"—was harsh. But Eisenhower's unassuming personal style and his interest in the men he commanded did as much to inspire the affection of Americans as did his purely military achievements.

After a brief period serving as Army Chief of Staff when the war was over, Eisenhower became the president of Columbia University in 1947. He had virtually no experience in academic life but the job gave him great visibility. In 1951, after he had declined overtures from both political parties to run for president in 1948, the general moved back into the military when Truman appointed him the first Commander of NATO.

When Eisenhower responded to the urging of Republican power brokers and agreed to be drafted as the party's presidential candidate in 1952, he did not even begin to campaign until June. In the fall, he left the dirty work to his running mate, Richard Nixon, and used his smile and his geniality to stand largely above the fray. He ran less as a Republican than as an emblem of American military greatness. He established himself as a firm but not zealous advocate of fiscal conservatism and anticommunism and an apostle of cautious moderate change. Many Americans apparently believed he would preserve the peace and restore tranquility to American society. For the most part, he did not disappoint them.

"What's Good for General Motors . . ."

The first Republican administration in twenty years staffed itself mostly with men drawn from the same quarter as those who had staffed Republican administrations in the 1920s: the business community. But many American businesses had developed a very different social and political outlook by the 1950s from that of their predecessors of earlier decades. Above all, many of them had reconciled themselves to at least the broad outlines of the Keynesian welfare state the New Deal had launched and, indeed, had come to see it as something that actually benefited them—by helping maintain social order, by increasing mass purchasing power, and by stabilizing labor relations.

To his cabinet, Eisenhower appointed wealthy corporate lawyers and business executives, who were unapologetic about their backgrounds—"eight millionaires and a plumber," the liberal *New Republic* magazine caustically remarked. (The plumber was Secretary of Labor Martin Durkin, president of the plumbers' union, who soon resigned.) Charles Wilson, president of General Motors, assured senators considering his nomination to be Secretary of Defense that he foresaw no conflict of interest between his new post and his old because he was certain that "what was good for our country was good for General Motors, and vice versa." But missing from most members of this business-oriented administration was the deep hostility to "government interference" that had so dominated corporate attitudes three decades before.

Eisenhower's leadership style, which stressed delegation of authority to subordinates, helped enhance the power of his cabinet officers and others. Secretary of State John Foster Dulles was widely believed to be running American foreign policy almost single-handedly (although it has since become clear that the president was far more deeply involved in international decisions than was often apparent at the time). Eisenhower's chief of staff, former New Hampshire governor Sherman Adams, exercised broad authority over relations with Congress and strictly controlled access to the president—until he left office in disgrace, near the end of Eisenhower's presidency, after he was discovered to have accepted gifts from a wealthy businessman.

Eisenhower's consistent inclination was to limit federal activities and encourage private enterprise. He opposed the Democrats in their bid to ensure

EISENHOWER AND DULLES. Although Eisenhower's likeable personality did not come across fully on television, his was the first administration to make extensive use of the new medium to promote its policies and dramatize its actions. The president's press conferences were frequently televised, and on several occasions Secretary of State John Foster Dulles reported to the president in front of the cameras. Dulles is shown in the Oval Office on May 17, 1955, reporting on a nine-day trip through western Europe, where he had signed a treaty restoring sovereignty to Austria.

federal control of atomic energy. Instead, Eisenhower approved legislation that allowed private companies to manufacture, own, and operate atomic power plants under the supervision of the Atomic Energy Commission. Soon after, the first private nuclear power plant in America was constructed in Pennsylvania. Eisenhower also supported the private rather than public development of natural resources (and once talked about selling the Tennessee Valley Authority to a private company). To the chagrin of farmers, he lowered federal support for farm prices. He also removed the last limited wage and price controls maintained by the Truman administration. He opposed the creation of new social welfare programs such as national health insurance. He strove constantly to reduce federal expenditures (even during the recession of 1958) and balance the budget. He ended 1960, his last full year in office, with a $1 billion budget surplus.

Federal Spending

The president took few new initiatives in domestic policy, but he resisted pressure from the right wing of his party to dismantle those welfare policies of the New Deal that had survived the conservative assaults of the war years and after. "Any political party" that tried to "abolish social security and eliminate labor laws and farm programs," he once told his brother, would not be heard from "again in our political history." While acknowledging that some extremist businessmen and politicians advocated such drastic measures, Eisenhower explained, "their number is negligible and they are stupid." Indeed, during his first term, Eisenhower agreed to extend the Social Security system to an additional 10 million people and unemployment compensation to an additional 4 million people. He also agreed to increase the minimum hourly wage from 75 cents to one dollar.

Perhaps the most significant legislative accomplishment of the Eisenhower administration was the Federal Highway Act of 1956, which authorized $25 billion for a ten-year effort to construct over 40,000 miles of interstate highways. It was the biggest public works project in American history. The program was to be funded through a highway "trust fund," whose revenues would come from new taxes on the purchase of fuel, automobiles, trucks, and tires. Highways were the one federal project Eisenhower seemed enthusiastic about funding throughout his presidency. He viewed their construction as a way of employing Americans, improving internal transportation, and strengthening national defense.

HIGHWAY CONSTRUCTION. In the 1950s massive outlays of federal funds for interstate highway construction began, resulting in the building of thousands of miles of new roadways. Here workmen in Topeka, Kansas spread wet burlap over newly poured concrete. After two days, the burlap would be removed and expansion joints would be sawed into the concrete.

Improved federal highways were important not only for travel and commerce. They would also be crucial, in the event of a nuclear war, for evacuating cities and moving military equipment.

Eisenhower displayed more fiscal conservatism in his attitude toward housing policies. In response to an enormous need for housing among the rapidly growing families of the postwar period, Democrats favored an expansive federal role in building and financing new homes. Republicans, however, believed such projects should be undertaken privately by the construction industry. Eisenhower, characteristically, attempted to forge a compromise. His Housing Act of 1954 established a four-year schedule for federal construction of some 140,000 homes, a number far smaller than that advocated by many Democrats. The time limit was designed to ensure that the federal government would gradually ease its way out of housing construction in favor of providing low-cost mortgages to new home owners.

In 1956, Eisenhower ran for a second term, even though he had suffered a serious heart attack the previous year. With Adlai Stevenson opposing him once again, he won by another, even greater landslide, receiving nearly fifty-seven percent of the popular vote and 442 electoral votes to Stevenson's eighty-nine. Still, Democrats retained the control of both houses of Congress they had won in 1954. And in 1958—during a serious recession—they increased that control by substantial margins.

Eisenhower and the Crusade Against Subversion

The Eisenhower administration did little in its first years in office to discourage the anticommunist furor that had gripped the nation. Indeed, in many ways it helped sustain it. The president intensified the search for subversives in the government, which Truman had begun several years earlier. More than 2,220 federal employees resigned or were dismissed as a result of security investigations. Among them were most of the leading Asian experts in the State Department, many of whom were harried from office because they had shown inadequate enthusiasm for the now exiled regime of Chiang Kai-shek.

Eisenhower also advanced legislation to increase federal control of the American Communist party. The Communist Control Act of 1954 cracked down hard on the party, stipulating, among other things, that citizens who advocated overthrow of the government by force be stripped of their citizenship and that labor organizations infiltrated by communists lose rights provided to them by the National Labor Relations Act.

Among the most celebrated controversies of the first year of the new administration was the case of J. Robert Oppenheimer, director of the Manhattan Project during the war and one of the nation's most distinguished and admired physicists. Although Oppenheimer was now out of government service, he continued as a consultant to the Atomic Energy Commission. But he had angered some officials by his public opposition to development of the new, more powerful hydrogen bomb, which Truman had launched toward the end of his presidency.

In 1953, the FBI distributed a dossier within the administration detailing Oppenheimer's prewar association with various left-wing groups. There was, in fact, nothing new about the information it contained. What was new was that Joseph McCarthy had acquired it. Fearful that McCarthy would exploit the issue, Eisenhower's advisers urged the president to act quickly to address the matter. Eisenhower privately expressed skepticism about the disloyalty charges. Even if the physicist had passed secrets to the Soviets, Eisenhower noted, ousting him now "would not be a case of merely locking the stable door after the horse is gone; it would be more like trying to find a door for a burned-down stable." Nonetheless the president ordered that a "blank wall" be placed between Oppenheimer and government secrets pending further official investigation. A federal inquiry, requested by Oppenheimer himself and conducted in an inflamed and confused atmosphere, confirmed the decision to deny him a security clearance not because he was disloyal but because he had "fundamental defects of character."

By 1954, however, such policies were beginning to produce significant popular opposition—an indication that the anticommunist passions of several years earlier were beginning to subside. The clearest signal of that change was the political demise of Senator McCarthy.

The Army-McCarthy Hearings

During the first year of the Eisenhower administration, McCarthy continued to operate with impunity. The president, who privately loathed him, nevertheless refused to speak out against him in public. Relatively few others—in the political world or in the press—were any more courageous. But McCarthy finally overreached himself in January 1954 when he attacked Secretary of the Army Robert Stevens and the armed services in general.

McCarthy spent much of the month of February 1954 hounding a decorated general, Ralph Zwicker, who had served with great valor in World War II. Among the things McCarthy was ostensibly attempting to learn was why a dentist who had been drafted into the army and who was alleged to be a communist had been promoted. When Zwicker disclaimed any knowledge of the event, McCarthy alternately ridiculed the general, whom the senator said did not possess "the brains of a five-year-old child," or vilified him as a man "unfit to wear that uniform." Army Secretary Stevens was outraged and instructed Zwicker not to reappear before McCarthy's committee. Now McCarthy demanded that Stevens himself appear to answer the charges.

At a private lunch, Stevens and McCarthy then worked out a compromise. Zwicker would return for testimony, Stevens would investigate further the promotion in question, and McCarthy would suspend his harassment of the army witness. Almost instantly, however, McCarthy turned the compromise to his ad-

THE ARMY-MCCARTHY HEARINGS. Senator Joseph McCarthy accuses Joseph Welch, chief counsel for the army, of a "smear" against members of McCarthy's office. Welch appears nonplussed. The televiséd hearings were called to mediate the dispute between McCarthy and the U.S. Army. They gave many Americans their first glimpse of McCarthy in action and contributed to McCarthy's 1954 censure by the Senate.

vantage by suggesting that Stevens and the Eisenhower administration had been bested. Eisenhower was furious and heatedly told an aide: "This guy McCarthy is going to get into trouble over this. I'm not going to take this lying down." Still, when a special congressional investigation of some of McCarthy's charges, known as the Army-McCarthy hearings got underway, Eisenhower continued to remain aloof. He believed that acting presidential and refusing to even address the "sideshow" was the best defense against McCarthy.

Meanwhile, however, McCarthy continued his attack on the army. He insisted upon playing a role in the Army-McCarthy hearings even though he and his own staff were now being investigated. The hearings were designed to explore the charge that McCarthy and Roy Cohn, counsel to McCarthy's subcommittee, had attempted to use their influence to procure special treatment for G. David Schine, another committee staffer who had been drafted into the army. McCarthy countercharged that the army was trying to stall his investigations of communist influence in the military.

The Army-McCarthy hearings, which began in late April 1954, were among the first congressional hearings to be nationally televised. For two months, much of the nation watched the spectacle with rapt attention. Eisenhower himself was riveted, although, he said, he found the events "close to disgusting. It saddens me that I must feel ashamed for the United States Senate." But it was less the Senate that reaped the popular disgust with the spectacle than McCarthy himself. The hearings had devastating results on the senator and his crusade against alleged communists in government. As the nation witnessed McCarthy in action—bullying witnesses, hurling groundless (and often cruel) accusations, evading issues—much of the public began to see him as a villain, and even a buffoon.

During the hearings, McCarthy met more than his match in Boston lawyer Joseph Welch, chief counsel for the army. With rapier wit and keen intelligence, Welch managed to turn the tables on McCarthy and expose his "cruelty," his "recklessness," and his ignorance. "Have you no sense of decency, sir, at long last?" Welch asked McCarthy in one of the most dramatic moments in the hearings. "Have you left no sense of decency?" McCarthy seemed unable to provide an answer. When the hearings came to a close, McCarthy had been badly discredited. In December 1954, the Senate voted sixty-seven to twenty-two to condemn him for "conduct unbecoming a senator." Three years later, with little public support left, he died—a victim, apparently, of complications arising from alcoholism.

In the midst of the hearings, Eisenhower made a crucial decision freighted with great future significance. In an effort to limit McCarthy's ability to subpoena military and personnel records and even officials from the executive branch to give testimony, Eisenhower invoked the doctrine of "executive privilege." Discussions among advisers to the president, Eisenhower asserted, were privileged. "It is not in the public interest," the president maintained, "that any of their conversations or communications, or any documents or reproductions, concerning such advice be disclosed." The president made it clear that his advisers should not offer any testimony before McCarthy's committee. Such a broad assertion of presidential power to withhold information from Congress was virtually unprecedented.

COLD WAR TENSIONS

The diminishing credibility of domestic anticommunist crusades occurred in the midst of continuing anxiety about American national security and the conflict with the Soviet Union. The threat of nuclear war with the Soviet Union, in particular, created a sense of real tension in international relations during the 1950s.

But the nuclear threat had another effect as well. With the potential costs of war now so enormous, both superpowers began to edge away from direct confrontations. Instead, the attention of both the United States and the Soviet Union gradually turned to the rapidly escalating instability in Third World nations. This would become the stage on which the superpowers would increasingly clash for the remainder of the Cold War.

"Massive Retaliation"

Among those who helped to define American foreign policy in the Eisenhower years was Secretary of State John Foster Dulles, an aristocratic corporate lawyer with a stern moral revulsion to communism. Second only to the president himself, Dulles was the dominant figure in the nation's foreign policy establishment in the 1950s. He entered office denouncing the containment policies of the Truman years as excessively passive, arguing that the United States should pursue an active program of "liberation," which would lead to a "rollback" of communist expansion. Once in power, however, he had to defer to the far more moderate views of the president, and he began to develop a new set of doctrines that reflected the impact of nuclear weapons on the world.

The most prominent of those doctrines was the policy of "massive retaliation," which Dulles announced early in 1954. The United States would, he explained, respond to communist threats to its allies not by using conventional forces in local conflicts (a policy that had led to so much frustration in Korea) but by relying on "the deterrent of massive retaliatory power" (by which he clearly meant nuclear weapons).

In part, the new doctrine reflected Dulles's inclination for tense confrontations, an approach he once defined as "brinksmanship"—pushing the Soviet Union to the brink of war in order to exact concessions. But the real force behind the massive retaliation policy was economics. With pressure growing both in and out of government for a reduction in American military expenditures, an increasing reliance on atomic weapons seemed to promise, as some advocates put it, "more bang for the buck."

At the same time, Dulles intensified the efforts of Truman and Acheson to "integrate" the entire noncommunist world into a system of mutual defense pacts modeled on NATO—but, without exception, far weaker than the European pact. By the end of the decade, the United States had become a party to almost a dozen such treaties in all areas of the world.

Korea and Vietnam

What had been the most troubling foreign policy concern of the Truman years—the war in Korea—plagued the Eisenhower administration only briefly. On July 27, 1953, negotiators at Panmunjom finally signed an agreement ending the hostilities. Each antagonist was to withdraw its troops a mile and a half from the existing battle line, which ran roughly along the thirty-eighth parallel, the prewar border between North and South Korea. A conference in Geneva was to consider means by which to reunite the nation peacefully—although, in fact, the 1954 meeting produced no agreement and left the cease-fire line as the apparently permanent border between the two countries.

Almost simultaneously, however, the United States faced a difficult choice in Southeast Asia where France was fighting to retain control of its one-time

THE FRENCH INDOCHINA WAR. These French soldiers keep watch for the enemy—
the Vietminh—at their fortress in Dienbienphu as others remain in their
trenches, visible only by their helmets. The disastrous battle of Dienbienphu marked
the end of the French war effort.

colony, Vietnam. Opposing the French, however, were the powerful nationalist
forces of Ho Chi Minh (who was both a committed nationalist and a committed
communist), determined to win independence for their nation. Concerned about
the potential for communist expansionism into Indochina, the Truman administration had supported the French, one of America's most important Cold War
allies, and the Eisenhower administration at first did the same.

Early in 1954, however, 12,000 French troops became surrounded in a disastrous siege in the valley of Dienbienphu. Only direct American military intervention, it was clear, could prevent the total collapse of the French war effort.
Yet despite the urging of Secretary of State Dulles, Vice President Nixon, and
others, Eisenhower refused to permit direct American military intervention in
Vietnam, claiming that neither Congress nor America's other allies would support such action. Without American aid, the French defense of Dienbienphu finally collapsed on May 7, 1954; and France quickly agreed to a settlement of the
conflict at the same conference in Geneva that summer that was considering the

Korean settlement. The agreement marked the end of the French commitment to Vietnam and the beginning of an expanded American presence there.

Israel and the Crises of the Middle East

The 1950s also produced critical changes in America's relationship with the Middle East. Especially important to the future were the ties between the United States and the young nation of Israel. For more than half a century before World War II, the establishment of a Jewish state in Palestine had been the dream of a powerful international Zionist movement. The plight of the homeless Jews uprooted by the war, and the international horror at revelations of the Holocaust gave new strength to Zionist demands in the late 1940s. So did the enormous immigration of European Jews into Palestine after 1945, despite the efforts of Britain (which had governed the region since World War I) to limit them.

Finally, Britain brought the problem to the United Nations, which responded by recommending the partition of Palestine into a Jewish and an Arab state. On May 14, 1948, British rule ended, and Jews proclaimed the existence of the nation of Israel. President Truman recognized the new government the following day. But the creation of Israel, while it resolved some conflicts, produced others. Palestinian Arabs, unwilling to accept being displaced from what they considered their own country, fought determinedly against the new state in 1948—the first of several Arab–Israeli wars.

America was also concerned about the stability and friendliness of the Arab regimes in the area. The reason was simple: The region contained the richest oil reserves in the world, reserves in which American companies had already invested heavily, reserves on which the health of the American (and world) economy would ultimately come to depend. Thus the United States reacted with alarm as it watched Mohammed Mossadegh, the nationalist prime minister of Iran, begin to resist the presence of western corporations in his nation in the early 1950s. In 1953, the American CIA joined forces with conservative Iranian military leaders to engineer a coup that drove Mossadegh from office. To replace him, the CIA helped elevate the young Shah of Iran, Mohammed Reza Pahlevi, from his position as a token constitutional monarch to that of a virtually absolute ruler. The Shah remained closely tied to the United States for the next twenty-five years.

American policy was less effective in dealing with the nationalist government of Egypt, under the leadership of General Gamal Abdel Nasser, which began to develop a trade relationship with the Soviet Union in the early 1950s. In 1956, to punish Nasser for his friendliness toward the communists, Dulles withdrew American offers to assist in building the great Aswan Dam across the Nile. A week later, Nasser retaliated by seizing control of the Suez Canal from the British, saying that he would use the income from it to build the dam himself. The repercussions of that seizure were quick and profound.

On October 29, 1956, Israeli forces struck a pre-emptive blow against Egypt. The next day the British and French landed troops in the Suez to drive the Egyptians from the canal. Dulles and Eisenhower feared that the Suez crisis would drive the Arab states toward the Soviet Union and precipitate a new world war. By refusing to support the invasion, and by joining in a United Nations denunciation of it, the United States helped pressure the French and British to withdraw and helped persuade Israel to agree to a truce with Egypt.

Nasser's continuing flirtation with the Soviet Union strengthened American resolve to resist the growth of communist influence in the Middle East. It also increased the tendency of American officials to equate Arab nationalism with communism. In 1958, as pan-Arab forces loyal to Nasser challenged the government of Lebanon, Eisenhower ordered 5,000 American Marines to land on the beaches of Beirut to protect the existing regime; British troops entered Jordan at about the same time to resist a similar threat there. The effect of the interventions was negligible. The governments of both countries managed to stabilize their positions on their own, and within months both the American and British forces withdrew.

Latin America and "Yankee Imperialism"

World War II and the Cold War had eroded the limited initiatives of the Good Neighbor Policy toward Latin America, as American economic aid now flowed increasingly to Europe. Latin American animosity toward the United States grew steadily during the 1950s, as more people in the region came to view the expanding influence of American corporations in their countries as a form of imperialism. Such concerns deepened in 1954, when the Eisenhower administration ordered the CIA to help topple the new, leftist government of Jacobo Arbenz Guzman in Guatemala, a regime that Dulles (responding to the entreaties of the United Fruit Company, a major investor in Guatemala fearful of Arbenz) argued was potentially communist. Four years later, the depths of anti-American sentiment became clear when Vice President Richard Nixon visited the region, to be greeted in city after city by angry, hostile, occasionally dangerous mobs.

No nation in the region had been more closely tied to America than Cuba. Its leader, Fulgencio Batista y Saldivar, had ruled as a military dictator since 1952, when with American assistance he had toppled a more moderate government. Cuba's relatively prosperous economy had become a virtual fiefdom of American corporations, which controlled almost all the island's natural resources and had cornered over half the vital sugar crop. American organized crime controlled much of the lucrative tourist industry. Beginning in 1957, a popular movement of resistance to the Batista regime began to gather power under the leadership of Fidel Castro. By late 1958, the Batista forces were in almost total disarray. And on January 1, 1959, with Batista now in exile in Spain, Castro marched into Havana and established a new regime.

At first, the American government reacted warmly to Castro, relieved to be rid of the corrupt and ineffective Batista, hopeful that Castro would be a mod-

FIDEL CASTRO. After a long struggle in the Cuban countryside, Castro's rebel forces marched toward Havana in the last days of 1958 and, as the government of Fulgencio Batista y Zaldivar fled the country, seized control of Havana on New Year's Day, 1959. Here Castro addresses some of his supporters as he makes his way to Havana.

erate, democratic reformer who would allow American economic activity to continue in Cuba unchallenged. But once Castro began implementing significant land reforms and expropriating foreign-owned businesses and resources, Cuban-American relations rapidly deteriorated. Of particular concern to Eisenhower and Dulles was the Cuban regime's growing interest in communist ideas and tactics. When Castro began accepting assistance from the Soviet Union in 1960, the United States cut back the "quota" by which Cuba could export sugar to America at a favored price. Early in 1961, as one of its last acts, the Eisenhower administration severed diplomatic relations with Castro. The American CIA had already begun secretly training Cuban expatriates for an invasion of the island to topple the new regime. Isolated by the United States, Castro soon cemented an alliance with the Soviet Union.

Europe and the Soviet Union

Although the problems of the Third World were moving slowly to the center of American foreign policy, the direct relationship with the Soviet Union and the effort to resist communist expansion in Europe remained the principal concerns of the Eisenhower administration.

Even as the United States was strengthening NATO and rearming West Germany, however, many Americans continued to hope for negotiated solutions to some of the remaining problems dividing the superpowers. Such hopes grew after the death of Stalin in 1953, especially when the Soviet Union extended a peace overture to the rebellious Tito government in Yugoslavia, returned a military base to Finland, signed a peace treaty with Japan, and ended its long military occupation of Austria by allowing that nation to become an independent, neutral state. In 1955, Eisenhower and other NATO leaders met with the Soviet premier, Nikolai Bulganin, at a cordial summit conference in Geneva. But when a subsequent conference of foreign ministers met to try to resolve specific issues, they could find no basis for agreement.

Relations between the Soviet Union and the West soured further in 1956 in response to the Hungarian Revolution. Inspired by riots in Poland a year earlier, Hungarian dissidents launched a popular uprising in November 1956 to demand democratic reforms. For several days, they had control of the Hungarian government. But before the month was out, Soviet tanks and troops entered Budapest to crush the uprising and restore an orthodox, pro-Soviet regime. The Eisenhower administration refused to intervene. But the suppression of the uprising convinced many American leaders that Soviet policies had not softened as much as the events of the previous two years had suggested.

HUNGARIAN REVOLUTION. In 1956, a popular uprising in Hungary threatened the pro-Soviet regime. Anti-Russian demonstrations swept the city of Budapest leaving bricks and other debris, as depicted in this photograph, in the streets. The rebellion prompted an invasion of Soviet troops and tanks and the restoration of rule by forces that answered to the Soviet Union.

The failure of conciliation brought renewed vigor to the Cold War and, among other things, greatly intensified the Soviet-American arms race. Both nations engaged in extensive nuclear testing. Both nations redoubled efforts to develop effective intercontinental ballistic missiles, which could deliver atomic warheads directly from one continent to another. The American military, in the meantime, developed a new breed of atomic-powered submarines, capable of launching missiles from under water anywhere in the world. Later, the Soviet Union did the same.

The arms race not only increased tensions between the United States and Russia; it increased tensions within each nation as well. In America, public concern about nuclear war was becoming a pervasive national nightmare, a preoccupation never far from popular thought. Movies, television programs, books, and popular songs all expressed the concern. Fear of communism, therefore, combined with fear of atomic war to create a persistent national anxiety.

The U-2 Crisis

In this tense and fearful atmosphere, the Soviet Union raised new challenges to the West in 1958, in Berlin. The continuing existence of an anticommunist West Berlin inside communist East Germany remained an irritant and embarrassment to the Soviets. In November 1958, Nikita Khrushchev, who had succeeded Bulganin as Soviet premier and Communist party chief earlier that year, renewed the demands of his predecessors that the NATO powers abandon the city. The United States and its allies refused.

Khrushchev declined to force the issue. Instead, he suggested that he and Eisenhower discuss the issue personally, both in visits to each other's countries and at a summit meeting in Paris in 1960. The United States agreed. Khrushchev's 1959 visit to America produced a cool but polite response, and plans proceeded for the summit conference and for Eisenhower's visit to Moscow shortly thereafter. Only days before the scheduled beginning of the Paris meeting, however, the Soviet Union announced that it had shot down an American U-2, a high-altitude spy plane, over Russian territory. Its pilot, Francis Gary Powers, was in captivity. The Eisenhower administration responded clumsily, at first denying the allegations and then, when confronted with proof of them, awkwardly admitting that they were true. Khrushchev lashed back angrily, breaking up the Paris summit almost before it could begin and withdrawing his invitation to Eisenhower to visit the Soviet Union. But the U-2 incident was probably only a pretext. By the spring of 1960, Khrushchev—under heavy pressure from hardliners within his own government—knew that no agreement was possible on the Berlin issue; the U-2 incident may have become an excuse to avoid what he believed would be fruitless negotiations.

The events of 1960 provided a somber backdrop for the end of the Eisenhower administration. After eight years in office, Eisenhower had failed to eliminate the tensions between the United States and the Soviet Union. He had failed to end the costly and dangerous armaments race. And he had presided over a transformation of the Cold War from a relatively limited confrontation with the Soviet Union in Europe to a global effort to resist communist subversion. Yet Eisenhower had brought to these matters his own sense of the limits of American power. He had resisted military intervention in Vietnam. And he had placed a measure of restraint on those who urged the creation of an enormous American military establishment, warning in his farewell address in January 1961 of the "unwarranted influence" of a vast "military-industrial complex." His caution, in both domestic and international affairs, stood in marked contrast to the attitudes of his successors, who argued that the United States must act more boldly and aggressively on behalf of its goals at home and abroad.

CHAPTER TWENTY-THREE

The Resurgence of Liberalism

∼

By the late 1950s, a growing restlessness was becoming visible beneath the apparently placid surface of American society. Anxiety about America's position in the world, growing pressures from African Americans and other minorities, the increasing visibility of poverty, the rising frustrations of women, and other problems were beginning to unsettle the nation's public life. Ultimately, that restlessness would make the 1960s one of the most turbulent eras of the twentieth century. But at first, it contributed to a bold and confident effort by political leaders to attack social and international problems within the framework of conventional liberal politics.

THE TRIUMPH OF LIBERAL IDEALS

Those who yearned for a more active government in the late 1950s, and who accused the Eisenhower administration of allowing the nation to "drift," looked above all to the presidency for leadership. The political scientist Richard Neustadt, for example, published an influential book in 1960 entitled *Presidential Power*, which stressed the importance of presidential action in confronting national problems. Presidents faced many constraints, he argued, but effective presidents must learn to break free of them. The two men who served in the White House through most of the 1960s—John Kennedy and Lyndon Johnson—seemed for a time to be the embodiment of these liberal ideals.

The Election of 1960

The campaign of 1960 produced two young candidates who claimed to offer the nation active leadership. The Republican nomination went almost uncontested to Vice President Richard Nixon, who abandoned the strident anticommunism that had characterized his earlier career and adopted a centrist position in favor of moderate reform. The Democrats, in the meantime, emerged from a hotly contested primary campaign united, somewhat uneasily, behind John Fitzgerald Kennedy, an attractive and articulate young senator from Massachusetts who had narrowly missed being the party's vice presidential candidate in 1956.

John Kennedy grew up in a world of ease and privilege, although he himself suffered from a series of grave physical ailments throughout his life. He was the son of the wealthy and powerful Joseph P. Kennedy, controversial American ambassador to Britain at the beginning of World War II. After graduating from Harvard, he served in the navy during World War II, was decorated for bravery, and returned to Massachusetts in 1946 to run for office. Making liberal use of his war record, his father's money, and his family's connections to Boston Irish politics that reached back to the nineteenth century, he won a seat in Congress. Six years later, he was elected to the United States Senate and, in 1958, reelected by a record margin. Within days of his triumph, he was planning a presidential campaign. He premised his candidacy, he said, "on the single assumption that the American people are uneasy at the present drift in our national course."

Three themes dominated his campaign. Kennedy stressed, first, (erroneously as it turned out) that the Soviet Union enjoyed an advantage over the

KENNEDY-NIXON DEBATES. The first televised presidential debates in American history took place during the campaign of 1960. Kennedy made masterful use of television, and the debates helped persuade many that the young candidate could be a forceful and effective president.

ELECTION OF 1960	(64% of electorate voting)	ELECTORAL VOTE	POPULAR VOTE (%)
John F. Kennedy (Democratic)		303	34,227,096 (49.9)
Richard M. Nixon (Republican)		219	34,108,546 (49.6)
Harry F. Byrd (Dixiecrat)		15	501,643 (0.7)
Other candidates (Socialist Labor; Prohibition; National States Rights, Socialist Workers, Constitution)		—	197,029

United States in military power. He argued, as well, that the level of growth in the American economy had begun to compare unfavorably to that of other leading western industrial nations. Finally, the Democratic candidate charged that the United States was "failing to modernize itself." Its cities, schools, and various other public services no longer met the needs of the nation's growing population. In the end, however, Kennedy's youthful, appealing, and carefully crafted public image would prove to be at least as important as his political positions in attracting popular support.

Kennedy also had significant liabilities. He was a Roman Catholic in a nation that had never elected a Catholic president, and that indeed had a long history of religious bigotry toward and suspicion of Roman Catholicism. Kennedy's age (he turned forty-three in 1960), while attractive to many, suggested to some a callow youth who lacked the statesmanlike qualities necessary for the presidency. In addition, his opponent was an experienced and widely known political figure. In the closing days of the campaign, President Eisenhower, who had earlier endorsed his vice president rather tepidly, mounted a vigorous effort on behalf of Nixon. That support, combined with continuing doubts about Kennedy's youth and religion, almost enabled the Republicans to overcome what had been a sizable Democratic lead.

Kennedy's strong performance in a series of televised presidential debates assisted his campaign greatly. Already skilled at dealing with the media, Kennedy proved especially adept in front of the camera as he managed to address most of his remarks to the public rather than to Nixon. Many who heard the debates on radio believed the two candidates had come out relatively evenly. But those who watched them on TV—as millions had—were impressed by Kennedy. In demonstrating the enormous importance of mass media, the first televised presidential debates left a mark on American politics that would be felt for the rest of the century. More immediately, they helped deliver the American presidency to John F. Kennedy, even if by an extraordinarily narrow margin. Kennedy won by only a tiny plurality—49.9 percent of the popular vote to Nixon's 49.6 percent—and only a slightly more comfortable electoral majority of 303 to 219.

If a few thousand voters in a few strategic states had voted differently, Nixon would have won the presidency in 1960.

The New Frontier

Kennedy had campaigned promising a program of domestic legislation more ambitious than any since the New Deal, a program he described as the "New Frontier." But the narrowness of his victory limited his political effectiveness, and throughout his brief presidency he had serious problems with Congress. Although Democrats remained in control of both houses, the party's majorities were heavily dependent on conservative southerners, who were far more likely to vote with the Republicans than with Kennedy. Many of those same southerners occupied powerful committee chairmanships. One after another of Kennedy's legislative proposals found themselves hopelessly stalled.

As a result, the president had to look elsewhere for opportunities to display positive leadership. One area where he believed he could do that was the economy. Economic growth was sluggish in 1961 when Kennedy entered the White House, with unemployment hovering at about six percent of the work force. Kennedy initiated a series of tariff negotiations with foreign governments—the "Kennedy Round"—in an effort to stimulate American exports. He began to consider an expanded use of Keynesian fiscal and monetary tools—culminating in his 1962 proposal for a substantial federal tax cut to stimulate the economy.

He also used his personal prestige to battle inflation. In 1962, several steel companies, led by U.S. Steel, announced that they were raising their prices by six dollars a ton, a move certain to trigger similar action by the rest of the steel industry. When U.S. Steel president Roger Blough appeared in the Oval Office to inform Kennedy, the president reacted with fury. "You have made a terrible mistake," Kennedy warned Blough, "You have double-crossed me." Kennedy then put heavy pressure on Blough and other steel executives to rescind the increase, in part by taking his case to the American people. How, Kennedy asked, could "a tiny handful of steel executives whose pursuit of private power and profit exceeds their sense of public responsibility . . . show such utter contempt for the interests of one hundred eighty-five million Americans." The steel companies soon relented. But it was a fleeting victory. Kennedy's relationship with the corporate community was now permanently strained.

The Charismatic President

More than any other president of the century (except perhaps the two Roosevelts and, later, Ronald Reagan), Kennedy made his own personality an integral part of his presidency and a central focus of national attention. His press conferences demonstrated Kennedy's quick wit and self-deprecating humor, and he relished them. His wife, Jacqueline, brought her natural beauty and her affinity for haute couture to drab political gatherings. His two young children enlivened the White House, where they played on the grounds and visited with their father in the Oval Office. Even the young president's emphasis on physical fitness suggested that a new kind of "vigor" had been brought, not just to the Washington, but to the nation. Although Kennedy in fact suffered from a serious chronic illness for much of his adult life—Addison's disease (a disorder of the adrenal glands)—his good looks and youth seemed to radiate health and energy.

Nothing illustrated Kennedy's impact on the nation more clearly than the popular reaction to the tragedy of November 22, 1963. Kennedy had traveled to Texas with his wife and Vice President Lyndon Johnson for a series of political appearances. While the presidential motorcade rode slowly through the streets of Dallas, shots rang out. Two bullets struck the president—one in the throat, the other in the head. He was sped to a nearby hospital, where minutes later he was pronounced dead. Lee Harvey Oswald, who appeared to be a confused and embittered Marxist, was arrested for the crime later that day. But within another two days he himself was mysteriously murdered by a Dallas nightclub owner, Jack Ruby, as police moved Oswald from one jail to another.

The popular assumption at the time was that both Oswald and Ruby had acted alone, assumptions endorsed by a federal commission, chaired by Chief Justice Earl Warren, that was appointed to investigate the assassination. In later years, however, many Americans—and in 1978 a congressional subcommittee—claimed that the Warren Commission report had not revealed the full story. *JFK*, a popular 1991 film by director Oliver Stone, endorsed one of the many conspiracy theories advanced over the previous decades to explain the assassination. But no solid evidence has ever appeared to confirm any such theories; and many informed observers continue to believe that the Warren Commission (hasty and sloppy as it undoubtedly was) had the story essentially right.

The enormous appeal of conspiracy theories in the more than thirty years after the Kennedy assassination reflected not just the reasonable doubts many Americans harbored about the official explanation of the tragedy. It reflected as well an unwillingness to accept that such a terrible event could have been as random an occurrence as the Warren Commission suggested it was. To many Americans it was almost unthinkable that a vital young president, who appeared in many ways larger than life, could have been felled by such an insignificant person.

In fact, whatever lay behind President Kennedy's murder in Dallas, there can be no question that the event itself left a deep mark on millions of Americans. Kennedy's assassination, like only a few other public events in national history, left most who experienced it with an indelible memory of where they were and how they felt when they heard the news on November 22. Over the next four days—as much of the nation suspended normal activity to watch the

THE DEATH OF KENNEDY. The assassination of President Kennedy on November 22, 1963 was a tragedy that profoundly touched millions of Americans. The elaborate state funeral, planned by his widow, was modeled on accounts of Lincoln's funeral in 1865. For days after the president's death, time seemed to stand still as Americans gathered around their televisions to watch as Kennedy was eulogized and finally brought to rest in Arlington Cemetery.

televised events surrounding the presidential funeral—images of Kennedy's widow, his small children, his funeral procession, his grave site at Arlington Cemetery with its symbolic eternal flame—all became deeply embedded in the public mind. In later years, when Americans looked back at the optimistic days of the 1950s and early 1960s and wondered how everything had subsequently seemed to unravel, many would think of November 22, 1963, as the beginning of the change.

President Johnson

At the time, however, much of the nation took comfort in the personality and performance of Kennedy's successor in the White House, Lyndon Baines Johnson. Johnson was a native of the poor "hill country" of west Texas and had risen to eminence by dint of extraordinary, even obsessive effort and ambition. He entered public life in the 1930s as an aide to a Texas congressman, then as the Texas director of the New Deal's National Youth Administration, and then, after 1937, as a young member of Congress fervently committed to Franklin Roosevelt. He rose steadily in Congress by working extraordinarily hard and by cultivating the favor of party leaders. In 1948, he narrowly won election to the United States Senate; a few years later he became the Senate Majority Leader, a job in which he displayed a legendary ability to persuade and cajole his colleagues into following his lead. Having failed to win the Democratic nomination for president in 1960, he surprised many who knew him—including it appears John F. Kennedy—by agreeing to accept the second position on the ticket. The events in Dallas thrust him into the presidency.

Johnson's rough-edged, even crude personality could hardly have been more different from Kennedy's. But like Kennedy, Johnson was a man who believed in the active use of power. And he proved, in the end, more effective than his predecessor in translating his goals into reality. Between 1963 and 1966, he compiled the most impressive legislative record of any president since Franklin Roosevelt. He was aided by the tidal wave of emotion that followed the Kennedy assassination, which helped win support for many New Frontier proposals. But Johnson also constructed a remarkable reform program of his own, one that he ultimately labeled the "Great Society." And he won approval of much of it through the same sort of skillful lobbying of Congress that had made him an effective majority leader.

Johnson envisioned himself, as well, as a great "coalition builder." He wanted the support of everyone, and for a time he very nearly got it. His first year in office was, by necessity, dominated by the campaign for reelection. There was little doubt that he would win—particularly after the Republican party fell under the sway of its right wing and nominated the conservative Senator Barry Goldwater of Arizona. Liberal Republicans abandoned Goldwater and openly supported Johnson. In the November election, the president received a larger plurality, over sixty-one percent, than any candidate before or since. Goldwater managed to carry only his home state of Arizona and five states in the deep South. Record Democratic majorities in both houses of Congress, many of whose members had been swept into office only because of the margin of Johnson's victory, ensured that the president would be able to fulfill many of his goals. Johnson seemed well on his way to achieving his cherished aim: becoming the most successful reform president of the century.

Health Care

The domestic programs of the Kennedy and Johnson administrations had two basic goals: maintaining the strength of the American economy and expanding the responsibilities of the federal government for social welfare. In the first, the two presidents were largely continuing a commitment that had been central to virtually every administration since early in the century. In the second, however, they were responding to a marked (and temporary) change in public attitudes. In particular, they were responding to what some described as the "discovery of poverty" in the late 1950s and early 1960s—the realization by Americans who had been glorying in prosperity that there were substantial portions of the population that remained destitute.

For the first time since the 1930s, the federal government took steps to create important new social welfare programs. The largest and most important of these was Medicare: a program to provide federal aid to the elderly for medical expenses. Kennedy initially proposed legislation to give Americans over sixty-five years old ninety days of hospital care and 180 days of nursing home assistance. But Kennedy's bill went down to defeat in the Senate in 1962. The president lambasted the Congress for delivering "a most serious defeat for every American family."

Lyndon Johnson finally made Medicare possible in 1965 bringing a temporary end to a bitter, twenty-year debate between those who believed in the concept of national health assistance and those who denounced it as "socialized medicine." The program, as crafted by the Kennedy and Johnson administrations, removed many objections. For one thing, it avoided the stigma of "welfare" by making Medicare benefits available to all elderly Americans, regardless of need (just as Social Security had done with pensions). That created a large middle-class constituency for the program. The legislation also defused the opposition of the medical community by allowing doctors serving Medicare patients to practice privately and to charge their normal fees; Medicare simply shifted responsibility for paying those fees from the patient to the government. In 1966, Johnson won passage as well of the Medicaid program, which extended federal medical assistance to welfare recipients of all ages. Criticism of both programs grew in subsequent years, both from those who thought Medicare and Medicaid were inadequate and from those who thought they were too expensive. But broad public support ensured their survival, and many liberals continued to hope for genuinely universal national health insurance.

The War on Poverty

Medicare and Medicaid were the first steps in a much larger assault on poverty—one that Kennedy had been contemplating in the last months of his life, and one that Johnson launched only weeks after taking office. It emerged out of a long debate within the administration, and within Congress, about the nature

ENACTING MEDICARE. With former President Harry Truman and Vice President Hubert Humphrey standing by, President Johnson signs legislation creating Medicare. Decades earlier, Truman had proposed national health insurance but had been unsuccessful in advancing that goal.

of poverty and the best way to fight it. And it reflected the views of those who believed that poverty was a result of more than lack of money; it was a product of institutional and cultural deficiencies that must be addressed to allow the poor to help themselves. That, in the end, was the key to the effort to end poverty: the effort to train the poor, to help the indigent climb the ladder of opportunity out of poverty. It was, as Johnson once put it, a "hand up, not a handout."

The centerpiece of this "war on poverty," as Johnson called it, was the Office of Economic Opportunity (OEO), which created an array of new educational, employment, housing, and health care programs. But the OEO was controversial from the start, in part because of its commitment to the idea of "Community Action." Community Action was an effort to involve members of poor communities themselves in the planning and administration of the programs designed to help them, to promote what some of its advocates called "maximum feasible participation." The Community Action programs provided some important benefits. In particular, they gave jobs to many poor people and gave them important experience in administrative and political work. Many men and women who went on to important careers in politics or community organizing, including many black and Hispanic politicians who would rise to prominence in the 1970s and 1980s, got their start in Community Action programs.

The programs were also important to Native Americans. They allowed tribal leaders to design and run programs for themselves and to apply for funds from the federal government on an equal basis with state and municipal authorities. Administering these programs helped produce a new generation of tribal leaders who learned much about political and bureaucratic power from the experience.

But despite its achievements, the Community Action approach proved impossible to sustain. Many programs fell victim to mismanagement or to powerful opposition from the local governments with which they were at times competing. Some activists in Community Action agencies employed tactics that mainstream politicians considered frighteningly radical. The apparent excesses of a few agencies damaged the popular image of the Community Action program as a whole. And even though Community Action was a relatively small part of the war on poverty, its growing unpopularity undermined support for the larger program as well.

The OEO spent nearly $3 billion during its first two years of existence, and it helped alleviate poverty in many ways. But it fell far short of eliminating poverty altogether. That was in part because of the weaknesses of the programs themselves and in part because funding for them, inadequate from the beginning, dwindled as the years passed and a costly war in Southeast Asia became the nation's first priority.

Still, the war on poverty left a number of significant legacies. A generation of minority men and women became politically active in the Community Action programs and continued to play a major role in public life for many years after. A series of programs—Head Start, a preschool program to help the children of poor families prepare for their educations; Food Stamps, which provided cash assistance to allow poor families to buy food; and others—were genuinely successful and had a permanent impact on poverty. Medicare and Medicaid, costly as they became, made major contributions to a long-term improvement in health care for the elderly and the poor.

Revitalizing American Cities and Schools

Closely tied to the antipoverty program were federal efforts to revitalize decaying cities and to strengthen the nation's schools. The Housing Act of 1961 offered $4.9 billion in federal grants to cities for the preservation of open spaces, the development of mass-transit systems, and the subsidization of middle-income housing. In 1966, Johnson established a new cabinet agency, the Department of Housing and Urban Development (led by Robert Weaver, the first African American ever to serve in a cabinet). Johnson also inaugurated the Model Cities program, which offered federal subsidies for urban redevelopment.

Kennedy had fought long and hard for federal aid to public education, but he had failed to overcome two important obstacles. Many Americans feared aid to education as the first step toward federal control of the schools. Many Catholics insisted federal assistance must extend to the parochial as well as public schools, a demand that raised serious constitutional issues and one that Kennedy (a Catholic himself) refused to consider. Johnson managed to circumvent both objections with the Elementary and Secondary Education Act of 1965 and a series of subsequent measures. The bills extended aid to both private and parochial schools and based the aid on the economic conditions of their students, not the needs of the schools themselves. Total federal expenditures for education and technical training rose from $5 billion to $12 billion between 1964 and 1967.

The Johnson administration also supported the Immigration Act of 1965, one of the most important pieces of legislation of the 1960s, even if largely unnoticed at the time. The law maintained a strict limit on the number of newcomers admitted to the country each year (170,000), but it eliminated the "national origins" system established in the 1920s, which gave preference to immigrants from northern Europe over those from other parts of the world. It continued to restrict immigration from some parts of Latin America, but it allowed people from all parts of Europe, Asia, and Africa to enter the United States on an equal basis. It meant that large new categories of immigrants—and especially large numbers of Asians—would begin entering the United States by the early 1970s and changing the character of the American population. Prior to the 1965 act, ninety percent of immigrants to the United States each year came from European countries. For more than twenty years after the act, only ten percent did.

The Impact of the Great Society

The great surge of reform during the Kennedy-Johnson years reflected a new awareness of social problems in America. It also reflected the confidence of many liberals that America's resources were virtually limitless and that purposeful public effort could surmount almost any obstacle—that it was possible, as Lyndon Johnson insisted, to create a "Great Society" through purposeful public action. By the time Johnson left office, legislation had been either enacted or initiated to deal with a remarkable number of social issues: poverty, health care, education, cities, transportation, the environment, consumer protection, agriculture, science, the arts.

Taken together, the Great Society reforms meant a significant increase in federal spending. For a time, rising tax revenues from the growing economy nearly compensated for the new expenditures. In 1964, Johnson managed to win passage of the $11.5 billion tax cut that Kennedy had first proposed in 1962. The cut increased the federal deficit, but it helped produce substantial economic growth over the next several years that made up for much of the revenue initially lost. As Great Society programs began to multiply, however, and particularly as they began to compete with the escalating costs of America's military ventures, the federal budget rapidly outpaced increases in revenues. In 1961, the federal government had spent just under $98 billion and had carried a deficit of $3.3 billion. By 1968, that sum had risen to $153 billion, with a $25 billion deficit.

The high costs of the Great Society programs, and the inability of the government to find the revenues to pay for them, contributed to a growing disillusionment in later years with the idea of federal efforts to solve social problems. By the 1980s, many Americans had become convinced that the Great Society efforts had not worked and that, indeed, government programs to solve social problems could not work. Others, however, argued equally fervently that social programs had made important contributions both to the welfare of the groups they were designed to help and to the health of the economy as a whole.

Whether because of economic growth or because of government antipoverty efforts—or, as seems most likely, because of both—the decade of the 1960s saw the most substantial decrease in poverty in the United States of any period in the nation's history. In 1959, according to the most widely accepted estimates, twenty-one percent of the American people lived below the officially established poverty line. By 1969, only twelve percent remained below that line. The improvements affected blacks and whites in about the same proportion: fifty-six percent of the black population had lived in poverty in 1959, while only thirty-two percent did so ten years later—a forty-two percent reduction; eighteen percent of all whites had been poverty-stricken in 1959, but only ten percent were living below the poverty line a decade later—a forty-four percent reduction.

THE CIVIL RIGHTS MOVEMENT IN TRIUMPH AND CRISIS

The nation's most important domestic initiative in the 1960s was the continuing struggle to address racial injustice and inequality. It was not an easy project, and it produced severe strains in American society. Although the initial aims of the civil rights movement fit comfortably with the ideals of American liberalism, tensions deepened as the movement advanced. There were important victories in the struggle to dismantle segregation in the South. But when the movement's attention turned to the racial problems in northern society, many of whose roots lay less in law than in economics, conflict between the moderate stance of most liberals and the growing impatience of many African Americans quickly grew.

Striking Down Segregation

John Kennedy had long been vaguely sympathetic to the cause of racial justice, but he was hardly a committed crusader. His intervention during the 1960 campaign to help win the release of Martin Luther King, Jr. from a Georgia prison won him a large plurality of the black vote. But like many presidents before him, he feared alienating southern Democratic voters and powerful southern Democrats in Congress. His administration set out to contain the racial problem by expanding enforcement of existing laws and supporting litigation to overturn existing segregation statutes. He hoped to make modest progress without creating politically damaging divisions.

But the pressure for more fundamental change was not so easy to resist in the 1960s. In February 1960, black college students in Greensboro, North Carolina staged a sit-in at a segregated Woolworth's lunch counter; and in the following months, similar demonstrations spread throughout the South, forcing many merchants to integrate their facilities. In the spring of 1960, some of those who had participated in the sit-ins formed the Student Nonviolent Coordinating Committee (SNCC), which worked to keep the spirit of resistance alive. Uneasy with the power of single charismatic individuals within the civil rights movement, and determined to marshall the commitment and daring of a younger generation, SNCC soon set off on its own course. It embraced participatory democracy as its model for decision making. And it set voter registration drives and citizen education as its priorities.

At the same time, other challenges to segregation continued and accelerated. In 1961, an interracial group of students, working with the Congress of Racial Equality (CORE), began what they called "freedom rides" (reviving a tactic CORE had tried, without much success, in the 1940s). Traveling by bus throughout the South, the freedom riders tried to force the desegregation of bus stations. In some places, they met with such savage violence at the hands of enraged whites that the president finally dispatched federal marshals to help keep the peace and ordered the integration of all bus and train stations. "Where are they getting these ideas?" Kennedy asked one African-American adviser with frustration as he observed the persistence of civil rights activists. "From you," came the answer.

In the meantime, SNCC workers began fanning out through African-American communities and even into remote rural areas to encourage blacks to challenge the obstacles to voting that white society had created. The Southern Christian Leadership Conference (SCLC) also created citizen education and other programs—many of them organized by the remarkable Ella Baker, one of the great grass-roots leaders of the movement—to mobilize black workers, farmers, housewives, and others to challenge segregation, disenfranchisement, and discrimination.

Continuing judicial efforts to enforce the integration of public education increased the pressure on national leaders to respond to the civil rights movement. In October 1962, a federal court ordered the University of Mississippi to enroll its first black student, James Meredith; Governor Ross Barnett, a strident segregationist, refused to enforce the order. When angry whites in Oxford, Mississippi, began rioting to protest the court decree, President Kennedy sent federal troops to the city to restore order and protect Meredith's right to attend the university.

BIRMINGHAM, ALABAMA IN 1963. During the spring of 1963, a series of peaceful civil rights demonstrations in Birmingham led to violence as Police Commissioner Eugene "Bull" Connor attempted to repress the protests. Here firemen direct their hoses on demonstrators who are attempting to protect themselves from the enormous pressure of the water.

Events in Alabama in 1963 helped bring the growing movement to something of a climax. In April, Martin Luther King, Jr. helped launch a series of nonviolent demonstrations in Birmingham, Alabama, a city unsurpassed in the strength of its commitment to segregation. Police Commissioner Eugene "Bull" Connor personally supervised a brutal effort to break up the peaceful marches, arresting hundreds of demonstrators and using attack dogs, tear gas, electric cattle prods, and fire hoses—at times even against small children—as much of the nation watched televised reports in horror. Two months later, Governor George Wallace—who had won election in 1962 promising staunch resistance to integration—pledged to stand in the doorway of a building at the University of Alabama to prevent the court-ordered enrollment of several black students. Only after the arrival of federal marshals and a visit from Attorney General Robert Kennedy did he give way. Even though the stand-off with the federal government was a victory for integration, tensions remained high, as did the threat of violence. In fact, the night of the University of Alabama confrontation, NAACP official Medgar Evers was murdered in Mississippi.

Civil Rights Legislation

The events in Alabama and Mississippi were a warning to the president that he could no longer contain or avoid the issue of racism. In an important television address on June 12 during the University of Alabama confrontation, Kennedy spoke eloquently of the "moral issue" facing the nation. "If an American," he asked, "because his skin is dark, . . . cannot enjoy the full and free life which all of us want, then who among us would be content to have the color of his skin changed and stand in his place? Who among us would then be content with the counsels of patience and delay?" Days later, he introduced a series of new legislative proposals prohibiting segregation in "public accommodations" (stores, restaurants, theaters, hotels), barring discrimination in employment, and increasing the power of the government to file suits on behalf of school integration.

MARTIN LUTHER KING, JR., IN 1963. On August 28, 1963 the greatest civil rights demonstration in American history was held in Washington, D.C. During the "March on Washington," as the event was known, over 200,000 people gathered in front of the Lincoln Memorial. Among the addresses they heard was the Reverend Martin Luther King, Jr.'s famous "I Have A Dream" speech—perhaps the most memorable oration in twentieth-century American history. King described his vision of a future in which racial harmony would prevail and all Americans would unite around the principle and practice of racial equality.

To generate support for the legislation, and to dramatize the power of the growing movement, more than 200,000 demonstrators marched down the Mall in Washington, D.C., in August 1963 and gathered before the Lincoln Memorial for the greatest civil rights demonstration in the nation's history. President Kennedy, who had at first opposed the idea of the march, in the end gave it his open support after receiving pledges from organizers that speakers would not criticize the administration. Martin Luther King, Jr., in one of the greatest speeches of his remarkable oratorical career, aroused the crowd with a litany of images prefaced again and again by the phrase "I have a dream." The march was the high-water mark of the peaceful, inter-racial civil rights movement—and one of the last moments of real harmony within it.

The assassination of President Kennedy three months later gave new impetus to the battle for civil rights legislation. The ambitious measure that Kennedy had proposed in June 1963 was stalled in the Senate after having passed through the House of Representatives with relative ease. Early in 1964, after Johnson applied both public and private pressure, supporters of the measure finally mustered the two-thirds majority necessary to close debate and end a filibuster by southern senators. The Senate then passed the most comprehensive civil rights bill in the history of the nation.

The Battle for Voting Rights

Having won a significant victory in one area, the civil rights movement shifted its focus to another: voting rights. During the summer of 1964, thousands of civil rights workers, black and white, northern and southern, spread out through the South, but primarily in Mississippi, to work on behalf of black voter registration and participation. The campaign was known as "Freedom Summer," and it produced a violent response from some southern whites. Before it had even begun, three participants—two whites, Andrew Goodman and Michael Schwerner, and one black, James Chaney—disappeared after traveling to Mississippi to investigate a church bombing. Their bodies were found later buried in an earthen dam. They had been murdered, an informant later revealed, by local police and Ku Klux Klansmen. This chilling event, and numerous other bombings during Freedom Summer, did much to transform the perspective of many civil rights activists, especially in SNCC. Although civil rights activists continued their efforts, many began to doubt the philosophy of passive resistance and nonviolence.

Freedom Summer also produced the Mississippi Freedom Democratic party (MFDP), an integrated alternative to the regular all-white state party organization. Under the leadership of Fannie Lou Hamer and others, the MFDP challenged the regular party's right to its seats at the Democratic National Convention that summer. President Johnson, eager to avoid antagonizing anyone (even southern white Democrats who seemed likely to support his Republican opponent) attempted to broker a compromise. The Democratic party leadership offered to seat two MFDP delegates along with the regular slate, with promises of party reforms later on. But the MFDP rejected the compromise measure, and many MFDP delegates walked out of the convention in protest.

A year later, in March 1965, King helped organize a major demonstration in Selma, Alabama to press the demand for the right of blacks to register to vote. Selma sheriff Jim Clark led local police in a brutal attack on the demonstrators—which, as in Birmingham, received graphic television coverage and horrified many viewers across the nation. Two northern whites participating in the Selma march were murdered in the course of the effort there—one, a minister, beaten to death in the streets of the town; the other, a Detroit housewife, shot as she drove along a highway at night with a black passenger in her car. The national outrage that followed the events in Alabama helped push Lyndon Johnson to propose and win passage of the Civil Rights Act of 1965, better known as the Voting Rights Act, which provided federal protection to blacks attempting to exercise their right to vote. But important as such gains were, they failed to satisfy the rapidly rising expectations of African Americans as the focus of the movement began to move from political to economic issues.

From De Jure *to* De Facto *Segregation*

For decades, the nation's African-American population had been undergoing a major demographic shift; and by the 1960s, the problem of race was no longer primarily southern or rural, as it had been earlier in the century. By 1966, sixty-nine percent of American blacks were living in metropolitan areas and forty-five percent outside the South. Although the economic condition of much of American society was improving, in the poor urban communities in which the black population was concentrated, things were getting significantly worse. Well over half of all American nonwhites lived in poverty at the beginning of the 1960s; black unemployment was twice that of whites.

By the mid-1960s, therefore, the issue of race was moving out of the South and into the rest of the nation. The legal battle against school desegregation had moved beyond the initial assault on *de jure* segregation (segregation by law) to an attack on *de facto* segregation (segregation in practice, as through residential patterns), thus carrying the fight into northern cities. Many African-American leaders (and their white supporters) were demanding, similarly, that the battle against job discrimination move to a new level. Employers should not only abandon negative measures to deny jobs to blacks; they should adopt positive measures to recruit minorities, thus compensating for past injustices. Lyndon Johnson gave his tentative support to the concept of "affirmative action" in 1965. Over the next decade, affirmative action guidelines gradually extended to virtually all institutions doing business with or receiving funds from the federal government (including schools and universities)—and to many others as well.

A symbol of the movement's new direction, and of the problems it would cause, was a major campaign in the summer of 1966 in Chicago, in which King played a prominent role. Organizers of the Chicago campaign hoped to direct national attention to housing and employment discrimination in northern industrial cities in much the same way similar campaigns had exposed legal racism in the South. But the Chicago campaign not only evoked vicious and at times violent opposition from white residents of that city; it failed to arouse the national conscience in the way events in the South had done. It did produce a weak agreement with the city government to end housing discrimination, but little changed as a result. The Chicago campaign was, on the whole, an exercise in frustration.

Urban Violence

Well before the Chicago campaign, the problem of urban poverty had thrust itself into the national consciousness when riots broke out in black neighborhoods in major cities. There were a few scattered disturbances in the summer of 1964, most notably in New York City's Harlem. The first large race riot since the end of World War II occurred the following summer in the Watts section of Los Angeles. In the midst of a seemingly routine traffic arrest, a white police officer

RIOT IN WATTS. A fire burns out of control during the 1965 riot in the Los Angeles neighborhood known as Watts. Firefighters, attempting to subdue the blaze, were fired upon by snipers, and National Guardsmen were called out to protect them as they tried to control the conflagration. The riot led to enormous destruction in Watts and the deaths of 34 people, almost all of them African Americans.

struck a protesting black bystander with his club. The incident triggered a storm of anger and a week of violence (and revealed how deeply blacks in Los Angeles, and in other cities, resented their treatment at the hands of local police). As many as 10,000 rioters were estimated to have participated—attacking white motorists, burning buildings, looting stores, and sniping at policemen. Thirty-four people died during the Watts uprising, which was eventually quelled by the National Guard; twenty-eight of the dead were African Americans. In the summer of 1966, there were forty-three additional outbreaks, the most serious of them in Chicago and Cleveland. And in the summer of 1967, there were eight major riots, including the largest of the decade—a racial clash in Detroit in which forty-three people (thirty-three of them black) died.

Televised reports of the violence alarmed millions of Americans and created both a new sense of urgency and a growing sense of doubt among those whites who had embraced the cause of racial justice only a few years before. A special Commission on Civil Disorders created by the president in response to the riots, known as the Kerner Commission, issued a celebrated report in the spring of 1968 recommending massive spending to eliminate the abysmal conditions of the ghettoes. "Only a commitment to national action on an unprecedented scale," the commission concluded, "can shape a future compatible with the historic ideals of American society." To many white Americans, however, the lesson of the riots was the need for stern measures to stop violence and lawlessness.

Black Power

Disillusioned with the ideal of peaceful change in cooperation with whites, an increasing number of African Americans were turning to a new approach to the racial issue: the philosophy of "black power." Black power meant different things to different people. But in all its forms, it suggested a move away from inter-racial cooperation and toward increased racial self-awareness and independence. It was part of a long nationalist tradition among African Americans that extended back into slavery and that had had its most visible twentieth-century expression in the Garvey movement.

Perhaps the most enduring impact of black-power ideology was a social and psychological one: instilling racial pride in African Americans, who lived in a society whose dominant culture generally portrayed blacks as inferior to whites. It encouraged the growth of black studies in schools and universities. It helped stimulate important black literary and artistic movements. It produced a new interest among many blacks in their African roots. It led to a rejection by some African Americans of certain cultural practices borrowed from white society: "Afro" hair styles began to replace artificially straightened hair; some blacks began to adopt African styles of dress, even to change their names.

But black power took political forms as well, most notably in creating a deep schism within the civil rights movement. Traditional black organizations that had emphasized cooperation with sympathetic whites—groups such as the NAACP, the Urban League, and King's Southern Christian Leadership Conference—now faced competition from more radical groups. The Student Nonviolent Coordinating Committee and the Congress of Racial Equality had both begun as relatively moderate, inter-racial organizations. By the mid-1960s, however, these and other groups were calling for more radical and occasionally even violent action against the racism of white society and were openly rejecting the approaches of older, more established black leaders.

Particularly alarming to many whites were organizations that existed entirely outside the mainstream civil rights movement. In Oakland, California, the Black Panther party (founded by Huey Newton and Bobby Seale) promised to defend African-American rights against oppression even if that required violence. Black Panthers organized along semimilitary lines and wore weapons openly and proudly. They were, in fact, more the victims of violence from the police than they were practitioners of violence themselves. But they created an image, quite deliberately, of militant blacks willing to fight for justice, in Newton's words, "through the barrel of a gun."

In Detroit, a once-obscure separatist group, the Nation of Islam, gained new prominence. Founded in 1931 by Elijah Poole (who converted to Islam and re-

MALCOLM X. Though criticized by many whites for his extremism, Malcolm X, stressed self-help and black independence. An outspoken critic of racism and a charismatic figure among Black Muslims, Malcolm X attracted a large following, especially among young African Americans in the inner-cities. Here he addresses a huge rally in Harlem.

named himself Elijah Mohammed), the movement taught blacks to take responsibility for their own lives, to be disciplined, to live by strict codes of behavior, and to reject any dependence on whites. The most celebrated of the Black Muslims, as whites often termed them, began his life as Malcolm Little, spent much of his youth as a drug addict and pimp and served time in prison. He rebuilt his life after joining the movement. He adopted the name Malcolm X ("X" to denote his lost African surname). And he became one of the movement's most influential spokesmen, particularly among younger blacks, as a result of his intelligence, his oratorical skills, and his harsh, uncompromising opposition to all forms of racism and oppression. He did not advocate violence, as his critics often claimed; but he insisted that black people had the right to defend themselves, violently if necessary, from those who assaulted their freedom. Malcolm died in 1965 when black gunmen, presumably under orders from rivals within the Nation of Islam, assassinated him in New York. But a book he had been working on before his death with the writer Alex Haley *(The Autobiography of Malcolm X)* attracted wide attention after its publication in 1965. Malcolm X remained an influential figure in many black communities long after his death—as important and revered a symbol to some African Americans as Martin Luther King, Jr., was to others.

By the mid-1960s, the struggle against racial discrimination and oppression was challenging many of the assumptions that had formed the core of postwar American liberalism. The persistent evidence of urban poverty in northern cities raised questions about the distribution of American abundance and the effectiveness of reform programs. The increasing violence, both among those who resisted change and those who were impatient to create it, suggested that deep fissures existed, which could not easily be healed by a common commitment to liberal ideals. The growing emphasis on self-help and black separatism disturbed many liberals who continued to emphasize the importance of peaceful integration. These conflicts would only grow deeper as the 1960s wore on.

CHAPTER TWENTY-FOUR

From Flexible Response to Vietnam

~

I n international as much as in domestic affairs, the optimistic liberalism of the Kennedy and Johnson administrations dictated a positive, active approach to dealing with the nation's problems. And just as the new activism in domestic reform proved more difficult and divisive than liberals had imagined, so too did it create frustrations and failures in foreign policy. Both Kennedy and Johnson shared their predecessors' concern about communist expansionism. During the 1960s, the effort to stop it enmeshed the United States in a disastrous war in Vietnam that shook the nation's confidence in the Cold War and strained its social fabric.

COLD WAR CONFRONTATIONS

John Kennedy's inaugural address was a clear indication of how central opposition to communism was to his and the nation's thinking. "In the long history of the world," he proclaimed, "only a few generations have been granted the role of defending freedom in its hour of maximum danger. I do not shrink from this responsibility; I welcome it." Yet the speech—which, significantly, made no mention whatsoever of domestic affairs—was also an indication of Kennedy's belief that the United States was not doing enough to counter the communist threat; that it needed to be able to resist aggression in more flexible ways than the atomic weapons–oriented defense strategy of the Eisenhower years permitted.

Diversifying American Foreign Policy

Kennedy remained committed to the nation's atomic weapons program. Indeed, he ran for president criticizing the Eisenhower administration for allowing an imbalance of nuclear weapons (a "missile gap") to develop between the

United States and the Soviet Union. In fact, as Kennedy discovered even before the election, whatever missile gap there was favored the United States. But Kennedy insisted on proceeding with an expansion of the nation's atomic arsenal nevertheless—and the Soviet Union, which several years earlier had slowed the growth of its own nuclear weapons stockpile, responded in kind.

Kennedy's unhappiness with the Eisenhower foreign policy was not simply that it relied too heavily on nuclear weapons; it was also that it developed too few other tools for countering aggression. Kennedy argued for a new and more versatile approach to containment that became known as "flexible response." He claimed that the United States lacked the capacity to respond quickly to problems for which nuclear weapons were inappropriate solutions. In particular, he was not satisfied with the nation's ability to meet the communist threat in "emerging areas" of the Third World where the Soviet Union was supporting wars of national liberation. In 1959, the Soviet Union endorsed such wars as a means of achieving global communism. Kennedy, likewise, concluded that the Third World would be the arena in which the real struggle against communism would be waged in the future. He gave enthusiastic support to the expansion of "counterinsurgency" training, and took a great interest in the Special Forces, a small branch of the army created in the 1950s to wage guerrilla warfare in limited conflicts. Kennedy expanded the unit, allowed its members to wear distinctive headgear (from which the Special Forces drew the informal name "the Green Berets"), and gave them an elite status within the military they had never had before.

Kennedy also favored expanding American influence through peaceful means. To repair the badly deteriorating relationship with Latin America, he proposed an "Alliance for Progress": a series of projects undertaken cooperatively by the United States and Latin American governments for peaceful development and stabilization of the nations of that region. Its purpose was both to spur social and economic development and to inhibit the rise of Castro-like movements in other Central or South American countries. Kennedy also inaugurated the Agency for International Development (AID) to coordinate foreign aid. And he established what became one of his most popular innovations: the Peace Corps, which sent young American volunteers abroad to work in developing areas.

The Bay of Pigs Invasion

Among the first foreign policy ventures of the Kennedy administration was a disastrous assault on the Castro government in Cuba. The Eisenhower administration had launched the project; and by the time Kennedy took office, the CIA had been working for months in Central America to train a small army of anti-Castro Cuban exiles to invade Cuba and overthrow the Castro regime. The operation proceeded under an assumed veil of secrecy, although news leaks compromised the planned invasion almost from its beginning. Kennedy had misgivings about the project, but in one of his first actions as president he decided to proceed.

PEACE CORPS. Among the many young Americans who responded to President Kennedy's call to devote their energy and talent to service in the developing world was this Peace Corps volunteer. He is instructing children in a school in Africa. The Peace Corps was one of the most popular programs undertaken during the Kennedy administration. It seemed to many to encapsulate the youthful idealism of the early 1960s.

Kennedy had warned that "communist domination in this hemisphere can never be negotiated." He believed that Castro represented a threat to the stability of other Latin American nations. For these reasons, and others, he accepted the CIA's optimistic assessments of the chances for success and approved the invasion.

On April 17, 1961, 2,000 of the armed exiles landed at the Bay of Pigs in Cuba, expecting first American air support and than a spontaneous uprising by the Cuban people on their behalf. They received neither. An initial bombing raid, flown by a Cuban exile who was a CIA operative in a plane painted with Cuban insignia, tried but failed to cripple the Cuban air force. As the exiles landed at the Bay of Pigs, the CIA requested that American planes cover the invading forces. Here Kennedy held the line—he was adamant that U.S. forces not be involved directly in the invasion. (Air support would not likely have changed the result in any case.) Not only did the expected uprising not occur, but well-armed Castro forces easily surrounded and crushed the invaders. Near the final moment, Kennedy permitted a few navy jets, with their markings blacked out, to fly cover but it was too late. Within two days the entire mission had collapsed.

Kennedy somberly took public responsibility for the fiasco. "How could I have been so stupid?" Kennedy rhetorically asked more than one of his confidantes. The president vowed privately never again to accept at face value the reassurances of the Joint Chiefs of Staff when they reported on planned military operations. But he refused to rule out further measures against the Castro regime. "We do not intend to abandon Cuba to the communists," he said only three days after the Bay of Pigs. In fact, after the failed invasion, the Kennedy administration redoubled its efforts to develop a strategy for removing Castro from power. Among the ideas being discussed within the government were various plans for assassinating Castro.

Confrontations with Khrushchev

In the grim aftermath of the Bay of Pigs, Kennedy traveled to Vienna in June 1961 for his first meeting with Soviet Premier Nikita Khrushchev. Their frosty exchange of views did little to reduce tensions between the two nations, nor did Khrushchev's continuing irritation over the existence of a noncommunist West Berlin in the heart of East Germany. The two men talked openly about each nation's ability to destroy the other. Kennedy appeared stunned by Khrushchev's belligerence and what he believed was a dismissive attitude toward him personally. When asked later how the summit went, Kennedy replied dejectedly, "worst thing in my life. He savaged me." Kennedy took away from the summit a nagging worry that Khrushchev had sized him up as a man who did not have the "guts" to stand up to the Soviet Union. "We have to see what we can do that will restore a feeling in Moscow that we will defend our national interest," Kennedy confessed to a reporter after the summit. "I'll have to increase the defense budget. And we will have to confront them. The only place we can do that is in Vietnam. We have to send more people there."

For the moment, however, the focus was Berlin. In Vienna, Khrushchev had threatened war if the West did not abandon its defense of Berlin. Later in the summer, however, he settled on a less dangerous—but still highly provocative—approach to the problem. Particularly embarrassing to the communists was the mass exodus of residents of East Germany to the West through the easily traversed border in the center of Berlin. Before dawn on August 13, 1961, the Soviet Union stopped the exodus by directing East Germany to construct a wall between East and West Berlin. Guards fired on those who continued to try to escape. For nearly thirty years, the Berlin Wall stood as the most potent physical symbol of the conflict between the communist and non-communist worlds. Although American troops were deployed to West Berlin to show American determination to protect its freedom, and although Kennedy himself paid a dramatic and supportive visit to the city, there was little the United States could do to change the Soviet determination to wall off West Berlin.

Rising tensions with the Soviet Union culminated the following October in the most dangerous and dramatic crisis of the Cold War. During the summer of 1962, American intelligence agencies had become aware of the arrival of a new wave of Soviet technicians and equipment in Cuba and of military construction in progress. On October 14, aerial reconnaissance photos produced

THE BERLIN WALL–1961. Constructed to prevent the exodus of refugees from East Germany to the West, the Berlin Wall served for nearly thirty years as a symbol of political repression. In this photograph, taken in September 1961, an East German policeman helps build the wall even higher to prevent Germans on either side from glimpsing those in the opposite sector.

clear evidence that the Soviets were constructing sites on the island for offensive nuclear weapons. To the Soviets, placing missiles in Cuba probably seemed a reasonable, and relatively inexpensive, way to counter the presence of American missiles in Turkey (and a way to deter any future American invasion of Cuba). But to Kennedy and most other Americans, the missile sites represented an act of aggression by the Soviets toward the United States. Almost immediately, the president decided that the weapons could not be allowed to remain.

On October 22, after nearly a week of tense deliberations by a special task force in the White House, Kennedy ordered a naval and air blockade around Cuba, a "quarantine" against all offensive weapons. Soviet ships bound for the island slowed down or stopped before reaching the point of confrontation. But work on the missile sites continued. Preparations were under way for an American air attack on Cuba when, late in the evening of October 26, Kennedy received a message from Khrushchev implying that the Soviet Union would remove the missile bases in exchange for an American pledge not to invade Cuba. Ignoring other, tougher Soviet messages, the president agreed. Privately, he also promised to remove American missiles from Turkey, a decision he had reached months earlier but had not yet implemented. The crisis was over.

The Cuban missile crisis brought the world closer to nuclear war than at any time since World War II. Both the United States and the Soviet Union had been forced to confront the momentous potential consequences of their rivalry. In the following months, both seemed ready to move toward a new accommodation. In June 1963, President Kennedy spoke at American University in Washington, D.C., and seemed for the first time to offer hope for a peaceful rapprochement with the Soviet Union. The United States did not seek, Kennedy said, a "Pax Americana enforced on the world by American weapons of war." He went on to strike an unusual conciliatory cord. "If we cannot end now all our differences, at least we can help make the world safe for diversity." That same summer, the United States and the Soviet Union concluded years of negotiation by agreeing to a treaty to ban the testing of nuclear weapons in the atmosphere—the first step toward de-escalating the arms race since the beginning of the Cold War.

In the longer run, however, the missile crisis had more ominous consequences. The humiliating retreat the United States forced upon the Soviet leadership undermined the position of Nikita Khrushchev and contributed to his fall from power a year later. His replacement, Leonid Brezhnev, was a much more orthodox party figure, less interested in reform than Khrushchev had been. Perhaps more important, the graphic evidence the crisis gave the Soviets of their military inferiority helped produce a dramatic Soviet arms buildup over the next two decades, a buildup that contributed to a comparable increase in the United States in the early 1980s and that for a time undermined American support for a policy of rapproachement.

Johnson and Containment

Lyndon Johnson entered the presidency lacking even John Kennedy's limited prior experience with international affairs. He was eager, therefore, not only to continue the policies of his predecessor but to prove quickly that he, too, was a strong and forceful world leader. Johnson relied upon many of Kennedy's foreign policy advisers as he worked to put together his own administration. He strongly shared his predecessor's belief that it was imperative to prevent communist aggression.

An internal rebellion in the Dominican Republic gave Johnson an early opportunity to demonstrate his anticommunist convictions. A 1961 assassination had toppled the repressive dictatorship of General Rafael Trujillo Molina, and for the next four years various factions in the country had struggled for dominance. In the spring of 1965, a conservative military regime began to collapse in the face of a revolt by a broad range of groups on behalf of the nationalist reformer Juan Bosch, who had been elected president in 1962 and deposed by the military after only seven months in office. Arguing (without any evidence) that Bosch planned to establish a pro-Castro, communist regime, Johnson dispatched 30,000 American troops to quell the disorder. Only after a conservative candidate defeated Bosch in a 1966 election were the forces withdrawn.

From Johnson's first moments in office, however, his foreign policy was almost totally dominated by the bitter civil war in Vietnam and by the expanding involvement of the United States there. In many respects, Johnson was on this issue simply the unfortunate legatee of commitments initiated by his predecessors. But the determination of the new president and of others within his administration to prove their resolve in the battle against communism helped produce the final, decisive steps toward a full-scale commitment.

THE WARS FOR INDOCHINA

George Kennan, who helped devise the containment doctrine in whose name the United States went to war in Vietnam, once called the conflict "the most disastrous of all America's undertakings over the whole 200 years of its history." In retrospect, few would now disagree. Yet at first, the Vietnam War seemed simply one more Third World struggle on the periphery of the Cold War, a struggle in which the United States would try to tip the balance against communism without becoming too deeply or directly engaged. No president really decided to go to war in Vietnam. The American involvement there emerged, rather, from years of slowly increasing commitments that gradually and imperceptibly expanded.

The First Indochina War

Vietnam had a long history both as an independent kingdom and a major power in its region, and as a subjugated province of China; its people were both proud of their past glory and painfully aware of their many years of foreign domination. In the mid-nineteenth century, Vietnam became a colony of France. And, like other European possessions in Asia, it fell under the control of Japan during World War II. After the defeat of Japan, the question arose of what was to happen to Vietnam in the postwar world.

There were two opposing forces attempting to answer that question, both of them appealing to the United States for help. The French were seeking to reassert their control over Vietnam. Challenging them was a powerful nationalist movement within Vietnam committed to creating an independent nation. The nationalists were organized into a political party, the Vietminh, which had been created in 1941 and led ever since by Ho Chi Minh, a communist educated in Paris and Moscow, and a fervent Vietnamese nationalist.

The Vietminh had fought against Japan throughout World War II (unlike the French colonial officials, who had remained in Vietnam during the war as representatives of the Vichy regime and had collaborated with the Japanese). In the fall of 1945, after the collapse of Japan and before the western powers had time to return, the Vietminh declared Vietnam an independent nation and set up a nationalist government under Ho Chi Minh in Hanoi.

Ho had worked closely during the war with American intelligence forces in Indochina in fighting the Japanese; he apparently considered the United States something of an ally. When the war ended in 1945, he began writing President Truman asking for support in his struggle against the French. He received no reply to his letters, probably because no one in the State Department had heard of him. At the same time, Truman was under heavy pressure from both the British and the French to support France in its effort to reassert control over Vietnam. The French argued that without Vietnam, their domestic economy would collapse. Since the economic revival of western Europe was quickly becoming one of the Truman administration's top priorities, the United States did nothing to stop (although, at first, also relatively little to encourage) the French as they moved back into Vietnam in 1946 and began a struggle with the Vietminh to reestablish control over the country.

At first, the French had little difficulty reestablishing control. They drove Ho Chi Minh out of Hanoi and into hiding in the countryside; and in 1949, they established a nominally independent national government under the leadership of the former emperor, Bao Dai—an ineffectual, westernized playboy unable to assert any real independent authority. The real power remained in the hands of the French. But the Vietminh continued to challenge the French-dominated regime and slowly increased its control over large areas of the countryside. The French appealed to the United States for support; and in February 1950, the Truman administration formally recognized the Bao Dai regime and agreed to provide it with direct military and economic aid.

For the next four years, during what has become known as the First Indochina War, Truman and then Eisenhower continued to support the French military campaign against the Vietminh; by 1954, according to some calculations, the United States was paying eighty percent of France's war costs. But the war went badly for the French anyway. Finally, late in 1953, Vietminh forces engaged the French in a major battle in the far northwest corner of the country, in a valley at Dienbienphu, an isolated and almost indefensible site. The Vietminh succeeded in seizing the hills around a garrison the French had established in the valley in a futile effort to lure the Vietminh into the open. The French wound up surrounded and unable to resupply their forces. The battle turned into a prolonged and horrible siege, with the French position steadily deteriorating. It was at this point that the Eisenhower administration decided not to intervene to save the French. The defense of Dienbienphu collapsed and the French government decided the time had come to get out. The First Indochina War had come to an end.

Geneva and the Two Vietnams

An international conference at Geneva, planned many months before to settle the Korean dispute and other controversies, now took up the fate of Vietnam as well. The United States was only indirectly involved in this part of the Geneva Conference. Secretary of State Dulles, who did not really believe in negotiating with communists, reluctantly attended (described by one observer as a "puritan in a house of ill repute") but left early; the United States never signed the accords. Even so, the Geneva Conference produced an agreement to end the Vietnam conflict. There would be an immediate cease-fire in the war; Vietnam would be temporarily partitioned along the seventeenth parallel, with the Vietminh in control of North Vietnam, and a pro-western regime in control of the South. In 1956, there would be elections to reunite the country under a single government. In the interim, no new military forces were to be introduced into Vietnam; nor was either section of the country to form any military alliances.

The partition of Vietnam was, essentially, an artificial one. But there were important differences between North and South Vietnam. North Vietnam, the area now to be controlled by the Vietminh, was the heart of traditional Vietnamese society, the area where French influence had been the weakest. Hence the North had remained a reasonably stable, reasonably homogeneous culture, most of whose people lived in very close-knit, traditional villages. Northern Vietnam was also the poorest region of the country: overpopulated, plagued by serious maldistribution of scarce land, and hit by a serious famine at the end of the war. The Vietminh had worked effectively to alleviate the great famine and had won strong popular allegiance to the regime as a result. (Later, in the early 1950s, it launched a disastrous land reform policy, which it soon repudiated.) The Hanoi government was also strengthened by the mass exodus, in 1954, at the time of the partition, of many of the Catholics and others in the North who might have opposed them had they stayed. The North Vietnamese were passionately committed to the unification of the nation, a commitment that had deep roots in Vietnamese history.

South Vietnam, by contrast, was a much more recently settled area. Until the early nineteenth century, in fact, very few Vietnamese had lived there. Even in the 1950s, most of its people had been there only three generations or less. It had for many years been something like the American West in the nineteenth century—the place where adventurous, opportunistic, or disenchanted people from the poor, overpopulated North would move in search of a new beginning, and in search of land (which was scarce in the North but plentiful in the South). It was a looser, more heterogeneous, more individualistic society. It was highly factionalized—religiously, politically, and ethnically—with powerful sects (and even a powerful mafia) all competing for power. It was also more prosperous and fertile than the North. It was not overpopulated. It had experienced no famine. It was the only region of the country producing a surplus for export.

South Vietnam had no legacy of strong commitment to the Vietminh and a much less fervent commitment to national unification. It was the area where the influence of the French (their language, culture, and values) had been strongest and where there was a substantial, westernized middle class. It was, in other words, a society much more difficult to unite and to govern than the society of the North.

America and Diem

As soon as the Geneva Accords established the partition, the French finally left Vietnam altogether. The United States almost immediately stepped into the vacuum and became the principal benefactor of the new government in the South, led by Ngo Dinh Diem.

Diem was an aristocratic Catholic from central Vietnam, an outsider in the South. But he was also a nationalist, uncontaminated by collaboration with the French. And he was, for a time, successful. With the help of the American CIA, Diem waged a successful campaign against some of the powerful religious sects and the South Vietnamese mafia, which had challenged the authority of the central government. As a result, the United States came to regard Diem as a powerful and impressive alternative to Ho Chi Minh. Lyndon Johnson once called him the "Churchill of Southeast Asia."

The American government supported Diem's refusal in 1956 to permit the elections called for by the Geneva Accords, reasoning, almost certainly correctly, that Ho Chi Minh would easily win any such election. Ho could count on the entire vote of the North, with its much larger population, and at least some support in the South. The United States, in the meantime, poured military and economic aid into South Vietnam. By 1956, it was the second largest recipient of American military aid in the world, after Korea.

Diem's early successes in suppressing the sects in Vietnam led him in 1959 to begin a similar campaign to eliminate the Vietminh supporters who had stayed behind in the South after the partition. He was quite successful for a time, so successful in fact that the North Vietnamese found it necessary to respond. A new policy emanating from Moscow beginning in 1959, emphasizing wars of national liberation (as opposed to direct confrontations in Europe), also encouraged Ho Chi Minh to resume his armed struggle for national unification. In 1959, the Vietminh cadres in the South reorganized and created the National

Liberation Front (NLF), known to many Americans as the Viet Cong (a derogatory shorthand for Vietnamese Communists). The National Liberation Front was closely allied from the start with the North Vietnam government who, of course, supported its goals to overthrow the "puppet regime" of Diem and reunite the nation. In 1960, under orders from Hanoi, and with both material and manpower support from North Vietnam, the NLF began military operations in the South. This marked the beginning of the Second Indochina War.

By 1961, NLF forces were very successfully destabilizing the Diem regime. They were killing over 4,000 government officials a year (mostly village leaders) and establishing effective control over many areas of the countryside. Diem was also by now losing the support of many other groups in South Vietnam, and he was even losing support within his own military. In 1963, the Diem regime precipitated a major crisis by trying to discipline and repress the South Vietnamese Buddhists in an effort to make Catholicism the dominant religion of

BUDDHIST PROTESTS. To protest the repression of their religion by the Diem regime, Buddhist monks staged a series of demonstrations in South Vietnam. Here a Buddhist monk has immolated himself in the streets of downtown Saigon in June 1963—the first in a series of such self-immolations. Photographs and videotape of these gruesome protests were disseminated around the world and only sharpened the Kennedy administration's growing conviction that Diem could no longer be trusted to lead South Vietnam.

the country. The Buddhists began to stage enormous antigovernment demonstrations; and after Diem launched a series of heavy-handed military and police actions against them—which included several massacres of demonstrators and violent government raids on their sacred pagodas—the demonstrations grew much larger. Several Buddhist monks doused themselves with gasoline, sat cross-legged in the streets of downtown Saigon, and set themselves on fire—in view of photographers and television cameras.

The Buddhist crisis was alarming and embarrassing to the Kennedy administration and caused the American government to reconsider its commitment to Diem—although not to the survival of South Vietnam; Kennedy had greatly increased the number of American personnel and the level of American assistance to the anticommunist regime. American officials pressured Diem to reform his government, but Diem made no significant concessions. As a result, in the fall of 1963, Kennedy gave his tacit approval to a plot hatched by a group of South Vietnamese generals, with CIA encouragement, to topple Diem. In early November 1963, the generals staged the coup, assassinated Diem and his brother and principal advisor, Ngo Dinh Nhu (something the United States had not wanted or expected), and established the first of a series of new governments. But these regimes, were, for over three years, even less stable than Diem's. A few weeks after the coup, John Kennedy, too, was dead.

Intervention

Lyndon Johnson, therefore, inherited what was already a substantial American commitment to the survival of an anticommunist South Vietnam. During his first two years in office, he expanded that commitment into a full-scale American war. Why he did so has long been a subject of debate.

Many factors played a role in Johnson's fateful decision. But the most obvious explanation is that the new president faced many pressures to expand the American involvement and only a very few to limit it. As the untested successor to a revered and martyred president, he felt obliged to prove his worthiness for the office by continuing the policies of his predecessor. Aid to South Vietnam had been one of the most prominent of those policies. Johnson also felt it necessary to retain in his administration many of the important figures of the Kennedy years. In doing so, he surrounded himself with a group of foreign policy advisers—Secretary of State Dean Rusk, Secretary of Defense Robert McNamara, National Security Adviser McGeorge Bundy, and others—who believed not only that the United States had an obligation to resist communism in Vietnam but that it possessed the ability and resources to make that resistance successful. A compliant Congress raised little protest to, and indeed at one point openly endorsed, Johnson's use of executive powers to lead the nation into war. And for several years at least, public opinion remained firmly behind him—in part because Barry Goldwater's bellicose remarks about the war during the 1964 campaign made Johnson seem by comparison to be a moderate on the issue.

The War in Vietnam and Indochina, 1964–1975

CHINA

Lao Cai

Than Uyen

Red River

Yen Bay

BURMA

Dienbienphu

NORTH VIETNAM

Hanoi

Red River Delta

Haiphong

Pak Seng

Luang Prabang

Ban Ban

Plain of Jars

Vang Vieng

L A O S

Vinh

Gulf of Tonkin

Hainan

Vientiane

Mekong River

Udon Thani

Phanom

Dong Hoi

Partition Line 1954

Vinh Linh

DMZ (Demilitarized Zone)

QUANG TRI PROVINCE

Khesanh

Hue

Phu Bai

Da Nang

Hoi An

Tamky

Chulai

My Lai

Quang Ngai

Dak To

THAILAND

Takhli

Don Muang

Lop Buri

Udon Ratchathani

Ratchasima

FRIENDSHIP HIGHWAY

Kontum

Pleiku

Ankhe

Plateau of Kontum

Quinhon

South China Sea

Bangkok

Angkor Wat

Battambang

Tonle Sap

CAMBODIA

Mekong River

Plateau of Darlac

Ban Me Thout

Sattahip

Nhatrang

Da Lat

Camranh Bay

Kompong Cham

Bo Duc

SOUTH VIETNAM

Phanrang

Phnom Penh

1970: U.S. and South Vietnam troops entered Viet Cong strongholds inside Cambodia

Prey Veng

Tay Ninh

Ben Cat

Gulf of Thailand

Sihanoukville

Tan Son Nhut Airbase

Bienhua

Saigon

Vung Tau

Rach Gia

Cantho

Quan Long

Mekong Delta

Ca Mau Peninsula

Con Son

| 0 | | 150 Miles |
| 0 | | 150 Kilometers |

■ U.S. bases

⬅ U.S. and South Vietnam invasion of Cambodia

← Ho Chi Minh Trail (communist supply route)

LYNDON JOHNSON AND ROBERT MCNAMARA. LBJ inherited the Vietnam War from his predecessors, and he relied especially upon advice from former Kennedy advisers such as Robert McNamara in determining how to proceed. As secretary of defense, McNamara played an important role in shaping the military effort in Vietnam. Here the strain shows in Johnson's face as he is briefed by McNamara in 1964.

Above all, intervention in South Vietnam was fully consistent with nearly twenty years of American foreign policy. An anticommunist ally was appealing to the United States for assistance; all the assumptions of the containment doctrine, as it had come to be defined by the 1960s, seemed to require the nation to oblige. Vietnam, Johnson believed, was a test of American willingness to fight communist aggression, a test he was determined not to fail. He was also acutely aware of the political costs a president who wavered in the face of communism might sustain. He was determined to ensure that his domestic agenda would not be jeopardized by critics who might pounce upon any show of weakness, particularly in the contested sphere of anticommunism.

During his first months in office, Johnson expanded the American involvement in Vietnam only slightly, sending an additional 5,000 military advisers there and preparing to send 5,000 more. Then, early in August 1964, the president announced that American destroyers on patrol in international waters in the Gulf of Tonkin had been attacked without provocation by North Vietnamese torpedo boats. Later information raised serious doubts as to whether the administration reported the attacks accurately. At the time, however, virtually no one questioned Johnson's portrayal of the incident as a serious act of aggression or his insistence that the United States must respond. By a vote of 416 to zero in the House and eighty-eight to two in the Senate, Congress hurriedly passed the Gulf of Tonkin Resolution, which authorized the president to "take all necessary measures" to protect American forces and "prevent further aggression" in Southeast Asia. The resolution became, in Johnson's view at least, an open-ended legal authorization for escalation of the conflict.

With the South Vietnamese leadership still in disarray, more and more of the burden of opposing the Viet Cong fell on the United States. In February 1965, seven marines died when communist forces attacked an American military base at Pleiku. Johnson retaliated by ordering American bombings of the North, which attempted to destroy the depots and transportation lines responsible for the flow of North Vietnamese soldiers and supplies into South Vietnam. The bombing continued intermittently until 1972. These bombing raids provided the rationale for introducing American ground forces into Vietnam. Military advisers warned the president that the bombing raids might well lead the Viet Cong to retaliate against the air bases from which the missions were flown. For this reason, initially, Johnson approved the introduction of troops to Vietnam. And in March 1965, two battalions of American marines landed at Da Nang in South Vietnam. There were now more than 100,000 American troops in Vietnam.

Four months later, the president finally admitted that the character of the war had changed. American soldiers would now, he announced, begin playing an active combat role in the conflict. By the end of the year, there were more than 180,000 American combat troops in Vietnam; in 1966, that number doubled; and by the end of 1967, there were over 500,000 American soldiers there—along with considerable civilian personnel working in various capacities and many American women (some enlisted, some not) who worked as nurses in military hospitals. In the meantime, the air war had intensified until the tonnage of bombs dropped on North Vietnam ultimately exceeded that in all theaters during World War II. And American casualties were mounting. In 1961, fourteen Americans had died in Vietnam. By the spring of 1966, more than 4,000 Americans had been killed.

Yet the gains resulting from the carnage were negligible. The United States had finally succeeded in 1965 in creating a reasonably stable government in the South under General Nguyen Van Thieu. But the new regime was hardly less corrupt or brutal than its predecessors, and no more able than they to establish its authority in its own countryside. The Viet Cong, not the Thieu regime, controlled the majority of South Vietnam's villages and hamlets.

The Quagmire

For more than seven years, American combat forces remained bogged down in a war that the United States was never able either to win or fully to understand. Combating a foe whose strength lay less in weaponry than in its infiltration of the population, the United States responded with heavy-handed technological warfare designed for conventional battles against conventional armies. American forces succeeded in winning most of the major battles in which they became engaged. Astounding (if not always reliable) casualty figures showed that far more communists than Americans were dying in combat. A continuous stream of optimistic reports poured forth from American military commanders, government officials, and others—including the famous statement of Secretary of Defense McNamara that he could see "the light at the end of the tunnel." But if the war was not actually being lost, neither was it being won.

Central to the American war effort was a commitment to what the military called "attrition," a strategy premised on the belief that the United States could inflict so many casualties and so much damage on the enemy that eventually they would be unable and unwilling to continue the struggle. But the attrition strategy failed because the North Vietnamese proved willing to commit many more

BOMBING CAMPAIGNS. Phantom jets drop a rain of bombs on North Vietnam in an effort to cripple Hanoi's capacity to wage war, prevent the movement of enemy supplies into South Vietnam along the Ho Chi Minh Trail, and persuade North Vietnam it could not win against the United States' superior military hardware and technology. In the end, although the bombing inflicted extensive damage, it did not succeed in defeating or demoralizing the North Vietnamese.

soldiers to the conflict than the United States had expected (and many more than America was willing to send).

It failed, too, because the United States relied heavily on its bombing of the North to eliminate the communists' warmaking capacity. American bombers struck at strategic targets in North Vietnam to weaken the material capacity of the communists to continue the war (factories, bridges, railroads, shipyards, oil storage facilities, depots, etc.); and they bombed jungle areas of Vietnam, Laos, and Cambodia to cut off the "Ho Chi Minh Trail," the infiltration routes by which Hanoi sent troops and supplies into the South. In addition, the Americans hoped bombing would weaken the will of North Vietnam to continue the war.

By the end of 1967, virtually every identifiable target of any strategic importance in North Vietnam had been destroyed. The bombing badly damaged the North Vietnamese economy, killed many soldiers and civilians, and made life difficult for those who survived. But it produced few of the effects that the United States had intended. North Vietnam was not a modern, industrial society; it did not have many of the sorts of targets that bombing is effective against. And in any case, the North Vietnamese responded to the air raids with enormous ingenuity: they created a great network of underground tunnels, shops, and factories. They also secured increased aid from the Soviet Union and China. Infiltration of the South was unaffected; the North Vietnamese just kept moving the Ho Chi Minh Trail. Nor did the bombing weaken North Vietnam's will to continue fighting. On the contrary, it seemed to increase the nation's resolve and strengthen its hatred of the United States. As one North Vietnamese leader later explained: "There was extraordinary fervor then. The Americans thought that the more bombs they dropped, the quicker we would fall to our knees and surrender. But the bombs heightened rather than dampened our spirit."

Another crucial part of the American strategy was the "pacification" program, whose purpose was to push the Viet Cong from particular regions and then "pacify" those regions by winning the "hearts and minds" of the people. Routing the Viet Cong was often possible, but the subsequent pacification proved more difficult. American forces appeared unable to establish the same kind of rapport with provincial Vietnamese that the Viet Cong had created; and the American military never gave that part of the program a very high priority in any case. Gradually, the pacification program gave way to the more heavy-handed relocation strategy, through which American troops uprooted villagers from their homes, sent them fleeing to refugee camps or into the cities (producing by 1967 more than 3 million refugees), and then destroyed the vacated villages and surrounding countryside. Saturation bombings (using conventional weapons), bulldozing settlements, chemically defoliating fields and jungles, and burning areas with napalm—were all tactics designed to eliminate possible Viet Cong sanctuaries. But the Viet Cong responded by moving to new sanctuaries elsewhere. The futility of the United States' effort was suggested by the statement of an American officer after flattening one such hamlet: it had been "necessary to destroy [the village] in order to save it."

As the war dragged on and victory remained elusive, some American officers and officials began to urge the president to expand the military efforts. Some argued for heavier bombing and increased troop strength; others insisted that the United States attack communist enclaves in surrounding countries; a few began to urge the use of nuclear weapons. The Johnson administration, however, resisted. Unwilling to abandon its commitment to South Vietnam for fear of destroying American "credibility" in the world, the government was also unwilling to expand the war too far, for fear of provoking direct intervention by the Chinese, the Soviets, or both. In the meantime, the president began to encounter additional obstacles and frustrations at home.

The Antiwar Movement

Few Americans, and even fewer influential ones, protested American involvement in Vietnam as late as the end of 1965. But as the war dragged on and its futility began to become apparent, political support for it began to erode. A series of "teach-ins" on university campuses, beginning at the University of Michigan in 1965, sparked a national debate over the war before such debate developed inside the government itself. Such pacifist organizations as the American Friends Service Committee and the Women's International League for Peace and Free-

ANTIWAR MARCH–1967. By 1967, protests against American involvement in the Vietnam War were growing. This demonstrator taunts a military policeman who is guarding the Pentagon during a massive antiwar march in Washington.

dom organized early protests. By the end of 1967, American students opposed to the war had become a significant political force. Enormous peace marches in New York, Washington, D.C., and other cities drew broad public attention to the antiwar movement. In the meantime, a growing number of journalists, particularly reporters who had spent time in Vietnam, helped sustain the movement with their frank revelations about the brutality and apparent futility of the war.

The growing chorus of popular protest soon was joined by opposition to the war from within the government. Senator J. William Fulbright of Arkansas, chairman of the powerful Senate Foreign Relations Committee, turned against the war and in January 1966 began to stage highly publicized and occasionally televised congressional hearings to air criticisms of it. Distinguished figures such as George F. Kennan and retired general James Gavin testified against the conflict, giving opposition to the war respectability in the minds of many Americans generally unwilling to question the government or the military. Other members of Congress joined Fulbright in opposing Johnson's policies—including, in 1967, Robert F. Kennedy, brother of the slain president, now a senator from New York. Even within the administration, the consensus seemed to be crumbling. Robert McNamara, who had done much to help extend the American involvement in Vietnam, quietly left the government, disillusioned, in 1968. His successor as secretary of defense, Clark Clifford, became a quiet but powerful voice within the administration on behalf of a cautious scaling down of the commitment.

In the meantime, the American economy began to suffer. Johnson's commitment to fighting the war while continuing his Great Society reforms—his promise of "guns and butter"—proved impossible to maintain. The inflation rate, which had remained at two percent through most of the early 1960s, rose to three percent in 1967, four percent in 1968, and six percent in 1969. In August 1967, Johnson asked Congress for a tax increase—a ten percent surcharge, widely labeled a "war tax"—which he knew was necessary if the nation was to avoid even more ruinous inflation. In return, congressional conservatives demanded and received a $6 billion reduction in the funding for Great Society programs.

By now it had become apparent that Vietnam was proving to be far costlier—in dollars, lives, and political capital—than anyone had anticipated. At home, dissent frayed the shared values so critical to the triumph of American liberalism. Even vociferous defenders of the president watched with dismay as his political support crumbled. The growing militancy of the antiwar movement created deep divisions, often generational, among many groups of Americans. In 1968, these divisions, and others, would erupt.

CHAPTER TWENTY-FIVE

Cultural Revolutions

~

The liberalism of the early 1960s rested on a series of optimistic assumptions about America's resources and about the essential stability of its society. The architects of the New Frontier and the Great Society, and the millions of Americans who supported their work, believed that rapid economic growth was now the normal condition of society. They believed that purposeful government action could erase poverty and solve social problems without creating serious conflict or requiring substantial sacrifice. They believed that most Americans embraced a shared set of social and cultural values, and that extending rights and freedoms to previously excluded groups would bring those groups into the national consensus.

By the late 1960s, all of those assumptions were in disarray. The American people were entering a period of profound change and unprecedented turmoil, and it may not be too much to say that the United States was in the throes of a series of cultural revolutions. The nation's political and economic institutions survived the turbulence of these years relatively unscathed. But American society and American culture were transformed.

THE TRAUMAS OF 1968

By the end of 1967, the twin crises of the war in Vietnam and the deteriorating racial situation at home, crises that fed upon and inflamed each other, had already unsettled American life. In the course of 1968, the tensions they had created suddenly burst to the surface and threatened the nation with chaos. Not since World War II had the United States experienced so profound a sense of crisis.

The Tet Offensive

On January 31, 1968, the first day of the Vietnamese New Year (Tet), communist forces launched an enormous, concerted attack on American strongholds
throughout South Vietnam. A few cities, most notably Hue, fell to the communists. Others suffered major disruptions. But in the end, the communists suffered
serious defeats in most of their engagements with the Americans. What made
the Tet Offensive so shocking to the American people, however, was the fierce
fighting of an enemy the American military command had said was weakening.

TET OFFENSIVE. Two American soldiers lie dead under a tarp
in the U.S. Embassy compound in Saigon on January 31,
1968. For several hours, the Embassy itself became a
battleground when Viet Cong guerrillas attacked the most
visible symbol of the American presence in South Vietnam as
well as outlying cities and towns. Although American military
forces eventually subdued the enemy, the surprise attack by
the Viet Cong undermined confidence among Americans that
the U.S. was really winning the war.

Through much of the Tet Offensive the nation witnessed on television the jarring sight of communist forces in the heart of Saigon, setting off bombs, shooting South Vietnamese officials and troops, and holding down fortified areas (including, briefly, the grounds of the American embassy).

The Tet Offensive also dramatized for the American public the brutality of the war in Vietnam. In the midst of the fighting, television cameras recorded the sight of a captured Viet Cong soldier being led up to a South Vietnamese officer in the streets of Saigon. Without a word, the officer pulled out his pistol and shot the young man in the head at point blank range, leaving him lying dead in the street, his blood pouring onto the pavement. It may be that no single event did more to undermine support for the war in the United States.

American forces soon dislodged the Viet Cong from most of the positions they had seized. Indeed, the Tet Offensive cost the communists such appalling casualties that they were significantly weakened for months to come. Tet would permanently deplete the ranks of the NLF and force North Vietnamese troops to take on a much larger share of the subsequent fighting. But all that had little impact on American opinion. Tet may have been a military victory for the United States; but it was a political defeat for the administration, a defeat from which it would never fully recover.

In the following weeks, opposition to the war grew substantially. Leading newspapers and magazines, television commentators, and mainstream politicians began taking public stands in favor of de-escalation of the conflict. Within weeks of the Tet Offensive, public opposition to the war had almost doubled. And Johnson's personal popularity rating slid to thirty-five percent, the lowest of any president since Harry Truman.

"Dumping" Johnson

Beginning in the summer of 1967, dissident Democrats (led by the talented activist Allard Lowenstein) tried to mobilize support behind an antiwar candidate who would challenge Lyndon Johnson in the 1968 primaries. When Robert Kennedy declined their invitation, they turned to Senator Eugene McCarthy of Minnesota. A brilliantly orchestrated campaign by Lowenstein and thousands of young volunteers in the New Hampshire primary produced a startling showing by McCarthy in March; he nearly defeated the president.

A few days later, Robert Kennedy finally entered the campaign, embittering many McCarthy supporters, but bringing his own substantial strength among African Americans, poor people, and workers to the antiwar cause. Polls showed the president trailing badly in Wisconsin, the next scheduled primary. Indeed, public animosity toward the president was now so intense that Johnson did not even dare to leave the White House to campaign. On March 31, he went on television to announce a limited halt in the bombing of North Vietnam—his first major concession to the antiwar forces—and, much more surprising, his withdrawal from the presidential contest.

For a moment, it seemed as though the antiwar forces had won. Robert Kennedy quickly established himself as the champion of the Democratic primaries, winning one election after another. In the meantime, however, Vice President Hubert Humphrey, with the support of President Johnson, entered the contest and began to attract the support of party leaders and of the many delegations that were selected not by popular primaries but by state party organizations. He soon appeared to be the front runner in the race.

The King and Kennedy Assassinations

In the midst of this bitter political battle, in which the war had been the dominant issue, attention turned suddenly back to the nation's enduring racial conflicts. On April 4, Martin Luther King, Jr., who had traveled to Memphis, Tennessee, to lend his support to striking black sanitation workers in the city, was shot and killed while standing on the balcony of his motel. The assassin, James Earl Ray, who was captured days later in London, had no apparent motive. Later evidence suggested that he had been hired by others to do the killing, but he never revealed the identity of his employers.

King's tragic death produced an outpouring of grief matched in recent memory only by the reaction to the death of John Kennedy. Among many African Americans, it also produced anger. In the days after the assassination, major riots broke out in more than sixty American cities. Forty-three people died; more than 3,000 suffered injuries; as many as 27,000 people were arrested.

In the midst of grief and turmoil, Robert Kennedy continued his campaign for the presidential nomination, raising the hopes of the many who believed he could heal some of the divisions in the nation. Late on the night of June 6, he appeared in the ballroom of a Los Angeles hotel to acknowledge his victory in that day's California primary. As he left the ballroom after his victory statement, Sirhan Sirhan, a young Palestinian apparently enraged by Kennedy's pro-Israel views, emerged from a crowd and shot him in the head. Early the next morning, Kennedy died.

By the time of his death, Robert Kennedy—who earlier in his career had been widely considered a cold, ruthless agent of his more attractive brother—had emerged as a figure of enormous popular appeal. More than John Kennedy, Robert identified his hopes with the American "dispossessed"—with African Americans, Hispanics, Native Americans, the poor—and with the many American liberals who were coming to believe that the problems of such groups demanded attention. Indeed, Robert Kennedy, much more than John, shaped what some would later call the "Kennedy legacy," a set of ideas that would for a time become central to American liberalism: the fervent commitment to using government to help the powerless. In addition, Robert had an impassioned following among many people who saw in him (and his family) the kind of glamour and hopefulness they had come, at least in retrospect, to identify with the martyred president. His campaign appearances inspired outbursts of public enthusiasm rarely seen in political life. The passions Kennedy aroused made his violent

ROBERT KENNEDY. Two weeks before his assassination, Robert Kennedy campaigns in California. The New York senator, and brother of the slain president, attracted adoring crowds throughout this last campaign. As he stood in this open car, he was virtually unprotected from potential assailants. Shortly after declaring his victory in the primary, Senator Kennedy was shot in the head by Sirhan Sirhan, a Palestinian enraged by Kennedy's pro-Israeli views on foreign policy. He died the following day.

death a particularly shattering experience for many Americans. The assassination helped spark a searching debate about violence in American society—why it occurred, how it could be stopped, what it said about the nation.

Chicago

Meanwhile, the presidential campaign continued gloomily during the last weeks before the convention. Hubert Humphrey, who had seemed likely to win the nomination even before Robert Kennedy's death, now faced only minor opposition—despite the embittered claims of many Democrats that Humphrey would simply continue the bankrupt policies of the Johnson administration. The approaching Democratic Convention, therefore, began to take on the appearance of an exercise in futility; and antiwar activists, despairing of winning any victories within the convention, began to plan major demonstrations outside it.

When the Democrats finally gathered in Chicago in August, even the most optimistic observers predicted a turbulent convention. Inside the hall, delegates bitterly debated an antiwar plank in the party platform that both Kennedy and

McCarthy supporters favored. Miles away, in a downtown park, thousands of antiwar protesters staged demonstrations. On the third night of the convention, as the delegates began their balloting on the now virtually inevitable nomination of Hubert Humphrey, demonstrators and police clashed in a bloody riot in the streets of Chicago. Hundreds of protesters were injured as police attempted to disperse them with tear gas and billy clubs. Aware that the violence was being televised to the nation, the demonstrators taunted the authorities with the chant, "The whole world is watching!" And Hubert Humphrey, who had spent years dreaming of becoming his party's candidate for president, received a nomination that appeared at the time to be almost worthless.

The Conservative Reaction

The turbulent events of 1968 persuaded many observers that American society was in the throes of revolutionary change. In fact, however, the response of most Americans to the turmoil was a conservative one.

The most visible sign of the conservative backlash was the surprising success of the campaign of George Wallace for the presidency. Wallace had established himself in 1963 as one of the nation's leading spokesmen for the defense of segregation when, as governor of Alabama, he had attempted to block the admission of black students to the University of Alabama. In 1964, he had run in a few Democratic presidential primaries and had done surprisingly well, even in several states outside the South. In 1968, after again running in several Democratic primaries and again showing striking strength, he became a third party candidate for president, basing his campaign on a host of conservative grievances, only some connected to race. He denounced the forced busing of students, the proliferation of government regulations and social programs, and the permissiveness of authorities toward race riots and antiwar demonstrations. There was never any serious chance that Wallace would win the election; but his standing in the polls rose at times to over twenty percent.

A more effective effort to mobilize the "silent majority" in favor of order and stability was under way within the Republican party. Richard Nixon, whose political career had seemed at an end after his losses in the presidential race of 1960 and a California gubernatorial campaign two years later, re-emerged as the preeminent spokesman for what he called "Middle America." Nixon recognized that many Americans were tired of hearing about their obligations to the poor, tired of hearing about the sacrifices necessary to achieve racial justice, tired of judicial reforms that seemed designed to help criminals. By offering a vision of stability, law and order, government retrenchment, and "peace with honor" in Vietnam, he easily captured the nomination of his party for the presidency. And after the spectacle of the Democratic Convention, he enjoyed a commanding lead in the polls as the November election approached.

That lead diminished greatly in the last weeks before the voting. Old doubts about Nixon's character continued to haunt the Republican candidate. A skillful

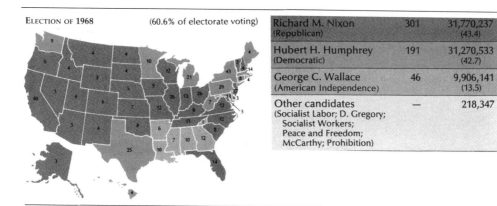

ELECTION OF 1968 (60.6% of electorate voting)		
Richard M. Nixon (Republican)	301	31,770,237 (43.4)
Hubert H. Humphrey (Democratic)	191	31,270,533 (42.7)
George C. Wallace (American Independence)	46	9,906,141 (13.5)
Other candidates (Socialist Labor; D. Gregory; Socialist Workers; Peace and Freedom; McCarthy; Prohibition)	—	218,347

last-minute surge by Hubert Humphrey, who managed to restore a tenuous unity to the Democratic party, narrowed the gap further. And the Wallace campaign appeared to be hurting the Republicans more than the Democrats. In the end, however, Nixon eked out a victory almost as narrow as his defeat in 1960. He received 43.4 percent of the popular vote to Humphrey's 42.7 percent (a margin of only about 500,000 votes), and 301 electoral votes to Humphrey's 191. George Wallace, who like most third-party candidates faded in the last weeks of the campaign, still managed to poll 13.5 percent of the popular vote and to carry five southern states with a total of forty-six electoral ballots—the best showing by a third party candidate since the 1920s. Nixon had hardly won a decisive personal mandate. But the election made clear that a majority of the American electorate was more interested in restoring stability than in promoting social change.

THE CRISIS OF AUTHORITY

The election of Richard Nixon in 1968 was the result of more than the unpopularity of Lyndon Johnson and the war. It was the result, too, of a strong public reaction against what many Americans considered a frontal assault on the foundations of their culture. Throughout the late 1960s and early 1970s, new interest groups were mobilizing to demand protections and benefits. New values and assumptions were emerging to challenge traditional patterns of thought and behavior. The United States was in the throes, some believed, of a genuine cultural revolution.

Some Americans welcomed the changes. But many—a clear majority, it seemed, on the basis of the 1968 election returns—feared them. There was growing resentment of the attention directed toward minorities and the poor, of the federal social programs that were funneling billions of dollars into the inner cities, of the increasing tax burden on the middle class, and of the "hippies" and radicals who were dominating public discourse with their bitter critiques of middle-class values. It was time, many men and women believed, for a restoration of stability and a relegitimization of traditional centers of authority.

In Richard Nixon, many Americans found a man who seemed perfectly to match their mood. Himself a product of a hard-working, middle-class family, Nixon had risen to prominence on the basis of his own unrelenting efforts; he projected an image of stern dedication to traditional values. Yet the presidency of Richard Nixon, far from returning calm and stability to American politics, coincided with, and in many ways helped to produce, more years of crisis.

What was perhaps most alarming to conservative Americans in the 1960s and 1970s was a pattern of social and cultural protest that was emerging from people, especially in the younger generation, who gave vent to two related impulses. One impulse, emerging from the political left, sought to create a new active community of the people that would rise up to break the power of elites—the "establishment"—and force the nation to end the war, pursue racial and economic justice, and transform its political life. The other, at least equally powerful, impulse appeared related to, but not entirely compatible with, the first: the vision of individual "liberation." It found expression in part through the efforts of particular groups—African Americans, Native Americans, Hispanics, women, homosexuals, and others—to define a place for themselves within the larger society. It also found expression through attempts to create a new culture—one that would permit escape from what some considered the dehumanizing pressures of modern "technocracy."

The New Left

In retrospect, it seems unsurprising that young Americans became so assertive and powerful in American culture and politics in the 1960s. The postwar baby-boom generation, the unprecedented number of people born in a few years during and just after World War II, was growing up. By 1970, more than half the American population was under thirty years old, and over eight million Americans (eight times the number in 1950) were attending college. This was the largest generation of youth in American history, one that came of age in a time of unprecedented affluence and opportunity. Young people are always more likely than their elders to challenge the existing order. And while relatively few young Americans embraced radical political causes or rebelled in any fundamental way against their culture in the 1960s, those who did were numerous enough, and assertive enough, to have a powerful impact on the nation's cultural and political climate.

The radicalization of many American young people was apparent in the rise of the New Left—a large, diverse group of men and women (many, but not all, of whom were students) energized by the polarizing developments of their time to challenge the political system. The New Left embraced the cause of African Americans and other minorities, but its own ranks consisted overwhelmingly of white Americans.

The New Left emerged from many sources. Some of its members were the children of radical parents (members of the so-called "Old Left" of the 1930s and 1940s) and grew up with an activist perspective on society and politics. Indeed, the New Left drew considerable support, and guidance, from groups and individuals from the Old Left; it was not as entirely "new" as its champions liked to claim. The New Left drew as well from the writings of some of the important social critics of the 1950s—among them C. Wright Mills, a sociologist at Columbia University who wrote a series of scathing and brilliant critiques of modern bureaucracies. And while relatively few members of the New Left were communists, many were drawn to the writings of Karl Marx and such other Marxist theorists as Antonio Gramsci and Herbert Marcuse. Some came to revere Third World Marxists such as Che Guevara, Mao Zedong, and Ho Chi Minh. For a while, left-leaning figures in the labor movement helped nurture the New Left—although relations between the two movements soon deteriorated.

But the New Left drew from nothing so much as the civil rights movement, in which many idealistic young white Americans had become involved in the early 1960s. Racism, oppression, and violence were nothing new to the many African Americans fighting for civil rights. But to white college students from middle-class backgrounds, the exposure to social injustice (and personal danger) in the South was shocking and disillusioning. It led many of them to question their assumptions about the basic values and institutions of American life. Within a few years, some white civil rights activists were beginning to consider broader political commitments.

In 1962, a group of college students gathered in Michigan (at a conference center owned by the United Auto Workers) to form an organization to give voice to their demands: Students for a Democratic Society (SDS). Their declaration of beliefs, the Port Huron Statement, expressed their disillusionment with the society they had inherited and their determination to build a new politics. "Many of us began maturing in complacency," the statement (most of it the work of student activist Tom Hayden) declared. "As we grew, however, our comfort was penetrated by events too troubling to dismiss." In the following years, SDS became the principal organization of student radicalism.

Some members of SDS moved into inner-city neighborhoods and tried for a time to mobilize poor and working-class people politically. But most members of the New Left were students, and over time they came to focus their radicalism on the modern university. One early indication of this emphasis was a 1964 dispute at the University of California at Berkeley over the rights of students to engage in political activities on campus. The Free Speech Movement, as it called itself, created turmoil at Berkeley, as students challenged campus police, occupied administrative offices, and produced a strike in which nearly three quarters of Berkeley students participated. The immediate issue focused on the right of students to pass out literature and recruit volunteers for political causes on campus. But the protest quickly evolved into a more basic critique of the university, and the society it seemed to represent. Mario Savio, a Berkeley graduate student and one of the leaders of the Free Speech Movement, captured something of the political anguish in a famous speech on campus, in which he said:

> There is a time when the operation of the machine becomes so odious, makes you so sick at heart, that you can't take part; you can't even passively take part, and you've got to put your bodies upon the gears and upon the wheels, upon the levers, upon all the apparatus and you've got to make it stop. And you've got to indicate to the people who run it, to the people who own it, that unless you're free, the machine will be prevented from working at all.

The revolt at Berkeley was the first outburst of what was to be nearly a decade of campus turmoil.

Students at Berkeley and elsewhere protested the impersonal character of the modern university. But their criticism also sought to expose the connections between academic institutions and the federal government. In particular, the university became for many activists a microcosm of many of the ills that existed in American society, most notably what they considered its corrupt and immoral public policies. The antiwar movement greatly inflamed the challenge to the universities and turned its focus to the ways in which they were complicit in the war in Vietnam: by having Reserve Officer Training Corps (ROTC) programs, by conducting research for the Defense Department, by facilitating the recruitment of students to work after graduation for companies engaged in producing arms and napalm.

Beginning in 1968, campus demonstrations, riots, and building seizures became almost commonplace. At Columbia University in New York, students seized the offices of the president and other members of the administration and faculty and occupied them for several days until local police forcibly (and violently) ejected them. Harvard University had a similarly violent experience a year later. Also in 1969, Berkeley became the scene of perhaps the most prolonged and traumatic conflict of any American college campus in the 1960s: a battle over the efforts of a few students to build a "People's Park" on land the university planned to use to build a parking garage.

This seemingly minor event precipitated weeks of impassioned and often violent conflicts between the university administration and its students and between students and police. By the end of the People's Park battle, which lasted for more than a week, the Berkeley campus was completely polarized; even students who had not initially supported or even noticed the People's Park (the great majority) were by the end committed to its defense; eighty-five percent of the 15,000 students who participated in a referendum voted to leave the park alone. Student radicals, for the first time, won large audiences for their heated rhetoric linking together university administrators, the police, and the larger political and economic system, describing them all as part of one, united, oppressive force. As one Berkeley activist said in the midst of the battle: "You've pushed us to the end of your civilization here, against the sea in Berkeley. Then you pushed us into a square-block area called People's Park. It was the last thing we had to defend, this square block of sanity amid all your madness. . . . We are now homeless in your civilized world. We have become the great American gypsies, with only our mythology for a culture." Over the next several years, hardly any major university was immune to some level of disruption. Small groups of especially dogmatic radicals—among them the "Weathermen," a violent offshoot of SDS—were responsible for a few cases of arson and bombing that destroyed campus buildings and claimed several lives.

Not many people ever accepted the radical political views that lay at the heart of the New Left. But many supported the position of SDS and other groups on particular issues, and above all on the Vietnam War. Between 1967 and 1969, student radicals organized some of the largest political demonstrations in American history. The march on the Pentagon of October 1967, where demonstrators were met by a solid line of armed troops; the "spring mobilization" of April 1968, which attracted hundreds of thousands of demonstrators in cities around the country; the Vietnam "moratorium" of the fall of 1969, during which millions of opponents of the war gathered in major rallies across the nation; and countless other demonstrations, large and small—all helped thrust the issue of the war into the center of American politics.

Closely related to opposition to the war—and another issue that helped fuel the New Left—was opposition to the military draft. The gradual abolition of many traditional deferments—for graduate students, teachers, husbands, fathers, and others—swelled the ranks of those faced with conscription (and thus likely to oppose it). Draft card burnings became common features of antiwar rallies on college campuses. Many draft-age Americans simply refused induction, accepting what were occasionally long terms in jail as a result. Thousands of others fled to Canada, Sweden, and elsewhere (where they were joined by many deserters from the armed forces) to escape conscription. Not until 1977, when President Jimmy Carter issued a general pardon to draft resisters and a far more limited amnesty for deserters, did the Vietnam exiles begin to return to the country in substantial numbers.

The Counterculture

Closely related to the New Left was a youth culture openly scornful of the values and conventions of middle-class society. The most visible characteristic of the counterculture, as it became known, was a change in lifestyle. As if to display their contempt for conventional standards, young Americans wore long hair and distinctive clothing (ragged or flamboyant by turns) and indicated a rebellious disdain for traditional speech and decorum. Central to the counterculture were drugs: marijuana smoking—which after 1966 became almost as common a youthful diversion as beer drinking—and the less widespread but still substantial use of other drugs, including potent hallucinogens such as LSD.

There was also a new, more permissive view of sexual behavior—the beginnings of what some called the "sexual revolution." To some degree, the emergence of more relaxed approaches to sexuality was a result less of the counterculture than of the new accessibility of effective contraceptives. The introduction of the birth control pill in 1960 and, a decade later, legalized abortion did much to diminish fear of unwanted pregnancy, a powerful force inhibiting female sexuality. But the new sexuality also reflected the counterculture's belief that individuals should strive for release from inhibitions and should give vent to their instincts—including the instinct for sensual pleasure.

The counterculture's iconoclasm and hedonism sometimes masked its implicit philosophy, which offered a fundamental challenge to the American middle-class mainstream. Like the New Left, with which it in many ways overlapped, the counterculture challenged the structure of modern American society, attacking its banality, its consumerism, its hollowness, its artificiality, and its isolation from nature. The most committed adherents of the counterculture—the hippies, who came to dominate the Haight-Ashbury neighborhood of San Francisco and other places, and social dropouts, many of whom retreated to rural communes—rejected modern society altogether and attempted to find refuge in a simpler, more "natural" existence. But even those whose commitment to the counterculture was less dramatic were attracted to the idea of personal fulfillment through rejecting the inhibitions and conventions of middle-class culture. In a corrupt and alienating society, the new creed seemed to suggest, the first responsibility of the individual was cultivation of the self, the unleashing of one's own full potential for pleasure and fulfillment.

Theodore Roszak, whose book *The Making of a Counter Culture* (1969) became a central document of the era, captured much of the spirit of the movement in his frank admission that "the primary project of our counter culture is to proclaim a new heaven and a new earth so vast, so marvelous that the inordinate claims of technical expertise must of necessity withdraw to a subordinate and marginal status in the lives of men." Charles Reich's *The Greening of America* (1970) created a short-lived sensation with its argument that the individual should strive for a new form of consciousness—"Consciousness III," as he called it—in which the self would be the only reality.

The effects of the counterculture reached out to the larger society and helped create a new set of social norms that many young people (and some adults) chose to imitate. Long hair and bohemian clothing became the badge not only of hippies and radicals but of an entire generation. The use of marijuana, the freer attitudes toward sex, the iconoclastic (and sometimes obscene) language—all spread far beyond the realm of the true devotees of the counterculture.

Perhaps the most pervasive element of the new youth society was one that even the least radical members of the generation embraced: rock music. Rock-'n'-roll first achieved wide popularity in the 1950s, on the strength of such early performers as Buddy Holly and, above all, Elvis Presley. Early in the 1960s, its influence began to spread, a result in large part of the phenomenal popularity of the Beatles, the English group whose first visit to the United States in 1964 created a remarkable sensation known at the time as "Beatlemania." For a time, most rock musicians—like most popular musicians before them—concentrated largely on romantic themes. One of the first great hits of the Beatles was a song with the innocuous title "I Want to Hold Your Hand." By the late 1960s, however, rock music had begun to reflect many of the new iconoclastic values of its time. The Beatles, for example, abandoned their once simple and seemingly innocent style for a new, experimental, even mystical approach that reflected their own growing fascination with drugs and Eastern religions. Other groups, such as the Rolling Stones, turned even more openly to themes of anger, frustration, and rebelliousness. Many popular musicians used their music to express explicit political radicalism as well—especially some of the leading folk singers of the era, such as Bob Dylan and Joan Baez. Rock's driving rhythms, its undisguised sensuality, and its sometimes harsh and angry tone all made it a compelling vehicle for expressing the unrest of the late 1960s.

A powerful symbol of the fusion of rock music and the counterculture was the great music festival at Woodstock, New York, in the summer of 1969, where 400,000 people gathered on a farm for nearly a week. Despite heavy rain, mud, inadequate facilities, and impossible crowding, the audience remained peaceful and harmonious. Champions of the counterculture spoke rhapsodically at the time of how Woodstock represented the birth of a new youth nation, the "Woodstock nation." The Beat poet Allen Ginsberg, revered by many enthusiasts of the counterculture and himself a champion of the "new consciousness," wrote an ecstatic poem proclaiming that at Woodstock "a new kind of man has come to his bliss/to end the cold war he has borne/against his own kind of flesh."

Virtually no Americans could avoid evidence of how rapidly the norms of their society were changing in the late 1960s. Those who attended movies saw a gradual disappearance of the banal, conventional messages that had dominated films since the 1920s. Instead, they saw explorations of political issues, of new sexual mores, of violence, and of social conflict. Television also began to turn (even if more slowly than the other media) to programming that reflected social and cultural conflict—as exemplified by the enormously popular *All in the Family*, whose working-class protagonist, Archie Bunker, displayed both obvious prejudice and, by episode's end, often some simple wisdom.

THE MOBILIZATION OF MINORITIES

The growth of black protest, and of a significant white response to it, both preceded the political and cultural upheavals of the 1960s and helped to produce them. It also encouraged other minorities to assert themselves and demand redress of their grievances. For Native Americans, Hispanic Americans, gay men and women, and others, the late 1960s and 1970s were a time of growing self-expression and political activism.

Seeds of Indian Militancy

Few minorities had deeper or more justifiable grievances against the prevailing culture than American Indians—or Native Americans, as many began to call themselves in the 1960s. Native Americans suffered enormous social and economic deprivations in American society. Average annual family income for Indians was 1,000 dollars less than that for blacks . The Native American unemployment rate was ten times the national rate. Joblessness was particularly high on the reservations, where nearly half of all Native Americans lived. But even most Native Americans living in cities suffered from their limited education and training and could find only menial jobs. Life expectancy among Indians fell twenty years below the national average. Suicides among Indian youths were a hundred times more frequent than among white youths. And while African Americans attracted the attention (for good or for ill) of many whites, Native Americans for many years remained largely ignored.

For much of the postwar era, and particularly after the resignation of John Collier as Commissioner of Indian Affairs in 1946, federal policy toward the tribes had been shaped by a determination to incorporate Indians into mainstream American society whether Indians wanted to assimilate or not. Two laws passed in 1953 established the basis of a new policy, which became known as "termination." Through termination, the federal government withdrew all official recognition of the tribes as legal entities, administratively separate from state governments, and made them subject to the same local jurisdictions as white residents. At the same time, the government encouraged Indians to assimilate into the larger society and worked to funnel Native Americans into cities, where, presumably, they would adapt themselves to the white world and lose their cultural distinctiveness.

To some degree, the termination and assimilation policies achieved their objectives. The tribes grew weaker as legal and political entities. Many Native Americans adapted to life in the cities, at least to a degree. On the whole, however, the new policies were a disaster for the tribes and a failure for the reformers who had promoted them. Termination led to widespread corruption and abuse. And the Indians themselves fought so bitterly against it that in 1958 the Eisenhower administration barred further "terminations" without the consent of the affected tribes. In the meantime, the struggle against termination had mobilized a new generation of Indian militants and had breathed life into the principal Native American organization, the National Congress of American Indians (NCAI), which had been created in 1944.

The Democratic administrations of the 1960s did not disavow the termination policy, but neither did they make any effort to revive it. Instead, they made modest efforts to restore at least some degree of tribal autonomy. The funneling of OEO money to tribal organizations through the Community Action program was one prominent example. In the meantime, the tribes themselves were beginning to fight for self-determination—partly in response to the black civil rights movement and partly in response to other social and cultural changes (among them, the expanding mobility and rising educational levels of younger Indians who refused to defer to the status quo and who fought inequalities aggressively.) The new militancy also benefited from the rapid increase in the Indian population, which was growing much faster than that of the rest of the nation (nearly doubling between 1950 and 1970 to a total of about 800,000).

The Indian Civil Rights Movement

In 1961, more than 400 members of sixty-seven tribes gathered in Chicago to discuss ways of bringing all Indians together in an effort to redress common wrongs. The manifesto they issued, the Declaration of Indian Purpose, stressed the "right to choose our own way of life" and the "responsibility of preserving our precious heritage."

The 1961 meeting was only one example of a growing Indian self-consciousness. Indians and others began writing books (for example, Vine Deloria, Jr.'s *Custer Died for Your Sins* and Dee Brown's *Bury My Heart at Wounded Knee*) and otherwise drawing renewed attention to the wrongs inflicted on the tribes by white people in past generations. One result was a gradual change in the way popular culture depicted Native Americans. By the 1970s, almost no films or television programs portrayed Indians as brutal savages attacking peaceful white people (as had been the norm for much of the 1950s). And Native American activists even persuaded some white institutions to abandon what they considered demeaning references to them, including some colleges who agreed to cease referring to their athletic teams as the "Indians." The National Indian Youth Council, created in the aftermath of the 1961 Chicago meeting, promoted the idea of Indian nationalism and intertribal unity. In 1968, a group of young, militant Indians established the American Indian Movement (AIM), which drew its greatest support from those Native Americans who lived in urban areas but soon established a significant presence on the reservations as well.

The new activism had some immediate political results. In 1968, Congress passed the Indian Civil Rights Act, which guaranteed reservation Native Americans many of the protections accorded other citizens by the Bill of Rights, but which also recognized the legitimacy of tribal laws within the reservations. But leaders of AIM and other insurgent groups were not satisfied and turned increasingly to direct action. In 1968, Native American fishermen, citing old treaty rights, clashed with Washington state officials on the Columbia River and in Puget Sound. The following year, members of several tribes occupied the abandoned federal prison on Alcatraz Island in San Francisco Bay, claiming the site "by right of discovery."

In response to the growing pressure, the new Nixon administration appointed a Mohawk-Sioux to the position of Commissioner of Indian Affairs in 1969; and in 1970, the president promised both increased tribal self-determination and an increase in federal aid. But the protests continued. In November 1972, nearly a thousand demonstrators, most of them Sioux Indians, forcibly occupied the building of the Bureau of Indian Affairs in Washington for six days. A more celebrated protest occurred later that winter at Wounded Knee, South Dakota, the site of the 1890 massacre of Sioux by federal troops.

In the early 1970s, Wounded Knee was part of a large Sioux reservation, two-thirds of which had been leased to white ranchers for generations as an outgrowth of the Dawes Act. Conditions for the Native-American residents were desperate, and passions grew quickly in 1972 in response to the murder of a Sioux by a group of whites, who were not, many Native Americans believed, adequately punished. In February 1973, members of AIM seized and occupied the town of Wounded Knee for two months, demanding radical changes in the administration of the reservation and insisting that the government honor its long-forgotten treaty obligations. A brief clash between the occupiers and federal

WOUNDED KNEE–1973. Oscar Running Bear, a member of the American Indian Movement, strikes a defiant stance during the confrontation between militant Native Americans and the federal government in Wounded Knee, South Dakota. For two months, members of AIM occupied the town of Wounded Knee to protest conditions on the large Sioux reservation and their unequal treatment in the larger society.

forces left one Native American dead and another wounded. Shortly thereafter the siege came to an end.

More immediately effective than these militant protests were the victories that various tribes were achieving in the 1970s in the federal courts. In *United States* v. *Wheeler* (1978), the Supreme Court confirmed that tribes had independent legal standing and could not be "terminated" by Congress. Other decisions ratified the authority of tribes to impose taxes on businesses within their reservations and perform other sovereign functions. In 1985, the U.S. Supreme Court, in *County of Oneida* v. *Oneida Indian Nation* supported Native American claims to 100,000 acres in upstate New York that the Oneida tribe claimed by virtue of treaty rights long forgotten by whites.

The Indian civil rights movement, like other civil rights movements of the same time, fell far short of winning full justice and equality for Native Americans. Nor did it ever resolve its own internal conflicts—conflicts similar to those facing other minority groups at the same time. To some Native Americans, the principal goal was to defend tribal autonomy, to protect the rights of Indians (and, more to the point, individual tribal groups) to remain separate and distinct. To others, the goal was equality—to win for Indians a place in society equal to that of other groups of Americans. This latter goal helped produce a new spirit of "pan-Indianism," an effort to persuade Native Americans to transcend tribal divisions and work together as "a Greater Indian America." But because there was no single Native American culture or tradition in America, pan-Indianism operated within strict limits.

For all its limits, however, the Indian civil rights movement helped the tribes win a series of new legal rights and protections that, together, gave them a stronger position than they had enjoyed at any previous time in the twentieth century. It helped many Native Americans gain a renewed awareness of and pride in their identity as Indians and as part of distinct communities within the larger United States. And it challenged patterns of discrimination that had prevented many Native Americans from advancing in the world outside the tribes.

Hispanic-American Activism

More numerous and more visible than Native Americans were Hispanic Americans (also known as Latinos), the fastest growing minority group in the United States. No more than Native Americans are they a single, cohesive group. Some—including the descendants of early Spanish settlers in New Mexico—have roots as deep in American history as those of any other group. Most are men and women who have immigrated since World War II. Nor are Latinos racially distinct. They can be descendants of Europeans, Africans, or Indians—or in most cases, some combination of all three.

Large numbers of Puerto Ricans had migrated to eastern cities, particularly New York. South Florida's substantial Cuban population began with a wave of middle-class refugees fleeing the Castro regime in the early 1960s. These first

Cuban migrants quickly established themselves as a successful and increasingly assimilated part of Miami's middle class. In 1980, a second, much poorer wave of Cuban immigrants—the so-called Marielistas, named for the port from which they left Cuba—arrived in Florida when Castro temporarily relaxed exit restrictions. (This group included a large number of criminals, whom Castro had, in effect, expelled from the country.) This second wave was less easily assimilated. Later in the 1980s, large numbers of immigrants (both legal and illegal) began to arrive from the troubled nations of Central and South America—from Guatemala, Nicaragua, El Salvador, Peru, and others. But the most numerous and important Hispanic group in the United States was Mexican Americans.

There had been a significant Mexican-American population in the West throughout the nineteenth and early twentieth centuries—descendants of Spanish and Mexican people who had settled in lands that once belonged to the Spanish empire and the Republic of Mexico. But the number grew rapidly and substantially during and after World War II. Large numbers of Mexican Americans entered the country during the war in response to the labor shortage, and many remained in the cities of the Southwest and the Pacific Coast. After the war, when legal agreements that had allowed Mexican contract workers to enter the country expired, large numbers of immigrants continued to move to the United States illegally. In 1953, the government launched what it called Operation Wetback to deport the illegals, but the effort failed to stem the flow of new arrivals. By 1960, there were substantial Mexican-American neighborhoods (or *barrios*) in American cities from El Paso to Detroit. The largest (with more than 500,000 people, according to census figures) was in Los Angeles, which by then had a bigger Mexican population than anyplace except Mexico City, Mexico.

But the greatest expansion in the Mexican-American population was yet to come. In 1960, the census reported slightly more than 3 million Hispanics (the great majority of them Mexican Americans) living in the United States. In 1970, that number had grown to 9 million and by 1990 to 20 million. Hispanics constituted more than a third of all legal immigrants to the United States after 1960. Since there was also an uncounted but very large number of illegal immigrants in those years (estimates ranged from 7 million to 12 million), the real percentage of Hispanic immigrants was undoubtedly much larger.

By the late 1960s, therefore, Mexican Americans were one of the largest population groups in the West (outnumbering African Americans) and had established communities in most other parts of the nation as well. They were also among the most urbanized groups in the population; almost ninety percent of them lived and worked in cities. Many of them (particularly members of the oldest and most assimilated families of Mexican descent) were wealthy and successful people. Affluent Cubans in Miami filled important positions in the professions and local government; in the Southwest, Mexican Americans elected their own leaders to seats in Congress and to governorships.

But most newly arrived Mexican Americans and others were less well educated than either "Anglos" or African Americans and hence found it difficult to secure high-paying jobs. The fact that some spoke little or no English further limited their employment prospects. Some found good industrial jobs in unionized industries, and some Mexican Americans became important labor organizers in the AFL-CIO. But many more (including the great majority of illegal immigrants) worked in low-paying service jobs with few if any benefits and no job security. And, like African Americans and other minorities, Mexican Americans encountered almost impossible obstacles when they attempted to move out of blue-collar or low-status service jobs. Almost nowhere were they able to establish themselves as managers or executives in the companies in which they worked; few were able to pursue successful professional careers.

Partly because of language barriers, partly because the family-centered culture of many Hispanic communities discouraged effective organization, and partly because of discrimination, Mexican Americans and others were slower to mobilize politically than were some other minorities. But many Latinos did respond to the highly charged climate of the 1960s by strengthening their ethnic identification and organizing. Young Mexican-American activists began to call themselves "Chicanos" (once a term of derision used by whites) as a way of emphasizing the shared culture of Spanish-speaking Americans; and the term quickly moved into widespread (although never universal) use among Mexican Americans. Some Chicanos advocated a form of nationalism not unlike the ideas of black power advocates. The Texas leaders of *La Raza Unida*, a Chicano political party in the Southwest, called for the creation of something like an autonomous Mexican-American state within a state; it demonstrated significant strength at the polls in the 1970s.

One of the most visible efforts to organize Mexican Americans occurred in California, where an Arizona-born Chicano farm worker, Cesar Chavez, created an effective union of itinerant farm workers. His United Farm Workers (UFW), a largely Mexican-American organization, launched a prolonged strike in 1965 against growers to demand, first, recognition of their union and, second, increased wages and benefits. When employers resisted, Chavez enlisted the cooperation of college students, churches, and civil rights groups (including CORE and SNCC) and organized a nationwide boycott, first of table grapes and then of lettuce. In 1968, Chavez campaigned openly for Robert Kennedy. Two years later, he won a substantial victory when the growers of half of California's table grapes signed contracts with his union.

Hispanic Americans were at the center of another controversy of the 1970s and beyond: the issue of bilingualism. It was a question that aroused the opposition not only of many whites but of some Hispanics too. Supporters of bilingualism in education (which included Hispanics, Asians, and others) argued that non–English speaking Americans were entitled to at least some schooling in their own language, that otherwise they would be at a grave disadvantage in comparison with native English speakers. Bilingualism, they argued, was the

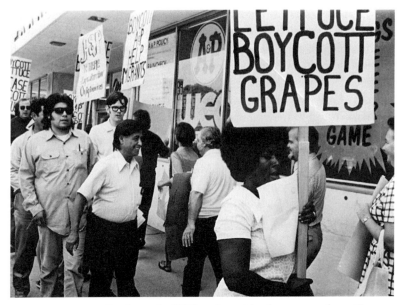

CESAR CHAVEZ. By the early 1970s, when this photo was taken, Cesar Chavez (at left, wearing a white short-sleeved shirt) was a nationally known champion of farm workers. His United Farm Workers (UFW) provided a voice, especially for Chicano migrant workers who picked crops under harsh conditions in California and had little power over the conditions of their labor. Chavez's national grape and lettuce boycotts succeeded in winning concessions from some employers, including recognition of the UFW by half the growers of California table grapes in 1970.

only way to overcome the language barrier that kept many students from making even minimal academic progress and the best way to move students into the English-speaking educational system. The United States Supreme Court confirmed the right of non–English speaking students to schooling in their native language in 1974. Opponents cited not only the cost and difficulty of bilingualism but the dangers they claimed it posed to the ability of students to become assimilated into the mainstream of American culture. Even many Hispanics feared that bilingualism might isolate their communities further from the rest of America and increase resentments toward them.

Challenging the "Melting Pot" Ideal

The efforts of blacks, Hispanics, Indians, Asians, and others to forge a clearer group identity seemed to challenge a long-standing premise of American political thought—the idea of the "melting pot." Older, European immigrant groups liked to believe that they had advanced in American society by adopting the values and accepting the rules of the world to which they had moved, by advancing within it on its own terms. The newly assertive ethnic groups of the 1960s and after were less willing to accept the standards of the larger society and more likely to demand recognition of their own ethnic identities. Many (although not all) African Americans, Indians, Hispanics, and Asians challenged the assimilationist idea and advocated instead a culturally pluralistic society, in which racial and ethnic groups would preserve not only a sense of their own heritage (which older, more "assimilationist" ethnic groups did as well) but also their own social and cultural norms.

To a large degree, the advocates of cultural pluralism succeeded. Recognition of the special character of particular groups was embedded in federal law through a wide range of affirmative action programs, which extended not only to blacks, but to Indians, Hispanics, Asians, and others. Ethnic studies programs proliferated in schools and universities. Eventually, this impulse led to an even more assertive (and highly controversial) cultural movement that in the 1980s and 1990s became known as "multiculturalism," which challenged the "Eurocentric" basis of American education and culture and demanded that non-European civilizations be accorded equal attention.

Gay Liberation

The last important liberation movement to emerge in the 1960s was the effort by homosexuals and lesbians to win political and economic rights and, equally important, social acceptance. Homosexuality had been an unacknowledged reality throughout American history; not until many years after their deaths did many Americans know, for example, that revered cultural figures such as Walt Whitman and Horatio Alger were homosexuals. Nonheterosexual men and women had long been forced either to suppress their sexual preferences, to exercise them surreptitiously, or to live within isolated and often persecuted communities. But by the late 1960s, the liberating impulses that had affected other groups helped mobilize gay men and women (as homosexuals and lesbians came to call themselves) to fight for their own rights.

On June 27, 1969, police officers raided the Stonewall Inn, a gay nightclub in New York City's Greenwich Village, and began arresting patrons simply for frequenting the place. The raid was not unusual; police had been harassing gay bars (and homosexual men and women) for years. It was, in fact, the accumulated resentment of this long history of assaults and humiliations that caused the extraordinary response that summer night. Gay onlookers taunted the police, then attacked them. Someone started a blaze in the Stonewall Inn itself, almost trapping the policemen inside. Rioting continued throughout Greenwich Village (the center of New York's gay community) through much of the night.

The "Stonewall Riot" marked the beginning of the gay liberation movement—one of the most controversial challenges to traditional values and assumptions of its time. New organizations—among them the Gay Liberation Front, founded in New York in 1969—sprang up around the country. Public discussion and media coverage of homosexuality, long subject to an unofficial taboo, quickly and dramatically increased. Gay activists had some success in challenging the long-standing assumption that homosexuality was "aberrant" behavior and argued that no sexual preference was any more "normal" than another.

Most of all, however, the gay liberation movement transformed the outlook of gay men and women themselves. It helped them to "come out," to express their preferences openly and unapologetically, and to demand from society a recognition that gay relationships were as significant and worthy of respect as heterosexual ones. Some gays advocated not only an acceptance of homosexuality as a valid and "normal" preference, but a change in the larger society as well: a redefinition of personal identity to give much greater importance to erotic impulses. Those changes did not quickly occur. But by the early 1980s, the gay liberation movement had made remarkable strides. Even the ravages of the AIDS epidemic, which in America affected the gay community first and for a time more disastrously than it affected any other group, failed to halt the growth of gay liberation. In many ways, it strengthened it.

By the early 1990s, homosexuals and lesbians were achieving some of the same milestones that other oppressed minorities had attained in earlier decades. Some openly gay politicians won election to public office. Universities established gay and lesbian studies programs. And laws prohibiting discrimination on the basis of sexual preference made slow, halting progress at the local level. But gay liberation produced a powerful backlash as well, as became evident when President Bill Clinton's 1993 effort to lift the ban on gays serving in the military fell victim to a storm of criticism from members of Congress and from within the military itself.

THE REVIVAL OF AMERICAN FEMINISM

Given the relative quiescence of the 1950s and its emphasis on domesticity, few would have predicted that the 1960s would give rise to a new, powerful wave of American feminism. But this was precisely what happened. At first haltingly, and then with increasing militancy, feminists began to direct attention to the place of women within American society and to attract millions of converts to their cause.

Sexual discrimination was deeply embedded in the fabric of society, and women faced many obstacles to equality. During the early 1960s, female professionals especially mobilized to improve the economic status of women in American society. As the decade wore on, however, a growing feminist movement expanded its agenda to attack deeper manifestations of "sexism"—as bias against women was increasingly known. Private life—woman's place within the family, her relationships to men, her sexuality—became especially important issues to those who advanced the "women's liberation movement" of the late 1960s and early 1970s. American women constituted fifty-one percent of the population and for that reason, among others, feminists succeeded in sparking a major debate and much legislative reform by the early 1970s. Public awareness of women's issues increased dramatically, and in many respects, the roles of women in American society—or at least prevailing conceptions of them—also changed fundamentally.

Rejecting the Feminine Mystique

Feminism had been a weak and often embattled force in American life for more than forty years after the adoption of the woman suffrage amendment in 1920. A few determined women kept feminist political demands alive in the National Woman's party and other organizations. Many more women expanded the acceptable bounds of female activity by entering new areas of the workplace or engaging in political activities. Nevertheless, through the 1950s active feminism seemed in retreat. That changed very dramatically in the early 1960s.

The 1963 publication of Betty Friedan's *The Feminine Mystique* is often cited as the first event of contemporary women's liberation. Friedan had traveled around the country interviewing the women who had graduated with her from Smith College in 1947. Most of these women were living out the dream that postwar American society had created for them; they were affluent wives and mothers living in comfortable suburbs. And yet many of them were deeply frustrated and unhappy. The suburbs, Friedan claimed, had become a "comfortable concentration camp," providing the women who inhabited them with no outlets for their intelligence, talent, and education. The "feminine mystique" was responsible for "burying millions of women alive." The only escape was for them to begin to fulfill "their unique possibilities as separate human beings." By chronicling their unhappiness and frustration, Friedan's book had a powerful impact. But it did not so much cause the revival of feminism as help give voice to a movement that was already stirring.

By the time *The Feminine Mystique* appeared, John Kennedy had established the President's Commission on the Status of Women. The president's motives in creating it probably had more to do with deflecting more substantive feminist demands than with real commitment to women's goals. Nonetheless, its creation reflected a growing recognition that a "problem" existed regarding women in American society. Furthermore, the commission brought national attention to sexual discrimination and helped create important networks of feminist activists who would lobby for legislative redress. Also in 1963, the Kennedy administration helped win passage of the Equal Pay Act, which barred the pervasive practice of paying women less than men for equal work. A year later, Congress incorporated into the Civil Rights Act of 1964 an amendment—Title VII—that extended to women many of the same legal protections against discrimination that were being extended to blacks.

The events of the early 1960s helped expose a contradiction that had been developing for decades between the image and the reality of women's roles in America. The image was what Friedan had called the "feminine mystique"— the ideal of women living happy, fulfilled lives in purely domestic roles. The reality was that increasing numbers of women (including, by 1963, over a third of all married women) had already entered the workplace and were encountering widespread discrimination there; and the reality was, too, that many other women were finding their domestic lives less than completely fulfilling. The conflict between the ideal and the reality was crucial to the rebirth of feminism.

In 1966, Friedan joined with other feminists to create the National Organization for Women (NOW), which was to become the nation's largest and most influential feminist organization. "The time has come," the founders of NOW maintained, "to confront with concrete action the conditions which now prevent women from enjoying the equality of opportunity and freedom of choice which is their right as individual Americans and as human beings." Like other movements for liberation, feminism drew much of its inspiration from the black struggle for freedom. "There is no civil rights movement to speak for women," the NOW organizers claimed, "as there has been for Negroes and other victims of discrimination."

The new organization reflected the varying constituencies of the emerging feminist movement. It responded to the complaints of the women Friedan's book had examined—affluent suburbanites with no outlet for their interests—by demanding greater educational opportunities for women and denouncing the ten-

BETTY FRIEDAN. At an April, 1975 rally in Chicago, feminist Betty Friedan exhorts her listeners to support the Equal Rights Amendment. One of the founders of the modern women's movement, Friedan helped provide intellectual and organizational leadership to the growing feminist movement.

dency to uphold the domestic ideal and the traditional concept of marriage as the singular goals of all women. But the heart of the movement, at least in the beginning, was directed toward the needs of women in the workplace. NOW denounced the exclusion of women from professions, from politics, and from countless other areas of American life. It decried legal and economic discrimination, including the practice of paying women less than men for equal work (a practice the Equal Pay Act had not eliminated). The organization called for "a fully equal partnership of the sexes, as part of the worldwide revolution of human rights." By the end of the decade, its membership had expanded to 15,000.

Women's Liberation

By the late 1960s, new and more radical feminist demands were also attracting a large following, especially among younger, affluent, white, educated women—although generally not among the older women whose lives Friedan had studied. The new feminists were mostly younger, the vanguard of the baby-boom generation. Many of them arrived at their commitment to feminism through their experience in the New Left and the civil rights movement. Even within those movements, dedicated as they claimed to be to freedom and equality, women faced discrimination and exclusion by male leaders. Indeed, in 1964 one of the first protests against sex discrimination within the civil rights movement came from African-American women in SNCC, who decried the automatic assignment of clerical duties to women. In SDS, women activists split off from the organization at one national conference to form small groups where they could openly discuss discrimination against women in "the movement." Soon what had begun as a growing awareness of gender discrimination gained coherence and emerged as a full-fledged drive to address the persistent inequality facing many American women.

Indeed, by the early 1970s, a significant change was visible in the tone and direction of the organization, and of the women's movement as a whole. New books by younger feminists expressed a harsher critique of American society than Friedan had offered. Kate Millett's *Sexual Politics* (1969) signaled the new direction by complaining that "every avenue of power within the society is entirely within male hands." The answer to women's problems, in other words, was not, as Friedan had suggested, for individual women to search for greater personal fulfillment; it was for women to band together to assault the male power structure. Shulamith Firestone's *The Dialectic of Sex* (1970) was subtitled "The Case for Feminist Revolution."

In its most radical form, the new feminism rejected the whole notion of marriage, family, and even heterosexual intercourse (a vehicle, some women claimed, of male domination). Not many women, not even many feminists, embraced such ideas. But by the early 1970s large numbers of women were coming to see themselves as an exploited group banding together against oppression and developing cultures and communities of their own. The women's liberation movement inspired the creation of grass-roots organizations and activities through which women not only challenged sexism and discrimination but created communities of their own. In cities and towns across the country, feminists opened women's bookstores, bars, and coffee shops. They founded feminist newspapers and magazines. They created centers to assist victims of rape and abuse, women's health clinics (and, particularly after 1973, abortion clinics), and daycare centers. These women-centered activities were crucial to the modern women's movement.

Expanding Achievements

By the early 1970s, the public and private achievements of the women's movement were already substantial. In 1971, the government extended its affirmative action guidelines to include women—linking sexism with racism as an officially acknowledged social problem. Women were making rapid progress, in the meantime, in their efforts to move into the economic and political mainstream. The nation's major all-male educational institutions began to open their doors to women. (Princeton and Yale did so in 1969, and most other once all-male colleges and universities soon did the same.) Some women's colleges, in the meantime, began accepting male students—although many remained committed to single-sex education, arguing for the value of the women's communities their campuses created. Passage of Title IX of the Higher Education Act in 1972 mandated that any co-educational college or university receiving federal funds could not discriminate against women in hiring, wages, admissions, access to instruction, or rules governing behavior, among other provisions.

Women were also becoming an important force in business and the professions. Nearly half of all married women held jobs by the mid-1970s, and almost nine-tenths of all women with college degrees worked. The two-career family, in which both the husband and the wife maintained active professional lives, was becoming a widely accepted norm; many women were postponing marriage or motherhood for the sake of their careers. There were also important symbolic changes, such as the refusal of many women to adopt their husbands' names when they married and the use of the term "Ms." in place of "Mrs." or "Miss" to denote the irrelevance of a woman's marital status in the professional world.

In politics, women were beginning to compete effectively with men by the early 1970s for both elected and appointive positions. By the early 1990s, women were serving in both houses of Congress, in numerous federal cabinet positions, as governors of several states, and in many other positions. Ronald Reagan named the first female Supreme Court Justice, Sandra Day O'Connor, in 1981; and Bill Clinton named the second, a self-proclaimed feminist, Ruth Bader Ginsburg, in 1993. In 1984, the Democratic party chose a woman, Representative Geraldine Ferraro of New York, as its vice presidential candidate. In academia, women were expanding their presence in traditional scholarly fields; they were also creating a field of their own—women's studies, which in the 1980s and early 1990s was the fastest growing area of American scholarship.

In professional athletics, in the meantime, women began to compete with men both for attention and for an equal share of prize money. Billie Jean King spearheaded the most effective female challenge to male domination of sports. Under her leadership, professional woman tennis players established their own successful tours and demanded equal financial incentives when they played in the same tournaments as men. By the late 1970s, the federal government was pressuring colleges and universities to provide women with athletic programs equal to those available to men. Women even joined what had previously been the most celebrated all-male fraternity in American culture: the space program. Sally Ride became the first woman astronaut to travel in space in 1983.

In 1972, Congress approved the Equal Rights Amendment to the Constitution, which some feminists had been promoting since the 1920s, and sent it to the states. For a while ratification seemed almost certain. By the late 1970s, however, the momentum behind the amendment had died. The ERA was in trouble not because of indifference but because of a rising chorus of objections to it from people (including many antifeminist women), who feared it would disrupt traditional social patterns. In 1982, the amendment finally died when the time allotted for ratification expired.

The Abortion Question

A vital element of American feminism since the 1920s has been the effort by women to win greater control of their own sexual and reproductive lives. This impulse helped produce an increasing awareness in the 1960s and 1970s of the problems of rape, sexual abuse, and wife beating. There continued to be some controversy over the dissemination of contraceptives and birth-control information; but that issue, at least, seemed to have lost much of the explosive character it had possessed in the 1920s, when Margaret Sanger had become a figure of public scorn for her efforts on its behalf. A related issue, however, stimulated as much popular passion as any question of its time: abortion.

Abortion had once been legal in much of the United States, but by the beginning of the twentieth century it was banned by statute in most of the country and remained so into the 1960s (although many abortions continued to be performed quietly, and often dangerously, out of sight of the law). But the women's movement created strong new pressures to legalize abortion and to give to women alone the right to choose whether or not to carry a pregnancy to term. Several states had abandoned restrictions on abortion by the end of the 1960s.

In 1973, the Supreme Court handed down a decision in *Roe* v. *Wade* based on a relatively new theory of a constitutional "right to privacy," first recognized by the Court only a few years earlier in *Griswold* v. *Connecticut* (1965). The Roe decision invalidated all laws prohibiting abortion during the first trimester—the first three months of pregnancy. Further, it supported the notion that the decision whether or not to have an abortion fell within the constitutional right of privacy. *Roe* v. *Wade* did not uphold the right to "abortion on demand." But it did stress that until a fetus was viable outside the womb, the abortion decision belonged to a woman and her physician; the state's interest in regulating abortion was restricted to protecting the health or life of the woman. The issue, it seemed, had been settled. But it soon became clear that it had not.

In many ways, feminism was much like other "liberation" movements of the 1960s and 1970s. But it differed in one fundamental respect: its success. The women's movement may not have fulfilled all its goals. But it achieved fundamental and permanent changes in the position of women in American life and promised to do much more.

CHAPTER TWENTY-SIX

The Imperial Presidency

≈

T he troubled social and cultural landscape of the late 1960s, and the powerful political reaction it created, shaped the presidency of Richard Nixon—one of the boldest and most divisive presidencies in American history. Nixon had been a familiar figure in American politics for more than a generation when he entered the White House in 1969. But nothing in his, or the nation's, past prepared him for the difficulties he would encounter in the turbulent years of the late 1960s and early 1970s.

The great majority of the voters had made clear in the 1968 election that they wanted a restoration of stability and order to American domestic life and to the nation's tortured adventures abroad. Nixon set out to provide both. He wanted to rebuild the legitimacy of traditional values and institutions at home. He wanted to bring "peace with honor" to Vietnam. And he wanted to build a new "structure of peace" in the world. In pursuing these bold goals, he took many risks and achieved many things. He also adopted a style of governance, rooted in his belief in the illegitimacy of the forces opposing him, that eventually led him to disaster.

THE VIETNAM WAR IN THE NIXON YEARS

Of all the ambitious goals Nixon carried with him into the White House, none was more important to him than creating a new and more stable international order. He knew from his long career in politics that the electorate cared first and foremost about domestic issues, and he was careful not to neglect them. But Nixon himself was most comfortable in the larger world, and foreign policy always remained his first and primary interest.

Central to his hopes for international stability was resolving the stalemate in Vietnam. Yet the new president felt no freer than his predecessor to abandon the

American commitment there. He realized that the endless war was undermining both the nation's domestic stability and its position in the world. But he feared that a precipitous retreat would destroy American honor and "credibility."

During the 1968 campaign, Nixon claimed to have formulated a plan to bring "peace with honor" in Vietnam, but he had refused to disclose its details. Once in office, however, he soon made clear that the plan consisted of little more than a vague set of general principles, not of any concrete measures to extricate the United States from the quagmire. American involvement in Indochina continued for four more years. And when a settlement finally emerged early in 1973, it produced neither peace nor honor. It succeeded only in removing the United States from the wreckage.

Vietnamization

Despite Nixon's own passionate interest in international affairs, he brought with him into government a man who often seemed to overshadow the president in the conduct of diplomacy: Henry Kissinger, a Harvard professor whom Nixon appointed as his special assistant for national security affairs. Kissinger quickly established dominance over both the Secretary of State, William Rogers, and the Secretary of Defense, Melvin Laird, although both were more experienced than he in public life. That was in part a result of Nixon's passion for concentrating decision making in the White House. But Kissinger's keen intelligence, his bureaucratic skills, and his success in handling the press were at least equally important. Together, Nixon and Kissinger set out to find an acceptable solution to the stalemate in Vietnam.

The new Vietnam policy moved along several fronts. One was an effort to limit domestic opposition to the war so as to permit the administration more political space in which to maneuver. Aware that the military draft was one of the most visible targets of dissent, the administration devised a new "lottery" system, through which only a limited group—those nineteen year olds with low lottery numbers—would be subject to conscription. Later, the president urged the creation of an all-volunteer army. By 1973, the Selective Service System was on its way to at least temporary extinction.

More important in stifling dissent, however, was the new policy of "Vietnamization" of the war—that is, the training and equipping of the South Vietnamese military to assume the burden of combat in place of American forces. In the fall of 1969, Nixon announced the withdrawal of 60,000 American ground troops from Vietnam, the first reduction in U.S. troop strength since the beginning of the war. The withdrawals continued steadily for more than three years, so that by the fall of 1972 relatively few American soldiers remained in Indochina. From a peak of more than 540,000 in 1969, the number had dwindled to about 60,000.

Vietnamization did help quiet domestic opposition to the war. It did nothing, however, to break the stalemate in the negotiations with the North Vietnamese in Paris. The new administration quickly decided that new military pressures would be necessary to do that.

Escalation

By the end of their first year in office, Nixon and Kissinger had concluded that the most effective way to tip the military balance in America's favor was to destroy the bases in Cambodia from which the American military believed the North Vietnamese were launching many of their attacks. Very early in his presidency, Nixon ordered the air force to begin bombing Cambodian territory to destroy the enemy sanctuaries. He kept the raids secret from Congress and the public. In the spring of 1970, possibly with American encouragement and support, conservative military leaders overthrew the neutral government of Cambodia and established a new, pro-American regime under General Lon Nol. Lon Nol quickly gave his approval to American incursions into his territory; and on

KENT STATE. The horrified expression on this young woman's face as she kneels over a slain student became a symbol of the tragedy of Kent State. Four students were killed at the university in May of 1970, when Ohio National Guardsmen fired into a crowd of anti-war demonstrators. Two days later, violence also broke out at Jackson State University in Mississippi when police fired on students during a demonstration, leaving two dead.

April 30, Nixon went on national television to announce that he was ordering American troops across the border into Cambodia to "clean out" the bases that the enemy had been using for its "increased military aggression."

Literally overnight, the Cambodian invasion restored the dwindling antiwar movement to vigorous life. The first days of May saw the most widespread and vocal antiwar demonstrations ever. Hundreds of thousands of protesters gathered in Washington to denounce the president's policies. Millions participated in countless smaller demonstrations on campuses and other sites nationwide. Antiwar frenzy was reaching so high a level that it was briefly possible for some Americans to believe (incorrectly) that a genuine revolution was imminent. The mood of crisis intensified greatly on May 4, when four college students were killed and nine others injured after members of the National Guard opened fire on antiwar demonstrators at Kent State University in Ohio. Ten days later, police killed two black students at Jackson State University in Mississippi during a demonstration there.

The clamor against the war quickly spread into the government and the press. Congress angrily repealed the Gulf of Tonkin Resolution in December, stripping the president of what had long served as the legal basis for the war. Nixon ignored the action. Then, in June 1971, first the *New York Times* and later other newspapers began publishing excerpts from a secret study of the war prepared by the Defense Department during the Johnson administration. The so-called Pentagon Papers, leaked to the press by former Pentagon official Daniel Ellsberg, provided confirmation of what many had long believed: that the government had been dishonest, both in reporting the military progress of the war and in explaining its own motives for American involvement. The administration went to court to suppress the documents, but the Supreme Court finally ruled that the press had the right to publish them.

Particularly troubling, both to the public and to the government itself, were signs of decay within the American military. Morale and discipline among U.S. troops in Vietnam, who had been fighting a savage and inconclusive war for more than five years, was rapidly deteriorating. The trial and conviction in 1971 of Lieutenant William Calley, who was charged with overseeing a massacre of more than 100 unarmed South Vietnamese civilians, attracted wide public attention to the dehumanizing impact of the war on those who fought it—and to the terrible consequences for the Vietnamese people of that dehumanization. Less publicized were other, more widespread problems among American troops in Vietnam: desertion, drug addiction, racial hostilities, refusal to obey orders, even the killing of unpopular officers by enlisted men.

The continuing carnage, the increasing savagery, and the social distress at home had largely destroyed public support for the war. By 1971, nearly two-thirds of those interviewed in public-opinion polls were urging American withdrawal from Vietnam. From Richard Nixon, however, there came no sign of retreat. On the contrary, the events of the spring of 1970 left him more convinced than ever of the importance of resisting what he once called the "bums" who opposed his military policies. With the approval of the White House, both the FBI and the CIA intensified their surveillance and infiltration of antiwar and radical groups, often resorting to blatant illegalities in the process. Administration officials sought to discredit prominent critics of the war by leaking damaging personal information about them. At one point, White House agents broke into the office of a psychiatrist in an unsuccessful effort to steal files on Daniel Ellsberg. During the congressional campaign of 1970, Vice President Spiro Agnew, using the acid rhetoric that had already made him the hero of many conservatives, stepped up his attack on the "effete" and "impudent" critics of the administration. The president himself once climbed on top of an automobile to taunt a crowd of angry demonstrators.

In Indochina, meanwhile, the fighting raged on. In February 1971, the president ordered the air force to assist the South Vietnamese army in an invasion of Laos—a test, as he saw it, of his Vietnamization program. Within weeks, the South Vietnamese scrambled back across the border in defeat. American bombing in Vietnam and Cambodia increased, despite its apparent ineffectiveness. In March 1972, the North Vietnamese mounted their biggest offensive since 1968 (the so-called "Easter Offensive"). American and South Vietnamese forces managed to halt the communist advance, but it was clear that without American support the offensive would have succeeded. At the same time, Nixon ordered American planes to bomb targets near Hanoi, the capital of North Vietnam, and Haiphong, its principal port, and called for the mining of seven North Vietnamese harbors (including Haiphong) to stop the flow of supplies from China and the Soviet Union.

"Peace with Honor"

As the 1972 presidential election approached, the administration stepped up its effort to produce a breakthrough in negotiations with the North Vietnamese. In April 1972, the president dropped his longtime insistence on a removal of North Vietnamese troops from the South before any American withdrawal. Meanwhile, Henry Kissinger was meeting privately in Paris with the North Vietnamese foreign secretary, Le Duc Tho, to work out terms for a cease-fire. On October 26, only days before the presidential election, Kissinger announced that "peace is at hand."

Several weeks later (after the election), negotiations broke down once again. Although both the American and the North Vietnamese governments were ready to accept the Kissinger-Tho plan for a cease-fire, the Thieu regime balked, still insisting on a full withdrawal of North Vietnamese forces from the South. Kissinger tried to win additional concessions from the communists to meet Thieu's objections; but on December 16, talks broke off.

The next day, December 17, American B52s began the heaviest and most destructive air raids of the entire war on Hanoi, Haiphong, and other North Vietnamese targets. Civilian casualties were high. And fifteen American B52s were shot down by the North Vietnamese; in the entire war to that point, the United

States had lost only one of the giant bombers. On December 30, Nixon terminated the "Christmas bombing." The United States and the North Vietnamese returned to the conference table. And on January 27, 1973, they signed an "agreement on ending the war and restoring peace in Vietnam." Nixon claimed that the Christmas bombing had forced the North Vietnamese to relent. At least equally important, however, was the enormous American pressure on Thieu to accept the cease-fire.

The terms of the Paris accords were little different from those Kissinger and Tho had accepted in principle a few months before. There would be an immediate cease-fire. The North Vietnamese would release several hundred American prisoners of war, whose fate had become an emotional issue of great importance within the United States. After that the agreement descended quickly into murky, unworkable arrangements. The Thieu regime would survive for the moment—the principal North Vietnamese concession to the United States—but North Vietnamese forces already in the South would remain there. An undefined committee would work out a permanent settlement.

PARIS ACCORDS–1973. Barely visible in this crowded room are representatives of the United States, North Vietnam, South Vietnam, and the Viet Cong as they sign the Paris accords officially ending the Vietnam War. Although the agreement created the outlines for a permanent settlement of the war and mandated a cease-fire, it broke down within months. It did, however, permit the United States to extricate itself from Vietnam after the long and bloody conflict.

Defeat in Indochina

American forces were hardly out of Indochina before the Pa... lapsed. During the first year after the cease-fire, the contending Vietn... armies suffered greater battle losses than the Americans had absorbed during ten years of fighting. In March 1975, finally, the North Vietnamese launched a full-scale offensive against the now greatly weakened forces of the South. Thieu appealed to Washington for assistance; the president (now Gerald Ford) appealed to Congress for additional funding; Congress refused. Late in April 1975, communist forces marched into Saigon, shortly after officials of the Thieu regime and the staff of the American embassy had fled the country in humiliating disarray. Communist forces quickly occupied the capital, renamed it Ho Chi Minh City, and began the process of reuniting Vietnam under the harsh rule of Hanoi. At about the same time, the Lon Nol regime in Cambodia fell to the murderous communists of the Khmer Rouge—whose genocidal policies led to the deaths of more than a third of the country's people over the next several years.

Such were the dismal results of more than a decade of direct American military involvement in Vietnam. More than 1.2 million Vietnamese soldiers had died in combat, along with countless civilians throughout the region. A beautiful land had been ravaged, its agrarian economy left in ruins; for many years after, Vietnam remained one of the poorest and most politically oppressive nations in the world. The United States had paid a heavy price as well. The war had cost the nation almost $150 billion in direct costs and much more indirectly. It had resulted in the deaths of 58,000 young Americans and the injury of 300,000 more. And the nation had suffered a blow to its confidence and self-esteem from which it would not soon recover.

NIXON, KISSINGER, AND THE WORLD

The continuing war in Vietnam provided a dismal backdrop to what Nixon considered his larger mission in world affairs: the construction of a new international order. The president had become convinced that old assumptions of a "bipolar" world—in which the United States and the Soviet Union were the only truly great powers—were now obsolete. America must adapt to the new "multipolar" international structure, in which China, Japan, and western Europe were becoming major, independent forces. "It will be a safer world and a better world," he said in 1971, "if we have a strong, healthy United States, Europe, Soviet Union, China, Japan—each balancing the other, not playing one against the other, an even balance."

Nixon and Kissinger believed it was possible to construct something like the "balance of power" that had permitted nineteenth-century Europe to experience nearly a century of relative stability. To do so, however, required a major change in several long-standing assumptions of American foreign policy.

China and the Soviet Union

For more than twenty years, ever since the fall of Chiang Kai-shek in 1949, the United States had treated China, the second largest nation on earth, as if it did not exist. Instead, America recognized the forlorn regime-in-exile on Taiwan as the legitimate government of mainland China. Nixon and Kissinger wanted to forge a new relationship with the Chinese communists—in part to strengthen them as a counterbalance to the Soviet Union. The Chinese, for their part, were eager to forestall the possibility of a Soviet-American alliance against China and to end China's own isolation from the international arena.

In July 1971, Nixon sent Henry Kissinger on a secret mission to Beijing. When Kissinger returned, the president made the startling announcement that

NIXON IN CHINA. President Nixon and Chou En-Lai review troops during Nixon's historic visit to China. A determined anticommunist for much of his political career, Nixon took bold steps as president toward normalizing U.S. relations in China.

he would visit China himself within the next few months. That fall, with American approval, the United Nations admitted the communist government of China and expelled the representatives of the Taiwan regime. Finally, in February 1972, Nixon paid a formal visit to China and, in a single stroke, erased much of the deep American animosity toward the Chinese communists. Nixon did not yet formally recognize the communist regime, but in 1972 the United States and China began low-level diplomatic relations.

The initiatives in China coincided with (and probably assisted) an effort by the Nixon administration to improve relations with the Soviet Union. In 1969, American and Soviet diplomats met in Helsinki, Finland to begin talks on limiting nuclear weapons. In 1972, they produced the first Strategic Arms Limitation Treaty (SALT I), which froze the nuclear missiles (ICBMs) of both sides at present levels. In May of that year, the president traveled to Moscow to sign the agreement. The next year, the Soviet premier, Leonid Brezhnev, visited Washington; and the two leaders pledged renewed efforts to speed the next phase of arms control negotiations.

The Problems of Multipolarity

The policies of rapprochement with communist China and detente with the Soviet Union reflected Nixon's and Kissinger's belief in the importance of stable relationships among the great powers. But great-power relationships could not alone ensure international stability, for the Third World remained the most volatile and dangerous source of international tension.

Central to the Nixon-Kissinger policy toward the Third World was the effort to maintain a stable status quo without involving the United States too deeply in local disputes. In 1969 and 1970, the president described what became known as the Nixon Doctrine, by which the United States would "participate in the defense and development of allies and friends" but would leave the "basic responsibility" for the future of those "friends" to the nations themselves. In practice, the Nixon Doctrine meant a declining American interest in contributing to Third World development; a growing contempt for the United Nations, where underdeveloped nations were gaining influence through their sheer numbers; and increasing support to authoritarian regimes attempting to withstand radical challenges from within.

In 1970, for example, the CIA poured substantial funds into Chile to help support the established government against a communist challenge. When the Marxist candidate for president, Salvador Allende, came to power through an honest election, the United States began funneling more money to opposition forces in Chile to help "destabilize" the new government. In 1973, a military junta seized power from Allende, who was subsequently murdered. The United States developed a friendly relationship with the new, repressive military government of General Augusto Pinochet.

CRISES IN THE MIDDLE EAST

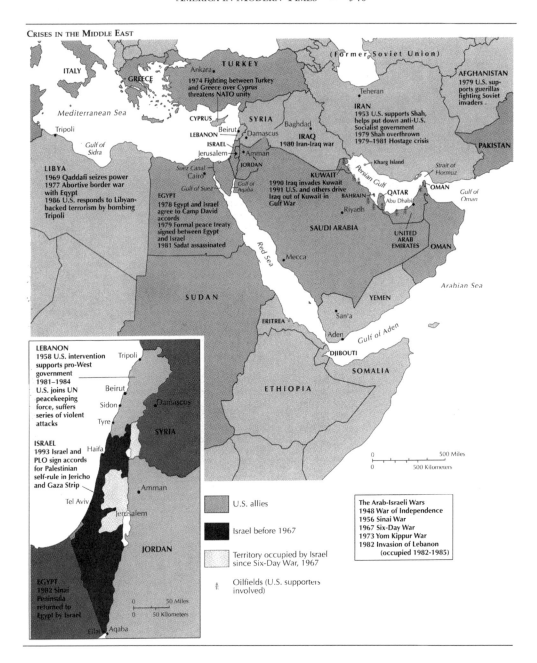

In the Middle East, conditions were growing more volatile in the aftermath of the 1967 "Six-Day War," in which Israel routed Egyptian, Syrian, and Jordanian forces and occupied substantial new territories: on the west bank of the Jordan River, the Gaza Strip, and elsewhere. The war also increased the number of refugee Palestinians—Arabs who claimed the lands now controlled by Israel and who, dislodged from their homes, became a source of considerable instability in

Jordan, Lebanon, and the other surrounding countries into which they now moved. Jordan's ruler, King Hussein, was particularly alarmed by the influx of Palestinians and by the activities of the Palestinian Liberation Organization (PLO) and other radical groups, which he feared would threaten Jordan's important relationship with the United States. After a series of uprisings in 1970, Hussein ordered the Jordanian army to expel the Palestinians. Many of them moved to Lebanon, where they became part of many years of instability and civil war.

In October 1973, on the Jewish high holy day of Yom Kippur, Egyptian and Syrian forces attacked Israel. For ten days, the Israelis struggled to recover from the surprise attack; finally, they launched an effective counteroffensive against Egyptian forces in the Sinai. At that point, the United States intervened, placing heavy pressure on Israel to accept a cease-fire rather than press its advantage.

The imposed settlement of the Yom Kippur War demonstrated the growing dependence of the United States and its allies on Arab oil. Permitting Israel to continue its drive into Egypt might have jeopardized the ability of the United States to purchase needed petroleum from the Arab states. A brief but painful embargo by the Arab governments on the sale of oil to supporters of Israel (including America) in 1973 provided an ominous warning of the costs of losing access to the region's resources. The lesson of the Yom Kippur War, therefore, was that the United States could no longer ignore the interests of the Arab nations in its efforts on behalf of Israel.

A larger lesson of 1973 was that the nations of the Third World could no longer be expected to act as passive, cooperative "client states." The United States could no longer depend on cheap, easy access to raw materials as it had in the past.

POLITICS AND ECONOMICS UNDER NIXON

For a time in the late 1960s, it had seemed to many Americans that the forces of chaos and radicalism were taking control of the nation. The domestic policy of the Nixon administration was an attempt to restore balance between the needs of the poor and the desires of the middle class, and between the power of the federal government and the interests of local communities. In the end, however, economic and political crises—some beyond the administration's control, some of its own making—sharply limited Nixon's ability to fulfill his domestic goals.

Domestic Initiatives

Many of Nixon's domestic policies were a response to what he believed to be the demands of his constituency—conservative, middle-class people whom he liked to call the "silent majority" and who wanted to reduce federal "interference" in local affairs. He tried, unsuccessfully, to persuade Congress to pass legislation prohibiting the use of forced busing to achieve school desegregation. He forbade the

Department of Health, Education, and Welfare to cut off federal funds from school districts that had failed to comply with court orders to integrate. At the same time, he began to reduce or dismantle many of the social programs of the Great Society and the New Frontier. In 1973, he abolished the Office of Economic Opportunity, the centerpiece of the antipoverty program of the Johnson years.

Yet Nixon's domestic efforts were also strikingly innovative. One of the administration's boldest efforts was an attempt to overhaul the nation's welfare system. Nixon proposed replacing the existing system, which almost everyone agreed was cumbersome, expensive, and inefficient, with what he called the Family Assistance Plan (FAP). It would in effect have created a guaranteed annual income for all Americans: $1,600 in federal grants, which could be supplemented by outside earnings up to $4,000. Even many liberals applauded the proposal as an important step toward expanding federal responsibility for the poor. Nixon, however, presented the plan in conservative terms: as something that would reduce the supervisory functions of the federal government and transfer to welfare recipients themselves daily responsibility for their own lives. Although the FAP won approval in the House in 1970, concerted attacks by welfare recipients (who considered the benefits inadequate), members of the welfare bureaucracy (whose own influence stood to be sharply diminished by the bill), and conservatives (who opposed a guaranteed income on principle) helped kill it in the Senate.

The Nixon Court

Of all the liberal institutions that had aroused the enmity of the "silent majority" in the 1950s and 1960s, none had evoked more anger and bitterness than the Supreme Court. Not only had its rulings on racial matters disrupted traditional social patterns in both the North and the South, but its staunch defense of civil liberties had, in the eyes of many Americans, contributed directly to the increase in crime, disorder, and moral decay. In *Engel* v. *Vitale* (1962), the Court had ruled that prayers in public schools were unconstitutional, sparking outrage among religious fundamentalists and others. In *Roth* v. *United States* (1957), the Court had sharply limited the authority of local governments to curb pornography. In a series of other decisions, the Court had greatly strengthened the civil rights of criminal defendants and had, in the eyes of many Americans, greatly weakened the power of law-enforcement officials to do their jobs. For example, in *Gideon* v. *Wainwright* (1963), the Court had ruled that every felony defendant was entitled to a lawyer regardless of his or her ability to pay. In *Escobedo* v. *Illinois* (1964), it had ruled that a defendant must be allowed access to a lawyer before questioning by police. In *Miranda* v. *Arizona* (1966), the Court had confirmed the obligation of authorities to inform a criminal suspect of his or her rights. By 1968, the Warren Court had become the target of Americans of all kinds who felt the balance of power in the United States had shifted too far toward the poor and dispossessed at the expense of the middle class, too far toward the rights of criminals at the expense of their victims.

Perhaps the most important decision of the Warren Court in the 1960s was *Baker* v. *Carr* (1962), which required state legislatures to apportion electoral districts so that the votes of all citizens would have equal weight. In dozens of states, systems of legislative districting had given disproportionate representation to sparsely populated rural areas, hence diminishing the voting power of urban residents. The reapportionment that the decision required greatly strengthened the voting power of African Americans, Hispanics, and other groups concentrated in cities.

Nixon was determined to use his judicial appointments to give the Court a more conservative cast. His first opportunity came almost as soon as he entered office. When Chief Justice Earl Warren resigned early in 1969, Nixon replaced him with a federal appeals court judge of known conservative leanings, Warren Burger. A few months later, Associate Justice Abe Fortas resigned his seat after the disclosure of a series of alleged financial improprieties. To replace him, Nixon named Clement F. Haynsworth, a respected federal circuit court judge from South Carolina. But Haynsworth came under fire from Senate liberals, African-American organizations, and labor unions for his conservative record on civil rights and for what some claimed was a conflict of interest in several of the cases on which he had sat. The Senate rejected him. Nixon's next choice was G. Harold Carswell, a judge of the Florida federal appeals court almost entirely lacking in distinction and widely considered unfit for the Supreme Court. The Senate rejected his nomination, too.

Nixon angrily denounced the votes, calling them expressions of prejudice against the South. But he was careful thereafter to choose men of standing within the legal community to fill vacancies on the Supreme Court: Harry Blackmun, a moderate jurist from Minnesota; Lewis F. Powell, Jr., a respected judge from Virginia; and William Rehnquist, a member of the Nixon Justice Department. In the process, he transformed the Warren Court into what some called the "Nixon Court" and others the "Burger Court."

The new Court, however, fell short of what the president and many conservatives had expected. Rather than retreating from its commitment to social reform, the Court in many areas actually moved further. In *Swann* v. *Charlotte-Mecklenburg Board of Education* (1971), it ruled in favor of the use of forced busing to achieve racial balance in schools. Not even the intense and occasionally violent opposition of local communities as diverse as Boston and Louisville, Kentucky, was able to weaken the judicial commitment to integration. In *Furman* v. *Georgia* (1972), the Court overturned existing capital punishment statutes and established strict new guidelines for such laws in the future. In *Roe* v. *Wade* (1973), it struck down laws forbidding abortions.

In other decisions, however, the Burger Court was more moderate. Although the justices approved busing as a tool for achieving integration, they rejected, in *Milliken* v. *Bradley* (1974), a plan to transfer students across district lines (in this case, between Detroit and its suburbs) to achieve racial balance. While the Court upheld the principle of affirmative action in its celebrated 1978 decision *Bakke* v. *Board of Regents of California*, it established restrictive new guidelines for such programs in the future. In *Stone* v. *Powell* (1976), the Court agreed to certain limits on the right of a defendant to appeal a state conviction to the federal judiciary.

The Election of 1972

However unsuccessful the Nixon administration may have been in achieving some of its goals, Nixon entered the presidential race in 1972 with a substantial reserve of strength. The events of that year improved his position immeasurably. His energetic re-election committee collected enormous sums of money to support the campaign. The president himself used the powers of incumbency, refraining from campaigning and concentrating on highly publicized international decisions and state visits. Agencies of the federal government dispensed funds and favors to strengthen Nixon's political standing in questionable areas.

Nixon was most fortunate in 1972, however, in his opposition. The return of George Wallace to the presidential fray caused some early concern. Nixon was delighted to see Wallace run in the Democratic primaries and had quietly encouraged him to do so. But he feared that Wallace would again launch a third party campaign; Nixon's own re-election strategy rested on the same appeals to the troubled middle class that Wallace was expressing. The possibility of such a campaign vanished in May, when a would-be assassin shot the Alabama governor during a rally at a Maryland shopping center. Paralyzed from the waist down, Wallace was unable to continue campaigning.

The Democrats, in the meantime, were making their own contributions to the Nixon cause by nominating for president a representative of their most liberal wing: Senator George S. McGovern of South Dakota. An outspoken critic of the war, a forceful advocate of advanced liberal positions on virtually every social and economic issue, McGovern seemed to embody those aspects of the turbulent 1960s that middle-class Americans were most eager to reject. McGovern profited greatly from party reforms (which he himself had helped to draft) that gave increased influence to women, blacks, and young people in the selection of the Democratic ticket. But those same reforms helped make the Democratic Convention of 1972 an unappealing spectacle to much of the public. The candidate then disillusioned even some of his own supporters by his indecisive reaction to revelations that his running mate, Senator Thomas Eagleton of Missouri, had undergone treatment for an emotional disturbance. Eagleton finally withdrew from the ticket. The remainder of the Democratic presidential campaign was an exercise in futility.

On election day, Nixon won re-election by one of the largest margins in history: 60.7 percent of the popular vote compared with 37.5 percent for the forlorn McGovern, and an electoral margin of 520 to 17. The Democratic candidate had carried only Massachusetts and the District of Columbia. The new commitments that Nixon had so effectively expressed—to restraint in social reform, to decentralization of political power, to the defense of traditional values, and to a new balance in international relations—had clearly won the approval of the American people. But other problems were already lurking in the wings.

The Troubled Economy

Although it was political scandal that would ultimately destroy the Nixon presidency, the most important national crisis of the early 1970s was the decline of the American economy. For three decades, the economic might of the United States had been the envy of the world. America had produced as much as a third of the world's industrial goods and had dominated international trade. The American dollar had been the strongest currency in the world, and the American standard of living had risen steadily from its already substantial heights. Most Americans assumed that this remarkable prosperity was the normal condition of their society. In fact, however, it rested in part on several artificial conditions that were rapidly disappearing by the late 1960s: the absence of significant foreign competition and easy access to raw materials in the Third World.

The most disturbing economic problem of the 1970s was inflation, which had been creeping upward for several years when Richard Nixon took office and which soon began to soar. Its most visible cause was a significant increase in federal deficit spending in the 1960s, when the Johnson administration tried to fund the war in Vietnam and its ambitious social programs without raising taxes. But there were other, equally important causes of the inflation and of the economic problems that lay behind it. No more did the United States have exclusive access to cheap raw materials around the globe; not only were other industrial nations now competing for increasingly scarce raw materials, but Third World suppliers of those materials were beginning to realize their value and demand higher prices for them.

The greatest immediate blow to the American economy was the increasing cost of energy. More than any nation on earth, the United States based its economy on the easy availability of cheap and plentiful fuels. No society was more dependent on the automobile; none was more wasteful in its use of oil and gas in its homes, schools, and factories. Domestic petroleum reserves were no longer sufficient to meet this demand, and the nation was heavily dependent on imports from the Middle East and Africa.

For many years, the Organization of Petroleum Exporting Countries (OPEC) had operated as an informal bargaining unit for the sale of oil by Third World (mostly Middle Eastern) nations but had seldom managed to exercise any real strength. But in the early 1970s, OPEC began to assert itself, to use its oil both as an economic tool and as a political weapon. In 1973, in the midst of the Yom Kippur War, Arab members of OPEC announced that they would no longer ship petroleum to nations supporting Israel—that is, to the United States and its allies in western Europe. At about the same time, the OPEC nations agreed to raise their prices 400 percent. These twin shocks produced momentary economic chaos in the West. The United States suffered its first fuel shortage since World War II. And although the crisis eased a few months later, the price of energy continued to skyrocket both because of OPEC's newly militant policies and because of the weakening competitive position of the dollar in world markets. No single factor did more to produce the soaring inflation of the 1970s.

But inflation was only one of the new problems facing the American economy. Another was the decline of the nation's manufacturing sector. American industry had flourished in the immediate aftermath of World War II, in part because of the new plant capacity the war had created, in part because it faced almost no competition from other industrial nations, all of them ravaged by war. American workers in unionized industries had profited from this postwar success by winning some of the most generous wage and benefits packages in the world.

By the 1970s, however, the climate for American manufacturing had changed significantly. Many of the great industrial plants were now many decades old, much less efficient than the newer plants that Japan and European industrial nations had constructed after the war. In some industries (notably steel and automobiles), management had become complacent and stultifyingly bureaucratic. Most importantly, U.S. manufacturing now faced major competition from abroad—not only in world trade (which still constituted only a small part of the American economy) but also at home. Automobiles, steel, and many other manufactured goods from Japan and Europe established major footholds in the United States markets. Some of America's new competitors benefited from lower labor costs than their U.S. counterparts; but that was only one of many reasons for their successes.

The 1970s marked the beginning, therefore, of a long, painful process of deindustrialization, during which thousands of factories across the country closed their gates and millions of workers lost their jobs. New employment opportunities were becoming available in other, growing areas of the economy: technology, information systems, and many other more "knowledge-based" industries. But many industrial workers were poorly equipped to move into those jobs. The result was a growing pool of unemployed and underemployed workers; the virtual disappearance of industrial jobs from many inner cities, where large numbers of minorities lived; and the impoverishment of communities dependent on particular industries. Some of the nation's manufacturing sectors ultimately revived, but few regained the size and dominance they had enjoyed in the 1950s and 1960s; and few employed a work force as large or as relatively well paid as they once had.

The Nixon Response

The Nixon administration responded to these mounting economic problems by focusing on the one thing it thought it could control: inflation. The government moved first to reduce spending and raise taxes. But those policies produced both congressional and popular protest, and Nixon turned increasingly to an economic tool more readily available to him: control of the currency. Placing conservative economists at the head of the Federal Reserve Board, he ensured sharply higher interest rates and a contraction of the money supply. But the tight money policy did little to curb inflation. The cost of living rose a cumulative fifteen percent during Nixon's first two and a half years in office. Economic growth, in the meantime, declined. The United States was encountering a new and puzzling dilemma: "stagflation," a combination of rising prices and general economic stagnation.

In the summer of 1971, Nixon imposed a ninety-day freeze on all wages and prices at their existing levels. Then, in November, he launched Phase II of his economic plan: mandatory guidelines for wage and price increases, to be administered by a federal agency. Inflation subsided temporarily, but the recession continued. Fearful that the recession would be more damaging than inflation in an election year, the administration reversed itself late in 1971: Interest rates dropped sharply, and government spending increased—producing the largest budget deficit since World War II. The new tactics helped revive the economy in the short term, but inflation rose substantially—particularly after the administration abandoned the strict Phase II controls and replaced them with a set of voluntary, and almost entirely ineffective, guidelines. In 1973, prices rose nine percent; in 1974, after the Arab oil embargo and the OPEC price increases, they rose twelve percent—the highest rate since the relaxation of price controls shortly after World War II. The value of the dollar continued to slide, and the nation's international trade continued to decline. The energy crisis, in the meantime, was quickly becoming a national preoccupation. But while Nixon talked often about the need to achieve "energy independence," he offered few concrete proposals.

The erratic economic programs of the Nixon administration were a sign of a broader national confusion about the prospects for American prosperity. The Nixon pattern—of lurching from a tight money policy to curb inflation at one moment to a spending policy to cure recession at the next—repeated itself during the two administrations that followed.

THE WATERGATE CRISIS

Although economic problems greatly concerned the American people in the 1970s, another stunning development almost entirely preoccupied the nation beginning early in 1973: the fall of Richard Nixon. The president's demise was a result in part of his own personality. Defensive, secretive, resentful of his critics, he brought to his office an element of mean-spiritedness that helped undermine even his most important accomplishments. But the larger explanation lay in Nixon's view of American society and the world, and of his own role in both. The president believed the United States faced grave dangers from the radicals and dissidents who were challenging his policies. He came increasingly to consider any challenge to his power a threat to "national security." By identifying his own political fortunes with those of the nation, Nixon was creating a climate in which he and those who served him could justify almost any tactics to stifle dissent and undermine opposition.

The Break-In

Nixon's outlook was in part a culmination of long-term changes in the presidency. Public expectations of the president had increased dramatically in the years since World War II; yet the constraints on the authority of the office had grown as well. In response, a succession of presidents had sought new methods for the exercise of power, often stretching the law, occasionally breaking it.

Nixon not only continued but greatly accelerated these trends. Facing a Democratic Congress hostile to his goals, he attempted to find ways to circumvent the legislature whenever possible. Saddled with a federal bureaucracy unresponsive to his wishes, he constructed a hierarchy of command in which virtually all executive power became concentrated in the White House. Operating within a rigid, even autocratic staff structure, the president became a solitary, at times brooding, figure whose contempt for his opponents and impatience with obstacles to his policies festered and grew. Unknown to all but a few intimates, the White House also became mired in a pattern of illegalities and abuses of power that late in 1972 began to break through to the surface.

Early on the morning of June 17, 1972, police arrested five men who had broken into the offices of the Democratic National Committee in the Watergate office building in Washington, D.C. Two others were seized a short time later and charged with supervising the break-in. When reporters for the *Washington Post* began researching the backgrounds of the culprits, they discovered that among those involved in the burglary were former employees of the Committee for the Re-Election of the President (CRP). One of them had worked in the White House itself. They had, moreover, been paid for the break-in from a secret fund of the re-election committee, a fund controlled by members of the White House staff.

Public interest in the disclosures grew slowly in the last months of 1972. Few Americans questioned the president's assurances that neither he nor his staff had any connection with what he called "this bizarre incident." Early in 1973, however, the Watergate burglars went on trial; and under relentless prodding from federal judge John J. Sirica, one of the defendants, James W. McCord, agreed to cooperate both with the grand jury and with a special Senate investigating committee recently established under Senator Sam J. Ervin of North Carolina. McCord's testimony opened a floodgate of confessions, and for months a parade of White House and campaign officials exposed one illegality after another. Foremost among them was a member of the inner circle of the White House, Counsel to the President John Dean, who leveled allegations against Nixon himself.

Two different sets of scandals emerged from the investigations. One was a general pattern of abuses of power involving both the White House and the Nixon campaign committee, which included, but was not limited to, the Watergate break-in. The other scandal, and the one that became the major focus of public attention for nearly two years, was the way in which the administration tried to manage the investigations of the Watergate break-in and other abuses— a pattern of behavior that became known as the "cover-up." There was never any conclusive evidence that the president had planned or approved the burglary in advance. But there was mounting evidence that he had been involved in illegal efforts to obstruct investigations of and withhold information about the episode. Testimony before the Ervin committee provided evidence of the complicity of Dean, Attorney General John Mitchell, top White House assistants H. R. Haldeman and John Ehrlichman, and others. As interest in the case grew to something approaching a national obsession, the investigation focused increasingly on a single question: In the words of Senator Howard Baker of Tennessee, a member of the Ervin committee, "What did the President know and when did he know it?"

Nixon accepted the departure of those members of his administration implicated in the scandals. But he continued to insist that he himself was innocent. There the matter might have rested had it not been for the disclosure during the Senate hearings of a White House taping system that had recorded virtually

WATERGATE HEARINGS. The testimony of White House advisers and officials during special Senate investigative hearings into the Watergate break-in proved devastating to President Nixon. Among those who inflicted the greatest damage was John Dean, counsel to the president, who testified that he believed President Nixon was involved in the cover-up of the break-in into the offices of the Democratic National Committee.

every conversation in the president's office during the period in question. All those investigating the scandals sought access to the tapes; Nixon, pleading "executive privilege," refused to release them. A special prosecutor appointed by the president to handle the Watergate cases, Harvard law professor Archibald Cox, took Nixon to court in October 1973 in an effort to force him to relinquish the recordings. Nixon, now clearly growing desperate, fired Cox and suffered the humiliation of watching both Attorney General Elliot Richardson and his deputy resign in protest. This "Saturday night massacre" made the president's predicament infinitely worse. Not only did public pressure force him to appoint a new special prosecutor, Texas attorney Leon Jaworski, who proved just as determined as Cox to subpoena the tapes; but the episode precipitated an investigation by the House of Representatives into the possibility of impeachment.

Nixon's Resignation

Nixon's situation deteriorated further in the following months. Late in 1973, Vice President Spiro Agnew became embroiled in a scandal of his own when evidence surfaced that he had accepted bribes and kickbacks while serving as governor of Maryland and even as vice president. In return for a Justice Department agreement not to press the case, Agnew pleaded no contest to a lesser charge of income-tax evasion and resigned from the government. With the controversial Agnew no longer in line to succeed to the presidency, the prospect of removing Nixon from the White House became less worrisome to his opponents. The new vice president (the first appointed under the terms of the Twenty-fifth Amendment, which had been adopted in 1967) was House Minority Leader Gerald Ford, an amiable and popular Michigan congressman.

The impeachment investigation quickly gathered pace. In April 1974, in an effort to head off further subpoenas of the tapes, the president released transcripts of a number of relevant conversations, claiming that they proved his innocence. Investigators and much of the public felt otherwise. Even these edited tapes seemed to suggest Nixon's complicity in the cover-up. In July, the crisis reached a climax. First the Supreme Court ruled unanimously, in *United States* v. *Richard M. Nixon*, that the president must relinquish the tapes to Special Prosecutor Jaworski. Days later, the House Judiciary Committee voted to recommend three articles of impeachment, charging that Nixon had, first, obstructed justice in the Watergate cover-up; second, misused federal agencies to violate the rights of citizens; and third, defied the authority of Congress by refusing to deliver tapes and other materials subpoenaed by the committee.

Even without additional evidence, Nixon might well have been impeached by the full House and convicted by the Senate. Early in August, however, he provided at last what some called the "smoking gun"—the concrete proof of his guilt that his defenders had long contended was missing from the case against him. Among the tapes that the Supreme Court compelled Nixon to relinquish were several that offered apparently incontrovertible evidence of his involve-

NIXON'S RESIGNATION. The President and
First Lady say goodbye to their successors,
Gerald and Betty Ford, on August 8, 1974, as
they board a helicopter on the White House
lawn moments after Richard Nixon's
unprecedented resignation from office.

ment in the Watergate cover-up. Only days after the burglary, the recordings
disclosed, the president had ordered the FBI to stop investigating the break-in.
Impeachment and conviction now seemed inevitable.

For several days, Nixon brooded in the White House, on the verge,
some claimed, of a breakdown. Finally, on August 8, 1974, he announced his
resignation—the first president in American history ever to do so. At noon the
next day, while Nixon and his family were flying west to their home in California, Gerald Ford took the oath of office as president.

Many Americans expressed relief and exhilaration that, as the new president
put it, "Our long national nightmare is over." Many were relieved to be rid of
Richard Nixon, who had lost virtually all of the wide popularity that had won
him his landslide re-election victory only two years before. And many were also
exhilarated that, as some boasted, "the system had worked." But the wave of
good feeling could not obscure the deeper and more lasting damage the Watergate crisis had done. In a society in which distrust of leaders and institutions of
authority was already widespread, the fall of Richard Nixon seemed to confirm
the most cynical assumptions about the character of American public life.

CHAPTER TWENTY-SEVEN

The Rise of American Conservatism

~

he frustrations of the early 1970s—the defeat in Vietnam, the Watergate crisis, the decay of the American economy—inflicted damaging blows to the confident, optimistic nationalism that had characterized so much of the postwar era. At first, many Americans responded to these problems by announcing the arrival of an "age of limits," in which America would have to learn to live with increasingly constricted expectations. By the end of the decade, however, the contours of another response to the challenges had become visible in both American culture and American politics. It was a response that combined a conservative retreat from some of the heady liberal visions of the 1960s with a reinforced commitment to the idea of economic growth, international power, and American exceptionalism.

POLITICS AND DIPLOMACY AFTER WATERGATE

In the aftermath of Richard Nixon's ignominious departure from office, many wondered whether faith in the presidency, and in the government as a whole, could easily be restored. The administrations of the two presidents who succeeded Nixon did little to answer those questions.

The Ford Presidency

Gerald Ford inherited the presidency under unenviable circumstances. He had to try to rebuild confidence in government in the face of the widespread cynicism the Watergate scandals had produced. And he had to try to restore prosperity in the face of major domestic and international challenges to the American economy. He enjoyed some success in the first of these efforts but very little in the second.

The new president's effort to establish himself as a symbol of political integrity suffered a setback only a month after he took office, when he granted Richard Nixon "a full, free, and absolute pardon" for any crimes he may have committed during his presidency. Ford explained that he was attempting to spare the nation the ordeal of years of litigation and to spare Nixon himself any further suffering. But much of the public suspected a secret deal with the former president. The pardon caused a decline in his popularity from which he never fully recovered. Nevertheless, most Americans considered Ford a decent man; his honesty and amiability did much to reduce the bitterness and acrimony of the Watergate years.

The Ford administration enjoyed less success in its effort to solve the problems of the American economy. In his efforts to curb inflation, the president rejected the idea of wage and price controls and called instead for largely ineffective voluntary efforts. After supporting high interest rates, opposing increased federal spending (through liberal use of his veto power), and resisting pressures for a tax reduction, Ford had to deal with a serious recession in 1974 and 1975. Central to the economic problems was the continuing energy crisis. In the aftermath of the Arab oil embargo of 1973, the OPEC cartel began to raise the price of oil—by 400 percent in 1974 alone. Even so, American dependence on OPEC supplies continued to grow—one of the principal reasons why inflation reached eleven percent in 1976.

At first it seemed that the foreign policy of the new administration would differ little from that of its predecessor. The new president retained Henry Kissinger as secretary of state and continued the general policies of the Nixon years. Late in 1974, Ford met with Leonid Brezhnev at Vladivostok in Siberia and signed an arms control accord that was to serve as the basis for SALT II, thus achieving a goal the Nixon administration had long sought. The following summer, after a European security conference in Helsinki, Finland, the Soviet Union and western nations agreed to ratify the borders that had divided Europe since 1945; and the Soviets pledged to increase respect for human rights within their own country. In the Middle East, in the meantime, Henry Kissinger helped produce a new accord by which Israel agreed to return large portions of the occupied Sinai to Egypt, and the two nations pledged not to resolve future differences by force. In China, finally, the death of Mao Zedong in 1976 brought to power a new, apparently more moderate government, eager to expand its ties with the United States.

Nevertheless, as the 1976 presidential election approached, Ford's policies were coming under attack from both the right and the left. In the Republican primary campaign, the president faced a powerful challenge from former California governor Ronald Reagan, leader of the party's conservative wing, who spoke for many on the right unhappy with any conciliation of communists.

The president only barely survived the assault to win his party's nomination. The Democrats, in the meantime, were gradually uniting behind a new and, before 1976, almost entirely unknown candidate: Jimmy Carter, a former governor of Georgia who organized a brilliant primary campaign and appealed to the general unhappiness with Washington by offering honesty, piety, and an outsider's skepticism of the federal government. And while Carter's once-mammoth lead in opinion polls dwindled to almost nothing by election day, unhappiness with the economy and a general disenchantment with Ford enabled the Democrat to hold on for a narrow victory. Carter emerged with 50 percent of the popular vote to Ford's 47.9 percent and 297 electoral votes to Ford's 240.

JIMMY CARTER.   Jimmy Carter campaigned for president by stressing that he was a Washington "outsider"—a message that appealed to many Americans after the political crisis of Watergate and the paralysis that seemed to grip government in its aftermath. The public image of a simple "peanut farmer" from Plains, Georgia did little to reveal, however, the depth of experience Carter brought to the White House. A graduate of the Naval Academy, a millionaire agricultural businessman, an engineer, and the reform governor of Georgia, Carter won admiration for his sincerity, intelligence, and informality. But he faced formidable challenges as president, including reversals in foreign policy, that would ultimately undermine public faith in him and lose him the presidency.

Jimmy Carter's Ordeal

Like Ford, Jimmy Carter assumed the presidency at a moment when the nation faced problems of staggering complexity and difficulty. Perhaps no leader could have thrived in such inhospitable circumstances. But Carter seemed at times to make his predicament worse by a style of leadership that many considered self-righteous and inflexible. He left office in 1981 one of the least popular presidents of the century.

Carter had campaigned for the presidency as an "outsider," representing Americans suspicious of entrenched bureaucracies and complacent public officials. He carried much of that suspiciousness with him to Washington. He surrounded himself in the White House with a group of close-knit associates from Georgia; and in the beginning, at least, he seemed deliberately to spurn assistance from more experienced political figures. Carter was among the most intelligent men ever to serve in the White House, but his critics charged that he provided no overall vision or direction to his government. His ambitious legislative agenda included major reforms of the tax and welfare systems; Congress passed virtually none of it.

Carter devoted much of his time to the problems of energy and the economy. Entering office in the midst of a recession, he moved first to reduce unemployment by raising public spending and cutting federal taxes. Unemployment declined, but inflation soared—less because of the fiscal policies he implemented than because of the continuing, sharp increases in energy prices imposed on the West by OPEC. During Carter's last two years in office, prices rose at well over a ten-percent annual rate. Like Nixon and Ford before him, Carter responded with a combination of tight money and calls for voluntary restraint. He appointed first G. William Miller and then Paul Volcker, conservative economists, to head the Federal Reserve Board, thus ensuring a policy of high interest rates and reduced currency supplies. By 1980, interest rates had risen to the highest levels in American history; at times, they exceeded twenty percent.

The problem of energy also grew steadily more troublesome in the Carter years. In the summer of 1979, instability in the Middle East produced a second major fuel shortage in the United States. In the midst of the crisis, OPEC announced another large price increase, clouding the economic picture still further. Faced with increasing pressure to act (and with public-opinion polls showing his approval rating at a dismal twenty-six percent, lower than Richard Nixon's lowest figures), Carter withdrew to Camp David, the presidential retreat in the Maryland mountains. Ten days later, he emerged to deliver a remarkable television address. It included a series of proposals for resolving the energy crisis. But it was most notable for Carter's bleak assessment of the national condition. Speaking with unusual fervor, he complained of a "crisis of confidence" that had struck "at the very heart and soul of our national will." The address became known as the "malaise" speech (although Carter himself had never used that word), and it helped fuel charges that the president was trying to blame his own problems on the American people. Carter's sudden firing of several members of his cabinet a few days later deepened his political problems.

Human Rights and National Interests

Among Jimmy Carter's most frequent campaign promises was a pledge to build a new basis for American foreign policy, one in which the defense of "human rights" would replace the pursuit of "selfish interests." Carter spoke out sharply and often about violations of human rights in many countries (including, most prominently, the Soviet Union). Beyond that general commitment, the Carter administration focused on several more traditional concerns. The president completed negotiations begun several years earlier on a pair of treaties to turn over control of the Panama Canal to the government of Panama. Domestic opposition to the treaties was intense, especially among conservatives who viewed the new arrangements as part of a general American retreat from international power. But the administration argued that relinquishing the canal was the best way to improve relations with Latin America and avoid violence in Panama. After an acrimonious debate, the Senate ratified the treaties by sixty-eight to thirty-two, only one vote more than the necessary two-thirds.

Less controversial, within the United States at least, was Carter's stunning success in arranging a peace treaty between Egypt and Israel—the crowning accomplishment of his presidency. Middle East negotiations had seemed hopelessly stalled when a dramatic breakthrough occurred in November 1977. The Egyptian president, Anwar Sadat, accepted an invitation from Prime Minister Menachem Begin to visit Israel. In Tel Aviv, he announced that Egypt was now willing to accept the state of Israel as a legitimate political entity. But translating these good feelings into an actual peace treaty proved more difficult.

When talks between Israeli and Egyptian negotiators stalled, Carter invited Sadat and Begin to a summit conference at Camp David in September 1978, holding them there for two weeks while he and others helped mediate the disputes between them. On September 17, Carter escorted the two leaders into the White House to announce agreement on a "framework" for an Egyptian-Israeli peace treaty. Carter intervened again several months later, when talks stalled once more and helped produce a vague compromise on the most sensitive issue between the two parties: the Palestinian refugee issue. On March 26, 1979, Begin and Sadat returned together to the White House to sign a formal peace treaty between their two nations.

In the meantime, Carter continued trying to improve relations with China and the Soviet Union and to complete a new arms agreement. He responded eagerly to the overtures of Deng Xiaoping, the new Chinese leader, who was attempting to open his nation to the outside world. On December 15, 1978, Washington and Beijing announced the resumption of formal diplomatic relations between the two nations. A few months later, Carter traveled to Vienna to meet with the aging and visibly ailing Brezhnev to finish drafting the new SALT

CAMP DAVID ACCORDS. Jimmy Carter gathered Egyptian President Anwar Sadat and Israeli Prime Minister Menachem Begin for a summit in September 1978 in the hopes of advancing peace in the Middle East. After two weeks of intense negotiation, a "framework" for peace between Israel and Egypt was agreed upon. Though further obstacles remained, in March 1979 Begin and Sadat came to the White House to sign a formal peace treaty. Carter considered the treaty one of the greatest achievements of his presidency.

II arms control agreement. The treaty set limits on the number of long-range missiles, bombers, and nuclear warheads on each side. Almost immediately, however, SALT II met with fierce conservative opposition in the United States. Central to the arguments was a fundamental distrust of the Soviet Union that nearly a decade of détente had failed to destroy; but specific provisions of the treaty—which even some supporters of détente felt were too favorable to the Soviets—also fueled the opposition. By the fall of 1979, with the Senate scheduled to begin debate over the treaty shortly, ratification was already in jeopardy. Events in the following months would provide a final blow, both to the treaty and to the larger framework of détente.

The Hostage Crisis

Ever since the early 1950s, the United States had provided political support and, more recently, massive military assistance to the government of the Shah of Iran, hoping to make his nation a bulwark against Soviet expansion in the Middle East. By 1979, however, the Shah was in deep trouble with his own people. Many Iranians resented the repressive, authoritarian tactics through which the Shah had maintained his autocratic rule. At the same time, Islamic clergy (and much of the fiercely religious majority of the populace) opposed his efforts to modernize and westernize a fundamentalist society. The combination of resentments produced a powerful revolutionary movement. In January 1979, the Shah fled the country.

The United States made cautious efforts in the first months after the Shah's abdication to establish cordial relations with the succession of increasingly militant regimes that followed. By late 1979, however, revolutionary chaos in Iran was making any normal relationships impossible. What power there was resided with a zealous religious leader, the Ayatollah Ruhollah Khomeini, whose hatred of the West in general and the United States in particular was intense.

In late October 1979, the deposed Shah arrived in New York to be treated for cancer. Days later, on November 4, an armed mob invaded the American embassy in Teheran, seized the diplomats and military personnel inside, and demanded the return of the Shah to Iran in exchange for their freedom. Fifty-three Americans remained hostages in the embassy for over a year. Coming after years of other international humiliations and defeats, the hostage seizure released a deep well of anger and emotion in the United States.

Only weeks after the hostage seizure, on December 27, 1979, Soviet troops invaded Afghanistan, the mountainous, Islamic nation lying between the USSR and Iran. The Soviet Union had, in fact, been a power in Afghanistan for years, and the dominant force since April 1978, when a coup had established a Marxist government there with close ties to the Kremlin. Challenges to that regime had sparked the Soviet intervention. But while some observers claimed that the Soviet invasion was a Russian attempt to secure the status quo, others—most notably the president—considered it a Russian "stepping stone to their possible control over much of the world's oil supplies." It was also, Carter claimed, the "gravest threat to world peace since World War II." Carter angrily imposed a series of economic sanctions on the Russians, canceled American participation in the 1980 summer Olympic Games in Moscow, and announced the withdrawal of SALT II from Senate consideration.

The combination of domestic economic troubles and international crises created widespread anxiety, frustration, and anger in the United States—damaging President Carter's already low standing with the public, and giving added strength to an alternative political force that had already made great strides.

THE RISE OF THE RIGHT

Much of the anxiety that pervaded American life in the 1970s was a result of jarring public events that left many men and women shaken and uncertain about their leaders and their government. But much of it was a result, too, of significant changes in the character of America's economy, society, and culture. Together these changes disillusioned many liberals, perplexed the already weak-

AMERICANS HELD HOSTAGE.   On November 4, 1979, Iranian militants overran the American Embassy in Teheran, took American personnel there hostage, and then paraded their captives in the streets while taunting and threatening them. Though a few hostages were subsequently released, fifty-five others were held captive for more than a year before they gained their freedom. This humiliating crisis put Jimmy Carter and his administration in an impossible position where the desire to gain the safe release of the Americans had to be weighed against the costs of negotiating with Iran's revolutionary regime. The crisis ended with the hostages' release on the last day of Carter's presidency.

ened left, and provided the right with its most important opportunity in generations to seize a position of authority in American life.

Sunbelt Politics

The most widely discussed demographic phenomenon of the 1970s was the rise of what became known as the "Sunbelt"—a term coined by the political analyst Kevin Phillips to describe a collection of regions that emerged together in the postwar era to become the most dynamically growing parts of the country. The Sunbelt included the Southeast (particularly Florida), the Southwest (particularly Texas), and above all, California, which became the nation's most populous state, surpassing New York, in 1964 and continued to grow in the years that followed. By 1980, the population of the Sunbelt had risen to exceed that of the industrial regions of the North and East, which were experiencing not only a relative, but in some cases an absolute, decline in population.

In addition to shifting the nation's economic focus from one region to another, the rise of the Sunbelt helped produce a change in the political climate. The strong populist traditions in the South and West were capable of producing progressive and even radical politics; but more often in the late twentieth century, they produced a strong opposition to the growth of government and a resentment of the proliferating regulations and restrictions that the liberal state were producing. Many of those regulations and restrictions—environmental laws, land-use restrictions, even the fifty-five-mile-per-hour speed limit created during the energy crisis to force motorists to conserve fuel—affected the West more than any other region. Both the South and the West, moreover, embraced myths about their own pasts that reinforced hostility to the liberal government of the mid- and late-twentieth century. White southerners equated the federal government's effort to change racial norms in the region with what they believed was the tyranny of Reconstruction. Westerners embraced an image of their region as a refuge of "rugged individualism" and resisted what they considered efforts by the government to impose new standards of behavior on them. Thus, the same impulses and rhetoric that populists had once used to denounce banks and corporations, the new conservative populists of the postwar era used to attack the government—and the liberals, radicals, and minorities whom they believed were driving its growth.

The so-called Sagebrush Rebellion, which emerged in parts of the West in the late 1970s, mobilized conservative opposition to environmental laws and restrictions on development. It also sought to portray the West (which had probably benefited more than any other region from federal investment) as a victim of government control. Its members complained about the very large amounts of land the federal government owned in many western states and demanded that they be opened for development.

The South as a whole was considerably more conservative than other parts of the nation, and its growth served to increase the power of the right in the 1960s and 1970s. The West was not, on the whole, a notably more conservative region than others; but its rise in the postwar period did help produce some of the most numerous and powerful conservative movements in the nation—particularly in southern California, where Orange County (a large suburban area south of Los Angeles) emerged as one of the most important centers of right-wing politics in the country. When the right rose to power in the 1970s and 1980s, westerners were among its most important leaders and constituents.

Religious Revivalism

In the 1960s, many social critics had predicted the virtual extinction of extensive religious influence in American life. *Time* magazine had reported such assumptions in 1966 with a celebrated cover emblazoned with the question, "Is God

Dead?" But religion in America was far from dead. Indeed, in the 1970s the United States experienced the beginning of a major religious revival, perhaps the most powerful since the second Great Awakening of the early nineteenth century. It continued in various forms into the 1990s.

Some of the new religious enthusiasm found expression in the rise of various cults and pseudo-faiths: the Church of Scientology; the Unification Church of the Reverend Sun Myung Moon; even the tragic People's Temple, whose members committed mass suicide in their jungle retreat in Guyana in 1978. But the most important impulse of the religious revival was the rise of evangelical Christianity.

Evangelicism is the basis of many forms of Christian faith. But evangelicals have in common a belief in personal conversion through direct communication with God. Evangelical religion had been the dominant form of Christianity in America through much of its history, and a substantial subculture since the late nineteenth century. In its modern form, it had been increasingly visible since at least the early 1950s, when fundamentalists such as Billy Graham and pentecostals such as Oral Roberts had begun to attract huge national (and international) followings for their energetic revivalism.

For many years, the evangelicals had gone largely unnoted by much of the media and the secular public, which had dismissed them as a limited, provincial phenomenon. By the early 1980s, it was no longer possible to do so. Earlier in the century, many (although never all) evangelicals had been relatively poor rural people, largely isolated from the mainstream of American culture. But the great capitalist expansion after World War II had lifted many of these people out of poverty and into the middle class, where they were more visible and more assertive. More than 70 million Americans now described themselves as "born-again" Christians—men and women who had established a "direct personal relationship with Jesus." Christian evangelicals owned their own newspapers, magazines, radio stations, and television networks. They operated their own schools and universities. They occupied positions of eminence in the worlds of entertainment and professional sports. And one of their number ultimately occupied the White House itself—Jimmy Carter, who during the 1976 campaign had spoken proudly of his own "conversion experience" and who continued openly to proclaim his "born-again" Christian faith during his years in office.

For Jimmy Carter and for some others, evangelical Christianity was the basis of a commitment to racial and economic justice and to world peace. For many evangelicals, however, the message of the new religion was very different—but no less political. In the 1970s, some Christian evangelicals became active on the political and cultural right. They were alarmed by what they considered the spread of immorality and disorder in American life; and they were concerned about the way a secular and, as they saw it, godless culture was intruding into their communities and families—through popular culture, through the schools, and through government policies. Many evangelical men and women feared the growth of feminism and the threat they believed it posed to the traditional family; and they resented the way in which government policies advanced the goals of the women's movement. Particularly alarming to them were Supreme Court decisions eliminating all religious observance from schools and, later, the decision guaranteeing women the right to an abortion.

By the late 1970s the "Christian right" had become a powerful and highly visible political force. Jerry Falwell, a fundamentalist minister in Virginia with a substantial television audience, launched a movement he called the Moral Majority, which attacked the rise of "secular humanism" in American culture. The Moral Majority and other organizations of similar inclination opposed federal interference in local affairs, denounced abortion, divorce, feminism, and homosexuality, defended unrestricted free enterprise, and supported a strong American posture in the world. Some evangelicals reopened issues that had long seemed closed. For example, many fundamentalist Christians questioned the scientific doctrine of evolution and urged the teaching in schools of the biblical story of the Creation instead. Others demanded various forms of censorship or control of television, movies, rock music, books, magazines, and newspapers. Their goal was a new era in which Christian values once again dominated American life.

The Emergence of the New Right

Evangelical Christians were an important part, but only a part, of what became known as the New Right—a diverse but powerful movement that enjoyed rapid growth in the 1970s and early 1980s. It had begun to take shape after the 1964 election, in which Barry Goldwater had suffered his shattering defeat. It was then that Richard Viguerie, a remarkable conservative activist and organizer, took a list of 12,000 contributors to the Goldwater campaign and used it to develop a formidable conservative communications and fund-raising organization. By the mid-1970s, he had gathered a list of 4 million contributors and 15 million supporters. Conservative campaigns had for many years been less well funded and organized than those of their rivals. Beginning in the 1970s, largely because of these and other organizational advances, conservatives found themselves almost always better funded and organized than their opponents. Gradually these direct-mail operations helped create a much larger conservative infrastructure, designed to match and even exceed what the right saw as the powerful liberal infrastructure. By the late 1970s, there were right-wing think tanks, consulting firms, lobbyists, foundations, and scholarly centers.

Another factor in the revival of the right was the emergence of a credible right-wing leadership in the late 1960s and early 1970s to replace the discredited (and somewhat erratic) conservative hero of the 1950s, Barry Goldwater. Chief among this new generation of conservative leaders was Ronald Reagan. Reagan had grown up in modest circumstances in the Midwest and attended a small college in Illinois. In 1937, at the age of twenty-six, he went to Hollywood and became a moderately successful actor, in westerns at times, but mostly in light romantic comedies. A liberal and a fervent admirer of Franklin Roosevelt as a young man, he later moved decisively to the right, especially when, as president of the Screen Actors Guild, he became embroiled in battles with communists in the union. In the early 1950s, he became a corporate spokesman for General Electric and won a wide following on the right with his smooth, eloquent speeches in defense of individual freedom and private enterprise.

In 1964, he delivered a memorable television address on behalf of Goldwater. After the Republican defeat that year, he worked quickly not only to seize the leadership of the conservative wing of the party but to denounce those Republicans who had repudiated Goldwater. "I don't think we should turn the high command over to leaders who were traitors during the battle just ended," Reagan said in 1965, when other Republicans were trying to push anti-Goldwater moderates into positions of leadership in the party. In 1966, with the support of a group of wealthy conservatives, he won the first of two terms as governor of California—which gave him a much more visible platform for promoting himself and his ideas.

The presidency of Gerald Ford also played an important role in the rise of the right by destroying the fragile equilibrium that had enabled the right wing and the moderate wing of the Republican party to coexist. Ford, probably without realizing it, touched on some of the right's rawest nerves. He appointed as vice president Nelson Rockefeller, the liberal Republican governor of New York and an heir to one of America's great fortunes; many conservatives had been demonizing Rockefeller and his family for more than twenty years. (Viguerie attributed the birth of the new right to this event alone.) Ford proposed an amnesty program for draft resisters, embraced and even extended the hated Nixon-Kissinger policies of détente, presided over the fall of Vietnam, and agreed to cede the Panama Canal to Panama. When Reagan challenged Ford in the 1976 Republican primaries, the president survived, barely, only by dumping Nelson Rockefeller from the ticket and replacing him with the more reliably conservative Robert Dole, a senator from Kansas, and by agreeing to a platform largely written by one of Reagan's principal allies, Jesse Helms. Reagan hailed that platform by saying that the party "must raise a banner of no pale pastels, but bold colors which make it unmistakably clear where we stand on all the issues troubling the people."

The Tax Revolt

At least equally important to the success of the new right was a new and potent conservative issue: the tax revolt. It had its public beginnings in 1978, when Howard Jarvis, a conservative activist, launched a major and successful citizens' tax revolt in California with Proposition 13, a referendum question on the state ballot rolling back property tax rates. Similar antitax movements soon began in other states and eventually spread to national politics.

The tax revolt became the solution to one of the right's biggest problems. For more than thirty years after the New Deal, Republican conservatives had struggled to halt and even reverse the growth of the federal government. Most of those efforts had ended in futility. Attacking government programs directly, as right-wing politicians from Robert Taft to Barry Goldwater discovered, was not the way to attract majority support. Every federal program had a political constituency. The biggest and most expensive programs had the broadest support. (Goldwater was plagued throughout the 1964 campaign by fears he would dismantle Social Security.)

In Proposition 13 and similar initiatives, members of the right found a better way to undermine government than by attacking specific programs: attacking taxes. By separating the issue of taxes from the issue of what taxes supported, the right found a way to achieve the most controversial elements of its own agenda (eroding the government's ability to expand and launch new programs) without openly antagonizing the millions of voters who supported specific programs. Virtually no one liked to pay taxes; and as the economy grew weaker and the relative burden of paying taxes grew heavier, that resentment naturally rose. The right exploited that resentment and, in the process, expanded its constituency far beyond anything it had known before. The 1980 presidential election propelled it to a historic victory.

The Campaign of 1980

By the time of the crises in Iran and Afghanistan, Jimmy Carter was in desperate political trouble—his standing in popularity polls lower than that of any president in history. Senator Edward Kennedy, younger brother of John and Robert Kennedy and one of the most magnetic figures in the Democratic party, was preparing to challenge him in the primaries. For a short while, the seizure of the hostages and the stern American response to the Soviet invasion revived Carter's candidacy. But as the hostage crisis dragged on, public impatience grew. Kennedy won a series of victories over the president in the later primaries. Carter managed in the end to stave off Kennedy's challenge and win his party's nomination. But it was an unhappy convention that heard the president's listless call to arms, and Carter's campaign aroused little popular enthusiasm as he prepared to face a powerful challenge.

The Republican party, in the meantime, had rallied enthusiastically behind the man who, four years earlier, had nearly stolen the nomination from Gerald Ford. Ronald Reagan was a sharp critic of the excesses of the federal government. He linked his campaign to the spreading tax revolt (something to which he had paid relatively little attention in the past) by promising substantial tax cuts. Equally important, he championed a restoration of American "strength" and "pride" in the world. Although he refrained from discussing the issue of the hostages, Reagan clearly benefited from the continuing popular frustration at Carter's inability to resolve the crisis. In a larger sense, he benefited as well from the accumulated frustrations of more than a decade of domestic and international disappointments.

On election day 1980, the anniversary of the seizure of the hostages in Iran, Reagan swept to victory with fifty-one percent of the vote to forty-one percent for Jimmy Carter, and seven percent for John Anderson—a moderate Republican congressman from Illinois who had mounted an independent campaign. Carter carried only five states and the District of Columbia, for a total of forty-nine electoral votes to Reagan's 489. The Republican party won control of the Senate for the first time since 1952; and although the Democrats retained a modest majority in the House, the lower chamber, too, seemed firmly in the hands of conservatives.

On the day of Reagan's inauguration, the American hostages in Iran were released after their 444-day ordeal. Jimmy Carter, in the last hours of his presidency, had concluded months of negotiations by agreeing to release several billion dollars in Iranian assets that he had frozen in American banks shortly after the seizure of the embassy. The government of Iran, desperate for funds to support its floundering war against neighboring Iraq, had ordered the hostages freed in return. Americans welcomed the hostages home with demonstrations of joy and patriotism not seen since the end of World War II. But while the celebration in 1945 had marked a great American triumph, the euphoria in 1981 marked something quite different—a troubled nation grasping for reassurance. Ronald Reagan set out to provide it.

THE "REAGAN REVOLUTION"

Ronald Reagan assumed the presidency in January 1981 promising a change in government more fundamental than any since the New Deal of fifty years before. While his eight years in office produced a significant shift in public policy, they brought nothing so radical as many of his supporters had hoped or his opponents had feared. But there was no ambiguity about the Reagan presidency's purely political achievements. Reagan succeeded brilliantly in making his own engaging personality the central fact of American politics in the 1980s.

The Reagan Coalition

Reagan owed his election to widespread disillusionment with Carter and to the crises and disappointments that many voters, perhaps unfairly, associated with him. But he owed it as well to the emergence of a powerful coalition of conservative groups. That coalition was not a single, cohesive movement. It was an uneasy and generally temporary alliance among several very different movements.

The Reagan coalition included a small but highly influential group of wealthy Americans associated with the corporate and financial world—the kind of people who had dominated American politics and government through much of the nation's history until the New Deal began to challenge their pre-eminence. What united this group was a firm commitment to capitalism and to unfettered economic growth; a deep hostility to most (although not all) government interference in markets; and a belief that most of what is valuable in American life depended on the health and strength of the corporate world, and thus that the corporate world was entitled to a special position of influence and privilege in society. Central to this group's agenda in the 1980s was opposition to what it considered the "redistributive" politics of the federal government (and especially its highly progressive tax structure) and hostility to the rise of what they believed were "antibusiness" government regulations. Reagan courted them carefully and effectively.

A second element of the Reagan coalition was even smaller, but also disproportionately influential: a group of intellectuals commonly known as "neoconservatives," who gave to the right something it had not had in many years—a firm base among "opinion leaders," people with access to the most influential public forums for ideas. Many of these people had once been liberals and, before that, socialists. But during the turmoil of the 1960s, they had become alarmed by what they considered a dangerous and destructive radicalism that they feared was destabilizing American life, and by the weakening of liberal ardor in the battle against communism. Neoconservatives were sympathetic to the complaints and demands of capitalists; but their principal concern was to reassert legitimate authority and reaffirm western democratic, anticommunist values and commitments. They considered themselves engaged in a battle to regain control of the marketplace of ideas—to "win back the culture"—from the crass, radical ideas that had polluted it. Some neoconservative intellectuals eventually became important figures in the battle against multiculturalism and "political correctness" within academia.

These two groups joined in an uneasy alliance in 1980 with the vast and growing movement known as the "new right" (or, to some, the populist right). Several things differentiated the new right from the corporate conservatives and the neoconservatives. Perhaps the most important was a fundamental distrust of the "eastern establishment": a suspicion of its motives and goals; a sense that it exercised a dangerous, secret power in American life; a fear of the hidden influence of such establishment institutions and people as the Council on Foreign Relations, the Trilateral Commission, Henry Kissinger, or the Rockefellers. These "populist" conservatives expressed the kinds of concerns that outsiders, non-elites, have traditionally voiced in American society: an opposition to centralized power and influence; a fear of living in a world where distant, hostile forces are controlling society and threatening individual freedom and community autonomy. It was a testament to Ronald Reagan's political skills and personal charm that he was able to generate enthusiastic support from these populist conservatives while at the same time appealing to more elite conservative groups whose concerns were in many ways antithetical to those of the new right.

RONALD REAGAN.   Ronald Reagan at his ranch in Santa Barbara, displaying the informal geniality that accounted for much of his remarkable popularity.

Reagan in the White House

Even many people who disagreed with Reagan's policies found themselves drawn to his attractive and carefully honed public image. Reagan was a master of television, a gifted public speaker, and—in public at least—rugged, fearless, and seemingly impervious to danger or misfortune. He turned seventy-years-old weeks after taking office and was the oldest man ever to serve in the White House. But through most of his presidency, he seemed vigorous, resilient, even youthful. He spent his many vacations on a California ranch, where he chopped wood and rode horses. When he was wounded in an assassination attempt in 1981, he joked with doctors on his way into surgery and appeared to bounce back from the ordeal with remarkable speed. Four years later, he seemed to re-bound from cancer surgery with similar zest. He had few visible insecurities. Even when things went wrong, as they often did, the blame seldom seemed to attach for long to Reagan himself (inspiring some Democrats to begin referring to him as "the Teflon president").

Reagan was not much involved in the day-to-day affairs of running the government; he surrounded himself with tough, energetic administrators who insulated him from many of the pressures of the office and apparently relied on him largely for general guidance, not specific decisions. At times, the president revealed a startling ignorance about the nature of his own policies or the actions of his subordinates. But Reagan did make active use of his office to generate support for his administration's programs, by appealing repeatedly to the public over television and by fusing his proposals with a highly nationalistic rhetoric.

"Supply-Side" Economics

Reagan's 1980 campaign for the presidency had promised, among other things, to restore the economy to health by a bold experiment that became known as "supply-side" economics or, to some, "Reaganomics." Supply-side economics operated from the assumption that the woes of the American economy were in large part a result of excessive taxation, which left inadequate capital available to investors to stimulate growth. The solution, therefore, was to reduce taxes, with particularly generous benefits to corporations and wealthy individuals, in order to encourage new investments. The result would be a general economic revival that would help everyone. Because a tax cut would reduce government revenues (at least at first), it would also be necessary to reduce government expenses. A cornerstone of the Reagan economic program, therefore, was a series of dramatic cuts in federal spending.

In its first months in office, accordingly, the new administration hastily assembled a legislative program based on the supply-side idea. It proposed $40 billion in budget reductions and managed to win congressional approval of almost all of them. In addition, the president proposed a bold, three-year rate reduction of thirty percent on both individual and corporate taxes. In the summer of 1981, Congress passed it too, after lowering the reductions slightly, to twenty-five percent. Not since Lyndon Johnson had a president compiled so impressive a legislative record in his first months in office. Reagan was successful because he had a disciplined Republican majority in the Senate, and because the Democratic majority in the House was weak and riddled with defectors. Shaken by the results of the 1980 election, dozens of Democrats from relatively conservative districts (mostly in the South) deserted the party's leadership; the defectors became known as "boll weevils."

Men and women appointed by Reagan fanned out through the executive branch of government committed to reducing the role of government in American economic life. "Deregulation," an idea many Democrats had begun to embrace in the Carter years, became the religion of the Reagan administration. Secretary of the Interior James Watt, who had been a major figure in the Sagebrush Rebellion, opened up public lands and water to development. The Environmental Protection Agency (before its directors were indicted for corruption) relaxed or entirely eliminated enforcement of critical environmental laws and regulations. The Civil Rights Division of the Justice Department eased enforcement of civil-rights laws. The Department of Transportation slowed implementation of new rules limiting automobile emissions and imposing new safety standards on cars and trucks. By getting government "out of the way," Reagan officials promised, they were ensuring economic revival.

By early 1982, however, the nation had sunk into the most severe recession since the 1930s. The Reagan economic program was not directly to blame for the problems. The recession was more a result of the high interest rates the Federal Reserve Board (run by Carter appointee William Volcker) had maintained since the late 1970s. The high rates made it difficult for businesses and individuals to borrow money for investment or consumer purchases. They also made the dollar attractive to overseas investors and significantly raised its value—thus making American products more expensive abroad and significantly reducing exports. By 1984, the U.S. trade deficit was $111 billion; in 1980, there had been a $25 billion surplus. The recession had particularly devastating effects on American industry, which had already been experiencing serious problems for a decade. Industrialists closed some plants, reduced the labor force in others, and eliminated millions of manufacturing jobs. In 1982, unemployment reached eleven percent, its highest level in over forty years. Farmers, even more dependent than manufacturers on the export trade, fared even worse. Hundreds of thousands of farmers lost so much money in the early 1980s that they could not keep their farms.

The recession convinced many people, including some conservatives, that the Reagan economic program (and thus the Reagan presidency) had failed. In fact, however, the economy recovered more rapidly and impressively than almost anyone had expected. By late 1983, unemployment had fallen to 8.2 percent, and it declined steadily for several years after that. The gross national product had grown 3.6 percent in a year, the largest increase since the mid-1970s. Inflation had fallen below five percent. The economy continued to grow, and both inflation and unemployment remained low (at least by the new and more pessimistic standards the nation seemed now to have accepted) through most of the decade.

The recovery was a result of many things. The years of tight-money policies by the Federal Reserve Board, however painful and destructive they may have been in other ways, had helped lower inflation; and equally important, the Board had lowered interest rates early in 1983 in response to the recession. A worldwide "energy glut" and the virtual collapse of the OPEC cartel had produced at least a temporary end to the inflationary pressures of spiraling fuel costs. And staggering federal budget deficits were pumping billions of dollars into the flagging economy. As a result, consumer spending and business investment both increased. And the stock market rose up from the doldrums of the late 1970s and began a sustained and historic boom. In August 1982, the Dow Jones Industrial Average stood at 777. Five years later, it had passed 2,000. Despite a frightening crash in the fall of 1987, the market continued to grow. In late 1996, the Dow Jones average was nearing 6,000.

The Fiscal Crisis

The economic revival did little, however, to reduce the staggering, and to many Americans alarming, deficits in the federal budget. By the mid-1980s, this growing fiscal crisis had become one of the central issues in American politics. Having entered office promising a balanced budget within four years, Reagan presided over record budget deficits and accumulated more debt in his eight years in office than the American government had accumulated in its entire

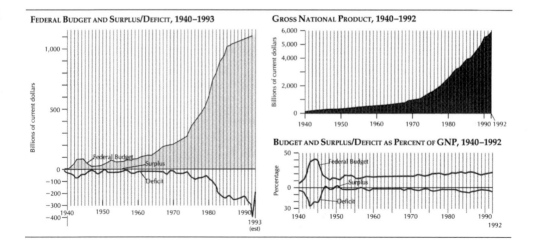

FEDERAL BUDGET AND SURPLUS/DEFICIT, 1940–1993

GROSS NATIONAL PRODUCT, 1940–1992

BUDGET AND SURPLUS/DEFICIT AS PERCENT OF GNP, 1940–1992

previous history. Before the 1980s, the highest single-year budget deficit in American history had been $66 billion (in 1976). Throughout the 1980s, the annual budget deficit consistently exceeded $100 billion (and in 1991 peaked at $268 billion). The national debt rose from $907 billion in 1980 to nearly $3.5 trillion by 1991.

The enormous deficits had many causes, some of them stretching back over decades of American public policy decisions. In particular, the budget suffered from enormous increases in the costs of "entitlement" programs (especially Social Security and Medicare), a product of the aging of the population and the dramatic increase in the cost of health care. But some of the causes of the deficit lay in the policies of the Reagan administration. The 1981 tax cuts, the largest in American history, eroded the revenue base of the federal government and accounted for a significant percentage of the deficit. The massive increase in military spending (a proposed $1.6 trillion over five years) on which the Reagan administration insisted added more to the federal budget than its cuts in domestic spending removed.

In the face of these deficits, the administration refused to consider raising income taxes (although it did agree to a major increase in the Social Security tax). It would not agree to reductions in military spending. It could not much reduce the costs of entitlement programs, and it could do nothing to reduce interest payments on the massive (and growing) debt. Its answer to the fiscal crisis, therefore, was further cuts in "discretionary" domestic spending, which included many programs aimed at the poorest (and politically weakest) Americans. There were reductions in funding for food stamps; a major cut in federal subsidies for low-income housing (which contributed to the radical increase in homelessness that by the late 1980s was plaguing virtually all American cities); strict new limitations on Medicare and Medicaid payments; reductions in student loans, school lunches, and other educational programs; and an end to many forms of federal assistance to the states and cities—which helped precipitate years of local fiscal crises as well.

By the end of Reagan's third year in office, funding for domestic programs had been cut nearly as far as Congress (and, apparently, the public) was willing to tolerate; and still no end was in sight to the rising deficits. Congress responded with the so-called Gramm-Rudman bill, passed late in 1985, which mandated major deficit reductions over five years and provided for automatic budget cuts in all areas of government spending should the president and Congress fail to agree on an alternative solution. Under Gramm-Rudman, the budget deficit did decline for several years from its 1983 high. But much of that decline was a result of a substantial surplus in the Social Security trust fund (which the sharply increased Social Security taxes had produced), not of the provisions of the law. By the late 1980s, some fiscal conservatives were calling for a constitutional amendment mandating a balanced budget—a provision the president himself claimed to support but did little to promote.

Reagan and the World

Reagan encountered a similar combination of triumphs and difficulties in international affairs. Determined to restore American pride and prestige in the world, he argued that the United States should once again become active and assertive in opposing communism and supporting friendly governments whatever their internal policies.

Relations with the Soviet Union, which had been steadily deteriorating in the last years of the Carter administration, grew still more chilly in the first years of the Reagan presidency. The president spoke harshly of the Soviet regime (which he once called the "evil empire"), accusing it of sponsoring world terrorism and declaring that any armaments negotiations must be "linked" to negotiations about Soviet behavior in other areas. Relations with the Russians deteriorated further after the government of Poland (under strong pressure from Moscow) imposed martial law on the country in the winter of 1981 to crush a growing challenge from an independent labor organization, Solidarity.

Although the president had long denounced the SALT II arms control treaty as unfavorable to the United States, he continued to honor its provisions. But the Reagan administration at first made little progress toward arms control in other areas. In fact, the president proposed the most ambitious new military program in many years: the so-called Strategic Defense Initiative (SDI), widely known as "Star Wars" (after a popular movie by that name). Reagan claimed that SDI, through the use of lasers and satellites, could provide an effective shield against incoming missiles and thus make nuclear war obsolete. The Soviet Union claimed that the new program would elevate the arms race to new and more dangerous levels and insisted that any arms control agreement begin with an American abandonment of SDI.

The escalation of Cold War tensions and the slowing of arms control initiatives helped produce an important popular movement in Europe and the United States calling for an end to nuclear weapons buildups. In America, the principal goal of the movement was a "nuclear freeze," an agreement between the two superpowers not to expand their atomic arsenals. In what many believed was the largest mass demonstration in American history, nearly a million people rallied in New York City's Central Park in 1982 to support the freeze. Perhaps in response to this growing pressure, the administration began tentative efforts to revive arms control negotiations in 1983.

It also began, rhetorically at least, to support opponents of communism anywhere in the world, whether or not the regimes or movements they were challenging had any direct connection to the Soviet Union. This new policy became known as the Reagan Doctrine, and it meant, above all, a new American activism in the Third World. The most conspicuous examples of the new activism came in Latin America. In October 1982, the administration sent American soldiers and Marines into the tiny Caribbean island of Grenada to oust an anti-American Marxist regime that showed signs of forging a relationship with Moscow. In El Salvador, where first a repressive military regime and later a moderate civilian one were engaged in murderous struggles with left-wing revolutionaries (who were supported, according to the Reagan administration, by Cuba and the Soviet Union), the president provided increased military and economic assistance. In neighboring Nicaragua, a pro-American dictatorship had fallen to the revolutionary "Sandinistas" in 1979; the new government had grown increasingly anti-American (and increasingly Marxist) throughout the early 1980s. The administration gave both rhetorical and material support to the so-called *contras*, a guerrilla movement drawn from several antigovernment groups and fighting (without great success) to topple the Sandinista regime. Indeed, support of the *contras* became a mission of special importance to the president, and later the source of some of his greatest difficulties.

In other parts of the world, the administration's bellicose rhetoric seemed to hide an instinctive restraint. In June 1982, the Israeli army launched an invasion of Lebanon in an effort to drive guerrillas of the Palestinian Liberation Organization from the country. The United States supported the Israelis rhetorically but also worked to permit PLO forces to leave Lebanon peacefully. An American peacekeeping force entered Beirut to supervise the evacuation. American Marines then remained in the city, apparently to protect the fragile Lebanese government, which was embroiled in a vicious civil war. Now identified with one faction in the struggle, Americans became the targets of a terrorist bombing of a U.S. military barracks in Beirut in 1983 that left 241 marines dead. Rather than become more deeply involved in the Lebanese struggle, Reagan withdrew American forces.

The tragedy in Lebanon was an example of the changing character of Third World struggles: an increasing reliance on terrorism by otherwise relatively powerless groups to advance their political aims. A series of terrorist acts in the 1980s—attacks on airplanes, cruise ships, commercial and diplomatic posts; the seizing of American and other western hostages—alarmed and frightened much of the western world. The Reagan administration spoke bravely about its resolve to punish terrorism; and at one point in 1986, the president ordered American planes to bomb sites in Tripoli, the capital of Libya, whose controversial leader Muammar al-Qaddafi was widely believed to be a leading sponsor of terrorism. In general, however, terrorists remained difficult to identify or control; and policymakers, in their frustration, began to search for new ways to deal with them.

The Election of 1984

Reagan approached the campaign of 1984 at the head of a united Republican party firmly committed to his candidacy. The Democrats, as had become their custom, followed a more fractious course. Former Vice President Walter

MONDALE-FERRARO. Walter Mondale made history when he selected Geraldine Ferraro, a member of the House of the Representatives from New York, as his running mate in 1984. Ms. Ferraro was the first woman nominated by a major political party for national office. Her historic selection, however, did not persuade voters to choose Mondale over Reagan, who won the election in a landslide.

Mondale established an early and commanding lead in the race by soliciting support from a wide range of traditional Democratic interest groups and survived challenges from Senator Gary Hart of Colorado (who claimed to represent a "new generation" of leadership) and the magnetic Jesse Jackson, a charismatic African-American leader who had established himself as the nation's most prominent spokesman for minorities and the poor. Mondale captured the nomination and brought momentary excitement to the Democratic campaign by selecting a woman, Representative Geraldine Ferraro of New York, to be his running mate and the first female candidate ever to appear on a national ticket.

The Republican party rallied comfortably behind its revered leader, who in his triumphant campaign that fall scarcely took note of his opponents and spoke instead of what he claimed was the remarkable revival of American fortunes and spirits under his leadership. His campaign emphasized such phrases as "It's Morning in America" and "America is Back." Reagan's victory in 1984 was decisive. He won approximately fifty-nine percent of the vote, and he carried every state but Mondale's native Minnesota and the District of Columbia. But Reagan was much stronger than his party. Democrats gained a seat in the Senate and maintained only slightly reduced control of the House of Representatives.

The triumphant re-election of Ronald Reagan was the high watermark of conservative, and Republican, fortunes in the postwar era to that point. It reflected satisfaction with the impressive performance of the economy under the Republican economic program and pride in the new assertiveness the United States was showing in the world. To many Reagan supporters, the 1984 election seemed to be the dawn of a new conservative era. But almost no one anticipated the revolutionary changes that would transform the world, and the United States's place in it, within a very few years. The election of 1984 was, therefore, not so much the first of a new era as it was the last of an old one. It was the final campaign of the Cold War.

CHAPTER TWENTY-EIGHT

Modern Times

~

On November 8, 1989, East German soldiers stood guard at the Berlin Wall—keeping westerners out and easterners in—as they had done every day for more than twenty-eight years. The next day they were gone. Within hours, thousands of citizens of both sides of the divided city were swarming over the wall in celebration. Within weeks, bulldozers were tearing it down. Within a year, East and West Germany—divided by the Cold War for forty-five years—had reunited.

The breaching of the Berlin Wall and the reunification of Germany were among the most dramatic of a series of changes between 1986 and 1991 that radically transformed the world. The Cold War, which as late as 1985 had seemed a permanent fact of international life, came to an end. A new world order, the outlines of which were still only dimly visible, was in the process of being born.

The Cold War had shaped the foreign policy and much of the domestic life of the United States for nearly half a century. Its sudden end changed the character of national politics, economics, and culture. But America in the late 1980s and early 1990s was also encountering a series of other important social and economic changes, many of them unrelated to the Cold War. As the end of the twentieth century approached, most Americans were uncertain whether the changes would bring a better, safer world or a harsher and more dangerous one.

THE END OF THE COLD WAR

Many factors contributed to the collapse of the Soviet empire. The long, stalemated war in Afghanistan proved at least as disastrous to the Soviet Union as the Vietnam War had been to America. The government in Moscow had failed to address a long-term economic decline in the Soviet republics and the eastern-bloc nations. Restiveness with the heavy-handed policies of communist police states was growing throughout much of the Soviet empire. But the most visible factor at the time was the emergence of a single man: Mikhail Gorbachev, who succeeded to the leadership of the Soviet Union in 1985 and, to the surprise of almost everyone, very quickly became the most revolutionary figure in world politics in at least four decades.

The Fall of the Soviet Union

Gorbachev quickly transformed Soviet politics with two dramatic new initiatives. The first he called *glasnost* (openness): the dismantling of many of the repressive mechanisms that had been conspicuous features of Soviet life for over half a century. The other policy Gorbachev called *perestroika* (reform): an effort to restructure the rigid and unproductive Soviet economy by introducing, among other things, such elements of capitalism as private ownership and the profit motive. He also began to transform Soviet foreign policy.

The severe economic problems at home evidently convinced Gorbachev that the Soviet Union could no longer sustain its extended commitments around the world. As early as 1987, he began reducing Soviet influence in eastern Europe. And in 1989, in the space of a few months, every communist state in Europe—Poland, Hungary, Czechoslovakia, Bulgaria, Romania, East Germany, Yugoslavia, and Albania—either overthrew its government or forced it to transform itself into an essentially noncommunist (and in some cases, actively anticommunist) regime. The communist parties of eastern Europe all but collapsed (although some of them later revived in altered form). Gorbachev and the Soviet Union actively encouraged the changes.

The challenges to communism were not successful everywhere. In May 1989, students in China launched a mass movement calling for greater democratization. But in June, hardline leaders seized control of the government and sent military forces to crush the uprising. The result was a bloody massacre on June 3, 1989, in Tiananmen Square in Beijing, in which a still-unknown number of demonstrators died. The assault crushed the democracy movement and restored the hardliners to power. It did not, however, stop China's efforts to modernize and even westernize its economy.

But China was an exception to the worldwide movement toward democratization, which even extended to parts of the world far removed from the Soviet empire. Early in 1990, the government of South Africa, long an international pariah for its rigid enforcement of "apartheid" (a system of legalized segregation of the races designed to protect white supremacy) began a cautious retreat from its traditional policies. Among other things, it legalized the chief black party in the nation, the African National Congress, which had been banned for decades, and on February 11, 1990, it released from prison the leader of the ANC, and a revered hero to black South Africans, Nelson Mandela, who had been in jail for twenty-seven years. Over the next several years, the South African government repealed its apartheid laws. And in 1994, there were national elections in which all South Africans could participate. As a result, Nelson Mandela became the first black president of South Africa.

In 1991, communism began to collapse at the site of its birth: the Soviet Union itself. An unsuccessful coup by hardline Soviet leaders on August 19 precipitated a dramatic unraveling of communist power. Within days, the coup itself collapsed in the face of resistance from the public and, more important, crucial elements within the military. Mikhail Gorbachev returned to power; but it soon became evident that the legitimacy of both the Communist party and the central Soviet government had been fatally injured. By the end of August, almost every republic in the Soviet Union had declared independence; the Soviet government was clearly powerless to stop the fragmentation. Gorbachev himself finally resigned as leader of the now virtually powerless Communist party and Soviet government, and the Soviet Union ceased to exist. Boris Yeltsin, the president of the Russian Republic who had led popular opposition to the coup, now emerged as the leader of the largest and most powerful part of the former Soviet empire. (In 1996, he staved off a strong challenge from unrepentant communists and won re-election.)

Reagan and Gorbachev

The last years of the Reagan administration coincided with the first years of the Gorbachev regime; and while Reagan was skeptical of Gorbachev at first, he gradually became convinced that the Soviet leader was sincere in his desire for reform. At a summit meeting with Reagan in Reykjavik, Iceland, in 1986,

THREE PRESIDENTS,1988   President-elect George Bush and President Ronald Reagan stand with Soviet President Mikhail Gorbachev before the Statue of Liberty on December 7, 1988, during a visit by Gorbachev to the United Nations.

Gorbachev proposed reducing the nuclear arsenals of both sides by fifty percent or more, although continuing disputes over Reagan's commitment to the SDI program derailed agreements. But in 1988, after Reagan and Gorbachev exchanged cordial visits to each other's capitals, the two superpowers signed a treaty eliminating American and Soviet intermediate-range nuclear forces (INF) from Europe—the most significant arms control agreement of the nuclear age. At about the same time, Gorbachev ended the Soviet Union's long and frustrating military involvement in Afghanistan, removing one of the principal irritants in the relationship between Washington and Moscow.

DOMESTIC POLITICS IN THE POST–COLD WAR PERIOD

As the Cold War came to an end, American political life also seemed to move toward a complex, ambiguous, and unpredictable stage in which neither of the major political parties appeared to provide a vision adequate for the new world. Americans remained preoccupied with the economy, less than confident in their future, and skeptical about the direction of change. In this context, political leaders had a difficult time maintaining power for long. The voters seemed to choose change whenever they had the opportunity.

The Fading of the Reagan Revolution

For a time, the dramatic changes around the world and Reagan's personal popularity deflected attention from a series of scandals that might well have destroyed another administration. There were revelations of illegality, corruption, and ethical lapses in the Environmental Protection Agency, the CIA, the Department of Defense, the Department of Labor, the Department of Justice, and the Department of Housing and Urban Development. A more serious scandal emerged within the savings and loan industry, which the Reagan administration had helped deregulate in the early 1980s. Many savings banks had responded by rapidly, often recklessly, and sometimes corruptly, expanding. By the end of the decade the industry was in chaos, and the government was forced to step in to prevent a complete collapse. Government insurance covered the assets of most savings and loan depositors; but the cost to the public of the debacle eventually ran to more than half a trillion dollars.

The most politically damaging scandal of the Reagan years came to light in November 1986, when the White House conceded that it had sold weapons to the revolutionary government of Iran as part of a largely unsuccessful effort to secure the release of several Americans being held hostage by radical Islamic groups in the Middle East. Even more damaging was the revelation that some of the money from the arms deal with Iran had been covertly and illegally funneled into a fund to aid the *contras* in Nicaragua.

In the months that followed, aggressive reporting and a highly publicized series of congressional hearings exposed a widespread pattern of covert activities orchestrated by the White House and dedicated to advancing the administration's foreign policy aims through secret and at times illegal means. The principal figure in this covert world appeared at first to be an obscure marine lieutenant colonel assigned to the staff of the National Security Council, Oliver North. But gradually it became clear that North was acting in concert with other, more powerful figures in the administration. The Iran-contra scandal, as it became known, did serious damage to the Reagan presidency—even though the investigations were never able decisively to tie the president himself to the most serious violations of the law. A blue ribbon commission appointed to explore Iran-contra painted a devastating picture of Reagan in its report. The president, the commission concluded, seemed detached, disinterested, and even unaware of events occurring in his own administration.

The Election of 1988

The fraying of the Reagan administration helped the Democrats regain control of the United States Senate in 1986 and fueled hopes in the party for a presidential victory in 1988. Even so, several of the most popular figures in the Democratic party refused to run. The nomination finally went to a previously little-known figure: Michael Dukakis, a three-term governor of Massachusetts. Dukakis was a dry, even dull campaigner with a reputation for honesty and competence and for presiding over an impressive economic revival in his home state, often called the "Massachusetts Miracle." Democrats were optimistic about their prospects in 1988, however, less because of Dukakis than because of the identity of their opponent, Vice President George Bush, who had captured the Republican nomination without great difficulty, but who had failed to spark any real public enthusiasm. He entered the last months of the campaign well behind Dukakis.

Beginning at the Republican convention, however, Bush staged a remarkable turnaround by transforming his campaign into a long, relentless attack on Dukakis, tying him to all the unpopular social and cultural stances Americans had come to identify with "liberals." Indeed, the Bush campaign was almost certainly the most savage of the twentieth century. It was also, apparently, one of the most effective, although the listless, indecisive character of the Dukakis effort contributed to the Republican cause as well. Bush won a substantial victory in November: fifty-four percent of the popular vote to Dukakis's forty-six, and 426 electoral votes to Dukakis's 112. But Bush carried few Republicans into office with him; the Democrats retained secure majorities in both houses of Congress.

The Bush Presidency

The Bush presidency was notable for a series of dramatic developments in international affairs and an almost complete absence of initiatives or ideas on domestic issues. For a time, Bush's achievements in foreign policy managed to obscure the absence of a domestic agenda. By early 1992, however, with the nation in the second year of a serious recession, the president's popularity had begun to fray.

The broad popularity Bush enjoyed during much of his first three years in office was partly because of his subdued, unthreatening public image. But it was primarily because of the wonder and excitement with which Americans viewed the dramatic events in the rest of the world. Bush moved cautiously at first in dealing with the changes in the Soviet Union. But like Reagan, he eventually embraced Gorbachev and reached a series of significant agreements with the Soviet Union in its waning years. In the three years after the INF agreement in 1988, the United States and the Soviet Union moved rapidly toward even more far-reaching arms reduction agreements, including major troop reductions in Europe and the dismantling of new categories of strategic weapons.

On domestic issues, the Bush administration was less successful—partly because the president himself seemed to have little interest in promoting a domestic agenda and partly because he faced serious obstacles. His administration inherited a staggering burden of debt and a federal deficit that had been out of control for nearly a decade. Any domestic agenda that required significant federal spending was, therefore, incompatible with the president's pledge to reduce the deficit and his 1988 campaign promise of "no new taxes." Bush faced a Democratic Congress with an agenda very different from his own. And he was constantly concerned about the right wing of his own party. In his eagerness to ingratiate himself with them, the president took divisive positions on such cultural issues as abortion and affirmative action that further damaged his ability to work with Congress.

Despite this political stalemate, Congress and the White House managed on occasion to agree on significant measures. They cooperated in producing a plan to salvage the floundering savings and loan industry. In 1990, the president bowed to congressional pressure and agreed to a large tax increase as part of a multiyear "budget package" designed to reduce the deficit. In 1991, after almost two years of acrimonious debate, the president and Congress agreed on a civil rights bill to combat job discrimination.

But the most politically damaging domestic problem facing the Bush administration was one to which neither the president nor Congress had any answer: a recession that began late in 1990 and slowly increased its grip on the national economy in 1991 and 1992. Because of the enormous level of debt that corporations (and individuals) had accumulated in the 1980s, the recession caused an unusual number of bankruptcies. It also created growing fear and frustration among middle- and working-class Americans and increasing pressure on the government to address such problems as the rising cost of health care.

The Gulf War

The events of 1989–1991 had left the United States in the unanticipated position of being the only real superpower in the world. The Bush administration, therefore, had to consider what to do with America's formidable political and military power in a world in which the major justification for that power—the Soviet threat—was now gone.

The events of 1989–1991 suggested two possible answers, both of which had some effect on policy. One was that the United States would reduce its military strength dramatically and concentrate its energies and resources on pressing domestic problems. And, indeed, there was considerable movement in that direction both in Congress and within the administration. The other was that America would continue to use its power actively, not to fight communism but to defend its regional and economic interests. In 1989, that impulse led the administration to order an invasion of Panama, which overthrew the unpopular military leader Mañuel Noriega (under indictment in the United States for drug trafficking) and replaced him with an elected, pro-American regime. And in 1991, that same impulse drew the United States into the turbulent politics of the Middle East.

On August 2, 1990, the armed forces of Iraq invaded and quickly overwhelmed their small, oil-rich neighbor, the emirate of Kuwait. Saddam Hussein, the militaristic leader of Iraq, soon announced that he was annexing Kuwait and set out to entrench his forces there. After some initial indecision, the Bush administration agreed to join with other nations to force Iraq out of Kuwait—through the pressure of economic sanctions if possible, through military force if necessary. Within a few weeks, Bush had persuaded virtually every important government in the world, including the Soviet Union and almost all the Arab and Islamic states, to join in a United Nations–sanctioned trade embargo of Iraq.

At the same time, the United States and its allies (including the British, French, Egyptians, and Saudis) began deploying a massive military force along the border between Kuwait and Saudi Arabia, a force that ultimately reached 690,000 troops (425,000 of them American) and that assembled the largest and most sophisticated collection of military technology ever used in warfare. On November 29, the United Nations, at the request of the United States, voted to authorize military action to expel Iraq from Kuwait if Iraq did not leave by January 15, 1991. On January 12, both houses of Congress voted to authorize the use of force against Iraq, although many Democrats opposed the resolution, arguing that sanctions should be given more time to work. And on January 16, American and allied air forces began a massive bombardment of Iraqi forces in Kuwait and of military and industrial installations in Iraq itself.

The allied bombing continued for six weeks, meeting only token resistance from the small Iraqi air force and ground defenses. And on February 23, allied (mostly American) forces under the command of General Norman Schwarzkopf began a major ground offensive—not primarily against the heavily entrenched Iraqi forces along the Kuwait border, as expected, but into Iraq itself. The allied armies encountered almost no resistance and suffered only light casualties (141 fatalities). There were no reliable figures for the number of Iraqi military casualties, but some estimated the deaths (most as a result of the bombing) to be 100,000 or more. There were also a significant, if unverifiable, number of civilian casualties. On February 28, Iraq announced its acceptance of allied terms for a cease-fire, and the brief war came to an end.

The quick and (for America) relatively painless victory over Iraq was highly popular in the United States. But the longer range results of the Gulf War were more difficult to assess. The tyrannical regime of Saddam Hussein survived, in a weakened form but showing few signs of retreat from its militaristic ambitions. And Kuwait returned to the control of its prewar government, an undemocratic monarchy increasingly unpopular with its own people.

The Election of 1992

President Bush's popularity reached a record high in the immediate aftermath of the Gulf War. But the glow of the Gulf War victory faded quickly as the recession worsened in late 1991, and as the administration declined to propose any policies for combatting it. The president's standing soon eroded.

Because the early maneuvering for the 1992 presidential election occurred when President Bush's popularity remained high, many leading Democrats declined to run. That gave Bill Clinton, the young five-term governor of Arkansas, the opportunity to emerge early as the front-runner, as a result of a skillful campaign that emphasized broad economic issues over the racial and cultural questions that had so divided the Democrats in the past. Clinton survived a bruising primary campaign and a series of damaging personal controversies to win his party's nomination. And George Bush withstood an embarrassing primary challenge from the conservative journalist Pat Buchanan to become the Republican nominee again.

Complicating the campaign was the emergence of Ross Perot, a blunt, forthright Texas billionaire who became an independent candidate by tapping popular resentment of the federal bureaucracy and by promising tough, uncompromising leadership to deal with the fiscal crisis and other problems of government. Particularly appealing to many voters were Perot's attacks on corruption in the political system and his insistence that his own campaign (funded by his personal fortune, not by special-interest lobbies) was a pure reflection of the will of the people. At several moments in the spring, Perot led both Bush and Clinton in public opinion polls. In July, as he began to face hostile scrutiny from the media, he abruptly withdrew from the race. But early in October, he re-entered and soon regained much (although never all) of his early support.

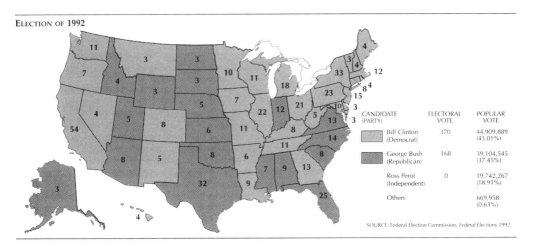

ELECTION OF 1992

CANDIDATE (PARTY)	ELECTORAL VOTE	POPULAR VOTE
Bill Clinton (Democrat)	370	44,909,889 (43.01%)
George Bush (Republican)	168	39,104,545 (37.45%)
Ross Perot (Independent)	0	19,742,267 (18.91%)
Others		669,958 (0.63%)

SOURCE: Federal Election Commission, *Federal Elections 1992.*

After a campaign in which the economy and the president's unpopularity were the principal issues, Clinton won a clear, but hardly overwhelming, victory over Bush and Perot. He received forty-three percent of the vote in the three-way race, to the president's thirty-eight percent and Perot's nineteen percent (the best showing for a third party or independent candidate since Theodore Roosevelt in 1912). Clinton won 370 electoral votes to Bush's 168; Perot won none. Democrats retained control of both houses of Congress.

Launching the Clinton Presidency

Bill Clinton was the first Democratic president since Jimmy Carter, and the first liberal activist to be president since Lyndon Johnson. He entered office carrying the extravagant expectations of liberals who had spent a generation in exile and with a domestic agenda more ambitious than that of any president since Lyndon Johnson. But Clinton also had significant political weaknesses. Having won the votes of well under half the electorate, he enjoyed no powerful mandate. Democratic majorities in Congress were frail, and Democrats in any case had grown unaccustomed to bowing to presidential leadership. The Republican leadership in Congress was highly adversarial and opposed the president with unusual unanimity on many issues.

The new administration compounded its problems with a series of missteps and misfortunes in its first months. The president's effort to end the longtime ban on gay men and women serving in the military met with ferocious resistance from the armed forces themselves and from many conservatives in both parties. He was forced to settle for a pallid compromise. Several of his early appointments—to the Justice Department, in particular—became so controversial he had to withdraw them. A longtime friend of the president from Arkansas serving in the office of the White House counsel committed suicide in

BILL CLINTON.   After a difficult campaign for the
Democratic nomination in which he was almost derailed
more than once in the primaries, Bill Clinton secured the
nomination and went on to defeat incumbent George Bush
in a harshly fought battle for the presidency. A member of
the "baby boom" generation, Clinton brought a youthful
energy to the presidency not seen since John F. Kennedy.
But, he soon learned how difficult advancing a
liberal reform agenda was in the political context
of the late twentieth century.

the summer of 1993. His death helped spark an escalating inquiry into some
banking and real estate ventures involving the president and his wife in the early
1980s; and the clumsy actions of some administration officials raised suspicions
that the White House was attempting to interfere with the investigation into
what became known as the Whitewater affair. A special prosecutor began examining these issues in 1993, and several congressional committees began hearings
that continued into 1996.

Despite its many problems, the Clinton administration could boast of some
significant achievements in its first year. The president narrowly (by a single vote
in the Senate) won approval of a budget that marked a significant turn away from
the policies of the Reagan-Bush years. It included a substantial tax increase on the
wealthiest Americans, a significant reduction in many areas of government spending, and a major expansion of tax credits to low-income working people, designed
to help lift many struggling families out of poverty. And after a long and difficult
battle against, among others, Ross Perot, the AFL-CIO, and most Democrats in
Congress, he won approval of the North American Free Trade Agreement, which
eliminated most trade barriers among the United States, Canada, and Mexico.

But the administration's substantial achievements were overshadowed by
a large failure. The president's most important and ambitious initiative—the

project that he hoped would define his presidency—was a major reform of the nation's health care system. Early in 1993, he appointed a task force chaired by his wife, Hillary Rodham Clinton, which proposed a sweeping reform designed to guarantee coverage to every American and hold down the costs of medical care. (In the process of heading the task force, Mrs. Clinton emerged as the most powerful First Lady in American history). The Clinton plan relied heavily on existing institutions, most notably private insurance companies; some critics from the left complained that the new system would be too closely tied to an unreliable market. But the most substantial opposition came from those who believed the reform would transfer too much power to the government; and that opposition—combined with the determination of Republican leaders to deny the president any kind of victory on this potent issue—doomed the plan. There was particular opposition to the proposed tax on employers to finance the plan, a tax that small businesses claimed would be too burdensome for them. But there were complaints, too, from doctors, drug companies, insurance companies, and many people who were content with their existing insurance plans and who feared the new system would treat them less favorably. In September 1994, after a series of compromises failed to attract majorities, Congress abandoned the health reform effort.

The foreign policy of the Clinton administration was at first cautious and even tentative—a reflection, perhaps, of the president's relative inexperience in international affairs, but also of the rapidly changing character of the world order. Gradually, however, the president seemed to gain assurance and secured a number of notable achievements. Clinton presided over (although his administration had played only a small role in creating) a historic agreement between Israel and the Palestinian Liberation Organization to end their long struggle over the lands Israel had occupied in 1967. His administration reached an agreement with Ukraine for an elimination of the nuclear weapons that had been positioned there when the republic had been part of the Soviet Union. And the president helped broker an agreement that led to the departure of a brutal military government from Haiti; American troops arrived to help preserve order as the elected president of Haiti returned from exile and established a new civilian regime.

The most troubling international question of the early 1990s emerged in eastern Europe. Yugoslavia, a nation created after World War I out of a group of small Balkan countries formerly part of the Austro-Hungarian empire, dissolved into several new nations in the wake of the collapse of European communism after 1989. Bosnia was among the new nations, and it quickly became embroiled in a bloody civil war between its two major ethnic groups: one Muslim, the other Serbian and Christian. All efforts by the other European nations and the United States to negotiate an end to the struggle failed until 1995, when the American negotiator Richard Holbrooke finally brought the warring parties together and crafted an agreement to partition Bosnia. The United States was among the nations to send peacekeeping troops to Bosnia to police the fragile settlement.

The Republican Resurgence

The trials of the Clinton administration, and the failure of the health care reform in particular, proved enormously damaging to the Democratic party as it faced the congressional elections of 1994. Few doubted that the Republicans would make significant gains that year, but almost everyone was surprised by the dimensions of their victory. Every Republican incumbent won re-election. Democrats lost in droves. For the first time in forty years, Republicans seized control of both houses of Congress.

Several months before the election, Representative Newt Gingrich of Georgia released a set of campaign promises signed by almost all Republican candidates for the House and labeled the "Contract With America." It called for dramatic changes in federal spending to produce a balanced budget, tax reductions, and a host of other promises consistent with the long-time goals of the Republican party's conservative wing. Opinion polls suggested that few voters in 1994 were aware of the "Contract" at the time they voted. But Gingrich and the new Republican congressional leadership nevertheless interpreted the election results as a mandate for their program.

Throughout 1995, the Republican Congress worked at a sometimes feverish pace to construct one of the most ambitious and even radical legislative programs in modern times. They proposed a series of measures to transfer important powers from the federal government to the states (including a proposal to abolish welfare as it had existed since the 1930s and replace it with block grants to state governments). They proposed dramatic reductions in federal spending, including a major restructuring of the once-sacrosanct Medicare program, to reduce costs. They attempted to scale back a wide range of federal regulatory functions. In all these efforts, they could count on an unprecedentedly disciplined Republican majority in the House and an only slightly less united Republican majority in the Senate. The Republican agenda, if successfully enacted, would have represented the most substantial shift in the distribution of public authority in at least fifty years.

President Clinton responded to the 1994 election results by shifting his own agenda conspicuously to the center and calling for his own plan to cut taxes and balance the budget. Indeed, the gap between the Democratic White House and the Republican Congress on most major issues was relatively small. But because the legislative politics of 1995 was becoming part of the presidential politics of 1996, compromise between the president and Congress became very difficult. At one point in November 1995, the federal government literally shut down for nearly a week because the president and Congress could not agree on a budget. There was another shutdown, for the same reason, in January. By the beginning of 1996, public opinion was turning against much of the Republican agenda—and against the man most clearly identified with it. Gingrich was one of the most unpopular political leaders in the nation, while Clinton was slowly improving his standing in the polls.

The 1996 Campaign

The 1996 campaign began with the president unopposed within his own party (the first Democratic incumbent to run for re-nomination unchallenged since Franklin Roosevelt) and holding a substantial lead in public opinion polls against most of his likely Republican opponents. The former chairman of the Joint Chiefs of Staff, Colin Powell, a widely revered man—all the more so, it seemed, because he was an African American— flirted for a time with running for president as a Republican but ultimately decided to stay out of the race. The remaining Republican candidates were far less popular. After some early setbacks that almost destroyed his candidacy, Robert Dole of Kansas, the Senate Majority Leader, emerged to secure his party's nomination. He approached his party's convention trailing the president in most polls by more than 20 points.

In the meantime, the 104th Congress was making its own bid for re-election. In the summer of 1996, after nearly two years of stalemate, it finally produced several significant measures—some through negotiations with the White House, some through an alliance of Democrats and moderate Republicans. They raised the minimum wage for the first time in more than a decade. They passed legislation, jointly sponsored by Senator Edward Kennedy of Massachusetts (a Democrat) and Senator Nancy Kassebaum of Kansas (a Republican), to ensure that laid-off workers could keep their health insurance after leaving their jobs. Most significantly, they passed a dramatic reform of the nation's welfare system that effectively ended the sixty-year federal entitlement, Aid to Families with Dependent Children. Instead, the new law provided for federal "block grants" to the states to use for welfare programs as they thought best; it denied benefits to illegal immigrants; it called for most welfare recipients to lose their benefits after two years; and it established a five-year lifetime maximum for benefits for the majority of the poor. Despite strong opposition from many Democrats, President Clinton agreed to sign the bill, even while expressing reservations about some of its harsher provisions. The flurry of legislation gave Republicans in Congress a list of accomplishments to take home as they campaigned for re-election. But it also permitted the president to take credit for some important legislative achievements.

As the party conventions approached in the summer of 1996, the Dole campaign—having failed to make any headway against the president—announced a bold proposal for a fifteen percent income tax cut. To burnish his previously weak credentials as a tax cutter, Dole chose as his running mate former congressman and cabinet secretary Jack Kemp, a leading advocate of "supply-side economics." Democrats ridiculed the Republican proposal as an election-year gamble that would increase deficits and raise interest rates, while President Clinton proposed a series of much more modest tax cuts, targeted at middle-class families. Republicans insisted their plan would restore dynamic growth to what they claimed was a sluggish economy. But as the last weeks of the campaign began, President Clinton remained comfortably in the lead.

AMERICAN SOCIETY AT THE CLOSE OF THE CENTURY

The widespread popular suspicion of politics and government that characterized American life in the 1980s and 1990s was in part a result of decades of crises and scandals in public life. But it reflected, too, a series of major changes in the character and behavior of the American economy and American society, changes more rapid—and more jarring—than those of any since at least the 1930s. As the United States approached the end of the twentieth century, formidable challenges remained.

The Two-Tiered Economy

Foremost among these changes was the dramatic transformation of the American economy, a transformation that had begun in earnest in the early 1970s and that continued unabated in the mid-1990s. The new economy created dazzling new miracles of technology that transformed the lives of almost everyone. It created enormous new wealth that enriched those talented, or lucky, enough to profit from the areas of growth. And it produced tremendous disparities in income, wealth, and opportunity that contributed to deep and increasingly corrosive divisions in American society.

The jarring changes in America's relationship to the world economy that had begun in the 1970s—the loss of cheap and easy access to raw materials, the penetration of the American market by foreign competitors, the restructuring of American heavy industry so that it produced fewer jobs and paid lower wages—continued and in some respects accelerated through the last decades of the century. Economic growth continued, but at a slower rate than before. In the twenty years after World War II, the gross national product grew, on average, by 3.8 percent a year. In the 1970s, 1980s, and 1990s, the GNP grew by an average of under 2.6 percent. Productivity grew 2.6 percent a year in the 1950s and 1960s; in the 1970s, 1980s, and 1990s, it grew by less than one percent. The national savings rate—the rate at which individuals and institutions saved income, which then became available for investment—peaked at around ten percent between 1948 and 1973. The highest single-year rate after that was 3.2 percent.

For many families and individuals, the results of these contractions were jarring. In the first twenty years after World War II, it was possible for many, perhaps most, Americans to sustain themselves on a single income. In later years, more and more families required two incomes to sustain their standards of living, and even that was often not enough. In the 1950s and 1960s, most Americans could expect to live more comfortably as adults than their parents had; in the 1980s and 1990s, increasing numbers of Americans were finding it impossible even to live as well as the generation before them. From 1973 to 1989, median family income increased under two percent after inflation (from

33,656 dollars a year to 34,213 in constant dollars), even though many families added a second income in those years. Incomes increased somewhat more rapidly in the 1990s, as the economy experienced a period of sustained, if less than robust, growth. But the problem of wage stagnation for most working people remained.

Poverty in America had declined steadily and at times dramatically in the years after World War II, so that by the end of the 1970s the percentage of people living in poverty had dropped to 12.3 percent (from 22.2 percent in 1960). By the early 1980s, the poverty rate was on the rise. It reached fifteen percent in 1993. As always, this increase in poverty affected women, children, and minorities more than any other groups.

The increasingly unequal distribution of wealth and income in the United States accentuated these changes. Between 1968 and 1994, the share of national income going to the wealthiest twenty percent of American households rose from 40.5 percent to 46.9 percent. That represented an average increase in income for this top group of forty-four percent after inflation. The poorest twenty percent of households in the same period saw their postinflation income rise by only seven percent during the same period. The vast majority of the new wealth the American economy created over this nearly thirty-year period went, in other words, to the most affluent fifth of the population. It was little wonder that the economic anxieties of the working and middle classes became one of the central issues in American politics in the late 1980s and 1990s.

The new economy caused a real decline in the standard of living of most working-class Americans and even of many members of the middle class. But it created enormous rewards for others. The most dramatic area of growth in the 1980s and 1990s was in technology, a field in which the United States continued to be highly competitive internationally. Biotechnology—which included pioneering new areas of medical research—was one sector of the economy that produced a bonanza. Even more important were computers, whose impact on American life exploded beginning in the 1980s and showed no signs of slowing as the century neared its close. Many of the greatest fortunes of the late twentieth century went to those men and women who capitalized on the growing market for computers and the services they provided. The wealthiest man in America in the mid-1990s was William Gates, the founder and president of Microsoft—the software company whose operating systems served the vast majority of the world's computers. But Gates was only the most fabulously successful of large numbers of people who earned great wealth through technology and, in the process, created flourishing new areas of the national and international economies.

It became a cliché of public rhetoric that the new economy rewarded education, skills, and knowledge; like many clichés, this one was largely true. Older sectors that relied on heavy machinery, large labor forces, and big corporate organizations did not disappear; in many cases, they restructured themselves and became more profitable—although often at the expense of their workers. But the "knowledge-based economy" was creating a disproportionate amount of wealth and the bulk of the highly paid jobs of the 1990s.

The result was what many began to call a "two-tiered economy"—an increasingly affluent group at the top, constituting a quarter of the population or less; a struggling middle class faced with stagnating incomes and increasing insecurity; and an impoverished bottom, at times approaching a quarter of the population, with decreasing prospects for advancement in a world in which unskilled and semiskilled labor had much less value than in the past.

"Globalization"

Perhaps the most important change, and certainly the one whose impact was the most difficult to gauge, was what became known as the "globalization" of the economy. The great prosperity of the 1950s and 1960s had rested on, among other things, the relative insulation of the United States from the pressures of international competition. As late as 1970, only nine percent of the goods made in America were exported. More importantly, less than a third of the goods produced in America faced competition from abroad for the domestic market. The United States was an important participant in international trade. But in 1970, international trade still played a relatively small role in the American economy as a whole, which thrived on the basis of the huge domestic market in North America.

By the end of the 1970s, the world had intruded into the American economy in profound ways, and that intrusion increased unabated for the next twenty years. Exports rose, both in absolute numbers and as a percentage of goods produced: from just under $43 billion in 1970 to nearly $513 billion in 1994. But imports rose even more dramatically: from just over $40 billion in 1970 to over $663 billion in 1994. As early as 1980, over seventy percent of American products faced foreign competition inside the United States, most notably some of the products whose role in creating and sustaining prosperity was especially important: steel and automobiles. America had made seventy-six percent of the world's automobiles in 1950 and forty-eight percent in 1960. By 1990, that share had dropped to twenty percent; and in 1994, even after a substantial revival of the automobile industry, the American share had risen only to twenty-five percent.

America was the largest exporter in the world in the 1980s and 1990s, and yet it had a huge trade imbalance (meaning it was importing much more than it was exporting). That was a reflection of how many competitors it faced and how deeply they had penetrated the U.S. market. The first American trade imbalance in the postwar era occurred in 1971; only twice since then, in 1973 and 1975, has the balance been favorable.

Globalization brought many benefits for the American consumer: new and more varied products, and lower prices for many of them. Most economists, and most national leaders, welcomed the process and worked to encourage it through lowering trade barriers. The North American Free Trade Agreement (NAFTA), ratified by the U.S. Senate in 1993, and the General Agreement on Trade and Tariffs (GATT), ratified a year later, were the boldest of a long series of treaties to lower trade barriers stretching back to the 1960s.

But globalization was also enormously destabilizing. It was particularly hard on industrial workers, who were affected in two important ways. First, American workers lost industrial jobs as American companies lost market share. As foreign, especially Japanese, competition cut into steel, automobiles, and other heavy industries in the 1970s and beyond, the work forces in those industries declined. Second, American workers lost jobs as American companies began exporting work: building plants in Mexico, Asia, and other lower wage countries to avoid having to pay the high wages workers had won in America. More than half of the production costs of making American cars were spent outside the United States by the 1990s. That was one reason for the rising unpopularity of free trade among many working-class people—an unpopularity effectively exploited by such self-proclaimed "populist" politicians as Ross Perot and Pat Buchanan, the conservative Republican who ran for president for the second time in 1996 and scored a startling victory in the New Hampshire primary that year but faded later on.

But it was not just the loss of market share or jobs to other countries that plagued industrial workers. It was also the downward pressure on wages and benefits that globalization imposed on those who remained employed in American factories. In almost every major industry, there was increasing pressure on workers and their unions to accept lower wage increases (or actual wage cuts); to contribute more to the cost of their health insurance; and to give up other economic benefits they had won earlier in the postwar era. Unions almost everywhere found themselves on the defensive, and union membership continued its fifty-year decline as a percentage of the work force. In 1945, 35.5 percent of the labor force had consisted of union members. By 1980, that figure had declined to 21.9 percent, and by 1994 to 15.5. The American work force grew from 90.6 million in 1980 to 108 million in 1994; the number of union members in the same period declined from just under 20 million to below 17 million. In 1995, Lane Kirkland, the long-time president of the AFL-CIO and a symbol to many of the complacent union leadership of much of the postwar era, resigned under pressure from his membership. His replacement, John Sweeney, was a much more aggressive figure determined to restore a sense of activism and even militancy to the union movement in an effort to help it regain its lost influence.

Globalization was also visible in the increasing presence of non-American investors and corporations within the American economy. Japanese and German automobile companies built new plants in the United States. European and Asian corporations established large presences in America and sometimes bought up major American companies. A group of Japanese investors bought the Columbia motion picture studio in 1989, and foreign companies purchased American corporations as large and visible as RCA, Goodyear, and Pillsbury.

The Graying of America

The new profile of the American population was also having profound effects on the economy and politics. After decades of steady growth, the nation's birth rate began to decline in the 1970s and remained low through the 1980s and early 1990s. In 1970, there were 18.4 births for every 1,000 people in the population. By 1975, the rate had declined to 14.6, the lowest in the twentieth century. And despite a modest increase in the 1980s, the rate remained below sixteen in the mid-1990s. The declining birth rate and a significant rise in life expectancy produced a substantial increase in the proportion of elderly citizens. There were 17 million Americans over sixty-five-years old in 1960 and 33 million in 1994. Over twelve percent of the population was more than sixty-five-years old by 1990, as compared with eight percent in 1970. That figure was projected to rise to over twenty percent by the end of the century as the members of the postwar baby boom began to enter old age. In 1994 the median age was 34 years, as compared with 28 in 1970.

The aging of the population had important political and economic implications. It was a cause of the increasing costliness of Social Security pensions, and of steadily rising payroll taxes to sustain the system. It helped cause dramatic increases in health costs, both for the federal Medicare and Medicaid systems and for private hospitals and insurance companies. One of the reasons for the enormous federal deficits that came to dominate American political life in the late twentieth century was the rapidly rising cost of these pensions and medical programs for the elderly. But the changing demography also ensured that the aged, who already formed one of the most powerful interest groups in America, would remain politically formidable well into the twenty-first century.

The Changing Profile of Immigration

Perhaps the most striking demographic change in America in the 1980s and 1990s, and one of those likely to have the farthest reaching consequences, was the enormous change in both the extent and the character of immigration. Immigration had steadily declined for sixty years until the 1970s, when it began sharply to increase. In the 1970s, more than 4 million legal immigrants entered the United States. In the 1980s and early 1990s, that number rose to more than 6 million. (In 1994 alone, over 800,000 legal immigrants entered the United States.) When the uncounted but very large numbers of illegal immigrants in those years are included, the wave of immigration in the quarter century after 1970 is the largest of the twentieth century. In 1994, 8.7 percent of the American population was foreign born—the largest percentage since 1940 and an eighty percent increase from 1970.

Equally striking was the character of the new immigration. The Immigration Reform Act of 1965 had eliminated quotas based on national origin; from then on, newcomers from regions other than Latin America were generally admitted on a first-come, first-served basis. In 1965, ninety percent of the immigrants to the United States came from Europe. Twenty years later, only ten percent of the new arrivals were Europeans, although that number began to rise slowly in the 1990s after the collapse of the Soviet empire, as increasing numbers of eastern Europeans began to move to America. The three largest groups of foreign-born Americans in 1994 were, in order, Mexicans, Filipinos, and Cubans. The extent and character of the new immigration was causing a dramatic change in the composition of the American population. Already by the early 1990s, people of white European background constituted under eighty percent of the population (as opposed to ninety percent a half century before). Some predicted that by the middle of the twenty-first century, whites of European heritage would constitute less than fifty percent of the population.

Hispanics and Asian Americans

Particularly important to the new immigration were two groups: Hispanics and Asians. Both had been significant segments of the American population for many decades—Hispanics since the very beginning of the nation's history, Asians since the waves of Chinese and Japanese immigration in the nineteenth century. But both groups experienced enormous, indeed unprecedented, growth after 1965.

People from Latin America—from Cuba, El Salvador, the Dominican Republic, and above all Mexico—constituted more than a third of the total number of legal immigrants to the United States in every year after 1965—and a much larger proportion of the total number of illegal immigrants. In California and the Southwest, in particular, they became an increasingly important presence. There were also substantial Hispanic populations in Illinois, New York, and Florida. High birth rates among Hispanic communities already in the United States further increased their numbers. In the 1980 census, six percent of the population was listed as being of Hispanic origin. The 1990 census showed an increase to nine percent—or 20 million people. (Twenty years earlier, the number had been 7 million.) Economic problems and political repression in Mexico and other Latin American and Caribbean nations propelled the new immigrants to move north; but in most of the areas of the United States to which they moved, opportunities were also hard to find. Mexican Americans had an official poverty rate of twenty percent in 1990 (and a real poverty rate that was probably much higher, given the number of illegal immigrants who evaded official statistics). The poverty rate among Puerto Ricans was thirty percent. For illegal immigrants, conditions were particularly dire. Because they were subject to deportation if they came to the attention of the government, they had no legal recourse when they were exploited by employers. Most worked for subsistence wages in menial jobs, constantly fearful of exposure. And both federal and state governments in the 1990s placed increasingly rigid restrictions on the public benefits they (and their children) received and the services they could use.

The growing Hispanic presence became a political issue of increasing importance in the 1980s and 1990s, both to "Anglos" and, of course, to Hispanics themselves. The Immigration Reform and Control (or Simpson-Mazzoli) Act of 1987 reflected the political power of both groups. Its principal goal was to respond to the demands of whites in the Southwest and California by stemming the flow of illegal immigrants (mostly from Mexico). To that end, it placed the burden on employers for the first time to confirm the legal status of their employees. Those who failed to do so faced economic and even criminal penalties. Hispanics charged that the bill would increase discrimination in hiring, and in the first years after its passage there was considerable evidence that such charges were well founded. At the same time, the act responded to the growing political influence of Hispanics by offering amnesty to all undocumented workers who had entered the country before 1982. By the early 1990s, however, it seemed clear that the law was failing. Illegal immigration from Mexico and elsewhere was continuing at near record levels.

White residents of areas in which the Hispanic populations were growing rapidly often reacted with alarm, fearing that they would soon become a minority in what they considered their own cities. Such fears lay behind efforts to bar the use of the Spanish language in public schools and other measures to force Hispanic immigrants to assimilate more quickly and completely.

In the 1980s and early 1990s, Asian immigrants arrived in numbers almost equal to those of Hispanics. Over six million of the foreign born in America in 1994 were from Asian nations (most notably the Philippines, China, Korea, Vietnam, and India). They swelled the already substantial Chinese communities in California and elsewhere. And they created substantial new communities of immigrants from other areas of Asia. By 1990, there were more than 7 million Asian Americans in the United States, more than twice the number of ten years before. Like Hispanics, they were concentrated mainly in large cities and in the West.

Like most new immigrant groups, Asian Americans found adjustment to the very different culture of the United States difficult and disorienting. They also experienced resentment and discrimination. Whites feared Asian competition in economic activities that they had been accustomed to controlling. For example, there were heated disputes between white and Vietnamese shrimpers on the Gulf Coast in Texas, Mississippi, and Louisiana. Some African Americans resented the success of Asian merchants in black neighborhoods (as the black filmmaker Spike Lee noted in his 1989 film *Do the Right Thing*). In New York, racial tensions led to a black boycott of some Korean grocery stores in African American neighborhoods in 1990.

VIETNAMESE REFUGEES. Nearly 500,000 Vietnamese refugees came to the United States after the fall of South Vietnam. Many quickly applied themselves with extraordinary determination to mastering the intricacies of their new country. These two immigrants stand in front of their grocery store in Arlington, Virginia, where they routinely spent thirteen hours a day meeting the needs of shoppers—especially those in the local Vietnamese community.

Resentment of Asian Americans may have been a result, in part, of their remarkable success. Indeed, some Asian groups (most notably Indians, Japanese, and Chinese) were by the 1980s earning larger average annual incomes than whites. Chinese and Japanese Americans consistently ranked at or near the top of high school and college classes in the 1980s. That was in part because Asian-American communities contained significant numbers of people who had been involved in business and the professions before coming to America and had arrived with a high degree of expertise. Many Asian families also placed an unusually high value on education.

African Americans in the Post-Liberal Era

The civil rights movement and the other liberal efforts of the 1960s had two very different effects on African Americans. On the one hand, there were increased opportunities for advancement available to those in a position to profit from them. On the other hand, as the industrial economy declined and government services dwindled, there was a growing sense of helplessness and despair among the large groups of nonwhites who continued to find themselves barred from upward mobility.

For the black middle class, which by the late 1970s constituted nearly a third of the entire black population of America, the progress was at times astonishing. Economic disparities between black and white professionals did not vanish, but they diminished substantially. Black families moved into more affluent urban communities and suburbs—at times as neighbors of whites, often into predominantly black communities. The number of African Americans attending college rose by 350 percent in the decade following the passage of the civil rights acts (in contrast to a 150 percent increase among whites); African Americans made up twelve percent of the college population in 1990 (up from five percent twenty-five years earlier), although by 1994 that figure had declined to just over ten percent. The percentage of black high-school graduates going on to college was by then virtually the same as that of white high-school graduates (although a far smaller proportion of blacks than whites completed high school). And African Americans were making rapid strides in many professions from which, a generation earlier, they had been barred or within which they had been segregated. They were becoming partners in major law firms and joining the staffs of major hospitals and the faculties of major universities. Nearly half of all employed blacks in the United States had white-collar jobs. There were few areas of American life from which blacks were any longer entirely excluded. Middle-class blacks, in other words, had realized great gains from the legislation of the 1960s, from a softening of many of the worst barriers imposed by racial discrimination, and from the creation of affirmative action programs.

But the rise of a black middle class also accentuated the increasingly desperate plight of other African Americans, whom many of the liberal programs of the 1960s had never reached. This growing "underclass" made up about a third of the nation's black population. It felt the impact of the economic troubles of the 1970s and 1980s with special force. As more successful blacks moved out of the inner cities, the poor were left virtually alone in decaying neighborhoods from which most jobs had disappeared. A third of all black families lived in poverty in 1993; at the same time, just over twelve percent of white families could be officially classified as poor. Less than half of young inner-city blacks finished high school; more than sixty percent were unemployed.

Exacerbating the problems imposed by urban poverty were the number of single-parent, female-headed black households in the 1970s and 1980s. In the early 1990s, over sixty percent of all black children were born into single-parent families, as opposed to only fifteen percent of white children (also a substantial increase over earlier eras). In 1960, only twenty percent of black children had lived in single-parent homes. In a society in which women continued to earn significantly lower wages than men, in which gender segregation in the labor market remained widespread, and in which many working mothers needed daycare many of them could not afford, families led by women were often poor families.

Nonwhites faced many disadvantages in the changing social and economic climate of the 1980s. Among them was a growing impatience with affirmative action and other programs designed to advance their fortunes, as symbolized by the Bakke case in 1978 and by a growing reluctance among federal officials after 1980 to move aggressively to enforce affirmative action guidelines. By the mid-1990s, the white assault on affirmative action had gained so much momentum that there was real doubt as to whether very much of it would survive. Nonwhites suffered as well from a steady decline in the number of unskilled jobs in the economy. They suffered from the long, steady deterioration of urban public education and of other social services, which made it more difficult for them to find opportunities for advancement. And they suffered, in some cases, from a sense of futility and despair, born of years of entrapment in poverty.

By the early 1990s, whole generations of nonwhites had grown to maturity living in destitute neighborhoods where welfare, drug dealing, and other crimes were virtually the only means of support for some. Violence was increasingly a part of daily life. While rates of violent crime were declining nationally in the late 1980s and early 1990s, violence (much of it entirely random) was escalating in many inner-city communities—a result of the drug trade, gang wars, and the proliferation of guns.

The anger and despair such conditions were creating among inner-city residents became clear in the summer of 1992 in Los Angeles. The previous year, a bystander had videotaped several Los Angeles police officers beating an apparently helpless black man whom they had captured after an auto chase. Broadcast repeatedly around the country, the tape evoked outrage among whites and blacks alike. But an all-white jury in a suburban community just outside Los Angeles acquitted the officers when they were tried for assault. African-American residents of South Central Los Angeles, one of the poorest communities in the city, erupted in anger—precipitating the largest racial disturbance of the twentieth century. There was widespread looting and arson. More than fifty people died. In the 1960s, urban uprisings had helped produce a major (if ultimately inadequate) government effort to deal with the problems of the inner city. But in the fiscally starved 1990s, the Los Angeles riot produced no such response.

What Americans had long called "race relations," the way in which white and black Americans viewed each other, grew increasingly sour in these difficult years. White impatience with black demands grew, as did a willingness to listen to old and long-discredited arguments about genetic differences between the races. A controversial book by two social scientists, *The Bell Curve*, published in 1994, helped reopen this bitter debate about the innate capacities of members of different races. Many African Americans, for their part, felt an intensified mistrust of the institutions of white society—of the government, the corporations, the universities, and perhaps above all the system of law enforcement.

Nowhere was this mutual suspicion more evident than in the celebrated trial of the former football star O. J. Simpson, who was accused of murdering his former wife and a young man in Los Angeles in 1994. The long and costly "O. J. trial" was an enormous media sensation for over a year; and throughout the proceedings, opinions about Simpson's guilt broke down along strikingly racial lines. A vast majority of whites believed that he was guilty, and a vast majority of blacks believed he was innocent. Simpson's defense focused on the issue of police corruption and succeeded, it appeared, in deflecting attention away from (or casting doubt upon) the defendant's record of domestic violence and the extensive DNA evidence tying him to the crime. Simpson's acquittal in the fall of 1995 caused great celebrations in many African-American communities and a quiet disgust among many whites.

Modern Plagues: Drugs, AIDS, and Homelessness

Poor African Americans and new immigrants found themselves clustered, often trapped, in cities being ravaged not just by economic decline but by two new and deadly epidemics. One was a dramatic increase in drug use, which penetrated nearly every community in the nation. The enormous demand for drugs, and particularly for "crack" cocaine, spawned what was in effect a multibillion dollar industry; and those reaping the enormous profits of the illegal trade fought strenuously and often savagely to protect their positions.

Political figures of both parties spoke heatedly about the need for a "war on drugs"; but in the absence of significant funding for such programs, government efforts appeared to be having little effect. Drug use declined significantly among middle-class people beginning in the late 1980s, but the epidemic showed no signs of abating in the poor urban neighborhoods, where it was doing the most severe damage.

The drug epidemic was directly related to another scourge of the 1980s and 1990s: the epidemic spread of a new and lethal disease first documented in 1981 and soon named AIDS (acquired immune deficiency syndrome). AIDS is the product of the human immunodeficiency virus (HIV), which is transmitted by the exchange of bodily fluids (blood or semen). The virus gradually destroys the body's immune system and makes its victims highly vulnerable to a number of diseases (particularly to various forms of cancer and pneumonia) to which they would otherwise have a natural resistance. Although many of those infected with the virus (i.e., people who are "HIV positive") lived for many years without developing AIDS, once they did become ill they were, until the mid-1990s at least, virtually certain to die—although new treatments for the disease were extending the life expectancy of many of the infected and showing some promise of giving them a relatively normal lifespan. The first American victims of AIDS (and in

The other night Charlie brought home a quart of milk, a loaf of bread and a case of AIDS.

Charlie always felt his bisexual affairs were harmless enough.

But Charlie did catch the AIDS virus. That's why his family's at risk. His wife risks losing her husband, and when she has sex with him, her own life. If she becomes pregnant she can pass the AIDS virus to her baby.

Charlie could have protected himself. Saying "No" could have done it, or using a condom.

Right now there's no vaccine for AIDS, and no cure in sight. With what we know today, and with the precautions that can be taken, no

AIDS one has to come home with a story like Charlie's.

If you think you can't get it, you're dead wrong.

AIDS EDUCATION.   This poster was prepared by the AIDS Action Committee of Massachusetts to educate the public about transmission and prevention of the disease. Many Americans mistakenly believed only those in the gay community, where the disease first appeared, were vulnerable to the disease. This poster stresses the threat to women and children through heterosexual transmission of the disease.

the early 1990s the group among whom cases remained the most numerous) were homosexual men. But by the late 1980s, as the gay community began to take preventive measures, the most rapid increase in the spread of the disease occurred among heterosexuals, many of them intravenous drug users, who spread the virus by sharing contaminated hypodermic needles. By the mid-1990s, U.S. government agencies were estimating that between 1 and 1.5 million Americans were infected with HIV. (Worldwide, the figure was over 18 million.) Over 400,000 Americans had actually contracted AIDS, and over 280,000 had died by the mid-1990s.

A large research effort produced a wealth of new knowledge about the virus and developed the drugs that were succeeding in delaying or limiting the effects of AIDS. But neither a cure nor a vaccine seemed imminent. Governments and private groups, in the meantime, began promoting AIDS awareness in increasingly visible and graphic ways—urging young people, in particular, to avoid "unsafe sex" through abstinence or the use of latex condoms. The spread of AIDS had a chilling effect on the sexual revolution that had transformed behavior beginning in the 1960s. Fear of infection caused many people to avoid casual sexual relations; but the more puritanical sexual standards against which many Americans had rebelled in the 1960s—and that some conservative Americans hoped to restore—did not return.

The increasing scarcity of housing for low-income people contributed to another urban crisis of the 1980s and 1990s: homelessness. There had always been homeless men and women in most major cities; but their numbers were clearly growing at an alarming rate in the face of rising housing costs, severe cutbacks in federal support for public housing, reduced welfare assistance, deinstitutionalization of the mentally ill, and the declining availability of unskilled jobs. An accurate number of the total homeless population was virtually impossible to determine. Still, the phenomenon of tens of thousands of homeless people at large in the cities put pressure on municipal governments to provide shelter and assistance for the indigent; but in an age of fiscal stringency and greatly reduced federal aid, cities found it difficult to respond adequately to the dimensions of the crisis.

Battles Against Feminism and Abortion

Among the principal goals of the New Right, as it became more powerful and assertive in the 1980s and 1990s, was to challenge feminism and its achievements. Leaders of the New Right had campaigned successfully against the proposed Equal Rights Amendment to the Constitution. And they played a central role in the most divisive issue of the late 1980s and early 1990s: the controversy over abortion rights.

For those who favored allowing women to choose to terminate unwanted pregnancies, the Supreme Court's decision in *Roe* v. *Wade* (1973) had seemed to settle the question. By the 1980s, abortion was the most commonly performed surgical procedure in the country. But at the same time, opposition to abortion was creating a powerful grassroots movement. The right-to-life movement, as it called itself, found its most fervent supporters among Catholics; and indeed, the Catholic church itself lent its institutional authority to the battle against legalized abortion. Religious doctrine also motivated the antiabortion stance of Mormons, fundamentalist Christians, and other groups. The opposition of some other antiabortion activists had less to do with religion than with their commitment to traditional notions of family and gender relations. To them, abortion was a particularly offensive part of a much larger assault by feminists on the role of women as wives and mothers. It was also, many foes contended, a form of murder. Fetuses, they claimed, were human beings who had a "right to life" from the moment of conception.

Although the right-to-life movement was persistent in its demand for a reversal of *Roe* v. *Wade* or, barring that, a constitutional amendment banning the procedure, it also attacked abortion in more limited ways, at its most vulnerable points. In the 1970s, Congress and many state legislatures began barring the use of public funds to pay for abortions, thus making them almost inaccessible for many poor women. The Reagan and Bush administrations imposed further restrictions on federal funding and even on the right of doctors in federally funded clinics to give patients any information on abortion. (President Clinton eliminated many of those restrictions in 1993.) Extremists in the right-to-life movement began picketing, occupying, and at times bombing abortion clinics. One antiabortion activist murdered a doctor in Florida who performed abortions; other physicians were subject to campaigns of terrorism and harassment—part of an effort to force them to abandon serving women who wanted abortions.

The changing composition of the Supreme Court in the 1980s to early 1990s (when five new conservative justices were named by Presidents Reagan and Bush) renewed the right-to-life movement's hopes for a reversal of *Roe* v. *Wade*. In *Webster* v. *Reproductive Health Services* (1989), the Court upheld a Missouri law that forbade any institution receiving state funds from performing abortions, whether or not those funds were used to finance the abortions. But the Court stopped short of overturning the 1973 *Roe* v. *Wade* decision.

Through much of the 1970s and much of the 1980s, defenders of abortion had remained confident that *Roe* v. *Wade* protected women's right to choose abortion and that the antiabortion movement was unlikely to prevail. But the changing judicial climate of the late 1980s and early 1990s mobilized defenders of abortion as never before. They called themselves the "pro-choice" movement, because they were defending not so much abortion itself as every woman's right to choose whether and when to bear a child. It quickly became clear that the pro-choice movement was in many parts of the country at least as strong as, and in some areas much stronger than, the right-to-life movement. With the election of President Clinton in 1992, the immediate threat to *Roe v. Wade* seemed to fade. In his first two years in office, Clinton named two pro-choice justices to the Court—Ruth Bader Ginsburg and Stephen Breyer. But the increasing strength of the Republican right, as demonstrated in the 1994 congressional elections, suggested that the issue was far from closed.

At times the pro-choice campaign overshadowed other efforts by feminists to protect and expand the rights of women. But such efforts continued. Women's organizations and many individual women worked strenuously in the 1980s and 1990s to improve access to childcare for poor women, and to win the right to caregiver leaves for parents. They also worked to raise awareness of sexual harassment in the workplace, with considerable success. Colleges, universities, government agencies, even many corporations established strict new standards of behavior for their employees in dealing with members of the opposite sex and created grievance procedures for those who believed they had been harassed.

Both the achievements and the limits of their progress on this issue were evident in the sensational controversy in 1991 over Judge Clarence Thomas, President Bush's nominee for a seat on the Supreme Court. Late in the confirmation proceedings, accusations of sexual harassment from Anita Hill, a law professor and former employee of Thomas, became public. Hill's testimony before the Senate Judiciary Committee dramatically polarized both the Senate and the nation. Feminists and others tended to believe the accusations, based in part upon their own experience in the labor force. They hailed Anita Hill for drawing national attention to the issue of harassment. But many other Americans (and most members of the virtually all-male Senate) apparently did not believe Hill—or at least concluded that the alleged activities should not disqualify Thomas from serving on the Court. Thomas was ultimately confirmed by a narrow margin. But the issue of sexual harassment remained a matter of debate and discussion, one that many American women especially believed deserved far more attention than it had heretofore received.

The Changing Left and the New Environmentalism

The New Left of the 1960s and early 1970s did not disappear after the end of the war in Vietnam, but it faded rapidly. Many of the students who had fought in its battles grew up, left school, and entered conventional careers. Some radical leaders, disillusioned by the unresponsiveness of American society to their demands, resignedly gave up the struggle and chose instead to work "within the system." Radical ideas continued to flourish in some academic circles, but to much of the public they came to appear dated and irrelevant— particularly as, beginning in 1989, Marxist governments collapsed in disrepute around the world.

ANITA HILL.   University of Oklahoma law professor Anita
Hill testifies before the Senate Judiciary Committee in
1991 about what she claimed was Supreme Court nominee
Clarence Thomas's sexual harassment of her when they
both worked at the EEOC (Equal Employment
Opportunities Commission). Thomas vigorously denied
the charges and was later confirmed by the Senate.

Yet a left of sorts did survive, giving evidence in the process of how greatly
the nation's political climate had changed. Where 1960s activists had rallied to
protest racism, poverty, and war, their counterparts in the 1980s and 1990s more
often fought to stop the proliferation of nuclear weapons and power plants, to
save the wilderness, to protect endangered species, to limit reckless economic
development, and otherwise to protect the environment.

Public concerns about the environment had arisen intermittently since the
beginning of the industrial era and had been growing in intensity since 1962,
when the publication of Rachel Carson's *Silent Spring* aroused widespread public concern about the effect of insecticides on the natural world. Several highly
visible environmental catastrophes in the 1960s and 1970s greatly increased that
concern. Among them were a major oil spill off Santa Barbara, California, in
1969; the discovery of large deposits of improperly disposed toxic wastes in a residential community in upstate New York in 1978; and a frightening accident at
the nuclear power plant on Three Mile Island, Pennsylvania in 1979. These and

other revelations of the extent to which human progress threatened the natural world helped produce a major popular movement.

In the spring of 1970, a nationwide "Earth Day" signaled the beginning of the modern environmental movement. It differed markedly from the "conservation" movements of earlier years. Modern environmentalists shared the concerns of such earlier figures as John Muir and Gifford Pinchot about preserving some areas of the wilderness and carefully managing the exploitation of resources. But the new activists went much further, basing their positions on the developing field of ecology, the study of the interconnections among all components of an environment. Toxic wastes, air and water pollution, the destruction of forests, the extinction of species—these were not separate, isolated problems, the new environmentalists claimed. All elements of the earth's environment were intimately and delicately linked. According to ecologists, damaging any one of those elements risked damaging all the others. Only by adopting a new social ethic, in which economic growth became less important than ecological health, or a new economics, in which environmental costs were factored into economic analyses, could humans hope to preserve a healthy world for themselves and their children.

In the twenty-five years after the first Earth Day, environmental issues gained increasing attention and support. The federal government passed important legislation in the early 1970s requiring measures to clean up the nation's environment, and over time these new requirements contributed to a dramatic improvement in the quality of the air and water in much of the country. The Environmental Protection Agency, a new federal bureau established in 1971, gave the federal government far more authority than it had ever had before to police the environment and force remedies to ecologically dangerous practices—although the vigor with which the EPA pursued its goals varied greatly from one administration to another. Other legislation gave the government the power to protect endangered species and to limit development in other ways—powers that became increasingly controversial in an age of slow economic growth and that helped spawn the powerful antienvironmental movements of the 1980s and 1990s. Environmentalists won significant victories in blocking the construction of roads, airports, and other projects (including American development of the supersonic transport airplane, or SST) that they believed would be ecologically dangerous. And they created wide alarm with their warnings that the release into the atmosphere of certain industrial pollutants (most notably chlorofluorocarbons) was depleting the ozone layer of the earth's atmosphere, which protects the globe from the most dangerous rays of the sun. They warned, too, of the related danger of global warming, a rise in the earth's temperature as a result of emissions from the burning of coal, oil, and other fossil fuels.

The concern for the environment, the opposition to nuclear power, the resistance to economic development—all were reflections of a more fundamental characteristic of the post-Vietnam left. In a sharp break from the nation's long commitment to growth and progress, many dissidents argued that only by limiting growth and curbing traditional forms of progress could society hope to survive. Some of these critics of the "idea of progress" expressed a gloomy resignation, urging a lowering of social expectations and predicting an inevitable deterioration in the quality of life. Other advocates of restraint believed that change did not require decline: human beings could live more comfortably and more happily if they learned to respect the limits imposed on them by their environment. But in either case, such arguments evoked strong opposition from conservatives and others, who ridiculed the no-growth ideology as an expression of defeatism and despair. Ronald Reagan, in particular, made an attack on the idea of "limits" central to his political success.

The rising popularity of environmental issues reflected another important shift both in the character of the American left and in the tone of American public life generally. Through much of the first half of the twentieth century, American politics had been preoccupied with debates over economic power and disparities of wealth. In the late twentieth century, with concentrations of wealth and power reaching unprecedented levels, such debates had largely ceased. There were, of course, economic implications to environmentalism and other no-growth efforts. But what drove such movements was less a concern about power and wealth than a concern about the quality of individual and community life.

The "Culture Wars"

As class-based controversies ceased to shape American public life, cultural battles took their place. Indeed, few issues attracted more attention in the 1990s than the battle over what became known as "multiculturalism." Multiculturalism meant different things to different people, but at its core was an effort to legitimize the cultural pluralism of the rapidly diversifying American population. That meant acknowledging that "American culture," which had long been defined primarily by white males of European descent, also included other traditions: female, African-American, Native American, and increasingly in the late twentieth century, Hispanic and Asian. Although such demands were often controversial, especially when they became the basis of assaults on traditional academic curricula, much greater acrimony emerged out of efforts by some revisionists to portray traditional western culture as inherently racist and imperialistic. A prolonged, if somewhat muted, dispute over how to commemorate the 500th anniversary of Columbus's first voyage to the "New World" illustrated how sharply ideas of multiculturalism had changed the way Americans discussed their past. In 1892, the Columbian anniversary had been the occasion of a boisterous national celebration—and a great world's fair in Chicago. In 1992, it produced agonizing debates over the impact of the European discovery on native peoples; and the only world's fairs were in Italy and Spain.

Debates over multiculturalism and related issues helped produce an increasingly strained climate in academia and in the larger American intellectual world. People on the left complained that the ascendancy of conservative politics placed new and intolerable limits on freedom of expression, as efforts to restrict grants by the National Endowment for the Arts to controversial artists suggested. Many on the right complained equally vigorously of a tyranny of "political correctness," by which feminists, cultural radicals, and others introduced a new form of intolerance to public discourse in the name of defending the rights of women and minorities.

The controversies surrounding multiculturalism and "political correctness" were illustrations of a painful change in the character of American society. Traditional patterns of authority faced challenges from women, minorities, and others. The liberal belief in tolerance and assimilation was fraying in the face of the growing cultural separatism of some ethnic and racial groups. Confidence in the nation's future was declining, and with it confidence in the capacity of American society to provide justice and opportunity to all its citizens.

Facing the New Century

The American people approached the end of the twentieth century filled with anxieties, doubts, and resentments. Faith in the nation's institutions—most notably government—was at its lowest point in many decades. Confidence in the nation's leaders had badly eroded. Economic resentments, which few Americans seemed able to translate into a coherent economic agenda, increased the nation's growing discontent.

And yet the United States in the 1990s, despite its many problems, remained a remarkably successful society—and one that had made dramatic strides in improving the lives of its citizens and dealing with many of its social problems since the end of World War II. The crisis of confidence that darkened the nation's public life in the waning years of the century was not irrational to be sure. There were many reasons for concern, even alarm, about the national condition. But the problems facing the United States as the twentieth century drew to a close were not unprecedented. Many Americans like to believe that the crises of our own time mark a sharp departure from the normal condition of our national life. But in reality, conflict and uncertainty are much more the normal condition of American history than the stability and consensus many critics of our present condition seek to restore. In the twentieth century alone, the United States has experienced two world wars and two agonizing conflicts in Asia. It has struggled through a decade of the worst economic depression in its history. It has survived revolutionary changes in the structure of international relations. It has experienced repeated racial and cultural conflict. It has seen dramatic increases, and then significant declines, in poverty, crime, and disease. It has worked repeatedly to protect the environment from the effects of economic growth. The nation's record in solving such problems has been decidedly mixed, to be sure. But the effort to confront seemingly insuperable obstacles has been a central part of American history.

The American people have never been wholly content about the condition of their nation. But they have also been extraordinarily resilient—and through much of their history they have clung resolutely to the belief that if they tried hard enough, they could, if not perfect, then at least improve their world. Strengthening the nation's waning faith in the possibility of progress—a faith at the heart of most of the many traditions that have shaped American history—is one of the great challenges of our time.

Suggested Readings

1: A NEW SOCIETY

General Studies of Late Nineteenth Century Economic and Social Changes. Daniel Boorstin, *The Americans: The Democratic Experience* (1973). Thomas C. Cochran and William Miller, *The Age of Enterprise* (1942). Carl Degler, *The Age of the Economic Revolution* (1977). John A. Garraty, *The New Commonwealth* (1968). Ray Ginger, *The Age of Excess* (1963). Samuel P. Hays, *The Response to Industrialism, 1885–1914* (1957). Robert L. Heilbroner, *The Economic Transformation of America* (1977). Robert Higgs, *The Transformation of the American Economy, 1865–1914* (1971). Edward C. Kirkland, *Industry Comes of Age: Business, Labor, and Public Policy, 1860–1897* (1961). Alan Trachtenberg, *The Incorporation of America: Culture and Society in the Gilded Age* (1982). Robert Wiebe, *The Search for Order, 1877–1920* (1968).

Railroads. Lee Benson, *Merchants, Farmers, and Railroads* (1955). Edward G. Campbell, *The Reorganization of the American Railroad System* (1938). Thomas C. Cochran, *Railroad Leaders* (1953). Robert Fogel, *Railroads and American Economic Growth* (1964). Edward C. Kirkland, *Men, Cities, and Transportation*, 2 vols. (1948). Gabriel Kolko, *Railroads and Regulation, 1877–1916* (1965). George H. Miller, *Railroads and the Granger Laws* (1971). Richard C. Overton, *Burlington West* (1941); *Gulf to Rockies* (1953). John F. Stover, *The Life and Decline of the American Railroad* (1970); *The Railroads of the South, 1865–1900* (1955). George R. Taylor and I. D. Neu, *The American Railroad Network, 1861–1890* (1956). Anthony F. C. Wallace, *St. Clair: A Nineteenth-Century Coal Town's Experience with a Disaster-Prone Industry* (1987).

Technology. Robert W. Bruce, *Bell* (1973). Roger Burlingame, *Engines of Democracy: Inventions and Society in Mature America* (1940); *Henry Ford* (1957). Robert Conot, *A Streak of Luck* (1979). Richard N. Current, *The Typewriter and the Men Who Made It* (1954). George Daniels, *Science and Society in America* (1971). Frank E. Hill, *Ford* (1954). Thomas P. Hughes, *Networks of Power: Electrification in Western Society, 1880–1930* (1983). Judith McGaw, *Most Wonderful Machine: Mechanization and Social Change in Berkshire Paper Making, 1801–1885* (1988). Martin V. Melosi, *Coping with Abundance: Energy and Environment in Industrial America* (1985). Elting E. Morison, *Men, Machines, and Modern Times* (1966). Lewis Mumford, *Technics and Civilization* (1934). Allan Nevins, *Ford*, 3 vols. (1954–1962). David F. Noble, *America by Design: Science, Technology, and the Rise of Corporate Capitalism* (1977). Leonard S. Reich, *The Making of American Industrial Research: Science and Business at GE and Bell, 1876–1926* (1985). Nathan Rosenberg, *Technology and American Economic Growth* (1972). Peter Temin, *Steel in Nineteenth Century America* (1964). Wyn Wachhorst, *Thomas Alva Edison: An American Myth* (1981). Frederick A. White, *American Industrial Research Laboratories* (1961).

Labor. Paul Avrich, *The Haymarket Tragedy* (1984). John Bodnar, *Immigration and Industrialization: Ethnicity in an American Mill Town* (1977). Stanley Buder, *Pullman* (1967). John T. Cumbler, *Working-Class Community in Industrial America* (1979). Henry David, *The Haymarket Affair* (1936). Ileen A. DeVault, *Sons and Daughters of Labor: Class and Clerical Work in Turn-of-the-Century Pittsburgh* (1990). Melvyn Dubofsky, *Industrialism and the American Worker, 1865–1920* (1975). Melvyn Dubofsky and Warren Van Tine, eds., *Labor Leaders in America* (1987). P. K. Edwards, *Strikes in the United States, 1881–1974* (1981). Leon Fink, *Workingmen's Democracy: The Knights of Labor and American Politics* (1983). Samuel Gompers, *Seventy Years of Life and Labor,*

2 vols. (1975). David M. Gordon, Richard Edwards, and Michael Reich, *Segmented Work, Divided Workers: The Historical Transformation of Labor in the United States* (1982). Brian Greenberg, *Worker and Community: Response to Industrialization in a Nineteenth-Century American City, Albany, New York, 1850–1884* (1985). Herbert G. Gutman, *Work, Culture, and Society in Industrializing America* (1976). Willam F. Hartford, *Working People of Holyoke: Class and Ethnicity in a Massachusetts Mill Town, 1850–1960* (1990). Stuart Kaufman, *Samuel Gompers and the Origins of the American Federation of Labor* (1978). Alexander Keyssar, *Out of Work: The First Century of Unemployment in Massachusetts* (1986). S. J. Kleinberg, *The Shadow of the Mills: Working-Class Families in Pittsburgh, 1870–1907* (1989). David Montgomery, *Beyond Equality* (1975); *Workers' Control in America: Studies in the History of Work Technology, and Labor Struggles* (1979); *The Fall of the House of Labor: The Workplace, the State, and American Labor Activism, 1865–1925* (1987). Daniel Nelson, *Managers and Workers: Origins of the New Factory System in the United States, 1880–1920* (1975). Richard J. Oestreicher, *Solidarity and Fragmentation: Working People and Class Consciousness: Detroit, 1875–1900* (1986). Henry Pelling, *American Labor* (1960). Peter Rachleff, *Black Labor in Richmond, 1865–1890* (1984). Roy Rosenzweig, *"Eight Hours for What We Will": Workers and Leisure in an Industrial City, 1870–1920* (1983). Steven J. Ross, *Workers on the Edge: Work, Leisure, and Politics in Industrializing Cincinnati, 1788–1890* (1985). Peter R. Shergold, *Working Class Life* (1982). Sheldon Stromquist, *A Generation of Boomers: The Pattern of Railroad Labor Conflict in Nineteenth-Century America* (1987). Philip Taft, *The A. F. of L. in the Time of Gompers*, 2 vols. (1957–1959). Kim Voss, *The Making of American Exceptionalism: The Knights of Labor and Class Formation in the Nineteenth Century* (1993). Daniel J. Walkowitz, *Worker City, Company Town: Iron and Cotton Workers Protest in Troy and Cohoes, New York, 1855–1884* (1978). Leon Wolff, *Lockout: The Story of the Homestead Strike of 1892* (1965).

Women Workers. Mary Blewett, *Men, Women, and Work Culture: Class, Gender, and Protest in the New England Shoe Industry* (1988). Patricia Cooper, *Once a Cigar Maker: Men, Women, and Work Culture in American Cigar Factories, 1900–1919* (1987). Tamara Hareven, *Family Time and Industrial Time: The Relationship Between the Family and Work in a New England Industrial Community* (1982). Paula Hyman, Charlotte Baum, Sonya Michel, *The Jewish Woman in America* (1975). Susan E. Kennedy, *If All We Did Was to Weep at Home: A History of White Working-Class Women in America* (1979). Alice Kessler-Harris, *Out to Work: A History of Wage-Earning Women in the United States* (1982). Susan Levine, *Labor's True Women: Carpet Weavers, Industrialization, and Labor Reform in the Gilded Age* (1984). Elizabeth Anne Payne, *Reform, Labor, and Feminism* (1988). Barbara Wertheimer, *We Were There: The Story of Working Women in America* (1977).

The Corporation. Alfred D. Chandler, Jr., *Strategy and Structure: Chapters in the History of the American Industrial Enterprise* (1962); *Pierre S. DuPont and the Making of the Modern Corporation* (1971); *The Visible Hand: The Managerial Revolution in American Business* (1977); *Scale and Scope: The Dynamics of Industrial Capitalism* (1990). David F. Hawkes, *John D.: The Founding Father of the Rockefellers* (1980). Matthew Josephson, *The Robber Barons* (1934). Maury Klein, *The Life and Legend of Jay Gould* (1986). Norma R. Lamoreaux, *The Great Merger Movement in American Business, 1895–1904* (1985). Harold C. Livesay, *Andrew Carnegie and the Rise of Big Business* (1975). Allan Nevins, *Study in Power: John D. Rockefeller*, 2 vols. (1953). Glenn Porter and Harold C. Livesay, *Merchants and Manufacturers* (1971). Joseph Wall, *Andrew Carnegie* (1970). Bernard Weisberger, *The Dream Maker* (1979). Olivier Zunz, *Making America Corporate, 1870–1920* (1990).

Urbanization. Howard Chudacoff, *The Evolution of American Urban Society*, rev. ed. (1981). Charles N. Glaab and Andrew T. Brown, *A History of Urban America* (1967).

Constance M. Green, *The Rise of Urban America* (1965). Blake McKelvey, *The Urbanization of America* (1963). Lewis Mumford, *The Culture of the Cities* (1938); *The City in History* (1961). Arthur M. Schlesinger, *The Rise of the City, 1878–1898* (1933). Jon C. Teaford, *City and Suburb: The Political Fragmentation of Urban America* (1979); *The Twentieth-Century American City: Problem, Promise, and Reality* (1986). Sam Bass Warner, Jr., *The Urban Wilderness* (1972); *Streetcar Suburbs* (1962).

Mobility and Race. Howard Chudacoff, *Mobile Americans: Residential and Social Mobility in Omaha, 1880–1920* (1972). Michael Frisch, *Town into City* (1972). Clyde Griffen and Sally Griffen, *Natives and Newcomers* (1977). Gerald D. Jaynes, *Branches Without Roots: Genesis of the Black Working Class in the American South, 1862–1882* (1986). Philip Kasinitz, *Caribbean New York: Black Immigrants and the Politics of Race* (1992). David M. Katzman, *Before the Ghetto* (1966). Kenneth L. Kusmer, *A Ghetto Takes Shape* (1976). Roger Lane, *The Roots of Black Violence in Philadelphia, 1860–1900* (1986). Gilbert Osofsky, *Harlem: The Making of a Ghetto* (1966). Richard Sennett, *Families Against the City* (1970). Allan H. Spear, *Black Chicago* (1967). Stephan Thernstrom, *Poverty and Progress* (1964); *The Other Bostonians* (1973). Stephan Thernstrom and Richard Sennett, eds., *Nineteenth Century Cities* (1969). Olivier Zunz, *The Changing Face of Inequality: Urbanization, Industrial Development, and Immigrants in Detroit, 1880–1920* (1982).

Immigration and Ethnicity. Thomas J. Archdeacon, *Becoming American: An Ethnic History* (1983). Josef Barton, *Peasants and Strangers: Italians, Rumanians, and Slovaks in an American City* (1975). John Bodnar, *The Transplanted: A History of Immigrants in America* (1985); *Immigration and Industrialization* (1977). John W. Briggs, *An Italian Passage* (1978). Jack Chen, *The Chinese of America* (1980). Robert D. Cross, *The Church and the City* (1967). Leonard Dinnerstein and David Reimers, *Ethnic Americans: A History of Immigration and Assimilation* (1975). John B. Duff, *The Irish in the United States* (1971). Elizabeth Ewen, *Immigrant Women in the Land of Dollars: Life and Culture on the Lower East Side, 1890–1925* (1985). Lawrence H. Fuchs, *The American Kaleidoscope: Race, Ethnicity, and the Civic Culture* (1990). Mario T. Garcia, *Desert Immigrants: The Mexicans of El Paso, 1880–1920* (1981). Nathan Glazer and Daniel P. Moynihan, *Beyond the Melting Pot* (1963). Susan A. Glenn, *Daughters of the Shtetl: Life and Labor in the Immigrant Generation* (1990). Milton M. Gordon, *Assimilation in American Life* (1964). Victor Greene, *For God and Country: The Rise of Polish and Lithuanian Ethic Consciousness in America* (1975). Oscar Handlin, *The Uprooted*, rev. ed. (1973). Marcus Hansen, *The Immigrant in American History* (1940). John Higham, *Strangers in the Land* (1955); *Send These To Me: Jews and Other Immigrants in Urban America* (1975). John Higham, ed., *Ethnic Leadership in America* (1978). Bill Ong Hing, *Making and Remaking Asian America through Immigration Policy* (1993). Francis L. K. Hsu, *The Challenge of the American Dream: The Chinese in the United States* (1971). Maldwyn A. Jones, *American Immigration* (1960). Edward R. Kantowicz, *Polish-American Politics in Chicago* (1975). Thomas Kessner, *The Golden Door: Italian and Jewish Immigrant Mobility* (1977). Harry Kitano, *Japanese-Americans: The Evolution of a Subculture* (1969). Alan M. Kraut, *The Huddled Masses: The Immigrant in American Society, 1880–1921* (1982); *Silent Travelers: Germs, Genes, and the "Immigrant Menace"* (1994). Matt S. Maier and Feliciano Rivera, *The Chicanos: A History of Mexican-Americans* (1972). Gwendolyn Mink, *Old Labor and New Immigrants in American Political Development: Union, Party, and State, 1875–1920* (1986). Ewa Morawska, *For Bread and Butter: The Life-Worlds of East Central Europeans in Johnstown, Pennsylvania, 1890–1940* (1985). Stanley Nadel, *Ethnicity, Religion, and Class in New York City, 1845–1880* (1990). Humbert S. Nelli, *The Italians of Chicago* (1970). Moses Rischin, *The Promised City: New York's Jews* (1962). Barbara Solomon, *Ancestors and Immigrants* (1965). Thomas Sowell, *Ethnic America*

(1981). Philip Taylor, *The Distant Magnet: European Emigration to the U.S.A.* (1971). David Ward, *Cities and Immigrants* (1965). Mark Wyman, *Round-Trip to America: The Immigrants Return to Europe, 1880–1900* (1993). Virginia Yans-McLaughlin, *Family and Community: Italian Immigrants in Buffalo, 1880–1930* (1977).

Urban Poverty and Reform. Robert H. Bremner, *From the Depths* (1956). Stephan F. Brumberg, *Going to America, Going to School* (1986). James H. Cassedy, *Charles V. Chapin and the Public Health Movement* (1962). Allen F. Davis, *Spearheads for Reform* (1967). Barbara Gutmann Rosencrantz, *Public Health and the State* (1972). Marvin Lazerson, *Origins of the Urban School* (1971). James T. Patterson, *America's Struggle Against Poverty* (1981). Thomas L. Philpott, *The Slum and the Ghetto* (1978). James F. Richardson, *The New York Police* (1970). Jacob Riis, *How the Other Half Lives* (1890); *Children of the Poor* (1892); *The Battle with the Slum* (1902). Selwyn K. Troen, *The Public and the Schools* (1975). David B. Tyack, *The One Best System: A History of American Urban Education* (1974).

2: THE POLITICS OF INDUSTRIAL SOCIETY

General Histories. Sean Dennis Cashman, *America and the Gilded Age* (1984). Carl N. Degler, *The Age of the Economic Revolution, 1976–1900*, 2nd. ed. (1977). John H. Dobson, *Politics in the Gilded Age* (1972). Harold U. Faulkner, *Politics, Reform, and Expansion* (1959). John A. Garraty, *The New Commonwealth* (1969). Samuel P. Hays, *The Response to Industrialism, 1885–1914* (1957). Morton Keller, *Affairs of State: Public Life in Late Nineteeth Century America* (1977). Nell Irvin Painter, *Standing at Armageddon: The United States, 1877–1919* (1987). Alan Trachtenberg, *The Intercorporation of America: Culture and Society in the Gilded Age* (1982). Robert Wiebe, *The Search for Order, 1877–1920* (1967). R. Hal Williams, *Years of Decision: American Politics in the 1890s* (1978).

Party Leaders. Harry Barnard, *Rutherford B. Hayes and His America* (1954). Herbert Croly, *Marcus Alonzo Hanna* (1912). Kenneth Davison, *The Presidency of Rutherford B. Hayes* (1972). Lewis L. Gould, *The Presidency of William McKinley* (1981). David Jordan, *Roscoe Conkling of New York* (1971). Margaret Leech, *In the Days of McKinley* (1959). Margaret Leech and Harry J. Brown, *The Garfield Orbit* (1978). Horace Samuel Merrill, *Bourbon Leader: Grover Cleveland and the Democratic Party* (1957). H. Wayne Morgan, *William McKinley and His America* (1963). Allan Nevins, *Grover Cleveland: A Study in Courage* (1933). Allan Peskin, *Garfield* (1978). Thomas C. Reeves, *Gentleman Boss: The Life of Chester Alan Arthur* (1975). Nick Salvatore, *Eugene V. Debs: Citizen and Socialist* (1982). Harry J. Sievers, *Benjamin Harrison*, 3 vols. (1952–1968).

Urban Politics. John M. Allswang, *Bosses, Machines and Urban Voters* (1977). Alexander B. Callow, *The Tweed Ring* (1966). Brian J. Cudahy, *Cash, Tokens, and Transfers: A History of Urban Mass Transit in North America* (1990). Lyle Dorsett, *The Pendergast Machine* (1968). Lori Ginzberg, *Women and the Work of Benevolence: Morality, Politics, and Class in the Nineteenth-Century United States* (1990). Roger Lane, *Policing the City: Boston, 1822–1885* (1967). Seymour Mandelbaum, *Boss Tweed's New York* (1965). Christine M. Rosen, *The Limits of Power: Great Fires and the Process of City Growth in America* (1986). John Sproat, *The Best Men* (1968). Zane L. Miller, *Boss Cox's Cincinnati: Urban Politics in the Progressive Era* (1968).

Politics, Reform, and the State. Geoffrey Blodgett, *The Gentle Reformers* (1966). Ruth Bordin, *Woman and Temperance: The Quest for Power and Liberty, 1873–1900* (1980). James Bryce, *The American Commonwealth*, 2 vols. (1888). Tony Freyer, *Regulating Big Business: Antitrust in Great Britain and America, 1880–1990* (1992). Ari Hoogenboom, *Outlawing the Spoils: The Civil Service Movement* (1961). Richard Jensen, *The Winning of the Midwest: Social and Political Conflict, 1888–1896* (1971).

Matthew Josephson, *The Politicos* (1963). Morton Keller, *Affairs of State* (1977). Paul Kleppner, *The Cross of Culture: A Social Analysis of Midwestern Politics, 1850–1900* (1970); *The Third Electoral System, 1853–1892* (1979). J. Morgan Kousser, *The Shaping of Southern Politics: Suffrage Restriction and the Establishment of the One-Party South, 1880–1910* (1974). Michael P. Malone, *The Battle for Butte: Mining and Politics on the Northern Frontier, 1864–1906* (1981). Robert D. Marcus, *Grand Old Party* (1971). Gerald W. McFarland, *Mugwumps, Morals, and Politics, 1884–1920* (1975). Michael E. McGerr, *The Decline of Popular Politics* (1986). H. Wayne Morgan, *From Hayes to McKinley* (1969). Walter T. K. Nugent, *Money and American Society, 1865–1880* (1968). David J. Rothman, *Politics and Power: The United States Senate, 1869–1901* (1966). Martin J. Sklar, *The Corporate Reconstruction of American Capitalism, 1890–1916* (1988). Theda Skocpol, *Protecting Soldiers and Mothers: The Political Origins of Social Policy in the United States* (1992); Stephen Skowronek, *Building a New American State: The Expansion of National Administrative Capacities, 1877–1920* (1982). John Sproat, *"The Best Men": Liberal Reformers in the Gilded Age* (1968). Tom E. Terrill, *The Tariff, Politics, and American Foreign Policy, 1874–1901* (1973). Irwin Unger, *The Greenback Era* (1964). Leonard D. White, *The Republican Era* (1958).

Labor. Melvyn Dubofsky and Warren Van Tine, eds., *Labor Leaders in America* (1987). P. K. Edwards, *Strikes in the United States, 1881–1974* (1981). Leon Fink, *Workingmen's Democracy: The Knights of Labor and American Politics* (1983). Stuart Kaufman, *Samuel Gompers and the Origins of the American Federation of Labor* (1978). David Montgomery, *The Fall of the House of Labor: The Workplace, the State, and American Labor Activism, 1865–1925* (1987). Richard J. Oestreicher, *Solidarity and Fragmentation: Working People and Class Consciousnesss: Detroit, 1875–1900* (1986). Sheldon Stromquist, *A Generation of Boomers: The Pattern of Railroad Labor Conflict in Nineteenth-Century America* (1987). Philip Taft,

The A. F. of L. in the Time of Gompers, 2 vols. (1957–1959). Kim Voss, *The Making of American Exceptionalism: The Knights of Labor and Class Formation in the Nineteenth Century* (1993). Daniel J. Walkowitz, *Worker City, Company Town: Iron and Cotton Workers Protest in Troy and Cohoes, New York, 1855–1884* (1978). Leon Wolff, *Lockout: The Story of the Homestead Strike of 1892* (1965).

Populism. Peter Argersinger, *Populism and Politics: William Alfred Peffer and the People's Party* (1974). O. Gene Clanton, *Populism: The Humane Preference in America, 1890–1900* (1991); *Kansas Populism: Ideas and Men* (1969). Robert F. Durden, *The Climax of Populism: The Election of 1896* (1965). Lawrence Goodwyn, *Democratic Promise* (1976); *The Populist Moment (an Abridgement of Democratic Promise)* (1978). Sheldon Hackney, *Populism to Progressivism in Alabama* (1969). Steven Hahn, *The Roots of Southern Populism: Yeoman Farmers and the Transformation of the Georgia Upcountry, 1850–1890* (1983). John D. Hicks, *The Populist Revolt* (1931). Richard Hofstadter, *The Age of Reform* (1954). Robert McMath, *Populist Vanguard* (1975); *American Populism: A Social History, 1877–1898* (1993). Theodore R. Mitchell, *Political Education in the Southern Farmers Alliance, 1887–1900* (1987). Walter T. K. Nugent, *The Tolerant Populists* (1960). Bruce Palmer, *Man over Money* (1980). Stanley Parsons, *The Populist Context: Rural Versus Urban Power on a Great Plains Frontier* (1973). Norman Pollack, *The Populist Response to Industrial America* (1962); *The Just Polity: Populism, Law, and Human Welfare* (1987). Martin Ridge, *Ignatius Donnelly: Portrait of a Politician* (1962). Theodore Saloutos, *Farmer Movements in the South, 1865–1933* (1960). Fred Shannon, *The Farmer's Last Frontier* (1945). Barton C. Shaw, *The Wool-Hat Boys: Georgia's Populist Party* (1984). Francis B. Simkins, *Pitchfork Ben Tillman* (1944). Allan Weinstein, *Prelude of Populism: Origins of the Silver Issue* (1970). C. Vann Woodward, *Origins of the New South* (1972); *Tom Watson, Agrarian Rebel* (1938). James E. Wright, *The Politics of Populism: Dissent in Colorado* (1974).

3: THE CRISIS OF THE 1890s

The Depression and Labor Unrest. Ray Ginger, *Altgeld's America* (1958); *The Bending Cross* (1949). Almot Lindsey, *The Pullman Strike* (1942). Donald McMurray, *Coxey's Army* (1929). Samuel McSeveney, *The Politics of Depression* (1972). Carlos A. Schwantes, *Coxey's Army* (1955). Mari Jo Buhle, *Women and American Socialism, 1870–1920* (1981). Melvyn Dubofsky, *We Shall Be All: A History of the Industrial Workers of the World* (1969). Gerald N. Grob, *Workers and Utopia* (1961). J. H. M. Laslett, *Labor and the Left* (1970). Nick Salvatore, *Eugene V. Debs: Citizen and Socialist* (1982).

Ideologies. Charles A. Baker, *Henry George* (1955). Robert C. Bannister, *Social Darwinism: Science and Myth in Anglo-American Social Thought* (1967). Samuel Chugerman, *Lester F. Ward: The American Aristotle* (1939). Sidney Fine, *Laissez Faire and the General Welfare State: A Study of Conflict in American Thought, 1865–1901* (1956). Louis Galambos, *The Public Image of Big Business in America, 1880–1940* (1975). Richard Hofstadter, *Social Darwinism in American Thought*, rev. ed. (1955). Edward C. Kirkland, *Dream and Thought in the Business Community, 1860–1900* (1956). T. J. Jackson Lears, *No Place of Grace: Antimodernism and the Transformation of American Culture, 1880–1920* (1981). Robert G. McCloskey, *American Conservatism in the Age of Enterprise* (1951). Arthur E. Morgan, *Edward Bellamy* (1944). Daniel T. Rodgers, *The Work Ethic in Industrial America, 1850–1920* (1978). David Thelen, *Paths of Resistance: Tradition and Dignity in Industrializing Missouri* (1986). John L. Thomas, *Alternative America: Henry George, Edward Bellamy, Henry Demarest Lloyd, and the Adversary Tradition* (1983). Irvin G. Wylie, *The Self-Made Man in America* (1954).

The "Battle of the Standards" and the Election of 1896. Paolo Coletta, *William Jennings Bryan*, 3 vols., (1964–1969). Milton Friedman and Anna J. Schwartz, *A Monetary History of the United States* (1963). Paul Glad, *McKinley, Bryan, and the People* (1964);

The Trumpet Soundeth (1960). J. Rogers Hollingsworth, *The Whirligig of Politics: The Democracy of Cleveland and Bryan* (1963). Stanley Jones, *The Presidential Election of 1896* (1964).

Native Americans and Race. Dee Brown, *Bury My Heart at Wounded Knee* (1970) Frederick Hoxie, *A Final Promise: The Campaign to Assimilate the Indians* (1984). Wilcomb E. Washburn, *Red Man's Lands/White Man's Law (1971); The Indian in America* (1975). Richard White, *The Roots of Dependency* (1983). Edward Ayers, *The Promise of the New South* (1992). Gavin Wright, *Old South, New South* (1986). Roger Ransom and Richard Sutch, *One Kind of Freedom* (1977). C. Vann Woodward, *The Strange Career of Jim Crow*, rev. ed. (1974). Joel Williamson, *The Crucible of Race* (1985).

4: IMPERIALISM AND EXPANSIONISM

General Histories. Robert L. Beisner, *From the Old Diplomacy to the New, 1865–1900*, 2nd ed. (1986). Charles S. Campbell, *The Transformation of American Foreign Relations, 1865–1900* (1976). John Dobson, *America's Ascent: The United States Becomes a Great Power, 1880–1914* (1978). Foster Rhea Dulles, *Prelude to World Power, 1865–1900* (1965). Walter LaFeber, *The Cambridge History of American Foreign Relations, Vol. 2: The Search for Opportunity, 1865–1913* (1993). J. A. S. Grenville and George Berkeley Young, *Politics, Strategy and American Diplomacy: Studies in Foreign Policy, 1873–1917* (1966). David F. Healy, *U.S. Expansionism: Imperialist Urge in the 1890s* (1970). Walter LeFeber, *The New Empire* (1963). Ernest May, *Imperial Democracy* (1961); *American Imperialism: A Speculative Essay* (1968). H. Wayne Morgan, *America's Road to Empire* (1965). Milton Plesur, *America's Outward Thrust: Approaches to Foreign Affairs, 1865–1890* (1971). David M. Pletcher, *The Awkward Years: American Foreign Relations under Garfield and Arthur* (1962). Julius W. Pratt, *Expansionists of 1898* (1936). Emily

S. Rosenberg, *Spreading the American Dream: American Economic and Cultural Expansion, 1890–1945* (1982). Albert K. Weinberg, *Manifest Destiny: A Study in Nationalist Expansion in American History* (1935). William Appleman Williams, *The Tragedy of American Diplomacy*, rev. ed. (1972).

The Spanish-American War. Richard Challener, *Admirals, Generals, and American Foreign Policy, 1889–1914* (1973). Graham A. Cosmas, *An Army for Empire: The United States Army in the Spanish-American War* (1971). Philip S. Foner, *The Spanish-Cuban-American War and the Birth of American Imperialism*, 2 vols. (1972). Frank Freidel, *The Splendid Little War* (1958). Willard B. Gatewood, Jr., *"Smoked Yankees": Letters from Negro Soldiers, 1898–1902* (1971); *Black Americans and the White Man's Burden, 1898–1903* (1975). Gerald F. Linderman, *The Mirror of War: American Society and the Spanish-American War* (1974). Walter Millis, *The Martial Spirit* (1931). Joyce Milton, *The Yellow Journalists* (1989). Edmund Morris, *The Rise of Theodore Roosevelt* (1979). John L. Offner, *An Unwanted War: The Diplomacy of the United States and Spain over Cuba, 1895–1898* (1992). Louis A. Perez, Jr., *Cuba Between Empires, 1868–1902* (1983). Hyman Rickover, *How the Battleship Maine Was Destroyed* (1976). David F. Trask, *The War with Spain in 1898* (1981). Richard S. West, Jr., *Admirals of the American Empire* (1948).

Imperialism and Anti-Imperialism. Robert L. Beisner, *Twelve Against Empire* (1968). Kendrick A. Clements, *William Jennings Bryan* (1983). James H. Hitchman, *Leonard Wood and Cuban Independence, 1898–1902* (1971). Frederick Merk, *Manifest Destiny and Mission in American History* (1963). Thomas J. Osborne, *"Empire Can Wait": American Opposition to Hawaiian Annexation, 1893–1898* (1991). William J. Pomeroy, *American Neo-Colonialism: Its Emergence in the Philippines and Asia* (1970). Julius W. Pratt, *America's Colonial Empire* (1950). Robert Seager, II, *Alfred Thayer Mahan* (1977). E. Berkeley Tompkins, *Anti-Imperialism in the United States, 1890–1920: The Great Debate* (1970).

The Pacific Empire. H. W. Brands, *Bound to Empire: The United States and the Philippines* (1992). John Morgan Gates, *Schoolbooks and Krags: The United States Army in the Philippines, 1898–1902* (1971). Stanley Karnow, *In Our Image: America's Empire in the Philippines* (1989). Paul M. Kennedy, *The Samoan Tangle* (1974). Glenn A. May, *Social Engineering in the Philippines* (1980). Stuart Creighton Miller, *"Benevolent Assimilation": The American Conquest of the Philippines, 1899–1903* (1982). Daniel B. Schirmer, *Republic or Empire? American Resistance to the Philippine War* (1972). Peter Stanley, *A Nation in the Making: The Philippines and the United States* (1974). Merze Tate, *The United States and the Hawaiian Kingdom* (1965). Richard E. Welch, Jr., *Response to Imperialism: The United States and the Philippine-American War, 1899–1902* (1979). Leon Wolff, *Little Brown Brother* (1961).

America and Asia. Warren Cohen, *America's Response to China*, rev. ed. (1980); *East Asian Art and American Culture: A Study in International Relations* (1992). Kenton Clymer, *John Hay: Gentlemen as Diplomat* (1975). Patricia Hill, *The World Their Household: The American Women's Foreign Mission Movement and Cultural Transformation* (1985). Michael Hunt, *The Making of a Special Relationship: The United States and China to 1914* (1983). Jane Hunter, *The Gospel of Gentility: American Women Missionaries in Turn-of-the-Century China* (1984). Akira Iriye, *Across the Pacific* (1967); *Pacific Estrangement: Japanese and American Expansion* (1972). Robert McClellan, *The Heathen Chinese: A Study of American Attitudes Toward China* (1971). Thomas J. McCormick, *China Market: America's Quest for Informal Empire, 1893–1901* (1967). Charles Neu, *The Troubled Encounter* (1975). James C. Thomsen, Jr., Peter W. Stanley, and John Curtis Perry, *Sentimental Imperialists: The American Experience in East Asia* (1981). Paul Varg, *Missionaries, Chinese and Diplomats* (1958); *The Making of a Myth: The United States and China, 1897–1912* (1968). Marilyn B. Young, *The Rhetoric of Empire: American China Policy, 1895–1901* (1968).

5: ORIGINS OF PROGRESSIVISM

Progressivism: Overviews. John D. Buenker, John C. Burnham, and Robert M. Crunden, *Progressivism* (1977). John W. Chambers II, *The Tyranny of Change: America in the Progressive Era, 1900–1917* (1980). John Milton Cooper, *The Pivotal Decades: The United States, 1900–1920* (1990). Alan Dawley, *Struggles for Justice: Social Responsibility and the Liberal State* (1991). Richard Hofstadter, *The Age of Reform: From Bryan to FDR* (1955). Gabriel Kolko, *The Triumph of Conservatism: A Reinterpretation of American History* (1963). Arthur S. Link and Richard L. McCormick, *Progressivism* (1983). Nell Irvin Painter, *Standing at Armageddon: The United States, 1877–1919* (1987). James Weinstein, *The Corporate Ideal in the Liberal State, 1900–1918* (1969). Robert Wiebe, *The Search for Order, 1877–1920* (1967).

The Muckrakers. David Chalmers, *The Social and Political Ideas of the Muckrakers* (1964). Louis Filler, *The Muckrakers*, rev. ed. (1980). Leon Harris, *Upton Sinclair* (1975). Justin Kaplan, *Lincoln Steffens* (1974). C. C. Regier, *The Era of the Muckrakers* (1932). Harold S. Wilson, *McClure's Magazine and the Muckrakers* (1970).

Progressive Thought. Richard Abrams, *The Burdens of Progress* (1978). Carl N. Degler, *In Search of Human Nature: The Decline and Revival of Darwinism in American Social Thought* (1991). Arthur Ekirch, *Progressivism in America* (1974). Charles V. Forcey, *The Crossroads of Liberalism: Croly, Weyl, Lippman* (1961). Sudhir Kakar, *Frederick Taylor* (1970). D. W. Marcell, *Progress and Pragmatism: James, Dewey, Beard and the American Idea of Progress* (1974). David W. Noble, ed., *The Progressive Mind*, rev. ed. (1981). Jean B. Quandt, *From the Small Town to the Great Community: The Social Thought of Progressive Intellectuals* (1970). Robert Westbrook, *John Dewey and American Democracy* (1991). Morton White, *Social Thought in America* (1949).

Social Work and the Social Gospel. Jane Addams, *Twenty Years at Hull House* (1910).

Paul Boyer, *Urban Masses and Moral Order, 1820–1920* (1978). Mina Carson, *Settlement Folk: Social Thought and the American Settlement Movement, 1885–1930* (1990). Robert M. Crunden, *Ministers of Reform: The Progressives' Achievement in American Civilization, 1889–1920* (1982). Susan Curtis, *A Consuming Faith: The Social Gospel and Modern American Culture* (1991). Allen F. Davis, *Spearheads of Reform: The Social Settlements and the Progressive Movement, 1890–1914* (1968); *American Heroine: The Life and Legend of Jane Addams* (1973). C. H. Hopkins, *The Rise of the Social Gospel in American Protestantism* (1940). William R. Hutchinson, *The Modernist Impulse in American Protestantism* (1982). Rivka Shpak Lissak, *Pluralism and Progressives: Hull House and the New Immigrants, 1890–1919* (1989). Roy Lubove, *The Progressives and the Slums: Tenement House Reform in New York City* (1962). Henry May, *Protestant Churches and Industrial America* (1949). Timothy Miller, *Following in His Steps: A Biography of Charles M. Sheldon* (1987).

Education and the Professions. Clyde W. Barrow, *Universities and the Capitalist State: Corporate Liberalism and the Reconstruction of American Higher Education, 1894–1928* (1990). Burton Bledstein, *The Culture of Professionalism* (1976). Lawrence A. Cremin, *The Transformation of the Schools: Progressivism in American Education, 1876–1957* (1971). Lynn D. Gordon, *Gender and Higher Education in the Progressive Era* (1990). Samuel Haber, *The Quest for Authority and Honor in the American Professions, 1750–1900* (1991). Barbara Harris, *Beyond Her Sphere: Women and the Professions in American History* (1978). Thomas L. Haskell, *The Emergence of Professional Social Science* (1977). Morton J. Horwitz, *The Transformation of American Law, 1870–1960: The Crisis of Legal Orthodoxy* (1992). Kenneth M. Ludmerer, *Learning to Heal: The Development of American Medical Education* (1985). Regina Markell Morantz-Sanchez, *Sympathy and Science: Women Physicians in American Medicine* (1985). Barbara Miller Solomon, *In the Company of Educated Women: A History of Women in Higher Education in*

America (1985). Paul Starr, *The Social Transformation of American Medicine* (1982). David Tyack and Elizabeth Hansot, *Managers of Virtue: Public School Leadership in America, 1820–1980* (1982). Lawrence Veysey, *The Emergence of the American University* (1970).

Women, Reform, and Suffrage.   Paula Baker, *The Moral Frameworks of Public Life: Gender, Politics, and the State in Rural New York, 1870–1930* (1991). Karen Blair, *The Clubwoman as Feminist* (1980). Mari Jo Buhle, *Women and American Socialism* (1983). Norman H. Clark, *Deliver Us From Evil: An Interpretation of American Prohibition* (1976). Mark T. Connelly, *The Response to Prohibition in the Progressive Era* (1980). Nancy Cott, *The Grounding of Modern Feminism* (1987). Ellen C. DuBois, *Feminism and Suffrage: The Emergence of an Independent Women's Movement in America, 1848–1869* (1978). Nancy Shrom Dye, *As Equal as Sisters: Feminism, The Labor Movement, and the Women's Trade Union League of New York* (1981). Eleanor Flexner, *Century of Struggle* (1959). Linda Gordon, *Woman's Body, Woman's Right: A Social History of Birth Control* (1976). Alan P. Grimes, *The Puritan Ethic and Woman Suffrage* (1967). Jacquelyn Dowd Hall, *The Revolt Against Chivalry* (1979). David M. Kennedy, *Birth Control in America: The Career of Margaret Sanger* (1970). Aileen S. Kraditor, *Ideas of the Woman Suffrage Movement* (1965). Ellen C. Lagemann, *A Generation of Women: Education in the Lives of Progressive Reformers* (1979). Elaine Tyler May, *Great Expectations: Marriage and Divorce in Post-Victorian America* (1980). David Morgan, *Suffragists and Democrats: The Politics of Woman Suffrage in America* (1972). Robyn Muncy, *Creating a Female Dominion in American Reform, 1890–1935* (1991). William O'Neill, *Divorce in the Progressive Era* (1967); *Everyone Was Brave: The Rise and Fall of Feminism in America* (1969). Ruth Rosen, *The Lost Sisterhood: Prostitutes in America, 1900–1918* (1982). Rosalind Rosenberg, *Beyond Separate Spheres: Intellectual Roots of Modern Feminism* (1982). Elyce J. Rotella, *From Home to Office: U.S. Women and Work,*

1870–1930 (1981). Sheila M. Rothman, *Woman's Proper Place* (1978). Anne F. Scott, *Making the Invisible Woman Visible* (1984).

Racial Issues.   John Dittmer, *Black Georgia in the Progressive Era, 1900–1920* (1977). George Frederickson, *The Black Image in the White Mind* (1968). Paula Giddings, *When and Where I Enter: The Impact of Black Women on Race and Sex in America* (1984). Louis Harlan, *Booker T. Washington: The Making of a Black Leader* (1856); *Booker T. Washington: The Wizard of Tuskegee, 1901–1915* (1983). Charles F. Kellogg, *NAACP* (1970). Jack Temple Kirby, *Darkness at Dawning: Race and Reform in the Progressive South* (1972). David L. Lewis, *W. E. B. DuBois: Biography of a Race, 1868–1919* (1993). William A. Link, *The Paradox of Southern Progressivism, 1880–1930* (1992). Ralph E. Luker, *The Social Gospel in Black and White: American Racial Reform, 1885–1912* (1991). James M. McPherson, *The Abolitionist Legacy: From Reconstruction to the NAACP* (1975). August Meier, *Negro Thought in America, 1880–1915* (1963). Cynthia Neverdon-Morton, *Afro-American Women of the South and the Advancement of the Race, 1885–1925* (1989). Elliott Rudwick, *W. E. B. DuBois* (1969). Donald Spivey, *Schooling for the New Slavery: Black Industrial Education* (1978). Joel Williamson, *The Crucible of Race: Black-White Relations in the American South Since Emancipation* (1985).

6: REFORMING POLITICS, MOBILIZING GOVERNMENT

Municipal Reform.   John D. Buenker, *Urban Liberalism and Progressive Reform* (1973). James B. Crooks, *Politics and Progress: The Rise of Urban Progressivism in Baltimore* (1968). Oscar Handlin, *Al Smith and His America* (1958). Melvin G. Holli, *Reform in Detroit: Hazen S. Pingree and Urban Politics* (1969). J. Joseph Huthmacher, *Senator Robert F. Wagner and the Rise of Urban Liberalism* (1971). Michael Kazin, *Barons of Labor: The San Francisco Building Trades and*

Union Power in the Progressive Era (1981). Zane Miller, *Boss Cox's Cincinnati* (1968). Martin J. Schiesl, *The Politics of Efficiency: Municipal Administration and Reform in America, 1880–1920* (1977).

State-Level Reform. Richard M. Abrams, *Conservatism in a Progressive Era: Massachusetts* (1964). Dewey Grantham, *Southern Progressivism: The Reconciliation of Progress and Tradition* (1983). Sheldon Hackney, *Populism to Progressivism in Alabama* (1969). Robert S. Maxwell, *La Follette and the Rise of Progressivism in Wisconsin* (1944). Richard L. McCormick, *From Realignment to Reform: Political Change in New York State, 1893–1910* (1981). George E. Mowry, *California Progressives* (1951). Russel B. Nye, *Midwestern Progressive Politics* (1951). David P. Thelen, *The New Citizenship: Origins of Progressivism in Wisconsin* (1972); *Robert M. La Follette and the Insurgent Spirit* (1976); *Paths of Resistance: Tradition and Dignity in Industrializing Missouri* (1986). Robert F. Wesser, *Charles Evans Hughes: Politics and Reform in New York State, 1905–1910* (1967). C. Vann Woodward, *Origins of the New South* (1951). Irwin Yellowitz, *Labor and the Progressive Movement in New York State* (1965).

National Issues. Ruth Bordin, *Woman and Temperance: The Quest for Power and Liberty, 1873–1900* (1980). Melvyn Dubofsky, *We Shall Be All* (1969). Sidney Fine, *Laissez Faire and the General Welfare State* (1956). Joseph Gusfield, *Symbolic Crusade: Status Politics and the Temperance Movement* (1963). John Higham, *Strangers in the Land* (1955). Michael E. McGerr, *The Decline of Popular Politics: The American North, 1865–1928* (1986). Bruno Ramirez, *When Workers Organize: The Politics of Industrial Relations in the Progressive Era, 1898–1916* (1978). James T. Timberlake, *Prohibition and the Progressive Movement* (1963). James Weinstein, *The Decline of Socialism in America* (1967). Robert Wiebe, *Businessmen and Reform: A Study of the Progressive Movement* (1962). Olivier Zunz, *Making America Corporate, 1870–1920* (1990).

7: NATIONAL REFORM

General Studies. John Milton Cooper, Jr., *The Warrior and the Priest: Woodrow Wilson and Theodore Roosevelt* (1983). Arthur Link, *Woodrow Wilson and the Progressive Era, 1910–1917* (1954). George E. Mowry, *The Era of Theodore Roosevelt* (1958).

Theodore Roosevelt. John Morton Blum, *The Republican Roosevelt* (1954). G. Wallace Chessman, *Theodore Roosevelt and the Politics of Power* (1969). John A. Garraty, *The Life of George W. Perkins* (1960). Lewis L. Gould, *The Presidency of Theodore Roosevelt* (1991). William H. Harbaugh, *Power and Responsibility* (1961); published in paperback as *The Life and Times of Theodore Roosevelt* (1975), Horace S. Merrill and Marion G. Merrill, *The Republican High Command* (1971). Edmund Morris, *The Rise of Theodore Roosevelt* (1979). Henry F. Pringle, *Theodore Roosevelt* (1931).

William Howard Taft. Donald E. Anderson, *William Howard Taft* (1973). Paolo E. Coletta, *The Presidency of William Howard Taft* (1973). George Mowry, *Theodore Roosevelt and the Progressive Movement* (1946). Henry F. Pringle, *The Life and Times of William Howard Taft*, 2 vols. (1939). Norman Wilensky, *Conservatives in the Progressive Era: The Taft Republicans of 1912* (1965).

Woodrow Wilson. John Morton Blum, *Joseph Tumulty and the Wilson Era* (1951); *Woodrow Wilson and the Politics of Morality* (1956). Alexander George and Juliette George, *Woodrow Wilson and Colonel House* (1956). L. J. Holt, *Congressional Insurgents and the Party System, 1909–1916* (1967). Arthur S. Link, *Woodrow Wilson*, 5 vols. (1947–1965). Edwin A. Weinstein, *Woodrow Wilson: A Medical and Psychological Biography* (1981).

National Issues. O. E. Anderson, *The Health of a Nation* (1958). Stephen R. Fox, *The American Conservation Movement: John Muir and His Legacy* (1981). Samuel P. Hays, *The Gospel of Efficiency: The Progressive*

Conservation Movement, 1890–1920 (1962). James Holt, *Congressional Insurgents and the Party System* (1969). John M. Jordan, *Machine Age Ideology: Social Engineering and American Liberalism, 1911–1939* (1994). Susan Kleinberg, *The Shadow of the Mills: Working Class Families in Pittsburgh, 1870–1907* (1989). Naomi Lamoreaux, *The Great Merger Movement in American Business, 1895–1904* (1985). Albro Martin, *Enterprise Denied: Origins of the Decline of the American Railroads, 1897–1917* (1971). Thomas K. McCraw, ed., *Regulation in Perspective* (1981). Roderick Nash, *Wilderness and the American Mind* (1967). James Penick, Jr., *Progressive Politics and Conservation: The Ballinger-Pinchot Affair* (1968). Harold T. Pinkett, *Gifford Pinchot: Private and Public Forester* (1970). Elmo P. Richardson, *The Politics of Conservation* (1962). David Sarasohn, *The Party of Reform: The Democrats in the Progressive Era* (1989). Martin J. Sklar, *The Corporate Reconstruction of American Capitalism, 1890–1916: The Market, the Law, and Politics* (1988). Peter Temin, *Taking Your Medicine: Drug Regulation in the U.S.* (1980). Melvin I. Urofsky, *Louis D. Brandeis and the Progressive Tradition* (1981). Bernard Weisberger, *The LaFollettes of Wisconsin: Love and Politics in Progressive America* (1994). Craig West, *Banking Reform and the Federal Reserve, 1863–1923* (1977). Robert Wiebe, *Businessmen and Reform: A Study of the Progressive Movement* (1962).

Roosevelt's Foreign Policy. Howard K. Beale, *Theodore Roosevelt and the Rise of America to World Power* (1956). David H. Burton, *Theodore Roosevelt: Confident Imperialist* (1969). Richard Challener, *Admirals, Generals, and American Foreign Policy, 1898–1914* (1973). Raymond A. Esthus, *Theodore Roosevelt and International Rivalries* (1970). Michael H. Hunt, *The Making of a Special Relationship: The United States and China to 1914* (1983). Akira Iriye, *Pacific Estrangement: Japanese and American Expansion, 1897–1911* (1972). Richard Leopold, *Elihu Root and the Conservative Tradition* (1954). Charles E. Neu, *An Uncertain Friendship: Roosevelt and Japan, 1906–1909* (1967). Bradford Perkins, *The Great Rapprochement:*

England and the United States, 1895–1914 (1968). Julius W. Pratt, *Challenge and Rejection: The United States and World Leadership, 1900–1921* (1967). Charles Vevier, *United States and China* (1955).

America and the Caribbean. P. Edward Haley, *Revolution and Intervention: The Diplomacy of Taft and Wilson with Mexico, 1910–1917* (1975). David Healy, *The United States in Cuba, 1898–1902* (1963). Walter LaFeber, *The Panama Canal* (1978). Lester E. Langley, *The Banana Wars: An Inner History of American Empire, 1900–1934* (1983). David McCullough, *The Path Between the Seas* (1977). Dwight C. Miner, *Fight for the Panama Route* (1966). Dana G. Munro, *Intervention and Dollar Diplomacy in the Caribbean, 1900–1921* (1964). Louis A. Perez, Jr., *Cuba under the Platt Amendment* (1988). Walter Scholes and Marie Scholes, *The Foreign Policies of the Taft Administration* (1970). John Womack, *Zapata and the Mexican Revolution* (1968).

Wilson's Foreign Policy. Kenneth Grieb, *The United States and Huerta* (1969). David Healy, *Gunboat Diplomacy in the Wilson Era: The U.S. Navy in Haiti, 1915–1916* (1976). Thomas J. Knock, *To End All Wars: Woodrow Wilson and the Quest for a New World Order* (1992). Arthur Link, *Wilson the Diplomatist* (1957); *Woodrow Wilson: Revolution, War, and Peace* (1979). Dana Munro, *Intervention and Dollar Diplomacy in the Caribbean, 1900–1914* (1964). Robert Quirk, *The Mexican Revolution, 1914–1915* (1960); *An Affair of Honor: Woodrow Wilson and the Occupation of Veracruz* (1962). James Reed, *The Missionary Mind and America's East Asian Policy, 1911–1915* (1983). Robert Freeman Smith, *The United States and Revolutionary Nationalism in Mexico, 1916–1932* (1972).

8: THE GREAT WAR AND THE
UNITED STATES

The Road to War. Thomas A. Bailey and Paul B. Ryan, *The Lusitania Disaster* (1975).

John Coogan, *The End to Neutrality* (1981). John Milton Cooper, Jr., *The Vanity of Power: American Isolation and the First World War* (1969). Patrick Devlin, *Too Proud to Fight: Woodrow Wilson's Neutrality* (1974). Ross Gregory, *The Origins of American Intervention in the First World War* (1971). Manfred Jonas, *The United States and Germany* (1984). C. Roland Marchand, *The American Peace Movement and Social Reform* (1973). Ernest R. May, *The World War and American Isolation* (1959). Emily Rosenberg, *Spreading the American Dream* (1982). Jeffrey J. Sanford, *Wilsonian Maritime Diplomacy* (1978). Daniel Smith, *Robert Lansing and American Neutrality* (1958); *The Great Departure: The United States and World War I, 1914–1920*, (1965). Barbara Tuchman, *The Zimmerman Telegram* (1958); *The Guns of August* (1962).

Military Histories. A. E. Barbeau and Florette Henri, *The Unknown Soldiers: Black American Troops in World War I* (1974). Christopher Campbell, *Aces and Aircraft of World War I* (1981). John Whiteclay Chambers, *To Raise an Army* (1987). J. Garry Clifford, *The Citizen Soldiers* (1972). Edward M. Coffman, *The War to End All Wars* (1969). Harvey A. DeWeerd, *President Wilson Fights His War* (1968). Frank Freidel, *Over There: The Story of America's First Great Overseas Crusade* (1964). Robert Jackson, *Fighter Pilots in World War I* (1977). Herbert B. Mason, Jr., *The Lafayette Escadrille* (1964). Donald Smythe, *Pershing* (1986). Lawrence Stallings, *The Doughboys: The Story of the AEF, 1917–1918* (1963). David Trask, *The United States in the Supreme War Council* (1961). Frank E. Vandiver, *Black Jack: The Life and Times of John J. Pershing* (1977). Russell Weigley, *The American Way of War* (1973).

Wartime Diplomacy. Kathleen Burk, *Britain, America, and the Sinews of War* (1985). W. B. Fowler, *British-American Relations, 1917–1918* (1969). John Lewis Gaddis, *Russia, the Soviet Union and the United States* (1978). George F. Kennan, *Russia Leaves the War* (1956); *Russia and the West Under Lenin and Stalin* (1961). Carl Parrini,

Heir to Empire: United States Economic Diplomacy, 1916–1923 (1969).

Politics and Government in Wartime. Ray H. Abrams, *Preachers Present Arms: The Role of the American Churches and Clergy in World Wars I and II* (1969). Daniel R. Beaver, *Newton D. Baker and the American War Effort, 1917–1919* (1966). George T. Blakey, *Historians on the Homefront* (1970). William J. Breen, *Uncle Sam at Home* (1984). Zechariah Chaffee, Jr., *Free Speech in the United States* (1941). Charles Chatfield, *For Peace and Justice: Pacifism in America, 1914–1941* (1971). Edward M. Coffman, *The Hilt of the Sword: The Career of Peyton C. Marsh* (1966). Valerie Jean Conner, *The National War Labor Board* (1983). Alfred E. Conrebise, *War as Advertised: The Four Minute Men and America's Crusade, 1917–1918* (1984). Wayne Cornelius, *Building the Cactus Curtain: Mexican Migration and U.S. Responses from Wilson to Carter* (1980). Robert D. Cuff, *The War Industries Board: Business-Government Relations During World War I* (1973). Charles DeBenedettis, *Origins of the Modern Peace Movement* (1978). H. A. DeWeerd, *President Wilson Fights His War* (1968). Charles V. Forcey, *The Crossroads of Liberalism* (1961). Charles Gilbert, *American Financing of World War I* (1970). Otis L. Graham, Jr., *The Great Campaigns* (1971). Ellis W. Hawley, *The Great War and the Search for a Modern Order* (1979). Sondra Herman, *Eleven Against War* (1969). Donald Johnson, *The Challenge to America's Freedoms* (1963). David M. Kennedy, *Over Here* (1980). Seward Livermore, *Politics Is Adjourned* (1966). J. R. Mock and Cedric Larson, *Words That Won the War* (1939). Paul L. Murphy, *World War I and the Origins of Civil Liberties* (1984). George Nash, *The Life of Herbert Hoover: The Humanitarian, 1914–1917* (1990). Harold C. Peterson, *Propaganda for War: The Campaign Against American Neutrality, 1914–1917* (1968). Harold C. Peterson and Gilbert Fite, *Opponents of War, 1917–1918* (1957). Richard Polenberg, *Fighting Faiths: The Abrams Case, the Supreme Court, and Free Speech* (1987). William Preston, Jr., *Aliens and Dissenters:*

Federal Suppression of Radicals, 1903–1933 (1963). Ronald Schaffer, *America in the Great War: The Rise of the War Welfare State* (1991). Harry N. Scheiber, *The Wilson Administration and Civil Liberties, 1917–1921* (1960). Jordan Schwarz, *The Speculator: Bernard M. Baruch in Washington, 1917–1965* (1981). John A. Thomas, *Reformers and War* (1987). Stephen Vaughn, *Holding Fast the Inner Lines: Democracy, Nationalism, and the Committee on Public Information* (1979). Neil A. Wynn, *From Progressivism to Prosperity: World War I and American Society* (1986).

Wartime Society and Culture. Allan M. Brandt, *No Magic Bullet: A Social History of Venereal Disease in the United States* (1985). Paul Chapman, *Schools as Sorters* (1988). Stanley Cooperman, *World War I and the American Novel* (1970). Alfred W. Crosby, Jr., *Epidemic and Peace, 1918* (1976). Maurine W. Greenwald, *Women, War, and Work* (1980). Carol S. Gruber, *Mars and Minerva* (1975). John Higham, *Strangers in the Land: Patterns of American Nativism* (1955). Michael T. Isenberg, *War on Film* (1981). Frederick C. Luebke, *Bonds of Loyalty: German-Americans and World War I* (1974). Elizabeth Payne, *Reform, Labor, and Feminism: Margaret Dreier Robins and the Women's Trade Union League* (1988). Michael Pearlman, *To Make Democracy Safe for America: Patricians and Preparedness in the Progressive Era* (1984). Barbara J. Steinson, *American Women's Activism in World War I* (1982).

Wilson and the Peace. Lloyd Ambrosius, *Woodrow Wilson and the American Diplomatic Tradition* (1987). John Morton Blum, *Woodrow Wilson and the Politics of Morality* (1956). Robert H. Ferrell, *Woodrow Wilson and World War I* (1985). Peter Filene, *Americans and the Soviet Experiment* (1967). Denna Fleming, *The United States and the League of Nations* (1932). Inga Floto, *Colonel House at Paris* (1980). John L. Gaddis, *Russia, the Soviet Union, and the United States* (1978). Lloyd C. Gardner, *Safe for Democracy: The Anglo-American Response to Revolution, 1913–1923* (1984). John A. Garraty, *Henry Cabot Lodge* (1953). Robert Jackson,

At War with the Bolsheviks: The Allied Intervention into Russia, 1917–1920 (1972). George Kennan, *Decision to Intervene* (1958). Thomas Knock, *To End All Wars: Woodrow Wilson and the Quest for a New World Order* (1992). Warren F. Kuehl, *Seeking World Order* (1969). Christopher Lasch, *The American Liberals and the Russian Revolution* (1962). N. Gordon Levin, Jr., *Woodrow Wilson and World Politics* (1968). Arthur S. Link, *Woodrow Wilson*, 5 vols. (1947–1965); *Wilson the Diplomatist* (1957); *Woodrow Wilson: War, Revolution, and Peace* (1979). Arno Mayer, *Wilson vs. Lenin* (1959); *Political Origins of the New Diplomacy, 1917–1918* (1963); *Politics and Diplomacy of Peacemaking: Containment and Counterrevolution* (1965). David W. McFadden, *Alternative Paths: Soviets and Americans, 1917–1920* (1993). Charles L. Mee, Jr., *The End of Order: Versailles 1919* (1980). Robert E. Osgood, *Ideals and Self-Interest in American Foreign Relations* (1953). Klaus Schwabe, *Woodrow Wilson, Revolutionary Germany, and Peacemaking, 1918–1919* (1985). Gene Smith, *When the Cheering Stopped* (1964). Ronald Steel, *Walter Lippman and the American Century* (1980). Ralph Stone, *The Irreconcilables: The Fight Against the League of Nations* (1970). Arthur Walworth, *Wilson and the Peacemakers* (1986). William C. Widenor, *Henry Cabot Lodge and the Search for an American Foreign Policy* (1980).

Postwar America. Wesley M. Bagby, Jr., *The Road to Normalcy* (1962). David Brody, *Steelworkers in America* (1960); *Labor in Crisis: The Steel Strike of 1919* (1965). Stanley Coben, *A. Mitchell Palmer* (1963). David Cronon, *Black Moses* (1955). Elton C. Fax, *Garvey* (1972). Roberta Strauss Feuerlicht, *Justice Crucified: The Story of Sacco and Vanzetti* (1977). Robert L. Friedheim, *The Seattle General Strike* (1965). Vanessa Northington Gamble, *Making a Place for Ourselves: The Black Hospital Movement* (1995). Amy J. Garvey, *Garvey and Garveyism* (1963). Robert V. Haynes, *A Night of Violence: The Houston Riot of 1917* (1976). Florette Henri, *Black Migration: Movement Northward, 1900–1920* (1975). Kenneth Kusmer, *A Ghetto Takes Shape* (1976). David

Montgomery, *The Fall of the House of Labor: The Workplace, the State, and American Labor Activism, 1865–1921* (1987). Robert K. Murray, *The Red Scare: A Study in National Hysteria, 1919–1920* (1955). Burl Noggle, *Into the Twenties* (1974). Stuart I. Rochester, *American Liberal Disillusionment in the Wake of World War I* (1977). Elliott Rudwick, *Race Riot at East St. Louis* (1964). Francis Russell, *A City in Terror* (1975). Alan Spear, *Black Chicago* (1967). Judith Stein, *The World of Marcus Garvey* (1986). William M. Tuttle, Jr., *Race Riot: Chicago in the Red Summer of 1919* (1970). Theodore Vincent, *Black Power and the Garvey Movement* (1971).

9: THE "NEW ERA" AND ITS DISCONTENTS

General Studies. Frederick Lewis Allen, *Only Yesterday* (1931). John Braeman, Robert Bremner, and David Brody, eds., *Change and Continuity in Twentieth Century America: The 1920s* (1968). Ellis Hawley, *The Great War and the Search for a Modern Order* (1979). John D. Hicks, *Republic Ascendancy* (1960). Isabel Leighton, ed., *The Aspirin Age* (1949). William E. Leuchtenburg, *The Perils of Prosperity*, rev. ed. (1994). Donald R. McCoy, *Coming of Age* (1973). Michael Parrish, *Anxious Decades: America in Prosperity and Depression, 1920–1941* (1992). Geoffrey Perrett, *America in the Twenties* (1982). Arthur M. Schlesinger, Jr., *The Crisis of the Old Order* (1957). George Soule, *Prosperity Decade: From War to Depression* (1947).

Labor, Agriculture, and Economic Growth. Guy Alchon, *The Invisible Hand of Planning: Capitalism, Social Science, and the State in the 1920s* (1985). Irving Bernstein, *The Lean Years: A History of the American Worker, 1920–1933* (1960). David Brody, *Steelworkers in America* (1960); *Workers in Industrial America* (1980). Alfred Chandler, *Strategy and Structure* (1962). Lisabeth Cohen, *Making a New Deal: Industrial Workers in Chicago, 1919–1930* (1990). Melvyn Dubofsky, *The State and Labor in Modern*

America (1994). Gilbert C. Fite, *George Peek and the Fight for Farm Parity* (1954); *American Farmers: The New Minority* (1981). Louis Galambos, *Competition and Cooperation* (1966). Louis Galambos and Joseph Pratt, *The Rise of the Corporate Commonwealth: U.S. Business and Public Policy in the Twentieth Century* (1988). Peter Gottlieb, *Making Their Own Way: Southern Blacks' Migration to Pittsburgh, 1916–1930* (1987). Jim Potter, *The American Economy Between the Wars* (1974). Theodore Saloutos and John D. Hicks, *Twentieth Century Populism* (1951). George Soule, *Prosperity Decade* (1947). Sharon Hartman Strom, *Beyond the Typewriter: Gender, Class, and the Origins of Modern American Office Work, 1900–1930* (1992). Mira Wilkins, *The Maturing of Multinational Enterprise: American Business Abroad from 1914 to 1970* (1974). Leslie Woodcock, *Wage-Earning Women* (1979). Gerald Zahavi, *Workers, Managers, and Welfare Capitalism* (1988). Robert Zieger, *Republicans and Labor* (1969).

Politics and Government. Kristi Andersen, *The Creation of a Democratic Majority, 1928–1936* (1979). LeRoy Ashby, *Spearless Leader* (1972). Christine Bolt, *American Indian Policy and American Reform* (1987). David Burner, *The Politics of Provincialism* (1967). David Burner, *Herbert Hoover* (1979). E. Paula Elder, *Governor Alfred E. Smith: The Politician as Reformer* (1983). Frank Freidel, *Franklin D. Roosevelt: The Ordeal* (1954); *Franklin D. Roosevelt: The Triumph* (1956). James N. Giglio, *H. M. Daugherty and the Politics of Expediency* (1978). James Gilbert, *Designing the Industrial State* (1972). Oscar Handlin, *Al Smith and His America* (1958). William Harbaugh, *Lawyer's Lawyer* (1973). Ellis Hawley, *Herbert Hoover as Secretary of Commerce: Studies in New Era Thought and Practice* (1974). Robert Herzstein, *Henry R. Luce: A Political Portrait of the Man Who Created the American Century* (1994). Robert F. Himmelberg, *The Origins of the National Recovery Administration: Business, Government, and the Trade Association Issue, 1921–1933* (1976). Morton Keller, *Regulating a New Society: Public Policy and Social Change in America, 1900–1933*

(1994). Alan Lichtman, *Prejudice and the Old Politics* (1979). Richard Lowitt, *George W. Norris*, vol. 2 (1971). Carol R. McCann, *Birth Control Politics in the United States, 1916–1945* (1994). Donald R. McCoy, *Calvin Coolidge* (1967). Robert K. Murray, *The Harding Era* (1969); *The Politics of Normalcy* (1973). Burl Noggle, *Teapot Dome* (1962). Elisabeth Israels Perry, *Belle Moskowitz: Feminine Politics and the Exercise of Power in the Age of Alfred E. Smith* (1987). Francis Russell, *The Shadow of Blooming Grove* (1968). Andrew Sinclair, *The Available Man* (1965). David P. Thelen, *Robert M. La Follette and the Insurgent Spirit* (1978). George B. Tindall, *The Emergence of the New South* (1967). Eugene Trani and David Wilson, *The Presidency of Warren G. Harding* (1977). G. Edward White, *Justice Oliver Wendell Holmes: Law and the Inner Self* (1993). William Allen White, *A Puritan in Babylon* (1940). John Hoff Wilson, *Herbert Hoover: Forgotten Progressive* (1975).

10: A MODERN CULTURE

The New Culture. Erik Barnouw, *A Tower in Babel: A History of American Radio to 1933* (1966). Daniel Boorstin, *The Americans: The Democratic Experience* (1973). Paul Carter, *The Twenties in America* (1968); *Another Part of the Twenties* (1977). Stanley Coben, *Rebellion Against Victorianism: The Impetus for Cultural Change in 1920s America* (1991). Ed Cray, *Chrome Colossus* (1980). Robert Creamer, *Babe* (1974). Kenneth S. Davis, *The Hero: Charles A. Lindbergh* (1959). Ann Douglas, *Terrible Honesty: Mongrel Manhattan in the 1920s* (1995). Susan J. Douglas, *Inventing American Broadcasting* (1987). Ronald Edsforth, *Class Conflict and Cultural Consensus: The Making of a Mass Consumer Society: Flint, Michigan* (1987). Melvin Patrick Ely, *The Adventures of Amos 'n Andy: A Social History of an American Phenomenon* (1991). Stewart Ewen, *Captains of Consciousness* (1976). James J. Flink, *The Car Culture* (1975); *The Automobile Age* (1988). Stephen Fox, *The Mirror Makers: A History of American Advertising and Its Creators* (1984). Dana Frank, *Purchasing Power: Consumer Organizing, Gender and Seattle Labor Movement, 1919–1929* (1994). Neal Gabler, *An Empire of Their Own: How the Jews Invented Hollywood* (1988). Harvey Green, *Fit for America* (1986). Allen Guttmann, *A Whole New Ball Game* (1988). Sumiko Higashi, *Virgins, Vamps, and Flappers: The American Silent Movie Heroine* (1978). Daniel Horowitz, *The Morality of Spending: Attitudes Toward the Consumer Society in America, 1875–1940* (1985). Jackson Lears, *Fables of Abundance: A Cultural History of Advertising in America* (1994). Robert Lynd and Helen Lynd, *Middletown* (1929). Roland Marchand, *Advertising the American Dream* (1985). Lary May, *Screening Out the Past* (1980). Fred J. McDonald, *Don't Touch That Dial* (1979). Clay McShane, *Down the Asphalt Path: The Automobile and the American City* (1994). Zane Miller, *The Urbanization of America* (1973). William Leach, *Land of Desire: Merchants, Power, and the Rise of a New American Culture* (1993). Kathy H. Ogren, *The Jazz Revolution: Twenties America and the Meaning of Jazz* (1989). Michael Oriard, *Reading Football: How the Popular Press Created an American Spectacle* (1993). Kathy Peiss, *Cheap Amusements* (1986). Daniel Pope, *The Making of Modern Advertising* (1983). Randy Roberts, *Jack Dempsey, The Manassa Mauler* (1979). Philip T. Rosen, *The Modern Stentors: Radio Broadcasting and the Federal Government, 1920–1933* (1980). Joan Shelley Rubin, *The Making of Middlebrow Culture* (1992). Robert Sklar, *Movie-Made America* (1975). Susan Smulyan, *Selling Radio: The Commercialization of American Broadcasting*, Smithsonian Institution Press (1994). Susan Strasser, *Satisfaction Guaranteed: The Making of the American Mass Market* (1989). Bernard A. Weisberger, *The Dream Maker* (1979).

Women, Family, and Youth. W. Andrew Achenbaum, *Shades of Gray: Old Age, American Values, and Federal Policies Since 1920* (1983). Beth L. Bailey, *From Back Porch to Front Seat* (1988). Lois Banner, *American Beauty* (1983). Susan Porter Benson, *Counter*

Cultures (1986). William H. Chafe, *The American Woman: Her Changing Social and Political Roles* (1972). Ellen Chesler, *Woman of Valor: Margaret Sanger and the Birth Control Movement in America* (1992). Howard P. Chudacoff, *How Old Are You? Age in American Culture* (1989). Nancy Cott, *The Grounding of American Feminism* (1987). Ruth Schwarz Cowan, *More Work for Mother* (1983). John D'Emilio and Estelle B. Friedman, *Intimate Matters: A History of Sexuality in America* (1988). Paula Fass, *The Damned and Beautiful* (1977). David H. Fischer, *Growing Old in America* (1977). Linda Gordon, *Woman's Body, Woman's Right* (1976). Helen Lefkowitz Horowitz, *Campus Life: Undergraduate Cultures from the End of the Eighteenth Century to the Present* (1987). Alice Kessler-Harris, *Out to Work: A History of Wage-Earning Women in America* (1982). J. Stanley Lemons, *The Woman Citizen: Social Feminism in the 1920s* (1973). Elizabeth Lunbeck, *The Psychiatric Persuasion: Knowledge, Gender, and Power in Modern America* (1994). Sheila Rothman, *Woman's Proper Place* (1978). Lois Scharf, *To Work and to Wed* (1980). Virginia Scharff, *Taking the Wheel* (1991). Susan Strasser, *Never Done: A History of American Housework* (1982). Winifred Wandersee, *Women's Work and Family Values, 1920–1940* (1981). Renold Wilk, *Henry Ford and Grass Roots America* (1972).

Intellectuals and the Arts. Charles C. Alexander, *Here the Country Lies: Nationalism and the Arts in Twentieth Century America* (1980). Houston Baker, Jr., *Modernism and the Harlem Renaissance* (1987). Loren Baritz, ed., *The Culture of the Twenties* (1970). Cleanth Brooks, *William Faulkner: The Yoknapatawpha Country* (1963). Paul Conkin, *The Southern Agrarians* (1988). Malcolm Cowley, *Exiles Return* (1934). Robert Crunden, *From Self to Society: Transition in American Thought, 1919–1941* (1972). George H. Douglas, *H. L. Mencken* (1978). Frederick J. Hoffman, *The Twenties* (1949). Nathan I. Huggins, *Harlem Renaissance* (1971). Gloria T. Hull, *Color, Sex, and Poetry: Three Women Writers of the Harlem Renaissance* (1987). David L. Lewis, *When Harlem Was in Vogue*

(1981). Roderick Nash, *The Nervous Generation: American Thought, 1917–1930* (1969). John Stewart, *The Burden of Time* (1965). Kenneth M. Wheeler and Virginia L. Lussier, eds., *Women, the Arts, and the 1920s in Paris and New York* (1982). Edmund Wilson, *The Twenties* (1975).

11: BATTLES FOR TRADITION AND ORDER

Efforts to Control Behavior. Charles C. Alexander, *The Ku Klux Klan in the Southwest* (1965). Paul Avrich, *Sacco and Vanzetti: The Anarchist Background* (1991). Herbert Asbury, *The Great Illusion* (1950). Kathleen M. Blee, *Women of the Klan: Racism and Gender in the 1920s* (1991). David Chalmers, *Hooded Americanism* (1965). Norman Clark, *Deliver Us From Evil* (1976). Joseph Gusfeld, *Symbolic Crusade* (1963). John Higham, *Strangers in the Land* (1963). Kenneth Jackson, *The Ku Klux Klan in the City* (1965). Morton Keller, *Regulating a New Society* (1994). K. Austin Kerr, *Organized for Prohibition: A New History of the Anti-Saloon League* (1985). Nancy MacLean, *Behind the Mask of Chivalry: The Making of the Second Ku Klux Klan* (1994). Leonard Moore, *Citizen Klansmen: The Ku Klux Klan in Indiana, 1921–1928* (1991). George J. Sanchez, *Becoming Mexican American: Ethnicity, Culture, and Identity in Chicano Los Angeles, 1900–1945* (1993). Andrew Sinclair, *The Era of Excess* (1962). Richard K. Tucker, *The Dragon and the Cross: The Rise and Fall of the Ku Klux Klan in Middle America* (1991).

Anti-Modernism. Norman Furniss, *The Fundamentalist Controversy* (1954). Ray Ginger, *Six Days or Forever?* (1958). Don Kirschner, *City and Country: Rural Responses to Urbanization in the 1920s* (1970). Lawrence Levine, *Defender of the Faith, William Jennings Bryan: The Last Decade, 1915–1925* (1965). George M. Marsden, *Fundamentalism and American Culture* (1980). William G. McLoughlin, *Modern Revivalism* (1959).

12: THE GREAT DEPRESSION AND AMERICAN SOCIETY

The Coming of the Depression. Michael Bernstein, *The Great Depression: Delayed Recovery and Economic Change in America, 1929–1939* (1987). Lester V. Chandler, *America's Greatest Depression* (1970). Milton Friedman and Anna Schwartz, Chapter 7 of *A Monetary History of the United States* (1963); *The Great Contraction* (1965). John Kenneth Galbraith, *The Great Crash* (1954). Susan E. Kennedy, *The Banking Crisis of 1933* (1973). Charles Kindelberger, *The World in Depression* (1973). Broadus Mitchell, *Depression Decade* (1947). Robert Sobel, *The Great Bull Market* (1968). Peter Temin, *Did Monetary Forces Cause the Great Depression?* (1976).

The Impact of the Depression. Francisco Balerman, *In Defense of La Raza: The Los Angeles Mexican Consulate and the Mexican Community, 1929–1936* (1982). Ann Banks, ed., *First-Person America* (1980). Irving Bernstein, *The Lean Years* (1960). Caroline Bird, *The Invisible Scar* (1966). Glen H. Elder, Jr., *Children of the Great Depression* (1974). Federal Writers' Project, *These Are Our Lives* (1939). James N. Gregory, *American Exodus: The Dust Bowl Migration and Okie Culture in California* (1989). Jacquelyn Dowd Hall, et al., *Like a Family: The Making of a Southern Cotton Mill World* (1987). Abraham Hoffman, *Unwanted Mexican-Americans in the Great Depression* (1974). Richard Lowitt and Maurine Beasley, eds., *One-Third of a Nation: Lorena Hickok Reports the Great Depression* (1981). Robert S. McElvaine, ed., *Down and Out in the Great Depression: Letters from the Forgotten Man* (1983). William Mullins, *The Depression and the Urban West Coast, 1929–1933* (1991). Janet Poppendieck, *Breadlines Knee-Deep in Wheat: Food Assistance in the Great Depression* (1986). Udo Sautter, *Three Cheers for the Unemployed: Government and Unemployment before the New Deal* (1991). Arthur M. Schlesinger, Jr., *The Crisis of the Old Order* (1957). Walter Stein, *California and the Dust Bowl Migration* (1973). Bernard Sternsher, *Hitting Home: The Great Depression in Town and Country* (1970). Catherine McNicol Stock, *Main Street in Crisis: The Great Depression and the Old Middle Class on the Northern Plains* (1992). Studs Terkel, *Hard Times* (1970). Tom Terrill and Jerrold Hirsch, *Such as Us: Southern Voices of the Thirties* (1978). Donald Worster, *Dust Bowl: The Southern Plains in the 1930s* (1979).

Depression-Era Culture and Society. Charles C. Alexander, *Nationalism in American Thought, 1930–1945* (1969). Frederick Lewis Allen, *Since Yesterday* (1940). Andrew Bergman, *We're in the Money: Depression America and Its Films* (1971). Vanessa Northington Gamble, *Making a Name for Ourselves: The Black Hospital Movement* (1995). Camille Guerin-Gonzales, *Mexican Workers and American Dreams: Immigration, Repatriation, and California Farm Labor, 1900–1939* (1994). Anthony Heilbut, *Exiled in Paradise: German Refugee Artists and Intellectuals in America from the 1930s to the Present* (1983). Richard Krickus, *Pursuing the American Dream* (1976). Robert Lynd and Helen Merrell Lynd, *Middletown in Transition* (1935). Alice Goldfarb Marquis, *Hopes and Ashes: The Birth of Modern Times, 1929–1939* (1986). Jeffrey Meikle, *Twentieth Century Limited: Industrial Design in America, 1925–1939* (1979). Gilbert Osofsky, *Harlem: The Making of a Ghetto* (1966). Gilman Ostrander, *American Civilization in the First Machine Age* (1970). David P. Peeler, *Hope Among Us Yet: Social Criticism and Social Thought in the Depression Years* (1987). Richard Pells, *Radical Visions and American Dreams: Culture and Social Thought in the Depression Years* (1973). Thomas Schatz, *The Genius of the System: Hollywood Film Making in the Studio Era* (1988). Ed Sikov, *Screwball: Hollywood's Madcap Romantic Comedies* (1989). Warren Susman, *Culture as History* (1984).

Women and the Depression. Julia K. Blackwelder, *Women of the Depression: Caste and Culture in San Antonio, 1919–1939* (1984). William Chafe, *The American Woman* (1972). Joan Jensen and Lois Scharf, eds., *Decades of Discontent: The Women's Movement, 1920–1940* (1983). Marjorie Rosen, *Popcorn*

Venus: Women, Movies, and the American Dream (1971). Vicki Ruiz, *Cannery Women, Cannery Lives: Mexican Women, Unionization, and the California Food Processing Industry, 1930–1950* (1987). Lois Scharf, *To Work and to Wed: Female Employment, Feminism, and the Great Depression* (1980). Susan Ware, *Holding Their Own: American Women in the 1930s* (1982). Jeane Westin, *Making Do: How Women Survived the '30s* (1976). Patricia Zavella, *Women's Work and Chicano Families* (1987). *Radicalism.* Robert Cohen, *When the Old Left Was Young: Student Radicals and America's First Mass Student Movement, 1929–1941* (1993). Dorothy Healey and Maurice Isserman, *Dorothy Healey Remembers: A Life in the American Communist Party* (1990). Irving Howe and Lewis Coser, *The American Communist Party: A Critical History* (1957). Robin D. G. Kelley, *Hammer and Hoe: Alabama Communists During the Great Depression* (1990). Harvey Klehr, *The Heyday of American Communism: The Depression Decade* (1984).

13: THE STRUGGLE FOR
RECOVERY

The Hoover Presidency. William J. Barber, *From New Era to New Deal: Herbert Hoover, The Economists, and American Economic Policy, 1921–1933* (1985). David Burner, *Herbert Hoover* (1978). Martin Fausold, *The Presidency of Herbert C. Hoover* (1985). Martin Fausold and George Mazuzun, eds., *The Hoover Presidency* (1974). *Herbert Hoover, The Great Depression* (1952). James S. Olsen, *Herbert Hoover and the Reconstruction Finance Corporation* (1977); *Saving Capitalism: The Reconstruction Finance Corporation and the New Deal, 1933–1940* (1988). Albert U. Romasco, *The Poverty of Abundance* (1965). Jordan Schwarz, *The Interregnum of Despair* (1970). Harris Warren, *Herbert Hoover and the Great Depression* (1959). Joan Hoff Wilson, *Herbert Hoover: Forgotten Progressive* (1975).

Politics and Protest. Gary Dean Best, *FDR and the Bonus Marchers, 1933–1935*

(1992). David Burner, *The Politics of Provincialism* (1967). Robert Cohen, *When the Old Left Was Young: Student Radicals and America's First Mass Student Movement, 1929–1941* (1993). Roger Daniels, *The Bonus March* (1971). Frank Freidel, *The Triumph* (1956); *Launching the New Deal* (1973). Donald Grubbs, *Cry from the Cotton* (1971). Dorothy Healey and Maurice Isserman, *Dorothy Healey Remembers: A Life in the American Communist Party* (1990). Irving Howe and Lewis Coser, *The American Communist Party: A Critical History* (1957). Robin D. G. Kelley, *Hammer and Hoe: Alabama Communists During the Great Depression* (1990). Thomas Kessner, *Fiorello H. La Guardia and the Making of Modern New York* (1989). Harvey Klehr, *The Heyday of American Communism: The Depression Decade* (1984). Donald Lisio, *The President and Protest: Hoover, Conspiracy, and the Bonus Riot* (1974). Mark Naison, *Communists in Harlem During the Depression* (1983). Eliot Rosen, *Hoover, Roosevelt, and the Brains Trust* (1977). Arthur M. Schlesinger, Jr., *The Crisis of the Old Order* (1957). John Shover, *Cornbelt Rebellion* (1965). Rexford G. Tugwell, *The Brains Trust* (1968).

Roosevelt and the New Deal: General and Biographical Studies. Anthony J. Badger, *The New Deal* (1989). John Braemen et al., eds., *The New Deal*, 2 vols. (1975). James MacGregor Burns, *Roosevelt: The Lion and the Fox* (1956). Blanche Wiesen Cooke, *Eleanor Roosevelt: Volume One, 1884–1933* (1992). Paul Conkin, *The New Deal*, 2nd ed. (1975). Kenneth Davis, *FDR: The New York Years: 1928–1933* (1985); *FDR: The New Deal Years, 1933–1937* (1986). Peter Fearon, *War, Prosperity, and Depression* (1987). Steve Fraser and Gary Gerstle, eds., *The Rise and Fall of New Deal Liberalism* (1988). Frank Freidel, *Franklin D. Roosevelt*, 4 vols. (1952–1973); *Franklin D. Roosevelt: A Rendezvouz with Destiny* (1990). Joseph P. Lash, *Eleanor and Franklin* (1971). William E. Leuchtenburg, *Franklin D. Roosevelt and the New Deal* (1963); *In the Shadow of FDR* (1983); *The FDR Years: On Roosevelt and His Legacy* (1995); Katie Louchheim, *The Making of the New Deal* (1983). Richard Lowitt,

The New Deal and the West (1984). Robert S. McElvaine, The Great Depression (1984). Gerald Nash, The Great Depression and World War II (1979). Edgar Robinson, The Roosevelt Leadership (1955). Arthur M. Schlesinger, Jr., The Age of Roosevelt, 3 vols. (1957–1960). Harvard Sitkoff, ed., Fifty Years Later: The New Deal Evaluated (1985). Geoffrey Ward, Before the Trumpet: Young Franklin Roosevelt, 1882–1905 (1985); A First-Class Temperament: The Emergence of Franklin Roosevelt (1989). J. H. Wilson and Marjorie Lightman, eds., Without Precedent: The Life and Career of Eleanor Roosevelt (1984).

Early New Deal Politics and Programs. Mimi Abramowitz, Regulating the Lives of Women (1988). Bernard Bellush, The Failure of the NRA (1975). Donald Brand, Corporatism and the Rule of Law (1988). William R. Brock, Welfare, Democracy, and the New Deal (1987). Searle Charles, Minister of Relief (1963). Ralph F. De Bedts, The New Deal's SEC (1964). Herbert Feis, Characters in Crisis (1966). Sidney Fine, The Automobile Under the Blue Eagle (1963). Kenneth Finegold and Theda Skocpol, Frank Freidel, Launching the New Deal (1973); State and Party in America's New Deal (1995). Gerald H. Gamm, The Making of New Deal Democrats: Voting Behavior and Realignment in Boston, 1920–1940 (1989). Colin Gordon, Otis Graham, Encore for Reform (1967); New Deals: Business, Labor, and Politics in America, 1920–1935 (1994). Nancy L. Grant, TVA and Black Americans: Planning for the Status Quo (1990). Ellis Hawley, The New Deal and the Problem of Monopoly (1966). Peter H. Irons, The New Deal Lawyers (1982). Mark Leff, The Limits of Symbolic Reform: The New Deal and Taxation, 1933–1939 (1984). Thomas K. McCraw, TVA and the Power Fight (1970). George McJimsey, Harry Hopkins: Ally of the Poor and Defender of Democracy (1987). Sidney M. Milkis, The Presidents and Their Parties: The Transformation of the American Party System Since the End of the New Deal (1993). Raymond Moley and Eliot Rosen, The First New Deal (1966). Michael Parrish, Securities Regulation and the New Deal (1970). James T. Patterson, Amer-

ica's Struggle Against Poverty, 1900–1980 (1981). Albert U. Romasco, The Politics of Recovery: Roosevelt's New Deal (1983). John Salmond, The Civilian Conservation Corps (1967). Bonnie Fox Schwartz, The Civil Works Administration, 1933–1934 (1984). Jordan Schwarz, The New Dealers: Power Politics in the Age of Roosevelt (1993). Studs Terkel, Hard Times (1970). Susan Ware, Beyond Suffrage (1981); Partner and I: Molly Dewson, Feminism, and New Deal Politics (1987).

Agriculture. Christina Campbell, The Farm Bureaus (1962). David Conrad, The Forgotten Farmers (1965). Lowell K. Dyson, Red Harvest: The Communist Party and American Farmers (1982). Gilbert Fite, George M. Peek and the Fight for Farm Parity (1954). David Hamilton, From New Day to New Deal: American Farm Policy from Hoover to Roosevelt, 1928–1933 (1991). Richard S. Kirkendall, Social Scientists and Farm Politics in the Age of Roosevelt (1966). Paul Mertz, The New Deal and Southern Rural Poverty (1978). Van L. Perkins, Crisis in Agriculture (1969). Bruce Shulman, From Cotton Belt to Sunbelt (1991).

14: CHALLENGING
THE NEW DEAL

Depression Dissidents. David H. Bennett, Demagogues in the Depression (1969). Alan Brinkley, Voices of Protest: Huey Long, Father Coughlin, and the Great Depression (1982). Donald Grubbs, Cry from the Cotton (1971). William Ivy Hair, The Kingfish and His Realm: The Life and Times of Huey P. Long (1991). Glen Jeansonne, Gerald L. K. Smith: Minister of Hate (1988). Abraham Holzman, The Townsend Movement (1963). R. Alan Lawson, The Failure of Independent Liberalism (1971). Donald McCoy, Angry Voices (1958). Leo Ribuffo, The Old Christian Right: The Protestant Far Right from the Great Depression to the Cold War (1983). Arthur M. Schlesinger, Jr., The Politics of Upheaval (1960). Charles J. Tull, Father Coughlin and the New Deal (1965). David Warren, Radio

Priest: Charles Coughlin, The Father of Hate Radio (1996). T. Harry Williams, Huey Long (1969). George Wolfskill, Revolt of the Conservatives (1962).

The "Second New Deal." Sidney Baldwin, Poverty and Politics: The Farm Security Administration (1968). Edward Berkowitz, Mr. Social Security: The Life of Wilbur J. Cohen (1995). Paul Conkin, Tomorrow a New World (1971). Linda Gordon, Pitied But Not Entitled: Single Mothers and the History of Welfare (1994). J. Joseph Huthmacher, Senator Robert Wagner and the Rise of Urban Liberalism (1968). Roy Lubove, The Struggle for Social Security (1968). William F. McDonald, Federal Relief Administration and the Arts (1968). Jerre Mangione, The Dream and the Deal (1972). Jane deHart Matthews, The Federal Theater (1967). W. D. Rowley, M. L. Wilson and the Campaign for Domestic Allotment (1970).

Labor. Jerold Auerbach, Labor and Liberty (1966). John Barnard, Walter Reuther and the Rise of the Auto Workers (1983). Irving Bernstein, Turbulent Years (1970); A Caring Society: The New Deal, the Worker, and the Great Depression (1985). David Brody, Workers in Industrial America (1980). Bert Cochran, Labor and Communism (1977). Lizabeth Cohen, Making a New Deal: Industrial Workers in Chicago, 1919–1939 (1990). Melvyn Dubofsky and Warren Van Tine, John L. Lewis (1977). Elizabeth Faue, Community of Suffering and Struggle: Women, Men, and the Labor Movement in Minnesota, 1915–1945 (1991). Sidney Fine, Sit-Down (1969). Joshua Freeman, In Transit: The Transport Workers Union in New York City, 1933–1966 (1989). Peter Friedlander, The Emergence of a UAW Local (1975). Gary Gerstle, Working-Class Americanism: The Politics of Labor in a Textile City 1914–1960 (1989). John W. Hevener, Which Side Are You On? The Harlan County Coal Miners, 1931–1939 (1978). Nelson Lichtenstein, The Most Dangerous Man in Detroit: Walter Reuther and the Fate of American Labor (1995). August Meier and Elliott Rudwick, Black Detroit and the Rise of the UAW (1979). David Milton, The Politics of U.S. Labor:

From the Great Depression to the New Deal (1980). Bruce Nelson, Workers on the Waterfront: Seamen, Longshoremen, and Unionism in the 1930s (1988). Daniel Nelson, American Rubber Workers and Organized Labor, 1900–1941 (1988). Annelise Orleck, Common Sense and a Little Fire: Women and Working-Class Politics in the United States, 1900–1965 (1995). Paula F. Pfeffer, A. Philip Randolph, Pioneer of the Civil Rights Movement (1990). Ronald W. Schatz, The Electrical Workers (1983). George G. Suggs, Jr., Union Busting in the Tristate: The Oklahoma, Kansas, and Missouri Metal Workers Strike of 1935 (1986). Christopher L. Tomlins, The State and the Unions (1985). Robert H. Zieger, American Workers, American Unions, 1920–1985 (1986); John L. Lewis: Labor Leader (1988).

The Late New Deal. Leonard Baker, Back to Back (1967). Alan Brinkley, The End of Reform: New Deal Liberalism in Recession and War (1995). Frank Freidel, FDR and the South (1965). Barry Karl, Executive Reorganization and Reform in the New Deal (1963). William E. Leuchtenburg, The Supreme Court Reborn: The Constitutional Revolution in the Age of Roosevelt (1995). Dean May, From New Deal to New Economics (1981). James T. Patterson, Congressional Conservatism and the New Deal (1967); The New Deal and the States (1969). Richard Polenberg, Reorganizing Roosevelt's Government (1966). Theodore Rosenof, Dogma and Depression (1972); Patterns of Political Economy in America (1983). Herbert Stein, The Fiscal Revolution in America (1969). Charles Trout, Boston: The Great Depression and the New Deal (1977). George Wolfskill and John Hudson, All But the People (1969).

Blacks, Hispanics, Indians. Rodolfo Acuna, Occupied America, rev. ed. (1981). Francisco E. Balerman, In Defense of La Raza (1982). Thomas Biolsi, Organizing the Lakota: The Political Economy of the New Deal on the Pine Ridge and Rosebud Reservations (1992). Ralph Bunche, The Political Status of the Negro in the Age of FDR (1973). Dan T. Carter, Scottsboro (1969). Vine DeLoria, Jr., The Nations Within (1984). Sarah Deutsch,

No Separate Refuge: Culture, Class, and Gender on the Anglo-Hispanic Frontier in the American Southwest, 1880–1940 (1987). John Dollard, *Caste and Class in a Southern Town* 3rd ed. (1957). James Goodman, *Stories of Scottsboro* (1994). Cheryl Lynn Greenberg, *"Or Does It Explode?": Black Harlem in the Great Depression* (1991). Laurence C. Kelly, *The Assault on Assimilation: John Collier and the Origins of Indian Policy Reform* (1983). John B. Kirby, *Black Americans in the Roosevelt Era* (1980). Clifford Lytle, *American Indians, American Justice* (1983). Carey McWilliams, *Factories in the Field* (1939). Donald L. Parman, *The Navajos and the New Deal* (1976). Kenneth R. Philp, *John Collier's Crusade for Indian Reform, 1920–1954* (1977). Harvard Sitkoff, *A New Deal for Blacks* (1978). Graham D. Taylor, *The New Deal and American Indian Tribalism* (1980). Nancy Weiss, *The National Urban League* (1974); *Farewell to the Party of Lincoln: Black Politics in the Age of FDR* (1983). Raymond Wolters, *Negros and the Great Depression* (1970). Robert L. Zangrando, *The NAACP Crusade Against Lynching* (1980).

Women and the New Deal. Mimi Abramowitz, *Regulating the Lives of Women* (1988). William Chafe, *The American Woman* (1972). Blanche Wiesen Cooke, *Eleanor Roosevelt: Volume One, 1884–1933* (1992). Joan Jensen and Lois Scharf, eds., *Decades of Discontent: The Women's Movement, 1920–1940* (1983). Vicki Ruiz, *Cannery Women, Cannery Lives: Mexican Women, Unionization, and the California Food Processing Industry, 1930–1950* (1987). Lois Scharf, *To Work and to Wed: Female Employment, Feminism, and the Great Depression* (1980). Susan Ware, *Beyond Suffrage* (1981); *Holding Their Own: American Women in the 1930s* (1982); *Partner and I: Molly Dewson, Feminism, and New Deal Politics* (1987). J. H. Wilson and Marjorie Lightman, eds., *Without Precedent: The Life and Career of Eleanor Roosevelt* (1984).

15: THE WORLD IN CRISIS

The 1920s. Thomas Buckley, *The United States and the Washington Conference* (1970).

Warren Cohen, *America's Response to China* (1971); *Empire Without Tears* (1987). Frank Costigliola, *Awkward Dominion: American Political, Economic, and Cultural Relations with Europe, 1919–1933* (1984). Roger Dingman, *Power in the Pacific* (1976). L. Ethan Ellis, *Republican Foreign Policy, 1921–1933* (1968). Robert H. Ferrell, *Peace in Their Time* (1952). Michael J. Hogan, *Informal Entente: The Private Structure of Cooperation in Anglo-American Economic Diplomacy, 1918–1928* (1977). Akira Iriye, *The Cambridge History of American Foreign Relations, vol. 3: The Globalizing of America, 1913–1945; After Imperialism* (1965). William Kamman, *A Search for Stability: United States Diplomacy Toward Nicaragua, 1925–1933* (1968). Melvyn P. Leffler, *The Elusive Quest: America's Pursuit of European Stability and French Security, 1919–1933* (1979). Merlo J. Pusey, *Charles Evans Hughes*, 2 vols. (1963). Joseph Tulchin, *The Aftermath of War* (1971). William Appleman Williams, *The Tragedy of American Diplomacy* (1962). Joan Hoff Wilson, *American Business and Foreign Policy, 1920–1933* (1968); *Ideology and Economics* (1974).

The Hoover Years. Alexander DeConde, *Hoover's Latin American Policy* (1951). Robert H. Ferrell, *American Diplomacy in the Great Depression* (1970). Elting Morison, *Turmoil and Tradition* (1960). Raymond O'Connor, *Perilous Equilibrium* (1962). Armin Rappaport, *Stimson and Japan* (1963).

New Deal Diplomacy. Edward E. Bennett, *Recognition of Russia* (1970). Dorothy Borg, *The United States and the Far Eastern Crisis of 1933–1938* (1964). Robert Browder, *The Origins of Soviet-American Diplomacy* (1953). Bruce J. Calder, *The Impact of Intervention* (1984). Robert Dallek, *Franklin D. Roosevelt and American Foreign Policy, 1932–1945* (1979). Beatrice Farnsworth, *William C. Bullitt and the Soviet Union* (1967). Peter Filene, *Americans and the Soviet Experiment, 1917–1933* (1967). Frank Freidel, *Launching the New Deal* (1973). Lloyd Gardner, *Economic Aspects of New Deal Diplomacy* (1964). Irwin F. Gellman, *Good Neighbor Diplomacy: United States Policies in*

Latin America, 1933–1945 (1979). David Green, *The Containment of Latin America* (1971). Warren F. Kimball, *The Juggler: Franklin Roosevelt as Wartime Statesman* (1991). Walter LaFeber, *Inevitable Revolutions* (1983). Lorenzo Meyer, *Mexico and the United States in the Oil Controversy* (1977). Bryce Wood, *The Making of the Good Neighbor Policy* (1961).

Isolationism and Pacifism. Selig Adler, *The Uncertain Giant* (1966); *The Isolationist Impulse* (1957). Charles Chatfield, *For Peace and Justice: Pacifism in America, 1914–1941* (1971). Warren I. Cohen, *The American Revisionists* (1967). Wayne S. Cole, *America First* (1953); *Senator Gerald P. Nye and American Foreign Relations* (1962); *Charles A. Lindbergh and the Battle Against American Intervention in World War II* (1974); *Roosevelt and the Isolationists, 1932–1945* (1983). Charles DeBenedetti, *Origins of the Modern American Peace Movement, 1915–1929* (1978); *The Peace Reform in American History* (1980). Robert Divine, *The Reluctant Belligerent* (1965). Thomas N. Guinsburg, *The Pursuit of Isolation in the United States Senate from Versailles to Pearl Harbor* (1982). Manfred Jones, *Isolationism in America* (1966). Thomas C. Kennedy, *Charles A. Beard and American Foreign Policy* (1975). William Langer and S. Everett Gleason, *The Challenge to Isolation* (1952); *The Undeclared War* (1953). Richard Lowitt, *George W. Norris*, 3 vols. (1963–1978). John K. Nelson, *The Peace Prophets* (1967). Lawrence Wittner, *Rebels Against War* (1984).

The Coming of World War II. James MacGregor Burns, *Roosevelt: The Soldier of Freedom* (1970). Peter N. Carroll, *Odyssey of the Abraham Lincoln Brigade: Americans in the Spanish Civil War* (1994). Garry Clifford and Samuel R. Spencer, Jr., *The First Peacetime Draft* (1986). Roger Dingman, *Power in the Pacific* (1976). Bernard F. Donahoe, *Private Plans and Public Dangers* (1965). Herbert Feis, *The Road to Pearl Harbor* (1950). Waldo H. Heinrichs, Jr., *Threshold of War* (1988). Akira Iriye, *After Imperialism: The Search for a New Order in the Far East, 1921–1933* (1965); *Across the Pacific* (1967);

The Origins of the Second World War in Asia and the Pacific (1987). Manfred Jonas, *The United States and Germany* (1984). Warren Kimball, *The Most Unsordid Act: Lend-Lease, 1939–1941* (1970). Joseph Lash, *Roosevelt and Churchill* (1976). James Leutze, *Bargaining for Supremacy* (1977). Martin V. Melosi, *The Shadow of Pearl Harbor* (1977). Arnold Offner, *The Origins of the Second World War* (1975). Gordon Prange, *At Dawn We Slept* (1981); *Pearl Harbor* (1986). Michael S. Sherry, *The Rise of American Airpower* (1987). David Reynolds, *The Creation of the Anglo-American Alliance, 1937–1941* (1982). David F. Schmitz, *The United States and Fascist Italy, 1922–1944* (1988). Jonathan Utley, *Going to War with Japan* (1985). Roberta Wohlstetter, *Pearl Harbor: Warning and Decision* (1962). David S. Wyman, *Paper Walls: America and the Refugee Crisis, 1938–1941* (1985).

16: FIGHTING A GLOBAL WAR

Wartime Military and Diplomatic Experiences. Stephen Ambrose, *The Supreme Commander* (1970); *Eisenhower: Soldier, General of the Army, President-Elect* (1983); *D-Day: June 6, 1944* (1994). Albert Russell Buchanan, *The United States and World War II*, 2 vols. (1962). James MacGregor Burns, *Roosevelt: The Soldier of Freedom* (1970). Winston S. Churchill, *The Second World War*, 6 vols. (1948–1953). Robert Divine, *Second Chance* (1967); *Roosevelt and World War II* (1969). Dwight D. Eisenhower, *Crusade in Europe* (1948). John S. D. Eisenhower, *Allies: Pearl Harbor to D-Day* (1982). Kenneth Greenfield, *American Strategy in World War II* (1963). Max Hastings, *Overlord: D-Day and the Battle for Normandy* (1984). Patrick Heardon, *Roosevelt Confronts Hitler: American Entry into World War II* (1987). Godfrey Hodgson, *The Colonel: The Life and Wars of Henry Stimson, 1867–1950* (1990). Michael Howard, *The Mediterranean Strategy in World War II* (1968). Margaret Hoyle, *A World in Flames* (1970). D. Clayton James, *A Time for Giants: Politics of the American High Command in World War II* (1987). John

Keegan, *Six Armies in Normandy: From D-Day to the Liberation of Paris, June 6–August 25, 1944* (1982). Warren Kimball, *The Juggler: Franklin Roosevelt as Wartime Statesman* (1991). E. J. Kind and W. M. Whitehill, *Fleet Admiral King* (1952). Charles B. McDonald, *The Mighty Endeavor* (1969). William Manchester, *American Caesar* (1979). Samuel Eliot Morison, *Strategy and Compromise* (1958); *History of United States Naval Operations in World War II*, 14 vols. (1947–1960); *The Two Ocean War* (1963). Geoffrey Perret, *There's a War to Be Won: The United States Army in World War II* (1991). Forrest Pogue, *George C. Marshall*, 2 vols. (1963–1966). Gordon W. Prange, *At Dawn We Slept: The Untold Story of Pearl Harbor* (1981). Fletcher Pratt, *War for the World* (1951). Cornelius Ryan, *The Longest Day* (1959); *The Last Battle* (1966). Ronald Schaffer, *Wings of Judgment: American Bombing in World War II* (1985). Michael Schaller, *The United States Crusade in China, 1938–1945* (1979). Michael Sherry, *Preparing for the Next War: American Plans for Postwar Defense, 1941–1945* (1977); *The Rise of American Air Power* (1987). Louis Simpson, "A Deadly Welcome", *New York Times Magazine*, 7 May 1995, pp. 75–77. Gaddis Smith, *American Diplomacy During the Second World War* (1964). Ronald H. Spector, *Eagle Against the Sun: The American War with Japan* (1985). James L. Stokesbury, *A Short History of World War II* (1980). Mark A. Stoler, *The Politics of the Second Front: Planning and Diplomacy in Coalition Warfare, 1941–1945* (1977). Studs Terkel, *The Good War* (1984). Christopher Thorne, *Allies of a Kind: The United States, Britain and the War Against Japan, 1941–1945* (1978). John Toland, *The Last Hundred Days* (1966); *The Rising Sun* (1970). Barbara Tuchman, *Stilwell and the American Experience in China* (1971). Russell Weigley, *The American Way of War* (1973); *Eisenhower's Lieutenants: The Campaign of France and Germany, 1944–1945* (1981). Gerhard Weinberg, *A World At Arms: A Global History of World War II* (1994). Chester Wilmot, *The Struggle for Europe* (1952). David S. Wyman, *The Abandonment of the Jews: America and the Holocaust, 1941–1945* (1984).

Atomic Warfare. Gar Alperovitz, *Atomic Diplomacy* (1965). Nuel Davis, *Lawrence and Oppenheimer* (1969). Robert Donovan, *Conflict and Crisis* (1977). Herbert Feis, *The Atomic Bomb and the End of World War II* (1966). Gregg Herken, *The Winning Weapon: The Atomic Bomb in the Cold War* (1980). John Hersey, *Hiroshima* (1946). Robert Jungk, *Brighter Than a Thousand Suns* (1958). Richard Rhodes, *The Making of the Atomic Bomb* (1987). W. S. Schoenberger, *Decision of Destiny* (1969). Martin Sherwin, *A World Destroyed* (1975). Leon V. Sigal, *Fighting to a Finish* (1988).

17: WARTIME SOCIETY AND CULTURE

War and American Society. John Morton Blum, *V Was for Victory* (1976). Lewis A. Erenberg and Susan E. Hirsch, *The War in American Culture: Society and Consciousness during World War II* (1996). Mark J. Harris et al., *The Homefront* (1984). Glen Jeansonne, *Women of the Far Right: The Mothers' Movement and World War II* (1996). Richard R. Lingeman, *Don't You Know There's a War On?* (1970). Gerald D. Nash, *The American West Transformed: The Impact of the Second World War* (1985). Geoffrey Perrett, *Days of Sadness, Years of Triumph: The American People, 1939–1945* (1974). Richard Polenberg, *War and Society* (1972). Studs Terkel, *"The Good War" An Oral History of World War II* (1984).

War Mobilization. Oscar E. Anderson, Jr., *The New World* (1962). Ellsworth Barnard, *Wendell Willkie* (1966). Chester Bowles, *Promises to Keep* (1971). Alan Brinkley, *The End of Reform: New Deal Liberalism in Recession and War* (1995). David Brinkley, *Washington Goes to War* (1987). James MacGregor Burns, *Roosevelt: The Soldier of Freedom* (1970). Bruce Catton, *War Lords of Washington* (1946). Lester V. Chandler, *Inflation in the United States, 1940–1948* (1951). Alan Clive, *State of War: Michigan in World War II* (1979). George Q. Flynn, *The Mess in Washington: Manpower Mobilization in World War II* (1979). Doris Kearns Goodwin, *No Ordinary Time: Franklin and*

Eleanor Roosevelt: The Home Front in World War II (1994). Leslie R. Groves, *Now It Can Be Told* (1962). Howell John Harris, *The Right to Manage* (1982). Maurice Isserman, *Which Side Were You On? The American Communist Party During World War II* (1982). Eliot Janeway, *Struggle for Survival* (1951). Paul A. C. Koistinen, *The Military-Industrial Complex: A Historical Perspective* (1980). Philip Knightley, *The First Casualty* (1975). Nelson Lichtenstein, *Labor's War at Home: The CIO in World War II* (1982). Donald Nelson, *Arsenal of Democracy* (1946). Joel Seidman, *American Labor from Defense to Reconversion* (1953). Bradley F. Smith, *The Shadow Warriors: The OSS and the Origins of the CIA* (1983). Richard Steele, *Propaganda in an Open Society* (1985). Patrick S. Washburn, *A Question of Sedition: The Federal Government's Investigation of the Black Press During World War II* (1986). Michi Weglyn, *Years of Infamy: The Untold Story of America's Concentration Camps* (1976). Alan M. Winkler, *The Politics of Propaganda: The Office of War Information, 1942–1945* (1978).

The War and Race. Beth Bailey and David Farber. *The First Strange Place: The Alchemy of Race and Sex in World War II Hawaii* (1993). Domenic J. Capeci, Jr., *The Harlem Riot of 1943* (1977); *Race Relations in Wartime Detroit* (1987). Richard M. Dalfiume, *Desegregation of the U.S. Armed Forces* (1969). Roger Daniels, *The Politics of Prejudice* (1962); *Concentration Camps, USA: Japanese Americans and World War II* (1971); *Prisoners Without Trial: Japanese Americans in World War II* (1993). John W. Dower, *War Without Mercy: Race and Power in the Pacific War* (1986). Mario T. Garcia, *Mexican-Americans: Leadership, Ideology, and Identity, 1930–1960* (1989). Herbert Garfinkel, *When Negroes March* (1959). Audrie Girdner and Anne Loftis, *The Great Betrayal* (1969). Bill Hosokawa, *Nisei* (1969). Peter Iorns, *Justice at War* (1983). Thomas James, *Exiles Within: The Schooling of Japanese-Americans, 1942–1945* (1987). Valerie J. Matsumoto, *Farming the Home Place: A Japanese American Community in California, 1919–1982* (1993). Philip McGuire, ed., *Taps for a Jim Crow Army: Letters from Black Soldiers in World War II* (1982). Mauricio Mazon, *The Zoot-Suit Riots* (1984). August Meier and Elliott Rudwick, *CORE* (1973). Louis Ruchames, *Race, Jobs, and Politics* (1953). Holly Cowan Shulman, *The Voice of America* (1991). Neil Wynn, *The Afro-American and the Second World War* (1976).

Women and the War. Karen Anderson, *Wartime Women: Sex Roles, Family Relations, and the Status of Women During World War II* (1981). D'Ann Campbell, *Women at War with America* (1984). Sherna B. Gluck, *Rosie the Riveter Revisited* (1987). Susan Hartmann, *The Homefront and Beyond: American Women in the 1940s* (1982). Margaret R. Higgonet et al., *Behind the Lines: Gender and the Two World Wars* (1987). Maureen Honey, *Creating Rosie the Riveter: Class, Gender, and Propaganda During World War II* (1984). Ruth Milkman, *Gender at Work: The Dynamics of Job Segregation by Sex During World War II* (1987). Susan M. Reverby, *Ordered to Care: The Dilemma of American Nursing, 1850–1945* (1987). Leila Rupp, *Mobilizing Women for War* (1978).

18: WAGING PEACE

Origins of the Cold War. Gar Alperovitz, *Atomic Diplomacy: Hiroshima and Potsdam*, rev. ed. (1985). Stephen Ambrose, *Rise to Globalism*, 5th ed. (1988). Terry H. Anderson, *The United States, Great Britain, and the Cold War, 1944–1947* (1981). H. W. Brands, *Inside the Cold War: Loy Henderson and the Rise of the American Empire, 1918–1961* (1991). Diane Clemens, *Yalta* (1970). Warren I. Cohen, *The Cambridge History of American Foreign Relations, vol. 4: America in the Age of Soviet Power, 1945–1991* (1991). Herbert Feis, *Churchill, Roosevelt, and Stalin* (1957); *Between War and Peace: The Potsdam Conference* (1960). John Lewis Gaddis, *The United States and the Origins of the Cold War, 1941–1947* (1972); *Strategies of Containment* (1982); *The Long Peace* (1987). Lloyd C. Gardner, *Spheres of Influence: The Great Powers Partition Europe, from Munich to Yalta* (1993). Gregg Herken, *The Winning*

Weapon: Then Atomic Bomb in the Cold War, 1945–1950 (1980). George C. Herring, Jr., *Aid to Russia* (1973). Timothy P. Ireland, *Creating the Entangling Alliance: The Origins of NATO* (1981). Bruce Kuniholm, *The Origins of the Cold War in the Middle East* (1980). Walter LaFeber, *America, Russia, and the Cold War, 1945–1967*, rev. ed. (1980). Melvyn P. Leffler, *A Preponderance of Power: National Security, the Truman Administration, and the Cold War* (1992). William NcNeill, *America, Britain, and Russia* (1953). Wilson D. Miscamble, *George F. Kennan and the Making of American Foreign Policy, 1947–1950* (1992). W. L. Neumann, *After Victory* (1969). Thomas G. Paterson, *Soviet-American Confrontation* (1974); *On Every Front: The Making of the Cold War* (1979); *Meeting the Communist Threat* (1988). Robert A. Pollard, *Economic Security and the Origins of the Cold War* (1985). Martin Sherwin, *A World Destroyed* (1975). Gaddis Smith, *American Diplomacy During the Second World War* (1965); *Dean Acheson* (1972). John L. Snell, *Illusion and Necessity* (1967). William Taubman, *Stalin's American Policy* (1982). Athan G. Theoharis, *The Yalta Myths* (1970). Adam Ulam, *The Rivals: America and Russia Since World War II* (1971). Bernard Weisberger, *Cold War, Cold Peace* (1984). Lawrence Wittner, *American Intervention in Greece, 1943–1949* (1982). Daniel Yergin, *Shattered Peace* (1977).

tain: Churchill, America, and the Origins of the Cold War (1986). Michael Hogan, *The Marshall Plan* (1987). Akira Iriye, *The Cold War in Asia* (1974). Laurence Kaplan, *The United States and NATO* (1984). George F. Kennan, *American Diplomacy, 1900–1950* (1952); *Memoirs, 1925–1950* (1967). Joyce Kolko and Gabriel Kolko, *The Limits of Power* (1970). Bruce R. Koniholm, *The Origins of the Cold War in the Middle East* (1980). William R. Louis, *The British Empire in the Middle East* (1984). Gary May, *China Scapegoat* (1979). David Mayer, *George Kennan and the Dilemmas of U.S. Foreign Policy* (1988). Wilson D. Miscamble, *George F. Kennan and the Making of American Foreign Policy, 1947–1950* (1992). Brenda Gayle Plummer, *Black Americans and U.S. Foreign Affairs, 1935–1960* (1996). Edwin O. Reischauer, *The United States and Japan*, rev. ed. (1965). Lisle Rose, *Roots of Tragedy* (1976). Michael Schaller, *Communists* (1971); *The U.S. Crusade in China* (1979); *The American Occupation of Japan: The Origins of the Cold War in Asia* (1985). Howard Schonberger, *Aftermath of War: Americans and the Remaking of Japan* (1989). Anders Stephanson, *Kennan and the Art of Foreign Policy* (1989). Michael B. Stoff, *Oil, War, and American Security* (1980). Christopher Thorne, *Allies of a Kind* (1978). Imanuel Wexler, *The Marshall Plan Revisited* (1983).

Truman's Foreign Policy.

Dean Acheson, *Present at the Creation* (1970). Hadley Arkes, *Bureaucracy, the Marshall Plan and National Interest* (1973). Richard J. Barnet, *The Alliance* (1983). Robert M. Blum, *Drawing the Line: The Origin of the American Containment Policy in East Asia* (1982). Russell D. Buhite, *Soviet-American Relations in Asia, 1945–1954* (1982). Warren I. Cohen, *America's Response to China*, rev. ed. (1980). Jeffrey Diefendorf, *American Policy and the Reconstruction of West Germany, 1945–1955* (1993). Robert Donovan, *Conflict and Crisis* (1977); *Tumultuous Years* (1982). John King Fairbank, *The United States and China*, rev. ed. (1971). Lloyd Gardner, *Architects of Illusion* (1970). Fraser J. Harbutt, *The Iron Cur-*

19: COLD WAR AMERICA

Truman's Domestic Policies.

Stephen K. Bailey, *Congress Makes a Law* (1950). Jack S. Ballard, *The Shock of Peace: Military and Economic Demobilization After World War II* (1983). William C. Berman, *The Politics of Civil Rights in the Truman Administration* (1970). Barton J. Bernstein, ed., *Politics and Policies of the Truman Administration* (1970). Allida M. Black, Richard Dalfiume, *Desegregation of the U.S. Armed Forces* (1969); *Casting Her Own Shadow: Eleanor Roosevelt and the Shaping of Postwar Liberalism* (1996). Richard O. Davies, *Housing Reform During the Truman Administration* (1966). John P.

Diggins, *The Proud Decades* (1988). Robert Donovan, *Conflict and Crisis* (1977); *Tumultuous Years* (1982). Andrew J. Dunar, *The Truman Scandals and the Politics of Morality* (1984). Robert H. Ferrell, *Harry S. Truman and the Modern American Presidency* (1983). Eric Goldman, *The Crucial Decade—and After: America, 1945–1960* (1961). Alonzo Hamby, *Beyond the New Deal: Harry S. Truman and American Liberalism* (1973). Susan Hartman, *Truman and the 80th Congress* (1971). Roy Jenkins, *Truman* (1986). R. Alton Lee, *Truman and Taft-Hartley* (1967); *Truman and the Steel Seizure Case* (1977). Arthur F. McClure, *The Truman Administration and the Problems of Postwar Labor* (1969). Donald R. McCoy, *The Presidency of Harry S. Truman* (1984). Donald McCoy and Richard Ruetten, *Quest and Response* (1973). David McCullough, *Truman* (1992). Maeva Marcus, *Truman and the Steel Seizure* (1977). Allen J. Matusow, *Farm Policies and Politics in the Truman Years* (1967). Merle Miller, *Plain Speaking* (1980). Richard L. Miller, *Truman: The Rise to Power* (1986). William O'Neill, *American High* (1986). William E. Pemberton, *Harry S. Truman* (1989). Monte S. Poen, *Harry S. Truman Versus the Medical Lobby* (1979). Gary Reichard, *Politics as Usual: The Age of Truman and Eisenhower* (1988). Christopher L. Tomlins, *The State and the Unions* (1985).

Cold War Politics and Culture. H. W. Brands, *The Devil We Knew: Americans and the Cold War* (1993). John P. Diggins, *The Proud Decades, 1941–1960* (1989). Steven M. Gillon, *Politics and Vision: The ADA and American Liberalism, 1947–1985* (1987). David Goldfield, *Black, White, and Southern: Race Relations and Southern Culture* (1990). Maurice Isserman, *If I Had a Hammer . . . : The Death of the Old Left and the Birth of the New Left* (1987). Norman Markowitz, *The Rise and Fall of the People's Century: Henry A. Wallace and American Liberalism, 1941–1948* (1973). James T. Patterson, *Mr. Republican* (1972). Richard Pells, *The Liberal Mind in a Conservative Age: American Intellectuals in the 1940s and 1950s* (1985). Irwin Ross, *The Loneliest Campaign* (1968). Richard Norton

Smith, *Thomas E. Dewey and His Times* (1982). Allan M. Winkler, *Life Under a Cloud: American Anxiety about the Atom* (1993). Allen Yarnell, *Democrats and Progressives* (1974).

The Korean War. Carl Berger, *The Korean Knot* (1957). Ronald Caridi, *The Korean War and American Politics* (1969). Bruce Cumings, *The Origins of the Korean War* (1980); Bruce Cumings, ed., *Child of Conflict: The Korean-American Relationship, 1943–1953* (1983). Charles W. Dobbs, *The Unwanted Symbol* (1981). Joseph C. Goulden, *Korea: The Untold Story of the War* (1982). John Halliday and Bruce Cumings, *Korea: The Unknown War* (1980). Robert Leckie, *Conflict* (1962). Glenn D. Paige, *The Korean Decision* (1968). Michael Schaller, *Douglas MacArthur* (1989). Robert R. Simmons, *The Strained Alliance* (1975). John Spanier, *The Truman–MacArthur Controversy* (1959). Allen Whiting, *China Crosses the Yalu* (1960). *Countersubversion.* Michael R. Belknap, *Cold War Political Justice: The Smith Act, the Communist Party, and American Civil Liberties* (1977). Eric Bentley, ed., *Thirty Years of Treason* (1971). David Caute, *The Great Fear* (1978). Larry Ceplair and Steven Englund, *The Inquisition in Hollywood* (1983). Richard Freeland, *The Truman Doctrine and the Origins of McCarthyism* (1971). Richard Fried, *Men Against McCarthy* (1976); *Nightmare in Red* (1990). Robert Griffith, *The Politics of Fear* (1970). Robert Griffith and Athan Theoharis, eds., *The Specter: Original Essays on the Cold War and the Origins of McCarthyism* (1974). Alan Harper, *The Politics of Loyalty* (1969). Stanley Kutler, *The American Inquisition* (1982). Harvey Levenstein, *Communism, Anticommunism, and the CIO* (1981). Mary Sperling McAuliffe, *Crisis on the Left* (1978). Victor Navasky, *Naming Names* (1980). William O'Neill, *A Better World* (1983). David M. Oshinsky, *A Conspiracy So Immense: The World of Joe McCarthy* (1983). Richard Gid Powers, *Secrecy and Power: The Life of J. Edgar Hoover* (1987). Ronald Radosh and Joyce Milton, *The Rosenberg File* (1983). Thomas C. Reeves, *The Life and Times of Joe McCarthy* (1982). Michael Paul

Rogin, *The Intellectuals and McCarthy* (1967). Richard Rovere, *Senator Joe McCarthy* (1959). Walter and Miriam Schneer, *Invitation to an Inquest*, rev. ed. (1983). Ellen Schrecker, *No Ivory Tower* (1986). Edward Shils, *The Torment of Secrecy* (1956). Joseph Starobin, *American Communism in Crisis* (1972). Athan Theoharis, *Seeds of Repression* (1971); *Spying on Americans* (1978). Athan Theoharis and John Stuart Cox, *The Boss: J. Edgar Hoover and the Great American Inquisition* (1988). Allen Weinstein, *Perjury: The Hiss-Chambers Case* (1978). Stephen J. Whitfield, *The Culture of the Cold War* (1991).

20: THE CULTURE OF POSTWAR PROSPERITY

General Studies. Numan V. Bartley, *The New South, 1945–1980* (1995). John Brooks, *The Great Leap* (1966). William Chafe, *The Unfinished Journey* (1986). Carl Degler, *Affluence and Anxiety* (1968). John P. Diggins, *The Proud Decades* (1989). Eric Goldman, *The Crucial Decade and After* (1960). David Halberstam, *The Fifties* (1993). Godfrey Hodgson, *America in Our Time* (1976). William Leuchtenburg, *A Troubled Feast* (1979). Douglas T. Miller and Marion Novak, *The Fifties* (1977). William O'Neill, *American High* (1986). James T. Patterson, *Grand Expectations: Postwar America, 1945–1974* (1996).

Economy and Labor in Postwar America. David P. Calleo, *The Imperious Economy* (1982). Gilbert C. Fite, *American Farmers* (1981). John K. Galbraith, *The Affluent Society* (1958); *The New Industrial State* (1967). Mark I. Gelfand, *A Nation of Cities* (1975). Robert Heilbroner, *The Limits of American Capitalism* (1965). John Hutchinson, *The Imperfect Union* (1970). C. Wright Mills, *The Power Elite* (1956). Loren J. Okroi, *Galbraith, Harrington, Heilbroner* (1986). Joel Seidman, *American Labor from Defense to Reconversion* (1953). David Stebenne, *Arthur J. Goldberg: New Deal Liberal* (1996). Harold

G. Vatter, *The U.S. Economy in the 1950s* (1963).

Culture and Ideas. Daniel Bell, *The End of Ideology* (1960); Daniel Bell, ed., *The Radical Right* (1963). Peter Biskind, *Seeing is Believing: How Hollywood Taught Us to Stop Worrying and Love the Fifties* (1983). Paul Boyer, *By the Bomb's Early Light* (1986). Howard Brick, *Daniel Bell and the Decline of Intellectual Radicalism* (1986). James L. Baughman, *The Republic of Mass Culture: Journalism, Filmmaking, and Broadcasting in America since 1941* (1992). Paul A. Carter, *Another Part of the Fifties* (1983). Ann Charters, *Kerouac* (1973). Bruce Cook, *The Beat Generation* (1971). Thomas Cripps, *Making Movies Black: The Hollywood Message Movie from World War II to the Civil Rights Era* (1993). Tom Engelhardt, *The End of Victory Culture: Cold War America and the Disillusioning of a Generation* (1995). Edward J. Epstein, *News from Nowhere* (1973). Herbert Gans, *The Levittowners* (1967). William Graebner, *The Age of Doubt: American Thought and Culture in the 1940s* (1991). David Halberstam, *The Powers That Be* (1979). Jeffrey Hart, *When the Going Was Good: American Life in the Fifties* (1982). Dolores Hayden, *Redesigning the American Dream* (1984). Kenneth T. Jackson, *The Crabgrass Frontier: The Suburbanization of the United States* (1985). Marty Jezer, *The Dark Ages: Life in the U.S. 1945–1960* (1982). Landon Y. Jones, *Great Expectations: America and the Baby Boom Generation* (1980). Neil Jumonville, *Critical Crossings: The New York Intellectuals in Postwar America* (1991). George Lipsitz, *Class and Culture in Cold War America* (1981). Roger W. Lotchin, *Fortress California, 1910–1961: From Warfare to Welfare* (1992). Mary Sperling McAuliffe, *Crisis on the Left* (1978). Walter A. McDougall, *The Heavens and the Earth: A Political History of the Space Age* (1985). Dennis McNally, *Desolate Angel* (1979). Margaret Marsh, *Suburban Lives* (1990). Douglas T. Miller and Marion Novak, *The Fifties* (1977). Zane L. Miller, *Suburb: Neighborhood and Community in Forest Park, Ohio, 1935–1976* (1981). C. Wright Mills, *White Collar* (1956). Richard H. Pells,

The Liberal Mind in a Conservative Age: American Intellectuals in the 1940s and 1950s (1985). David Potter, *People of Plenty* (1954). David Riesman, *The Lonely Crowd* (1950). Leila Rupp and Verta Taylor, *Survival in the Doldrums* (1987). Arthur M. Schlesinger, Jr., *The Vital Center* (1949). Lynn Spigel, *Make Room for TV* (1992). Walter Sullivan, ed., *America's Race for the Moon* (1962). John Tytell, *Naked Angels* (1976). Alan M. Wald, *The New York Intellectuals* (1987). Stephen J. Whitfield, *The Culture of the Cold War* (1991). William Whyte, *The Organization Man* (1956). Tom Wolfe, *The Right Stuff* (1979). Gwendolyn Wright, *Building the American Dream: A Social History of Housing in America* (1981).

Women and Families. William Chafe, *The American Woman: Her Changing Social, Economic, and Political Roles, 1920–1970*, rev. ed. (1988). Ruth Cowan, *More Work for Mothers: The Irony of Household Technology* (1983). Eugenia Kaledin, *Mothers and More: American Women in the 1950s* (1984). Susan Estabrook Kennedy, *If All We Did Was to Weep at Home: A History of White Working-Class Women in America* (1979). Alice Kessler-Harris, *Out to Work: A History of Wage-Earning Women in the United States* (1982). Elaine Tyler May, *Homeward Bound: American Families in the Cold War* (1988). Susan Strasser, *Never Done: A History of American Housework* (1982).

Minorities and the Poor. Rodolfo Acuña, *Occupied America: A History of Chicanos* (1981). Larry W. Burt, *Tribalism in Crisis: Federal Indian Policy, 1953–1961* (1982). Donald Fixico, *Termination and Relocation: Federal Indian Policy, 1945–1970* (1986). J. Wayne Flint, *Dixie's Forgotten People: The South's Poor Whites* (1979). Michael Harrington, *The Other America* (1962). Jacqueline Jones, *The Dispossessed: America's Underclasses from the Civil War to the Present* (1992). Nicholas Lemann, *The Promised Land: The Great Black Migration and How It Changed America* (1991). Elena Padilla, *Up from Puerto Rico* (1958). Linda Reed, *Simple Decency and Common Sense* (1992).

21: THE FIGHT FOR RACIAL JUSTICE

Overviews and Early Days. Taylor Branch, *Parting the Waters* (1988). Thomas Brooks, *The Walls Came Tumbling Down* (1974). William Chafe, *Civilities and Civil Rights* (1980). John Egerton, *Speak Now Against the Day: The Generation Before the Civil Rights Movement in the South* (1994). David Garrow, *Bearing the Cross* (1986). Kevin Gaines, *Uplifting the Race: Black Leadership, Politics, and Culture in the Twentieth Century* (1996). Darlene Clark Hine, *Black Victory* (1979). Richard H. King, *Civil Rights and the Idea of Freedom* (1992). Steven Lawson, *Black Ballots* (1976). Steven Lawson, *Running for Freedom* (1991). Nicholas Lehman, *The Promised Land* (1991). Anthony Lewis, *Portrait of a Decade: The Second American Revolution* (1964). Douglas McAdam, *Political Process and the Development of Black Insurgency* (1982). Benjamin Muse, *The American Negro Revolution* (1970). Manning Marable, *Race, Reform, and Rebellion* (1984). Robert J. Norrell, *Reaping the Whirlwind: The Civil Rights Movement in Tuskegee* (1985). Howell Raines, *My Soul Is Rested* (1977). Harvard Sitkoff, *The Struggle for Black Equality, 1954–1980* (1981). Patricia Sullivan, *Days of Hope: Race and Democracy in the New Deal Era*. Juan Williams, *Eyes on the Prize* (1988).

School Desegregation. John W. Anderson, *Eisenhower, Brownell, and the Congress* (1964). Numan V. Bartley, *The Rise of Massive Resistance* (1969). Jack Bass, *Unlikely Heroes* (1981). Daniel Berman, *It is So Ordered* (1966). Robert F. Burk, *The Eisenhower Administration and Black Civil Rights* (1984). Clarence Clyde Ferguson, Jr., *Desegregation and the Law*. Jack Greenberg, *Race Relations and American Law* (1959). Elizabeth Huckaby, *Crisis at Central High* (1980). Richard Kluger, *Simple Justice* (1976). Melvin Tumin, *Desegregation* (1957).

Montgomery. Taylor Branch, *Parting the Waters* (1988). Virginia Foster Durr, *Outside the Magic Circle* (1985). David Garrow,

Bearing the Cross (1986). David Garrow, ed., *The Montgomery Bus Boycott and the Women Who Started It: A Memoir of Jo Ann Gibson Robinson* (1987). Martin Luther King, Jr., *Stride Toward Freedom* (1958). David Lewis, *King: A Critical Biography* (1970). Aldon Morris, *The Origins of the Civil Rights Movement* (1984). Stephen B. Oates, *Let the Trumpet Sound* (1982). Earl and Miriam Selby, *Odyssey: Journey Though Black America* (1971).

22: EISENHOWER REPUBLICANISM

Politics in the Eisenhower Years. Sherman Adams, *Firsthand Report* (1961). Charles C. Alexander, *Holding the Line* (1975). Stephen Ambrose, *Eisenhower the President* (1984). John W. Anderson, *Eisenhower, Brownell, and the Congress* (1964). Jean Baker, *The Stevensons: A Biography of an American Family* (1996). Brian Balogh, *Chain Reaction: Expert Debate and Public Participation in American Nuclear Commercial Power, 1945–1975* (1991). Piers Brendon, *Ike* (1986). Jeff Broadwater, *Eisenhower and the Anti-Communist Crusade* (1992). Robert F. Burk, *Dwight D. Eisenhower* (1986). Barbara B. Clowse, *Brainpower for the Cold War: The Sputnik Crisis and the National Defense Education Act of 1958* (1981). Dwight D. Eisenhower, *The White House Years*, 2 vols. *(1963–1965)*. Fred Greenstein, *The Hidden-hand Presidency* (1982). Emmet John Hughes, *The Ordeal of Power* (1963). Peter Lyon, *Eisenhower: Portrait of a Hero* (1974). Richard Nixon, *Six Crises* (1962). Herbert S. Parmet, *Eisenhower and the American Crusades* (1972). Nicol C. Rae, *The Decline and Fall of the Liberal Republicans* (1989). Gary Reichard, *The Reaffirmation of Republicanism* (1975); *Politics as Usual* (1988). David W. Reinhard, *The Republican Right Since 1945* (1983). Elmo Richardson, *The Presidency of Dwight D. Eisenhower* (1979). Mark H. Rose, *Interstate: Express Highway Politics, 1941–1956* (1979). R. L. Rosholt, *An Administrative History of NASA* (1966).

Foreign Policy. Stephen Ambrose, *Ike's Spies* (1981). David L. Anderson, *Trapped by Success: The Eisenhower Administration and Vietnam, 1953–1961* (1991). Howard Ball, *Justice Downwind: America's Nuclear Testing Program in the 1950s* (1986). Michael Beschloss, *MAYDAY* (1986). Henry W. Brands, *Cold Warriors* (1988); *The Spector of Neutralism: The United States and the Emergence of the Third World, 1947–1960* (1989). Blanche W. Cooke, *The Declassified Eisenhower* (1981). Chester Cooper, *Lost Crusade* (1970); *The Lion's Last Roar* (1978). Cecil Currey, *Edward Lansdale: The Unquiet American* (1988). Robert A. Divine, *Foreign Policy and U.S. Presidential Elections*, 2 vols. (1974); *Blowing in the Wind: The Nuclear Test Ban Debate, 1954–1960* (1978); *Eisenhower and the Cold War* (1981). William J. Duiker, *U.S. Containment Policy and the Conflict in Indochina* (1992). Frances Fitzgerald, *Fire in the Lake* (1972). Steven Z. Freiberger, *Dawn over Suez: The Rise of American Power in the Middle East, 1953–1957* (1992). Louis Gerson, *John Foster Dulles* (1967). Gregg Herken, *Counsels of War* (1985). George Herring, *America's Longest War* (1979). Richard G. Hewlett and Jack M. Hall, *Atoms for Peace and War, 1953–1961* (1989). Townsend Hoopes, *The Devil and John Foster Dulles* (1973). Richard Immerman, *The CIA in Guatemala* (1982). Burton Kaufman, *The Oil Cartel Case* (1978). Gabriel Kolko, *Confronting the Third World* (1988). Walter LaFeber, *Inevitable Revolutions* (1983). John T. McAlister, Jr., *Vietnam: The Origins of Revolution* (1969). Richard A. Melanson and David A. Mayers, eds., *Reevaluating Eisenhower* (1986). Stephen G. Rabe, *Eisenhower and Latin America* (1988). Kermit Roosevelt, *Counter-coup* (1980). Andrew Rotter, *The Path to Vietnam* (1987). Richard Smoke, *National Security and the Nuclear Dilemma* (1988). Hugh Thomas, *Suez* (1967). Mira Wilkins, *The Maturing of Multinational Enterprise* (1974).

Legal and Constitutional Issues. Alexander Bickel, *Politics and the Warren Court* (1965); *The Supreme Court and the Idea of Progress* (1970). Phillip Kurland, *Politics, the Constitution, and the Warren Court* (1970).

Paul Murphy, *The Constitution in Crisis Times* (1972). Bernard Schwartz, *Super Chief: Earl Warren and His Supreme Court* (1983). Philip Stern, *The Oppenheimer Case* (1969). Michael Straight, *Trial by Television* (1954). John Weaver, *Earl Warren* (1967).

23: THE RESURGENCE OF LIBERALISM

General Studies. William Chafe, *The Unfinished Journey: America Since World War II*, rev. ed. (1991). Godfrey Hodgson, *America in Our Time* (1976). Allen J. Matusow, *The Unraveling of America: A History of Liberalism in the 1960s* (1984). Charles R. Morris, *A Time of Passion* (1984). Theodore H. White, *America in Search of Itself* (1982).

Kennedy and Johnson. Vaughn D. Bornet, *The Presidency of Lyndon B. Johnson* (1983). Thomas Brown, *JFK: The History of an Image* (1988). David Burner, *John F. Kennedy and a New Generation* (1988). Robert Caro, *The Years of Lyndon B. Johnson: The Path to Power* (1982); *Means of Ascent* (1990). Paul K. Conkin, *Big Daddy from the Pedernales* (1986). Robert Dallek, *Lone Star Rising: Lyndon Johnson and His Times, 1908–1960* (1991). Robert A. Divine, *The Johnson Years* (1987). Ronnie Dugger, *The Politician* (1982). Edward J. Epstein, *Inquest* (1966); *Legend* (1978). Henry Fairlie, *The Kennedy Promise: The Politics of Expectation* (1973). Richard Reeves, *President Kennedy: Profile of Power* (1993). Eric Goldman, *The Tragedy of Lyndon Johnson* (1968). Richard N. Goodwin, *Remembering America* (1988). Jim Heath, *Decade of Disillusionment* (1975). Henry Hurt, *Reasonable Doubt* (1985). Lyndon B. Johnson, *Vantage Point* (1971). Doris Kearns, *Lyndon Johnson and the American Dream* (1976). Donald Lord, *John F. Kennedy: The Politics of Confrontation and Conciliation* (1977). William Manchester, *The Death of a President* (1967). Bruce Miroff, *Pragmatic Illusions: The Presidential Politics of JFK* (1976). Lewis Paper, *The Promise and the Performance* (1975). Herbert

Parmet, *Jack* (1980); *JFK* (1983). George Reedy, *The Twilight of the Presidency* (1970). Richard Reeves, *President Kennedy* (1992). Thomas Reeves, *A Question of Character: The Life of John F. Kennedy in Image and Reality* (1991). Arthur M. Schlesinger, Jr., *A Thousand Days* (1965). Theodore Sorensen, *Kennedy* (1965). Anthony Summers, *Conspiracy* (1980). Warren Commission, *The Report of the Warren Commission* (1964). Theodore H. White, *The Making of the President, 1960* (1961). Garry Wills, *The Kennedy Imprisonment* (1982).

Domestic Policies and Politics. Henry J. Aaron, *Politics and the Professors* (1978). William H. Chafe, *Never Stop Running: Allard Lowenstein and the Struggle to Save American Liberalism* (1993). Greg J. Duncan, *Years of Poverty, Years of Plenty* (1984). Mark Gelfand, *A Nation of Cities* (1975). James Giglio, *The Presidency of John F. Kennedy* (1991). Hugh Davis Graham, *Uncertain Trumpet* (1984). Robert H. Haveman, ed., *A Decade of Federal Antipoverty Programs* (1977). Jim Heath, *John F. Kennedy and the Business Community* (1969). Daniel Knapp and Kenneth Polk, *Scouting the War on Poverty* (1971). Sar Levitan, *The Great Society's Poor Law* (1969). Sar Levitan and Robert Taggart, *The Promise of Greatness* (1976). Allen J. Matusow, *The Unraveling of America: A History of Liberalism in the 1960s* (1984). Charles Morris, *A Time of Passion* (1984). Charles Murray, *Losing Ground* (1984). Victor Navasky, *Kennedy Justice* (1971). James T. Patterson, *America's Struggle Against Poverty, 1900–1980* (1981). Frances Fox Piven and Richard Cloward, *Regulating the Poor* (1971). John E. Schwarz, *America's Hidden Success* (1983). James L. Sundquist, *Politics and Policy: The Eisenhower, Kennedy, and Johnson Years* (1968). Tom Wicker, *JFK and LBJ* (1968).

Race Relations and Civil Rights. Taylor Branch, *Parting the Waters: America in the King Years* (1988). Carl Brauer, *John F. Kennedy and the Second Reconstruction* (1977). Paul Burstein, *Discrimination, Jobs, and Politics* (1985). James Button, *Black Violence: Political Impact of the 1960s Race Riots* (1978).

Stokely Carmichael and Charles Hamilton, *Black Power* (1967). Clayborne Carson, *In Struggle: SNCC and the Black Awakening of the 1960s* (1981). William Chafe, *Civilities and Civil Rights: Greensboro, North Carolina, and the Black Struggle for Freedom* (1980). Joe R. Feagin and Harlan Hahn, *Ghetto Revolts* (1973). Robert Fogelson, *Violence as Protest* (1971). David Garrow, *Protest at Selma* (1978); *The FBI and Martin Luther King* (1981); *Bearing the Cross* (1986). Hugh Davis Graham, *The Civil Rights Era* (1990). Alex Haley, *The Autobiography of Malcolm X* (1966). Martin Luther King, Jr., *Why We Can't Wait* (1964). Steven Lawson, *Black Ballots: Voting Rights in the South, 1966–1969* (1976). Nicholas Lemann, *The Promised Land: The Great Black Migration and How It Changed America* (1991). David L. Lewis, *King: A Critical Biography* (1970). Doug McAdam, *Freedom Summer* (1988). Benjamin Muse, *The American Negro Revolution* (1969). United States Kerner Commission, *Report of the National Advisory Commission on Civil Disorders* (1968). Stephen Oates, *Let the Trumpet Sound* (1982). Harvard Sitkoff, *The Struggle for Black Equality, 1954–1992* (1992). James R. Ralph Jr., *Northern Protest: Martin Luther King Jr., Chicago, and the Civil Rights Movement* (1993). Mark Stern, *Calculating Visions: Kennedy, Johnson, and Civil Rights* (1992). Abigail Thernstrom, *Whose Votes Count? Affirmative Action and Minority Voting Rights* (1987). Robert Weisbrot, *Freedom Bound: A History of America's Civil Rights Movement* (1990). Nancy J. Weiss, *Whitney M. Young, Jr., and the Struggle for Civil Rights* (1989). Roy Wilkins, *Standing Fast* (1982). Harris Wofford, *Of Kennedy and Kings* (1980). Eugene Wolfenstein, *The Victims of Democracy: Malcolm X and the Black Revolution* (1981). Howard Zinn, *SNCC: The New Abolitionists* (1981).

24: FROM FLEXIBLE RESPONSE TO VIETNAM

Foreign Policy. Elie Abel, *The Missile Crisis* (1966). Graham Allison, *Essence of Decision* (1971). Richard Barnet, *Intervention and Revolution* (1968). Michael Bechloss, *The Crisis Years* (1990). McGeorge Bundy, *Danger and Survival* (1989). Warren Cohen, *Dean Rusk* (1980). Herbert Dinerstein, *The Making of a Missile Crisis* (1976). Bernard Firestone, *The Quest for Nuclear Stability* (1982). Louise Fitzsimmons, *The Kennedy Doctrine* (1972). Philip Geyelin, *Lyndon B. Johnson and the World* (1966). John Girling, *America and the Third World* (1980). Trumball Higgins, *The Perfect Failure: Kennedy, Eisenhower, and the CIA at the Bay of Pigs* (1987). Roger Hilsman, *To Move a Nation* (1965). Haynes Johnson, *The Bay of Pigs* (1964). Robert Kennedy, *Thirteen Days* (1969). Dan Kurzman, *Santo Domingo* (1966). Walter LaFeber, *Inevitable Revolutions: The United States in Central America* (1985). Thomas J. McCormick, *America's Half Century: United States Foreign Policy in the Cold War* (1989). Richard D. Mahoney, *JFK: Ordeal in Africa* (1983). Gerald T. Rice, *The Bold Experiment: JFK's Peace Corps* (1985). Jerome Slater, *Intervention and Negotiation* (1970). Richard Walton, *Cold War and Counterrevolutions* (1972). Peter Wyden, *Bay of Pigs* (1969).

Vietnam. Mark Baker, Christian G. Appy, *Nam* (1982); *Working-Class War: American Combat Soldiers and Vietnam* (1993). Lawrence Baskir and William Strauss, *Chance and Circumstance* (1978). Larry Berman, *Planning a Tragedy* (1982); *Lyndon Johnson's War* (1989). Peter Braestrup, *Big Story* (1977; abridged ed. 1978). William Broyles, Jr., *Brothers in Arms: A Journey from War to Peace* (1986). Philip Davidson, *Vietnam at War* (1991). Gloria Emerson, *Winners and Losers* (1976). Frances Fitzgerald, *Fire in the Lake* (1972). John Galloway, *The Gulf of Tonkin Resolution* (1970). Leslie Gelb and Richard Betts, *The Irony of Vietnam: The System Worked* (1979). David Halberstam, *The Best and the Brightest* (1972). Michael Herr, *Dispatches* (1977). George C. Herring, *America's Longest War*, rev. ed. (1986). George McT. Kahin, *Intervention* (1986). Stanley Karnow, *Vietnam* (1983). Alexander Kendrick, *The Wound Within* (1974). Gabriel Kolko, *The Anatomy of a War* (1985). Robert W. Komer, *Bureaucracy at War*

(1986). David Levy, *The Debate over Vietnam* (1991). Guenter Lewy, *America in Vietnam* (1978). Don Oberdorfer, *Tet* (1971). Bruce C. Palmer, Jr., *The 25-Year War* (1984). *The Pentagon Papers*, Senator Gravel edition (1975). Norman Podhoretz, *Why We Were in Vietnam* (1982). Thomas Powers, *Vietnam: The War at Home* (1973). Al Santoli, *Everything We Had* (1981). Herbert Schandler, *The Unmaking of a President: Lyndon Johnson and Vietnam* (1977). Neil Sheehan, *A Bright Shining Lie* (1988). R. B. Smith, *An International History of the Vietnam War: The Kennedy Strategy* (1985). Ronald Spector, *Advice and Support* (1983). Col. Harry Summers, *On Strategy* (1981). Wallace Terry, *Bloods* (1984). Thomas C. Thayer, *War Without Fronts* (1985). Wallace J. Thies, *When Governments Collide* (1980). James Thompson, *Rolling Thunder* (1980). Kathleen J. Turner, *Lyndon Johnson's Dual War: Vietnam and the Press* (1981). Irwin Unger, *The Movement* (1974). Marilyn Young, *The Vietnam Wars* (1991).

25: CULTURAL REVOLUTIONS

General Studies. John Morton Blum, *Years of Discord: American Politics and Society, 1961–1974* (1991). Peter N. Carroll, *It Seemed Like Nothing Happened* (1982). Allen J. Matusow, *The Unraveling of America* (1984). Kim McQuaid, *The Anxious Years* (1989). William O'Neill, *Coming Apart* (1971).

1968. Dan T. Carter, *The Politics of Rage: George Wallace, The Origins of the New Conservatism, and the Transformation of American Politics* (1995). David Caute, *The Year of the Barricades* (1988). Lewis Chester, Godfrey Hodgson, and Lewis Page, *American Melodrama* (1969). David Farber, *Chicago 68* (1988). Marshall Frady, *Wallace*, rev. ed. (1976). Godfrey Hodgson, *America in Our Time* (1976). Charles Kaiser, *1968 in America* (1988). Norman Mailer, *Miami and the Siege of Chicago* (1968). Arthur M. Schlesinger, Jr., *Robert Kennedy and His Times* (1978). Ben Stavis, *We Were the Campaign*

(1969). Theodore White, *The Making of the President, 1968* (1969).

The New Left and the Counterculture. Edward Bacciocco, Jr., *The New Left in America* (1974). Ronald Berman, *America in the Sixties* (1968). Wini Breines, *Community and Organization in the New Left* (1983). Peter Clecak, *Radical Paradoxes* (1973). Peter Collier and David Horowitz, *Destructive Generation: Second Thoughts About the Sixties* (1989). Margaret Cruikshank, *The Gay and Lesbian Liberation Movement in America* (1992). Morris Dickstein, *Gates of Eden* (1977). Joan Didion, *Slouching Towards Bethlehem* (1967); *The White Album* (1979). John Diggins, *The American Left in the Twentieth Century* (1973). Sara Evans, *Personal Politics* (1979). Lewis Feuer, *The Conflict of Generations* (1969). Richard Flacks, *Youth and Social Change* (1971). Todd Gitlin, *The Whole World Is Watching* (1981); *The Sixties: Years of Hope, Days of Rage* (1987). Paul Goodman, *Growing Up Absurd* (1960). David Harris, *Dreams Die Hard* (1983). Maurice Isserman, *"If I Had a Hammer . . .": The Death of the Old Left and the Birth of the New Left* (1987). Joseph Kelner and James Munves, *The Kent State Coverup* (1980). Kenneth Keniston, *Young Radicals* (1968); *Youth and Dissent* (1971). Richard King, *The Party of Eros* (1972). James Kunen, *The Strawberry Statement* (1968). Lawrence Lader, *Power on the Left* (1979). Klaus Mehnert, *Twilight of the Young* (1978). James Miller, *"Democracy in the Streets": From Port Huron to the Siege of Chicago* (1987). Charles Reich, *The Greening of America* (1970). W. J. Rorabaugh, *Berkeley at War* (1989). Theodore Roszak, *The Making of a Counter Culture* (1969). Kirkpatrick Sale, *SDS* (1973). Irwin Unger, *The Movement* (1974). Milton Viorst, *Fire in the Streets* (1979). Jon Wiener, *Come Together: John Lennon and His Time* (1984).

Indians, Hispanics, Asians. Rodolfo Acuña, *Occupied America*, 2nd ed. (1981). Larry W. Burt, *Tribalism in Crisis: Federal Indian Policy, 1953–1961* (1982). Vine Deloria, Jr., *Custer Died for Your Sins* (1969); *Behind the Trail of Broken Treaties* (1974).

Ronald Dewing, *Wounded Knee: The Meaning and Significance of the Second Incident* (1985). Douglas E. Foley, *From Peones to Politicos: Class and Ethnicity in a South Texas Town, 1900–1987* (1988). Peter Iverson, *The Navajo Nation* (1981). Oscar Lewis, *La Vida* (1969). D'Arcy McNickle, *Native American Tribalism* (1973). Matt Meier and Feliciano Rivera, *The Chicanos* (1972). David M. Reimers, *Still the Golden Door: The Third World Comes to America* (1985). Julian Samora, *Los Mojados* (1971). Stan Steiner, *The New Indians* (1968). Ronald Takaki, *Strangers from a Distant Shore: A History of Asian Americans* (1989); *A Different Mirror: A History of Multicultural America* (1993). Ronald Taylor, *Chavez and the Farm Workers* (1975). Wilcomb Washburn, *Red Man's Land/White Man's Law* (1971). Charles F. Wilkinson, *American Indians, Time, and the Law* (1987).

Feminism. William Chafe, *The American Woman* (1972). Nancy Cott, *The Grounding of Modern Feminism* (1987). Marian Faux, *Roe v. Wade* (1988). Jo Freeman, *The Politics of Women's Liberation* (1975). Betty Friedan, *The Feminine Mystique* (1963). Carol Gilligan, *In A Different Voice* (1982). Cynthia Harrison, *On Account of Sex: The Politics of Women's Issues, 1945–1968* (1988). Susan M. Hartmann, *From Margin to Mainstream: Women and American Politics Since 1960* (1989). Alice Kessler-Harris, *Out to Work: A History of Wage-Earning Women in the United States* (1982). Ethel Klein, *Gender Politics* (1984). Kristin Luker, *Abortion and the Politics of Motherhood* (1984). Robin Morgan, ed., *Sisterhood Is Powerful* (1970). Rosalind Petchesky, *Abortion and Women's Choice* (1984). Sheila Rothman, *Woman's Proper Place* (1978). Winifred Wandersee, *On the Move: American Women in the 1970s* (1988). Gayle Yates, *What Women Want* (1975).

26: THE IMPERIAL PRESIDENCY

Nixon and the World. Seyom Brown, *The Crisis of Power* (1979). Lloyd Gardner, *The Great Nixon Turnaround* (1973); *A Covenant with Power* (1984). Seymour Hersh, *The Price of Power* (1983). Roger Hilsman, *The Crouching Future* (1975). Arnold Isaacs, *Without Honor: Defeat in Vietnam and Cambodia* (1983). Walter Isaacson, *Kissinger* (1992). Marvin Kalb and Bernard Kalb, *Kissinger* (1974). Henry A. Kissinger, *White House Years* (1979); *Years of Upheaval* (1982); *Diplomacy* (1994). David Landau, *Kissinger: The Uses of Power* (1972). Robert S. Litwak, *Detente and the Nixon Doctrine: American Foreign Policy and the Pursuit of Stability* (1984). Timothy Lomperis, *The War Nobody Lost—and Won* (1984). Roger Morris, *Uncertain Greatness* (1977). Harland Moulton, *From Superiority to Parity* (1973). John Newhouse, *Cold Dawn* (1973). Michael Oksenberg and Robert Oxnam, eds., *Dragon and Eagle* (1978). Gareth Porter, *A Peace Denied* (1975); *Vietnam* (1979). Thomas Powers, *The Man Who Kept the Secrets* (1979). William Quandt, *Decade of Decision* (1977). Franz Schurman, *The Foreign Policies of Richard Nixon* (1987). William Shawcross, *Sideshow: Nixon, Kissinger, and the Destruction of Cambodia* (1978). Richard Stevenson, *The Rise and Fall of Detente* (1985). John Stockwell, *In Search of Enemies* (1977). Robert Stookey, *America and the Arab States* (1975). Robert D. Schulzinger, *Henry Kissinger: Doctor of Diplomacy* (1989). Tad Szulc, *The Illusion of Peace* (1978).

Nixon and His Presidency. Stephen Ambrose, *Nixon: The Triumph of a Politician, 1962–1972* (1989). Richard Barnet, *The Lean Years* (1980). Fawn Brodie, *Richard Nixon: The Shaping of His Character* (1981). Vincent Burke and Vee Burke, *Nixon's Good Deed* (1974). John Ehrlichman, *Witness to Power* (1982). John R. Greene, *The Limits of Power: The Nixon and Ford Administrations* (1992). H. R. Haldeman, *The Haldeman Diaries: Inside the Nixon White House* (1994). Joan Hoff, *Nixon Reconsidered* (1994). J. C. Hurewitz, ed., *Oil, the Arab-Israeli Dispute, and the Industrial World* (1976). R. L. Miller, *The New Economics of Richard Nixon* (1972). Daniel P. Moynihan, *The Politics of a Guaranteed Income* (1973). R. P. Nathan et al., *Monitoring Revenue Sharing* (1975). Richard

Nixon, *RN: The Memoirs of Richard Nixon* (1978). Herbert Parmet, *Richard Nixon and His America* (1989). Raymond Price, *With Nixon* (1977). James Reichley, *Conservatives in an Age of Change: The Nixon and Ford Administrations* (1981). William Safire, *Before the Fall* (1975). Joan Edelman Spero, *The Politics of International Economic Relations* (1977). Michael Tanzer, *The Energy Crisis* (1974). Theodore H. White, *The Making of the President, 1972* (1973). Bob Woodward and Scott Armstrong, *The Brethren* (1980).

Nixon and Watergate. Fawn Brodie, *Richard Nixon: The Shaping of His Character* (1981). Richard Cohen and Jules Witcover, *A Heartbeat Away* (1974). Len Colodny and Robert Gettlin, *Silent Coup* (1991). John Dean, *Blind Ambition* (1976). James Doyle, *Not Above the Law* (1977). Fred Emery, *Watergate: The Corruption of American Politics* (1994). Stanley J. Kutler, *The Wars of Watergate* (1990). J. Anthony Lukas, *Nightmare: The Underside of the Nixon Years* (1976). Bruce Mazlish, *In Search of Nixon* (1972). Richard M. Nixon, *RN: The Memoirs of Richard Nixon* (1978). Jonathan Schell, *The Time of Illusion* (1975). Arthur M. Schlesinger, Jr., *The Imperial Presidency* (1973). Michael Schudson, *Watergate in American Memory: How We Remember, Forget, and Reconstruct the Past* (1992). William Sirica, *To Set the Record Straight* (1979). Maurice Stans, *The Terrors of Justice* (1984). Theodore H. White, *Breach of Faith* (1975). Garry Wills, *Nixon Agonistes* (1970). Bob Woodward and Carl Bernstein, *All the President's Men* (1974); *The Final Days* (1976).

27: THE RISE OF AMERICAN CONSERVATISM

The Ford Presidency. James M. Cannon, *Time and Chance: Gerald Ford's Appointment with History* (1994). Gerald Ford, *A Time to Heal* (1979). John R. Greene, *The Limits of Power: The Nixon and Ford Administrations* (1992). Robert T. Hartmann, *Palace Politics* (1990). Gerald Ter Horst, *Gerald Ford* (1975). Richard Reeves, *A Ford Not a Lin-*

coln (1976). A. James Reichley, *Conservatives in an Age of Change: The Nixon and Ford Administrations* (1981). Edward and Frederick Schapsmeier, *Gerald R. Ford's Date with Destiny: A Political Biography* (1989). James L. Sundquist, *The Decline and Resurgence of Congress* (1981).

The Carter Presidency. Jack Bass and Walter Devries, *The Transformation of Southern Politics* (1976). James Bill, *The Eagle and the Lion* (1988). Zbigniew Brzezinski, *Power and Principle* (1983). Jimmy Carter, *Why Not the Best?* (1975); *Keeping Faith* (1982). Rosalynn Carter, *First Lady from Plains* (1984). Steven Gillon, *The Democrats' Dilemma: Walter Mondale and the Liberal Legacy* (1992). Betty Glad, *Jimmy Carter* (1980). Erwin Hargrove, *Jimmy Carter as President* (1989). Steven B. Hunt, *The Energy Crisis* (1978). Haynes Johnson, *In the Absence of Power* (1980). Charles O. Jones, *The Trusteeship Presidency* (1988). Hamilton Jordon, *Crisis* (1982). Walter LaFeber, *Panama Canal* (1978). Clark Mollenhoff, *The President Who Failed* (1980). A. Glenn Mower, Jr., *Human Rights and American Foreign Policy* (1987). William B. Quandt, *Decade of Decisions* (1977); *Camp David* (1986). Barry Rubin, *Paved with Good Intentions* (1983). Lars Schoultz, *Human Rights and U.S. Policy Toward Latin America* (1981). Gaddis Smith, *Morality, Reason, and Power* (1986). Strobe Talbott, *Endgame* (1979). Jules Witcover, *Marathon* (1977). James Wooten, *Dasher* (1978). Cyrus Vance, *Hard Choices* (1983).

The New Right. Sidney Blumenthal, *The Rise of the Counter-Establishment* (1986). George Nash, *The Conservative Intellectual Movement in America Since 1945* (1979). Burton Yale Pines, *Back to Basics* (1982). David W. Reinhard, *The Republican Right Since 1945* (1983). Kirkpatrick Sale, *Power Shift: The Rise of the Southern Rim and Its Challenge to the Eastern Establishment* (1975). Peter Steinfels, *The Neo-Conservatives* (1979). John K. White, *The New Politics of Old Values* (1988). Clyde Wilcox, *God's Warriors: The Christian Right in Twentieth Century America* (1992). John Woodridge, *The Evangelicals* (1975).

The Reagan Presidency. Frank Ackerman, *Reaganomics* (1982). Laurence I. Barrett, *Gambling with History* (1984). Bill Boyarsky, *The Rise of Ronald Reagan* (1968). Paul Boyer, ed., *Reagan as President: Contemporary Views of the Man, His Politics, and His Policies* (1990). William J. Broad, *Teller's War: The Top-Secret Story Behind the Star Wars Deception* (1992). Lou Cannon, *Reagan* (1982); *President Reagan: The Role of a Lifetime* (1990). Joan Claybrook, *Retreat from Safety: Reagan's Attack on American Health* (1984). Robert Dallek, *Ronald Reagan: The Politics of Symbolism* (1984). Ronnie Dugger, *On Reagan* (1983). Thomas Byrne Edsall, *The New Politics of Inequality* (1984). Anne Edwards, *Early Reagan* (1987). Rowland Evans and Robert Novak, *The Reagan Revolution* (1981). Benjamin Friedman, *Day of Reckoning: The Consequences of American Economic Policy Under Reagan and After* (1988). Jack Germond and Jules Witcover, *Blue Smoke and Mirrors: How Reagan Won and Why Carter Lost the Election of 1980* (1981); *Wake Us When It's Over: Presidential Politics of 1984* (1985). George Gildner, *Wealth and Poverty* (1981). Fred I. Greenstein, ed., *The Reagan Presidency* (1983). William Greider, *The Education of David Stockman and Other Americans* (1982). Haynes Johnson, *Sleepwalking Through History: America in the Reagan Years* (1991). Jonathan Lash, *A Season of Spoils: The Story of the Reagan Administration's Attack on the Environment* (1984). Robert Lekachman, *Greed Is Not Enough: Reaganomics* (1982). Jane Mayer and Doyle McManus, *Landslide: The Unmaking of the President, 1984–1988* (1988). Charles Noble, *Liberalism at Work: The Rise and Fall of OSHA* (1986). Peggy Noonan, *What I Saw at the Revolution: A Political Life in the Reagan Era* (1990). John L. Palmer and Isabel V. Sawhill, eds., *The Reagan Experiment* (1982). Michael J. Piore and Charles F. Sabel, *The Second Industrial Divide* (1984). Frances Fox Piven and Richard A. Cloward, *The New Class War: Reagan's Attack on the Welfare State and Its Consequences* (1982). Nancy Reagan, *My Turn* (1989). Richard Reeves, *The Reagan Detour* (1985). Donald T. Regan, *For the Record* (1988). Michael Rogin, *Ronald Reagan: The Movie* (1987). Michael

Schaller, *Reckoning with Reagan: America and Its President in the 1980s* (1992). C. Brant Short, *Ronald Reagan and the Public Lands: America's Conservation Debate, 1979–1984* (1989). Hedrick Smith, *The Power Game* (1988). Hedrick Smith et al. *Reagan: The Man, the President* (1980). David A. Stockman, *The Triumph of Politics* (1986). Sidney Weintraub and Marvin Goodstein, eds., *Reaganomics in the Stagflation Economy* (1983). F. Clifton White and William Gil, *Why Reagan Won* (1982). Theodore H. White, *America in Search of Itself* (1982). Garry Wills, *Reagan's America* (1987).

Reagan and the World. Seweryn Bialer and Michael Mandelbaum, eds., *Gorbachev's Russia and American Foreign Policy* (1988). Raymond Bonner, *Weakness and Deceit: U.S. Policy and El Salvador* (1984). Tom Buckley, *Violent Neighbors* (1984). Steven Emerson, *Secret Warriors: Inside the Covert Military Operations of the Reagan Era* (1988). Thomas L. Friedman, *From Beirut to Jerusalem* (1989). Alexander Haig, *Caveat: Realism, Reagan and Foreign Policy* (1984). Jane Hunter et al., *The Iran-Contra Connection* (1987). David E. Kyvig, ed., *Reagan and the World* (1990). Walter LaFeber, *Inevitable Revolutions*, rev. ed. (1984). Richard A. Melanson, *Reconstructing Consensus: American Foreign Policy Since the Vietnam War* (1991). John Newhouse, *War and Peace in the Nuclear Age* (1989). Robert O. Pastor, *Condemned to Repetition: The United States and Nicaragua* (1987). Charles D. Smith, *Palestine and the Arab-Israeli Conflict*, 2nd ed. (1992). Strobe Talbott, *Deadly Gambits* (1984); *The Master of the Game: Paul Nitze and the Nuclear Peace* (1988). Daniel Wirls, *Buildup: The Politics of Defense in the Reagan Era* (1992). Bob Woodward, *Veil: The Secret Wars of the CIA* (1987).

28: MODERN TIMES

The Post Cold-War World. Bernard Gwertzman and Michael T. Kaufman, eds., *The Collapse of Communism* (1990). Paul Kennedy, *The Rise and Fall of the Great Pow-*

ers (1987). Robert Kuttner, *The End of Laissez Faire: National Purpose and the Global Economy After the Cold War* (1991). John Mueller, *Policy and Opinion in the Gulf War* (1994). Henry R. Nau, *The Myth of America's Decline: Leading the World Economy in the 1990s* (1990). Joseph Nye, *Bound to Lead: The Changing Nature of American Power* (1990) H. Norman Schwarzkopf, *It Doesn't Take a Hero* (1992).

Politics After Reagan. E. J. Dionne, *Why Americans Hate Politics* (1991). Thomas Ferguson and Joel Rogers, *Right Turn* (1986). William Greider, *Who Will Tell the People?* (1992). Robert S. McElvaine, *The End of the Conservative Era: Liberalism After Reagan* (1987). Kevin Phillips, *The Politics of Rich and Poor: Wealth and the American Electorate in the Reagan Aftermath* (1990). Adolph L. Reed, Jr., *The Jesse Jackson Phenomenon* (1986). Bob Woodward, *The Agenda* (1994).

Post-Liberal Culture. Peter N. Carroll, *It Seemed Like Nothing Happened* (1982). Pete Clecak, *America's Quest for the Ideal Self* (1983). Jim Hougan, *Decadence: Radical Nostalgia, Narcissism, and Decline in the Seventies* (1975). Christopher Lasch, *The Culture of Narcissism* (1978). Edwin Schur, *The Awareness Trap* (1976). Daniel Yankelovich, *New Rules: Search for Self-Fulfillment in a World Turned Upside Down* (1981).

Economy and Society. Carl Abbott, *The New Urban America: Growth and Politics in the Sunbelt Cities* (1981). Michael A. Bernstein and David E. Adler, *Understanding American Economic Decline* (1994). Barry Bluestone and Bennett Harrison, *The Deindustrializing of America* (1982). Connie Bruck, *The Predator's Ball: The Junk Bond Raiders and the Man Who Staked Them* (1988). Bryan Burroughs and John Helyar, *Barbarians at the Gate: The Fall of RJR Nabisco* (1990). Elizabeth Fee and Daniel M. Fox, eds., *AIDS: The Burdens of History* (1988); *AIDS: The Making of a Chronic Disease* (1992). Gerald N. Grob, *From Asylum to Community: Mental Health Policy in Modern America* (1991). Robert Heilbroner and Lester Thurow, *Five Economic Challenges*

(1983). John Langone, *AIDS: The Facts* (1988). Frank Levy, *Dollars and Dreams: The Changing American Income Distribution* (1987). Michael Lewis, *Liar's Poker* (1989). Eric Marcus, *Making History: The Struggle for Gay and Lesbian Equal Rights, 1945–1990* (1992). Robert Reich, *The Work of Nations: Preparing Ourselves for Twenty-first-Century Capitalism* (1991). Kirkpatrick Sale, *Power Shift* (1975). Jonathan Schell, *The Fate of the Earth* (1982). Arthur Schlesinger, Jr., *The Disuniting of America* (1992). Bruce J. Schulman, *From Cotton Belt to Sunbelt: Federal Policy, Economic Development, and the Transformation of the South, 1938–1980* (1991). Randy Shilts, *And the Band Played On: Politics, People, and the AIDS Epidemic* (1987). James B. Stewart, *Den of Thieves* (1991). Studs Terkel, *The Great Divide* (1988). John Woodridge, *The Evangelicals* (1975). Daniel Yergin, *The Prize* (1991).

Gender and Family. Mary Francis Berry, *Why ERA Failed* (1986). Susan M. Bianchi, *American Women in Transition* (1987). Nancy Caraway, *Segregated Sisterhood: Racism and the Politics of American Feminism* (1991). Andrea Dworkin, *Right-Wing Women* (1983). Barbara Ehrenreich, *The Hearts of Men: American Dreams and the Flight from Commitment* (1983). Jonathan Kozol, *Rachel and Her Children: Homeless Families in America* (1988). Kristin Luker, *Abortion and the Politics of Motherhood* (1984). Jane Mansbridge, *Why We Lost the ERA* (1986). Donald G. Mathews and Jane Sherron De Hart, *Sex, Gender, and the Politics of E.R.A.: A State and the Nation* (1990). Rosalind Pechesky, *Abortion and Woman's Choice* (1984). Harrell R. Rodgers, Jr., *Poor Women, Poor Families* (1986). Hilda Scott, *Working Your Way to the Bottom: The Feminization of Poverty* (1985). Ruth Sidel, *Women and Children Last* (1986). Suzanne Staggenborg, *The Pro-Choice Movement: Organization and Activism in the Abortion Conflict* (1991). Winifred D. Wandersee, *On the Move: American Women in the 1970s* (1988).

Nonwhites in the 1970s and 1980s. Ken Auletta, *The Underclass* (1981). Frank D. Bean and Marta Tienda, *The Hispanic Population of the United States* (1987). Derrick

Bell, *And We Were Not Saved: The Elusive Quest for Racial Justice* (1987). James D. Cockcroft, *Outlaws in the Promised Land: Mexican Immigrant Workers and America's Future* (1986). John Crewden, *The Tarnished Door: The New Immigrants and the Transformation of America* (1983). Vine Deloria, Jr., *American Indian Policy in the Twentieth Century* (1985). Leslie W. Dunbar, ed., *Minority Report* (1984). Marian Wright Edelman, *Families in Peril* (1987). Douglas Glasgow, *The Black Underclass* (1980). Andrew Hacker, *Two Nations: Black and White, Separate, Hostile, Unequal* (1992). Michael Katz, *The Undeserving Poor: From the War on Poverty to the War on Welfare* (1989). Nicholas Lemann, *The Promised Land: The Great Black Migration and How It Changed America* (1989). Carl Nightingale, *On the Edge: A History of Poor Black Children and Their American Dreams* (1993). David M. Reimers, *Still the Golden Door* (1985). Carol B. Stack, *All Our Kin: Strategies for Survival in a Black Community* (1975). Stan Steiner, *The New Indians* (1968). William Julius Watson, *The Truly Disadvantaged* (1987); *When Work Disappears* (1996).

Picture Credits

Index

Page references followed by "f" indicate illustrations and photographs. Page references followed by "m" indicate maps.